Third Edition _____

Majority-Minority Relations _____

John E. Farley

Southern Illinois University
at Edwardsville

PRENTICE HALL, Upper Saddle River, New Jersey 07458

Library of Congress Cataloging-in-Publication Data

Farley, John E.
    Majority-minority relations / John E. Farley. — 3rd ed.
        p. cm.
    Includes bibliographical references and index.
    ISBN 0-13-106675-7 (hardcover)
    1. Ethnology—United States.   2. United States—Race relations.
    3. United States—Ethnic relations.   I. Title
    E184.A1F34   1995
    305.8'00973—dc20   94-39956
                                    CIP

Editorial/production supervision
    and interior design: *Virginia Livsey*
Editor in Chief: *Nancy Roberts*
Associate editor: *Sharon Chambliss*
Editorial assistant: *Pat Naturale*
Cover designer: *Rose Marie Votta*
Cover art: Romare Bearden, "New Orleans Ragging Home, 1974."
    Courtesy Estate of Romare Bearden.
Photo researcher: *Diane Kraut*
Photo editor: *Lorinda Morris-Nantz*
Copy editor: *Carol Browne*
Buyer: *Mary Ann Gloriande*

This edition is dedicated to the children of Bosnia and Rwanda: Never again can we honestly say "never again."

© 1995, 1988, 1982 by Prentice-Hall, Inc.
A Simon & Schuster Company
Upper Saddle River, New Jersey 07458

Printed in the United States of America
10   9   8   7   6   5   4

ISBN 0-13-106675-7

Prentice-Hall International (UK) Limited, *London*
Prentice-Hall of Australia Pty. Limited, *Sydney*
Prentice-Hall Canada Inc., *Toronto*
Prentice-Hall Hispanoamericana, S.A., *Mexico*
Prentice-Hall of India Private Limited, *New Delhi*
Prentice-Hall of Japan, Inc., *Tokyo*
Simon & Schuster Asia Pte. Ltd., *Singapore*
Editora Prentice-Hall do Brasil, Ltda., *Rio de Janeiro*

Contents _____

Preface *ix*

1 Orientation: Basic Terms and Concepts *1*

Why Study Race and Ethnic Relations? *1*
Emphasis and Approach of the Book *3*
Basic Terms and Concepts *4*   Race and Ethnicity *5*   Majority
and Minority Groups *6*   Racism *8*
Summary and Conclusion *11*

Part I   Social-Psychological Perspectives
on Majority-Minority Relations: The Study of Prejudice

2 Prejudice: Its Forms and Causes *13*

What Is Prejudice? *13*
Forms of Prejudice *14*
Stereotypes *14*
Causes of Prejudice *16*
Theories About Personality and Prejudice *16*   Is Prejudice Generalized? *17*
The Authoritarian Personality *18*   Explaining Prejudice: Scapegoating
and Projection *20*   The Development of Prejudiced Personalities *21*
Evaluation of the Personality Theory of Prejudice *22*
Social Learning and Conformity as Causes of Prejudice *24*   Personality
Theory Versus Social Learning Theory *26*
Socioeconomic Status and Prejudice *27*   Effects of Education *28*
Economic Insecurity and Prejudice *28*
Summary and Conclusion *29*

3 Reducing Prejudice: How Achievable?
How Important? *30*

Reducing Prejudice: Some Principles and Approaches *30*   Persuasive
Communications *31*   Education *34*   Intergroup Contact *37*
Simulation Exercises *42*   Therapy *43*   Overview *44*
How Important Is Prejudice? *44*   Merton's Typology on Prejudice
and Discrimination *45*   Can Behavior Determine Attitudes? *46*
Prejudice and Discrimination in America Today *47*   Do Attitudes Cause
Intergroup Inequality? *51*
Summary and Conclusion *55*

Part II Social-Structural Perspectives on Majority-Minority Relations

4 Sociological Perspectives: The Order and Conflict Models 56

Sociological Versus Social-Psychological Approaches to Majority–Minority Relations *56* Factors Shaping Patterns of Majority–Minority Relations: The Sociological View *57*
Perspectives in Sociology *58*
Order and Conflict: Two Sociological Perspectives *59* The Order (Functionalist) Perspective *59* The Conflict Perspective *60* A Comparison *63*
The Social-Structural Perspectives and Social Problems *63* The Definition of Social Problems *64* The Location of Social Problems *64*
The Social-Structural Perspectives and Majority–Minority Relations *65* Functionalist Theories About Majority–Minority Relations *66* Conflict Theories About Majority–Minority Relations *69* *BOX: Ethnocentrism and War* *71* Varieties of Conflict Theory in Race and Ethnic Relations *72* Competing Perspectives: Is Synthesis Possible? *73*
An Illustration of the Debate: Culture of Poverty Theory and African American Families *75* Culture of Poverty Theory *75* Family Structure, Poverty, and African American Families *76* Evaluation: Is the Black Family Responsible for Disproportionate Black Poverty? *78* Teenage Pregnancy and the Black Family *82* Overview *84*
Summary and Conclusion *85*

5 Origins and Causes of Ethnic Inequality 86

Patterns of Race/Ethnic Relations *87* Caste Versus Class Systems of Stratification *87* Three Common Patterns of Race Relations *87*
The Development of Ethnic Stratification *92* Initial Contact Between Racial/Ethnic Groups *94* Origins of Ethnic Inequality *94*
Origins of Racial and Ethnic Inequality in the United States *95* African Americans *95*
Life Under Slavery *100* *BOX: The Peculiar Institution: Slavery in the Ante-Bellum South* *100* Native Americans *106* The Indian Reservation and the Slave Plantation: A Comparison *111* Mexican Americans *113*
Summary and Conclusion *119*

6 Changing Patterns of Majority–Minority Relations in the United States 121

Origins of Contact and Modern-Day Race Relations: A Theory of Internal Colonialism *121*
Evolving Patterns of Black–White Race Relations *125* Caste Relations Become Unstable: The Development of Rigid Competitive Race Relations, 1860–1945 *125* *BOX: The Ethics of Living Jim Crow* *130*

Rigid Competitive Race Relations and Other Racial/Ethnic Groups   *139*
Asian Americans   *139*   Mexican Americans   *140*   Overview   *141*
A Shift to Fluid Competitive Race Relations: America Since World War II   *142*
Changes in the Law: The Banning of Discrimination   *143*   Changes
in Economics: The Development of Substantial Middle Classes Among Minority
Groups   *145*   Changes in Attitudes: Changes in the Kind and Degree of
Prejudice Among Whites   *146*
**Factors Causing the Changes: The Effects of Urbanization
and Industrialization**   *147*   Requirement of Greater Mobility and the
Economic Irrationality of Discrimination   *147*   Generally Rising Educational
Levels   *148*   Postwar Economic Growth and Easing of Intergroup Competition
148   Increased Assertiveness on the Part of Minorities   *149*
Summary and Conclusion   *149*

7   Minority-Group Movements, Values, and Contemporary Intergroup Relations   *150*

Adaptive Responses   *150*   Acceptance   *151*   Displaced Aggression   *151*
Avoidance   *152*   Seeking Assimilation   *152*
Change-oriented Responses   *153*
A Shift Toward Change-oriented Responses   *154*
The Rising Tide of Protest   *154*
Necessary Conditions for Social Movements   *158*   Dissatisfaction (Relative
Deprivation)   *158*   Communication Network   *158*   Resources   *158*
Sense of Efficacy   *159*   Leadership   *159*
**Development of These Conditions and the Formation of Minority Social
Movements in the United States After World War II**   *159*   Urbanization and
Industrialization   *160*   Economic Expansion   *161*   Mass Communications
162   Rising Educational Levels   *163*   International Changes   *163*
**Changing Values and Goals: Racial and Ethnic Group Movements
from the 1960s to the 1990s**   *164*
Three Ideal Models of Intergroup Relations   *165*   Model 1: Assimilation   *165*
Model 2: Pluralism   *166*   Model 3: Separatism   *167*
Assimilation, Pluralism, and Separatism in American Society   *168*   Assimilation
and Anglo-Conformity   *168*   Critique: Have Social Scientists Exaggerated
the Degree of Assimilation in American Society?   *171*
Changing Attitudes Toward Assimilation and Pluralism   *172*   African
Americans   *172*   Pluralism and Militancy Among Chicanos, Latinos, and
American Indians   *184*   The "Ethnic Revival" Among White Americans   *188*
Summary and Conclusion   *189*

8   Cross-cultural Studies of Majority–Minority Relations   *191*

Cross-cultural Evidence on the Effects of Colonization   *191*   South
Africa   *192*   Northern Ireland   *194*   Quebec, Canada   *195*   The
Former Soviet Union   *196*   Former Yugoslavia   *199*   *BOX: Irma: The Story
of One Bosnian Child*   *202*   The Middle East   *204*   Some Comparisons and
Contrasts   *207*   Great Britain: Another Effect of Colonialism   *207*

Societies with Peaceful Intergroup Relations *208*
Cross-cultural Evidence on the Effects of Urbanization and Modernization *209*
Industrialized Countries *209*   Increasing Fluidity? Or Rigidity with Conflict?
211   Third World Countries: Two Major Trends *214*
Combined Effects of Colonialism and Degree of Modernization *216*
Number of Racial and Ethnic Groups *216*
Cultural and Demographic Characteristics of Majority and Minority Groups:
The Examples of Brazil and Mexico *218*
Overlapping Versus Crosscutting Cleavages *220*
Territorial Ethnic Base *222*
Language *223*
International Relationships *223*   Surges of Immigration *224*
Racial Versus Ethnic Divisions *226*
International Pressure *226*
Summary and Conclusion *227*

Part III   Majority-Minority Relations in America Today:
The Role of Institutional Discrimination

9 The Status of Majority and Minority Groups in the United States Today *229*

Major Racial and Ethnic Groups: Overview and General Statistics *229*
Minority Groups—African Americans, Latinos, and Native Americans *229*
Groups with Intermediate Status: Asian, Jewish, and "White Ethnic"
American *235*   Whites from Western and Northern Europe:
A Dominant Group Within a Dominant Group *238*
Status of Minority Groups in America Today *240*   Evidence of Improvement
in Minority Status *240*   Evidence of Continuing Majority–Minority
Inequality *242*
Summary and Conclusion *250*

10 The American Economic System and the Status of Minority Groups Today *252*

The Economics of Discrimination: Three Theories *253*   Gary Becker's
Theory *254*   Split Labor Market Theory *255*   Marxist Theory *256*
Evaluating Theories About the Economics of Discrimination *257*
Discrimination and Economic Productivity *260*
Recent Trends and Their Effects on Racial Economic Inequality *261*
Rising Educational Demands and the Employment of Minorities *261*
Job Decentralization and Housing Segregation *262*
Housing Discrimination and Segregation *266*   Housing Segregation
Between Blacks and Whites *266*   Economic Explanations of Housing
Segregation *268*   Black Preferences *270*   White Preferences *270*
Practices in the Real-Estate Business *273*   Housing Segregation Among
Latinos and Asian Americans *276*   Impacts of Segregation *277*

The Fiscal Crisis of Cities and Its Impact on Minorities *279* BOX: *Supporting Integrative Moves: One State's Initiative* *279*
Health Care and Minorities *282* Cost of Health Care *284* Frequency of Seeking Medical Care *285* Availability of Health-Care Personnel *287* Lack of Minority Physicians *288* Places and Types of Care: Race and Class Differentials *289* The Medicaid Program *291* The American Health-Care Institution: A Conclusion *294*
Summary and Conclusion *295*

11 The American Political and Legal System and Majority–Minority Relations 297

Government in America: Agent of the White Oppressor or Protector of Minority Rights? *299* Historical Patterns: Governmental Policies of Discrimination *299* Contemporary Patterns: Government and Majority–Minority Relations Today *305* Barriers to Greater Minority Political Power *311* Voting and Political Participation *312*
The American Legal System and Majority–Minority Relations *316* The Criminal-Justice System and the Minority Accused *316* Conclusion *328* Protecting Minority Rights *329*
Summary and Conclusion *334*

12 Education and American Minority Groups 336

A Brief History of School Segregation Since 1954 *337*
The Role of Education: Two Views *339*
Funding of Schools *342*
Cultural and Behavioral Factors in the Education of Minorities *346* Cultural Deprivation? *347* Cultural Bias? *348* Biased or Limited Coverage of Minority Groups in School Materials *349* Teacher Expectations and Tracking *352* Linguistic Differences *356* Test Bias *361* Testing Bias: Summary *365* Lack of Minority Role Models *367*
Racial Bias in the Educational System: An Evaluation *367*
Resolving Problems of Majority–Minority Inequality in Education: Four Approaches *369* Approach 1: The Problem Does Not Lie in the Educational System *369* Approach 2: Assimilation *369* Approach 3: Multiculturalism and Cultural Immersion *378* Approach 4: The Interactionist Approach *382*
Summary and Conclusion *384*

Part IV Values, Goals, and Issues of the Present and Future in Majority-Minority Relations

13 Majority–Minority Relations Based on Gender, Sexual Orientation, and Disability 385

The Nature of Gender Inequality *385*
Causes of Gender Inequality *387* Functionalist Explanations of Gender Inequality *387* Conflict-Theory Explanations of Gender Inequality *389*
The Intersection of Race, Gender, and Class Inequality *391* The Meaning

of Gender for Women of Color   *391*   Black Males in American Society   *393*
BOX: *Opportunity for Inner-City Black Males: The Difference
a Generation Makes   397*
Prejudice, Inequality, and Discrimination Based on Sexual Orientation   398
The Applicability of the Majority–Minority Model to Sexual Orientation   *398*
Causes of Discrimination Against Gay Men and Lesbians   *402*
People with Disabilities as a Minority Group   404   Access and the Americans
with Disabilities Act   *406*
Summary and Conclusion   407

14   Current Trends in Majority–Minority Relations   409

Diversity and Multiculturalism in Work and Education   409   Diversity
Management in the Workplace   *411*   Characteristics of Effective
Diversity Management Programs   *413*   Diversity Management
and Multiculturalism   *415*
Hate-Group Activity and Hate Crime in the 1990s   416   Causes of Increased
Hate-Group Activity   *419*
Combating Hatred: Debates over Speech Codes and "Political Correctness"   424
The Discrimination-Testing Movement   427
Summary and Conclusion   431

15   Selected Issues for the Future of Majority–Minority Relations in the United States   433

Alternative Models for Intergroup Relations   433   Assimilation   *434*
Pluralism   *435*   Racial/Ethnic Separatism   *437*
Affirmative Action   438   Undoing Discrimination   *440*   Reverse
Discrimination   *440*   Considering the Net Outcome   *441*   Practical
Consequences of Affirmative Action: Empirical Evidence   *444*   Legal Aspects
of the Affirmative-Action Controversy   *447*   Minority Set-Aside Programs   *451*
Immigration Policy   453   Illegal Immigration and the 1986 and 1990
Immigration Reform Laws   *454*
The Relative Importance of Race and Class in American Society   458
Summary and Conclusion   463

Glossary   464

References   470

Index   504

Preface

This book is designed to enable the reader to understand the principles and processes that shape the patterns of relations between racial, ethnic, and other groups in society. It is not a study of any one racial or ethnic group, though a wide variety of information is indeed provided about a number of groups. Rather, it is intended to enhance the reader's understanding of why such groups interact as they do. The primary emphasis is on the relationships between dominant (majority) and subordinate (minority) racial and ethnic groups in the United States. However, thorough understanding of the dynamics of intergroup relations cannot be obtained by looking at only one society. Accordingly, a full chapter is devoted to the examination of intergroup relations in societies other than the United States. There is also attention, particularly in Chapter 13, to minority groups other than racial and ethnic ones.

The book is divided into four major parts. In Part I (Chapters 2 and 3) the attitudes and beliefs of the individual concerning intergroup relations are explored using a variety of social-psychological approaches. The concept of prejudice is examined, and various theories about the causes of prejudice are presented and evaluated. There is also attention to ways in which prejudice may be combated and to the relationship between intergroup attitudes and intergroup behavior. In Part II (Chapters 4–8) the emphasis shifts to the larger societal arena. Two major sociological perspectives, order and conflict, are introduced here. These perspectives, and more specific kinds of theories arising from them, are used throughout the book as a means of understanding intergroup relations in society. In the balance of Part II, the history of U.S. majority-minority relations is explored and analyzed using the two perspectives, and the theories arising from the perspectives are tested and refined using this historical material. Also introduced here are the concepts of assimilation and pluralism along with a discussion of their roles in the history of American intergroup relations. The theories are further refined through examination of cross-cultural variations in intergroup relations in the closing chapter of Part II.

The major concern in Part III of the book (Chapters 9–12) is with present-day intergroup relations in the United States. This part begins with a compilation of data concerning the numbers, characteristics, and social statuses of a wide range of American racial and ethnic groups. The remainder of Part III consists of an extensive discussion of institutional discrimination in America. Analysts of intergroup relations are in relatively broad agreement that institutional discrimination has become more important than individual discrimination in the maintenance of racial and ethnic inequality in America. That fact is not, however, reflected in the content of most of the general works on intergroup relations now available. This book attempts to remedy that deficiency through extensive discussion of processes that create or maintain such inequality of the political, legal, economic, health care, and educational institutions. All of these areas, as well as housing discrimination and its causes and effects, are discussed and analyzed in Chapters 9–12.

In Part IV of this book, key issues, trends, and controversies in the present and future of intergroup relations are explored. Part IV of the book has been expanded from earlier editions and includes two entirely new chapters. Chapter 13 addresses majority-minority relations based on gender, sexual orientation, and disability, with special attention to ways in which racial inequality and gender inequality interact and overlap, thus presenting special concerns and dilemmas for women and men of color. Chapter 14 addresses current trends in majority-minority relations, including diversity and multiculturalism in work and education; the resurgence of hate group activity and hate crime in the 1990s; debates about how to combat hatred, including issues centering around speech codes and "political correctness"; and the discrimination-testing movement. Chapter 15 explores selected issues in the future of race and ethnic relations in the United States, including the continuing controversy over affirmative action; debates concerning the desirability of assimilation, pluralism, and separatism; the relative importance of race and class in American society; and the current and future immigration policy of the United States.

For the most part, the basic approach and organization of the first and second editions have been retained. However, the book has been revised extensively, and, as noted above, two entirely new chapters have been added in Part IV. Because of growing attention in our society to majority-minority relations based on social characteristics other than race and ethnicity, a full chapter (Chapter 13) is now devoted to issues of gender, people with disabilities, and sexual orientation. Important new societal trends pertaining to race and ethnic relations that have emerged since the previous edition are addressed in the entirely new Chapter 14. Much of the material that formerly appeared in Chapter 13 now appears in updated form in Chapter 15. Throughout the book, material has been revised to reflect new developments, new research, and up-to-date statistics. Dramatic social changes in the Middle East, South Africa, and eastern Europe have rendered much of what appeared in Chapter 8 of the second edition totally out of date. Large portions of this chapter have been entirely rewritten to reflect new developments, and the coverage of different parts of the world has been both shifted and expanded to cover the ethnic trouble spots of the 1990s. In particular, there is extensive new coverage of ethnic relations in the former Soviet Union and eastern Europe.

While the chapters discussed above represent the biggest changes in the third edition, there are substantial revisions and updates in every chapter. A measure of the amount of new and revised material can be seen in the fact that well over 400 new sources are cited in the third edition. Some of the bigger changes in the third edition include the following: New material on education and simulation exercises as ways of reducing prejudice in Chapter 3; new sections on different varieties of conflict theories about majority-minority relations and on family structure, poverty, and African American families in Chapter 4; a new discussion of recent research on "oppositional identity" in Chapter 6; extensive new material on current trends in Chapter 7 addressing such issues as the 1992 Los Angeles riot, resurgent black nationalism, Afrocentrism, and environmental racism along with expanded and updated coverage of the Nation of Islam. Virtually every statistic in Chapter 9 (The Status of Majority and Minority Groups in the United States Today) is updated, with large sections of the chapter entirely rewritten, including detailed discussion and analysis of the 1990 census. In Chapter 10, there is new material on the effects of discrimination on economic productivity, extensively updated and expanded material on housing segregation and discrimination, and discussion of the possible effects on the Clinton health-care reform proposals on health care for people of color in the United States. New sections in Chapter 12 discuss multiculturalism in education and immersion schools for students of color, particularly black males; an update on research concerning Head Start and similar early childhood education programs; and numerous updates on the subject of school desegregation.

Finally, new boxed material has been added in several chapters. In Chapter 8, a new box addresses the plight of children in war-torn Bosnia. In Chapter 10, a new box describes one state's innovative efforts to promote residential integration. And in Chapter 13, a box uses the experiences of a successful black journalist returning to his old inner-city neighborhood to illustrate the worsening conditions that people living in many such neighborhoods face.

To enhance the reader's awareness of essential concepts used throughout the book, important new terms are defined in a glossary at the end of the book. Major ideas throughout the book have been illustrated photographically, and the substantial list of references has been grouped together at the end of this book so any reference can be easily located. For the instructor, a test item file is also available.

An undertaking such as the writing of this book would be impossible without the assistance of many people. In the early stages of developing ideas for this book I received encouragement and helpful advice from Hugh Barlow, Joel Charon, and Charles Tilly. Donald Noel, Howard Schuman, Lyle Shannon, Richard Cramer, David Willman, Katherine O'Sullivan See, and Betsey Useem each read and commented upon part or all of earlier versions of the manuscript. Reviewers for the second edition were Darnell F. Hawkins of the University of Illinois at Chicago and Katherine O'Sullivan See of Michigan State University. The book has benefited greatly from their insightful observations; the shortcomings that remain are entirely the responsibility of the author. Portions of the manuscript were typed by Sherrie Williams, Kathy Howlatt, Lynn Krieger, Krista Wright, and Marilyn Morrison. Brenda Eich assisted in the compilation of the reference list. The capable editorial staff at Prentice Hall, including past Sociology Editors Ed Stanford and Bill Webber, their assistants Irene Fraga and Kathleen Dorman, and past Production Editors Alison Gnerre and Marianne Peters, have been a pleasure to work with.

In the third edition, I am grateful to Acquisitions Editors Nancy Roberts and Sharon Chambliss for their continued work and commitment on behalf of this book, as well as to Project Manager Virginia Livsey. Helpful suggestions on portions of the book were received from Thomas D. Hall, DePauw University; David N. Lawyer, Jr., Santa Barbara City College; Pranab Chatterjee, Case Western Reserve University; Alan Siman, San Diego State University; and Vernon McClean, William Paterson College. I am grateful to graduate students Craig Hughey, Cheryl Riggs, and Michelle Ruffner for library assistance during the revision of the third edition, and to Michelle Ruffner and Gina Goodwin for assistance in combining the new references for the third edition with the reference list from the second edition. As usual, support and ideas from my colleagues in the Department of Sociology and Social Work at Southern Illinois University at Edwardsville have made an important contribution to the third edition. Finally, the most important support of all is the emotional support that I have received from my daughter Megan, who celebrated her tenth birthday the day before I wrote this revised preface.

1

Orientation: Basic
Terms and Concepts

WHY STUDY RACE AND ETHNIC RELATIONS?

At the beginning of the second edition of this book, I commented on an apparent resurgence of hate groups such as the Ku Klux Klan, the Order, the Aryan Nations, and the Posse Comitatus. I pointed to that as an indication that race relations in America are perhaps the nation's most intractable problem; simply put, the problem that won't go away. This resurgence is no longer apparent but patently obvious. According to the Klanwatch program, which keeps track of the actions of hate groups like these, there were more bias-motivated murders, assaults, and acts of vandalism—and more cross burnings—in 1992 than in any year since such records were first kept in 1979 (Southern Poverty Law Center, 1993a).

For the first time in my life, I personally witnessed hooded, torch-bearing Klan members when I joined with fellow faculty, staff, and students from the university where I teach to protest a Ku Klux Klan rally held just fifteen miles from campus. A few weeks later, the White Aryan Resistance (WAR), a group whose leader was ordered to pay damages of $12.5 million for inciting a group of skinheads to murder an African college student in Oregon, surreptitiously plastered the campus with racist literature, then sent letters filled with racial slurs to people who dared to speak out against them. The same group also placed its calling cards on the windshields of people attending a local racial-harmony meeting. All of these events occurred within a two-month period in the fall of 1992.

Such events are not peculiar to the town where I live or the campus where I teach. Rather, they are simply the local manifestations of the national trend described in the Klanwatch report. Similar events occurred in other cities and towns and on other college campuses throughout the United States. The results were sometimes deadly: In St. Louis, for example, two white men ran over a black man with their pickup truck for no reason other than that the man was black. And as everyone knows, the violence of 1992 took other forms as well. In Los Angeles, the deadliest riot of the twentieth century followed the acquittal of four police officers in the videotaped beating of Rodney King. Serious outbreaks of violence occurred in several other cities as well. Preliminary studies indicate that this violence was directed toward individual civilians to a far greater extent than was the case in the riots of the 1960s (McPhail, 1993).

Hate violence in 1992 was not always racial. The year brought record numbers of attacks on gay and lesbian Americans, including a fatal beating administered to a gay man by off-duty naval enlistees. Nor was the violence limited to the United States. In fact, America's intergroup violence, although the worst in decades, paled in comparison with that of a number of other countries. In former Yugoslavia, for example, systematic genocide was practiced in ways that brought chilling reminders of Nazi Germany, and in Germany itself, violent attacks against Turks, Gypsies, refugees from former Yugoslavia, and other minorities and immigrants caused scores of deaths and left hundreds of people homeless.

The fact is that conflict, discrimination, and inequality among racial and ethnic groups are deeply entrenched in American society, as they are in many other multiethnic and multiracial societies. In the United States, this remains true in spite of a decline in open discrimination; in spite of hundreds of civil rights laws, ordinances, and court decisions at the federal, state, and local levels; and in spite of the fact that conditions have substantially improved for some minority group members. In spite of all this, the aggregate pattern remains one of racial and ethnic inequality. This is true whether we talk about income, education, political representation, or any other measure of status in American society. Furthermore, for many minority group members conditions have not improved, and for some they have actually gotten worse.

These basic facts carry serious implications for all Americans. For some minority group members, they mean that life is a day-to-day struggle for survival. For all minority group members, they mean facing socially imposed disadvantages that they would not face if they were white. For majority group members, they mean the continued dilemma of living in a society that preaches equality but in large part fails to practice it. Furthermore, they mean facing the near certainty of turmoil and social upheaval in the future. As long as the fundamental inequalities that have led to past and present upheavals remain, the potential—indeed the strong likelihood—of future turmoil remains. All that is needed is the right mix of precipitating social conditions to set off the spark. The conclusion is inescapable: The issue of racial and ethnic relations will somehow affect the life of nearly every American in the coming years.

Another reason that racial and ethnic relations continue to be of concern can be found in the changing racial and ethnic composition of the United States. For a number of reasons, a growing percentage of the American population will be composed of racial and ethnic minorities in coming years. Of particular importance is the growing percentage of Spanish-speaking ethnic groups. Increasingly, the United States—particularly in certain regions—may become a bilingual society. This is something largely new to this country, a situation that will require sizable adjustments. It will also require a greater understanding by all Americans of the ethnic and cultural issues that are raised when two linguistically different groups interact in one society.

As America becomes more diverse—and as it continues to face increased international competition in the world economy—every American has a growing economic stake in reducing racial inequality in the United States. Today, the talents of millions of Americans are being wasted. Poor education, concentrated poverty, and rising unemployment in the country's predominantly black and Hispanic inner cities are making it increasingly difficult for the people who live there to develop the skills needed in today's high-tech economic environment. Conditions on many Indian reservations, as well as for rural African Americans, Hispanics, and poor whites, are as bad or worse. Moreover, the situation of those people of color who live in areas of concentrated poverty has become increasingly bleak since the 1970s (Wilson, 1987, 1991a; Massey, 1990). In addition to the potential for social turmoil that this creates, it has a direct bearing on our present and future productivity. Today, about 25 percent of the American population is composed of people of color (African Americans, Hispanic or Latino Americans, Asian Americans, and Native Americans). By 2020, this is projected to increase to 35 percent, and by 2050, to over 45 percent (O'Hare, 1992; Passel and Edmonston, 1992; U.S. Bureau of the Census, 1992a). As pointed out in the *Workforce 2000* report (U.S. Department of Labor, 1987), failing to fully utilize the human resources of a group this large will seriously harm America's productivity precisely at a time when international competition is at an all-time high—and continuing to increase. The consequences of such a decline in competitiveness in today's global economy are clear: Fewer people will buy American products, with the result that jobs will be lost and wages will fall. This will affect all Americans, not just people of color. One recent study estimated the cost of racial discrimination to the U.S. economy (in the form of reduced gross domestic product) in 1991 at $215 billion—nearly ten times what it was in 1967 (Brimmer, 1993). And as the minority share of the population grows and international competition intensifies, this cost can only grow.

For all of these reasons, there remains a critical need for understanding racial and ethnic dynamics in America. The goal of this book is to contribute to such understanding. In the remainder of this chapter, we describe the emphases of the book and the approaches to the study of racial and ethnic relations that it stresses. Finally, we define and discuss some basic concepts that will be used throughout the book and that one must thoroughly understand to study racial and ethnic relations effectively.

EMPHASIS AND APPROACH OF THE BOOK

As is evident by now, the primary emphasis of this book is on race and ethnic relations in the United States. Nonetheless, this is not exclusively a book about American race relations. The fundamental objective of the book is to understand the dynamics of race and ethnic relations. This could never be accomplished by looking at only one society. How ethnic groups interact with one another varies from one society to another according to the social, economic, cultural, and political conditions found in those societies. Racial and ethnic relations—including those in America—can therefore be best understood by comparing what has happened in different times and places. Moreover, patterns and problems similar to some of those in the United States are evident in a number of other industrialized countries with diverse populations. For all these reasons, the emphasis of this book on the American situation cannot and does not exclude a comparative analysis of racial and ethnic relations in other societies.

A second major characteristic of this book is that it is concerned with analysis and explanation rather than merely description. In other words, the major concern is with understanding *why* race relations work the way they do, not merely with describing the pattern of American race relations or with presenting a detailed descriptive history of various ethnic groups. (The size of the book would not permit us to do justice to the varied and rich histories of the multiplicity of American ethnic groups, in any case.)[1] If we are to understand and deal with racial and ethnic problems, we must know not only what those problems are, but how they developed and what the social forces are that cause them to persist. Thus, ours is a search for principles and regularities in patterns of ethnic relations: For example, what are the social conditions under which segregation develops? What changes are associated with declines in segregation? Only through this approach, which stresses the whys of race relations, can we begin to understand and deal with the problems we face today.

A third important characteristic of this book is that it will enable us to examine race and ethnic relations on both the individual and societal levels. Some people who study race relations look mainly at the behaviors and prejudices of individuals, asking why a person is prejudiced and what we can do about it. Others look mainly at groups and societies, stressing economic and political systems or such trends as urbanization and industrialization, asking how these large-scale factors influence the interaction of the ethnic groups in a society. This book begins at the individual level then moves to analyzes on a larger scale. We shall examine theory and research about individual thinking and behavior regarding race and ethnicity, then theories and research about the larger societal factors and their relationship to race and ethnicity. Having laid this groundwork, we will consider the status of various racial and ethnic groups in American society today and the ways in which major American social institutions influence the status of these groups. The book concludes with an examination of contemporary trends in majority–minority relations and issues likely to shape future intergroup relations in the United States.

BASIC TERMS AND CONCEPTS

In any field of study, one must understand certain terms and concepts to make sense of the subject. The field of racial and ethnic relations is certainly no exception. Unfortunately, in this field more than most, any particular term may be given a wide variety of meanings by different scholars. Therefore, it is probably impossible to come up with definitions on which all would agree. Still, we must know what is meant by the terms we are using. Accordingly, we present the following definitions with the understanding that

1. It is unlikely that every social scientist who studies race and ethnic relations would agree on all of these definitions, or on any set of definitions.

---

[1] For those interested in historical information on a wide variety of racial and ethnic groups in America, an excellent source is the *Harvard Encyclopedia of American Ethnic Groups* (Thernstrom et al., 1980).

2. The definitions, insofar as possible, reflect current trends in common usage among those who study race and ethnic relations.

3. The reasons for using a particular definition will be explained.

4. The definitions are stated in such a way that, once they are understood, it should be quite possible for any reader to say who or what fits the definition and who or what does not.

Race and Ethnicity

A **race** can be defined as a group of people who (1) are generally considered to be physically distinct in some way, such as skin color, hair texture, or facial features, from other groups and (2) are generally considered by themselves and/or others to be a distinct group. Thus, the concept of race has two components: physical and social. The physical component involves the fact that every race is generally regarded as being somehow different in appearance from other races. The social component involves group identity: The group must in some way be recognized by its own members or by others as a distinct group, or at least as having some characteristics (physical and perhaps other characteristics) in common. Without such social recognition, a group of people will not be identified as a race.

This sense of the term conflicts with that used by many members of the general public (and, at one time, many scientists as well). Race was considered entirely a matter of physical or biological characteristics, something that is genetically determined. Although it is true, as we have seen, that race is *partly* a matter of physical characteristics, that it is not entirely physical or genetic can be readily shown. The best illustration of this is the inability of geneticists, anthropologists, or sociologists to agree on how many races there are in the world's population. The estimates range anywhere from the common notion of three races (black, white and yellow) to thirty-four races (Dobzhansky, 1962) to over a hundred. Furthermore, the particular physical characteristics that are used to define a race are arbitrary and vary from one classification scheme to the next. Finally, long-term interbreeding between races has in many cases made the notion of race as a discrete biological category meaningless. All in all, it is hard to avoid concluding that social factors are at least as important as physical or biological ones in determining the meaning of race. Physical characteristics partially define race, *but only in the context of a decision by society to consider those physical characteristics relevant.* This illustrates an important fact: Race is a *socially constructed concept.* In other words, race is meaningless as a purely biological concept; rather, it is based upon societal choices about what physical characteristics to pay attention to and how to classify people on the basis of those characteristics. Such societal choices can and do vary over time and from one society to another.

Some social scientists make a distinction between a race and a **racial group.** This distinction is illustrated by Spencer (1979, p. 274), who presents the example of an Eskimo girl raised in a white American family in the South, never exposed to Eskimo culture or society. This girl's race might be considered Eskimo (she has physical features and parentage that would define her as Eskimo), but she is not part of Eskimo society or culture and would not, on first contact with Eskimo society, understand it any more than anyone else in the South would. She would not, therefore, be considered a member of the Eskimo racial group. Thus, a racial group can be defined as a group of people of the same race who interact with one another and who develop some common cultural characteristics. In practice, however, many sociologists question the distinction between a race and a racial group. Pointing out that race is a socially constructed concept, they maintain that races, as well as racial groups, are social groups, not biological ones. One could also note that others in society may treat the Eskimo girl in Spencer's example as an Eskimo, even if she is not familiar with Eskimo culture. For these reasons, "race" and "racial group" will be used interchangeably in this book, though we shall follow what appears to be a growing tendency in the discipline toward using the term *racial group* in preference to *race.* This reflects sociology's recognition of the fact that races and racial groups are socially defined and constructed. Nonetheless, it is important to keep Spencer's basic point in mind: Whether or not one makes a distinction between a race and a racial group, it is important to recognize that groups and individuals do vary in the degree of their identification with a racial group and the degree to which they develop cultural characteristics shared by other members of the same racial group.

A concept closely related to race is that of ethnic group. An **ethnic group** can be defined as a group of people who are generally recognized by themselves and/or by others as a distinct group, with such recognition based on social or cultural characteristics. The most common of these characteristics are nationality, language, and religion. Ethnic groups tend to be, at least to some degree, biologically self-perpetuating, so that ethnicity, like race, is a social characteristic that passes from generation to generation. In the United States, Irish Americans, Jewish Americans, and Italian Americans are examples of ethnic groups. Unlike races or racial groups, physical traits are not necessarily characteristics of an ethnic group. In the case of ethnic groups, it is impossible to reliably tell on the basis of appearance alone who belongs and who does not. It is perhaps ironic that Adolf Hitler, who always insisted that Jews are a race, ultimately turned to a classification based on parentage to determine who was Jewish (one was Jewish if one or more of one's grandparents identified with the Jewish faith), since it was impossible to tell by appearance. To tell who was Jewish, Hitler required Jews to wear identifying marks such as buttons with the Star of David.

Sociologists disagree on whether ethnicity is a broad concept that includes racial groups or whether racial and ethnic groups are two different entities. Some (Gordon 1964; Glazer, 1971) argue that races are a particular type of ethnic group. By this definition, some ethnic groups are not racial groups (for example, Mennonites, Polish Americans), but all races are ethnic groups. Other social scientists make a distinction, arguing that if physical characteristics are involved, the group is a race (blacks, whites), but if the group is based solely on social or cultural characteristics, the group is an ethnic group (French Canadians, German Americans). Examples of this can be seen in the writings of Warner and Srole (1945) and Van de Berghe (1978). Because it makes a good deal of difference in terms of intergroup relations whether or not a group is identifiable on the basis of appearance, we shall use this approach in this book unless expressly indicated otherwise. Thus, for purposes of this book, racial groups are defined on the basis of both physical and social characteristics; ethnic groups purely on the basis of social or cultural characteristics.

Majority and Minority Groups

Two terms used throughout this book are **majority group** and **minority group.** When sociologists use these terms, they are not speaking strictly in the numerical sense in which the terms *majority* and *minority* are ordinarily used. The sociological meaning of **majority group,** as used in this book, is any group that is dominant in society, that is, any group that enjoys more than a proportionate share of the wealth, power, and/or social status in that society. Typically, a majority group is in a position to dominate or exercise power over other groups in society. A **minority group** can be defined as any group that is assigned an inferior status in society, that is, any group that has less than its proportionate share of wealth, power, and/or social status. Frequently, minority group members are discriminated against by those in the majority.

A number of important points can be made about majority and minority groups. First, majorities and minorities are frequently determined by race or ethnicity, but they can also be determined on the basis of many other factors, such as sex, physical disability, lifestyle, or sexual orientation (homosexuality or heterosexuality). Much of what is true about relations between blacks and whites, for example, is also true about relations between males and females, disabled and nondisabled, gays and straights. We have chosen to title this book in terms of majority–minority relations precisely for this reason: The dynamics of relations between majority groups and minority groups are in many ways similar, regardless of how those groups are defined. Accordingly, it should be kept in mind that although this book is mainly about race and ethnic relations, many of the principles apply to other kinds of majority–minority relations, or intergroup relations, as well.

Second, as we noted above, that the sociological usage of the terms *majority* and *minority* differs from the common numerical usage. It is quite possible for a group to be a numerical majority but still a minority group in the sociological sense. Several familiar examples come to mind. Perhaps the best-known is that of blacks in South Africa. Although over 80 percent of the population is black, the political system was, until very recently, completely under the control of whites since the country was created in 1949. Racial separation and discrimination were written into the laws at that time, and these laws remained in effect for forty years. Even when many of them were repealed in the late 1980s and early 1990s, nearly every aspect of South African society remained, for the most part, segregated and unequal. In 1993, an agreement was reached to hold free elections in 1994, in which people of all races could, for the first time, vote to elect a parliament. These elections were held in April, 1994, and Nelson Mandela, the leader of the African National Congress, was elected and inaugurated as South Africa's first black president. However, even with such free elections, it is likely that a disproportionate share of the country's wealth will remain in the hands of the white minority for many years. Thus, although blacks are an overwhelming majority numerically, they are a minority group in the sociological sense because they were forced into a *subordinate* role in South Africa's social system.

Another instance of a numerical majority that is a sociological minority group is women in the United States. Women make up slightly over half of the U.S. population but relatively few hold offices in the nation's higher political governing bodies (such as the U.S. Congress). They have long been subject to discrimination, and a proposed U.S. constitutional amendment to ban sexual discrimination still has not been enacted. Even today, full-time working women are paid only about 70 percent of the wages of similarly educated working men. Thus, even though they are a numerical majority, women have in many ways been relegated to a subordinate role in American society. Accordingly, they can be regarded as a minority group in the sociological sense.

The important point to keep in mind, then, is that it is a group's role and

Ethnicity is based on cultural, rather than physical, characteristics. Could you identify the ethnicity of this group of people without the ethnic dress?

status, not its numbers, that make it a majority group or a minority group. A helpful way to think of this, suggested by Yetman (1991, p. 11), is to think of *majority* as a synonym for **dominant,** and *minority* as a synonym for **subordinate.** Occasionally, a society may have relatively peaceful and egalitarian relations among its racial or ethnic groups, so that no group is dominant or subordinate. The more common pattern in diverse societies, however, is for some groups to dominate others; thus, in such societies majority (dominant) and minority (subordinate) groups can be identified.

Accordingly, interracial and interethnic relations usually fall into the larger category of majority–minority relations. Unless we are talking specifically about cases in which the three concepts—race and ethnic relations, majority–minority relations, and intergroup relations—do *not* overlap, we shall use these terms more or less interchangeably to avoid fatigue from repeated use of the same term. This is not meant in any way to negate the important facts that not *all* race and ethnic relations are marked by domination and subordination and that many intergroup relations besides race and ethnic relations operate according to the majority–minority model.

Racism

Perhaps no term in recent years has been used in as many different ways as the term **racism.** Any definition of this term is subject to controversy; for this reason, we have chosen to give this term a very broad definition and then to present further definitions to identify different forms of racism. Accordingly, **racism** can be defined as any attitude, belief, behavior, or institutional arrangement that favors one race or ethnic group (usually a majority group) over another (usually a minority group). By favoring one group over another, we are talking not only about intentions but also about consequences: If the result of an action or social arrangement is that one race or ethnic group receives a disproportionate share of scarce resources (for example, money, education, political power, social status), it is an example of racism. It is also a case of racism if the consequence of an arrangement is to give one group greater freedom than another. Thus, by this broad definition, something or someone can be racist either on the basis of intentions or on the basis of results. Accordingly, it follows that sometimes racism (and similar phenomena such as sexism) are conscious and deliberate; at other times they are not. The unfortunate fact is that if one is the victim of racism or sexism, it makes relatively little difference whether the disadvantage was intentionally imposed or not—it is still a disadvantage. (For further discussion of this broad concept of racism, see U.S. Commission on Civil Rights, 1970b; Jones, 1972; and Yetman, 1991, pp. 19–29).

Within this broad definition of racism, we can identify several specific kinds of racism. One kind of racism is attitudinal; this kind is referred to as racial prejudice. A second, more narrowly-defined kind of racism is ideological racism, also called racist ideology. A third type involves individual behavior, and is referred to as racial discrimination. A fourth type involves institutional or societal patterns; this type is called institutional racism or institutional discrimination.

Racial Prejudice.   **Racial prejudice,** the attitudinal form of racism, refers to people's thinking: their attitudes and beliefs which tend to favor one group over another, or to cause unequal treatment on the basis of race. Prejudice can be direct or overt, such as disliking a group or believing that it is inherently inferior. However, it also can be subtle. Examples of subtle prejudice include the belief that a group that has been discriminated against is to blame for its own troubles; the feeling that a group protesting its subordinate status is "causing trouble"; and the practice of stereotyping, of assuming that "all of them are alike." Thus, two critical points should be kept in mind about the meaning of *prejudice*. First, the term refers to people's thinking—their attitudes and beliefs—not their behavior. Second, prejudice can be overt and very obvious or it can be subtle and indirect. A more detailed definition of racial prejudice is presented in Chapter 2; the purpose here is to distinguish it from other forms of racism.

Ideological Racism.   Closely related to the concept of prejudice is the more specific concept of **ideological racism,** or **racist ideology.** These terms refer specifically to the belief that some races are biologically, intellectually, or culturally inferior to others. The term *racism* was originally used to mean this type of ideology that views various races as superior or inferior to one another, and some social scientists continue to prefer this narrower definition. Racist ideology has been widely advocated and widely believed, particularly in Europe and North America. Frequently, such racist ideology has been elevated to the status of "scientific theory," giving rise to what has been called *scientific racism*. The idea here is that science supposedly proves that some groups are innately superior to others. It is significant that such ideologies always define the race of the "scientist" as superior. An example of this can be seen in social Darwinism, which argues on the basis of "survival of the fittest" that the wealthiest and most powerful groups are biologically the "most fit."

This ideology was widely used to justify domination and colonization of the natives of Asia, Africa, the Americas, and Oceania by white Europeans. In fact, it is an important characteristic of ideological racism that its main function is to justify domination and exploitation of one group by another by showing that group superiority/inferiority is the natural way of things (Wilson, 1973, pp. 32–35). When it has served dominant-group interests to do so, claims of innate inferiority have been made at various times in the United States against a wide variety of groups, including Irish, Italian, Polish, Portuguese, and Jewish Americans, as well as blacks, Chicanos, and American Indians. The rise of the anti-immigration and anti-Catholic Know Nothing Party around 1850 and the Ku Klux Klan in the early twentieth century marked high points of ideological racism in the United States. Elsewhere, ideological racism was at the heart of German Nazism, whose ideology consisted of beliefs that Germans were part of the superior "Aryan" race and that Jews, blacks, and others were innately inferior. Notions of racial superiority were also used by the Japanese to justify expansionism during World War II.

Despite the advocacy of scientific racism in Europe, America, and elsewhere for over a hundred years (Gobineau, 1915; Grant, 1916; Stoddard, 1920; Hitler, 1940), careful scientific analysis does not support the notion of innate biological, intellectual, cultural, temperamental, or moral superiority of any racial or ethnic group over another (see UNESCO, 1950, 1952; Montagu, 1963, 1964).[2] It is also significant that science has discredited not only the notion of racial superiority but also—as we have noted—the concept that races can even be defined on a purely biological basis. Ideological racism is best understood as a means by which members of dominant groups attempt to make acceptable their domination of other groups. Unfortunately, the stamp of science has often been used to legitimize such ideological racism.

Obviously, ideological racism is in many regards similar to some types of racial prejudice. The difference is that ideological racism has become institutionalized (in other words, it has become a widely accepted element within a culture) and/or it is used to justify behavior whereby one group dominates or exploits another. Prejudice, on the other hand, can exist in the absence of both of these conditions.

Individual Discrimination.   When we talk about discrimination, we are referring to behavior, not beliefs or attitudes. **Individual discrimination** can be defined as any behavior on the part of an individual that leads to unequal treatment on the basis of race or ethnicity. Examples could include a homeowner refusing to sell his or her home to a Jew, a taxi driver refusing to pick up blacks, or an employer paying lower wages to Chicanos than to Anglos for comparable work. The important distinction here is what people actually do—their behavior—rather than what they think. The two are not always the same.

Institutional Discrimination.   It has been pointed out by Carmichael and Hamilton (1967) that not all—and perhaps not even most—discrimination is perpetrated by individuals. Our basic **social institutions**—well established structures such as the family, the state, the educational system, the economic system, and reli-

---

[2]It is true that average scores on particular tests designed to measure intelligence and achievement vary from group to group. As we shall see in a later chapter, however, these differences are best explained by the testing process and by cultural variations between groups, rendering any one test useless as a measure for all groups.

gion, which perform basic functions in our society—play a critical role in the creation and perpetuation of racial inequality. Accordingly, we can define **institutional racism** or **institutional discrimination** as arrangements or practices in social institutions and their related organizations that tend to favor one racial or ethnic group (usually the majority group) over another. Institutional racism is sometimes conscious and deliberate, as in the legally required school segregation that existed in some southern states before the 1954 Supreme Court decision banning such segregation. Frequently, however, institutional practices develop without any conscious racist intent; nonetheless, these practices tend to place or keep minority groups in a subordinate position.

An example can be seen in today's high costs of college tuition. The cost of college is one reason that African Americans and Hispanic Americans remain less than half as likely to become college graduates as whites. College tuition is the product of a political decision that students should pay a significant part of the cost of a college education. It has not always been this way: At one time, California's public colleges were tuition-free, and high school—which early in the twentieth century was sufficient for most good jobs—has always been free. But today, students are expected to pay much of the cost of college, which has more of an impact on blacks and Hispanics because of their lower average incomes. This may not be the result of any intent to discriminate, and tuition costs keep many whites from attending college as well. The results of this policy, however, *are* discriminatory, because a higher proportion of blacks and Hispanics than of Anglos (non-Hispanic whites) are kept out of college by its high cost.

Sometimes, such unconscious institutional discrimination operates by perpetuating the effects of past, more deliberate discrimination. Minorities today have low incomes partly because of past discrimination. The cost of college thus often deprives them of education, which in turn deprives them of access to good jobs. Thus, inequality resulting from past discrimination is perpetuated.

Institutional racism—including that which is not necessarily conscious or deliberate—plays a critical role in the continuing pattern of racial and ethnic inequality in the United States. Every available measure shows significant reductions in prejudice in general and in the belief in racist ideologies in particular over the past forty years in the United States. Deliberate racial discrimination in virtually every form has been illegal for years. Yet, as indicated at the beginning of the chapter, racial inequality continues in America today, and for many minority group members, the situation is getting worse. In the judgment of the author, the explanation for this is to be found largely in our social institutions and related organizations. Thus, our concern in this book cannot focus exclusively on prejudice, racist ideology, or deliberate instances of individual discrimination. We must also examine our political, economic, educational, and other institutions to identify ways in which they unconsciously serve to perpetuate racial inequality. Without such analysis, the problem of racial inequality in the America of the 1990s can be neither understood nor effectively attacked.

SUMMARY AND CONCLUSION

In this chapter, we have examined some of the reasons for studying race relations in contemporary America and discussed some of the ways this book approaches the study of majority–minority relations. We have also defined some of the basic terms that will be encountered throughout the book. Your understanding of the terms presented in this chapter is critical, both because the terms are used throughout the book and because you must understand their meaning if you are to understand the principles of intergroup relations in later parts of the book. As you proceed through the book, you will encounter additional definitions related to each topic. The concepts presented in this chapter, however, are crucial to your understanding of virtually all topics in the book. To facilitate your understanding of the concepts presented here and in later chapters, a glossary is provided at the end of the book. The key terms that appear in boldface print in each chapter are defined in the Glossary. It is hoped that this will be a handy reference to help you keep track of concepts that are critical to your understanding of majority–minority relations.

In the next two chapters, we will be concerned primarily with the first of the four kinds of racism: racial or ethnic prejudice. We shall try to identify what causes prejudice, what can be done about it, and how it is related to the problem of racial and ethnic discrimination.

2

Prejudice: Its Forms and Causes

WHAT IS PREJUDICE?

One of the first things most people think of when they think about race and ethnic relations is *prejudice*. We are all familiar with the concept of prejudice, and we have all seen numerous examples of it, both in individuals we know and in examples from the popular media. At the most basic level, nearly everyone knows that the term **prejudice** means just what it suggests: attitudes and beliefs involving a tendency to prejudge people, usually negatively and usually on the basis of a single personal characteristic (such as race, sex, religion, hair length, etc.), without any objective basis for making such a judgment. This prejudgment takes the form of *overcategorization*—the tendency to think of or react to everyone in some category (for example, black, Chinese, female, gay) in a more or less fixed way, based on the category. Prejudice differs from objective observations about average differences among categories. It would not be prejudice, for example, to state that Mexican Americans have a higher rate of unemployment than Anglos, because that is true. It would, however, be prejudice to automatically assume that because a person is Mexican American, he or she is unemployed. Such overcategorization can take several forms, and thus there are several types of prejudice, not all of which are found in the same people. The objectives of this chapter are to investigate those different types of prejudice, illustrate some of the ways they differ, and try to find at least some tentative answers to the ever-present question, Why are people prejudiced?

FORMS OF PREJUDICE

As described in the previous chapter, prejudice is basically in the mind: The term refers not to behavior but rather to beliefs and attitudes, to what people think. What people think can be divided into at least three dimensions: what they believe is true (*cognitive*), what they like or dislike (*affective*), and how they are inclined to behave (*conative*). This suggests three types of prejudice, each slightly different from the others. Prejudice toward a group may take the form of having negative beliefs concerning what is true about a group (cognitive prejudice), disliking a group (affective prejudice), or wanting to discriminate against or show aggression toward a group (conative prejudice) (Kramer, 1949; Triandis, 1971). Although the three are related, it is quite possible for an individual to be prejudiced in one way without being prejudiced in the others (Williams, 1992; Stangor, Sullivan, and Ford, 1991). An individual might, for example, believe that most members of a particular race lack intelligence yet feel no dislike toward them and have no desire to discriminate. Or someone might dislike a particular ethnic group because he or she is in intense competition with members of the group (for scarce jobs, for example) without believing that members of the group are stupid, clannish, greedy, immoral, or anything else bad. The distinction among these types of prejudice can be important, because sometimes it is possible to reduce one type without having much effect on another. We might, for example, correct a white person's incorrect beliefs about black people without reducing his or her dislike for them. Moreover, recent research indicates that such affective prejudices may have stronger effects on people's overall racial attitudes than cognitive prejudices (Stangor, Sullivan, and Ford, 1991). The common factor in each type of prejudice—cognitive, affective, and conative—is that the beliefs, attitudes, or tendencies toward discrimination are overcategorized: They are applied to the group as a whole, without recognition of wide variations that exist in individuals in any group (Allport, 1954, chap. 1).

STEREOTYPES

Of special interest to those who study race relations is the form of cognitive prejudice called *stereotyping*. Various definitions of *stereotype* are possible, but Allport's (1954) will do quite well: A **stereotype** is an exaggerated belief associated with a category (a group of people, such as a racial, ethnic, or religious group). This short definition implies several important characteristics. First, it refers to *exaggerated* beliefs. Occasionally, groups are stereotyped in ways that bear absolutely no resemblance to reality. Often, though, there are real cultural differences between racial and ethnic groups, and some stereotypes do contain, as Allport puts it, a "kernel of truth." It is true, for example, that African Americans are more likely to support liberal political candidates than are white Americans. That does not, however, justify the stereotype that all blacks are liberals—many are not. The difference between a stereotype and a legitimate observation about group differences is that the latter allows for the considerable variation in cultural traits that occurs from one individual to another in any group; the former does not.

A second characteristic of a stereotype is that, like other forms of prejudice, it is associated with a *category* of people: blacks, whites, Jews, Americans, Germans, homosexuals, or whatever. The stereotyped thinker tends to categorize people, assuming that they have whatever characteristic he or she associates with the category. For example, if John believes that Jewish people are money-hungry (a common stereotype among people prejudiced against Jews), he will tend, more or less without thinking about it, to assume that any Jewish person he encounters is money-hungry. In other words, he has come to more or less automatically associate the characteristic "money-hungry" with the category "Jew."

Not all stereotypes are negative or derogatory. Frequently, we tend to form positive or complimentary stereotypes of our own group (what social psychologists call the **in-group**) and negative or derogatory stereotypes of groups of which we are not a member and that are different from our own (the **out-groups**). An example of this is illustrated by surveys of college students in the United States (Katz and Braly, 1933; Gilbert 1951), in which students chose highly positive adjectives to describe "Americans" but much less positive and frequently negative terms to describe "Chinese," "Jews," "Negroes," and "Turks." (Interestingly, more recent studies have shown drastic changes in these stereotyping patterns. These changes will be discussed in a later chapter.) It is also true that the identical trait may be given positive connotations for an in-group but negative connotations for an out-group. A widely used example suggested by Merton (1949, pp. 426–30) highlights the characteristics admired in Abraham Lincoln: thrift, ambition, hard work. Stereotyped thinkers often see these same characteristics in Jews, for example, or Asian Americans. In these out-groups, however, the characteristics are seen not as admirable traits but as greed, tightfistedness, pushiness, being unfairly competitive. In other words, the *same* stereotypes that make Abraham Lincoln admirable are labeled so as to make Jewish or Asian Americans objects of disdain. To summarize then, a stereotype can be either favorable or unfavorable. Frequently, we stereotype so as to create a positive image of our own group and a negative image of others—sometimes even when the stereotypes of in-groups and out-groups refer to essentially the same traits.

In some cases, stereotypes of out-groups are positive. Blacks, for example, are often stereotyped by whites as being "musical" or "good dancers." Such stereotypes, however, are at best mixed blessings for the group to which they are applied. First, they serve to rationalize the more common negative stereotypes and make the prejudiced person appear a bit more "reasonable." Second, they deny individuals in the group the freedom to be what they are, demanding instead that they live up to the stereotypical expectation. This was graphically illustrated in the television epic *Roots, Part II,* in which a black college president was made to tap dance to please a group of white benefactors.

Positive stereotypes can also be used to justify more negative ones and to channel minorities away from other areas of activity in which they could potentially excel. For example, the sports sociologist Harry Edwards (1994) has pointed out that the stereotype that blacks are superior athletes goes hand in hand with the stereotype that they are not as good as other groups at intellectual endeavors. In addition, he points out that the false belief among many young African Americans that sports is the best route to success leads many black youths to pursue sports goals that only a tiny percentage will attain while at the same time pulling young blacks away from careers such as medicine, law, economics, science, and business. Thus, Edwards argues convincingly that what many might view as a positive stereotype of African Americans has actually contributed to economic and professional underdevelopment in the black community.

CAUSES OF PREJUDICE

It has often been suggested that people form prejudices because they observe characteristics they do not like in members of the group against whom they are prejudiced; in other words, that prejudice should be explained not in terms of the characteristics of those who are prejudiced but rather in terms of the characteristics of the group they are prejudiced against. If this were true, a researcher who wanted to find out why people are prejudiced against, for example, Turks, might study Turks rather than the people who are prejudiced. There are several problems with this line of reasoning. Although it is undoubtedly true that individual encounters shape many people's thinking about out-groups, prejudice involves unfounded generalizations about groups and does not allow for individual variations within those groups. Many people may have unpleasant experiences with individual members of out-groups, but only *some* of those individuals respond with the irrational generalizations that we call prejudice. Another fact that calls into question the view that the cause of prejudice is to be found in the out-group is illustrated in a fascinating study by Hartley (1946). In this study, respondents were asked about their attitudes concerning a variety of ethnic groups, including "Danireans," "Piraneans," and "Wallonians." The study found that people who were antagonistic toward blacks and Jews were also antagonistic toward these other three groups, sometimes even advocating that restrictive measures be taken against them. The catch is that none of the three groups exist! In other words, people who are prejudiced against real groups are also quite capable of being prejudiced against nonexistent groups. This suggests very strongly that the causes of prejudice must be sought in the characteristics and experiences of those who are prejudiced—*not* in the characteristics of those they are prejudiced against.

In our discussion of causes of prejudice, we shall focus on three general kinds of theories. One of these approaches, which applies some basic ideas from Freudian psychology to the problem of prejudice, views prejudice primarily as a means of meeting the personality needs of individuals with certain kinds of experiences. A second approach views prejudice as an attitude learned from others and that develops largely out of the need to conform to group pressures. A third approach sees the source of prejudice primarily in a person's position in the larger social structure (one's economic position, for example). In the remainder of this chapter, we shall discuss and evaluate each of these three major kinds of theories about why people are prejudiced.

THEORIES ABOUT PERSONALITY AND PREJUDICE

One of the most influential studies ever done on the subject of prejudice was published in 1950 in a book by Theodor Adorno, Else Frenkel-Brunswick, and associates entitled *The Authoritarian Personality*. This book, which today remains a basic study in the understanding of prejudice, made the fundamental argument that people are prejudiced because their prejudices meet certain personality needs. The questions these researchers sought to answer were (1) Is a particular personality type associated with prejudice? and (2) If so, how is such a personality acquired?

Is Prejudice Generalized?

Adorno and his associates began with the assumption that, if there is a prejudiced personality type, it ought to be possible to show that a person prejudiced against one out-group is likely to be prejudiced against out-groups in general. In other words, if being prejudiced is a personality characteristic, as the researchers thought, we would expect that a person with this personality characteristic would be prejudiced not just against one particular out-group but against people or groups in general who are culturally or ethnically different. To test this assumption, they developed questionnaires designed to measure two forms of prejudice. One measured **anti-Semitism,** which refers to prejudice against Jews.[1] The other measured a somewhat more complex and generalized form of prejudice called *ethnocentrism.* **Ethnocentrism** refers to a tendency to view one's own group as the norm and other groups not only as different but also as strange and, usually, inferior. Thus, one's own ways of doing things are seen not only as the best but as the normal, natural way of doing things, a standard against which the ways of other groups are to be judged. (The concept of ethnocentrism is extremely important in the study of majority–minority relations and is widely utilized throughout this book.)

Both questionnaires consisted of sets of statements to which respondents could choose one of six responses ranging from strong agreement to strong disagreement. There was no "neutral" choice. The anti-Semitism, or AS, scale included such items as the following:

1. One trouble with Jewish businessmen is that they stick together and connive so that a Gentile doesn't have a fair chance in competition.
2. I can hardly imagine myself marrying a Jew.
3. No matter how Americanized a Jew may seem to be, there is always something different and strange, something basically Jewish underneath.
4. The trouble with letting Jews into a nice neighborhood is that they gradually give it a typical Jewish atmosphere.

The last item above is suggestive of the sometimes subtle nature of prejudice. Certainly it does not indicate a fierce hatred of Jewish people or a malicious intent to do harm. Nonetheless, it does reflect some deep-seated prejudices. The phrase *letting into,* for example, suggests that Gentiles are or should be in a position of greater power and also suggests a belief that Jews have a certain "pushiness" or intrusiveness. The term *nice neighborhood* suggests that the neighborhood might become otherwise if Jewish people move in, and the word *typical* is indicative of stereotyped thinking.

The ethnocentrism, or E-scale, items are of a similar nature, but they are designed to measure both the in-group's feelings of superiority and its distrust of out-groups, traits that characterize enthocentrism. Examples of items include

1. Negroes have their rights, but it is best to keep them in their own districts and schools and to avoid too much contact with whites.

[1] Actually, the term *Semitic* properly refers to a variety of people of eastern Mediterranean stock, including both Jews and Arabs, but in common usage, *anti-Semitism* has come to refer to prejudice against Jews.

2. Certain religious sects who refuse to salute the flag should be forced to conform to such a patriotic action or else be abolished.

3. America may not be perfect, but the American Way has brought us about as close as human beings can get to a perfect society.

If prejudice is a generalized attitude, as Adorno believed, then a person prejudiced against Jews would also be prejudiced against blacks, Mexican Americans, immigrants, and so on. If this were the case, we would expect two things to be true with regard to the AS and E scales. First, the E-scale (ethnocentrism) items should be highly correlated with one another, that is, a person agreeing with one of them should tend to agree with most of the rest of them. Second, we would expect that people scoring high on the AS scale would tend to score high on the E scale, and that people scoring low on one would tend to score low on the other. It turns out indeed that *both* of these things were true. In fact, a high correlation (0.80) between E-scale and AS-scale scores was obtained.[2] This finding (along with other similar findings) supports the view that prejudice is largely a personal characteristic of the prejudiced person directed at a variety of out-groups rather than an attitude resulting from a person's particular experiences with one specific group. If a person is prejudiced against one group, she or he is likely to be prejudiced to some degree against a number of groups. Although Adorno's research was done nearly fifty years ago, today's studies continue to show the same pattern. For example, recent studies have shown that prejudices against homosexuals and against people with AIDS are correlated with racial prejudice, anti-Semitism, and sexism (Ficarrotto, 1990; Larsen, Ommundsen, and Elder, 1991).

Adorno and his colleagues also developed a measure of political and economic conservatism to see if prejudice might simply be an indication of conservatism. They found that it was not. Conservative people did tend to be somewhat more prejudiced, but it was far from a perfect relationship: Some conservatives turned out to be not at all prejudiced and some liberals turned out to be quite prejudiced. More recent research findings support the view that conservatism and prejudice are clearly two different things (Sniderman et al., 1991).

The Authoritarian Personality

At this point, Adorno and his colleagues were ready to test their theory that prejudice is produced by some particular personality pattern or type. They were able to identify certain themes that appeared with some regularity in the speeches and writings of fascists and anti-Semitic agitators, and they hypothesized that these themes might be indicative of the characteristics of a prejudiced or authoritarian personality type. A questionnaire similar to the E and AS scales was developed to test for and measure this personality type. This questionnaire was called the F scale (for potential for fascism); it is now commonly referred to as the authoritarianism scale (Brown, 1965). They referred to this personality type as the authoritarian personal-

---

[2]A correlation, or correlation coefficient, is a statistical measure of the strength and direction of a relationship between any two variables that can be expressed as numbers. It can range from +1.0 (perfect positive relationship) through 0 (no relationship) to −1.0 (perfect negative relationship). Since many studies in the social sciences base their findings on correlations as weak as .20 to .40, a correlation of .80 is considered a very strong positive relationship.

ity, because they felt that people with it would be likely to support authoritarian political movements espousing prejudice, such as the Nazis in Germany, who Adorno had fled to the United States to escape. The basic characteristics Adorno believed are associated with the authoritarian personality and some of the F-scale items used to measure them follow:

1. Conventionalism: Rigid adherence to conventional values
   a. Obedience and respect for authority are the most important virtues children should learn.
   b. A person who has bad manners, habits, and breeding can hardly expect to get along with decent people.
   c. The businessman and the manufacturer are much more important to society than the artist and the professor.
2. Authoritarian submission: Uncritical acceptance of authority
   a. Every person should have complete faith in some supernatural power whose decisions he obeys without question.
   b. Young people sometimes get rebellious ideas, but as they grow up, they ought to get over them and settle down.
3. Authoritarian aggression: Aggressiveness toward people who do not conform to authority or conventional norms.
   a. An insult to our honor should always be punished.
   b. There is hardly anything lower than a person who does not feel a great love, gratitude, and respect for his parents.
4. Anti-intraception: Opposition to the subjective or imaginative; rejection of self-analysis
   a. When a person has a problem or worry, it is best for him not to think about it but to keep busy with more cheerful things.
   b. Nowadays more and more people are prying into matters that should remain personal and private.
5. Superstition and stereotypical thinking
   a. Some people are born with an urge to jump from high places.
   b. Someday it will probably be shown that astrology can explain a lot of things.
6. Concern with power and toughness
   a. An insult to our honor should always be punished.
   b. People can be divided into two distinct classes: the weak and the strong.
7. Destructiveness and cynicism
   a. Human nature being what it is, there will always be war and conflict.
   b. Familiarity breeds contempt.
8. Projectivity: Projection outward of unconscious emotions; belief that the world is a wild and dangerous place
   a. Nowadays when so many different kinds of people move around and mix together so much, a person has to protect himself especially carefully against catching an infection or disease from them.
   b. Most people don't realize how much our lives are controlled by plots hatched in secret places.
9. Exaggerated concern with sexual "goings-on"
   a. Sex crimes, such as rape and attacks on children, deserve more than imprisonment; such criminals ought to be publicly whipped or worse.

b. The wild sex life of the old Greeks and Romans was tame compared with some of the goings-on in this country, even in places where people might least expect it.

Unlike the AS scale, which measured attitudes toward Jews, and the E scale, which measured attitudes toward out-groups in general, the F scale does not attempt to measure any one type of attitude. Rather, it measures a *set* of attitudes and beliefs that do not necessarily follow *logically* from one another (one does not logically have to be superstitious to be submissive to authority) but nonetheless are believed to occur together in the same people. It is this fact that makes the F scale a *personality* measure, which the others are not; only the F scale measures a set of logically diverse or unrelated attitudes and beliefs that are nonetheless found together in the same persons. Adorno and his colleagues were able to show that the F scale was indeed a valid measure of personality: The various attitudes and beliefs measured by the scale did tend to "hang together" as they expected. Specifically, they were able to show that if a person agreed with one of the items, he or she was likely to agree with most of the rest. Furthermore, Adorno was able to show that people who scored high on the F scale were substantially more likely than others to be prejudiced: High F-scale scores tended to be strongly associated with high AS-scale (anti-Semitism) and E-scale (ethnocentrism) scores. Accordingly, Adorno had established significant evidence supporting the following generalizations:

1. Prejudice is an attitude or set of attitudes that tends to be generalized to a wide variety of out-groups rather than a specific attitudinal response based on experiences with members of a particular out-group.
2. There is a personality type (he called it the authoritarian personality) that tends to be associated with prejudice.

Explaining Prejudice: Scapegoating and Projection

It should be noted here that Adorno is not without his critics, and some of the major criticisms will be discussed as we look at other theories about the causes of prejudice. Nonetheless, it appears that Adorno was able to mount substantial, if not conclusive, evidence in support of the generalizations above. If we were to stop here, however, something would be fundamentally dissatisfying or incomplete about the knowledge. While it may be interesting (and perhaps self-satisfying to the unprejudiced person, if such exists) to know that prejudice is associated with a personality type, it leaves unanswered the basic question of how that personality type comes into being. Fortunately, Adorno did not stop with the conclusion that there is a personality type associated with prejudice. Indeed, probably the most useful—and most controversial—part of his work addresses the question of how people acquire the personality pattern associated with prejudice. Adorno's theories in this regard illustrate two of the most widely analyzed processes that lead to prejudice: *scapegoating,* or *displaced aggression,* and *projection.* **Scapegoating,** or **displaced aggression** (the terms are used almost interchangeably), refers to a tendency to take out one's feelings of frustration and aggression on someone other than the true source of the frustration. Often, this someone is an out-group or a relatively powerless minority group. The process of projection is related but somewhat different. **Projection** is a process in which one forgets about, minimizes, or denies undesirable characteristics in oneself by exaggerating those same characteristics in others. Again, the others in whom those "undesirable" characteristics are exaggerated are often members of cultural or ethnic groups other than one's own. Adorno argues—based largely on the theories of Sigmund Freud—that people with authoritarian personalities have unusually strong personality needs for scapegoating and projection. Like Freud, Adorno felt that adult personalities largely reflect childhood experiences. A major aspect of Freudian theory is the notion that people are born with strong innate needs or drives, such as aggressiveness and sexuality. Freud felt that if these drives are too severely repressed in childhood, frustrations result that remain throughout life and are reflected in adult personality problems (see Freud, 1962 [1930]).

The Development of Prejudiced Personalities

Using this as a theoretical starting point, Adorno explored the childhood experiences and the personalities of highly prejudiced and relatively unprejudiced subjects through open-ended questions and projective methods. The latter included the Thematic Apperception Test (TAT), in which subjects were shown pictures and asked to tell stories about them, and questions such as, We all have times when we feel below par. What moods or feelings are most unpleasant or disturbing to you? This part of Adorno's study revealed a number of additional findings that are useful in explaining how people may develop a personality type that predisposes them toward prejudice. Among these findings:

1. Prejudiced subjects were generally unwilling to acknowledge faults in themselves, whereas unprejudiced subjects tended to be more objective in self-evaluation, seeing both good and bad in themselves.
2. Perhaps to an even greater degree, prejudiced subjects tended to idealize their parents. These subjects appeared unable to view their parents critically; unprejudiced subjects, on the other hand, tended to be able to talk about both desirable and undesirable characteristics in their parents.
3. On those occasions when prejudiced subjects did say something that might appear critical of themselves or their parents, they tended to quickly qualify it or explain it away. In themselves, they tended to view negative qualities as coming from some external force, making statements such as "I let my carnal self get away from me," "It's the Latin in me," or "I got that from the other side of the family." When they criticized their parents, they tended to withdraw or qualify the criticism quickly: "He forced some decisions on me," followed quickly by, "but he allowed me to do as I pleased."
4. While prejudiced subjects were unlikely to see faults in themselves or their parents or quickly downplayed or explained away such faults, they were *very* likely to find faults in out-groups. Their references, for example, to "oversexed Negroes" and "pushy Jews" showed up in this open-ended part of the research as well as on the fixed-response questionnaires discussed earlier.

These four findings strongly support the notion that projection is an important process in the thinking of prejudiced people. They downplay faults in themselves and those close to them by exaggerating the same characteristics in others, particularly in others who are culturally, racially, ethnically, or religiously different. Indeed, a wide variety of research (for a thorough review, see Ehrlich, 1973) shows that people who are insecure about their own qualities or are inwardly lacking in self-esteem are the people who are most often prejudiced. It is among such people that the need for projection is likely to be greatest—particularly if they are unable to accept the negative aspects of their personalities. The relationship between feelings of insecurity and prejudice has been documented not only in the United States but in other countries as well (Sharma and Zafar, 1989). Two other findings from the subjective part of Adorno's research cast additional light on the dynamics of prejudice.

First, the responses to open-ended and projective questions indicated that the prejudiced subjects were highly concerned about status. They appeared to have a strong need to rank people and showed evidence of having learned at an early age to be very concerned about their own status. Frequently, they talked about the importance of never doing anything that would reflect negatively on their family.

Second, Adorno noticed that nearly all the prejudiced subjects came from very strict homes. As children, they had been severely punished and taught to obey without arguing or asking way.

Through these findings, Adorno and his colleagues felt that they had identified the process by which prejudiced persons develop personality needs for projection and scapegoating. The process can be sketched as follows:

1. Very strict child-rearing practices generate feelings of frustration and aggression. This occurs because of the severity of punishment and the highly restrictive rules characteristic of very strict families.
2. At the same time, children are taught strong norms (rules) about respecting authority. They are also taught to believe in the justness and legitimacy of society's ranking systems. Eventually, they come to internalize (accept in their own minds) these norms and beliefs.
3. These conditions create a situation in which feelings of frustration and aggression build up but cannot be released against the authority figures who are the source of the strict rules and severe punishment.
4. As a consequence, a process of displacement, or scapegoating, occurs: The aggression is taken out against those who are low in the individual's ranking system (racial, ethnic, or religious minorities, or other out-groups).
5. Because of the concern with ranking and the learned need to avoid bringing shame on themselves or their families, faults in the self are minimized (or the admission of them is avoided entirely) by exaggerating those faults in out-groups (this is the process of projection discussed earlier). This projection is especially noticeable in the areas of sexual behavior and aggression.

Evaluation of the Personality Theory of Prejudice

Certainly, Adorno's authoritarian personality study has been subjected to considerable criticism, both of the methods employed and the underlying theories on which they are based. Methodologically, for example, the study has been criticized because, on three of the four scales, the prejudiced or authoritarian response was always to "agree" with the statements presented. Some people, commonly known as "yeasayers," will agree with almost any statement that they are presented with (Cronbach, 1946; Babbie, 1992, p. 156). Thus, the scales to some degree probably measured yeasaying rather than prejudice or authoritarianism (Cohn, 1953; but cf. Ray, 1980). A common substantive criticism has been that the theory deals only with right-wing or fascist authoritarianism, when it may be true that those on the left— liberals and radicals—can be rigid and authoritarian, too. This has sparked consid-

Overly strict childrearing may be an important cause of the development of prejudiced personalities, because it frequently leads to a tendency toward displacement of aggression. Frequently, minority groups become scapegoats toward whom such displaced aggression is expressed.

erable sociological and psychological debate over whether there are authoritarians of the left as well as of the right (for detailed discussions of these and other criticisms, see Brown, 1965, pp. 509–44; Kirscht and Dillehay, 1967; Simpson and Yinger, 1985, pp. 78–88). Despite these criticisms, few social scientists would deny that prejudice meets basic personality needs in some individuals. It is also widely agreed that displacement, or scapegoating, and projection are important processes leading to prejudice (see, for example, Allport, 1954, chap. 21 and 24; Simpson and Yinger, 1985, pp. 73–78). Research has continued to show that authoritarian, restrictive child rearing often leads children to be more prejudiced when they grow up (Hassan, 1987; Hassan and Khalique, 1987). A need to see the world in oversimplified terms has also been clearly linked to prejudice (Hamilton, 1981). Debate continues on the precise means by which people develop authoritarian personality patterns and how such patterns contribute to prejudice. Numerous studies in a wide variety of countries and time periods, however, have linked authoritarianism with prejudice and have shown that this linkage holds for a number of different types of prejudice including racial prejudice (Morris and Heaven, 1986; Heaven and Furnham, 1987; Ray, 1988); prejudice against people with AIDS (Witt, 1989; Cunningham et al., 1991); sexism (Rigby, 1988); hostility toward the disabled (Jabin, 1987); and anti-Arab prejudice (Johnson, 1992).

The major debate today centers around the relative importance of personality needs compared with other factors in causing prejudice. One example of this can be found in the observation that people who feel insecure about their status are more likely to be prejudiced. Although this can be readily interpreted as evidence that personality problems lead to prejudice, there are other views as well. It could be argued that people who feel insecure about their status frequently *are* in more insecure social and economic positions and that they will feel (perhaps with some justification) that any gains by minority groups are likely to come at their expense rather than at the expense of those who are better off. Indeed, people who are in marginal economic positions do tend to be more prejudiced. It is also hard for personality theory to account for sudden upsurges of prejudice, such as that of anti-Semitism in Germany before and during World War II: Are we to believe that massive numbers of Germans suddenly acquired the authoritarian personality type? Although this is not plausible, some other ideas associated with this theory are: Germany had experienced defeat in World War I, followed by economic depression—certainly a situation conducive to frustration, aggression, and even collective scapegoating. In this case, however, the experiences producing these conditions occurred on a societal, not individual, scale. It is reasonable then to conclude that some of the patterns observed by Adorno may be the result of the larger social structure rather than entirely the product of individual personalities. We shall turn now to some of the other possible causes of prejudice.

SOCIAL LEARNING AND CONFORMITY AS CAUSES OF PREJUDICE

Rather than focus on the personality needs of the individual, social scientists who study social learning and conformity as causes of prejudice usually look at the social environment. Their belief is that an environment in which prejudice is the norm tends to produce prejudiced individuals—even if those individuals have no particular personality need to be prejudiced.

One way this happens is through the childhood socialization process. In a variety of ways, agents of socialization—parents, peers, schools, the media—transmit *their* values and behavior patterns to the child. One of the most important transmission processes is that of selective exposure and modeling. In this process, children are exposed to certain kinds of values and behaviors but not others. Sometimes this reflects a deliberate effort on the part of parents seeking to "protect" or shelter children. However, such exposure is often quite unintentional, reflecting homogeneity among peer groups, parents, and other agents of socialization. In any case, if a child is exposed over a long period of time to one set of values or one way of doing things, he or she is likely to eventually come to view that as the natural way or the only way. This is particularly true when the models (those from whom the values or behaviors are learned) are people with whom the child feels a close identification, such as parents or close friends (Allport, 1954; Bandura and Walters, 1963). Parents, for example, can do a great many things that a young child cannot and of course are the main source of assistance and support. Frequently, young children see their parents as all-knowing and all-powerful. Thus, the parents' prejudices are taken for truth by the children, often with very little thought or awareness that they have been taught to be prejudiced (Allport, 1954, chap. 17).

In addition to these effects of selective exposure and modeling, we may add patterns of reward and punishment. All agents of socialization reward behavior and expression of attitudes that conform to their norms and punish those that do not. As with selective exposure, these patterns of reward and punishment are sometimes very deliberate and planned but at other times very informal and impromptu. Among peer groups, it may be as simple as mild derision or "kidding" when non-conforming views are expressed. Thus, the message gets across: Conform and you will be rewarded; dissent and you will be punished. Research on moral and cognitive development of children, moreover, shows that while children may initially conform merely to get rewards or avoid punishment, they will eventually internalize (come to accept on their own) the conforming beliefs, values, and norms about behavior (Piaget, 1965 [1932]; Kohlberg, 1969).

Prejudice can be seen as just one of many kinds of beliefs and attitudes that are learned through such socialization processes as selective exposure, modeling, re-ward and punishment, and internalization. This suggests that one source of preju-dice is a prejudiced environment: families, peer groups, schools, and other places where prejudice is the norm. Children growing up in such environments are in fact likely to express considerable prejudice (see, for example, Blake and Dennis, 1943; Allport, 1954; Richert, 1974; Hassan and Khalique, 1987); to the degree that they in-ternalize prejudiced beliefs and attitudes, they may retain these biases into their adult lives. Indeed, it has been shown by numerous studies that people's ethnic atti-tudes—even in adulthood—are substantially influenced by the attitudes of their par-ents. (For a review of this literature, see Ehrlich, 1973). Of course, many other fac-tors in adult life will determine the actual level of prejudice, but it does appear that social learning from parents and other agents of childhood socialization lays a groundwork that significantly predisposes people to being prejudiced or unpreju-diced later on.

Not all social learning and pressure for conformity occur in childhood, how-ever. Indeed, social scientists today recognize that socialization is a lifelong process. Moreover, it seems fair to say that the attitudes prevailing in an adult's *present* social environment can be at least as important in shaping her or his attitudes as anything learned in childhood. Put simply, most people are concerned about what others think of them and tend to conform to gain or keep the acceptance of others. The strength of this pressure for conformity has been demonstrated in a famous experi-ment by Asch (1956) showing that people will give a description contrary to what they can plainly see if the pressure for conformity is strong enough. In Asch's ex-periment, seven confederates (the researcher's accomplices who posed as subjects) gave an obviously wrong answer concerning the relative length of lines shown to re-search subjects. When the real subjects were asked the answer, about a third of them conformed to the unanimous opinion of the others and agreed with the clearly wrong answer given by the others. (In a control group where no confederate gave a wrong answer, less than 1 percent of subjects gave wrong answers.) This tendency toward conformity has been widely confirmed by other research.

These general principles about the tendency of attitudes to conform to those of *reference others* (other people with whom we have contact, who are meaning-ful to us, and whose judgments are important to us) have been shown to be true for prejudice as well as for other types of attitudes and beliefs. This can be illustrated in several ways. First, it appears that in settings in which strong prejudice is the norm, personality factors are less valid predictors of one's level of prejudice. In the south-ern United States in the 1950s, for example, the pressure to conform was so strong that the overwhelming majority expressed prejudiced views (see, for example,

Prothro, 1952). In that setting, one definitely did not have to have an authoritarian personality to score high on a scale measuring antiblack or anti-Semitic attitudes and beliefs (Pettigrew, 1971, chap. 5). For similar reasons, authoritarian personality theory does not appear very useful for explaining racial prejudice among whites in South Africa (Louw-Potgieter, 1988).

The tendency to conform to the norms of reference others on racial and ethnic issues can also be seen in a set of studies in which college students were asked to commit themselves to public actions supporting harmonious race relations. Examples included appearing with a person of the opposite race and sex in a newspaper ad supporting tolerance, participating in a civil rights demonstration, and giving a speech on television advocating tolerance. (For examples of this type of research, see DeFleur and Westie, 1958; Fendrich, 1967; Ewens and Ehrlich, 1969). These studies found that individual attitudes and beliefs could not completely predict willingness to take such actions. Furthermore, the perceived attitudes of reference others—friends, parents, acquaintances—were a significant factor influencing such willingness. Taken together, the various studies on conformity and prejudice suggest that ethnic attitudes, beliefs, and predisposition to behave are all shaped by the dominant norms of one's reference others. In other words, they are significantly influenced by pressure for conformity.

This suggests two generalizations about prejudice. First, as we have already observed, people who grow up in social settings in which prejudice is the norm tend to be prejudiced both in childhood and in their adult lives. Second, anyone in an environment in which prejudice is the norm experiences pressure to be prejudiced. Thus, people in such settings tend to be more prejudiced than people in settings without norms favoring prejudice. There are of course rebels: Some people in prejudiced environments are unprejudiced, and some people in tolerant settings are prejudiced. Social learning and conformity clearly do not totally explain human behavior. Nonetheless, people do, in the absence of some social or psychological force to the contrary, usually tend to conform.

Personality Theory Versus Social Learning Theory

It is difficult to evaluate the relative importance of personality needs as opposed to social learning and conformity pressure as causes of prejudice. Some have suggested that social learning offers a simpler explanation for some of the relationships observed in the authoritarian-personality studies than the rather complex Freudian theories suggested by Adorno. If, as Adorno found, authoritarian people are prejudiced, and prejudiced people tend to have been raised in authoritarian homes, is it not possible that they simply learned prejudice from their parents? This is an appealing suggestion and probably is of merit in some cases. The problem with it is that some people who grow up in prejudiced homes retain their prejudices throughout life and others do not. One explanation of this is that people who have a strong personality need to be prejudiced tend to remain prejudiced even when the social environment is *not* supportive, whereas people who are prejudiced mainly for reasons of conformity tend more often to change as the environment changes. There is in fact good evidence that many people of both types exist (Pettigrew, 1976, pp. 486–89). Personality needs, then, suggest one reason why, in spite of the general tendency toward conformity, many people do not conform, even when the social environment offers clear norms.

Of course, it is more often than not true that in homes where children are strictly raised and severely punished (which leads to personality types that are prone to prejudice), the parents also tend to be more prejudiced (see, for example, Allport, 1954, chap. 18; Hassan and Khalique, 1987). Thus, both personality dynamics *and* social learning patterns tend to create prejudice in the same individuals, and it is often difficult to sort out the influences of the two factors. In spite of this difficulty, it does seem clear that prejudice that meets some basic personality needs (such as scapegoating and projection) is more difficult to change than prejudice that is mainly the result of social learning and conformity. The latter can frequently be unlearned in an unprejudiced environment; the former cannot.

Before moving on, we should point to one further pattern that suggests that neither personality theory nor social learning–conformity theory can give us the whole picture of prejudice. This pattern is easy to understand and quite well known: Various social groups differ drastically in their degree of prejudice toward groups and individuals who differ from them. Such group differences cannot be explained on the basis of individual personality differences, and social learning and conformity do not offer a very good explanation either. They can, of course, explain why people *within* a group tend to hold similar attitudes, but they cannot explain how different groups developed different attitudes and beliefs in the first place. In other words, why is it that some social, economic, cultural, and religious groups tend generally to be open and tolerant toward others, while other groups tend to be narrow and intolerant? It appears that the answer to this must be sought in variations in the collective experiences of the groups, or in the larger social structure within which the groups exist. This approach is given greater emphasis in later chapters, but we shall explore one aspect of it in the remainder of this chapter.

SOCIOECONOMIC STATUS AND PREJUDICE

One of the fundamental criteria by which people in any society tend to group themselves is socioeconomic status (often abbreviated SES). By *socioeconomic status,* we mean one's position in society's ranking system as represented particularly by such criteria as income, educational level, and occupation. It has been shown quite consistently that the various forms of prejudice are quite strongly related to socioeconomic status. Persons in lower SES groups tend to report more negative views toward out-groups, to be more ethnocentric, and to express more-stereotyped thinking (see, for example, Brown, 1965, pp. 518–23; Simpson and Yinger, 1985, pp. 66–70). Some critics of this view have suggested that the relationships researchers have found reflect sophistication more than actual prejudice: Middle- and upper-class participants in present-day social research "know better" than to make strongly or clearly prejudiced statements (Brewer and Kramer, 1985, p. 231). There are, however, several reasons to believe that the SES-prejudice relationship cannot be entirely dismissed. First, many characteristics known to be related to prejudice are also related to social class: Authoritarianism and its related dimensions, rigidity of thinking, and status concern coupled with insecurity are examples (MacKinnon and Centers, 1956; Lipset, 1959). Furthermore, there are two important ways in which socioeconomic status can logically be expected to influence levels of prejudice. The first is through the direct effects of education on prejudice, and the second concerns the nature of one's economic or social position: how secure it is and whether or not it involves the appearance or the reality of competition with other groups.

Effects of Education

Education is widely seen as a way of breaking down stereotyped, oversimplified thinking. This may directly affect how people think about out-groups, but it may also influence prejudice in other ways. As has been noted earlier, by its very nature, prejudice involves oversimplification. Prejudiced people react to others on the basis of one characteristic—race, ethnicity, gender, sexual orientation, disability, religion, or whatever. It is certainly true that if we could know everything there is to know about a person on the basis of one or more of these characteristics, our world would be tremendously simplified. Of course, reality is much more complex than that. But for people who cannot tolerate ambiguity or uncertainty, prejudice becomes a way of simplifying reality. It is no coincidence that prejudice is correlated with a lack of tolerance for ambiguity and uncertainty. And this helps to explain an important reason why education might reduce prejudice: As we become more educated, we become better able to understand complex ideas and situations, and our tolerance for complexity and ambiguity increases. On this basis alone, we might expect more educated people to be less prejudiced.

Research suggests strongly that this is the case. People with higher levels of education score lower on most measures of prejudice, although the relationship is not always strong (Allport, 1954; Bagley and Verma, 1979). Recent studies show that this relationship holds for a number of different types of prejudice, in the United States as well as in a number of other societies (Morris and Heaven, 1986; Case, Greeley, and Fuchs, 1989; Dyer, Vedlitz, and Worchel, 1989; Bolvin, Donkin, and Darling, 1990; D'Alessio and Stolzenberg, 1991; Gibson and Duch, 1992; Johnson, 1992).

Economic Insecurity and Prejudice

Prejudice can arise from both the perception of and the reality of status insecurity. If persons who feel insecure about their status are indeed more prejudiced, it is hardly surprising that persons of lower SES are more prejudiced: Their position in life is in fact more marginal and insecure than that of people who are economically "better off." As a result, they may attempt to make themselves feel better about their status by invidious comparisons with minority group members: "I may not be much, but at least I'm better than a lousy [fill in the blank]." Still another explanation for the tendency toward an inverse relationship between SES and prejudice is to be found in the structural position of the lower- or working-class person. As we shall show in considerable detail in subsequent chapters, society is organized so that most of the time it is the *least advantaged* members of the majority group who are forced to compete with minority group members for such resources as jobs, education, and housing. This view suggests that the source of working-class prejudice may not be found mainly in personality or psychological factors but rather in the fact that working-class whites are structured into competing with minorities in a way that others are not (Ransford, 1972). For this reason, lower-status members of majority groups sometimes see minorities as threats, even enemies, and develop the prejudiced attitudes consistent with that view.

Research findings are inconclusive regarding the extent to which perceived or real competition contributes to prejudice (Case, Greeley, and Fuchs, 1989; Lynch and Beer, 1990). Some studies, however, do indicate higher levels of prejudice among lower-income persons (Dyer, Vedlitz, and Worchel, 1989), and racist organizations such as the Ku Klux Klan have historically drawn most of their support from working-class and poor whites. Moreover, there is evidence that societies that provide higher levels of social and economic security to their citizens are characterized by lower levels of aggression between groups within their societies (Marmor, 1992).

SUMMARY AND CONCLUSION

In this chapter we have examined the meaning of the concept of prejudice and seen the various forms that prejudice can take. We have seen that one reason people are prejudiced is that prejudice meets some people's personality needs, which have developed as a result of certain kinds of experiences in life. Nonetheless, not all people who are prejudiced have a psychological need for prejudice: Some are prejudiced either because they learned prejudice from their parents, peers, or other agents of socialization or because they live in a social environment in which prejudice is the norm. Finally, we have introduced the idea—to be explored in greater detail in later chapters—that prejudice can be a result of one's position in the socioeconomic hierarchy. This can occur either because of effects of education, which is believed to make people more open-minded, or because of structured competition between minority groups and lower-status, majority group members. In addition, downgrading of minorities may serve the psychological function of easing dissatisfaction with one's own low status.

   This chapter has concerned itself mainly with the nature of prejudice and with its causes; the next chapter turns to two important questions about prejudice that we have not yet discussed: First, how can existing prejudice be effectively combated or reduced? Second, what is the relationship between prejudiced attitudes and discriminatory behavior?

3

Reducing Prejudice:
How Achievable?
How Important?

Having examined some of the causes of prejudice and the ways in which people become prejudiced, we shall now examine two other important issues. First, we shall examine and evaluate various approaches to combating or reducing prejudice. Second, we shall look at the relationship between prejudice and behavior and attempt to answer the question, How important is prejudice as a cause of racial and ethnic discrimination?

REDUCING PREJUDICE: SOME PRINCIPLES AND APPROACHES

Two important principles were presented in the previous chapter: (1) There are three different kinds of prejudice: cognitive (involving beliefs), affective (involving dislike), and conative (involving a desire to discriminate); and (2) prejudice of any kind has multiple causes, such as personality needs, social learning and conformity, and the nature of a society and its institutions. Taken together, these facts suggest some important principles about combating or reducing prejudice. First, no one approach is *the* solution to the problem of prejudice in society. There are simply too many kinds of prejudice, and too many reasons why people are prejudiced, for any one approach to always work. Thus, such statements as "The answer is education" or "If only people would get to know each other, they'd get along" are oversimplifications. They are true in some situations but clearly not in others.

A second general principle about combating prejudice is that the approaches that work best vary from individual to individual, depending on the *type* of prejudice and its main causes in any given case. An example may help to illustrate this. If some personality need underlies a person's prejudice, neither education nor contact with minorities is likely to reduce that prejudice. The most effective approach in such a case may be some type of individual or group therapy to resolve the personality problem causing the prejudice. If a person is prejudiced mainly as a result of social learning or pressure for conformity, however, personal therapy aimed at personality change may be quite ineffective. A better solution in this case could be either an educational effort aimed at correcting false stereotypes or an effort to change the environment to make it more conducive to open-mindedness, either by reducing pressure to discriminate or express prejudiced views or by creating counterpressure (conformity pressure can tend to make people unprejudiced as well as prejudiced). Another important situation is one in which prejudice serves mainly as a mechanism to justify or support discriminatory behavior. In this case, direct attempts to change the prejudice may not be effective at all: The behavior is the source of the problem, and it is the behavior that needs to be changed. The important point is that what works to eliminate one type of prejudice may be ineffective against another type; therefore, the approach used must always be geared to the particular situation.

We can identify at least five major approaches that are frequently suggested as possible ways of reducing racial and ethnic prejudice. These are persuasive communications, education, intergroup contact, simulation exercises, and therapy. All share the common assumption that, while prejudice may serve some important individual or social functions, it fundamentally involves invalid or irrational thinking and is therefore vulnerable to attack. In addition to examples of this shown in Chapter 2 (for example, prejudice against nonexistent groups), it has also been shown that stereotyping frequently is contradictory. Anti-Semitic persons, for example, view Jews as "pushing in where they don't belong" but also "sticking to themselves and refusing to assimilate," or as being "ruthless capitalists and unfair businessmen" but also "communistic" (Adorno et al., 1950; Allport, 1954). In theory, then, pointing out the fallacies of prejudiced thinking ought to have some potential for reducing the level of prejudice. All five methods seek to do this in some way. Therapy, in addition, may seek to resolve personality problems that may be causing prejudice. In practice, the effectiveness of each of these techniques varies widely. They can be used well or used poorly, and their effectiveness varies with different types and causes of prejudice. In the following pages, we shall discuss and evaluate each of these five approaches to the reduction of prejudice.

Persuasive Communications

A **persuasive communication** can be broadly defined as any communication—written, oral, audiovisual, or whatever—that is specifically intended to influence attitudes, beliefs, or behavior. The key defining characteristic here is intent. A speech, movie, or book clearly aimed at reducing prejudice is a persuasive communication; a college course on race relations, designed only to impart information, is not, even if it did bring about a change in students' attitudes. (Of course, this example is not an accurate description of all college courses; some are designed with the intent of changing people's minds.) Some social scientists, such as Simpson and Yinger (1985, pp. 387–90) further subdivide persuasive communications into such categories as exhortation (direct pleading or argument of a viewpoint to a person or audience) and propaganda (large-scale and organized efforts, frequently involving the mass media). Although such a distinction is useful for some purposes, the general principles regarding the effectiveness of the communication are quite similar for either type. Accordingly, in this chapter we shall treat these two subtypes together under the general heading of persuasive communications.

Perhaps the best way to begin our evaluation of persuasive communications as a means of reducing prejudice is to examine what is known about the effectiveness of persuasive communications in general. We can start with some principles that establish minimum conditions necessary for a persuasive communication to be successful (Flowerman, 1947; Hovland, Janis, and Kelley, 1953; McGuire, 1968). First, a communication must be heard and paid attention to. This is no small requirement, because in a society in which advertising and propaganda are pervasive, most people have developed considerable skill at avoiding or ignoring persuasive communications. Second, the message must be correctly understood. If a pleasant story with the moral that prejudice is bad is understood only as a pleasant story—that is, if the message about prejudice is totally missed—it cannot be effective in changing people's minds. (For recent research on message reception and persuasion, see Tesser and Shaffer, 1990; Rhodes and Wood, 1992; Eagley and Chaiken, 1993, pp. 505–7). Third, receiving the communication must in some way be a positive experience: The message must be enjoyed or seen as presenting "a good idea." Finally, the message must be retained and internalized so that the desired effect lasts more than a few minutes after the end of the communication. A failure at any one of these points means that the communication is not going to be successful in changing attitudes or beliefs. The likelihood that these conditions will be met depends on a number of factors, including (1) the source of the communication, (2) the content of the message, (3) the process in which the message is presented, and (4) the characteristics of the audience, that is, the person or persons receiving the message (Triandis, 1971).

Having outlined these general principles about persuasive communications and attitude change, we can move to several more specific observations. One is that people tend to expose themselves to messages that are consistent with what they already believe. They also tend to pay better attention to, and to retain longer, messages that support their preexisting viewpoints. These tendencies vary according to personality and situation (Triandis, 1971, chap. 6), but overall, we see, pay attention to, and remember things that reinforce what we already believe. Thus, those who are most likely to accept an antiprejudice communication tend to be people who are already least prejudiced. Furthermore, the tendency is for those who are *most* strongly prejudiced to be the least exposed and the most resistant to antiprejudice communications. The reasons for this are that people tend to dislike having their beliefs seriously challenged (so they avoid communications that do so), and they tend to resolve inconsistencies by ignoring or rationalizing away communications that are inconsistent with their attitudes and beliefs rather than by changing their thinking. Prejudiced people, moreover, frequently do not think of themselves as prejudiced and thus see the message as applicable to someone else. Moreover, as prejudices have become more subtle, such rationalizations have probably become easier (Pettigrew, 1985, p. 338). In short, attitudes tend to be resistant to change, even if they are, *logically* speaking, vulnerable to attack. Thus, the prospect for changing a strongly prejudiced person through persuasion is usually not good. The potential of persuasive communication appears to be greatest as a means of reinforcing open-mindedness in relatively unprejudiced persons. It can sometimes reduce prejudice in mildly prejudiced persons, but not usually in ones with strong prejudices (Simpson and Yinger, 1985).

A further point relating to the question of exposure is that the main sources of information for most people—books, newspapers, television, and movies—are generally privately controlled and enjoy constitutional guarantees of freedom of expression. Thus, there is no easy way to force these media to expose people to antiprejudice communications. In fact, the messages people receive tend to reflect the interests and values of those who produce the media as well as the values already present in the larger culture (since the media producers want to sell their product). The likelihood that people will be exposed to antiprejudice messages depends very much on the wishes of media owners and producers and on the general social and cultural atmosphere at any given time. It follows, unhappily, that in times when prejudice is most widespread, the media will be least likely to send antiprejudice messages.

The personality characteristics of the person receiving the message also influence the effectiveness of persuasive communication aimed at reducing prejudice. In general, people who have a strong personality need for prejudice tend to be resistant to persuasion. Such people are prejudiced mainly because prejudice serves a psychological function for them, not because they are persuaded by the logic of prejudiced arguments. There may, however, be some effective ways to use persuasion in such cases. One is to persuade the person to adopt some other viewpoint that meets his or her personality needs more effectively than prejudice, though this can in practice be difficult if the personality need is related to self-image (Triandis, 1971, p. 144), as it often is in prejudiced persons. With authoritarian personalities, another approach is to alter the source of the communication. In this case, a message from a respected authority figure might be better received than a message from some other source.

As the last illustration suggests, the source can be highly important in determining the effectiveness of antiprejudice persuasion. The prestige, credibility, attractiveness, and power of the person or source presenting the message can all influence how the message is received (DeBono and Harnish, 1988; Chebat, Filiatrault, and Perrien, 1990). Of course, the kind of speaker with prestige and power varies with the audience. For conservative whites, the American Legion has high prestige, and a message from the Legion would usually be more effective for such an audience than an identical one from the National Association For the Advancement of Colored People or the American Civil Liberties Union.

The effects of source credibility, attractiveness, and power, as well as those of message content, intensity, and approach, all vary, however, with the personality, attitudes, and experience of the person being persuaded. Among the attributes that influence how people respond to a message or its source are their degree of involvement with the issue (Chebat, Filiatrault, and Perrien, 1990), the extent to which they monitor their own thinking (DeBono and Harnish, 1988), their sense that they can control their situation (Chebat, Filiatrault, and Perrien, 1990), their degree of experience with the issue being addressed (Wu and Shaffer, 1987), the personal relevance of the issue being addressed (Petty, Cacioppo, and Goldman, 1981), and their self-esteem (Baumeister and Covington, 1985). To a large extent, the message of this research is that to maximize persuasion, the source, the approach used, and the content of a persuasive message must all to some extent be tailored to the audience. If the audience is diverse or if the person doing the persuading has limited knowledge of the audience's characteristics, it is almost inevitable that any approach to reducing prejudice through persuasion will work better for some people in the audience than for others.

Research suggests that of the various factors mentioned, the most important one for bringing about long-term attitude change is the credibility of the source (Kelman, 1958). The expertise of the source is especially influential (Cooper and Croyle, 1984, p. 418). Power is less so, because it matters only as long as the source of the message has some control over the audience. Finally, research shows that messages are especially effective when their content is unexpected, such as when a well-known segregationist argues in favor of integration (Wood and Eagley, 1981).

To summarize, antiprejudice persuasion appears to be most effective when the audience is initially not highly prejudiced, when the message is enjoyable and does not conflict with personality needs of the recipient, and when the source of the communication is seen as highly credible by the recipient. Repetition of the message over an extended period is also helpful. Research shows that getting the same message from several sources increases persuasion—if the sources are (or at least appear to be) independent of one another (Harkins and Petty, 1987). All of this suggests that the effectiveness of persuasion as a way of reducing prejudice, while variable, is quite limited, particularly among the most prejudiced people. They are least likely to be exposed to the message, and if they are exposed, they are least likely to understand it (Cooper and Jahoda, 1947; Kendall and Wolf, 1949), enjoy it, or be persuaded by it. They are particularly resistant to persuasion if their prejudices are meeting basic personality needs.

We should not conclude, however, that persuasion can never lead people to become less prejudiced. Studies have shown, for example, that people can become somewhat less prejudiced as a result of viewing a film with a theme of tolerance. In one instance, students shown a popular Hollywood movie that took a strong stand against anti-Semitism became somewhat less prejudiced against not only Jews but also blacks, even though antiblack prejudice was not dealt with in the film (Middleton, 1960). As expected, persons highly concerned about status—a characteristic associated with authoritarian personalities—were least affected by the film. There was, however, no follow-up to see whether the reduction of prejudice remained over an extended time. A similar study (Mittnick and McGinnies, 1958) indicated that, if a film was followed by a discussion of prejudice, some of the reduction in prejudice resulting from the film remained a month later.

All in all, we can conclude that persuasive communications can—under certain circumstances—lead to some reduction in prejudice and can reinforce open-mindedness in those who are already relatively unprejudiced. However, the effectiveness of this approach seems very limited when prejudice is strong and when prejudice is meeting some personality need.

Education

Intergroup education works in ways somewhat similar to persuasion, in that it imparts information that may help to break down incorrect stereotypes and irrational prejudices. Certainly, it is subject to some of the same limitations as persuasion; for example, it cannot by itself resolve personality needs that cause people to be prejudiced. The main definitional difference between persuasion and education is that education does not, per se, attempt to change people's attitudes. Its objective is to bring about learning, to impart information. As it is actually practiced, it often does have a latent objective of changing people's minds. For the purposes of definition, however, the objective of education is to teach rather than persuade. Nevertheless, in real life, much of what is called education is in fact a mixture of education and persuasion.

Many of the principles pertaining to persuasion also apply to education, but we can make some generalizations that apply specifically to education. Our focus here is mainly on education about intergroup relations; we discuss the effects of educational level later in this chapter when we examine the influence of social structure, including socioeconomic status, on intergroup relations, and in the chapter on education and intergroup relations.

One principle is that education about intergroup relations is most effective in reducing prejudice when it minimizes the stress associated with admitting previous error (this also applies to persuasion). In other words, such education should not make people feel defensive or threaten their egos. The best results are obtained if the person feels he or she is participating in the process of learning new ideas that may be contrary to old ones (Lewin, 1948; Fineberg, 1949).

Teachers, like other people, are sometimes themselves prejudiced—a fact that potentially limits the effect of intergroup-relations education. Also, minority-group members are underrepresented in the teaching profession. Although minority representation on teaching staffs improved somewhat during the 1960s and 1970s, there have been setbacks since. As other occupations have opened somewhat to people of color, fewer of them have chosen to enter the teaching profession. During the 1980s, for example, the proportion of African American elementary and secondary teachers declined, even as the proportion of African American students rose. The underrepresentation of African Americans and Hispanic Americans as college and university faculty members is even more of a problem. The evident presence of prejudice or discrimination in the teacher or a teaching staff that is all or mostly white can offset any positive effects of the educational program. Thus, it is important that minorities be appropriately represented on intergroup-relations teaching staffs and that the teachers in such courses be as free from racial and ethnic prejudices as is humanly possible. School materials must also be free of stereotypical portrayals of minorities and of the equally common pattern of ignoring minorities altogether (see, for example, Lessing and Clark, 1976). These principles apply not only to intergroup-relations courses and materials but to the entire curriculum. If the learning that occurs in the race relations course if offset by prejudiced teachers, discriminatory practices, and stereotypical books and materials elsewhere in the curriculum, it is unlikely that students will become less prejudiced.

Another problem with the use of education to reduce prejudice—particularly at the college level, where courses are frequently taken on an elective basis—is the familiar one of self-selection. People who take courses in majority–minority relations or related topics probably tend to be less prejudiced than others to begin with. Thus, as with persuasion, education frequently does not reach the most prejudiced people. A similar pattern may develop at the elementary and secondary levels, although for different reasons. At those levels, the school districts that do the most to teach intergroup relations tend to be the more liberal ones in which prejudice may be somewhat less widespread to begin with. School districts in which prejudice is more widespread (among parents as well as children) may do less to teach intergroup relations simply because the decisionmakers generally reflect those views of the people in the school district. Those residents frequently tend to view intergroup-relations education as unnecessary and perhaps even undesirable, since it detracts from time spent on "reading, writing, and arithmetic" and might lead children to develop "unconventional" ideas, ones contrary to those of their parents. *The Autobiography of Malcolm X* (Haley, 1964), for example, has been a frequent target of protesting parents who object to their children's being exposed to that important work concerning white racism, the black experience, and the Black Power movement.

Nonetheless, increasing numbers of elementary and secondary schools and colleges have been including intergroup or multicultural education as a mandatory part of their curriculum in recent years. In part, this is in response to the increasing number of racial incidents in schools and on college campuses during the late 1980s. At the elementary- and secondary-school levels, for example, programs such as A World of Difference and Teaching Tolerance have been used in a growing number of school districts to teach students about cultural differences and to encourage them to value and respect diversity (Golub, 1989).

At the college level, more and more colleges and universities have established requirements that all students take at least one course in intergroup relations or minority-group studies. Some states have passed legislation mandating that all public colleges and universities have such a requirement. These courses are designed to show why majority and minority groups often have different experiences, perceptions, and beliefs that can become sources of tension if left unaddressed. For example, students of color often experience discrimination and social isolation that white students do not experience. These differences in experiences lead to very different beliefs among minority- and majority-group students about the extent of discrimination in society and the fairness of the social system. By showing how these different experiences lead to different beliefs among students of color and white students, such courses are designed to alleviate some of the causes of tension between students of different racial and cultural backgrounds.

For the most part, research indicates that well-designed educational programs are an effective means of reducing prejudice. Early reviews of such research showed that studies that showed a reduction in prejudice outnumbered ones that did not by about two to one (Harding et al., 1969; Ashmore, 1970). More-recent studies support this conclusion, if such educational programs are comprehensive and designed to address various sources of prejudice, including personality, social structure, culture, and the environment (Lynch, 1987, 1988). Some research suggests that prejudice is most easily changed in young children (Rooney-Rebek and Jason, 1986). Common techniques used in such programs include factual teaching about race and ethnic relations; value-based approaches, including statements that prejudice and discrimination are unacceptable and will not be tolerated; experiential simulations (discussed in greater detail later in this chapter); intergroup contact; and confrontational strategies designed to bring prejudice into the open (Andreoni and Nihas, 1986; see also Beswick, 1990). Care must be taken with the latter strategy; it may be counterproductive, especially if teachers are not adequately prepared to deal with prejudiced statements by students (Fenton and Nancarrow, 1986). In some cases, education programs have also been used to reduce prejudice in teachers and to encourage them to develop multicultural skills and incorporate the experiences of diverse social groups in their classroom teaching. Evaluation studies indicate that such programs have positive effects on teachers' knowledge, attitudes, and behaviors, though the extent of these effects on different teachers varies widely (Bennett, 1989).

As it has become more common for intergroup-relations courses to be required at the college level, researchers have begun to evaluate the effects of these courses. A study of education students in a required intergroup-relations course, showed, for example, that after taking the course, students had become more supportive of policies to increase opportunities for minorities (Davine and Bills, 1992). An advantage of required college courses in intergroup relations is that they avoid the problem of self-selection discussed earlier. On the other hand, in the short term such required courses may trigger intergroup conflicts by bringing latent racial tensions to the surface. This clearly has happened on occasion. Most educators believe, however, that over the long term it is better to get the issues on the table and deal with them as fairly and sensitively as possible. Such an approach may have a long-term effect of reducing prejudices and improving intergroup relations. Moreover, if the tensions are there, it is likely that they will come to the surface in some context anyway, and the chances of addressing them effectively are greater in a classroom setting in which they can be dealt with in the presence of an instructor with training and expertise in intergroup relations. Of course, it is important to stress again that instructors must be both knowledgeable about their subject matter and free from prejudices themselves, and that the teaching staff should be diverse so that teaching occurs by example as well as through course content.

As with other methods of reducing prejudice, intergroup education appears to be most effective when prejudices are relatively mild and communities are not highly polarized and tension-ridden (Litcher and Johnson, 1969; Lessing and Clarke, 1976). And as suggested earlier, the educational approach appears to be more effective when prejudice does not arise out of personality needs. Dent (1975), for example, found that an education program in intergroup relations was somewhat effective in lowering prejudice in persons with relatively low F-scale (authoritarianism) scores, but among those with high F-scale scores, education made no significant difference. These results suggest that—like persuasion—the educational approach to reducing prejudice can be effective, but only up to a point and only in certain situations. For cases in which prejudice is strongest and most deeply entrenched, the educational approach is least effective.

Intergroup Contact

One of the remedies most frequently suggested for reducing racial and ethnic prejudices is intergroup contact. It is generally believed that intergroup contact, perhaps even more than persuasion and education, can break down people's prejudices by showing them that their stereotypes or fears about out-groups are unfounded. Indeed, some impressive findings from social science lend support to this notion (often referred to as the "contact hypothesis"). Studies have shown, for example, that people living in integrated public housing projects are less prejudiced and interact more closely with persons of the opposite race than people who live in segregated (all-white or all-black) projects (Deutsch and Collins, 1951; Wilner et al., 1955). Similar results have been obtained in studies of military personnel: It was found that a change from segregated to integrated troop units and living quarters led to substantial declines in prejudice among white soldiers (Stouffer et al., 1949; Mandelbaum, 1952). In studies of other areas of life, the results have been less consistent, but there is considerable evidence that reductions in prejudice—or increased acceptance of racial and ethnic groups other than one's own—result from contact in educational, employment, recreational, and other settings. A national survey, for example, showed that school desegregation is associated with increased racial tolerance in both blacks and whites (Scott and McPartland, 1982). One problem, however, is that increased contact in a particular setting may lead to increased acceptance only in that situation (Ashmore, 1970; Wilder and Thompson, 1980; Jackman and Crane, 1986). For example, a white person who works with black people might come to favor integrated workplaces but continue to object to integrated neighborhoods.

Contact between two racial or ethnic groups does not always lead to reduced prejudice or improved relations between the groups. An example can be seen in the intense and sometimes violent conflicts accompanying school desegregation in Boston; Louisville; Pontiac, Michigan; and elsewhere. Accordingly, research exploring the contact hypothesis has sought to identify the conditions under which contact is likely to reduce prejudice. One essential condition is *equal status*. In other words, people from the racial or ethnic groups involved must be similar in status and power and must not be in a position where one can dominate or exercise authority over the other. Persons working on the same jobs for the same pay or renting similar apartments in the same building are an example of equal-status contact. A supervisor–employee relationship is a clear case of unequal-status contact. If the people are not of equal status, contact is likely to foster resentment for those in the subordinate role and to reinforce stereotypes about group superiority and dominance, and inferiority and submission. Since in a society marked by racial inequality

Intergroup contact often leads to intergroup friendships, as with these children in a Bronx, New York, school. Under the right circumstances, such contact can lead to improved intergroup relations and to reduced prejudice. *United Nations/Marcia Weinstein.*

much intergroup contact is on an unequal basis, often the effectiveness of inter-group contact as a way of reducing prejudice is limited. In some cases, contact situations designed to create equal status fail to do so because cultural or institutionalized status differences carry over into the situation. Thus, groups designed to create equal-status, majority–minority contact frequently end up being dominated by majority group members (Cohen, 1972, 1982). Accordingly, special efforts may be necessary to ensure that truly equal status is created. Research by Cohen et al. (1976) suggests that one way to do this may be to present role models or experiences that contradict the generalized cultural pattern, such as having black students act as teachers and white students as learners in training exercises involving unfamiliar tasks or knowledge. In situations in which the minority group is perceived as academically disadvantaged, equal-status contact may be possible only if the minority group is highly influential in some other arena, such as the social. Such influence may be enhanced by minority-group teachers and administrators and by emphasis in the school on minority-group culture (Cohen, 1984).

Another essential condition is that contact be noncompetitive and non-threatening for both groups involved. Any contact that evokes fear and defensiveness runs the risk of making intergroup relations worse, not better. Racial prejudice is sometimes strong in working-class whites because they fear they will lose their jobs or lose control of their schools or neighborhoods to blacks, Chicanos, Puerto Ricans, or other minorities. Contact that intensifies such fears often makes prejudiced people even more prejudiced. Some school desegregation conflicts illustrate this. The city of Boston experienced intense conflict and a number of violent incidents during the implementation of a school desegregation plan in the mid 1970s. Although the plan involved numerous neighborhoods and schools, the violence centered around a very few schools and neighborhoods. The conflict was most intense in the white districts of South Boston, and to a lesser degree, Charlestown, East Boston, and Hyde Park, and in the black neighborhood of Roxbury. Most of these neighborhoods shared certain characteristics that explain why they experienced great turbulence while the rest of the city remained quiet. Most were poor or near-poor neighborhoods, where people had little security or control in their jobs and their economic situations. Most of them were also ethnic neighborhoods (South Boston, for example, was heavily Irish), and ethnicity formed a basis for solidarity. In addition, the neighborhoods were grossly underrepresented in the city's political and educational power structure. There was, however, a strong sense of community within the neighborhood—perhaps even a sense of "turf." Indeed, the residents (whites particularly) perceived their immediate neighborhood—symbolized by the neighborhood school—as one of the very few places where they did have control. Finally, there was a widespread belief, both among the poor blacks in Roxbury and the poor whites in South Boston and similar neighborhoods, that they were in intense job competition with the other race. As is frequently the case with the urban working and lower classes, each race tended to see the other as a threat to already-limited employment opportunities. To whites in South Boston, school desegregation took away one of the few remaining areas in which they felt they had control. When combined with their generally insecure position and their fears and prejudices toward blacks, an explosive mix was created. Antiblack feelings soared and exploded into violence. Blacks, who felt equally threatened and powerless, responded with violence of their own. The result was several mass attacks on black people in South Boston, followed by attacks on whites in Roxbury. As we shall see when we study the busing issue in a later chapter, it is questionable whether much could have been gained by including such poverty-stricken white neighborhoods in the busing plan. The particular character-istics of the neighborhoods made them ones where desegregation was viewed as an intense threat and where intergroup contact led to worse, not better, race relations, at least in the first year or two of the plan. The difference between these neighbor-hoods and most Boston neighborhoods (where little or no real conflict accompa-nied desegregation) illustrates well the point that intergroup contact must be non-competitive and nonthreatening to both groups. If this condition is not met, the contact is unlikely to lead to improved attitudes and can, in fact, make racial atti-tudes much less favorable.

Before moving on, it should be pointed out that even a situation in which intergroup contact is highly threatening to both groups does not have to remain that way forever. If the initial storm can be weathered, people can sometimes overcome their fears so that they see less threat or no threat in a particular kind of contact. An example can be seen in another northern school desegregation case, this one in Pon-tiac, Michigan. Several years before the Boston controversy, a desegregation plan that, like Boston's, involved busing was implemented in Pontiac under court order. The plan brought intense conflict, climaxed by a bombing of several school buses by Ku Klux Klan members. Within a few years, however, people had accommodated themselves to the plan, and many felt that, although they would rather have done without it, it did not really pose a great threat to the quality of their lives. Many ob-servers in the community also felt that racial conflict in Pontiac was greatly reduced in the several years following implementation of the desegregation plan. Thus, con-tact must be noncompetitive and nonthreatening if it is to lead to improved inter-group attitudes and beliefs, but what is initially a threatening contact does not always have to remain so.

Intergroup contact must also be more than superficial if it is to lead to re-duced prejudice. Studies of interracial camping situations have shown, for example, that sharing a room or tent led to a greater reduction in prejudice and stereotyping than merely playing games together. This is probably because—given their preex-isting prejudices—people tend to avoid getting to know members of the other race very well if the situation permits such avoidance. This is probably why interracial housing arrangements generally lead to a greater reduction in prejudice than other forms of contact (Harding et al., 1969).

It has become increasingly clear that the most effective contact in reducing prejudice is contact that not only meets all of the above conditions but also makes members of the two groups dependent on one another and demands cooperation. This principle was illustrated in a fascinating study by Sherif et al. (1961) known as the robbers cave experiment. Sherif and his colleagues divided a group of boys at-tending scout camp into two groups (the Rattlers and the Eagles), then placed the groups in numerous competitive and sometimes frustrating situations. In addition, situations were arranged such as one in which one group arrived first at a party and ate most of the food before the other arrived. This caused strong group identities to form within each group and considerable hostility to develop between the groups. Eventually, the experimenters ended the competition and brought the groups to-gether in noncompetitive situations. This had no effect. The groups continued to maintain their identities, and members of each remained hostile and cold toward members of the other. It was not until a third stage of the experiment that a signifi-cant change occurred. In this stage, the experimenters cleverly created situations in which members of the two groups *had* to cooperate to achieve some shared goal. For example, on a trip a truck stalled and members of both groups had to cooperate in pulling it up a hill until it would start. In another instance, the experimenters secretly disrupted the camp's water supply, and members of the two groups had to cooperate in restoring it. After a series of similar incidents, the hostility had almost entirely melted away. No longer were members of the opposite group shunned and ridiculed; instead, friendships developed between members of opposite groups. In this experiment, equal-status contact alone was not sufficient to break down the intense intergroup hostility that had developed. Only when the two groups were *interdependent* and had to cooperate did the hostilities break down.

Although the Sherif experiment involved groups "artificially" created by an experimenter rather than real racial and ethnic groups, there is ample evidence that interdependency is important in reducing real-life racial and ethnic prejudices. This is illustrated, for example, by the reductions in racial prejudice among black and white soldiers who have depended on one another in combat situations (Stouffer et al., 1949)—perhaps the prototypical case of a situation demanding cooperation for a common goal. Similarly, a series of studies has shown that use of interracial work groups whose tasks required cooperation led to improved intergroup acceptance (Johnson, Johnson, and Maruyama, 1984) and that this acceptance extends beyond the immediate work setting. A cautionary note should be added that such benefits may occur only if the task is completed successfully (Brewer and Miller, 1984). A wide variety of research since Sherif's experiment has confirmed that equal-status, cooperative intergroup contact reduces prejudice. Recent studies, for example, have shown this to be the case among young elementary-school children (Rooney-Rebek and Jason, 1986); whites who have previously indicated prejudice toward blacks (Cook, 1990); and high-school students (McWhirter et al., 1988).

To summarize, then, under the right conditions, contact can be an important force for reducing prejudice. To be effective, intergroup contact must be on an equal-status basis, it must be more than superficial, and it must be nonthreatening and noncompetitive. It is most effective when the contact is such that members of the groups must cooperate to reach some common goal. Unfortunately, much of the contact between racial and ethnic groups in America today does not meet these conditions. Moreover, because of the largely segregated nature of American social institutions, many whites have very little contact other than that of the most superficial type with minority group members.

Many of the research studies we have discussed have focused mainly on the prejudices of majority-group members. Indeed, the intergroup attitudes of whites have been studied much more extensively than those of minority-group members. This is partly because the problem of racial discrimination is by its nature mainly a majority group problem. Subordinated minorities simply do not have comparable power to discriminate, even if they are so inclined. Nonetheless, the research that has recently been undertaken in the area of minority-group attitudes has yielded some interesting findings. One is that the attitudes of blacks toward whites appear less subject to change by education (Robinson and Preston, 1976) and by intergroup contact (Ford, 1973; Robinson and Preston, 1976) than do the attitudes of whites about blacks. This could be interpreted as meaning that blacks are less flexible in their thinking than whites, but the studies suggest that other explanations are more plausible. These studies showed that blacks were less prejudiced to begin with and so had less room for improvement. It also turns out that what whites see as equal-status contact does not seem equal to blacks, who perceive—often with some basis in fact—subtle acts of condescension or superiority and dominance on the part of whites (see Cohen and Roper, 1972; Riordan and Ruggiero, 1980; Cohen, 1982). Finally, the "prejudices" among blacks turn out to be mainly the perception that whites will behave in a discriminatory, paternalistic, or egotistical manner toward blacks. Since whites have a disproportionate share of power, and since many (though certainly not all) whites do behave in these ways, the negative interracial attitudes of blacks appear to be largely a cautious approach of withholding trust until they are confident that trust is warranted. If this is prejudice, it is certainly qualitatively different from the kinds of prejudice whites frequently display toward blacks. In any case, research on minority group attitudes toward the majority group is increasingly showing that processes by which ethnic attitudes are formed and altered can be quite different for minority group members than for majority group members.

Simulation Exercises

Another approach to reducing prejudice that has come into increasing use in recent years involves simulation exercises. These sometimes combine aspects of several other techniques, including education, intergroup contact, and therapy. The exercises set up a situation in which people experience discrimination, so people learn about the feelings that result from being discriminated against, and they see in a direct way the irrationality of prejudice and discrimination. Simulation games such as Star Power and Urban Dynamics, in which people are randomly assigned to what turn out to be advantaged and disadvantaged groups, are one example of this approach. Another is the "Brown Eyes–Blue Eyes" exercise, first developed by Jane Elliott, a teacher in a small, rural, all-white town in northern Iowa. In this exercise, participants are randomly assigned to advantaged and disadvantaged groups according to eye color. Hostility and discrimination quickly develop, and people who had been friends in the past become instant enemies. The effects of the hostility created were so profound that, among Elliott's students, there were substantial increases in achievement among the advantaged group and declines among the disadvantaged group, which were reversed the next day when the groups were switched. First used with elementary-school students, this exercise has since been used by a wide variety of groups ranging from college students to prison guards. A study of the effects of this exercise among teacher education students confirmed that it reduced racial prejudice (Byrnes and Kiger, 1990). Many years after participating in the exercise, Elliott's own students said that it had had lasting effects, making them less prejudiced and more accepting of diversity (Public Broadcasting Service, 1985).

Another simulation exercise designed to reduce prejudice is one in which participants are excluded from group exercises, which simulates the exclusion that occurs with discrimination. Evaluations of this exercise with a group of eight- to ten-year-olds revealed that after being excluded, the children became more sensitive to the feelings of children from other ethnic groups (Ciullo and Troiani, 1988). While much of the research on simulation exercises is encouraging, this approach shares some of the same shortcomings as others we have examined. One is that the most prejudiced people are least likely to be involved in such exercises, unless the exercises are mandatory, as has been the case in some schools and among some public-employee groups. Another is that relatively little carefully controlled research on the long-term effects of such exercises has been done.

Therapy

To a large degree, various forms of therapy are aimed at a different kind of prejudice than are the methods previously discussed. Persuasion, education, and intergroup contact, as we have seen, all appear to be most useful when prejudice arises from causes other than personality needs. When prejudice serves mainly as a way of handling personal feelings of insecurity or low self-esteem, undermining the logic of prejudice is unlikely to have much effect. It simply does not deal with the needs and functions that prejudice serves for the person. Rather, when prejudice arises from personality needs, many social psychologists feel that some form of individual or group therapy may be the best approach. Such therapy may be aimed at resolving the personality problems that are causing the prejudice or, more conservatively, at convincing the prejudiced person that prejudice is not a rational way of dealing with one's problems and insecurities. Although there is some evidence that individual therapy can sometimes reduce prejudice (Allport, 1954, chap. 30), group therapy is most commonly used to reduce prejudice, partly because persons rarely if ever seek individual therapy primarily to change their ethnic attitudes. When individual therapy does deal with ethnic attitudes, it is usually in relation to some other problem that caused the person to seek therapy. Another reason for the emphasis on group therapy is that the intense, one-to-one, and frequently long-term interaction between patient and therapist necessary in individual therapy simply does not permit the method to reach any sizeable proportion of the large number of prejudiced persons in the population. Accordingly, group therapy is more widely used to reduce prejudice, and its use for that purpose has been more widely evaluated. There is evidence that both group therapy aimed at personality change (Haimowitz and Haimowitz, 1950; Pearl, 1954; Rubin, 1967) and group therapy that shows that prejudice is a poor way of adjusting by revealing the personality dynamics of prejudice (Katz, Sarnoff, and McClintock, 1956; Stotland, Katz, and Patchem, 1959) can be effective in reducing prejudice.

Research by Grossarth-Maticek, Eysenck, and Vetter (1989) has shown that, among people with prejudice-prone personality types, cognitive-behavior therapy aimed at changing personality patterns can reduce prejudice. Another study evaluated weekly group therapy sessions conducted in a therapeutic residential setting with nine- to sixteen-year olds who had a history of maladjustment problems. The therapy, which addressed topics such as racial tolerance, led to declines in prejudice that were sustained three and six months later and at the time the youths left the residential community (Lowenstein, 1985). Another type of therapy sometimes used to reduce prejudice is rational-emotive therapy, which uses experimental methods to help people achieve peaceful human relationships and reduce anger and hostility, which are common causes of prejudice (Ellis, 1992).

While group therapy can be effective in reducing prejudice, the effects of the therapy itself as opposed to the effects of intergroup contact occurring in the therapeutic group can be difficult to sort out. Ashmore (1970), for example, has pointed out that since groups used in many studies of group therapy are racially diverse, some of the reduction in prejudice is probably a result of the effects of intergroup contact. In some of the studies, the people in the groups were relatively well educated and may have been more motivated than the typical person to reduce their prejudices. More typically, highly prejudiced people tend to avoid any kind of therapy because they do not believe they are prejudiced and, as noted in Chapter 2, anti-

intraception is a characteristic of authoritarian personalities. Thus, even group therapy probably does not reach many of the people who need it most, and when it does,
the reasons for entering therapy may have little to do with prejudice.

Another way that has been suggested to reduce personality-related prejudice is to induce people to change their child-rearing practices. As we saw in Chapter 2, those with prejudiced personalities have frequently grown up in an overly strict,
authoritarian home. Unfortunately, however, those parents who are most authoritarian are least likely to be influenced by the child-rearing advice of psychologists
and sociologists.

Overview

We have seen that—depending on the situation, the kind of prejudice, the
reasons a person is prejudiced, and other factors—persuasion, education, contact,
simulation exercises, and therapy can be effective in reducing prejudice. None of
these approaches, however, offer great promise for making inroads on the strongest
or most deeply entrenched kinds of prejudice. Many sociologists believe that the
causes of prejudice are largely to be found in features of the larger society, such as
competition between blacks and whites for scarce jobs. These sociologists believe
that the most promising approach to reducing prejudice is to alter the features of
society that cause people to be prejudiced. This view is explored extensively in later
portions of this book.

Another, closely related, view is that prejudiced attitudes are largely produced by discriminatory behavior (Raab and Liset, 1959). According to this view,
prejudiced attitudes develop largely to support or rationalize discriminatory behavior that has become institutionalized in some social settings. According to this view,
such strategies as persuasion, therapy, and education are unlikely to succeed unless
accompanied by efforts to prevent discriminatory behavior, because it is largely the
discrimination that causes the prejudice.

A question that follows from this one is whether or not prejudice is really an
important cause of discriminatory behavior. Although it is popularly believed that
attitudes cause behavior, there is some reason to question the extent to which they
really do. In the remainder of the chapter, we shall focus on questions relating to the
importance of prejudice as a cause of discrimination and to the reverse possibility,
that discrimination may in some cases be a cause of prejudice.

HOW IMPORTANT IS PREJUDICE?

Just how important is prejudice as a cause of discriminatory behavior? A classic study
by La Piere (1934) illustrates dramatically that discrimination does not always follow
from prejudice. La Piere, a white man, traveled around the United States with a Chinese couple. They visited 66 hotels and motels and 184 restaurants. Of all the establishments, only one refused them service. Six months later, he sent a letter to each
establishment asking whether it would serve Chinese guests. Only about half answered the letter, but of those that did, 92 percent indicated that they would *not* serve
Chinese guests. (Obviously, such a response would be illegal today, but at that time
it was not.) Kutner and his colleagues (1952) obtained substantially the same results
in visits to restaurants by a group of blacks and whites. It is evident that the opera-

tors of the establishments had some racial prejudices and *preferred* not to serve Chinese Americans or blacks. When presented with an actual fact-to-face encounter, however, they did. Why is this so? There are several possibilities. Perhaps in the actual face-to-face situation, the proprietors did not have the nerve to say no. Other values—the desire to avoid a hassle or to avoid seeming unkind—may have outweighted the prejudice. Perhaps, too, the presence of a white person with the Chinese or black persons made a difference. It could be that when the operators of the establishments answered the letters, they did not envision the possibility of a racially mixed group of customers. To a prejudiced white, a Chinese person with a white person along to "keep an eye on him or her" may not have seemed as bad as a Chinese person alone.

Ironically, recent research has indicated that behavioral intentions like those measured by La Piere and Kutner may be the kind of attitudes that *best* predict behavior (Fishbein and Ajzen, 1975; Ajzen and Fishbein, 1980). Recent studies indicate a correlation of up to .70 between stated behavioral intentions and actual behavior (Sheppard, Hartwick, and Warshaw, 1988; Tesser and Shaffer, 1990). Nonetheless, even a correlation of this magnitude means that intentions predict behavior only half the time. In some cases, as demonstrated by the La Piere and Kutner studies, the specific nature of the situation in which the behavior occurs has a greater effect on behavior than plans or intentions about how to behave. In addition, generalized attitudes, such as prejudice, have been shown to be much weaker predictors of behavior, in part because they do not directly prescribe any given behavior (Eagly, 1992, pp. 695–97). Thus, it is not surprising that prejudiced attitudes—even ones that directly support discrimination—do not always lead to discrimination.

Merton's Typology on Prejudice and Discrimination

Merton (1949) developed a useful typology based on the principle that prejudice and discrimination do not always occur together. He developed four classifications concerning prejudice and discrimination (see Figure 3.1). Type 1, the unprejudiced nondiscriminator, or all-weather liberal, behaves consistently with his or her beliefs, as does Type 4, the prejudiced discriminator. Many people—perhaps most—do not fit into either of these categories, however. Some (Type 2) are fair-weather liberals: They are not prejudiced, but they discriminate anyway. Others (Type 3) are timid bigots: They are prejudiced but do not discriminate. How can the behavior of fair-weather liberals and timid bigots be explained? In both cases, the answer is likely to be found in social pressures that influence people's behavior so

Figure 3.1   Merton's Typology on Prejudice and Discrimination

	DOES NOT DISCRIMINATE	DISCRIMINATES
UNPREJUDICED	1. Unprejudiced nondiscriminator. (all-weather liberal)	2. Unprejudiced discriminator. (fair-weather liberal)
PREJUDICED	3. Prejudiced nondiscriminator. (timid bigot)	4. Prejudiced discriminator. (all-weather bigot)

that it does not always reflect their beliefs. The fair-weather liberal (unprejudiced discriminator) may discriminate because his or her friends or work associates discriminate and expect others to. It is simply easier to discriminate than to risk the ridicule or criticism that could result from doing otherwise. For fair-weather liberals, social policies that create counterpressure *not* to discriminate or that reduce the pressure to discriminate may be very effective in reducing or eliminating discriminatory behavior. Greater contact with all-weather liberals may also reduce discrimination among such people, since such contact would strengthen and reinforce their unprejudiced attitudes and perhaps make them aware of the inconsistency of their behavior. The timid bigots (prejudiced nondiscriminators) are also inconsistent in their behavior. Although they would like to discriminate, they don't because they fear running afoul of civil rights laws or, like La Piere's subjects, they are simply too uncomfortable to discriminate in the face-to-face situation. If they are businesspeople, they might avoid discrimination for fear of losing minority business. When such people have the opportunity and/or power to discriminate without suffering any consequences, they usually will—but in the face of consequences, they usually will not. Antidiscrimination laws are thus probably an important means of preventing such people from discriminating.

Very few people, of course, fit unambiguously into any one category all of the time. The lines between categories can be fuzzy, behavior often varies from one incident to the next, and both prejudice and discrimination are partly a matter of degree. Also, prejudice today is often more subtle than in the past and thus harder to detect. Even so, prejudice and discrimination do not always go together. In any particular case, the presence or absence of discrimination is influenced by a number of factors other than prejudice. The pressures of any given situation can influence behavior as much as or more than personal attitudes. Furthermore, other personal attitudes—for example, the desire to please others—may conflict with one's ethnic attitudes. How one behaves in such situations may be largely determined by which of the conflicting attitudes is stronger or more salient in the situation at hand.

Can Behavior Determine Attitudes?

We have established that attitudes do not always determine behavior. We can now go a step further and ask whether behavior can sometimes determine attitudes. A social-psychological theory known as **cognitive dissonance theory** (Festinger, 1957) is relevant to this question. Dissonance theory says that we want to believe that our behavior is consistent with our attitudes. Accordingly, if—because of social pressure or for some other reason—we repeatedly behave in a manner inconsistent with our attitudes, we tend to unconsciously change our *attitudes* so that the attitudes and behavior are again consistent. Festinger and Carlsmith (1959) found, for instance, that laboratory subjects who were asked to do a boring task and did so decided afterward that the task had really been quite interesting—even when given very little reward for doing it. Moreover, other subjects who had been paid more for doing the same task later said that it had been dull and boring. The difference was that these subjects could say "It was stupid, but I did it for the money," but the poorly paid subjects could make no such rationalization. They could either say "I did this dumb task and got almost nothing for doing it" or "That was really fun." Most chose the latter. Since Festinger's original research, a variety of studies have confirmed the principle that behavior influences attitudes. Researchers continue to debate what precise thought processes lead to such attitudinal change, but the general principle that people often change their attitudes in response to how they have already behaved has received strong support from social-psychological research (Eagly, 1992; Eagly and Chaiken, 1993).

The application of these findings to race relations can perhaps be best seen in the American South. The most dramatic declines in prejudice and discrimination in the United States since World War II have been in the South. The decline did not occur as a result of voluntary attitude change; rather, the South was more or less forced to change by federal legislation, court orders, and at times intervention of federal marshals and federal troops under the order of the president. *After* overt discrimination had been outlawed and had largely disappeared, attitudes changed to become consistent with behavior. In effect, it was easier to say "We don't discriminate because we know now that discrimination is wrong" than to say "We really want to discriminate, but we don't because the Washington bureaucrats told us we can't." Indeed, the new viewpoint even puts southerners in a position to tell whites protesting school desegregation in Boston or Michigan to "practice what you preach; we are." In fact, something very similar to that happened in the 1970s, as students from desegregated schools in North Carolina were invited to assist students in northern states adapt to school desegregation. Indeed, the experiences of the United States South since World War II seriously challenge the old truism that "legislation can't change people's minds." Although prejudice has not been eliminated in the South or elsewhere, it has been substantially reduced, and an important cause of this reduction was legislation that forced behavior to change by banning open and deliberate forms of discrimination. In short, a change in behavior led to a change in attitudes (for further discussion of these issues, see Sheatsley, 1966; Bem, 1970, pp. 68–69).

Prejudice and Discrimination in America Today

Because prejudice is not always accompanied by discrimination and because a reduction in discrimination can cause a reduction in prejudice, many social scientists believe that prejudice is not really an important cause of discrimination. More important, they argue, are characteristics of the larger society, such as the relative power and numbers of different races and ethnic groups and the degree of competition between groups for scarce resources such as jobs and housing. Furthermore, a strong argument can be made that both prejudice and open, deliberate discrimination are much less important today as causes of racial and ethnic inequality than they were in the past.

For one thing, we know that at least the more open forms of prejudice are less prevalent today. This is evident in several ways. Studies of cognitive forms of prejudice show, for example, that negative stereotyping of minority groups, once commonplace, clearly declined sharply between about 1930 and 1970. A series of studies of Princeton University students in 1933, 1951, and 1967 graphically illustrates the change. Students were given lists of traits and asked to mark those that were true of each of a variety of ethnic groups. Data from these studies showing a steady decline in negative stereotyping of blacks are presented in Table 3.1. The same studies showed similar tendencies regarding stereotypes of Chinese (sharp reductions in checking of "superstitious" and "sly"), Jews (greatly reduced tendency to mark "shrewd" and "mercenary"), and Turks (large reduction in marking of "cruel"). On

Table 3.1 Characteristics Assigned to Blacks by White Princeton University Students

	1993	1951	1967
Superstititious	84%	41%	13%
Lazy	75	31	26
Happy-go-lucky	38	17	27
Ignorant	38	24	11
Musical	26	33	47

Source: Adapted from Marvin Karlins, Thomas Coffman, and Gary Walters, "On the Fading of Social Stereotypes: Studies of Three Generations of College Students," *Journal of Personality and Social Psychology* 13:1–6. Copyright 1969 by the American Psychological Association. Reprinted by permission.

the other hand, there appears to have been an increased tendency to attribute more positive stereotypes to minority groups such as "musical" for blacks, "ambitious" for Jews, and "loyal to family ties" for Chinese. This suggests that people still think in stereotypes, but they are considerably less willing today than in the past to stereotype minority groups negatively. The opposite may be true of stereotypes of the majority group. There was a large reduction in the marking of "industrious" and "intelligent" for "Americans," and an even larger increase in marking of "materialistic" for them: By 1967, this trait was marked more than twice as often as any other. A reduction in cognitive prejudices toward minorities—at least the negative type—can also be seen in the first part of Table 3.2, which shows a huge increase in the percentage of whites agreeing that blacks are as intelligent as whites. In 1942, fewer than half of white Americans agreed with such a statement; since the mid 1950s, studies have consistently shown 70 to 80 percent of whites agreeing with it.

On the one hand, this change is encouraging because it suggests real attitude change: If you express racial stereotypes, you are more likely to anger your friends or colleagues than would have been the case fifty years ago, because more people today genuinely disapprove of racial stereotyping. On the other hand, the fact that stereotyping is less socially acceptable today leads some people to mask their stereotyped thinking. This is clear from surveys that ask about racial stereotypes in subtler ways. For example, a national survey on racial attitudes in 1990 showed reductions in prejudice compared with 1972, but it also revealed that stereotyping may be more widespread than previous surveys suggested (National Opinion Research Center, 1991). Rather than asking people to agree or disagree with a stereotype of a particular group, as earlier surveys had done, this survey asked respondents to rank various groups on a scale of one to seven on how well they fit each of six stereotypes. The result: 78 percent ranked blacks higher than whites on likelihood of preferring welfare, and 74 percent ranked Hispanics higher than whites. In sharp contrast to the findings of surveys using the old methodology, 55 percent ranked Hispanics as less intelligent than whites, and 53 percent ranked blacks as less intelligent. Blacks and Hispanics were also seen as lazier and less patriotic than whites. Thus, subtler forms of stereotyping remain much more widespread than pre-1990 surveys might suggest.

Table 3.2   Percentage of Whites Agreeing with Statements About Blacks
in U.S. National Samples

Blacks are as intelligent as whites.*	
1942:	42%
1956:	78
1976:	72
1978:	75
I would not object if a black of the same income and education as mine moved onto my block.†	
1942:	35%
1956:	51
1968:	65
1972:	84
1986–1987:	79
White children and black children should attend the same schools.††	
1942:	30%
1956:	48
1968:	60
1970:	73
1972:	84
1977:	85
1980:	87
1983:	89
Combined 1982, 1984, 1985:	91

Sources: * 1942–1956: Hyman and Sheatsley, 1964. 1976–1978: *Newsweek*, 1979.
† 1942–1968: Skolnick, 1969, pp. 179–82. 1972: R. Farley, 1977. 1986–87: Schuman and Bobo, 1988.
†† 1942–1968: Skolnick, 1969; 1970: Greeley and Sheatsley, 1971; 1972: R. Farley, 1977. 1977–1982, 85: Tuch, 1988.

Another study also suggests caution in the use of survey data on stereotyping. In this study, respondents were asked about stereotypes of "blacks," "Negroes," and "Afro-Americans." While these terms all apply to the same racial group, people responded to them differently. They were most stereotypical in their responses to blacks, least so to Afro-Americans, with responses to Negroes in between (Fairchild, 1985).

As indicated in Chapter 2, another slightly different form of prejudice is conative prejudice, a tendency to behave in a particular way toward a group. The findings in Table 3.2 show that there has been a major change here too, at least for some types of conative prejudice. Compared with the early 1940s, far fewer whites in recent years indicated a preference to discriminate in the areas of schools and housing. Note, however, that this trend occurred mainly between 1942 and 1972, with less change thereafter. A trend toward less prejudice can be seen in measures of *social distance* as well. The concept of social distance refers to a preference to avoid certain kinds of contact with minority groups. In general, the closer the contact (for example, living next door as opposed to shopping in the same store), the greater the tendency to maintain social distance or avoid contact. One commonly used measure of social distance developed by Bogardus was administered to U.S. college students in 1926, 1946, 1956, 1966, and 1977. The items on this scale range from "would marry into group" to "would debar from my nation." The results of these studies for se-lected groups are presented in Table 3.3. The larger the average social distance score shown in the table, the less accepting the students were of a group. These studies show a substantial decline in social distance for minority groups over the fifty-year period. An especially sharp decline occurred for blacks between 1966 and 1977, though, consistent with the stereotyping studies, social distance increased during that period for the dominant group (white Americans) and also increased slightly for Japanese Americans.

Trends in Prejudice Since 1980.   Some of the studies cited earlier indicate relatively little change in prejudiced attitudes after about 1972. We also noted in a previous chapter that the number of racial incidents as well as hate-group activ-ity increased during the late 1980s and early 1990s. These observations have led some researchers to question whether or not there may have been a resurgence in racial prejudice during the 1980s. Several studies have tracked trends in preju-dice during this time, and all of them suggest that this is not the case. However, there may well be some leveling off in earlier downward trends in prejudice; the ex-tent to which this appears to be the case depends on what aspects of prejudice are measured and how they are measured. Research by Firebaugh and Davis (1988) revealed that in the overall population, levels of antiblack prejudice showed a fairly steady decline from 1972 to 1984. This survey mainly used conative measures of prej-udice, measuring attitudes toward housing discrimination, willingness to invite blacks to one's home, laws on intermarriage, and so forth. Declines in prejudice occurred both because people's attitudes were changing and because less prejudiced younger generations were replacing more prejudiced older ones. However, the generational effect was bigger than the attitude change for several measures of prej-udice.

More-recent research reports (National Opinion Research Center, 1991) indicate that the trend toward reduction in some kinds of conative prejudice con-

Table 3.3   Bogardus Social-Distance Scores for Selected Groups, U.S. National Samples of College Students

	1926	*1946*	*1956*	*1966*	*1977*
White Americans	1.10	1.04	1.08	1.07	1.25
Negroes	3.28	3.60	2.74	2.56	2.03
Mexican Americans	—	2.52	2.51	2.37	2.17
American Indians	2.38	2.45	2.35	2.12	1.84
Japanese Americans	—	2.90	2.34	2.14	2.18
Mean, 30 groups	2.14*	2.12	2.08	1.92	1.93

Sources: Emory Bogardus, 1968, "Comparing Racial Distance in Ethiopia, South Africa, and the United States," *Sociology and Social Research* 52:149–156; Carolyn Owen, Howard C. Eisner, and Thomas R. McFaul, 1981, "A Half Century of Social Distance Research: National Replication of the Bogardus Studies," *Sociology and Social Research* 66:80–98.

* 28 groups in 1926.

tinued through 1990. The proportion of whites opposing laws against racial intermarriage, for example, rose to 76 percent, compared with 48 percent in 1972. Also, white support for busing to desegregate schools more than doubled, from 14 percent to 29 percent, though the majority of whites still disapproved of this policy.

A recent study used similar policy questions to measure the trend in racial attitudes of young white adults between 1984 and 1990 (Steeh and Schuman, 1992). The study showed no significant trend, either upward or downward, in racial tolerance among this group. Overall, the results of these various studies show that there was no resurgence in prejudice in the overall population during the 1980s. Whether prejudice declined or stayed the same appears to depend on what types of prejudice are measured, and how. Of course, if overall prejudice did not increase, we are faced with the question of why racial incidents and hate-group activity did increase after the mid 1980s. The answer appears to be that, for reasons we shall explore soon, prejudiced people became more comfortable or bolder about expressing and acting on their prejudices.

Symbolic Racism.   Despite these indications of declining prejudice, a case can be made that more subtle forms of prejudice remain widespread in the American population. One example is a slightly different type of conative prejudice called "symbolic racism" (Kinder and Sears, 1981) or sometimes "modern racism" (McConahay, Hardeen, and Batts, 1981). While rejecting stereotypes and blatant discrimination, this form of racism, involves opposition to any social policy that would enable minorities to escape their disadvantaged position in American society (Pettigrew, 1985). This form of prejudice appears to be based on a belief, apparently learned in childhood socialization, the blacks are getting unfair advantages that violate basic American norms such as individualism and self-reliance. A key element of this form of prejudice appears to be a denial of the presence of racial inequality in society: Kluegel and Smith (1982, 1986; Kluegel, 1990) showed that the majority of white Americans believe that blacks have equal or greater chances to get ahead in life compared with whites. In a society in which nearly one black child out of two lives in poverty (to cite just one of many relevant statistics), this belief is preposterous—yet many whites believe it anyway, apparently because it absolves whites of responsibility for problems of racial inequality. Thus, a case can be made that prejudice has changed its form but is still around, and may even be more insidious because it is less obvious.

Do Attitudes Cause Intergroup Inequality?

Attitude surveys over the past thirty years—those mentioned here and others—consistently indicate a reduction in the expression of stereotyped thinking and in the desire to openly discriminate. In spite of this change, racial and ethnic inequalities in America persist. In Chapter 8, we shall explore in detail the status of a variety of American minority groups. A fair summary of that material is that, despite improvement in some areas, very substantial inequalities persist, and in some areas there has been no real improvement. This brings us back to the question raised at the beginning of this chapter: If prejudice has declined but inequality persists, just how important can majority-group attitudes be as a cause of racial inequality? Social scientists answer this question in two ways, and there is no unanimous belief about which answer is better.

The Affirmative Answer: Attitudes Do Cause Inequality. Several kinds of arguments are made by those who support the view that white attitudes are an important cause of minority disadvantage, even today when surveys indicate that majority-group prejudices have decreased. First, people of this viewpoint are quick to point out that the prejudice has by no means been eliminated, despite the changes. The social distance scores for blacks, Chicanos, American Indians, and Japanese Americans remain much higher than those for white Americans and for European groups, despite the decreases. Furthermore, and consistent with the notion of symbolic racism, there is a notable unwillingness on the part of whites to support efforts aimed at *undoing* the effects of discrimination. Busing, and hiring and admissions programs giving preference to minorities who have been victimized by discrimination are opposed by the great majority (many surveys indicate about 80 percent) of whites. Moreover, when whites, who generally deny the existence of black disadvantage, are pressed to account for whatever disadvantage blacks do experience, they usually maintain that blacks themselves are mainly responsible, as shown in Table 3.4 (Schuman, 1975; see also Feagin, 1972). Like the belief that blacks have no disadvantage, this belief is not based in reality. The effects of growing up in poverty are alone enough to greatly reduce the opportunities one has in life, and black children are about four times as likely as white children to live below the poverty level. Rather than being based on facts, the belief that blacks are responsible for their own disadvantages appears deeply rooted in an American ideology of individualism, a belief that each individual determines his or her own situations (Sniderman and Hagen, 1985; Kluegel and Smith, 1986). Although it conflicts with reality, the belief that blacks are largely responsible for their own disadvantages appears to be shared even by a large number of blacks (Parent, 1980).

Research shows that beliefs such as these have an important effect on people's views about public policy on race relations. Recent research by Kluegel (1990) shows that when people believe that the system is fair, that is, that African Americans and Latinos have the same opportunity as white Americans, they will usually do two things. First, they will view any disadvantage minorities experience as being the minorities' own fault rather than that of white discrimination or of unfairness in the system. Second, they will oppose policies designed to increase minority opportunities, such as busing for school desegregation, affirmative action in hiring and college admissions, minority scholarships, and so forth (Kluegel, 1990; see also Sears et al., 1980; McConahay, 1982). In one regard, such reasoning seems to make sense: If the system is fair and everyone has equal opportunities, then such programs would amount to an unfair advantage for minority groups. The problem, however, is that

Table 3.4   White Opinions About Who Is Mainly to Blame for Black Disadvantage

Discrimination (by whites)	19
Negroes themselves	54
Mixture of both	19
Denied disadvantage/refused to answer	4
Don't know	4

Source: Schuman, 1975.

the system *is not* fair: As is shown in several later chapters, numerous discriminatory processes exist that make it harder for some groups to get ahead in American society than it is for the white majority group.

Of course, this does suggest a way in which attitudes might be changed so that people would be more supportive of policies to increase opportunities for minority groups: show them convincing evidence that minorities do not today enjoy equal opportunity. In my own classes and in diversity workshops. I have done this by showing a video of a series of "hidden-camera" tests for discrimination that were conducted in the St. Louis area in the early 1990s (ABC News, 1991). In these tests, a black man and a white man of similar age and education level visited a number of businesses and agencies in the St. Louis area over a period of two weeks. Every day, the camera captured incidents in which the black man was discriminated against. This happened in stores, auto dealerships, employment agencies, rental offices, and even on the streets and sidewalks of St. Louis. Before showing the video, I gave many of these groups a questionnaire similar to the one used by Kluegel (1990; Kluegel and Smith, 1986) and obtained similar results to those obtained by Kluegel: whites typically perceive the American system to be a good deal fairer than blacks perceive it to be. After viewing the video, however, many of the whites indicated that they would have answered the questionnaire differently, having observed more discrimination in the video than they had expected to see.

Opinion pools show that most whites today perceive that blacks have the same opportunities as do whites in the United States.
The Image Works/Rhoda Sidney

Beliefs that African Americans enjoy greater opportunities than they actually do have also been associated with unwillingness among some whites to vote for black political candidates (Kinder and Sears, 1981; Farley, 1992a). With a few notable exceptions, such as Carol Moseley-Braun's successful 1992 Illinois U.S. Senate campaign and the election of L. Douglas Wilder as governor of Virginia in 1989, it remains relatively uncommon for African Americans to be elected by predominantly white constituencies. In fact, Moseley-Braun is the only African American woman ever elected to the U.S. Senate, and Wilder was the first African American elected governor of any state. The reluctance of many whites to vote for black candidates in large part explains why there are only one-tenth as many elected black officials as would be expected based on the size of the black population. Thus, a strong case can be made that white attitudes, translated into votes and political pressure, still make a difference by blocking policy changes that could break the cycle of racial inequality and by limiting minority political representation.

Research also indicates that racial attitudes are an important factor influencing the behavior of whites in the workplace toward minority coworkers and subordinates (Harding et al., 1969). Since blocked mobility in the workplace—being trapped in low-status, low-paying jobs—is an important source of minority disadvantage, it appears that majority group attitudes may contribute to racial inequality in this area. Finally, research also indicates that one of the areas in which attitudes are most related to behavior toward minorities is that of friendly association (Harding et al., 1969). Prejudiced people simply avoid friendly contact with members of groups other than their own. To the degree that this promotes separate institutions and the exclusion of minorities, it may contribute to racial inequality.

All in all, it is clearly an overstatement to say that racial attitudes have no effect on racial inequality: We have seen several areas in which they do have an effect. On the other hand, how large and how important this effect is, is open to serious question. Attitudes should not be ignored as a cause of racial and ethnic inequality, but neither should they be overplayed. Other factors may be of equal or greater importance than attitudes, as we shall see in the next section.

The Negative Answer: Attitudes Are Not an Important Cause of Inequality. Social scientists who do not see individual attitudes as an important cause of inequality generally tend to see larger-scale characteristics of ethnic groups and entire societies as the main cause of inequality. This idea is explored in detail in the next few chapters; the main objective here is to outline why individual attitudes are not in this view an important cause of racial and ethnic stratification and conflict. Basically, two kinds of arguments are made, and both have already at least been hinted at. One argument centers around a fact we examined earlier in the chapter: Attitudes and beliefs often change to conform to behavior (as they have in the South since discrimination was made illegal) rather than the other way around. Social scientists who hold this view tend to ask, What came first, the attitude or the behavior? If racist attitudes develop merely as a way of rationalizing racist behavior that is already present for some other reasons, such as personal gain, then the attitudes cannot be the cause of the racist behavior; they are merely a supporting mechanism.

The other argument acknowledges that racist attitudes can sometimes lead to racist behavior but questions where the attitudes came from in the first place. If intergroup competition or social and economic insecurity, for example, are the ultimate causes of people's prejudices, then it is not productive to point fingers at prejudice as the cause of racial inequality and conflict. The cause runs deeper, Social scientists who hold this view generally tend to downplay the study of prejudice and in particular do not emphasize personality needs or social learning as the root causes of prejudice. Instead, they see prejudice, discrimination, and intergroup conflict as all being caused by larger social forces that can be understood only by being aware of how entire societies operate. Thus, to blame racial inequality entirely on prejudice is, at best, an oversimplification. Whatever importance prejudice may have, we cannot have a full understanding of majority–minority relations without also understanding how the characteristics of whole societies shape the relations between the racial and ethnic groups within them.

SUMMARY AND CONCLUSION

In the latter part of this chapter we have seen that, while there is some relationship between prejudiced attitudes and discriminatory behavior, it is far from a one-to-one relationship. In any given case, a person's prejudice is only one of several factors that determine whether or not that person actually discriminates. Moreover, at the larger societal level, there is far from a one-to-one relationship between the degree or prevalence of prejudice and the degree of actual racial inequality. Prejudices, at least of some kinds, have greatly declined in the United States compared with forty years ago, but inequality persists. Thus, factors other than prejudice may account at least for the persistence, if not the original development, of racial inequality. Finally, we have seen that attitudes sometimes change to conform to behavior rather than the other way around. For all these reasons, prejudice *alone* cannot totally explain racial and ethnic inequality and conflict. We must also look at larger societal forces, which we shall do in the next part of the book.

4

Sociological
Perspectives:
The Order
and Conflict Models

SOCIOLOGICAL VERSUS SOCIAL-PSYCHOLOGICAL
APPROACHES TO MAJORITY–MINORITY RELATIONS

In Chapters 2 and 3, we primarily employed a *social-psychological* approach to race and ethnic relations. In other words, our concern was with socially learned attitudes and beliefs in *individuals*. We looked at how individuals develop negative attitudes and beliefs concerning out-groups, how those attitudes and beliefs can be changed once they have become established, and how they relate to an individual's behavior toward out-groups. Throughout the discussion, we talked mainly about individuals: their attitudes and beliefs, their experiences, their behavior.

In this chapter, we introduce an alternative approach. This approach is **sociological** because, rather than studying individuals, it focuses on *collectivities* of people: groups and societies. It suggests that the nature of interaction between racial and ethnic groups is determined not by the characteristics of individuals in such groups but rather by the nature of the groups themselves and the society in which they are found. Those who study majority–minority relations from a sociological, or social-structural, perspective are concerned with such variables as the social, political, and economic organization of a society; the roles played by various ethnic groups within that society; the social organization within the ethnic groups; and the cultures of both the society as a whole and the various groups that compose that society.

The sociological approach assumes that the attitudes of individuals are for the most part shaped by these larger social forces and that the patterns of ethnic relations also are largely determined by such social forces. In other words, the general characteristics of a society at a given point in time, and the position of a social group (for example, Chinese-Americans) within that society determine (1) the relationship between Chinese-Americans and other groups in society, (2) the pattern of attitudes held by individual Chinese-Americans toward other groups, and (3) the attitudes of individuals elsewhere in society toward Chinese-Americans. The sociological view, then, views individual attitudes as relatively unimportant in *causing* patterns of intergroup relations to develop. Instead, it sees these patterns as caused by the nature of the society as a whole and the nature and social positions of the groups within it. Furthermore, these societal and group characteristics are viewed as the major factors determining individual attitudes. Thus, although attitudes may act to perpetuate inequalities, the ultimate cause of the attitudes is the structure of society.

Accordingly, those who take this sociological, or social-structural, approach toward studying race relations analyze groups and societies rather than individuals. They seek, first, to describe accurately the patterns of relations between the racial and ethnic groups in a society and, second, to explain the reasons for the particular pattern of relationships found in a society. In making such explanations, they emphasize characteristics of the society and characteristics and positions within society of the groups in that society—not the characteristics of individuals, which are seen for the most part as resulting from, not causing, the group- and societywide patterns.

Perhaps an example will help to illustrate this principle. Let us imagine a hypothetical society in which there are two ethnic groups—let us say Wallonians and Piraneans. The first task of a social scientist studying intergroup relations in this society would be to describe the nature of the relationship between the two ethnic groups. It might be the case, for example, that the Wallonians generally dominate the Piraneans. Most of the better jobs and positions of authority are held by Wallonians, and Wallonians have higher incomes and better education. Furthermore, although not all Wallonians are wealthy, nearly all the means of production (such as factories, land, and natural resources) are owned by Wallonians. Furthermore, Wallonians frequently discriminate against Piraneans, though there is no formal code requiring such discrimination. Sometimes the Piraneans respond to their subordinate position with organized protest, but usually they try to adapt and make the best of their situation.

The above would be an example (abbreviated and simplified) of a description of a relationship between two ethnic groups in a society. Indeed, if one were to substitute "whites" for Wallonians and "blacks" for Piraneans, the description would be similar in several regards to the relationship between blacks and whites in the United States during recent decades. As you can see, the emphasis is not on individual behavior but on group characteristics and on interaction between the two groups, including their roles and statuses in the larger society. In this case, we might summarize the relationship as being one of subtle but nonetheless real domination of one group by another, with the subordinate group responding to the domination with a mixture of protest and adaptation.

Factors Shaping Patterns of Majority–Minority Relations: The Sociological View

The next task of the sociologist is to explain the *reasons* for the particular relationship that exists in the society. These reasons would similarly be sought in the characteristics of the society and of the two ethnic groups. Among the features a sociologist would look for are the following:

1. *The basis of economic production in the society:* Is the society an industrial society? an agricultural society? a colony? Closely related, what is the level of technology and productivity in the society? Is the society highly complex and specialized or small and simple without great specialization? Such factors influence the roles that may be played by the social groups within that society and thereby influence the way the groups relate to one another.

2. *The nature of the political system:* Is it, for example, a democracy, dictatorship, or monarchy? What are the power relationships between groups? What degree of political freedom is permitted in the society?

3. *The nature of the economic system:* Is it capitalist, feudal, socialist, or some other system? Of particular importance is the overall distribution of income and wealth, particularly ownership of the basic means of production.

4. *Characteristics of other basic institutions in society:* These include religion, the family, and education.

5. *The predominant culture in the society:* Particularly relevant are the shared beliefs about reality and the value systems in the society.

6. *Internal cultural and social characteristics of the various ethnic groups that make up the society:* Examples might be the existence of aggressive or warlike values, a history of doing a certain kind of work, a shared belief in a particular religion, and so on.

7. *Historical conditions:* For example, if there are different racial or ethnic groups, did they come into contact with one another as a result of voluntary immigration, or did one group conquer or impose its rule on another?

If we wanted, then, to explain why in our imaginary society Wallonians and Piraneans relate to one another as they do, and if our approach was a sociological or social-structural one, we would ask questions such as these. All of the questions pertain to characteristics either of the society as a whole or to entire groups within that society—*not* to the characteristics of individual members of the society.

PERSPECTIVES IN SOCIOLOGY

Those who study racial and ethnic relations from a social-structural approach may be further divided into at least two differing and often clashing groups. These groups are said to represent competing *perspectives* within sociology. In this section we shall briefly explain what is meant by a perspective; in the remainder of the chapter we shall describe, illustrate, and compare the two dominant perspectives used by those who take a sociological approach to the study of majority–minority relations.

In the most literal sense, a **perspective** is a way of looking at a question or problem. In large part, that is what the term means when it is applied to sociology. A "way of looking at a problem" may, however, be broken down into at least three parts. The first part involves the questions we ask about a problem or issue. (In a sense, the "answer" we get always depends in part on the question we ask.) The second involves what we believe to be true about the issue. When we put together a complex set of propositions that we believe to be true about some topic, we say we have developed a *theory* about that topic. Ideally, a theory is testable: We can gather evidence to evaluate the degree to which it accurately describes reality. The third part of a "way of looking at a problem" often implies that we may like or dislike what we see; that is, we may believe that it is "good" or "bad." This opinion is *not* something that can be proved or disproved; it is a matter of personal preference, perhaps a personal moral code. When we talk about personal preferences and opinions that carry notions of good or bad, right or wrong, we are talking about **values.** A perspective, then, is usually composed of three elements:

1. An approach to a topic that helps to determine the kinds of questions that are asked about the topic.
2. A theory or set of theories describing what are believed to be the realities of the topic.
3. Stated or unstated values concerning potentially controversial issues related to the topic.

It is, of course, sometimes asserted that the social sciences are or should be free of values. In real life, however, this is rarely possible. Even the topic a researcher chooses and the questions he or she asks about it are always determined at least partly by personal values. Furthermore, it will become evident as we discuss and illustrate the major perspectives in sociology and how they apply to race relations that these perspectives are far from value-free. This does not imply, of course, that they are *only* value judgments or "just a matter of opinion": They do reflect actual theories about the reality of how societies in general and majority–minority relations in particular work. However, they—like most human creations—also reflect the values of the people who developed them. (For further discussion of the role of values in the sociology of majority–minority relations, see Abalos, 1986).

ORDER AND CONFLICT: TWO SOCIOLOGICAL PERSPECTIVES

In macrosociology (the study of large-scale social-structural issues), two perspectives—order and conflict—have been particularly influential. Furthermore, in the specific area of racial and ethnic relations, most social theorizing has utilized one or the other of the two perspectives or has attempted to achieve a synthesis of the two. We shall describe in general terms each of the two perspectives, then attempt to show the major ways in which each has been applied to the study of race and ethnic relations.

The Order (Functionalist) Perspective

The first perspective we will discuss is known by a variety of names. It has at various times been called the **order perspective,** the **functionalist perspective,** structural functionalism, consensus theory, equilibrium theory, and system theory. It arises largely from the theories of Emile Durkheim; however, it has been further developed and greatly elaborated on by Talcott Parsons and numerous other contemporary sociologists. As we shall also see, it has been widely applied to race and ethnic relations, particularly but not exclusively in the United States. This perspective, like others, should not be seen as one clear, unified, all-encompassing theory but rather as a set of related theories (and sometimes value judgments) arising from certain common premises. We shall attempt to state those premises as concisely as possible, keeping in mind that different theorists stress different aspects of the general perspective. In the most basic sense, the common notion underlying this perspective is that society is the way it is not by chance but for very specific reasons. Social arrangements exist because they perform some *function* for society: They meet some need of the society or somehow enable the society to operate more smoothly and efficiently than would otherwise be possible. This perspective involves a number of assumptions related to this basic premise; most important are the following:

1. Society is made up of a number of interdependent parts. The functioning of society depends on the operation and coordination of all these interdependent segments. Because different parts of society depend on one another, a change at one point in society will have impacts elsewhere. This is especially true in large, modern, complex, specialized societies.

2. Every element of society performs some function for the social system: Somehow, it meets a need or contributes to making the system work or holding it together. A frequently unstated but implicit notion is that society usually tends to work for the greatest good of the largest number of its members.

3. Societies tend toward stability and equilibrium. This is the case because each part of society is performing a function (making a contribution to society) and is interrelated with other parts. A drastic change anywhere would usually be dysfunctional for the entire system (preventing it from meeting its basic needs).

4. Society tends toward consensus, at least on certain basic values. This consensus is necessary for cooperation, which in turn is necessary because the people and groups in the social system depend on one another to meet their basic needs.

5. Consensus and stability are desirable in society (a value judgment) because they facilitate the cooperation necessary to meet individual, group, and system needs.

In large part because of the final assumption, the order, or functionalist, perspective is frequently associated with political conservatism, or at most with a cautious type of liberalism advocating minor adjustment but not wholesale change in the social, political, and economic system. Because of its emphasis on stability and its belief that social structure as it is meets basic social needs, the order perspective frequently values stability over social equality, the attainment of which often requires conflict, change, and struggle. For this reason, critics point out that the perspective reflects certain values as well as sociological theory (see, for example, Horton, 1966), even though some of its proponents purport it to be value-free. The functionalist perspective was dominant throughout much of the history of American sociology, particularly from the end of World War II into the early 1960s. For a variety of reasons, however, including the fact that order theory did not predict (and had a hard time explaining) the social upheavals of the 1960s and early 1970s, its alternative, the conflict perspective, was "rediscovered" in the 1960s and has taken on increased importance in American sociology since then. It has become particularly influential in the study of race and ethnic relations.

The Conflict Perspective

The major competing approach to the order perspective is known as the **conflict perspective.** This approach arises largely, though not entirely, out of the theories of Karl Marx and has been elaborated on by such modern sociologists as C. Wright Mills and Ralf Dahrendorf. As with the order approach, the conflict perspective is best seen not as one unified, totally coherent theory but as a set of related theories that share certain common premises and assumptions. The basic premise underlying this approach is that society is made up of groups with conflicting self-interests. Often, one such group dominates, and society in that case takes on the form that best serves the interests of that dominant group. The conflict perspective involves the following assumptions:

1. Conflict is built into society; that is, societies naturally tend toward conflict. This is because wealth and power are distributed unequally; therefore, different social groups have different and conflicting self-interests.

2. Because competing interest groups have unequal power, one group usually becomes dominant. This group uses its power so that most or all aspects of the social structure operate in a way that serves its interest. As a result, this group (usually small relative to the entire population) controls a vastly disproportionate share of such scarce resources as wealth and social status.

3. When consensus does appear in society, it is artificial and unlikely to persist over the long run. The usual causes of apparent consensus in society are either coercion and repression by the dominant group or an acceptance by disadvantaged groups of ideologies not in their self-interest. The latter occurs because dominant groups exert disproportionate control over the sources of influence over public opinion. In either case, the consensus lacks a fundamental stability and is unlikely to persist over the longer run.

4. Conflict in society is desirable (a value judgment) because it makes possible social change, which may lead to a more equitable distribution of wealth and power.

As can be seen from the last assumption, the conflict perspective also makes value judgments. Because social change and equality are valued over stability, the conflict perspective tends toward a radical (or at the very least, strongly reformist) political orientation: It argues that if the social structure promotes the interests of a dominant few at the expense of others, it must be changed—often in very basic and fundamental ways.

As noted, one social theorist, Karl Marx, has had an especially strong influence on the conflict perspective. Although by no means are all conflict-oriented theories based on Marx's thought, his theories are relevant to race and ethnic relations, and they have influenced many modern conflict theories. Hence, some elaboration of these theories appears useful. A central assumption of Marxist theory is that the distribution of wealth by and large determines other aspects of society, such as the political system and the culture, including social norms, values, and beliefs (Marx, 1964, 1967, [1867–1894], 1971 [1859]), which Marx referred to as *ideology*. In particular, Marx focused on ownership of the **means of production** by which he meant whatever one had to own or control to produce things of economic value. This varies with technology and the system of production. For example, in an agricultural society the means of production is mainly land; in an industrial society it is *capital;* ownership of factories, stores, natural resources, and such, or the money with which to purchase them. According to Marx, then, the political system, social institutions, and culture all tend to support the economic system: Specifically, they serve the interests of those who control the means of production. In effect, the system by which wealth (means of production) is distributed determines the political system, social institutions, and culture. These in turn support and reinforce the economic system and protect the interests of those who control the means of production.

Consider the following example of this principle. In the Middle Ages, there was a common religious belief known as the divine right of kings. According to this principle, kings were appointed to their royal positions through the will of God. Ac-

Some sociologists would look at this picture and see cooperation, exchange, and interdependency. Others would look at it and see unequal power, possibly even domination. What do you see? *Photo Researchers, Inc./Guy Gillette, 1990*

cordingly, anyone who challenged the right of a king to rule, or objected to the system of royalty and nobility, was opposing the will of God. In effect, the royalty and nobility, who amassed wealth by controlling the means of production (land), were able to create an ideology—the divine right of kings—that served their own economic interests. Furthermore, this belief was generally accepted in the societies of the time—even by the peasant class, which provided the labor that enriched the landowners but provided very little reward for its members.

According to Marx and his followers, this pattern of a subordinate group's acceptance of an ideology that goes against its own self-interest is not unusual. It is, in fact, common enough that they have a name for it—**false consciousness.** The existence of false consciousness among subordinate groups is not limited to societies in the past. In fact, an example can be seen in recent American history. In the 1972 presidential election, the Democratic candidate, Senator George McGovern, proposed a 100 percent tax on all inheritance over $500,000—an amount equivalent in purchasing power to $1.6 million today. The practical effect of the proposal would have been to make that the maximum amount an individual could inherit. Although this would have sharply limited the perpetuation of concentrated wealth through inheritance and would probably have benefited the working class through lower taxes or improved services, the *strongest* opposition to it came not from the elite, which had the most to lose, but from the working class, which stood to gain (Dushkin Publishing Group, 1977). Apparently, blue-collar workers wanted to *believe* they had the chance of amassing such a fortune and passing it along to their children—even though the real chance of any particular blue-collar worker ever attaining such wealth was very close to zero. The consequence, of course, is that the attitudes of the masses helped to preserve the right of a very wealthy few to pass their wealth down from generation to generation.

A Comparison

Before moving on to apply the order and conflict perspectives more specifically to majority–minority relations, several general observations will be useful. First, the two are in many ways competing perspectives. The order approach sees society as basically stable and orderly, arranged in ways that meet its basic needs and marked by value consensus. The conflict approach, on the other hand, sees society as being arranged in ways that meet the needs of a powerful few, often marked by sharply conflicting values and power conflicts that arise from the unequal distribution of resources. Conflict theorists believe that because of these struggles, society tends toward change, sometimes drastic change. Furthermore, the two approaches often involve conflicting values and political orientations. Nonetheless, the fact that the two perspectives frequently compete and disagree does not necessarily make them completely incompatible—a fact that leading social theorists increasingly emphasize (Williams, 1977; Schermerhorn, 1978). This is true in several ways. First, it is quite possible that any given aspect of social structure or of culture may operate the way both perspectives say it should. It other words, it may *both* meet some need—say, contributing to overall efficiency—of the society as a whole *and* tend to keep wealth and power in the hands of a few. The task of the serious researcher is to try to answer the question, How much of each? and to identify the process by which it works both ways. Second, it is evident even to a casual student of history that in any given society—take the United States as an example—there are periods of relative stability and periods marked by conflict and upheaval. Obviously, then, there are both forces for stability and forces for change at work in the same society, albeit in different amounts at different times. Again, then, the task of the serious student of society is to identify these forces and determine why some predominate at one time and others predominate at another time. Similarly, some societies have relatively equal intergroup relations; others are marked by brutal exploitation and intense conflict. Again, it becomes a matter of identifying basic differences that cause one society to have peace and the other to have conflict. Throughout much of the rest of this book, we will engage in analyses such as those described previously, using the order and conflict approaches together to identify the basic dynamics of interaction between different racial and ethnic groups in different societies. Because it is anticipated that most readers of this book will be Americans, the greatest emphasis is on intergroup relations in the United States.

THE SOCIAL-STRUCTURAL PERSPECTIVES AND SOCIAL PROBLEMS

The sociology of racial and ethnic relations is viewed by many sociologists as one part of a somewhat larger area: the study of social problems. We, too, shall begin our study of how the order and conflict perspectives are applied to intergroup relations by determining how they apply more generally to the study of social problems. In the study of social problems, the two perspectives tend strongly toward disagreement in two particular areas. One is in the *definition* of social problems, which is mostly a matter of values; the other is in the *location*, or *cause*, of social problems, which is—or should be—an issue of scientific theory and empirical research.

The Definition of Social Problems

When we talk about defining social problems, we simply mean asking, What is considered to be a problem? At this point, we are primarily talking about a value judgment: Something is a problem if it has (or can be expected to have) some consequence that people don't like or consider undesirable (for elaboration, see Farley, 1992b, chap. 1). What people "don't like" is not always the same, however. On the one hand, it is primarily the human reaction to some fact or event (i.e., a substantial number of people "do not like" its consequences) that makes it a problem. However, this reaction is not the same for everyone. Some people may see a condition as a social problem, while others do not. Such disagreement often occurs among sociologists of the order and conflict perspectives. What the order perspective sees as a social problem is not necessarily a problem from the conflict perspective. Furthermore, even when both agree that something is a problem, they may not agree on *how serious* that problem is, or even *why* it is a problem.

In general, to the order, or functionalist, sociologist, the most serious social problems are those that threaten the smooth or efficient functioning of society or that threaten to cause such drastic social change that a new, less well adapted form of society may result. For this reason, social protest—especially if it is violent or demands radical change—is seen as potentially a very serious problem. Conflict in society is usually seen as a problem for the same reason (for an example of this viewpoint, see Lipset and Raab's 1973 analysis of social conflicts underlying the Watergate case). To the conflict sociologist, on the other hand, the most serious social problems involve such concerns as poverty, racism, and, more generally, exploitation of subordinate groups and inequitable distributions of scarce resources. Conflict and social movements are generally *not* considered significant social problems. In part, this is because conflict and change are seen as built into society. Conflict theorists view conflict as an ordinary part of society that does not threaten the existence of a smoothly operating society. More fundamentally, however, the conflict theorist believes *only* conflict and change can bring about a fairer and more equitable distribution of resources. For this reason, then, many conflict theorists view protest and conflict as *desirable,* offering the possibility of reducing the social inequality that the conflict theorist usually sees as the most serious social problem.

The Location of Social Problems

While the definition of social problems is mainly a matter of values, the *location* of social problems involves a theoretical or empirical question: Where should we look to find the source of a social problem? or, put differently, What is the *cause* of some phenomenon that we have decided is a problem? Since this is a *factual* question, it is—in the ideal sense—a theoretical–empirical question not a matter of values. However, values still have some influence. First, one can look in different places or ask different questions in seeking the cause of some social problem. An order sociologist and a conflict sociologist probably would begin their analysis of a problem by asking different questions. Second, almost any problem in real life has multiple causes, and functionalists and conflict theorists are apt to emphasize different causes.

Concretely, the major differences between the order and conflict perspectives concerning the location of social problems can be summarized as follows: The order, or functionalist, sociologist tends to seek the causes of a social problem mainly in the characteristics of a disadvantaged group. Such a group might be disadvantaged because it collectively *lacks* the necessary skills to perform a function for which it would be rewarded, or perhaps because its culture is incompatible with the general culture that exists in a society. In each case, the burden of change is placed mainly on the disadvantaged group, not on the dominant group, and certainly not on the society as a whole. In fact, the functionalist would counsel *against* major changes in the society itself: The society is the way it is because it works well that way (its various elements perform functions necessary to the system as a whole), and if it is substantially changed, this functioning is likely to be disrupted or impaired.

The conflict theorist, on the other hand, does not seek the source of social problems in the characteristics of disadvantaged groups. These groups are seen as the victims of exploitation by the powerful: Seeking the causes of social problems in these subordinate groups is somewhat akin to blaming the victim of a crime for the crime (for a forceful statement of this view, see Ryan, 1971). In the view of the conflict theorist, the source of social problems is to be found in the exploitative behavior of the dominant or ruling class: It is assumed that if someone is suffering or placed in a disadvantaged position, more than likely someone else more powerful is benefiting from it (see, for example, Gans's 1971 analysis of who benefits from poverty). Furthermore, since, as we have seen, conflict theorists frequently assume that a society's institutions are arranged so that they serve the needs of the dominant elite, these institutions are seen as an important source of the problem. If such social problems as poverty and racism are to be effectively combated, argue conflict sociologists, the only workable solution is to make fundamental changes in the social, political, and economic institutions that are believed to be an important source of the problems.

With regard to the location of social problems, the positions argued by the order and conflict perspectives are, at least in theory, empirically testable. A supporter of the functionalist view should be able to identify what characteristics of a subordinate group cause it to be disadvantaged, to show that these are genuine characteristics of the group, and to demonstrate how these characteristics place the group at a disadvantage. A conflict theorist should be able to show that someone else is indeed benefiting from the disadvantaged position of a subordinate group and to show the means by which social institutions actually work both to benefit the dominant group and to hold down the subordinate group. Of course, supporters of each view will frequently advance their position by trying to disprove arguments made in support of the opposite view. Once again, it should be emphasized that in most instances, neither one perspective nor the other is "totally right." Social problems may well be caused in part by the behavior of subordinate groups and in part by the behavior of dominant groups and by the structure of society's institutions. The job of the researcher is to answer the question, How much of each, and in what ways? The present state of sociological knowledge about the answer leaves room for a spirited debate between functionalist and conflict sociologists. In the remainder of this chapter, we shall examine this debate as it applies to race and ethnic relations.

THE SOCIAL-STRUCTURAL PERSPECTIVES AND MAJORITY–MINORITY RELATIONS

As was the case when we spoke of social problems in the more general sense, we can best start a discussion of the order and conflict approaches to majority–minority relations by looking at their definitions of the problem. In other words, *why* do majority–minority relations constitute a social problem? (Keep in mind that when we talk about *definitions* of social problems, we are primarily talking about value judgments.) Before we address this question, we should stress that the different answers given by the order, or functionalist, and conflict perspectives are more a matter of *emphasis* than of total disagreement. In general, however, functionalist sociologists tend to be *most* concerned about majority–minority problems because of their potential for serious disruption—and in severe cases, even the destruction—of society. In other words, it is simply not rational or functional for society to become severely divided along lines of race, ethnicity, or religion. When such division becomes sufficiently deep, a society can simply no longer function normally. One might point to Northern Ireland, Lebanon, Bosnia–Herzegovina, the former Soviet Union, or Rwanda in recent years as examples to support this viewpoint.

Conflict theorists tend to see majority–minority relations as a source of social problems for somewhat different reasons. The conflict sociologist looks at majority–minority relations as a case of domination and exploitation. The problem is that the majority group—or some elite within the majority group—enhances its own position by placing or keeping the minority group in a disadvantaged position. The conflict sociologist is likely to view intergroup relations as a problem because the minority group is treated unfairly or because its members are harmed by the exploitative behavior of the dominant group. From this perspective, racial or ethnic conflict is often seen as desirable because the position of the minority group may be improved through such conflict.

We turn now to the actual theories about intergroup relations the two sociological perspectives offer. Of all the substantive areas in sociology, race and ethnic relations is one of the areas in which the two theoretical perspectives have been most widely applied. As with other areas in sociology, the order, or functionalist, approach to race and ethnic relations was the much more widely used of the two, especially in American sociology, until the changes of the 1960s challenged many assumptions of this approach. This is not to say that the conflict approach had no adherents; some important analyses of intergroup relations did use this approach (see, for example, Cox, 1948). On the whole, however, approaches to the study of intergroup relations using the conflict perspective have been much more common since the mid 1960s. Today, it is fair to say that in the area of race and ethnic relations, each approach has many adherents, though the conflict approach probably predominates. At the same time, there is also a large and growing number of sociologists attempting to achieve a synthesis of the two approaches.

Functionalist Theories About Majority–Minority Relations

Such phenomena as racial and ethnic inequality, prejudice, and ethnocentrism can be explained along quite different lines, depending on one's theoretical perspective. Let us first examine the approach taken by the order, or functionalist, perspective. We shall begin with the example of *ethnic stratification*. By **ethnic stratification,** or **ethnic inequality,** we mean any system that distributes scarce resources (such as wealth, income, and power) on an unequal basis according to race or ethnicity. *Racial inequality* is a special case of ethnic stratification in which the inequality is based on race. While the conflict theorist tends to see such inequality as mainly a case of domination and exploitation, the functionalist is more likely to suggest that if a society has ethnic inequality, one of two conditions is present. Either (1) the inequality itself is meeting some kind of social need in the society, or more likely,

(2) the inequality is a result of some social condition that is in some way useful to the society.

We can start by examining social inequality in the *general* sense (that is, stratification or inequality not necessarily based on race or ethnicity). In one of the best-known (and most controversial) sociological articles ever written, Davis and Moore (1945) presented a functionalist theory of stratification (social inequality). They argued that the existence of social inequality is necessary to create incentives. Some jobs are more critical to the functioning of society and require longer, more difficult periods of training than others. To ensure that these more critical and more demanding jobs are filled by competent individuals, they must carry greater rewards. Accordingly, socioeconomic inequality is necessary and inevitable in a modern society. This, of course, does not explain why stratification should occur on the basis of race or ethnicity (in fact, we will see later that it suggests this should *not* be the case), but it does clearly suggest that any modern society needs and will tend to have socioeconomic inequality.

Taking it as a given (from the functionalist perspective) that a society will have socioeconomic inequality, we still face the question of why that inequality falls along the lines of race. There are several reasons why this may be the case, according to sociologists who identify with the functionalist perspective. One argument suggests that ethnic minorities fill an important need in society by their willingness to work at jobs and/or wages that are unattractive to others. This may be particularly true of immigrant minorities who view such positions as better than those available in their place of origin; the same argument is applied to rural migrants to the city. Were it not for such minorities, these jobs—ones that need to be done but are unattractive—would go unfilled.

An example of this can be seen in Germany's guest-worker program. Germans—particularly those from what used to be West Germany—have enjoyed a high standard of living and have often been unwilling to work low-wage jobs. To get certain jobs done that native Germans were not willing to do, guest workers from other countries, such as Turkey, were admitted on the condition that they accept these jobs. Many did, because jobs in their home countries paid even less, or could not be found at all. The results, however, included ethnic inequality and ethnic conflict. People of Turkish and other non-German ethnic groups experienced a lower standard of living than ethnic Germans. Moreover, when Germany's economy worsened in the early 1990s, many native Germans found it increasingly difficult to find work. They began to perceive Turks and other minorities as taking their job opportunities, even though most Germans were in fact unwilling to work for the wages paid to the guest workers. These resentments contributed to a series of riots and attacks against Turks and other immigrants, guest workers, and minority groups in Germany.

Ethnocentrism and Ethnic Stratification. This case presents an example of the argument that ethnic inequality can be directly useful to a society: It may enable the filling of essential jobs. The *most* important explanation of ethnic stratification offered by the functionalist perspective, however, sees ethnic stratification not so much as something that is useful to society itself but rather as a product of another condition that is useful to society. That condition is *ethnocentrism,* which was introduced in Chapter 2. (It might be helpful to review that section if you are at all unclear about the meaning of *ethnocentrism.*) Although ethnocentrism obviously can be dysfunctional if it causes ethnic conflict that threatens to tear a society apart, a manageable amount of it is often seen as functional, or useful, for society (Sumner, 1906, p. 13; Catton, 1961; Simpson and Yinger, 1985, chap. 3). The reason is found in a society's need for consensus and a shared identity, or a "we" feeling. Durkheim (1964, 1965) and numerous order theorists since his time have argued that cooperation within a society is possible only when the members of the society share certain basic values and feel a sense of common or shared identity. Ethnocentrism can contribute to this in several ways. First, it highlights the nature of that common culture and group identity. It helps to illustrate, for example, what is "true American" by illustrating what is "un-American." Furthermore, it can create unity and cooperation within the in-group by defining the out-group as a threat or by promoting hostility toward the out-group. Perhaps the best example of this is the characterization of "the enemy" in times of war. For all these reasons there is some tendency for ethnocentrism to develop in any society (see, for example, Williams, 1977, pp. 18–19). But however functional or necessary this may or may not be, it also can create problems. The two most obvious are that it can push a society into conflict with another society when such conflict might not otherwise happen, and—our present concern—it can lead to ethnic stratification (and therefore ethnic conflict) within any society that is racially, ethnically, or culturally diverse. This is because ethnocentrism in reality is directed not only at other societies perceived as enemies but also at minority groups within the society. As a result of such generalized ethnocentrism, the minority groups against whom it is directed are placed in a disadvantaged position. In other words, ethnic stratification results.

Most functionalist sociologists agree that ethnic stratification is a problem and that it ought to be minimized. However, many of them see it as inevitable as long as there is diversity within society. Because of the need for consensus and group identity, ethnocentrism will always tend to occur. As long as there are cultural minorities[1] within the society, they will tend to become the objects of enthocentrism. The best ways to minimize this, then, are (1) to reduce the cultural differences between the dominant group and the minorities, (2) to eliminate legal and other barriers set up by the dominant group to exclude the minorities, and (3) to develop in the minority groups any skills they may be lacking to enable them to participate in the society. This approach will result in **assimilation:** The minority group will gradually become integrated into the system, and the need for drastic changes that threaten the system will be avoided. Furthermore, by becoming culturally similar to the majority group, the minority group eliminates itself as a potential target of ethnocentrism. Since both stratification and ethnocentrism are considered by functionalists to be necessary for society, however, this view sees ethnic stratification as more or less unavoidable in any culturally diverse society—the only possible way out is through assimilation. According to functionalists, assimilation offers a way out because once all groups become culturally similar, their differences no longer become the basis for ethnocentrism and prejudice among different groups within the society. When all groups share a common culture, ethnocentrism will no longer divide them; rather, with one common culture, it will unify them, according to the functionalist view.

Because they emphasize the need for assimilation, functionalist theories about majority–minority relations have frequently been criticized for placing most of the burden of change on minority groups. If stratification and ethnocentrism are

---

[1]Keep in mind that here and throughout the chapter we are using the term *minority* in the sociological sense as explained in Chapter 1.

indeed more or less inevitable in any society, it seems to follow that minorities will experience hostility (and probably subordination) as long as they remain different from the majority group. Therefore, it appears to follow from this viewpoint that for equality to occur, minorities must become more similar to the majority. It is not particularly surprising that some people, particularly minority-group members, find this view offensive; furthermore, not all sociologists accept this view. For an alternative interpretation, we now turn to the conflict perspective.

Conflict Theories About Majority–Minority Relations

Compared with order theorists, conflict theorists are much less supportive of the notions that ethnic stratification and ethnocentrism are functional and necessary in any society. Ethnic stratification is seen not as an unfortunate byproduct of social diversity but rather as a pattern that exists mainly because it serves the interests of some dominant elite. According to this view, the basic cause of the problem is to be found in the exploitative behavior of either the majority group as a whole or some very wealthy and powerful (though possibly very small) segment of that group. Minority groups are subordinated because doing so provides some benefit to the elite and because the minority either lacks the power or the awareness to prevent such exploitation.

As suggested above, conflict theorists are generally unconvinced by functionalist arguments about the necessity of economic stratification for a productive, efficient society. Tumin (1953) and others have raised a number of criticisms, arguing that Davis and Moore's functionalist theory cannot explain the degree of stratification that is found in most societies, that of the United States particularly, which has greater economic inequality than most other industrialized countries. First of all, they argue, economic stratification cannot possibly act as an incentive in the way Davis and Moore argue, because most inequality is inherited rather than earned. For the system to work as the functionalists claim, there would have to be free mobility between generations so that, for example, a well-qualified son or daughter of a sharecropper would have the same chance of becoming a medical doctor as anyone else. In reality, this rarely happens. In addition, ethnic stratification itself acts as a barrier to the mobility necessary for inequality to work as an incentive in the way that the functionalists argue. If high income is to reward hard work, it must be equally available to anyone who is capable and works hard, regardless of ethnicity.

Tumin and other critics also argue that shortages of personnel in highly demanding jobs often exist because professional organizations restrict entry into the profession, not because there is a shortage of motivated and capable people seeking entry. Two other observations can be made. First, some occupations that carry relatively little economic reward in relation to the training required are nonetheless crowded because they are rewarding in themselves or because they carry prestige. Social workers and college professors are frequently cited as examples. Second, it can be demonstrated that there is considerable variation in the degree of stratification in societies with similar levels of productivity. Several industrialized countries, for example, have lesser extremes of wealth and poverty than the United States, yet similar levels of productivity. Examples include Norway, Sweden, and Japan, whose per capita gross national product in 1991 ranged from $1,500 to $4,000 *higher* than that of the United States (Population Reference Bureau, 1993). Considering all these arguments, conflict theorists conclude that stratification is much less neces-

sary than the functionalist view suggests and that it exists mainly because it benefits the wealthy and powerful elite at the upper end of the scale. It is doubtful whether the society as a whole—and particularly those, including racial and cultural minorities, who are in the lower part of the wealth and income distributions—really benefits from the degree of social inequality that exists.

According to conflict theorists, then, stratification exists not because it meets the needs of society as a whole but because it serves the interests of some group that is dominant in terms of wealth, income, and/or power. Similarly, if inequality occurs along the lines of race or ethnicity, it is because such ethnic stratification

ETHNOCENTRISM AND WAR

One of the best illustrations of the functions of ethnocentrism can be seen in characterizations of the enemy during periods of war. Baldridge (1976, pp. 110–111) uses war posters to illustrate this. Note the threatening, distorted appearance of the German soldiers in this poster. Similarly, a British World War I poster read "Wounded and a Prisoner, Our Soldier Cries for Water. The German 'Sister' Pours It on the Ground Before His Eyes. There is No Woman in Britain Who Will Forget." Of course, in wartime situations such ethnocentrism is usually mutual. One German poster, for example, depicted U.S. president Woodrow Wilson as a dragon.

serves the interests of some advantaged group—usually either the majority group as a whole or some elite among the majority group. This viewpoint does not see ethnocentrism primarily as a way of promoting social solidarity and thereby contributing to society's ability to function. Rather, it claims that ethnocentrism and other forms of prejudice develop as a way of rationalizing exploitation of minority groups.

In fact, ethnocentrism and prejudice can be seen as just one example of a general principle discussed earlier in this chapter: According to Marx and other conflict theorists, a society's ideology (system of beliefs and values) tends to support its distribution of resources. In general, the elite or advantaged group will—consciously or otherwise—promote the beliefs and values that serve its own self-interests, which usually conflict with those of subordinate groups.

For this reason, among others, many conflict theorists—and many members of minority groups themselves—are skeptical of the argument that racial or ethnic equality can best be brought about by assimilation. If the Marxist theory that a society's ideology generally supports the interests of an elite over all others is correct, then it would be foolhardy for any disadvantaged or exploited group to buy into that ideology. Indeed, it would be a classic case of false consciousness: supporting a system of beliefs and values that goes against one's own self-interests. Fundamentally, if a social system is built on inequality, domination, and exploitation, the best way for a minority group to achieve equality is not to try to become part of that system, not to adopt the ideologies created by that system. Rather, according to the conflict theorist, the answer is to take action to make fundamental changes in the way the system works and in the way resources are distributed in the system. In effect, this means a challenge to the power of the dominant group.

Because the self-interests of subordinate groups (ethnic or otherwise) lie in challenging the power structure, conflict theorists believe that any society with stratification (ethnic or otherwise) will sooner or later experience social conflict. Thus, if there is racial or ethnic stratification in a society, that society will very likely experience conflict along racial or ethnic lines. Conflict theorists do not see anything wrong with this; indeed, they tend to view it as desirable. The most effective strategy for a minority group, they argue, is to challenge the power structure that keeps the minority group disadvantaged. To accept the ideologies of the dominant society, which may actually be used against the minority group, is not considered a viable strategy; rather it is counterproductive.

There is a further reason why many conflict theorists are skeptical of assimilation. Fundamentally, this comes down to the notion of "blaming the victim" discussed earlier. If, as those who support the conflict perspective believe, racial inequality results from exploitation of the minority group by the majority group, then the cause of the inequality is primarily to be found in the behavior of the majority group. Assimilation, however, typically demands that the minority group make most or all of the changes in behavior; it must change its ways to "fit in." Many see this as both being illogical and making an unfair demand on minority groups whose subordinate position is, after all, not their fault.

Varieties of Conflict Theory in Race and Ethnic Relations

In general, conflict theorists agree that (1) there are competing interests in society with unequal power and unequal shares of scarce resources; (2) in diverse societies, power and money are distributed unequally along the lines of social class, race, and ethnicity; and (3) it is not usually in the interests of subordinate groups to adopt the ideology of the dominant group. There are a number of specific points about which in conflict theorists do not agree, however, which resulted in the development of a number of competing conflict theories about race and ethnic relations. One of the areas in which they disagree most intensely concerns the degree to which social inequality is based on social class (i.e., economics) as opposed to race. This disagreement distinguishes three of the most important types of conflict theory about race: Marxist theory (Cox, 1948), split labor market theory (Bonacich, 1972, 1975, 1976), and internal colonialism theory (Blauner, 1972). While all of these theories are discussed in greater detail in later chapters, they are briefly introduced here to illustrate the range of conflict theories about race and ethnic relations. These theories can be arranged in a continuum based on the relative importance they attribute to class and race as bases of inequality in society.

Marxist Theory. At one end is Marxist theory, which, as we have seen, maintains that inequality is based mainly on class; specifically, who owns the means of production. Marxist theory considers racism to be a mechanism used by the wealthy to prevent the working class (to Marxists, everyone who works for a wage or salary) from recognizing its own interests. Marxists believe that there are only two true interest groups in society: those who own the means of production and the rest of society, which works for wages for those who own the means of production. Marxists view racism as a means by which wage earners are manipulated and divided. If, for example, white, African American, and Latino workers spend all of their time and energy fighting one another, there is little chance that the working class will unite and demand a bigger share from employers. This keeps wages low and profits high. Thus, Marxists believe that the working class would best be served by putting aside racial divisions. Doing so would enable its members to think of themselves as workers first and to act on their common class interests.

Split Labor Market Theory. In the middle of the continuum is split labor market theory, which sees both race and class as the bases of inequality in society. Split labor-market theorists divide society into three classes—rather than the two envisioned by Marxist theorists. The three classes are those who own the means of production, higher-paid laborers, and lower-paid laborers. The owners have an interest in getting the best worker for the lowest price, while the higher-paid workers are seeking to protect their jobs from competition from lower-paid workers. For this reason, higher-paid workers, who tend to be either from the middle and working classes of the dominant group or from ethnic groups with a "middle" status, feel that they have an interest in protecting their position and often demand discrimination against the minority groups that encompass much of lower-paid labor. Thus, split labor market theory proposes that the working class of the majority group may often demand discrimination to protect its "middle" position, particularly in bad economic times, when that position may be particularly threatened.

Internal Colonialism Theory.   At the opposite end of the continuum from Marxist theory is internal colonialism theory. Internal colonialism theory sees societal inequality as being largely racial and ethnic, resulting from a dominant racial group establishing a system of racial inequality for its own benefit. It emphasizes the fact that groups such as African Americans, Mexican Americans, and Native Americans were involuntarily brought under the rule of white Americans of European ancestry and that this was done so that persons within the white population could benefit economically. To establish such a system, whites used force, promoted racist ideologies, attacked the cultures of people of color, and isolated those peoples from mainstream labor markets. These experiences became the basis of the racial inequality that continues today and were rationalized by beliefs about the cultural inferiority of the groups that were exploited. This theory sees race as the primary basis of social inequality and the primary issue dividing societies such as the United States. According to this view, minority groups would be best served by rejecting attacks on their culture, rejecting calls for assimilation, and promoting and maintaining their own set of values supportive of economic development and control by people of color of the resources of their own communities.

Though these theories will all be discussed in greater detail later in this book, they are introduced here to show that there are certain things that conflict theories have in common and other issues about which they disagree. On the one hand, all of these conflict theories emphasize the ideas that racial and socioeconomic inequalities exist because there are interest groups that benefit from them and that it is often not in the interests of disadvantaged groups to accept the ideology of the dominant group in society. On the other hand, they disagree with one another on the relative importance of race and class as a cause of inequality in the United States and on whether class consciousness or race consciousness is the best way for subordinate groups to advance their self-interests.

Competing Perspectives: Is Synthesis Possible?

To briefly summarize the chapter thus far, we have outlined two competing perspectives in sociology and examined how they apply to majority–minority relations. One, the order, or functionalist, perspective, sees society as basically stable and orderly. Society does tend to have inequality and ethnocentrism, but they exist because they perform certain functions for society. This often leads to ethnic stratification, which is seen as a social problem for several reasons, most particularly because the resultant conflict can inhibit the effectiveness and productivity of the society and, in severe cases, can even destroy the society. The functionalist perspective considers the best solution to the problem to be a gradual process of assimilation, whereby minorities come to accept and be accepted into the dominant society and culture.

Conflict theory, on the other hand, sees society as tending—over the long run—toward instability and change. This is because most societies have marked inequality between those who own and control resources and those who do not. This comes about mainly because such an arrangement favors the interests of the elite, which is powerful enough to hold on to what it has. A society's institutions and culture (ideology) tend to serve the interests of that elite. Accordingly, acceptance of dominant ideologies and institutions is not in the interests of those who lack resources, including racial and ethnic minority groups. Rather, their interests are best served by challenging the power structure and seeking to alter the distribution of resources. Such conflict is both natural and desirable. Rather than viewing it as a threat to society, conflict theorists see it as a way to create a better, more egalitarian society, free of inequality and racism.

Obviously, the two perspectives are fundamentally opposed in many ways. By now you may be wondering if any synthesis is possible. Many strong adherents of each perspective would say no: They are stating opposite views, and one is right and the other wrong. Yet, as we have mentioned, many sociologists, including race- and ethnic-relations specialists such as Williams (1977) and Schermerhorn (1978), have been seeking to attain such a synthesis. There are probably two ways such common ground might be found. First, it is possible that the two perspectives could, on any given point, each be partially correct. For example, a given institution or ideology might both promote the efficiency of the society as a whole (as functionalists argue) *and* serve the interests of the dominant elite in particular (as conflict theorists argue). The task here is to identify, as precisely as possible, the ways in which it does each.

The second source of common ground can be found in the fact that under different circumstances, people and societies behave differently. Thus, as Schermerhorn (1978) points out, a society may at one point in its history and under one set of circumstances be stable and orderly, with ethnic minorities seeking—and to some extent gaining—equality through assimilation. At another point in time, the same society might be marked by disorder and conflict, with minority groups seeking—and again to some extent gaining—equality through conflict and use of power. Here, the key task for sociologists is to identify the circumstances that produce one outcome or the other.

In much of the rest of this book, we will seek to answer the following questions:

1. In what ways are racial and ethnic relations consistent with the predictions of order theories? of conflict theories?
2. Under what circumstances do racial and ethnic relations tend to follow patterns predicted by order theorists? by conflict theorists?

In the remainder of the chapter, we shall present an example that concretely illustrates the differences and disagreements between the two perspectives and that shows some ways in which sociological research can be used to test competing theories arising from the two perspectives.

AN ILLUSTRATION OF THE DEBATE: CULTURE OF POVERTY THEORY AND AFRICAN AMERICAN FAMILIES

A debate that illustrates the arguments of the two sociological perspectives as well as any centers around a concept known as the "culture of poverty" and, in particular, African American families. We begin our discussion of this debate with a general overview of culture of poverty theory, then proceed to a more specific analysis of the debate over African American family structure.

Culture of Poverty Theory

The term *culture of poverty* arises from the work of Oscar Lewis (1959, 1965). Lewis and other social researchers have observed certain cultural characteristics among poor people in industrial capitalist societies. These characteristics have been observed in a number of such societies and across a wide variety of racial and ethnic groups. Furthermore, according to Lewis and other culture of poverty theorists, poor people in such societies display cultural characteristics and values that are not held by the nonpoor in those same societies. Among these characteristics are

> the absence of childhood as a specially prolonged and protected stage in the life-cycle, early initiation into sex, free unions or consensual marriages, a relatively high incidence of abandonment of wives and children, a trend toward female- or mother-centered families, a strong predisposition toward authoritarianism, lack of privacy, verbal emphasis upon family solidarity which is only rarely achieved because of sibling rivalry, and competition for limited goods and maternal affection. (Lewis, 1965, p. xvii)

According to culture of poverty theory, such cultural characteristics are predominant among the poor because they enable poor people to adapt to difficulties arising from poverty. At the same time as they permit people to adapt, however, it is argued that they make escape from poverty more difficult. Therefore, the net effect of the culture of poverty is to keep poor people poor and to cause poverty to be passed from generation to generation. Accordingly, many culture of poverty theorists conclude that as long as poor people retain the culture of poverty, they will remain poor. The way to enable poor people to escape poverty, therefore, is to change the culture of poverty.

As you can see, this theory is closely associated with the functionalist perspective. Poor people are kept poor because their culture deviates from the norm; therefore, the solution to the problem of poverty is to change the culture of poor people so that it more closely fits the dominant culture. In other words, poor people need to be assimilated. Not surprisingly, this view has come under both ideological and theoretical attack from social scientists associated with the conflict perspective. They argue that this approach (1) blames the poor for their poverty, when the true cause is to be found in the exploitative behavior of those who benefit from poverty, and (2) suggests an ineffective approach to solving the problems of poverty, since acceptance of an ideology and system that serves mainly the interests of the "haves" cannot possibly serve the interests of the "have-nots." Examples of such criticism can be seen in the writings of Valentine (1968), Ryan (1971), and Gans (1973, chap. 4).

Family Structure, Poverty, and African American Families

Beginning with a government report written in the mid 1960s, known as the Moynihan Report (U.S. Department of Labor, 1965), and continuing until today in the form of the "family values" debate that has played an important role in the politics of the 1990s, both social scientists and the general public have debated the extent to which changing family structure is an important cause of poverty and other social problems in America today. Because African American families have changed the most from the traditional model of the two-parent family in which the parents raise their children together and stay married until death, much of this debate has centered on African American families and the extent to which family structure is a cause of poverty and other problems in the African American community.

The Moynihan Report is named for its author, Daniel Patrick Moynihan, a social scientist, advisor to four presidents, and U.S. senator from New York since 1976. In the report, Moynihan presented statistics showing above-average rates of divorce, separation, and unwed motherhood in the black community, which together resulted in an above-average proportion of single-parent, female-householder families.

It was not Moynihan's statistics but rather his conclusions, however, that made the report controversial. In effect, Moynihan concluded that the structure of the black family was the most important cause of continuing black poverty and that blacks would not be able to escape poverty until their family structure changed. Consider the following quotations from the Moynihan Report:

> At the heart of the deterioration of the fabric of Negro society is the deterioration of the Negro family.
> It is the fundamental source of the weakness of the Negro community at the present time. (U.S. Department of Labor, 1965, p. 5)
> The evidence—not final, but powerfully persuasive—is that the Negro family in urban ghettoes is crumbling. So long as this situation persists, the cycle of poverty and disadvantage will continue to repeat itself. (U.S. Department of Labor, 1965, introduction)

Although the Moynihan Report was written three decades ago and was greeted by a hail of criticism when it appeared, the basic argument it made continues to enjoy the support of a number of sociologists today. Some have even seen it as prophetic, since the proportion of single-parent families in the black population is far higher today than it was when Moynihan wrote the report. In 1991, just over half of all black families with children under eighteen were single-parent families with a female householder (U.S. Bureau of the Census, 1992). In fact, the incidence of such families has risen considerably among all racial and ethnic groups since the 1960s. However, the rate remains higher among African Americans (one family out of two) than among other groups. About one out of four Hispanic families and one out of six white families is headed by an unmarried female householder.

A number of sociologists have pointed out that female-householder families have a very high poverty rate (Bianchi, 1981; Reimers, 1984; Wilson, 1987; Mare and Winship, 1991). In fact, their poverty rate is nearly five times as high as that of married-couple families, and more than half of all African American families with a female householder have incomes below the poverty level. In addition to Moynihan,

An impoverished black family. The Moynihan Report argued that black poverty is perpetuated by certain features of the black family. Critics of this view suggest that if the black family is different from the white family, the difference is a result of poverty rather than a cause of poverty. *United Nations/S. Rotner*

other sociologists have recently argued that the growing incidence of divorce and single parenthood is detrimental to children as well as an important cause of poverty (Sampson, 1987; McLanahan, 1988; McLanahan and Bumpass, 1988; Popenoe, 1988; for an update of Moynihan's views, see Moynihan, 1986). These arguments, like Moynihan's original report, have often generated significant sociological controversy, and in the political arena, family structure and family values debates have been very intense, as illustrated, for example, by the flap over unwed childbearing by the television character Murphy Brown, which occurred during the 1992 presidential campaign.

This issue is a good example of a situation in which statistics show the presence of a certain pattern but the meaning of that pattern is intensely debated. The statistics show racial and ethnic variation in the rates of single-parenthood, which are highest among blacks, intermediate among Hispanics, and lowest among non-Hispanic whites. They show a rising incidence of single parenthood among all groups, and they show that the poverty rate of single-parent families is much higher than that of married-couple families among all racial and ethnic groups. But what does this mean? Does it mean that single-parent families are a *cause* of poverty? Does it mean that the family structure of African Americans is a major reason why the poverty rate of African Americans is higher than that of whites? In general, functionalists tend to answer these questions yes, while conflict theorists are much more likely to answer no.

In general, those who see black family structure as a major cause of poverty operate largely from the order perspective, broadly speaking, and, more specifically, from culture of poverty theory. They argue that black family structure places blacks at a disadvantage partly for the simple reason that it is different from the typical American family structure; that is, it does not "fit in" (U.S. Department of Labor, 1965). Thus, although it may have evolved partly in response to a high rate of poverty (a point culture of poverty theorists generally acknowledge), it now becomes a barrier to blacks' escaping poverty. In fact, some sociologists have argued that the high rate of female-householder families is the most important reason why the poverty rate among African Americans is three times as high as among whites. The solution, in this view, is to alter black family structure so that it corresponds more closely to the American ideal of the two-parent family.

Critics of this view, largely associated with the conflict perspective, argue that it puts the blame for black poverty on blacks. Citing the black family as the primary cause of continuing black poverty, critics argue, deflects people's attention from what they regard as the real causes of disproportionate black poverty, such as higher unemployment, lower wages, and poorer educational opportunities. This latter group of factors, they point out, is associated with processes at work in the larger society—a point that is lost or forgotten when the blame is focused on the black family. It has also been pointed out that the mere fact that female-householder families are correlated with poverty does not establish that they *cause* poverty—and the Moynihan Report did not present any actual evidence of a mechanism by which this might occur.

Besides their sociological criticisms, conflict theorists and others have also expressed concern about the political effects of emphasizing the black family as a cause of poverty. They point out that there is a real risk that whites will conclude, "There is nothing our society can do about the problem of black poverty; it is entirely the product of black family structure, which is up to blacks to take care of." Certainly, to say that black family structure contributes to black poverty is not to say that society can do nothing about it, but the risk is all too real that it will be interpreted in this manner by those who have a vested interest in doing so. Finally, with all this emphasis on single-parent families in the black community, it is easy to forget that married-couple families remain common among African Americans. For example, it is still true today that about half of all black family households consist of married couples (O'Hare, 1992). It would also be a mistake to associate single parenthood only with African Americans: The percentages of single-parent households today among whites and Hispanics are very similar to that observed among blacks when Moynihan first wrote his report on the black family. In sheer numbers, there are in fact more single-parent households among white Anglos than among any other group.

Evaluation: Is the Black Family Responsible for Disproportionate Black Poverty?

To evaluate the competing arguments of the order and conflict theories concerning the black family and poverty, it is helpful to consider some statistics. We can get some idea of the importance of family type as an *immediate* cause of poverty

Table 4.1 Median Family Income by Race, Hispanic Origin, and Type of Family, 1990

	ALL FAMILIES	MARRIED-COUPLE FAMILIES		MALE HOUSEHOLDER, NO WIFE	FEMALE HOUSEHOLDER, NO HUSBAND
		Wife in Paid Labor Force	Wife Not in Paid Labor Force		
U.S. Total	$35,353	$46,777	$30,265	$29,046	$16,932
White	36,915	47,247	30,781	30,570	19,528
Black	21,423	40,038	20,333	21,848	12,125
Hispanic	23,431	34,778	21,166	22,744	11,914

Source: U. S. Bureau of the Census, 1991b.

by considering the income data in Table 4.1. As we would expect from the preceding discussion, the table shows that female-householder families have lower incomes than other families, and black and Hispanic female-householder families have the lowest incomes of all. It is clear, however, that the income difference by race persists even among those with the same family type. Note that *in every type of family,* blacks (and, for that matter, Hispanics as well) have much lower incomes than whites. Thus, race clearly is associated with income and poverty above and beyond any effect of family type.

Still, it is true that for each racial group, female-householder families have the lowest incomes, suggesting that they may account for *part* of the racial difference in income, since they are more common among African Americans than among whites. Does that suggest that there is something "pathological" about the single-parent family, to use Moynihan's (U.S. Department of Labor, 1965) rather value-laden term? To answer this question, we must address several issues.

Poverty as a Cause of Single Parenthood.   First, given that there is a correlation between single parenthood and poverty, we must ask about the possible direction of cause and effect. The argument that single parenthood causes poverty assumes that single parenthood is the cause and poverty is the effect. Yet there is a good deal of convincing evidence that poverty causes single parenthood. Poverty both prevents and disrupts marriages. Our society continues to expect males to support their families, or at least to be the primary source of support. Yet as poverty and joblessness have grown in America's inner cities, this has become increasingly difficult for many African American males to do (Wilson, 1987, forthcoming; Mare and Winship, 1991; Massey and Denton, 1993). This has several consequences. First, it disrupts marriages: Low socioeconomic status is associated with higher divorce rates (Waite and Lillard, 1991) and much higher separation rates than occur among middle- and upper-class families.

Poverty is even more strongly associated with births outside marriage (Jencks, 1991). Poor inner-city women—particularly African Americans—experience a severe shortage of men who would make suitable marriage partners because many of the men in their community are unemployed, imprisoned, or prematurely dead (Wilson, 1987; Lichter, LeClere, and McLaughlin, 1991). Yet, like single women of all social classes and ethnic backgrounds in 1990s America, most of these women are sexually active. This fact, together with the low marriage rates of inner city women due to a shortage of employed men who could serve as marriage part-ners, contributes to an elevated rate of childbirth outside marriage. An additional factor is that many of these women have limited knowledge about and access to con-traceptives: Like nearly everything else, health care is inadequate in areas of con-centrated poverty. And as black poverty in particular, but Hispanic poverty to some extent, too, has become increasingly concentrated, the problem has become worse. More and more, African Americans and Hispanic Americans who live in large cities live in areas where a large proportion of the population is poor (Wilson, 1987; Massey, 1990; Massey and Denton, 1993). This contributes to the hardships young women experience in their attempt to find employed, nonpoor males who would be in a position to provide economic support for a family. For these reasons, it is clear that poverty does contribute to single parenthood, which clearly accounts for at least part of the correlation between the two.

The Wages of Women and Minority Groups.   A second part of the answer can be found by comparing the two kinds of single parent families shown in Table 4.1. Note that the incomes of the single-parent, male-householder family are con-sistently higher than those of the female-householder family for all racial groups. In fact, the male version of the single-parent family enjoys very similar incomes to the most traditional American family, a married-couple family in which only the father works outside the home. Why do single-parent, male-householder families do so much better than ones with female householders? Obviously, one reason is that women's wages are far below those of men. Thus, a single-parent, male-householder family can enjoy a fairly comfortable income, while a single-parent, female-house-holder family experiences a high risk of poverty. This suggests strongly that the low wages of women (about two-thirds those of men, regardless of level of education) may be at least as important a cause of poverty as anything inherent in the family. In short, living in a female-headed family would not carry nearly the risk of poverty that it does if sexual inequality in wages were eliminated. In fact, sociologist Cordella Reimers (1984) has pointed out that "the most important single reason for the lower family incomes of Hispanics and blacks than of white non-Hispanics is lower wage rates even after differences in age, education, and regional distribution are con-trolled." As this suggests, black and Hispanic female-householder families experi-ence a double disadvantage in income—the low wages and high unemployment rates associated with minority group status *and* the low wages of women. Significantly, neither of these has anything to do with the effects of one-parent, female-headed families per se.

Longer-Term Effects of Single-Parent Families.   A third argument is that the disproportionate number of female-headed families in the black population has longer-term effects—that children who grow up in single-parent families are disad-vantaged in ways that put them at a high risk of poverty when they grow up. This was a key point made in the Moynihan Report, yet Moynihan presented no direct evi-dence of any such disadvantage (Gans, 1967; Ryan, 1967). Gans pointed out a num-ber of studies showing that single-parent families are not strongly linked to such problems as poor school performance (mentioned by Moynihan) and mental ill-ness. Research since that time has added greatly to our knowledge of the effects of growing up in single-parent families. The most comprehensive research to date, a series of studies of California children whose parents were divorced, is fairly representative of what such research shows. In these studies, Wallerstein and Kelly (1980) found that about one-fourth of these "children of divorce" were very well adjusted, about one-fourth had real problems, and the rest were coping adequately but not totally free from difficulties—a mix probably not much different from the population of children as a whole. In fact, these researchers concluded that a "divorced family *per se* is neither more or less beneficial for children than an unhappy marriage."

In a later study extending ten years after divorce, results were not much different (Wallerstein and Blakeslee, 1989). A number of the children did report long-term problems such as low self esteem, anger, and underachievement. Yet many others developed into well-balanced, competent adolescents or young adults. The authors of the study did note, however, that it was not at all clear that these young people would have been better off if their parents had stayed married: Continued exposure to open conflict between parents is usually even worse for children than divorce (Wallerstein and Blakeslee, 1989, p. 305; see also Peterson and Zill, 1986; Demo and Acock, 1988).

Lieberson (1980, pp. 183–93) conducted research concerned specifically with the effect of black family structure on the educational achievement of black children. He found that very little of the racial gap in school success could be explained by racial differences in family structure. In a way, such findings are hardly surprising—families have ways of adapting, and a female-headed family cannot be equated with an unstable family. In particular, the role of the extended family as a source of strength and stability in the black family has been noted by many sociologists, with grandmothers and aunts playing a particularly important role (Frazier, 1966; Gans, 1967; Hill, 1972; Staples, 1973).

Some recent research does suggest that single parenthood may have some damaging long-term effects (McLanahan, 1988; McLanahan and Bumpass, 1988). These include a greater risk of early and premarital childbearing, a greater risk of divorce, and lower education and income. Sampson (1987) also found in a study of African American families that family disruption led to increased rates of juvenile crime. These differences, though real, are often offset by other factors, most notably family size. In general, children with more brothers and sisters do more poorly in several regards, perhaps because their parents, like single parents, are busier (Featherman and Hauser, 1978; Jencks, 1991, p. 87). Since one-parent families have fewer children than two-parent families, particularly among the poor, the disadvantages of a one-parent family are largely offset by the advantages of a smaller family (Jencks, 1991).

What does this information, taken as a whole, tell us? First, much of the correlation between single parenthood and poverty occurs because poverty prevents and disrupts marriage. Thus, to a large extent, poverty causes single parenthood rather than the reverse. Second, gender inequality in wages is a major cause of the high poverty rates of single-parent families, and for black and Hispanic single mothers, this is aggravated by racial inequalities. Third, the long-term effects on children of growing up in single-parent families, though real, are limited and partially offset by other factors. All of this together suggests the following: While the high rate of single-parent families among poor African Americans may contribute somewhat to the perpetuation of poverty, it is not the main cause of their high poverty rates. To a large extent, it is a consequence of those rates. Finally, its importance has been overstated in the many discussions of minority poverty that have appeared in the media, and some that have been written by sociologists. While single parenthood may play some role in perpetuating poverty among African Americans, it is not the main cause and—equally important—high rates of single parenthood among African Americans are not likely to decline much as long as many African Americans live in areas of concentrated poverty and unemployment. The latter point is backed by historical analyses. Although female-headed families were somewhat more common among blacks than whites as early as 1900 (Morgan et al., 1993), most of the racial difference in the incidence of single parenthood developed after African Americans began to urbanize on a large scale and consequently encounter the concentrated poverty of inner-city ghettos. Until the mid twentieth century, the vast majority of black families were two-parent families (Lammermeier, 1973; Furstenburg, Hershberg, and Modell, 1975; Gutman, 1976; Wilson, 1987). Taken together, these findings do not offer strong support for the culture-of-poverty theory's argument that differences in family structure play a major role in the perpetuation of poverty, though they may well play a minor role.

Teenage Pregnancy and the Black Family

In recent years, increased attention has been devoted to another aspect of black family life—a high rate of teenage pregnancy and childbirth. In 1989, the birthrate among unmarried teenagers was 103.4 per thousand among blacks aged fifteen to nineteen, compared with 28.4 among whites in this age group (National Center for Health Statistics, 1991a). Because such teenagers and their children are at a very high risk of poverty—even compared with other female-householder families—this is seen as a serious problem affecting the black community.

Again, however, there is considerable debate whether or not a high rate of teenage pregnancy is a cultural characteristic of black and/or poor Americans that perpetuates poverty, as has been suggested by culture-of-poverty theorists. It is true that teenage pregnancy and childbirth are disproportionately common among poor people of all races, and in large part they happen more often among blacks because blacks are much more likely to be poor than whites. However, is teenage pregnancy a product of the *culture* of the poor (as culture of poverty theory argues), or is it a response to the *situation* of poor teenagers (as conflict theory would argue)?

We do know several things about teenage pregnancy that may be relevant to answering this question. First, racial and social-class differences in the teenage-pregnancy rate are *not* mainly due to differences in sexual activity. Although black teenagers, for example, may be initiated into sex at a slightly younger age than whites, the overall amount of teenage sexual activity today does not vary much by race: Large numbers of U.S. teenagers of all races are sexually active (National Research Council, 1987, pp. 40–46).

Thus, racial and class differences in teenage-pregnancy and childbearing rates are not, by and large, the product of differences in the amount of sexual activity. Rather, they are mostly the product of differences in the likelihood that sexual activity will result in a pregnancy. Anderson (1991) examined social factors that contribute to high teenage-pregnancy rates. He found that in poor neighborhoods, where people experience less control over many aspects of their lives than the non-poor, teenagers felt less control over whether or not they got pregnant and thus were less likely to try to prevent pregnancy. Also, to some impoverished teenaged girls, having a baby can be a rare source of self-estten, a sign of growing up. Among poor teenaged boys, sexual conquest (which is valued to some extent among young males of all social classes) can be one of the few ways they have to attain a feeling of accomplishment, given that most opportunities for legitimate achievement are blocked. Thus, some teenage pregnancies may well result from cultural values that arise as ways of adapting to poverty. It seems unlikely, however, that these values will change for teenagers growing up in neighborhoods where nearly everyone is poor and where unemployment is the norm. Unfortunately, as the black and Hispanic urban poor have become more and more concentrated in such neighborhoods, the proportion who grow up in situations that tend to breed such responses has grown in recent years (Wilson, 1987, forthcoming; Massey and Denton, 1993).

While the desire to have a child may account for some teenage pregnancies, it clearly does not account for *most* teenage pregnancies, even among the urban poor. Research continues to show that most teenage pregnancies among the poor are unintentional. In particular, the rate of *unintended* pregnancies among African American and Latino teenagers and among poor teenagers of any race is considerably higher than in the teenaged population as a whole. In fact, about 80 percent of single black and Hispanic teenagers who have become pregnant did not intend to become pregnant (National Research Council, 1987, p. 52). Instead, they became pregnant because they (1) did not know how to keep from becoming pregnant, (2) did not have access to the contraceptives that could have kept them from becoming pregnant, or (3) did not have a real sense of control over whether or not they got pregnant.

For those who become pregnant, racial and class differences affect decisions regarding becoming a single parent. African American teenaged girls, and poor teenaged girls of any race, are less likely than their white, nonpoor counterparts to marry the father to make the baby "legitimate." We have already seen one reason for this: Given the high unemployment rates of those living in the inner city, the father is unlikely to have a steady job enabling him to provide financial support. (It should be noted, however, that getting married to "legitimize" a baby born out of wedlock, though more common among the white middle class than among other groups, is becoming less common among all groups.) Though the difference is declining, a black or poor teenager who conceives outside marriage is thus more likely than a white teenager in the same situation to be unmarried when the baby is born. In the past, black teenagers who became pregnant were also less likely than their white counterparts to have an abortion. This, too, meant that a black teenage pregnancy was more likely to result in single parenthood than a white teenage pregnancy. In recent years, however, this difference has narrowed, so there is no longer much racial difference in the incidence of abortion among pregnant adolescents (National Center for Health Statistics, 1991b).

The fact that most teenage pregnancies among the minority urban poor are unintentional suggests that greater information and better access to contraceptives might reduce the incidence of teenage pregnancies. In some urban neighborhoods, the severity of the teenage-pregnancy problem has led to the distribution of contraceptives through clinics in high schools and junior high schools. This decision has been controversial because some people, particularly religious traditionalists, have argued that such distribution promotes teenage sexual activity. Studies of clinics show, however, that the incidence of pregnancy is reduced and that sexual activity does not increase (Schorr, 1988, p. 53). One reason for this may be that such clinics often provide information about human sexuality and advice that teens do not have to be sexually active if they don't want to (Hayes, 1987a, 1987b). This empowers them to say "no" in situations in which they are pressured to have sex but do not want to.

In fact, we live in a society that continuously receives subtle and not-so-subtle sexual messages from the media and culture but that strongly discourages frank discussion of sex and contraception. Thus, teenagers become sexually active without being prepared for the consequences of that activity. Those with the least education and the least sense of control over their lives—often black, Hispanic, and the poor—are most affected. This is not necessarily because of their culture, as culture-of-poverty theory would argue, but because their situation makes them especially vulnerable to society's mixed message about sex. The role of this mixed message can be seen in the fact that teenage pregnancy in the United States is very high compared with other industrialized countries. In fact, even if one considers only the lower teenage-pregnancy rate of white U.S. teenagers, it is still higher than the teenage-pregnancy rate in such countries as Canada, Great Britain, France, Sweden, and the Netherlands—even though teens here are no more sexually active than teens in these other countries (Jones et al., 1986). One reason is that in most of these countries, sex and contraception are discussed more frankly than in the United States, so that teenagers do not get the kind of mixed message that American teenagers often get. Thus, what culture-of-poverty theorists see as a problem of the black and/or poor turns out to be largely a product of how our society treats sexuality—which has a disproportionate effect on black, Hispanic, and poor U.S. teenagers because of their lower educational level and lesser sense of control over their lives.

Overview

What, then, would conflict theorists argue is the best approach to the issue of race and poverty? Rather than focusing on characteristics of blacks (or, more generally, of any disadvantaged or exploited group), they would have sociologists direct their attention to aspects of the social structure that place the group at a disadvantage. Conflict theorists argue that blacks are disproportionately poor because whites (at least some) are benefiting from that fact and have been for years. By Moynihan's own admission, the differences in structure that do exist between black and white families are largely a product of racial discrimination and the historic exploitation of black people in the United States. Among these factors are the deliberate disruption of black families under slavery, discrimination and violence against black males (which certainly has weakened their ability to act as "leaders" of traditional families), and high black unemployment. To these factors one might add welfare laws that encourage the breakup of husband–wife families by denying benefits to poor mothers if an adult male is present in the household. For all these reasons, it is highly unrealistic to treat the black family as if it were independent of the social forces acting on it.

The solution, in the view of the conflict theorist, is to make fundamental changes in the aspects of the economic and political system that place blacks at a disadvantage. This would involve a challenge to the existing power structure. Whatever difficulties this may entail, conflict theorists prefer it to urging blacks (or other minorities) to conform to the majority group's cultural and institutional patterns. They believe there is no reason to conclude that such conformity will lead to an improvement in the group's situation or even that there is much chance that such conformity could happen, given the structural conditions that many blacks encounter on a daily basis.

SUMMARY AND CONCLUSION

We began this chapter by contrasting a sociological approach to majority–minority relations, which stresses social organization, institutions, and culture, with a social-psychological approach, which stresses individual attitudes and beliefs, including racial and ethnic prejudice. We then outlined two major perspectives within the sociological, or social-structural, approach. The order, or functionalist, perspective stresses order, stability, interdependency, and the need for shared values and beliefs in society. The conflict perspective stresses inequality, conflict, and biases supporting the dominant group in a society's social structure and culture. We examined how these approaches disagree on definitions and the causes of social problems, first in general, then specifically in the area of race relations. The culture of poverty issue and, specifically, the controversy over the black family illustrates this disagreement. The culture of poverty approach, represented, for example, by Moynihan, focuses on ways minority groups (or the poor in general) do not conform to a society's culture or institutions. This view is closely aligned with the functionalist perspective. The critics of the culture of poverty approach—mostly aligned more closely with the conflict perspective—argue that an emphasis on assimilation or "fitting in" is misplaced and that minority groups (and disadvantaged groups in general) can improve their position only by challenging the power structure and attempting to change the social institutions and/or dominant group behavior.

Having outlined and illustrated these two major sociological perspectives in this chapter, we shall use them (and, where appropriate, the social-psychological approach as well) in following chapters to enhance our understanding of how minorities and majorities relate to one another in a variety of situations.

5

Origins and Causes
of Ethnic Inequality

We all know that in societies with more than one ethnic or racial group—such as the United States—there is frequently inequality and/or conflict along the lines of race and ethnicity. We know, too, that the basic patterns of intergroup relations vary over time in any given society and also vary from one society to another. Black–white relations in the United States, for example, are quite different from black–white relations in Brazil. Today's race relations in the United States are also quite different from what they were before the Civil War, and both today's race relations and antebellum (before the Civil War) race relations differ markedly from those of the period between World War I and World War II.

In the next four chapters, we will examine some of the major ways in which race relations differ in various time periods and various societies. We will also try to find some of the reasons for these variations. In this chapter, we will be introduced to some major patterns of race and ethnic relations that have been identified by social scientists and seem to appear repeatedly in a number of societies. We will also examine the circumstances associated with the development of racial inequality in early American history. Using the theoretical perspectives outlined in previous chapters, we will try to answer the question, How and why did racial and ethnic inequality (also sometimes called *stratification*) first develop in the United States? In Chapters 6 and 7, we shall examine how and why race relations have changed in the United States, and in Chapter 8, how and why intergroup relations vary from one country to another in today's world.

PATTERNS OF RACE/ETHNIC RELATIONS

Caste Versus Class Systems of Stratification

Sociologists who study stratification, or social inequality, frequently try to place societies along a continuum or range that runs from *caste systems* at one end to *class systems* at the other. A **caste system** is one that has two or more rigidly defined and unequal groups in which membership is passed from generation to generation. The group into which one is born determines one's status for life. In this type of system, one's legal rights, job, marriage partner, and even where and when one may be present are all determined by caste membership. Caste membership is rigid and cannot be changed at any time throughout life. **Ascribed status**—the group into which one is born—totally determines one's opportunities throughout life. In caste systems, caste membership may be determined according to religious criteria, as it was in the caste system once legally in effect (and today far from totally eradicated) in India. However, many of the more rigid systems of racial inequality, such as that of South Africa from the late 1940s until the early 1990s, have operated in much the same way as caste systems. In fact, many social scientists consider them to be a slightly different form of caste system and refer to them as *racial caste systems*.

At the opposite end of the scale is the **class system.** In a class system, there is also inequality, but—ideally at least—one's status is not determined by birth. In a class system, **achieved status** is emphasized. This refers to status one gains through one's own actions, not the status one is born into. Theoretically, in class societies people are not born into rigid groups that influence their statuses for life. Rather, ideally everyone has the same chance, depending on what they do in life.

In reality, however, ascribed status does make a difference, even in class societies. Both the caste system and the class system, in their pure, abstract forms, are "ideal types," or hypothetical conceptualizations, that do not exist in such a pure form in real life. Most societies lie somewhere between a pure caste system and a pure class system. And in all societies that are commonly regarded as class systems, ascribed statuses do have important influences on the social and economic positions that people attain in their lives. Even though this is the case, caste and class are still useful concepts in describing real societies. In comparisons of two societies, for example, it is often quite possible to describe one as being more castelike, the other as more classlike.

Three Common Patterns of Race Relations

Borrowing from the work of sociologists Pierre L. Van den Berghe (1958, 1978) and William J. Wilson (1973, 1978), we can identify three major patterns of race and ethnic relations that are found in various societies. Initially, van den Berghe outlined two patterns, which he called paternalistic and competitive systems of race relations. Wilson expanded on the competitive system, dividing it into relatively rigid competitive and fluid competitive systems. We shall discuss in turn each of the three patterns: *paternalistic* race relations, *rigid competitive* race relations, and *fluid competitive* race relations. As with caste and class, keep in mind that these terms represent ideal types and that in real life societies exist along a continuum. Roughly speaking, paternalistic systems are at one end of the continuum, fluid competitive systems are at the other end, and rigid competitive systems are somewhere between.

Paternalistic Race Relations.   A **paternalistic** system of race relations can be seen as a kind of caste system. In this system, one's race pretty well determines one's status for life, and that of one's children as well. In a paternalistic system, the roles and status that belong to each race or ethnic group are known and understood by all in both the majority group and the minority group. These roles and statuses are supported by a complex system of "racial etiquette," which specifies the manner in which minority group members can speak to and behave toward majority group members. As the terminology suggests, there is a great deal of paternalism toward minority group members. It is frequently claimed that members of the subordinate group are childlike and helpless, so that dominant group members are doing them a great favor by providing them with shelter and work and teaching them the ways of civilization. The roles of majority and minority groups are structured in such a way that minorities are not permitted to compete with the dominant group for jobs, housing, and such. In societies of this type, there is usually little or no visible racial conflict or competition. There are two important reasons for the lack of conflict. Most important is the fact that the penalty for anyone who steps out of line is severe—often death. Another reason is that the ideology of dominant-group superiority, along with the idea that the dominant group is doing the minority group a favor by sheltering and civilizing its members, is sometimes accepted even by some minority group members. In some instances, it is the only mode of thinking to which they have been exposed. Of course, it is frequently true that minority group members may play along with the system to gain favors or avoid punishment without ever really accepting it.

Competitive Race Relations.   In competitive systems of race relations, on the other hand, conflict and competition occur between the races. This is true of both the rigid and fluid forms of competitive race relations. On a number of other criteria, however, these two patterns are quite different.

RIGID COMPETITIVE RACE RELATIONS.   The **rigid competitive** form of race relations, like the paternalistic form, closely resembles a caste system: For the most part, one's social status is determined by one's race. This system differs from the paternalistic system in some very important ways, however. First, majority and minority group members compete in some important areas. They may, for example, work at similar jobs in the same factory. Typically, the jobs held by minority group members have different job titles and lower pay than those held by majority group members. There is still at least implicit competition, however, because the two groups are doing much the same kind of work. Thus, there is always the possibility that the factory owner might fire members of the majority group and replace them with lower-paid minority group members. The two groups may also compete for housing if the population of either group (or both) increases rapidly in an area with limited housing. When such competition threatens the dominant group, it often responds by demanding increased discrimination against the subordinate group. In fact, one of the main ways this pattern differs from the paternalistic one is that the dominant group usually feels more immediately threatened by minority group competition. Partly for this reason, conflict between majority and minority groups is much more open under this system. This tendency toward conflict is a second major way the rigid competitive system is different from the paternalistic system. In rigid competitive race relations, both groups are aware that, despite the discrimination and racial inequality in the system, there is always the possibility of majority–minority competition, which was not the case in the paternalistic system. This makes the dominant group feel more threatened, and it makes the minority group feel more powerful and therefore assertive. Hence, there is more conflict. This conflict carries the possibility of mass violence between majority and minority groups and also the possibility of severe repression of the minority by the majority. Perhaps this pattern can be best described as an unstable form of caste system. There is still gross racial inequality and formalized discrimination, but the system is beginning to come under attack by the minority and the majority knows it. As a result, this pattern, unlike the paternalistic one, is marked by extensive open conflict.

FLUID COMPETITIVE RACE RELATIONS.   Considerable conflict and intergroup competition are also found under the **fluid competitive** pattern of majority–minority relations. This pattern, however, has more of the elements of a class system, though some castelike qualities remain. The main difference between fluid and rigid competitive race relations is that, under the fluid pattern, formalized discrimination has been largely eliminated—perhaps even outlawed. In *theory*, members of both the minority and majority group are free to pursue any endeavor and to be judged on their own merits. In practice, however, it doesn't quite work that way. Typically, minority groups start out with fewer resources because of past discrimination. Furthermore, the majority group usually controls the major social institutions and runs them in ways that serve its own interests first. Finally, for a variety of reasons, some majority group members do discriminate, even though discrimination is not socially approved. People also certainly continue to think of themselves in terms of their racial identity, so that when jobs, housing, or educational opportunities are in short supply, there is competition between racial groups for those resources. Frequently, this leads to racial or ethnic conflict. Another source of conflict comes from protests by minority group members against their generally disadvantaged position in the system, even in the absence of formalized discrimination. To summarize, under the fluid competitive system, minorities are much less restricted than under either the paternalistic or rigid competitive systems, but the fluid competitive system is still a system of racial inequality. Like the rigid competitive system, there is considerable racial competition and conflict. In fact, the fluid competitive pattern usually has even more competition and conflict, because minorities are freer both to compete with the majority and to protest their generally disadvantaged position.

Some Further Comparisons of Paternalistic, Rigid Competitive, and Fluid Competitive Race Relations.
In the preceding sections we have seen some of the basic elements of each of the three "ideal type" patterns of majority–minority relations. We shall now compare the three patterns on the basis of a number of characteristics on which they differ.

ECONOMIC SYSTEMS.   Patterns of majority–minority relations tend to differ according to a society's economic system, or system of production. The paternalistic system is most commonly found in rural, agricultural societies with large-scale land ownership. Typically, these are plantation or feudal economies in which much of the population serves as a source of cheap labor for the small elite that owns the land. In a paternalistic system of race relations, minority groups become the source of this cheap labor. As you may have surmised, the system of slavery in the United States before the Civil War is frequently given as an example of a paternalistic system of race relations. For reasons we will explore in considerable detail in the next two chapters, a society tends to move to competitive race relations when it urbanizes and industrializes. The rigid competitive pattern is associated with early stages of urbanization and industrialization. As society becomes more complex, diverse, and technologically sophisticated, it tends to move toward fluid competitive relations.

STRATIFICATION.   In paternalistic systems of race relations, stratification is very much linked to race. A very large gap exists between the social and economic status of the majority and minority groups, with very little difference within the minority group, where status is quite uniformly low. In the rigid competitive system, there is also considerable racial stratification. Typically, a few members of the minority group attain relatively high status, but the great majority remain near the "bottom of the ladder." Under the fluid competitive pattern there is also racial stratification, but the variation of status within both the majority group and the minority group is wide. A sizable proportion of the subordinate group may attain relatively high status, but the *average* status remains substantially lower for the subordinate group than for the dominant or majority group.

RELATIVE SIZE OF MAJORITY GROUP AND MINORITY GROUP.   Sociohistorical studies have shown that the paternalistic pattern occurs most often when the majority group in the sociological sense (the dominant group) is small in size relative to the subordinate, or minority, group. Frequently in paternalistic systems, the dominant group is actually a numerical minority. It is also not unusual for the dominant group to be a numerical minority in rigid competitive systems. In general, when a numerical minority is dominant, race relations tend to be castelike. When a dominant group is outnumbered, it requires more stringent social control to maintain its advantaged position. Any strengthening of the position of the subordinate group could lead to a breakdown of the dominant group's advantaged position. In the fluid competitive pattern of race relations, on the other hand, the dominant group is usually also the numerical majority. Here, superior numbers are often enough to assure a somewhat advantaged position, even without formal discrimination.

DIVISION OF LABOR.   In general, under the paternalistic pattern of majority–minority relations, division of labor is relatively simple because the society is not complex or highly specialized. Furthermore, division of labor is very much along racial lines, so that certain types of work are always or almost always done by members of the subordinate group and other kinds of work are done by members of the dominant group. In rigid competitive race relations, specialization of labor is more complex, and division of labor is less along the lines of race or ethnicity. Although the jobs may carry different titles and pay, members of the majority and minority groups may do quite similar kinds of work. As a society moves toward the fluid pattern of race relations, division of labor becomes more complex and less tied to race, although even at the fluid competitive end of the continuum, one's race has some influence on the kind of work one does.

MOBILITY.   Both geographic and socioeconomic mobility tend to increase as one moves from paternalistic race relations through rigid competitive toward more fluid race relations. Under the paternalistic pattern, the majority group generally determines where members of the minority group will live. It is a rural agricultural society in which there is little residential movement; people know what their social status is from early childhood and pass that same status on to their children.

Status tends to be less tied to birth as one moves through the competitive pattern, particularly toward the fluid competitive. Geographic mobility also increases as one moves through rigid competitive relations toward the fluid competitive pattern. However, there can still be considerable restrictions on where minorities can live under the rigid competitive system and in a less formal way under the fluid competitive system as well.

RACIAL INTERACTION.   One of the major differences among the three systems involves how the races interact with one another. As noted, in the paternalistic system, a complex racial etiquette specifies exactly how minority group members can speak to and behave toward majority group members. This system also permits majority group members—within certain limits—to give orders to minority group members and to extract favors from them. This system can best be described as one in which there is a great deal of contact between majority and minority, but the contact is always unequal, reminding the minority of its subordinate status. There is relatively little racial separation or segregation, other than living in separate homes: It is so clearly understood that the dominant and subordinate groups have unequal status that the dominant group feels no need to impose segregation to prove it. Even sexual contact is commonplace, but it reflects both racial and sexual inequality. Minority women must submit to the sexual desires of dominant group men, while subordinate group males are strictly forbidden sexual access to majority group females; violation of this rule results in severe punishment.

In the rigid competitive system the races become much more separated. Frequently, jobs and other statuses are not as sharply delineated as under the paternalistic pattern. Consequently, the majority group tries to protect and maintain its favored status by mandating a doctrine of "separate and unequal." It is under a system of rigid competitive race relations that **segregation**—enforced separation of racial groups—becomes most intense, as the majority group tries to protect its threatened status. What the majority group has lost in social deference and advantaged social standing automatically conferred by race it tries to make up for by requiring the minority to live in separate (and physically inferior) neighborhoods and to use separate and inferior public facilities.

Under the fluid competitive system, strict segregation has broken down under the pressures of a modern, complex, mobile society, and there is more interracial contact than under the rigid competitive pattern. That contact tends much more to be equal-status contact than under either of the other patterns. Still, to a large degree the majority and minority groups form separate subsocieties and often live in separate neighborhoods. Thus, close personal contact between racial groups outside work and business settings is more the exception than the rule.

VALUE CONSENSUS VERSUS CONFLICT.   As we have already noted, there is usually little or no open conflict under the paternalistic pattern. It is difficult to tell to what degree this reflects a value consensus and to what degree it results from forced conformity. Quite likely it is some of both. In such societies, people are usually exposed to only one way of thinking, so they come to accept it as the natural way of things. All institutions—scientific, religious, legal, educational—support the dominant group ideology. Even if people are inclined to disagree with the accepted mode of thought and behavior, the penalties for expressing such disagreement are severe enough to discourage most people. As we have noted, it is not unusual for minority group members to play along to avoid punishment or get what favors they can from the dominant group, even when they do not really believe in the dominant ideology. Thus, what appears to be consensus may in fact be conformity for the sake of survival. This question is explored further in a later part of this chapter when we discuss the experiences of specific minority groups in American society.

Under competitive patterns of majority–minority relations, there is usually a good deal of open conflict, and the value systems of majority and minority groups tend to differ on some key points. Although conflict occasionally reaches great intensity in rigid competitive systems, with outbreaks of mass violence between majority and minority groups, it is probably more widespread and continuous under the fluid competitive pattern. Societies of this type frequently have *institutionalized mechanisms of conflict resolution,* such as courts, civil rights commissions, and collective bargaining. These mechanisms acknowledge the regularity of conflict and also serve to keep it within acceptable bounds, preventing it from threatening the basic operation of the social system. Nonetheless, conflict sometimes becomes too intense for these mechanisms to handle, and it spills over into collective violence, as happened in many U.S. cities in the middle and late 1960s, and again in Miami in the 1980s and Los Angeles and several other cities in 1992.

These patterns are summarized in Table 5.1; in addition, countries and time periods that offer examples of each pattern are listed. In the next four chapters, we shall examine American history and compare different countries in today's world to find some reasons why each pattern has appeared in the times, places, and situations that it has.

THE DEVELOPMENT OF ETHNIC STRATIFICATION

As Table 5.1 indicates, each of the three patterns described above has been found in some times and places in American history. In fact, a strong argument can be made that in the history of the United States and some other societies, some very regular sequences of events can be found in which the three patterns appear in fairly regular order. This can be summarized as follows:

1. Diverse racial or ethnic groups come into contact with one another. Usually the initial contact is marked by curiosity and some degree of accommodation. Often, early contact has elements of both conflict and cooperation.
2. Under certain circumstances, one group becomes subordinated. When this happens, relations between the dominant and subordinate group quickly become castelike, and, depending on the social setting, either a paternalistic or rigid competitive system is established.
3. As the society modernizes, urbanizes, and industrializes, race relations become more classlike, with competitive systems replacing paternalistic ones and becoming increasingly fluid. Fewer and fewer formal restrictions are placed on the minority group, and its social movements become larger and stronger.

In the United States, three of the groups that best fit the definition of *minority group,* or *subordinate group,* presented in Chapter 1, are African Americans; American Indians, or Native Americans; and Chicanos, or Mexican Americans. We shall examine the history of these groups to see to what degree the general pattern described above fits their particular histories. We shall also try to identify some of

Table 5.1 Summary of Characteristics Associated with Three Patterns of Race/Ethnic Relations

	PATERNALISTIC	RIGID COMPETITIVE	FLUID COMPETITIVE
1. System of Production	Agricultural, usually plantation or feudal	Early urban industrial	Advanced industrial/corporate
2. Stratification	Caste; group determines status	Unstable caste, group usually determines status with some exceptions	Mixture of caste and class, considerable within-group status variation, but still racial stratification
3. Relative Size of Group	Dominant group usually numerical minority	Variable, but dominant group often numerically small	Dominant group usually numerical majority
4. Division of Labor	By race; simple division of labor	Mostly by race, but some jobs done by both dominant and subordinate groups; more complex division of labor	Complex specialization; race moderately related to type of work done; wide variation within all racial groups
5. Mobility	Very low	Low to moderate	Relatively high but not unlimited
6. Racial Interaction	Much interaction, but highly unequal; little separation of races	Little and mostly unequal interaction, almost total separation of races	More interaction than rigid, less than paternalistic; more equal interaction than either of the others
7. Consensus vs. Conflict	Little outward conflict, apparent consensus on most issues	Some racial conflict, occasional violent outbursts	Diverse values; institutionalized conflict in racial and other areas
8. Examples	United States South during slavery; many South American countries during slavery	United States South after slavery; South Africa after World War II	United States today; Great Britain today

Note: Material presented in this table is drawn primarily from Van den Berghe, 1958, 1967; and Wilson, 1973, 1978.

the reasons *why* these groups experienced the history of subordination that they did, and we shall use this knowledge to test competing theories about the causes of ethnic stratification.

Initial Contact Between Racial/Ethnic Groups

Obviously, before any kind of intergroup relations can occur, two or more racial or ethnic groups must come in contact with one another. This can happen in a number of ways, and how it happens can have a big effect on the subsequent relations between the two groups (Blauner, 1972; Schermerhorn, 1978, chap. 3; Feagin, 1984, pp. 20–26; Zweigenhaft and Domhoff, 1991). Essentially, for any two groups to come into contact, one or both of them must migrate: Either one group must move into an area where the other group is already present, or both groups must move into the same area. When these migration patterns occur, they can result in several types of contact, which can be classified as colonization, voluntary and involuntary annexation, and voluntary and involuntary immigration. **Colonization** occurs when one group migrates into an area where another group is present and conquers and subordinates that indigenous group. **Annexation** occurs when one group expands its territory to take over control of an area formerly under the control of another group. This can occur by military action (conquest), in which case the outcome may be very similar to colonization, or it can be voluntary, as when residents of an area petition to be annexed. Many cases of annexation, such as land purchases, fall somewhere between fully voluntary and fully involuntary actions. **Immigration** occurs when a group migrates into an area where another group is established and becomes a part of the indigenous group's society. Like annexation, migration may be voluntary, as when people move to a new country in search of better economic opportunity, or involuntary, as when they are imported as slaves. Again, there are intermediate cases, such as contract or indentured labor and political refugees. As we shall see, the degree to which an ethnic group is voluntarily a part of a society has a major influence on that group's status in the society. There is a tendency for greater stratification to exist when contact originally occurred through colonization, involuntary annexation, or involuntary migration. This alone does not *always* determine the outcome of contact, however, and it is certainly true that contact does not *always* lead to ethnic stratification.

Origins of Ethnic Inequality

Perhaps there is no better way to identify the causes of racial or ethnic inequality than to examine how it begins. You will recall from previous chapters that the different theoretical perspectives we have discussed offer different explanations of why there is racial inequality. The social-psychological approach stresses individual prejudices and suggests that inequality can occur if a sufficient number of individuals are racially or ethnically prejudiced. The order, or functionalist, approach also stresses attitudes and beliefs, but on a larger scale: It suggests that ethnocentrism toward out-groups becomes generalized in a society because it meets the society's needs for cohesiveness and cooperation. This ethnocentrism tends to cause discrimination against those who are racially or culturally different from the majority. Hence, stratification, which occurs in all societies, occurs along the lines of race or ethnicity in societies that are racially or culturally diverse. The conflict perspective, unlike the other two, does not stress prejudice or ethnocentrism as important causes of ethnic stratification. Rather, it stresses the idea that the dominant group benefits from ethnic stratification and is in a position to impose a subordinate role on the minority group. Thus, majorities subordinate minorities because they can gain from doing so.

Noel (1968) has drawn on both the order and conflict perspectives to develop an important theory of the origins of ethnic stratification. According to Noel, three conditions must be present for intergroup contact to lead to ethnic stratification. First, there must be *ethnocentrism,* as the order perspective suggests. This alone, however, will not cause ethnic stratification: Noel cites examples of initially ethnocentric groups that have lived side by side in peace over long periods. Second, there must be *competition* or opportunity for exploitation between ethnic groups. This occurs whenever two groups both desire the same scarce resource or have mutually exclusive needs or desires, or when one group has some resource (such as land or labor) that the other group wants. In short, the situation must be such that one group can benefit by subordinating the other. This, of course, is one of the main explanations given by the conflict perspective for social inequality. However, even the presence of ethnocentrism and competition does not guarantee that there will be ethnic stratification. If the groups involved have relatively equal power—if neither can impose its will on the other—ethnic stratification will not occur. Accordingly, a third condition that must be present for ethnic stratification to occur is *unequal power:* One group must be powerful enough to dominate or subordinate the other. To summarize, Noel's theory argues that we cannot explain racial/ethnic inequality on the basis of prejudice or ethnocentrism alone, as the social psychological or functionalist perspectives suggest. There must also be competition or opportunity for exploitation *and* unequal power, as suggested by the conflict perspective. In short, notions arising from *both* the order and the conflict approaches must be used to understand how racial or ethnic inequality initially develops.

ORIGINS OF RACIAL AND ETHNIC INEQUALITY IN THE UNITED STATES

We have argued that initial contact between diverse racial or ethnic groups frequently does not involve stratification. Ethnic stratification—the dominance of one group by another—occurs only when certain conditions are met, namely, ethnocentrism, competition, and unequal power. When ethnic stratification first occurs, the pattern is frequently castelike: paternalistic or rigid competitive. In the remainder of this chapter, we shall examine the history of interactions between whites and the three minorities mentioned earlier, African Americans, Native Americans, and Chicanos, to see to what degree the history of each group actually fits the theoretical pattern outlined above.

African Americans

Historians generally agree that blacks first arrived in what is now the United States in 1619 in the colony of Virginia. Since they were brought here involuntarily, racial inequality existed from the start. Considerable evidence suggests, however, that the racial inequality in the first few decades that blacks were present in North

America was quite mild compared with that which developed later. During the first generation or two of black presence here, many and perhaps all blacks had a status comparable to that of English indentured servants (Franklin, 1969, p. 71). While this was certainly involuntary servitude, it was not comparable to the system of chattel slavery that existed later. First, many blacks were servants for a limited period of time, after which they became free and received land of their own (Franklin, 1969, p. 71). Furthermore, the status of blacks was not very different from that of a great many whites, who frequently were under some form of involuntary servitude and were sometimes brought involuntarily to the New World. Handlin and Handlin (1950) note, for example, that "nearly everyone" in the Virginia colony in the mid seventeenth century was under some form of indenture or involuntary servitude. Thus, although blacks were generally not free, their status was also not very different from that of many whites. The amount of racial inequality was quite small *compared with what was to come later.* (For further discussion of this point see Degler, 1959a, 1959b; Elkins, 1959; and Jordan, 1962, 1968.)

Within two or three generations of the first arrival of blacks, the situation had changed drastically. By the 1660s, several colonies had passed laws sanctioning the enslavement of blacks, and the principle was rapidly evolving that slaves were property and therefore had few or no legal rights. By this time, slavery had become a status from which one could not escape and that was automatically passed on to one's children.

Why the change? Most sociologists and historians focus on two major factors. First, the plantation system that was evolving in the South could be most profitable only under a system that provided massive amounts of low-cost labor. Second, other groups were, for various reasons, not as easy to enslave and force to do plantation work as were blacks involuntarily imported from Africa. A third factor was ethnocentrism, though it alone would not have been sufficient to bring about slavery. Let us examine each of these factors in greater detail.

The Plantation System. The economic predominance of the plantation system coupled with the fact that the economic elite that controlled the system was dependent on slavery as a means of amassing wealth is probably the most important reason for the development of chattel slavery in the southern United States. In fact, it is probably safe to say that without the plantation system, slavery in this country would never have developed as it did. As the plantation system became the dominant mode of economic production in the South, two important changes occurred. First, the plantation-owning class became the dominant economic and political elite in the South. W. J. Wilson (1978, p. 25) tells us that "by the end of the eighteenth century, the Southern slaveholders had clearly established themselves as a regional ruling class. The economic system, the political system, and the juridical system were all controlled and shaped by the slaveholding elite." The plantation system owned by this elite required cheap and dependable labor to produce wealth for its owners. This explains why slavery was never institutionalized in the North to the degree that it was in the South: In the North, slaves were largely a luxury for a few wealthy individuals; they were not crucial to the power elite for amassing its wealth. Consequently, northern states never passed laws—as the South did—legislating all blacks into slavery. The plantation's need for labor also explains why most southern whites did not own any slaves at all and why most slaves belonged to plantation owners. Only one-fourth of all southern white families owned slaves, and over half the slaves were owned by "planter-class" white families that owned more than twenty slaves. Only about 3 percent of the white southern population owned this many slaves, yet this small group, almost all plantation owners, owned over half the slaves (Stampp, 1956, pp. 29–31). It seems clear that the self-interests of a small, wealthy, powerful elite were a critical factor leading to the creation of black slavery. In short, slavery was created because an elite could benefit from it. This indicates that one of Noel's three conditions for the development of ethnic stratification was clearly present: The elite group among the whites could benefit from the subordination and enslavement of blacks in the South.

Why Blacks?   But the question remains: Why were blacks rather than some other groups ultimately enslaved in the United States? One of Noel's other two conditions, ethnocentrism, suggests part of the answer: The elite required cheap labor, and blacks became the source because people were prejudiced against them. The answer, however, is not that simple. As Noel (1968) demonstrates, the prejudice and ethnocentrism among the British colonists were not directed toward blacks particularly more than toward some other groups, though there were certainly antiblack prejudices (Jordan, 1968, chap. 1). Certainly there was a comparable amount of ethnocentrism toward Indians, and the overriding prejudice of the period was against non-Christian "heathens," be they black, Indian, or otherwise (Boskin, 1965, p. 453; Jordan, 1968, pp. 85–92). Even non-English white Christians such as the Irish were

Although popular illustrations like this one often portrayed slavery in a somewhat benign manner, the reality was that it was a harsh institution in which slaves were forced to work at hard labor for many hours, and few escaped the whip. *Bettmann*

subjected to some, though less, ethnocentrism. Thus, while ethnocentrism undoubtedly played an important role in the enslavement of blacks, it alone cannot account for their enslavement. Noel's third factor, unequal power, appears to complete the explanation. The most obvious alternative groups that might have been enslaved on the plantations were white indentured servants and American Indians. However, both of these groups were in a better position to resist enslavement than were blacks. If indentured servants were permanently enslaved, there was the very real possibility that the supply of servants would be cut off: English debtors would no longer be willing to come to the colonies to work off their debts. Indeed, the supply of servants was in fact threatened by rumors of harsh treatment and permanent enslavement. Besides, white indentured servants were not racially identifiable if they ran away. Enslavement of Indians also proved difficult due to the ease with which they could run away and rejoin their tribal groups and the constant threat that Indians would attack the plantations to free their people. Furthermore, whites were often dependent on Indians for trade. None of these problems existed with blacks: There was nothing voluntary about their immigration, and once here they were in a strange land with no possibility of running off to rejoin their people. They lacked the group cohesion of the Indian tribes, since black family and tribal groupings were often deliberately broken up. In short, the power balance was so heavily weighted against blacks that they were the easiest group to enslave. Thus, we see that Noel's third condition, unequal power, was also a crucial factor in the development of black slavery. An additional factor was that black Africans knew hot-weather farming techniques unknown to either the Indians or Europeans, which made them even more desirable as a source of plantation labor. Finally, they were available in much larger numbers than were Indians. Thus, it seems safe to conclude that black enslavement was only in part due to ethnocentrism: The labor needs of the economic elite and blacks' relative lack of power to avoid enslavement were the crucial factors. Thus, we see that neither the order perspective, stressing cultural differences and ethnocentrism, nor the conflict perspective, stressing the dominant group's self-interests and the unequal power between races, is sufficient by itself to understand slavery: Both theories must be used to understand the origins of black–white inequality in the United States.

Institutionalization of Paternalistic Caste Relations. Over the two hundred or so years after slavery was legally established in the 1660s, it became increasingly more institutionalized and the plantation became even more the dominant mode of economic production in the South. The invention of the cotton gin in 1793, for example, altered the economics of southern agriculture further in favor of the large-scale plantation, thereby increasing the demand for black slaves (Franklin, 1969, p. 149). During the era of slavery, antiblack racism gradually intensified so that by the mid nineteenth century a pervasive racist ideology had developed in the South unlike anything that existed when slavery was first established (Jordan, 1968, chap. 2; Wilson, 1973, pp. 76–81).

Among the ideologies that became widespread *after* the establishment of slavery were the beliefs that blacks were innately inferior to whites, lacking in intelligence, and incapable of developing a civilized society. As is usually true of racist ideologies, these beliefs came into being mainly to justify slavery, which was beginning to come under attack from northern abolitionists. As Davis (1966) notes, many whites would find unacceptable the enslavement of human beings with the same abilities and human rights as themselves. If, however, they could convince themselves that slaves were less than human, heathens and savages incapable of being civilized, they might be able to convince themselves and others that slavery was not so bad. Indeed, they could even claim it was morally good, since it taught the slaves about as much as they could learn about the ways of "civilized" society. Thus, we see that ideological racism and intense antiblack prejudice were not so much the cause of slavery as the result of it: They developed in large part as a way for whites to rationalize or justify to themselves and others the brutal and total subjugation of other human beings that was slavery. This illustrates again that racial attitudes are as often the result of behavior as the cause and that a common function of racist ideology is to justify racist behavior (see, for example, Noel, 1972a).

In most regards, slavery in the South between the mid seventeenth and mid nineteenth centuries closely resembled Van den Berghe's concept of a paternalistic system of race relations. The status of slave was totally determined by race, with laws in most southern states aimed at assigning slave status to all blacks. A complex racial etiquette developed, specifying when and how blacks could approach and address whites. In general, there was little outward racial conflict, although serious slave uprisings did occasionally occur. Certainly, the planter class lived in constant fear of such uprisings. Especially during the latter portion of the period of slavery, the fear sometimes approached paranoia. This concern was increased by the realization that, in some parts of the South, blacks substantially outnumbered whites, as is frequently true under the paternalistic pattern of majority–minority relations.

Some historians have made much of the fact that there were relatively few slave revolts in the United States compared with Latin America. The major reason why so few slaves revolted appears not to be that most blacks accepted the status of slave, though in the controlled ideological setting of the southern plantation, some probably did.[1] Rather, the main reason is probably found in the power situation: There was virtually no opportunity for successful revolt. This was true for several reasons. First, blacks in the southern United States were, overall, a numerical minority, even though they outnumbered whites in some smaller areas. Being outnumbered, and with whites controlling the guns, blacks were in a poor position to revolt. Second, blacks were highly fragmented and scattered about in a white-dominated region. Families and tribal or linguistic groups were deliberately broken up to inhibit the planning of rebellions. Probably for similar reasons, it was against the law in most southern states for anyone to teach a black person to read or write. Slave codes also forbade slaves to travel except when authorized or accompanied by whites, so they lacked the mobility necessary to plan revolts on any regional scale. Even contact with slaves on a nearby plantation was very difficult. Furthermore, nearly half the slaves were on small plantations with fewer than twenty slaves, unlike South America, where the average plantation had about two hundred slaves. Finally, the agricultural development of the southern United States was such that runaway slaves could never be far from whites who supported slavery (including nonslaveholders). Escaping and plotting a rebellion was very difficult. The rebellions that did occur all ultimately ended in failure, and they were frequently followed by witch hunts in which any slave even suspected of supporting the uprising was in danger of losing his or her life. For these reasons, there was—as is typically the case with paternalistic, castelike race re-

---

[1]A related factor noted by Wilson (1973) is the relative lack in the United States of newly imported slaves who remembered their freedom, compared with the predominance of such slaves in Latin America.

lations—relatively little open conflict in the South during the era of slavery. This does not mean that most slaves willingly accepted their status. Subtle resistance in the form of sabotage, playing on white prejudices to avoid work or gain favor, and even self-mutilation that made it impossible to do some kinds of work were not uncommon. In addition, thousands of slaves ran away, despite the severe punishment they faced if caught.

LIFE UNDER SLAVERY

To understand majority–minority relations in the United States, one must be aware of the reasons for the emergence of black slavery; however, a sociological analysis cannot describe what slavery was like on a day-to-day basis, nor can it adequately depict what a dehumanizing institution slavery was. To truly understand the black experience in America, some awareness of the day-to-day operation of that institution is necessary. Such a description is presented vividly in the following excerpt from *The Peculiar Institution* (1956) by Kenneth Stampp.

THE PECULIAR INSTITUTION: SLAVERY IN THE ANTE-BELLUM SOUTH*

It would not be too much to say that masters usually demanded from their slaves a long day of hard work and managed by some means or others to get it. The evidence does not sustain the belief that free laborers generally worked longer hours and at a brisker pace than the unfree. During the months when crops were being cultivated or harvested the slaves commonly were in the fields fifteen or sixteen hours a day, including time allowed for meals and rest.[1] By ante-bellum standards this may not have been excessive, but it was not a light work routine by the standards of that or any other day.

In instructions to overseers, planters almost always cautioned against overwork, yet insisted that the hands be made to labor vigorously as many hours as there was daylight. Overseers who could not accomplish this were discharged. An Arkansas master described a work day that was in no sense unusual on the plantations of the Deep South: "We get up before day every morning and eat breakfast before day and have everybody at work before day dawns. I am never caught in bed after day light nor is any body else on the place, and we continue in the cotton fields when we can have fair weather till it is so dark we can't see to work, and this history of one day is the history of every day."[2]

Planters who contributed articles on the management of slaves to southern periodicals took this routine for granted. "It is expected," one of them wrote, "that servants should rise early enough to be at work by the time it is light. . . . While at work, they should be brisk. . . . I have no objection to their whistling or singing some lively tune, but no *drawling* tunes are allowed in the field, for their motions are almost certain to keep time with the music."[3] These planters had the businessman's interest in maximum production without injury to their capital.

The work schedule was not strikingly different on the plantations of the Upper South. Here too it was a common practice to regulate the hours of labor in accordance with the amount of daylight. A former slave on a Missouri tobacco and hemp plantation recalled that the field-hands began their work at half past four in the morning. Such rules were far more common on Virginia plantations than were the customs of languid patricians. An ex-slave in Hanover County, Virginia, remembered seeing slave women hurrying to their work in the early morning "with their shoes and stockings in their hands, and a petticoat wrapped over their shoulders, to dress in the field the best way they could."[4] The bulk of the Virginia planters were businessmen too.

Planters who were concerned about the physical condition of their slaves permitted them to rest at noon after eating their dinners in the fields. "In the Winter," advised one expert on slave management, "a hand may be pressed all day, but not so in Summer. . . . In May, from one and a half to two hours; in June, two and a half; in July and August, three hours rest [should be given] at noon."[5] Except for certain essential chores, Sunday work was uncommon but not unheard of if the crops required it. On Saturdays slaves were often permitted to quit the fields at noon. They were also given holidays, most commonly at Christmas and after the crops were laid by.

But a holiday was not always a time for rest and relaxation. Many planters encouraged their bondsmen to cultivate small crops during their "leisure" to provide some of their own food. Thus a North Carolina planter instructed his overseer: "As soon as you have laid by the crop give the people 2 days but . . . they must work their own crops." Another planter gave his slaves a "holiday to plant their potatoes," and another "holiday to get in their potatoes." James H. Hammond once wrote in disgust: "Holiday for the negroes who fenced in their gardens. Lazy devils they did nothing after 12 o'clock." In addition, slave women had to devote part of their time when they were not in the fields to washing clothes, cooking, and cleaning their cabins. An Alabama planter wrote: "I always give them half of each Saturday, and often the whole day, at which time . . . the women do their household work; therefore they are never idle."[6]

Planters avoided night work as much as they felt they could, but slaves rarely escaped it entirely. Night work was almost universal on sugar plantations during the grinding season, and on cotton plantations when the crop was being picked, ginned, and packed. A Mississippi planter did not hesitate to keep his hands hauling fodder until ten o'clock at night when the hours of daylight were not sufficient for his work schedule.[7]

Occasionally a planter hired free laborers for such heavy work as ditching in order to protect his slave property. But, contrary to the legend, this was not a common practice. Most planters used their own field-hands for ditching and for clearing new ground. Moreover, they often assigned slave women to this type of labor as well as to plowing. On one plantation Olmsted saw twenty women operating heavy plows with double teams: "They were superintended by a male negro driver, who carried a whip, which he frequently cracked at them, permitting no dawdling or delay at the turning."[8]

Among the smaller planters and slaveholding farmers there was generally no appreciable relaxation of this normal labor routine. Their production records, their diaries and farm journals, and the testimony of their slaves all suggest the same dawn-to-dusk regimen that prevailed on the large plantations.[9] This was also the experience of most slaves engaged in nonagricultural occupations. Everywhere, then, masters normally expected from their slaves, in accordance with the standards of their time, a full stint of labor from "day clean" to "first dark."

Some, however, demanded more than this. Continuously, or at least for long intervals, they drove their slaves at a pace that was bound, sooner, or later, to injure their health. Such hard driving seldom occurred on the smaller plantations and farms or in urban centers; it was decidedly a phenomenon of the large plantations. Though the majority of planters did not sanction it, more of them tolerated excessively heavy labor routines than is generally realized. The records of the plantation regime clearly indicate that slaves were more frequently overworked by calloused tyrants than overindulged by mellowed patriarchs.

That a large number of southern bondsmen were worked severely during the colonial period is beyond dispute. The South Carolina code of 1740 charged that "many owners . . . do confine them so closely to hard labor, that they have not sufficient time for natural rest."[10] In the nineteenth century conditions seemed to have improved, especially in the older regions of the South. Unquestionably the ante-bellum planter who coveted a high rank in society responded to subtle pressures that others did not feel. The closing of the African slave trade and the steady rise of slave prices were additional restraining influences. "The time has been," wrote a planter in 1849, "that the farmer could kill up and wear out one

Negro to buy another; but it is not so now. Negroes are too high in proportion to the price of cotton, and it behooves those who own them to make them last as long as possible."[11]

But neither public opinion nor high prices prevented some of the bondsmen from suffering physical breakdowns and early deaths because of overwork. The abolitionists never proved their claim that many sugar and cotton growers deliberately worked their slaves to death every seven years with the intention of replacing them from profits. Yet some of the great planters came close to accomplishing that result without designing it. In the "race for wealth" in which, according to one Louisiana planter, all were enlisted, few proprietors managed their estates according to the code of the patricians.[12] They were sometimes remarkably shortsighted in the use of their investments.

Irresponsible overseers, who had no permanent interest in slave property, were frequently blamed for the overworking of slaves. Since this was a common complaint, it is important to remember that nearly half of the slaves lived on plantations of the size that ordinarily employed overseers. But planters could not escape responsibility for these conditions simply because their written instructions usually prohibited excessive driving. For they often demanded crop yields that could be achieved by no other method.

Most overseers believed (with good reason) that their success was measured by how much they produced, and that merely having the slave force in good condition at the end of the year would not guarantee re-employment. A Mississippi overseer with sixteen years of experience confirmed this belief in defending his profession: "When I came to Mississippi, I found that the overseer who could have the most cotton bales ready for market by Christmas, was considered best qualified for the business—consequently, every overseer gave his whole attention to cotton bales, to the exclusion of everything else."[13]

More than a few planters agreed that this was true. A committee of an Alabama agricultural society reported: "It is too commonly the case that masters look only to the yearly products of their farms, and praise or condemn their overseers by this standard alone, without ever once troubling themselves to inquire into the manner in which things are managed on their plantations, and whether he may have lost more in the diminished value of his slaves by over-work than he has gained by his large crop." This being the case, it was understandably of no consequence to the overseer that the old hands were "worked down" and the young ones "overstrained," that the "breeding women" miscarried, and that the "sucklers" lost their children. "So that he has the requisite number of cotton bags, all is overlooked; he is re-employed at an advanced salary, and his reputation increased."[14]

2

A wise master did not take seriously the belief that Negroes were natural-born slaves. He knew better. He knew that Negroes freshly imported from Africa had to be broken in to bondage; that each succeeding generation had to be carefully trained. This was no easy task, for the bondsman rarely submitted willingly. Moreover, he rarely submitted completely. In most cases there was no end to the need for control—at least not until old age reduced the slave to a condition of helplessness.

Masters revealed the qualities they sought to develop in slaves when they singled out certain ones for special commendation. A small Mississippi planter mourned the death of his "faithful and dearly beloved servant" Jack: "Since I have owned him he has been true to me in all respects. He was an obedient trusty servant. . . . I never knew him to steal nor lie and he ever set a moral and industrious example to those around him. . . . I shall ever cherish his memory." A Louisiana sugar planter lost a "very valuable Boy" through an accident: "His life was a very great one. I have always found him willing and obedient and never knew him to fail to do anything he was put to do."[15] These were "ideal" slaves, the models slaveholders had in mind as they trained and governed their workers.

How might this ideal be approached? The first step, advised those who wrote discourses on the management of slaves, was to establish and maintain strict discipline. An Arkansas master suggested the adoption of the "Army Regulations as to the discipline in Forts." "They must obey at all times, and under all circumstances, cheerfully and with alacrity," affirmed a Virginia slaveholder. "It greatly impairs the happiness of a negro, to be allowed to cultivate an insubordinate temper. Unconditional submission is the only footing upon which slavery should be placed. It is precisely similar to the attitude of a minor to his parent, or a soldier to his general." A South Carolinian limned a perfect relationship between a slave and his master: "that the slave should know that his master is to govern absolutely, and he is to obey implicitly. That he is never for a moment to exercise either his will or judgment in opposition to a positive order."[16]

The second step was to implant in the bondsmen themselves a consciousness of personal inferiority. They had "to know and keep their places," to "feel the difference between master and slave," to understand that bondage was their natural status. They had to feel that African ancestry tainted them, that their color was a badge of degradation. In the country they were to show respect for even their master's nonslaveholding neighbors; in the towns they were to give way on the streets to the most wretched white man. The line between the races must never be crossed, for familiarity caused slaves to forget their lowly station and to become "impudent."[17]

Frederick Douglass explained that a slave might commit the offense of impudence in various ways: "in the tone of an answer; in answering at all; in not answering; in the expression of countenance; in the motion of the head; in the gait, manner and bearing of the slave." Any of these acts, in some subtle way, might indicate the absence of proper subordination. "In a well regulated community," wrote a Texan, "a negro takes off his hat in addressing a white man. . . . Where this is not enforced, we may always look for impudent and rebellious negroes."[18]

The third step in the training of slaves was to awe them with a sense of their master's enormous power. The only principle upon which slavery could be maintained, reported a group of Charlestonians, was the "principle of fear." In his defense of slavery James H. Hammond admitted that this, unfortunately, was true but put the responsibility upon the abolitionists. Antislavery agitation had forced masters to strengthen their authority: "We have to rely more and more on the power of fear. . . . We are determined to continue masters, and to do so we have to draw the reign tighter and tighter day by day to be assured that we hold them in complete check." A North Carolina mistress, after subduing a troublesome domestic, realized that it was essential "to make them stand in fear"![19]

In this the slaveholders had considerable success. Frederick Douglass believed that most slaves stood "in awe" of white men; few could free themselves altogether from the notion that their masters were "invested with a sort of sacredness." Olmsted saw a small white girl stop a slave on the road and boldly order him to return to his plantation. The slave fearfully obeyed her command. A visitor in Mississippi claimed that a master, armed only with a whip or cane, could throw himself among a score of bondsmen and cause them to "flee with terror." He accomplished this by the "peculiar tone of authority" with which he spoke. "Fear, awe, and obedience . . . are interwoven into the very nature of the slave."[20]

The fourth step was to persuade the bondsmen to take an interest in the master's enterprise and to accept his standards of good conduct. A South Carolina planter explained: "The master should make it his business to show his slaves, that the advancement of his individual interest, is at the same time an advancement of theirs. Once they feel this, it will require but little compulsion to make them act as it becomes them."[21] Though slaveholders induced only a few chattels to respond to this appeal, these few were useful examples for others.

The final step was to impress Negroes with their helplessness, to create in them "a habit of perfect dependence" upon their masters.[22] Many believed it dangerous to train slaves to be skilled artisans in the towns, because they tended to become self-reliant. Some thought it equally dangerous to hire them to factory owners. In the Richmond tobacco factories they were alarmingly independent and "insolent." A Virginian was dismayed to find that his bondsmen, while working at an iron furnace, "got a habit of roaming about and *taking care of themselves*." Permitting them to hire their own time produced even worse results. "No higher evidence can be furnished of its baneful effects," wrote a Charlestonian, "than the unwillingness it produces in the slave, to return to the regular life and domestic control of the master."[23]

"Chains and irons," James H. Hammond correctly explained, were used chiefly to control and discipline runaways. "You will admit," he argued logically enough, "that if we pretend to own slaves, they must not be permitted to abscond whenever they see fit; and that if nothing else will prevent it these means must be resorted to."[24] Three entries in Hammond's diary, in 1844, indicated that he practiced what he preached. July 17: "Alonzo runaway with his irons on." July 30: "Alonzo came in with his irons off." July 31: ". . . re-ironed Alonzo."

Hammond was but one of many masters who gave critics of the peculiar institution a poignant symbol—the fettered slave. A Mississippian had his runaway Maria "Ironed with a shackle on each leg connected with a chain." When he caught Albert he "had an iron collar put on his neck"; on Woodson, a habitual runaway, he "put the ball and chain." A Kentuckian recalled seeing slaves in his state wearing iron collars, some of them with bells attached. The fetters, however, did not always accomplish their purpose, for numerous advertisements stated that fugitives wore these encumbrances when they escaped. For example, Peter, a Louisiana runaway, "Had on each foot when leaving, an iron ring, with a small chain attached to it."[25]

But the whip was the most common instrument of punishment—indeed, it was the emblem of the master's authority. Nearly every slaveholder used it, and few grown slaves escaped it entirely. Defenders of the institution conceded that corporal punishment was essential in certain situations; some were convinced that it was better than any other remedy. If slavery were right, argued an Arkansas planter, means had to be found to keep slaves in subjugation, "and my opinion is, the lash—not used murderously, as would-be philanthropists assert, is the most effectual." A Virginian agreed: "A great deal of whipping is not necessary; *some* is."[26]

The majority seemed to think that the certainty, and not the severity, of physical "correction" was what made it effective. While no offense could go unpunished, the number of lashes should be in proportion to the nature of the offense and the character of the offender. The master should control his temper. "Never inflict punishment when in a passion," advised a Louisiana slaveholder, "but wait until perfectly cool, and until it can be done rather in sorrow than in anger." Many urged, therefore, that time be permitted to elapse between the misdeed and the flogging. A Georgian required his driver to do the whipping so that his bondsmen would not think that it was "for the pleasure of punishing, rather than for the purpose of enforcing obedience."[27]

Planters who employed overseers often fixed the number of stripes they could inflict for each specific offense, or a maximum number whatever the offense. On Pierce Butler's Georgia plantation each driver could administer twelve lashes, the head driver thirty-six, and the overseer fifty. A South Carolinian instructed his overseer to ask permission before going beyond fifteen. "The highest punishment must not exceed 100 lashes in one day and to that extent only in extreme cases," wrote James H. Hammond. "In general 15 to 20 lashes will be a sufficient flogging."[28]

The significance of these numbers depended in part upon the kind of whip that was used. The "rawhide," or "cowskin," was a savage instrument requiring only a few strokes to provide a chastisement that a slave would not soon forget. A former bondsman remembered that it was made of about three feet of untanned ox hide, an inch thick at the butt end, and tapering to a point which made it "quite elastic and springy."[29]

Many slaveholders would not use the rawhide because it lacerated the skin. One recommended, instead, a leather strap, eighteen inches long and two and a half inches wide, fastened to a wooden handle. In Mississippi, according to a visitor, the whip in general use consisted of a "stout flexible stalk" covered with a tapering leather plait, about three and a half feet in length, which formed the lash. "To the end of the lash is attached a soft, dry, buckskin cracker, about three eighths of an inch wide and ten or twelve inches long, which is the only part allowed to strike, in whipping on the bare skin. . . . When it is used by an experienced hand it makes a very loud report, and stings, or 'burns' the skin smartly, but does not bruise it."[30]

How frequently a master resorted to the whip depended upon his temperament and his methods of management. On some establishments long periods of time elapsed with relatively few whippings—until, as a rice planter explained, it seemed "as if the devil had got into" the hands, and for a time there was "a good deal of it." Or, occasionally, a normally amiable slave got out of hand and had to be flogged. "Had to whip my Man Willis for insolence to the overseer," wrote a Tennesseean. "This I done with much regret as he was never whipped before."[31]

On other establishments the whip was in constant use. The size of the estate may have had some relationship to the amount of whipping, but the disposition of the proprietor was decidedly more crucial. Small farmers, as well as large planters, often relied upon corporal punishment as their chief method of enforcing discipline. Southern women were sometimes equally prone to use the lash upon errant domestics.

Some overseers, upon assuming control, thought it wise to whip every hand on the plantation to let them know who was in command. Some masters used the lash as a form of incentive by flogging the last slave out of his cabin in the morning.[32] Many used it to "break in" a young slave and to "break the spirit" of an insubordinate older one. "If the negro is humble and appears duly sensible of the impropriety of his conduct, a very moderate chastisement will answer better than a severe one," advised a planter. "If, however, he is stubborn . . . a slight punishment will only make bad worse." Slaves had to be flogged, explained an Alabamian, until they manifested "submission and penitence."[33]

In short, the infliction of stripes curbed many a bondsman who could not be influenced by any other technique. Whipping had a dispiriting effect upon most of them. "Had to administer a little rod to Bob this morning," reported a Virginian. "Have seen for more than 3 months I should have to humble him some, hope it may benefit him."[34]

[*]Copyright© 1959 by Kenneth Stampp. Reprinted by permission of Alfred A. Knopf, Inc.

[1]Gray, *History of Agriculture,* I, pp. 556–57.

[2]Gustavus A. Henry to his wife, November 27, 1860, Henry Papers.

[3]*Southern Cultivator,* VIII (1850), p. 163.

[4]William W. Brown, *Narrative of William W. Brown, a Fugitive Slave* (Boston, 1847), p. 14; Olmsted, *Seaboard,* p. 109; *De Bow's Review,* XIV (1853), pp. 176–78; Benjamin Drew, *The Refugee: or the Narratives of Fugitive Slaves in Canada* (Boston, 1856), p. 162.

[5]*Southern Cultivator,* VIII (1850), p. 163.

[6]Henry K. Burgwyn to Arthur Souter, August 6, 1843, Henry King Burgwyn Papers; John C. Jenkins Diary, entries for November 15, 1845; April 22, 1854; Hammond Diary, entry for May 12, 1832; *De Bow's Review,* XIII (1852), pp. 193–94.

[7]Jenkins Diary, entry for August 7, 1843.

[8]Olmsted, *Back Country,* p. 81; Sydnor, *Slavery in Mississippi,* p. 12.

[9]See, for example, Marston Papers; Torbert Plantation Diary; *De Bow's Review,* XI (1851), pp. 369–72; Drew, *Refugee;* Douglass, *My Bondage,* p. 215; Trexler, *Slavery in Missouri,* pp. 97–98.

[10]Hurd, *Law of Freedom and Bondage,* 1, p. 307; Flanders, *Plantation Slavery in Georgia,* p. 42.

[11]*Southern Cultivator,* VII (1849), p. 69.

[12]Kenneth M. Clark to Lewis Thompson, December 29, 1859, Thompson Papers.

[13]*American Cotton Planter and Soil of the South,* II (1858), pp. 112–13.

[14]*American Farmer,* II (1846), p. 78; *Southern Cultivator,* II (1844), pp. 97, 107.

[15]Baker Diary, entry for July 1, 1854; Alexander Franklin Pugh Ms. Plantation Diary, entry for June 21, 1860.

[16]*Southern Cultivator,* IV (1846), pp. 43–44; XVIII (1860), pp. 304–305; *Farmers' Register,* V (1837), p. 32.

[17]*Southern Planter,* XII (1852), pp. 376–79; *Southern Cultivator,* VIII (1850), p. 163; *Farmers' Register,* I (1834), pp. 564–65.

[18]Douglass, *My Bondage,* p. 92; Austin *Texas State Gazette,* October 10, 1857.

[19]Phillips (ed.), *Plantation and Frontier,* II, pp. 108–11; *De Bow's Review,* VII (1849), p. 498; Mary W. Bryan to Ebenezer Pettigrew, October 20, 1835, Pettigrew Family Papers.

[20]Douglass, *My Bondage,* pp. 250–51; Olmsted, *Back Country,* pp. 444–45; [Ingraham], *South-West,* II, pp. 260–61.

[21]*Farmers' Register,* IV (1837), p. 574.

[22]*Southern Cultivator,* IV (1846), p. 44.

[23]*Southern Planter,* XII (1852), pp. 376–79; Olmsted, *Seaboard,* pp. 58–59; Charleston *Courier,* September 12, 1850.

[24]*De Bow's Review,* VII (1849), p. 500.

[25]Nevitt Plantation Journal, entries for November 9, 1827; March 28, 1831; July 18, 1832; Coleman, *Slavery Times in Kentucky,* pp. 248–49; New Orleans *Picayune,* December 26, 1847.

[26]*Southern Cultivator,* XVIII (1860), pp. 239–40; *Southern Planter,* XII (1852), p. 107.

[27]*De Bow's Review,* XXII (1857), pp. 376–79; *Southern Agriculturist,* IV (1831), p. 350.

[28]Kemble, *Journal,* pp. 42–43; Phillips (ed.), *Plantation and Frontier,* I, pp. 116–22; Plantation Manual in Hammond Papers.

[29]Douglass, *My Bondage,* p. 103.

[30]*Southern Cultivator,* VII (1849), p. 135; [Ingraham], *South-West,* II, pp. 287–88.

[31]Olmsted, *Seaboard,* pp. 438–39; Bills Diary, entry for March 30, 1860.

[32]*Southern Cultivator,* II (1844), pp. 169–70; Davis, *Cotton Kingdom in Alabama,* pp. 54–55.

[33]*Southern Cultivator,* VIII (1850), p. 164; William P. Gould Ms. Plantation Rules.

[34]Adams Diary, entry for July 2, 1860.

We have seen, then, that ethnocentrism, competition, and unequal power combined to take blacks from a status not too different from that of white indentured servants to that of white people's property with no recognized human rights. When it was profitable for the white power elite (remember, most slaves were owned by a tiny percentage of the white population) to do so, and they had the power to do so, blacks were relegated to the status of a minority group in a paternalistic system of race relations. Only after this system of racial inequality and exploitation was established did intense antiblack prejudices become widespread, apparently as a way of justifying the exploitation. (For further discussion of the origins of black–white inequality, including reprints of several articles cited in this section, see Noel, 1972b.)

Native Americans

Early Contact. The first thing to keep in mind about the history of relations between Native Americans and European whites in North America is that it is an incredibly complex history, with considerable variations in events from one area to another. When the Europeans first arrived, North America's native population numbered at least one million (Collier, 1947, p. 172), and probably several times that many (Josephy, 1992; 1968, pp. 50–51; Garbarino, 1976, p. 72). One of the more widely accepted estimates is that of Thornton (1987), who placed the Native American population at around 7 million. This population was composed of about six hundred independent nations that varied tremendously in culture, social organization, and mode of economic production. Three major national groups of Europeans—Spanish, French, and British—were involved in the conquest and settlement of North America by whites, and here, too, there was great variation within the three groups. Because of this historical complexity, almost any generalization one might make has its exceptions. Nonetheless, certain patterns and regularities in Indian–white relations in North America held more often than not, and these may enable us to understand some of the causes of the oppression and subordination of Indian people in the United States. Of the three major European colonial groups that settled in the United States, the one that had the greatest direct influence on Indian–white relations was the British. The Spanish played an important role in Florida and the Southwest, and had an important effect over a wider area because of the spread of horses—first introduced by the Spanish among a variety of Native American groups. The French played an important role for a time in the Northeast. In this country, however, most white contact with Native Americans involved British colonists or their descendants.

The Spanish, French, and British all had somewhat different objectives in coming to the New World. The Spanish came mainly to seek wealth, and secondarily to convert souls to Christianity (Garbarino, 1976). In Latin America, the Spanish also sought to conquer and control land (and the land's population), but basically to extract its wealth rather than to establish a self-supporting system of production (Josephy, 1968, chap. 25). This led them to immediately conquer whatever populations they encountered in Latin America; plunder the highly developed and often wealthy cities of the Aztecs, Incas, and Mayas; and force the natives into slavery or peonage. This was less common in North America, though it did occur to some extent both in the Southwest and in Florida (Hall, 1993). More often, Spanish contact with native peoples in North America tended to take one of two forms. When the Spanish periodically sent expeditions through North America seeking wealth, such as those of De Soto and various slave catchers in Florida, Indian people were sometimes brutally attacked, tortured, and killed. (Coronado's famous expedition in the western and plains states was a notable exception to this rule.) The other type of contact was more benevolent and took the form of missionaries seeking to convert the native peoples to Christianity.

Among both the French and British, trading with the Indians was an important objective. Accordingly, both groups enjoyed relatively harmonious relations with Indian people at first, and in these early years, both groups largely depended on Indian people for their survival. It is unlikely, for example, that the Pilgrims at Plymouth could have survived the winter of 1621–1622 without Indian assistance (Josephy, 1968, p. 301). The French depended largely on the fur trade as a source of economic support, and many British settlers also relied on trade with the Indians. Indian people, too, often found the early contact beneficial, particularly those tribes that were hunters and could benefit from the fur trade (Lurie, 1991). This relationship, marked by substantial but not total cooperation, did not last long, however. It soon changed to one of conflict and led to the conquest of the native people by the Europeans, particularly the British. However, the existence of this period of relative cooperation does illustrate one sociological point: Even where there are two greatly different cultural groups and considerable ethnocentrism, ethnic conflict and stratification do not automatically occur. It is clear that the British, especially, took a highly ethnocentric view of Native Americans, sometimes seeing them as ungodly heathens worthy neither of conversion nor human association. Under the influence of Calvinism, the Protestant British regarded conversion largely as a matter of predestination—either one was part of God's chosen people or one was not, and attempting to convert those who were not chosen was a waste of time. For the most part, this led to the view that the British were chosen and the Indians were not. Indeed, the same generalized prejudice against non-Christians that shaped British at-titudes toward blacks also shaped their attitudes toward Indians.

The Catholic French, on the other hand, were like the Catholic mission-aries from Spain: They viewed the Indians as fellow human beings with souls, and hence, they were obligated to give them the message of Christianity. Accordingly, the French had a milder prejudice against the Indians than did the British. Another fact, however, was of even greater importance in shaping the history of these two Euro-pean groups' relations with Native Americans. The French were for the most part uninterested in settling land: They were traders. Thus, their livelihood depended on reasonably good relations with the native hunting peoples, who provided them with their source of wealth. The British, on the other hand, mainly wanted to settle land. They were largely agriculturalists, and for British settlers, the opportunity to own land was one of the major attractive features of North America (Garbarino, 1976, p. 44). When *added to* their ethnocentrism, this factor made it inevitable that conflict would eventually break out between the British colonists and Indian people. As more and more British settlers arrived, Indian people began to be forced off their land (Josephy, 1968, chap. 26). Since the Europeans controlled the firearms, the balance of power was grossly unequal. The outcome could never have been in serious doubt once the British began to arrive in large numbers. Accordingly, the seeds of over two centuries of conquest and domination had now been sown. The basic approaches of making treaties with Indians to gain their land and of establishing Indian reserva-tions were largely established under the British before the Revolutionary War (Gar-barino, 1976, p. 440; Lurie, 1991, p. 136).

One disastrous effect of the displacement of Indian people by whites was an increase in rivalries between the various Indian nations (Abler, 1992). At first, con-flicts arose over who would have control of trading with the whites. Later, as Indian people began to be displaced from their homelands, conflicts over land flared be-tween various Indian tribes. A tragic consequence was a tremendous escalation of warfare among the various Native American groups. In the past, conflict had been controlled and somewhat ritualistic. Now, struggle was a matter of life and death. An-other reason this conflict became more deadly is that it now often included the use of firearms obtained from the Europeans (Abler, 1992). In addition to the deaths di-rectly resulting from the struggle, tribal warfare made it nearly impossible for Indian people to mount a unified defense against the incursions of the whites. Largely be-cause of animosities that had built up against Indian allies of the French, the Iro-quois nations supported (in fact, if not openly) the British in the French and Indian War (Josephy, 1968, pp. 311–12; Garbarino, 1976, p. 437). This support was critical for the British, and as a result of this war, the French lost control of eastern North America.

In addition to intertribal conflicts, another disastrous result of Indian–white contact was disease. Indian people had no immunity to European diseases. Most his-torians agree that more Indians died of white people's diseases than were killed in warfare. In some areas, 90 percent of the indigenous population was lost (Garbarino, 1976, p. 438), and in at least one case, an entire tribe was wiped out (Debo, 1970). This was not always accidental: In some cases, Europeans deliberately exposed Indi-ans to disease.

A Trail of Broken Treaties.   An American Indian protest campaign in the 1970s referred to itself as the "trail of broken treaties." This name is a fitting description of Indian–white relations from before the Revolutionary War until the end of the nineteenth century. Again and again, treaties were made with Indian nations, requiring the Indian people to give up their land with only the smallest compensation and move to new land, which was promised to be theirs forever. Again and again, the demands for land by a swelling white population and by white land speculators led to displacement of the Indian people from these "promised lands." This system of treaties was fundamentally deceptive to Indian people, for two major reasons. First, Indian nations generally had a system of common ownership of land. Often, they believed they were letting whites *use* commonly owned land, not giving it up. Whites, of course, saw the land as strictly theirs and did not even permit Indians to pass through it (see Guillemin, 1978, p. 320). Second, Indian people generally signed treaties in good faith, expecting them to be kept. In Indian societies, a person's word was enough. Whites, on the other hand, often saw the treaties as stopgap measures to get the Indians out of the way. Treaties could always be renegotiated later when whites needed more land (Lurie, 1991, pp. 139–41). Gradually, as whites increased their population and their desire for land, Indian nations were forced to move farther and farther west, often displacing others in the process. Some were ultimately forced to move as far as from Georgia to Oklahoma. One-fourth of the Cherokees died on one such forced trek (Josephy, 1968, p. 323). Certainly, it is one of history's worst examples of the forced migration of an indigenous population by an invading population.

Causes of the Subordination of Indian People. In analyzing the causes of this forced migration and subordination of America's native peoples, the same three factors stand out as with the establishment of slavery. First, there was ethnocentrism, as there usually is when two very different cultures come into contact. This in and of itself did not lead to widespread subordination of the Native American peoples. Only when population pressures in the land-settling British (and later American) population brought this group into competition with the Indians over land did subordination occur. In other words, whites had something to gain—land—by subordinating the Indians, just as the southern plantation owners had something to gain by enslaving blacks. Firearms gave the whites the power to take land from Indians, and they used this power. Thus, the same three factors—ethnocentrism, competition, and unequal power—seem important in explaining the displacement and conquest of Indians as in explaining the enslavement of blacks. As Lurie (1991, pp. 136–41) points out, this can be illustrated by comparing Indian–white relations in the United States with those in Canada, where white pressure for land was never as great. There, too, Indian people were often deprived of their land, but they were given more desirable land than the American Indian, with reserves "located in the tribes' homelands or nearby ecologically similar areas" (Lurie, 1991, p. 136). Furthermore, once treaties were established, they were generally honored, and Indian people were not forced to move repeatedly from place to place as they were in the United States. One reason for this milder treatment of the native population in Canada appears to be that there has always been much less pressure for land in that country, which has both a much smaller population and less reliance on the land-based enterprise of agriculture than the United States (see Guillemin, 1978).

The Reservation System. As Native Americans were forced off their land in the United States from the late eighteenth through the nineteenth century, more

Fort Union on the Missouri. Note the process of white encroachment on Indian land. Gradually, Indians were displaced from most of the desirable locations and forced into small areas on the least desirable land. *New York Public Library*

and more of them found themselves living on reservations. As the white population increased, the reservations were increasingly relegated to land the whites considered worthless or uninhabitable. The reservations also became more and more prison-like, with Indian people having fewer and fewer recognized legal rights. In 1871, Congress abolished the practice of making treaties with the Indians. This even further stripped Indians of their rights, since whites tended to view the "agreements" made after this exchange as legally and morally even less binding than the earlier treaties (Lurie, 1991). Another development during this period was the government's designation of Indian people as "wards" of the government in 1862. While paternalism and a general effort to press Indians to surrender their own culture and adopt the white man's ways had always been a key part of European colonial and, later, American policy toward Indian people, this became even more prevalent from the 1860s on. By the latter 1800s, most Indians had been forced onto reservations, often after ferocious warfare and great bloodshed on both sides. In California, for example, it is estimated that seventy thousand Indian people lost their lives in the ten years immediately after the 1849 gold rush, the period of greatest white population expansion (Garbarino, 1976; see also Hurtado, 1988). By the end of this period, most of those who survived had been forced onto Indian reservations.

The Indian reservation of the latter nineteenth century, if it existed today, would probably be called a concentration camp. The reservations more often than not were heavily guarded by U.S. Army troops, and Indian people could not leave the reservation without a pass. Practice of native religions and other displays of Indian culture were forbidden. The Sun Dance, an annual religious ritual practiced by many plains tribes, was banned (Jorgensen, 1972). The reason given was that the ceremony frequently involved some elements of self-torture, but the fact remains that it was a freely chosen and crucial aspect of the culture and belief of many tribes and nobody was compelled to participate in the self-torture aspect. Indian children on reservations were frequently taken from their homes and forced to attend boarding schools run by whites. At these schools, they were required to speak only English; if they were caught speaking their native language, they were severely punished. Finally, Indian people were denied the right to vote. They could not vote in state and federal elections because they were not regarded as U.S. citizens, and they were allowed no input into the running of reservations, either, even though the reservations were supposedly their land.

Even those who sought to help Indian people usually ended up exercising social control over them instead. Philanthropists, some policymakers, and missionaries who meant well generally assumed that the best way to improve the conditions of Indian people was to convince them to accept the "civilized" ways of the whites. Beginning in 1887, a policy known as "allotment" was initiated. The purpose of this program was to set Indians up as individual landowning farmers who would make a living growing and selling agricultural products from their own land. Because it simply attempted to model itself after the social and economic organization of white culture without understanding the situation of the people it was supposed to help, the program was a miserable failure (Garbarino, 1976, p. 442). To begin with, it was applied indiscriminately to all tribes, whether they had any history of agriculture or not. Second, it imposed the white concept of land ownership, which was different from the usual Indian concept of commonly owned land. Also, in many Indian cultures, women cultivated while men hunted or were warriors, so European-style farming was contrary to long-held notions about gender roles. Finally, many Indians were encouraged to become indebted to whites, who then took the land for payment (Lurie, 1991, p. 142). All of these factors combined to make this well-intended but highly ethnocentric program a failure: Its main result was to transfer millions of acres of Indian land to whites. Thus, we see that even when intentions were good (and they usually were not), the white people's behavior and policy toward Indian people was so shaped by paternalism and ethnocentrism that it ended up serving white interests rather than those of Native Americans (Guillemin, 1978, pp. 322–23).

The Indian Reservation and the Slave Plantation: A Comparison

We end our discussion of American Indian history up to 1900 by comparing the Indian reservation of the late nineteenth century with the slave plantation of the early nineteenth century. In some regards, the reservation fits the model of the paternalistic pattern of race relations almost as well as the slave plantation, though it is less often given as an example and there are some differences. In both systems, status was determined totally on the basis of racial or ethnic identity. Indians were expected to go to the reservations, just as antebellum southern blacks were automatically slaves. Moreover, neither group could freely travel. In both cases, group culture was severely repressed, and ideologies of paternalism—"we're doing them a favor by civilizing them"—were pervasive. Although such paternalism was typical even among well-intentioned people, it developed first and foremost as a way of justifying the exploitation that was occurring. Thus, the use of paternalism as a justifying ideology was another common element between the slave plantation and the Indian reservation.

Despite these similarities, there was at least one important difference between the two systems. Blacks were exploited totally for their labor; they had no land in this country that could be taken away. Indian people, on the other hand, were exploited mostly for their land. Although a few were made slaves by both British settlers in the Southeast and Spanish settlers in the Southwest; most Indians were not enslaved, for the reasons mentioned earlier in the discussion of slavery. This explains the other major difference between the two systems. Under slavery, there was continuous contact between whites and blacks, who, as indicated earlier, lived in close proximity to one another in a hierarchical system in which everyone was expected to know her or his place. This was necessary if whites were to exploit blacks for their labor on the plantation. The effort in the case of Native Americans, however, was to separate them from the white population; to force them onto white-controlled reservations. The main objective was to get them out of the way, so whites could safely farm or develop the land that had been taken from the Indian people.

Thus, the different economic objective of the dominant group—land versus labor—led to a difference in the pattern of racial inequality that resulted. The black–white pattern almost totally resembled the paternalistic form; the Indian–white pattern might best be described as basically paternalistic with the one difference being the racial separation that is more characteristic of the rigid competitive model. The important fact remains that when whites were in a position to benefit and when, with their firearms, they had the power to do so, they set up rigid systems of inequality, subordinating both black people and Indian people. Despite the many differences in the two histories, the crucial elements of ethnocentrism, competition or potential gain, and unequal power were present in both. In the case of black people, the objective was labor; in the case of Indian people, it was land. In both cases, too, intense racist ideologies developed as a way of rationalizing or justifying the exploitation. The original ethnocentrism greatly increased after the pattern of exploitation developed.[2] As Nash (1970, chap. 1) points out, the English settlers were aware that they were taking land away from an established people. To justify this, they developed an image of the Native American as a helpless savage who could only benefit from being Christianized, civilized, and brought into a modern agricultural system. As pressures for land increased, so did racist stereotyping of Indian people, and the image of the Indian as a lawless barbarian replaced the earlier image of the "noble savage."

---

[2]The different nature of the contact with and exploitation of the two groups resulted in somewhat different racist stereotypes. For further discussion of this point, see Nash, 1970, chap. 1.

Mexican Americans

Early Contacts. The first contact between Mexicans and Anglo Americans came about in what is now the southwestern United States. This contact began to occur on a sizable scale in the early 1800s, as the Mexican population expanded northward and the Anglo American population expanded westward. This Mexican population was mostly mestizo, a mixture of Spanish and Indian, which by that time made up the overwhelming majority of the Mexican population. There were also, however, some recent white immigrants from Spain who preferred to think of themselves as Spanish rather than Mexican and were generally so recognized. At this time, the present-day states of Texas, California, New Mexico, Arizona, Nevada, and Utah were all part of Mexico, as were most of Colorado and small parts of three other states. The relationship between white Americans, or Anglos, and Mexicans during this period might best be described as displaying elements of both cooperation and competition. There was a certain amount of competition, but there was little ethnic stratification between Mexicans and Anglos. Both groups were landowners, farmers, and ranchers; Mexicans were operating ranches on a large scale in Texas by the late eighteenth century, and later in California, especially after Mexico became independent from Spain in 1822 (Meier and Rivera, 1972, chap. 3). In addition to the general absence of ethnic inequality, the competition between Anglos and Mexicans was limited and, as mentioned, was counterbalanced by significant elements of cooperation. One example can be seen in the occasional instances of "filibustering" by some Anglo settlers in Texas. This refers to insurrections aimed at separating from the authority of the Mexican government. When these uprisings occurred, however, other Anglos generally helped the Mexican authorities put them down. One influential U.S. citizen who received a number of land grants from the Mexican government, Stephen Austin, was instrumental in helping control a revolt of this type in 1826, the Fredonia Revolt, which had the support of a number of recent American immigrants. Austin also ensured that immigrants respected the terms of their land grants and swore an oath of loyalty to Mexico (Meier and Rivera, 1972, p. 58). The relationship was such that one expert in Chicano (Mexican American) history has observed that "the *general* tone of the times was one of intercultural cooperation" (Alvarez, 1973, p. 922). In California in the 1820s and 1830s, there is similar evidence of cooperation. In fact, the Anglo immigrants of this period were often quite completely assimilated into Mexican life. Frequently, they became Mexican citizens, married Mexicans, and received land grants; occasionally they even held public office (Meier and Rivera, 1972, p. 67).

To summarize, then, Mexican and Anglo residents in the early stages of southwestern settlement lived side by side in relatively equal status, with relatively cooperative relationships. In each of the three major areas (Texas, California, and Nuevo Mexico, which largely comprised present-day Arizona and New Mexico) the lifestyle and mode of production were somewhat different, but in all three, the pattern was one of relative equality with substantial elements of cooperation. Of course, both groups in different ways oppressed the southwestern Indian people, but they treated and regarded one another as relative equals.

Origins of Ethnic Stratification. TEXAS. During the 1830s, a chain of events began that was to prove disastrous for Mexicans living in Aztlan, as the region of Mexico that became part of the United States is sometimes called. By the early

1830s, conflict had arisen in Mexico over the role of that country's national government. Some Mexicans, the centralists, wanted a strong national government that would exercise close administrative control over all of Mexico. Others, the federalists, wanted a looser confederation with greater local autonomy, not unlike the system of the United States. Most Texans—both Mexican and Anglo—favored the latter approach and sided with the federalists. However, centralists came to control Mexico's national government. This led to conflict with Texas, conflict that was heightened by the Mexican government's 1829 decision to abolish slavery: Many Anglos who immigrated to Texas were southern slaveowning cotton growers (Mirande, 1985, pp. 23–25; Estrada et al., 1985, p. 163). The Mexican army came to Texas to control the dissident federalists but in the process spilled so much blood that a revolution was started and Texas ended up—for a short time—as an independent nation (Alvarez, 1973). This chain of events upset the balance of power, creating new demands for land by whites in Texas in a way that resulted almost overnight in gross social inequality between Anglos and Mexicans. Why did this happen? First, Texas's independence from Mexico accelerated the influx of white immigrants, mostly from the United States South. This influx began in earnest when Mexico opened its northern border to non-Mexicans in 1821 (Nostrand, 1992), and continued after Texas declared independence from Mexico in 1836. The Mexican population of Texas fell to 20 percent in 1830, 10 percent in 1840, and just 6 percent by 1860 (Grebler, Moore, and Guzman, 1970, p. 40; Mirande, 1987, p. 31). The growing numbers of Anglo immigrants brought with them the prejudices of the South as well as a tremendous demand for land. Outnumbering the Mexicans as they did, they soon appealed for admission to the United States (as a slave state), and in 1845 Texas was annexed. The situation now was totally changed, and the past cooperation of the Mexicans with the Anglos was forgotten. Most Mexicans were quickly deprived of their land, either by force or by American law (backed by force), which consistently served Anglo, not Mexican, interests (Mirande, 1987, chap. 2). By 1900, even the largest and wealthiest Mexican landowners had generally been deprived of their land (Alvarez, 1973).

During this period, there was also a great upsurge in anti-Mexican prejudice, which further contributed to the subordination of the now Mexican American people in Texas. Alvarez (1973) cites three major reasons for this upsurge. First, the warfare with Mexico had led most Anglos to view *all* Mexicans as former enemies, even though most of them had also opposed Mexico's centralist government and many had fought for Texas's independence from Mexico. Second, as noted, many had learned intense racial prejudice in the United States South and readily applied notions of racial inferiority to Mexicans. Finally, racist ideology served an economic purpose in supporting and rationalizing the Anglos' actions of taking land from the Mexicans.

CALIFORNIA AND NUEVO MEXICO.   Most of the rest of the Southwest—California and Nuevo Mexico—became part of the United States in 1848 as a result of the Treaty of Guadalupe Hidalgo, which ended the Mexican War. This war was the result of a number of factors, particularly Mexican objections to the annexation of Texas by the United States, American desire to expand westward into Nuevo Mexico and California, and border disputes all along the U.S.–Mexican border (Meier and Rivera, 1972, chap. 4). During this war, Nuevo Mexico surrendered itself to the United States without a fight, in part because of opposition to the centralist government of Mexico. In California, the situation was somewhat different. The cooperation between Anglos and Californios (Mexican settlers in California) during the 1820s and 1830s increasingly turned to conflict during the 1840s, as more and more Anglo settlers came to northern California via the Oregon Trail. Here, too, opposition to the centralists among both Anglos and Mexicans was strong enough that California declared its independence from Mexico in 1836. In 1840, however, California returned to Mexican control. But increasingly, the influx of white settlers caused Anglo–Californio conflicts that ended any cooperation between the two, even though both had opposed the centralists in Mexico. In 1846, a new independence movement known as the Bear Flag Revolt took place. This movement came to be controlled mainly by Anglos, who soon antagonized Californios in Los Angeles so strongly that they rebelled against the Anglos, who by now were openly proclaiming California to be U.S. territory. This led to the only serious fighting of the part of the Mexican War that occurred in what is now the United States and by 1847 led to effective American control of California. Meanwhile, the major fighting of the war was taking place in Mexico, which had been invaded by U.S. troops. In 1847, Mexico City was captured, and a year later the Treaty of Guadalupe Hidalgo was signed and ratified. This treaty ceded most of California and Nuevo Mexico to the United States, formally recognized American sovereignty over Texas, and resolved the border disputes along the Texas–Mexico boundary in favor of the United States. In a protocol accompanying the treaty, the United States agreed in writing to recognize the land ownership of Mexicans in the ceded territories. The eighty thousand Mexicans living in the ceded territories also were given U.S. citizenship rights, and most became citizens.[3] A few years later, the present U.S.–Mexican border was established when the Gadsden Purchase (1853) ceded the southern parts of present-day Arizona and New Mexico to the United States.

As was the case a few years earlier in Texas, the annexation of Nuevo Mexico and California caused a critical change in the power structure, which would sooner or later prove disastrous for the Mexican people living in these two territories. The familiar pattern was repeated: Once there was a sizable influx of Anglos into an area, the Anglos and Mexican Americans came into competition over land. The Mexican Americans were nearly always deprived of their land, despite the international agreement (and numerous verbal promises) that this would not happen. Sometimes the land was simply taken by force; at other times, the legal system accomplished the same result. This was possible because the Mexican and American concepts of land ownership were different, as were the methods for legally proving a land claim (Meier and Rivera, 1972). Thus, many Mexicans who could easily have proven their claims in Mexican courts could not do so in American courts. It is also true, of course, that judges and magistrates were usually Anglo and protected Anglo interests and that Anglo landowners were often better able to afford quality lawyers. Furthermore, even when Mexican Americans did eventually win their claims, they would up so deeply in debt from the cost of the legal battle—some of which dragged on for as long as seventeen years—that they often lost part or all of their land because of the debt (Meier and Rivera, 1972, p. 80). Put simply, the balance of power was totally on the side of the Anglo Americans (Mirande, 1987).

As already stated, this process of competition for land and displacement of

---

[3]However, Indians in the ceded territories, who previously had the right of Mexican citizenship, did not receive the right of U.S. citizenship (Meier and Rivera, 1972, p. 70).

Mexican American landowners was closely associated with the influx of Anglo population into an area. This first occurred on a large scale in northern California during the gold rush, which began in 1849. In southern California, few Anglos were present; the process occurred more slowly. Californios and new immigrants from Mexico were in the majority until the 1870s, but the building of transcontinental railroads brought more whites to the region; by 1880, three-fourths of the population was Anglo (Meier and Rivera, 1972, chap. 5). With this influx of whites, Californio wealth, land ownership, and cultural influence over the region were largely lost. The process was sped up in the 1860s by floods, droughts, and declining farm prices, which put many Californio landowners in debt (Grebler, Moore, and Guzman, 1970, pp. 49–50). By the 1880s, Anglos were quite solidly in control of the region. The area slowest to come under Anglo domination was the present-day state of New Mexico, largely because there were fewer whites and a larger Mexican American population there than elsewhere. In 1848, about sixty thousand of the eighty thousand or so Mexican Americans lived in New Mexico (Moore, 1976, pp. 12, 15). Except on the ranchlands of eastern New Mexico near Texas, there was no influx of whites like that seen in Texas and California. A wealthy class of Mexican American urbanites—who usually preferred to think of themselves as Spanish rather than Mexican—was present in New Mexico and highly influential in the region's politics past the turn of the century. Even today, a larger and more powerful Hispanic elite lives there than anywhere else in the country. Even there, however, Anglos eventually came to dominate, though often only after strong resistance by Mexicans (Rosenbaum and Larson, 1987). One example of this domination can be seen in the fact that by 1910, fewer than a third of the parcels of land owned by Mexicans before annexation to the United States remained in the hands of the Mexican owners (Gonzales, 1967, p. 29). It is easy to see why. Between 1891 and 1904, New Mexico *Hispanos* claimed land grant rights on nearly 35 million acres, but less than 2 million acres of these claims were confirmed by the U.S. courts (Nostrand, 1992, p. 124). Nonetheless, more Hispanic landowners in New Mexico were able to hang on to some of their land than anywhere in the Southwest, and a major reason why was that Anglos did not become a majority of the population until after the turn of the century. In New Mexico in 1900, only about 30 percent of the population was Anglo (Nostrand, 1992).

Causes of Anglo–Chicano Inequality. This brief discussion of the early history of Anglo–Chicano relations is sufficient to confirm that Noel's (1968) theory about the origins of ethnic stratification can be applied to Mexican Americans as well as to other U.S. minorities.[4] Only in the presence of all three elements cited by Noel—ethnocentrism, competition, and unequal power—did patterns of near-total domination of Chicanos by Anglos emerge. Early competition for land and the whites' superior power and numbers brought this about first in Texas. The Treaty of Guadalupe Hidalgo gave political and legal power to whites throughout the Southwest, but this did not immediately cause great ethnic inequality except in northern California, where the gold rush began almost immediately after the treaty. In other areas, subordination of the Mexican American population tended to come when there was a sizable influx of whites—the 1870s and 1880s in much of southern Cali-

---

[4]For more complete discussions of Chicano history, see the previously cited publications as well as McWilliams, 1949, which is considered by some to be the best general work on Mexican American history in the Southwest.

fornia, later in New Mexico. This influx added the element of competition as whites wanting land deprived Mexican Americans of their land claims. It also increased both white ethnocentrism and the inequality of the power balance. As with blacks and Indians, racist stereotypes developed and were used to justify mistreatment of Chicanos. Another form of ethnocentrism was the concept of "Manifest Destiny," which was used to justify annexation of Mexican territory and to displace both Mexican Americans and Indians from their lands. This view was that the white man's supernaturally willed destiny was to rule and "civilize" all of North America, from coast to coast. Thus, the conquest of indigenous Indian and Mexican American populations and the taking of their lands could be justified—it was God's will. The other factor, unequal power, was also increased with a large influx of whites. Whites became a numerical majority, which augmented the legal and political power they already held. For all these reasons, there was a close association between the numerical balance of Anglos and Chicanos and the amount of inequality between the two groups in various times and places throughout the Southwest.

In the words of Mirande (1987, p. 29), "As the Anglo population expanded, so did it gain in political power. Loss of political control by the Californios went hand in hand with economic and occupational displacement." In some regards, the history of Chicanos is very different from that of blacks and Native Americans. Only Chicano history involves the conquest by force of a sovereign, internationally recognized nation-state and the abrogation of rights accorded to its citizens by that nation. In spite of this and other differences, however, the origin of Anglo–Chicano inequality seems to involve the same three elements as the other two groups we have examined.

Exploitation of Chicanos for Labor. Another way in which Mexican Americans are unique among the three groups discussed is that only they were exploited on a large scale for *both* their land and their labor in this country. Blacks had no land here because they were not indigenous. For reasons discussed earlier in the chapter, Indians were never enslaved on a large scale, and their resistance to forced assimilation, as well as their forced isolation on the reservation, generally kept white employers from seeing them as a source of cheap labor. Mexican Americans, however, soon came to be exploited for their labor as well as their land. We have already discussed at length the exploitation of Chicanos for their land and the reasons behind it. In the remainder of this section, we shall examine the ways in which Anglos took advantage of Mexican Americans as a source of cheap labor.

As Mexican Americans were being displaced from their land by whites during the 1850–1900 period, whites in the Southwest were developing an economic system largely built around mining, large-scale agriculture, and railroad transportation. These types of economic activity, especially mining and large-scale agriculture, are highly labor-intensive and are most profitable when there is a large labor supply. The owners of the ranches and mines accordingly sought a supply of laborers willing to do hard, dirty work for low wages (Grebler, Moore, and Guzman, 1970, p. 51). Although bonded laborers from Asia were brought to the West to do some of this work, Mexican Americans became the most important source of such labor. Those Mexican Americans who were displaced from their land when the United States took over the Southwest were placed in a desperate economic position and became a major source of farm and mine labor during the latter half of the nineteenth century. After the turn of the century, the Mexican Revolution of 1909–1910 caused massive displacement and widespread economic distress in Mexico. For political and economic reasons, as well as simply for reasons of personal safety, thousands of Mexicans fled to this country during and after that upheaval. This massive wave of immigration continued through the 1920s and made even more Mexican Americans available as a source of cheap labor. Furthermore, fears about competition with whites had led to tight restrictions on Asian immigration, so Asians were now less available as an alternative source of labor (see, for example, Camarillo, 1979).[5]

By the early twentieth century, the Chicano agricultural laborer was in a position only marginally better than a slave, in a system that in some ways resembled the paternalistic pattern of race relations. To a large degree, Mexican Americans were restricted to certain low-paying, low-status jobs, so that ethnicity largely determined one's status and economic position. Frequently, the total control over minority group life associated with paternalistic systems was present for farm and mine workers, who were required to buy their goods at inflated prices at the company or ranch store and were closely supervised by labor contractors. Frequently, too, the system of labor was more unfree than free, since workers were often bound to their employers to work off the debts incurred at these company stores or for housing. Finally, there was the paternalism—the constant assertion by ranch, farm, and mine owners that their Mexican American workers were happy, that the owners had their best interests at heart, and that the workers needed "close supervision" because they were incapable of functioning on their own. And, of course, there was the oft-repeated claim that Mexican Americans were incapable of work other than unskilled labor or farmwork and that they were especially suited to this type of work. Consider the following quote about Mexican farmworkers from a white cotton farmer in the 1930s: "Picking cotton, that's their lot. It don't make any difference whether you pay them 15 or 35 cents an hour. Their women only wear shoes when someone will see them. They buy Buicks and don't know how to spend their money intelligently. They're stupid" (Taylor and Kerr, 1935, quoted in Chacon, 1984, pp. 348–49).

It should be pointed out that in other regards, the pattern did not resemble Van den Berghe's paternalistic system. For one thing, there was typically a good deal of geographic mobility. Although one's movement might be quite restricted while working at any one ranch, Chicano farm labor in the early twentieth century (and since) was highly migratory, with movement from job to job as different crops came due to be planted or harvested. There was also much movement between the city and rural areas, with many of the farmworkers spending much of the off-season in the city, working at low-skill jobs and living in Mexican American neighborhoods known as *barrios* (Grebler, Moore, and Guzman, 1970). Regardless of just how closely it resembled the paternalistic pattern, it is clear that for Chicano farmworkers and many mine and railroad workers, the situation was highly exploitative. Hours were long, pay exceedingly low, food and housing poor, and education practically nonexistent. Especially in the rural areas, few Chicanos were permitted to rise above this status. The system of stratification thus closely fits the caste model. In the mining and railroad industries and in the city, the pattern was often more like the rigid competitive pattern than the paternalistic, but here, too, Mexican Americans were seen

---

[5]Similar efforts were also directed at Mexicans but had less effect. Immigration across the border was harder to control, and—especially in agriculture—Chicanos largely held jobs whites were unwilling to accept, so whites were somewhat less concerned about their competition.

Chicanos are unique in that they were exploited first for their land and later for their labor. Most Chicanos today live in cities, but it is still true that a disproportionate number of farm workers are Chicano. Farmworkers are still among the lowest paid of all workers, and are often exposed to dangerous pesticides. *Stock Boston, Inc.*

by employers as a source of cheap labor (Camarillo, 1979; Mirande, 1987).[6] In either case, most Mexican Americans in the latter nineteenth and early twentieth centuries found themselves in a caste system with little chance of advancement.

SUMMARY AND CONCLUSION

In this chapter, we have examined different patterns of race relations and the conditions under which these patterns tend to appear. We have discussed a theory of ethnic stratification that argues that three conditions must be present for ethnic stratification or racial inequality to develop: ethnocentrism; competition, or the opportunity for one group to gain at the other's expense; and unequal power. The order perspective stresses ethnocentrism as the major reason for racial inequality when different cultures come into contact. This approach suggests that to reduce racial inequality, assimilation must come about: Minority groups must be absorbed into the system and become culturally similar to the majority (though the majority may also borrow from the minority culture). The conflict perspective argues that racial inequality occurs because one group is in a position to gain by dominating or exploiting another and because groups are not equal in power. In such a context, the more powerful group will gain and the less powerful group will become subordinate. This approach suggests that assimilation cannot solve the problem of racial inequality, be-

[6]The experience of this segment of the Mexican American population is discussed in Chapter 6.

cause cultural differences are not the cause of the problem. Only a change in the balance of power or a redistribution of resources can solve the problem.

Our examination suggests that each view is partially correct. The histories of the three American groups we have examined, while varying greatly in many regards, all support Noel's thesis that ethnocentrism, competition, and unequal power must *all* be present before substantial racial or ethnic inequality will appear. Thus, the once-common view that eliminating prejudices and encouraging assimilation can by themselves eliminate racial inequality seems dubious: Prejudices and cultural differences did not *by themselves* cause racial inequality. It is only in the context of competition and unequal power that ethnocentrism seems to result in racial stratification. In other words, racial or ethnic inequality occur only when, in addition to the presence of ethnocentrism, one group can benefit from dominating or oppressing another and is powerful enough to do so. This suggests that part of the solution to the problem of racial inequality must be sought in the basic power structure of a society and that changes deeper than simple attitudinal and cultural change may be necessary to solve the problem.

To illuminate the origins and causes of racial and ethnic inequality in the United States, our discussion focused on three of the minority groups that have encountered the greatest exploitation and discrimination and that continue to occupy a disadvantaged status in American society today. It is, of course, true that intergroup inequality based on factors other than race or ethnicity (e.g., inequality based on gender or sexual orientation) may or may not have causes similar to the causes of racial and ethnic inequality. It is also true that the causes of racial and ethnic inequality may differ in different countries and thus may not be the same elsewhere as they have been in the United States. In later chapters, we shall explore the causes of types of majority–minority inequality other than racial and ethnic inequality as well as the causes of racial and ethnic inequality in other societies around the world.

In the next chapter, we shall examine more recent American history to identify some of the factors associated with change in patterns of racial inequality once they have been established. It is clear that majority–minority relations today are different from those fifty or one hundred years ago. In the next chapter, we will find out some of the reasons why.

6

Changing Patterns
of Majority–Minority
Relations in the
United States

In the previous chapter, we examined the origins of racial and ethnic inequality in the United States. We traced the early development of relations between whites and three minority groups—blacks, American Indians, and Chicanos—through an era of castelike relationships with gross racial inequality. In this chapter and the next, we shall examine changes over the past seventy-five to one hundred years, a period in which American race relations have gradually changed to a more fluid, classlike pattern. While still marked by great inequality, race relations today are in a number of ways fundamentally different from what they were in the late nineteenth century. In these chapters, we shall try to find out how and why we got from where we were then to where we are now.

Where we are now, of course, has been partly determined by our earlier patterns of racial inequality. Accordingly, we shall start this chapter by examining how the origins of ethnic stratification discussed at length in the previous chapter have influenced majority–minority relations through American history and to the present time. We shall then examine how we got from the castelike patterns discussed in the previous chapter to the more classlike race relations of today.

ORIGINS OF CONTACT AND MODERN-DAY RACE RELATIONS:
A THEORY OF INTERNAL COLONIALISM

In the previous chapter, we discussed a number of different ways that two groups can come in contact, ranging from voluntary to involuntary. Blauner's (1972) theory about the development of American race relations places crucial importance on the nature of this initial contact. Blauner's theory of **internal colonialism** distinguishes between those conquered peoples who became part of the United States (or any country) involuntarily and those who entered voluntarily. A group that is conquered, or annexed by force, is referred to as a **colonized minority;** one that entered willingly is called an **immigrant minority.** As we have seen, African Americans, Mexican Americans, and Native Americans all fit the category of colonized minorities. The Chicano and Indian people were conquered and forced into subordinate status in much the same way as native peoples in Asia, Africa, Latin America, and Oceania when the Europeans colonized those areas. A major difference is that in the United States, the white Europeans became a majority more quickly and declared independence from the mother country more quickly than in some of the other areas. They treated the indigenous populations they conquered—Indians and Mexicans—much as colonizers did in other parts of the world, however.

Some critics argue that blacks do not fit the model because they were not conquered and enslaved on their own land. Blauner replies that this does not change the basic fact that they were conquered and forced into a subordinate status in this country. Puerto Ricans (Boricuas) also largely fit the model, since America gained control over Puerto Rico, then a Spanish colony, through warfare. When Puerto Rico and Cuba fought for independence from Spain, the United States eventually joined the conflict in 1898, opposing Spain in what is now known as the Spanish–American War. Once the United States entered the conflict, Spain was quickly defeated. This resulted, eventually, in Cuba becoming independent, but Puerto Rico has remained under American rule as a U.S. territory ever since. For Puerto Rico, the result of this conflict was not its objective of independence but rather a transformation, in effect, from being a Spanish colony to being a U.S. colony. In one sense, however, Puerto Ricans on the U.S. mainland do not fully fit the definition of a colonized minority: Their presence is the result of a decision to immigrate, even though they did not voluntarily come under U.S. rule (Blauner, 1972). Moreover, though Puerto Rico's initial status as a U.S. territory was involuntary, it now has the legal right, if it chooses to do so, to become independent.

Nonetheless, the fact that Puerto Ricans first came under American rule by conquest has been a dominant factor in their experiences since, both in Puerto Rico and on the mainland. The experience of forced entry into American society distinguishes blacks, Chicanos, Indians, and, to a large extent, Puerto Ricans from all other American ethnic groups. However much discrimination various immigrant groups may have suffered, their entry here was voluntary. They did not take on the status of a conquered people. Blauner argues that this difference between immigrant and colonized minorities created vast differences in their position in American society, some of which persist today. According to Blauner, certain things always happen to ethnic or racial groups when they are conquered and colonized. First, they are forced to participate in somebody else's society, whether they want to or not. Second, they are subjected to some form of unfree labor, which "greatly restricts the social mobility of the group and its participation in the political arena" (Blauner, 1972, p. 53). Often, the colonized group is isolated in the least advanced sector of the society, away from the areas of growth and opportunity. Finally, the culture and social institutions of the colonized group are subjected to attack by the colonizer. The colonizer's objective is to *force* the group to give up its ways and accept the "superior" ways of the colonizer. As a result, the colonized minority is frequently subjected to the castelike patterns of intergroup relations discussed in the previous chapter. All of these things happened to blacks, Chicanos, and American Indians. (For further discussion of how this model applies to American Indians, see Snipp, 1986a, 1986b; Hall, 1989.)

It has been argued by some (see, for example, Murguia, 1975, chap. 3) that Mexican Americans fall somewhere between the colonial and immigrant classifications, largely because, despite their initial involuntarily presence, they have voluntarily been immigrating into the United States ever since the Southwest was annexed. However, the initial mode of contact—which for Chicanos was involuntary—shapes all subsequent contact. Even those who came as immigrants, for example, are influenced by the prejudice and the system of discrimination targeted toward a conquered people. For this reason, including the distinct Chicano history of subordination and subjection to unfree labor, many argue that the internal colonialism model describes very well the Chicano experience (Moore, 1970; Barrera, 1979; Mirande, 1985, 1987). Thus, despite some debate, Mexican Americans appear to fit the description of a colonized minority more closely than that of an immigrant minority.

The experience of blacks, American Indians, and Chicanos presents a sharp contrast when compared with that of European ethnic immigrants. For whatever reason, these immigrants came voluntarily. In some cases, their culture was closer to America's dominant culture than that of the other groups, but the critical difference is that they *chose* to enter and learn American culture. However much they may have been discriminated against, they never experienced the complete social control of the plantation or Indian reservation. They never experienced the unfree labor situation of the slave or the migrant farmworker. Their families and religious institutions were never systematically attacked as were those of black people and Indian people. Finally, they were never restricted to jobs outside the industrial mainstream, as were so many African Americans, Native Americans, and Chicanos. To all of these differences, we must add that a majority tends to have different and more intense prejudices toward a conquered and subordinated people than it has toward an immigrant people. Blauner's main point is actually quite simple: These tremendous historical differences place modern-day African Americans, Chicanos, Puerto Ricans, and Native Americans in a very different social position than their counterparts among the European ethnics. They have been, and are, subject to a number of socially imposed disadvantages that the immigrant groups are not, no matter how much they may have been discriminated against. Furthermore, the colonized minorities' relationship to the dominant society is and always has been fundamentally different. Blauner and others feel this offers one answer to two oft-repeated questions: (1) Why have blacks, Puerto Ricans, Chicanos, and Indians not assimilated to the degree that other groups have? and (2) Why do these four groups remain socially and economically disadvantaged when other groups, such as Irish Americans and Italian Americans, have enjoyed rising status? These sociologists believe that these differences result from the different historical experiences of *immigrant minorities* and *colonized minorities*. (Blauner, 1972, discusses all of these differences between European immigrant groups and colonized minorities at greater length.)

We have considered blacks, Puerto Ricans, Chicanos, Indians, and European immigrants in terms of the immigrant versus colonized minority dichotomy. By now, you may be wondering where the various Asian American groups fit in. The answer seems to be somewhere between an immigrant minority and a colonized minority. It is hard to classify their original presence in the United States as either completely voluntary or completely involuntary. The majority of Chinese immigrants during the peak period of migration in the nineteenth century came as indentured laborers or contract laborers. These immigrants were bound to creditors in China, to whom they had to pay off debt incurred for travel to the United States. Some of the contract laborers, who were referred to as "coolies," were actually forced into their servitude (Barth, 1964, pp. 50–59). The same was true of some, though far fewer, Japanese immigrants—mostly those who came by way of Hawaii (Ichihashi, 1969, chap. 5). The early immigration of Filipinos, whose homeland was in fact made into a colony of the United States, was also often less than voluntary. More recently, Vietnamese immigrants arrived as refugees—and served as a reminder of a war that many Americans would rather forget.

These groups might be classified as falling somewhere between immigrant and colonized minorities, and their experiences since their arrival in America support that view. Their labor was often unfree, with many tied to job and employer until their debts, contracts, or indentures were paid off. They were largely isolated in low-paying, labor-intensive sectors of the economy, as were blacks and Chicanos. On the other hand, they were not forcibly deprived of their land or subjected to the total control of slavery or the Indian reservation as were the other groups,[1] so they were in a more favorable position to retain their social organization and ways of life. Since many of them did come voluntarily, they were also more inclined to make some voluntary adaptation to American culture and institutions. Moreover, many of the more recent immigrants from Asia have been well-educated professional and managerial workers, who have had little trouble finding an economic niche. In short, both the nature of their arrival and their experiences after arriving in America suggest that the experiences of Asian Americans fall somewhere between the colonialized experience of blacks, Puerto Ricans, Chicanos, and Indians and the immigrant experience of the European ethnics.

Regardless of the exact position of any group on the immigrant-versus-colonized-minority continuum, Blauner's basic point seems to be correct. The experiences of those who entered America voluntarily have been quite different from the experiences of those who did not. Not only were they forced into American society against their will in the first place, but colonized minorities have also had imposed on them disadvantages, social control, and attacks on their culture that immigrant groups have not (see Lieberson, 1980, on this point with respect to blacks). Even the earliest immigrants from eastern and southern Europe experienced better social conditions in urban America than did their black counterparts (Lieberson, 1980). These differences have led to less assimilation, greater exploitation, and lower status, even to the present day, among colonized minorities as compared with immigrant minorities. To summarize, the position of any racial or ethnic group in America today cannot be understood without some examination of that group's history, going all the way back to how it first came into contact with American society.

Studies by Ogbu (1988), Zweigenhaft and Domhoff (1991), and Gibson and Ogbu (1992) show that this is the case not just in the United States, but in other countries as well. For example, in Japan, Koreans and the Burakumin—groups colonized and stigmatized in Japan—do poorly in Japanese schools. Yet in the United States, Koreans and descendants of the Burakumin (not recognized as a distinct group here but simply considered Japanese American) do as well as or better than

---

[1]A notable exception is the imprisonment of Japanese Americans in concentration camps during World War II, which is discussed later in this chapter.

white American children. This suggests very strongly that it is not the characteristics of a group or its traditional culture that determines success but rather how it is treated and viewed in the society in which it lives. Simply put, voluntary or immigrant minorities and involuntary or colonized minorities are treated very differently.

These researchers also suggest another reason why colonized minorities tend to be less successful than immigrant ones: The harsh treatment they receive produces in them an "oppositional identity," including rejection of the dominant group's values and cultural traits, that allows them to maintain a positive self-identity in the face of that treatment and the attacks on their culture. Whites, in turn, use that oppositional identity as a rationalization for rejecting minorities and keeping them in a low status, arguing that "they won't cooperate" or "they can't be trusted" (Fordham and Ogbu, 1986; Matute-Bianchi, 1986; Zweigenhaft and Domhoff, 1991, pp. 148–53). Thus, in addition to its other harmful effects on minorities, colonization tends to create a vicious cycle of reactions that create other disadvantages that immigrant minorities do not face. And, as these researchers show, these effects are found not only in the United States but in a number of other countries as well, including, for example, Japan and Sweden (Zweigenhaft and Domhoff, 1991).

EVOLVING PATTERNS OF BLACK–WHITE RACE RELATIONS

Caste Relations Become Unstable: The Development of Rigid Competitive Race Relations, 1860–1945

As America moved through the latter half of the nineteenth century and into the twentieth century, a number of important social changes were taking place. Throughout the Western world, including the United States, urbanization, industrialization, and an increase in the complexity of social organization were occurring. The dominant mode of production was shifting from agriculture, for which ownership of land was crucial, to industry and commerce, for which ownership of capital was crucial. In some ways it was a gradual, evolutionary process. In other ways, there were abrupt, cataclysmic changes. The Civil War, for example, is seen by most historians not simply as a struggle to free the slaves but as a more basic conflict between the rural, agrarian, landowning interests of the South and the rising industrial and commercial interests of the North. The North's victory is sometimes seen as a triumph of capitalism over feudalism, analogous in some ways to the outcome of the French Revolution. Both the abrupt changes that came with the Civil War and the more gradual changes that took place over a longer time caused important changes in the pattern of majority–minority relations in America, changes that are the main subject of this chapter.

The main effect of these changes was a destabilization of castelike race relations, but not—for a very long time—a real move toward their elimination. During the latter part of the nineteenth and early part of the twentieth centuries, the dominant pattern of American race relations came to resemble the rigid competitive pattern. This was most clearly true with regard to African Americans, but it was also largely true for Mexican Americans and Asian Americans and partially true for Native Americans and Puerto Ricans. Although the characteristics of rigid competitive patterns of race relations were described in some detail in the previous chapter, they can be briefly listed here:

1. Status is determined mostly, but not totally, by race. Small elites appear among generally disadvantaged minority groups.
2. Division of labor is largely but not totally by race. In some situations, both majority and minority group members are doing the same kind of work, although the minority group members are nearly always paid less for the same work. (This is called a *dual-wage market.*) Also, the job titles are frequently different for majority and minority group members even when the work is the same.
3. Separation of the races, or *segregation,* is extensive. The majority group imposes this segregation as a way of protecting its threatened status against the upward mobility of the minority group.
4. The competition over jobs (since in some situations both majority and minority are seeking and doing similar work) and other scarce resources carries the potential for severe conflict. Major outbursts of violence—usually attacks by majority group members against minorities—occur periodically.

The Antebellum North.   Perhaps the development of this pattern can be seen most clearly by examining the history of black–white relations of the nineteenth century and the first half of the twentieth century. The rigid competitive pattern was already well developed in the North before the Civil War. After slavery was abolished in the North—by 1804 in most of those areas where it had ever existed—blacks and whites, particularly lower-status whites who had recently immigrated from Europe, began to compete for jobs. Numerous discriminatory laws and practices were developed to protect white workers from black competition. In 1862, Irish longshoremen threatened to shut down the port of New York unless all black workers were fired (Bloch, 1969, p. 34). Earlier, laws had been passed in Illinois, Indiana, and Oregon banning black people from entering those states (Wilson, 1973, p. 95). By the time of the Civil War, a pattern of race riots was also becoming established in the North. In 1863, the worst riot in American history occurred in New York City as thousands of whites went on a rampage to protest being drafted to fight in the Civil War. It is estimated that up to two thousand people died in the violence (Bahr et al., 1979). Although this was not ostensibly a race riot, it had considerable racial overtones. First, it was largely a protest by whites against what they saw as being forced to fight a war to free black slaves. Second, like later race riots, it involved numerous attacks against blacks. Many blacks were beaten to death, and their homes destroyed. Clearly, then, racial resentment was a major factor in the violence. (For further discussion of northern race relations before the Civil War, see Litwack, 1961.)

The Postbellum South.   When the Civil War brought an end to slavery in the South, many hoped that it would result in major changes for the better in the pattern of race relations in the South. For a brief period of time known as Reconstruction, there were indications that such a positive change was happening. This period did not last, however, and before long, prejudice and racist ideology in the South intensified, and black–white segregation increased to a level beyond anything that existed under slavery. There are several important reasons why the Civil War did not bring an end to pervasive racial inequality in the South.

First, the elite planter class did not disappear at the end of the Civil War, though its power was certainly reduced. It still retained enough influence immediately after the war to pass a series of laws in southern states sometimes called Black Codes, aimed at keeping the black population in a subordinate status and, more specifically, at keeping blacks as a cheap source of labor (Woodward, 1971, pp. 251–52; Wilson, 1973, p. 99, 1978, pp. 52–53). These laws, passed in 1865–1866, were designed to force all blacks to work whether they wanted to or not, by providing for arrest and imprisonment of blacks who quit their jobs and by permitting those who refused to work to be fined and/or bound out to labor contractors (Franklin, 1969, p. 303; Wilson, 1973, p. 99). Laws were also passed that deprived blacks of the right to vote, hold office, serve in the military, sit on a jury, testify against whites in court, and travel freely (Gossett, 1963; Meier and Rudwick, 1970a).

These laws were quickly nullified by federal (that is, northern) intervention, which initiated Reconstruction. Partly for ideological reasons, but also in large part for political purposes (to strengthen their position nationally by giving the vote to southern blacks), the Republicans who controlled the U.S. Congress passed a series of laws in 1866 and 1867 protecting the rights of southern blacks. These civil rights laws and Reconstruction bills not only guaranteed protection of the rights of southern blacks and nullified the Black Codes but also established martial law in the South to enforce the federal policy. In addition, the Freedmen's Bureau was established to provide food, education, medical care, transportation, and, in some cases, land to freed slaves (and to many needy whites as well).

Reconstruction substantially improved the condition of southern blacks, both economically and politically. Blacks, for example, served in legislatures of southern states, occasionally in large numbers. At various times between 1869 and 1901, two blacks (Hiram R. Revels and Blanche K. Bruce, both from Mississippi) served in the U.S. Senate, and twenty blacks served in the U.S. House of Representatives. In spite of these improvements, Reconstruction did not last very long, and was soon replaced by a new version of the old order of racial inequality.

After about 1875, it became evident that Reconstruction was on its way out. In the North, political changes caused the federal government to lose its will to enforce the policies of Reconstruction. In the South, two important changes occurred. First, old Confederate officials and supporters—many of whom lost the right to vote at the start of Reconstruction—were given back the vote under amnesty or policies of universal male suffrage. This strengthened the political power of antiblack southern white Democrats. Second, southern whites opposed to Reconstruction took the law into their own hands by forming the Ku Klux Klan and a host of other violent secret societies that kept blacks from voting and exercising other rights. After Rutherford Hayes became president in 1876, federal troops were withdrawn from the South, and the reforms of Reconstruction were gradually undone. During the 1880s, blacks gradually lost the vote; segregation appeared and gradually became widespread in education and public facilities (Franklin, 1969, pp. 330–43). The Supreme Court began to strike down civil rights legislation that had been passed during Reconstruction and finally gave its full stamp of approval to segregation in the *Plessy* v. *Ferguson* case in 1896. In this ruling, the Court established the "separate-but-equal" doctrine, which upheld segregated facilities as long as the facilities available to each race were equal. As a practical matter, however, very little attention was paid to the "equal" part, and separate and *unequal* facilities became the rule throughout the South. By thirty-five years after the Civil War, a system of segregation existed that was unlike anything that had existed before, even under slavery. Prejudice and ideological racism (the belief that blacks are innately inferior) also rose to levels of intensity beyond even those of the slavery period.

Although historians debate which segment of the white population was responsible for and benefited from the establishment of racial segregation in the South, it is clear that both the upper and lower segments of the white population felt that they were benefiting from the reestablishment of strict racial inequality. There is little doubt that the main strength of the Ku Klux Klan and the greatest demand for segregation laws came from poor and working-class whites in the South. It was these whites who were in direct competition with freed blacks for land, under the sharecropping system, and for jobs. Thus, they sought to shield themselves from such competition through discrimination. The reaction of poorer whites to such competition was all the stronger because they had never had to compete directly with blacks in these ways before.

At the same time, the ruling class of the South—now composed both of the old planter class and a growing industrial elite—was happy to sit back and benefit from racism. As long as working-class whites and blacks saw each other as the enemy, there was little chance of a united, class-based movement against those who controlled the real wealth of the South. Thus, although the elite was willing to side at times with blacks against working-class whites to keep the latter under control, it was most definitely *not* willing to act effectively to prevent the emergence of a system of racial inequality that divided the poor and the working class along racial lines. Thus, both competition between lower-status whites and freed blacks *and* the desire of the upper economic class to protect its position by dividing its potential opposition helped to create and maintain the rigid system of segregation that developed in the South following the brief period of Reconstruction after the Civil War. (For further discussion of this period, see Woodward, 1966, 1971; W. J. Wilson, 1978, chap. 3.) Divisions and competition between poorer members of the majority group and minority group members are critical elements in a rigid competitive system of race relations and are a crucial reason for the emergence of such a system after Reconstruction.

There was, however, also an attempt by whites more generally to maintain a system in which whiteness conferred status; a system of **social distance.** Under slavery, doing so had been easy—everyone knew that whites were masters and blacks were slaves. This in itself created an unequal relationship from which the whites gained psychological and material benefit. If whites were to maintain such a relationship *after* slavery, however, they would have to find a new way to proclaim and enforce the norm of racial inequality. They did this by establishing segregation—in effect by replacing social distance with physical distance. Now, white superiority was proclaimed by setting up places and situations where only whites could go—and where blacks were defined as unworthy and unacceptable. In effect, society would be remade into a private club that only whites were good enough to enter. Special privilege and physical separation rather than a master–slave relationship were now the indicators of a system of white dominance and white superiority. Along with the policy of segregation came an intensified ideology of racism, as whites tried, through promoting notions of biological superiority, to retain the image of dominance and superiority that being a slaveowner race had given them. In short, the intensified racism and the rise of segregation after the Civil War represented an attempt by whites to hang onto the favored social and economic status that was threatened by the end of slavery.

There were some attempts during the post–Civil War period to break through the racial division and unify poor whites and blacks on the basis of class. Probably the most notable of these was the Populist party, which had some degree of success

Streetcar terminal in Oklahoma City, July 1939. Separate and usually unequal facilities were a predominant characteristic of the period of rigid competitive race relations in the United States. *Russell Lee, FSA, Library of Congress*

in getting the votes of both blacks and poor whites. The Populist appeal was clearly class-based, arguing that the rural poor of both races should unite to defeat the wealthy elite that ruled them. Consider, for example, the following statement by Populist leader Tom Watson: "You are made to hate each other because upon that hatred is rested the keystone of the arch of financial despotism which enslaves you both. You are deceived and blinded that you may not see how this race antagonism perpetuates a monetary system which beggars you both" (quoted in Woodward, 1966, p. 63). Watson gained substantial black support in Georgia, and a coalition of Populists and the remnants of Reconstruction-era liberal Republican organizations briefly gained control of the North Carolina legislature in 1894, resulting in the appointment of numerous black public officials (Franklin, 1969, p. 337). Ultimately, however, the Populists did not succeed. It became clear to them that the wealthy, southern Democratic elite could use laws designed to deny blacks the vote against poor whites, too. The elite's implicit threat to do so if the Populists continued to appeal to the black vote caused the Populists to back off this strategy in most areas. In addition, the Populists in many areas were hurt by the fraudulent use of black votes by conservative Democrats. Thus, the Populists were both weakened and frightened away from the black vote. In short, the strategy of the wealthy white elite to divide and conquer, though briefly challenged, was ultimately successful. As a consequence, black political power was thwarted, and the white working class was kept largely powerless and increasingly resentful of the threat of competition from blacks (for further discussion of the Populists, see Woodward, 1966, pp. 60–65; Franklin, 1969, pp. 335–38; Wilson, 1973, pp. 102–3, 1978, pp. 58–59).

In short, then, the power of the elite to divide and conquer the poor on the basis of race, combined with the real fear of the black population by working-class and poor whites who were forced into competition with it after the Civil War, led to a pattern of intensified prejudice, racism, and segregation by about thirty years after the Civil War. We can see again that the social-structural factors of unequal power, intergroup competition, and the opportunity for one group to gain by subordinating another played a crucial role in maintaining racial inequality in the South. Because the competition took a new form (the competition between poor whites and blacks for land and jobs) and because of federal intervention, which ended slavery, racial inequality took a new form. The old paternalistic system of slavery was replaced by a rigid competitive system of race relations, marked by strict segregation, heightened prejudice and ideological racism, and more intergroup conflict.

During the 1890s, most southern states went the final step and took measures to deprive blacks of the right to vote. Thus, on top of the new system of total segregation and the intensification of prejudice and racial ideologies already mentioned, blacks in the South lost virtually all of their political power. Before long, nearly all of the many blacks who had been elected to public office were gone. In effect, the racial caste system of the South was rather quickly restored in a new form. Because their status had been threatened by the end of slavery and the competition that entailed, whites now resorted to more violence against blacks than ever. According to Franklin (1969, p. 439), there were over twenty-five hundred lynchings in the last sixteen years of the nineteenth century. The great majority of the victims were black, and most of the lynchings took place in the South.

The following selection, drawn from the African American author Richard Wright's essay "The Ethics of Living Jim Crow," provides a graphic description of what black people experienced during the era of Jim Crow segregation, as the strict, legally-mandated segregation of blacks and whites came to be known. It also illustrates a number of features we have identified as characteristic of rigid competitive race relations: the white working class's fear of minority competition, the ideology of racial superiority, the segregation of blacks and whites, and the exclusion of blacks from white society.

THE ETHICS OF LIVING JIM CROW*

There is but one place where a black boy who knows no trade can get a job, and that's where the houses and faces are white, where the trees, lawns, and hedges are green. My first job was with an optical company in Jackson, Mississippi. The morning I applied I stood straight and neat before the boss, answering all his questions with sharp yessirs and nosirs. I was very careful to pronounce my *sirs* distinctly, in order that he might know that I was polite, that I knew where I was, and that I knew he was a *white* man. I wanted that job badly.

He looked me over as though he were examining a prize poodle. He questioned me closely about my schooling, being particularly insistent about how much mathematics I had had. He seemed very pleased when I told him I had had two years of algebra.

"Boy, how would you like to try to learn something around here?" he asked me.

"I'd like it fine, sir," I said, happy. I had visions of "working my way up." Even Negroes have those visions.

"All right," he said, "Come on."

I followed him to the small factory.

"Pease," he said to a white man of about thirty-five, "this is Richard. He's going to work for us."

Pease looked at me and nodded.

I was then taken to a white boy of about seventeen.

"Morrie, this is Richard, who's going to work for us."

"Whut yuh sayin' there, boy!" Morrie boomed at me.

"Fine!" I answered.

The boss instructed these two to help me, teach me, give me jobs to do, and let me learn what I could in my spare time.

My wages were five dollars a week.

I worked hard, trying to please. For the first month I got along O.K. Both Pease and Morrie seemed to like me. But one thing was missing. And I kept thinking about it. I was not learning anything and nobody was volunteering to help me. Thinking they had forgotten that I was to learn something about the mechanics of grinding lenses, I asked Morrie one day to tell me about the work. He grew red.

"Whut yuh tryin' t' do, nigger, get smart?" he asked.

"Naw; I ain' tryin' t' git smart," I said.

"Well, don't, if yuh know whut's good for yuh!"

I was puzzled. Maybe he just doesn't want to help me, I thought. I went to Pease.

"Say, are yuh crazy, you black bastard?" Pease asked me, his gray eyes growing hard.

I spoke out, reminding him that the boss had said I was to be given a chance to learn something.

"Nigger, you think you're *white,* don't you?"

"Naw, sir!"

"Well, you're acting mighty like it!"

"But, Mr. Pease, the boss said . . ."

Pease shook his fist in my face.

"This is a *white* man's work around here, and you better watch yourself!"

From then on they changed toward me. They said good-morning no more. When I was just a bit slow in performing some duty, I was called a lazy son-of-a-bitch.

Once I thought of reporting all this to the boss. But the mere idea of what would happen to me if Pease and Morrie should learn that I had "snitched" stopped me. And after all the boss was a white man, too. What was the use?

The climax came at noon one summer day. Pease called me to his workbench. To get to him I had to go between two narrow benches and stand with my back against a wall.

"Yes, sir," I said.

"Richard, I want to ask you something." Pease began pleasantly, not looking up from his work.

"Yes, sir," I said again.

Morrie came over, blocking the narrow passage between the benches. He folded his arms, staring at me solemnly.

I looked from one to the other, sensing that something was coming.

"Yes, sir," I said for the third time.

Pease looked up and spoke very slowly.

"Richard, *Mr.* Morrie here tells me you called me *Pease.*"

I stiffened. A void seemed to open up in me. I knew this was the show-down.

He meant that I had failed to call him Mr. Pease. I looked at Morrie. He was gripping a steel bar in his hands. I opened my mouth to speak, to protest, to assure Pease that I had never called him simply *Pease,* and that I had never had any intentions of doing so, when Morrie grabbed me by the collar, ramming my head against the wall.

"Now, be careful, nigger!" snarled Morrie, baring his teeth. "*I* heard yuh call 'im *Pease!* 'N' if yuh say yuh didn't, yuh're callin' me a *lie,* see?" He waved the steel bar threateningly.

If I had said: No sir, Mr. Pease, I never called you *Pease,* I would have been automatically calling Morrie a liar. And if I said: Yes sir, Mr. Pease, I called you *Pease,* I would have been pleading guilty to having uttered the worst insult that a Negro can utter to a southern white man. I stood hesitating, trying to frame a neutral reply.

"Richard, I asked you a question!" said Pease. Anger was creeping into his voice.

"I don't remember calling you *Pease,* Mr. Pease," I said cautiously. "And if I did, I sure didn't mean . . ."

"You black son-of-a-bitch! You called me *Pease,* then!" he spat, slapping me till I bent sideways over a bench. Morrie was on top of me, demanding:

"Didn't yuh call 'im *Pease?* If yuh say yuh didn't, I'll rip yo' gut string loose with this bar, you black granny dodger! Yuh can't call a white man a lie 'n' git erway with it, you black son-of-a-bitch!"

I wilted. I begged them not to bother me. I knew what they wanted. They wanted me to leave.

"I'll leave," I promised, "I'll leave right *now.*"

They gave me a minute to get out of the factory. I was warned not to show up again, or tell the boss.

I went.

When I told the folks at home what had happened, they called me a fool. They told me that I must never again attempt to exceed my boundaries. When you are working for white folks, they said, you got to "stay in your place" if you want to keep working.

II

My Jim Crow education continued on my next job, which was portering in a clothing store. One morning, while polishing brass out front, the boss and his twenty-year-old son got out of their car and half dragged and half kicked a Negro woman into the store. A policeman standing at the corner looked on, twirling his night-stick. I watched out of the corner of my eye, never slackening the strokes of my chamois upon the brass. After a few minutes, I heard shrill screams coming from the rear of the store. Later the woman stumbled out, bleeding, crying, and holding her stomach. When she reached the end of the block, the policeman grabbed her and accused her of being drunk. Silently, I watched him throw her into a patrol wagon.

When I went to the rear of the store, the boss and his son were washing their hands at the sink. They were chuckling. The floor was bloody and strewn with wisps of hair and clothing. No doubt I must have appeared pretty shocked, for the boss slapped me reassuringly on the back.

"Boy, that's what we do to niggers when they don't want to pay their bills," he said, laughing.

His soon looked at me and grinned.

"Here, hava cigarette," he said.

Not knowing what to do, I took it. He lit his and held the match for me. This was a gesture of kindness, indicating that even if they had beaten the poor old woman, they would not beat me if I knew enough to keep my mouth shut.

"Yes, sir," I said, and asked no questions.

After they had gone, I sat on the edge of the packing box and stared at the bloody floor till the cigarette went out.

That day at noon, while eating in a hamburger joint, I told my fellow Negro porters what had happened. No one seemed surprised. One fellow, after swallowing a huge bite, turned to me and asked:

"Huh! is tha' all they did t' her?"

"Yeah. Wasn't tha' enough?" I asked.

"Shucks! Man, she's a lucky bitch!" he said, burying his lips deep into a juicy hamburger. "Hell, it's a wonder they din't lay her when they got through."

III

I was learning fast, but not quite fast enough. One day, while I was delivering packages in the suburbs, my bicycle tire was punctured. I walked along the hot, dusty road, sweating and leading my bicycle by the handle-bars.

A car slowed at my side.

"What's the matter, boy?" a white man called.

I told him my bicycle was broken and I was walking back to town.

"That's too bad," he said. "Hop on the running board."

He stopped the car. I clutched hard at my bicycle with one hand and clung to the side of the car with the other.

"All set?"

"Yes sir," I answered. The car started.

It was full of young white men. They were drinking. I watched the flask pass from mouth to mouth.

"Wanna drink, boy?" one asked.

I laughed as the wind whipped my face. Instinctively obeying the freshly planted precepts of my mother, I said:

"Oh, no!"

The words were hardly out of my mouth before I felt something hard and cold smash me between the eyes. It was an empty whisky bottle. I saw stars, and fell backwards from the speeding car into the dust of the road, my feet becoming entangled in the steel spokes of my bicycle. The white men piled out and stood over me.

"Nigger, ain' yuh learned no better sense'n tha' yet?" asked the man who hit me. "Ain' yuh learned t' say *sir* t' a white man yet?"

Dazed, I pulled to my feet. My elbows and legs were bleeding. Fists doubled, the white man advanced kicking my bicycle out of the way.

"Aw, leave the bastard alone. He's got enough," said one.

They stood looking at me. I rubbed my shins, trying to stop the flow of blood. No doubt they felt a sort of contemptuous pity, for one asked:

"Yuh wanna ride t' town now, nigger? Yuh reckon yuh know enough t' ride now?"

"I wanna walk," I said, simply.

Maybe it sounded funny. They laughed.

"Well, walk, yuh black son-of-a-bitch!"

When they left they comforted me with:

"Nigger, yuh sho better be damn glad it wuz us yuh talked t' tha' way. Yuh're a lucky bastard, 'cause if yuh'd said tha' t' somebody else, yuh might've been a dead nigger now."

IV

Negroes who have lived South know the dread of being caught alone upon the streets in white neighborhoods after the sun has set. In such a simple situation as this the plight of the Negro in America is graphically symbolized. While white strangers may be in these noighborhoods trying to get home, they can pass unmolested. But the color of a Negro's skin makes him easily recognizable, makes him suspect, converts him into a defenseless target.

Late one Saturday night I made some deliveries in a white neighborhood. I was pedaling my bicycle back to the store as fast as I could, when a police car, swerving toward me, jammed me into the curbing.

"Get down and put up your hands" the policemen ordered.

I did. They climbed out of the car, guns drawn, faces set, and advanced slowly. "Keep still!" they ordered.

I reached my hands higher. They searched my pockets and packages. They seemed dissatisfied when they could find nothing incriminating. Finally, one of them said:

"Boy, tell your boss not to send you out in white neighborhoods after sundown."

As usual, I said:

"Yes, sir."

V

My next job was a hall-boy in a hotel. Here my Jim Crow education broadened and deepened. When the bell-boys were busy, I was often called to assist them. As many of the rooms in the hotel were occupied by prostitutes, I was constantly called to carry them liquor and cigarettes. These women were nude most of the time. They did not bother about clothing, even for bell-boys. When you went into their rooms, you were supposed to take their nakedness for granted, as though it startled you no more than a blue vase or a red rug. Your presence awoke in them no sense of shame, for you were not regarded as human. If they were alone, you could steal sidelong glimpses at them. But if they were receiving men, not a flicker of your eyelids could show. I remember one incident vividly. A new woman, a huge, snowy-skinned blonde, took a room on my floor. I was sent to wait upon her. She was in bed with a thickset man; both were nude and uncovered. She said she wanted some liquor and slid out of bed and waddled across the floor to get her money from a dresser drawer. I watched her.

"Nigger, what in hell you looking at?" the white man asked me, raising himself upon his elbows.

"Nothing," I answered, looking miles deep into the blank wall of the room.

"Keep your eyes where they belong, if you want to be healthy!" he said.

"Yes, sir."

VI

One of the bell-boys I knew in this hotel was keeping steady company with one of the Negro maids. Out of a clear sky the police descended upon his home and arrested him, accusing him of bastardy. The poor boy swore he had had no intimate relations with the girl. Nevertheless, they forced him to marry her. When the child arrived, it was found to be much lighter in complexion than either of the two supposedly legal parents. The white men around the hotel made a great joke of it. They spread the rumor that some white cow must have scared the poor girl while she was carrying the baby. If you were in their presence when this explanation was offered, you were supposed to laugh.

VII

One of the bell-boys was caught in bed with a white prostitute. He was castrated and run out of town. Immediately after this all the bell-boys and hall-boys were called together and warned. We were given to understand that the boy who had been castrated was a "mighty, mighty lucky bastard." We were impressed with the fact that next time the management of the hotel would not be responsible for the lives of "trouble-makin' niggers." We were silent.

VIII

One night, just as I was about to go home, I met one of the Negro maids. She lived in my direction, and we fell in to walk part of the way home together. As we passed the white nightwatchman, he slapped the maid on her buttock. I turned around, amazed. The watchman looked at me with a long, hard, fixed-under stare. Suddenly he pulled his gun and asked:

"Nigger, don't yuh like it?"

I hesitated.

"I asked yuh don't yuh like it?" he asked again, stepping forward.

"Yes, sir," I mumbled.

"Talk like it, then!"

"Oh, yes, sir!" I said with as much heartiness as I could muster.

Outside, I walked ahead of the girl, ashamed to face her. She caught up with me and said:

"Don't be a fool! Yuh couldn't help it!"

This watchman boasted of having killed two Negroes in self-defense.

Yet, in spite of all this, the life of the hotel ran with an amazing smoothness. It would have been impossible for a stranger to detect anything. The maids, the hall-boys, and the bell-boys were all smiles. They had to be.

IX

I had learned my Jim Crow lessons so thoroughly that I kept the hotel job till I left Jackson for Memphis. It so happened that while in Memphis I applied for a job at a branch of the optical company. I was hired. And for some reason, as long as I worked there, they never brought my past against me.

Here Jim Crow education assumed quite a different form. It was no longer brutally cruel, but subtly cruel. Here I learned to lie, to steal, to dissemble. I learned to play that dual role which every Negro must play if he wants to eat and live.

For example, it was almost impossible to get a book to read. It was assumed that after a Negro had imbibed what scanty schooling the state furnished he had no further need for books. I was always borrowing books from men on the job. One day I mustered enough courage to ask one of the men to let me get books from the library in his name. Surprisingly, he consented because he was a Roman Catholic and felt a vague sympathy for Negroes, being himself an object of hatred. Armed with a library card, I obtained books in the following manner: I would write a note to the librarian, saying: "Please let this nigger boy have the following books." I would then sign it with the white man's name.

When I went to the library, I would stand at the desk, hat in hand, looking as unbookish as possible. When I received the books desired I would take them home. If the books listed in the note happened to be out, I would sneak into the lobby and forge a new one. I never took any chances guessing with the white librarian about what the fictitious white man would want to read. No doubt if any of the white patrons had suspected that some of the volumes they enjoyed had been in the home of a Negro, they would not have tolerated it for an instant.

The factory force of the optical company in Memphis was much larger than that in Jackson, and more urbanized. At least they liked to talk, and would engage the Negro help in conversation whenever possible. By this means I found that many subjects were taboo from the white man's point of view. Among the topics they did not like to discuss with Negroes were the following: American white women; the Ku Klux Klan; France, and how Negro soldiers fared while there; French women; Jack Johnson; the entire northern part of the United States; the Civil War; Abraham Lincoln; U.S. Grant; General Sherman; Catholics; the Pope; Jews; the Republican party; slavery; social equality; Communism; Socialism; the 13th and 14th Amendments to the Constitution; or any topic calling for positive knowledge or manly self-assertion on the part of the Negro. The most accepted topics were sex and religion.

There were many times when I had to exercise a great deal of ingenuity to keep out of trouble. It is southern custom that all men must take off their hats when they enter an elevator. And especially did this apply to us blacks with rigid force. One day I stepped into an elevator with my arms full of packages. I was forced to ride with my hat on. Two white men stared at me coldly. Then one of them very kindly lifted my hat and placed it upon my armful of packages. Now the most accepted response for a Negro to make under such circumstances is to look at the white man out of the corner of his eye and grin. To have said: "Thank you!" would have made the white man *think* that you *thought* you were receiving from him a personal service. For such an act I have seen Negroes take a blow in the mouth. Finding the first alternative distasteful, and the second dangerous, I hit upon an acceptable course of action which fell safely between these two poles. I immediately—no sooner than my hat was lifted— pretended that my packages were about to spill, and appeared deeply distressed with keeping them in my arms. In this fashion I evaded having to acknowledge his service, and, in spite of adverse circumstances, salvaged a slender shred of personal pride.

How do Negroes feel about the way they have to live? How do they discuss it when alone among themselves? I think this question can be answered in a single sentence. A friend of mine who ran an elevator once told me:

"Lawd, man! Ef it wuzn't fer them polices 'n' them ol' lynch-mobs, there wouldn't be nothin' but uproar down here!"

*Selected excerpt from "The Ethics of Living Jim Crow" from *Uncle Tom's Children* by Richard Wright. Copyright 1937 by Richard Wright. Copyright renewed 1965 by Ellen Wright. Reprinted by permission of HarperCollins Publishers, Inc.

The Postbellum North.   In the North as in the South, the period immediately after the Civil War brought a short-lived easing of racial restrictions. The federal government's Reconstruction policies, aimed at transforming the South, had their effects in the North, too. For a time, from about 1870 to 1890, race relations in the North became more fluid, that is, less restrictive. Accounts of racial violence during this period (see, for example, Grimshaw, 1959a) focus mainly on the South, and Spear (1971, p. 154) reports that "there was probably more contact between the races [in the North] during this time than at any other time before or since." Following 1890, however, northern race relations took an abrupt turn for the worse, with a great upsurge in both prejudice and discrimination. Discriminatory devices of every type were used to keep blacks at a distance from whites and to protect whites from the perceived threat of black competition. It is significant to note that during this period there was also intensified prejudice and discrimination against other racial and ethnic minorities, notably Chinese Americans, Japanese Americans, and Mexican Americans in the West and Jewish Americans and Catholic Americans in the East. Sentiment against immigration was strong, and ideologies of racial superiority/inferiority were given legitimacy by scientific racists, who argued that science "proved" racial superiority (of their own race, of course).

There seem to be a number of reasons for this change, and it is striking that most of them in some way arose from the economics of the era, from some form of competition for scarce resources. To begin with, this was a period of unrestricted capitalism that led to some of the grossest exploitation of labor in American history. Accordingly, deep resentment developed among the working class (which in the North was still overwhelmingly white), and the beginnings of the American labor union movement were under way. At the same time, difficult conditions in the South were causing an increasing number of blacks to migrate to the North. They came to northern cities in sufficient numbers to be seen as a threat by whites but not yet in sufficient numbers to be a major political force. At the same time, large numbers of immigrants were arriving or had recently arrived on the East and West coasts.

The consequence was intense competition for jobs and housing, especially between white immigrants and blacks. This was made worse by labor and management practices. Most white workers saw blacks as a threat and tried to keep them out of the workplace. As a consequence, most of the labor unions discriminated against blacks and would not accept them as members. Blacks arriving from the South, desperately poor, were often willing to work for lower wages than whites. Even white immigrants at this time came from countries where opportunities were greater than those of southern blacks, and in the presence of racial discrimination were able to get better-paying jobs (Lieberson, 1980). For these reasons, dual-wage systems developed, in which blacks were paid less than whites for doing the same work. In other cases, blacks were kept out of certain "white jobs," at least until the white workers went on strike. For several reasons, blacks newly arriving in northern cities often ended up working as strikebreakers. First, their poverty often placed them in a position where they had little choice but to work any job that was offered. Second, because most unions excluded blacks, blacks were distrustful of and unsympathetic toward unions and therefore were sometimes willing to break their strikes. Third, being a strikebreaker was often the only way to move into certain better jobs that were normally reserved for whites. Finally, many employers actively sought out blacks to break their employees' strikes, realizing that their bargaining position would be enhanced if the working classes could be divided along the lines of race. In some cases, blacks in the South were promised jobs if they moved north, without being told that they would be breaking a strike.

For all these reasons, the use of blacks as strikebreakers stirred up racial tensions in northern cities large and small in the early twentieth century. In 1910, blacks were brought to Waterloo, Iowa, by the Illinois Central Railroad to break a strike by white workers (Kloss, Roberts, and Dorn, 1976). Railroads repeated that tactic in Chicago in 1916, and in the following ten years blacks were used to break six more strikes in that city (Bonacich, 1976). In East St. Louis, Illinois, use of blacks as strikebreakers in the meat-packing industry in 1916 and in the aluminum industry in 1917 was a significant factor contributing to that city's bloody race riot of 1917 (Rudwick, 1964). The most widespread instance of this practice occurred in 1919, when a nationwide steel strike was broken largely by the use of black strikebreakers. The steel companies brought an estimated thirty thousand to forty thousand blacks into the mills, mostly from the South, to break the strike (Foster, 1920). Of course, not all strikebreakers were blacks, and most black workers were not strikebreakers. Still, the use of blacks as strikebreakers was common enough to worsen the already tense relations of the era. Of course, the only real winners in these situations were the owners of the plants, mills, railroads, and so on. Because of their mutual fear and mistrust of one another—and their inherently weak bargaining position in an era of low wages and surplus labor—black and white workers were easily played off against one another.

These conflicts and similar ones over housing and other resources led whites—especially working-class and immigrant whites—to take drastic measures to protect their status from the real or perceived threats that blacks represented. Blacks were forced out of white neighborhoods by every means from boycotts to bombs. Juries and public officials stopped enforcing civil rights laws (Wilson, 1973, p. 104), and most public and private facilities became segregated. Even churches pushed out their black members. In short, there was in the North from 1890 on a shift toward the segregation that characterizes rigid competitive systems of race relations. Another characteristic of this pattern that was sadly evident was periodic severe outbursts of violence. Lynchings increased in the North, and the period from 1917 to 1919 included some of the bloodiest race riots in American history. Unlike the riots of the 1960s and 1970s, these riots involved mass fighting between blacks and whites, and the targets of the mobs were people, not property. Usually the riots broke out in cities where the black population was increasing and blacks and whites were competing for jobs. Fears of a sexual nature were also significant: Some of the riots started after rumors of attacks by blacks on white women were circulated in the white community. Nearly always the riots began with white mobs attacking blacks, and most of the victims were black. The two worst were in the Illinois cities of East St. Louis in 1917 and Chicago in 1919. The East St. Louis riot had the highest death toll of any U.S. riot clearly classifiable as a race riot until the 1992 Los Angeles riot, and among American riots of all types, it was, until 1992, exceeded in carnage only by the New York draft riot of 1863, discussed earlier in the chapter. The East St. Louis riot took forty-eight lives—thirty-nine black and nine white. The chilling accounts of this riot described the actions of whites as having a visible coolness and premeditation about it: "This was not the hectic and raving demonstration of men suddenly gone mad" (Rudwick, 1964, quoting reporters describing the violence). Two years later in Chicago, the violence was repeated. This riot was touched off when a group of black children swam into a white area on a Lake Michigan beach and were attacked by a white mob. Three days of violence ensued, with white mobs attacking blacks and black mobs striking back at whites. In this mayhem, thirty-eight people were killed: fifteen whites and twenty-three blacks. In both the Chicago and East St. Louis riots— and most of the other two dozen or so riots that occurred during this era—police did little or nothing to stop the white mobs from attacking blacks; they moved in only when the blacks began to strike back.

Although the tensions eased somewhat after 1920, the general pattern of discrimination, segregation, and periodic violent outbursts associated with the rigid competitive pattern of race relations continued until World War II. In 1943, in a situation of racial competition similar to the earlier situation in East St. Louis and Chicago, a bloody race riot erupted in Detroit. In this violence, twenty-five blacks and nine whites were killed.

It is notable that racial violence in the United States has closely corresponded with periods of war (Grimshaw, 1959b, 1969; Rudwick, 1964; Farley, 1994b). In fact, one study showed that of 210 major outbreaks of racial violence in the United States in the twentieth century, 202 occurred in just nine years during and immediately after World War I, World War II, and the Vietnam War (Schaich, 1975). While the specific causes of racial violence have varied in different periods, there do appear to be some ways in which war precipitates racial violence (Farley, 1994b). During World War I and World War II, for example, growth of wartime industries led to large-scale migrations of African Americans to several American cities, which in turn led whites in those cities to feel threatened. This was probably a factor in the East St. Louis, Chicago, and Detroit riots. Wars may also lead to heightened minority-group assertiveness, with minorities feeling that if they fight and risk their lives for their countries, they should receive some measure of equal opportunity in return. This may lead them to be more assertive, which in turn makes them seem more threatening to the dominant group. Sometimes, the dominant group responds to this perceived threat with violence and repression. Finally, war may heighten feelings of aggression, as well as a vicarious desire to participate. Under such conditions, domestic minority groups may be substituted for "the enemy," and attacked, a behavior pattern Mazón (1984) has referred to as "symbolic annihilation." It is important to stress, though, that war does not by itself *cause* racial violence—but it may make it more likely when conditions are otherwise favorable, as was the case during the era of rigid competitive race relations that prevailed in the North during the first half of the twentieth century.

RIGID COMPETITIVE RACE RELATIONS AND OTHER RACIAL/ETHNIC GROUPS

We have discussed the pattern of rigid competitive race relations mainly in terms of black–white relations, but from about 1880 to 1945 the pattern applied to a number of other minorities as well. In both the East and West, immigration was seen as a threat to the status of white workers and was widely opposed. Eastern Europeans and—largely by association—Catholics and Jews were the target in the East, Asian Americans and Mexican Americans in the West. In the East, strong opposition to immigration and accompanying surges of anti-Catholicism and anti-Semitism arose during periods of economic instability or downturn. Such periods occurred in the 1830s and the 1850s, from 1880 to 1900, and in the 1920s and 1930s (Simpson and Yinger, 1985).

Asian Americans

It was in the West that anti-immigrant sentiments were the strongest. The opposition to Asian immigrants became so strong that the U.S. Congress eventually passed laws forbidding Asians to immigrate to the United States. The first such law, passed in 1882, banned Chinese immigration. It was to last ten years but was repeatedly renewed until 1904, when it was made permanent. Immigration by Japanese was also gradually restricted after 1900, until it was ended entirely in 1924 by a quota system that banned all Asians from migrating to the United States.

While ethnic prejudices per se played an important role in the development of exclusionist sentiment, economic competition between whites and Asian Americans was probably the biggest cause. Of course, this competition was also a major cause of the prejudice. In any case, there was intense competition for jobs between whites and Asian Americans from the 1870s on. Asians, often in debt for passage to the United States, were frequently willing to work for lower wages than whites. This greatly aggravated the tensions between the two groups, and among most whites highly negative stereotypes ("deceitful," "opium smugglers," "clannish") replaced the earlier, more positive stereotypes. As had happened with blacks, considerable violence and mob action was directed against Asian Americans. Anti-Chinese riots broke out in San Francisco, Los Angeles, and a number of other areas. In San Francisco, white laborers rioted against the presence of Chinese workers in certain industries (Barth, 1964, p. 143). The Los Angeles riot of 1871 resulted in the death of twenty Chinese Americans (Kitano, 1985, p. 220). The Japanese were also sometimes the victims of violence: In 1890, fifteen Japanese cobblers were violently attacked by members of the shoemaker's union (Ichihashi, 1969). Boycotts of Japanese restaurants and other businesses were common in the early 1900s; in one case, the boycotters handed out matchboxes bearing the slogan "White men and women, patronize your own race" (Ichihashi, 1969, p. 235).

In 1906, the city of San Francisco banned all Japanese, Chinese, and Korean children from attending school with white students. Asian American students were required to attend a separate "Oriental school." In general, not only in education but in a number of areas, whites enforced a system that segregated Asian Americans much as had been done to blacks in other areas. These events set the stage for one of the most disgraceful events in all American history. During World War II, all persons of Japanese ancestry (defined as one-eighth or more Japanese) in the western United States were required by presidential order to be relocated to prison camps. By November 1942, nine months after the order, some 110,000 West Coast Japanese—most of them American citizens—were in the camps. They remained there for over two years. Many lost their incomes and possessions during the ordeal. One did not have to show any evidence of questionable loyalty to be in the camps—one only had to be Japanese. It is also significant that no such imprisonment was used against German Americans, even though the country was also at war with Germany. Racism appears to have been a crucial factor in the imprisonment of Japanese Americans (Grodzius, 1949; Hane, 1990).

With the one very serious exception of the internment of Japanese Americans, it is important to note that the severity of discrimination against Asians living in the United States gradually subsided after Asian immigration was banned. The apparent reason for this is that, as the banning of Asian immigration brought an end to rapid growth in the Asian population, the tendency of whites to see Asians as a serious economic threat subsided (Lieberson, 1980).

Mexican Americans

The patterns of competition, segregation, and occasional violent attacks that marked Asian–white relations also were evident in Anglo–Chicano relations. As with other groups, competition for jobs was an important cause of friction. Since many employers used a dual-wage system, paying Mexican Americans less than Anglos, many whites believed that Mexicans were responsible for low wages. Anglo labor unions also opposed Mexican immigration on the grounds that such immigration created a labor surplus that held down wages and raised unemployment. As had happened with blacks and Asian Americans, segregation in housing, schools, and public accommodations was imposed on Chicanos. Chicanos were sometimes the victims of mass violence, as other minorities had been. The worst was a week-long series of disturbances in Los Angeles in 1943, which have come to be called the "zoot-suit riots." The trouble began when gangs of white servicemen attacked Chicano youth wearing "zoot suits," a form of dress especially popular among young Mexican Americans. To many whites, zoot suits were a symbol of disrespect and lawlessness at a time when, because of World War II, national unity and sacrifice seemed especially important (Mazón, 1984). As the riots worsened, civilian whites joined the servicemen, and Mexican Americans were indiscriminately set on and beaten, whether or not they were wearing the zoot suits that supposedly were the target of the rioters. Chicanos—and some blacks and Filipinos as well—were dragged from streetcars and theaters and beaten. The police generally did not interfere with the rioters, but they did arrest a number of injured Mexican Americans after they had been beaten.

The press played a major role in inciting the race riot—for more than a year it had been headlining crime by Mexican youths and appealing to white fears. During the riots, the servicemen were presented in the papers as heroes, giving the "lawless youth gangs" a well-deserved lesson. The press also announced that Mexican "gangs" were planning a counterattack and even announced the times and places! These places then became the assembling points for mobs of whites who rampaged through the downtown area and Chicano neighborhoods beating and stripping people. The newspapers did not present the events as a race riot but rather as the action of servicemen attempting to restore law and order. The true character of these events—a race riot initiated and sustained by whites and in which only about half the Chicano victims were even wearing zoot suits—came out later. A committee appointed by the governor of California to investigate the riot concluded that it was a race riot, that Anglos were the main aggressors, and that the newspapers were largely to blame for the whole thing. This riot in Los Angeles triggered a number of similar disturbances in other western and midwestern cities and is seen by some as a contributing factor to Detroit's bloody race riot in 1943. (For a full account and analysis of the zoot-suit riots, see McWilliams, 1949, chaps. 12 and 13; the psychological factors contributing to this riot, including those related to World War II, are explored by Mazón, 1984.)

Overview

To summarize briefly, we can say that the general period from the end of the Civil War to World War II is a classic case of rigid competitive race relations. Urban populations of blacks, Asian Americans, and Chicanos increased rapidly at various places and times during this period, but their numbers were not yet great enough to give them much political power. All these groups were seen by whites as competitors for jobs, housing, education, and public facilities. All were limited to restricted, low-wage job markets as whites attempted to maintain the advantages they received in a racial caste system. The maintenance of that caste system, however, was threatened by the increasing industrialization of this period. Employers saw the advantage in playing white and minority workers off against one another. Dual-wage systems were set up in which minorities were paid less for the same work than whites. In addition to blatantly exploiting minority workers, this pattern also angered whites, who saw their wages and jobs threatened. They tried to protect their status by segregating and excluding minorities; blacks, Asian Americans, and Mexican Americans all experienced segregation during at least part of this period. White ethnocentrism, combined with fears of minority competition, and white economic and political power produced not only segregation but also violent outbursts against minorities, with the minorities receiving little or no protection or support from the law or the news media (for a summary, see Table 6.1). Thus, all the minorities mentioned above became the targets of race riots, suffered most of the casualties, and frequently ended up getting blamed for the riots, which were in fact initiated by whites. These riots tended to occur during periods when a city's minority population was growing rapidly and when white and minority workers were competing for jobs (Allport, 1954, pp. 59–61). As noted earlier, they were also particularly frequent around World Wars I and II, when ethnocentrism reached a fever pitch. While more peaceful at

Table 6.1   Major Riots in Which Whites Attacked Minority Group Members, 1860–1945

DATE	PLACE	NOTES
1863	New York	Draft riot, mass attacks by whites on blacks; total death toll, 1,000 to 2,000 (see text)
1871	Los Angeles	White mobs attacked Chinese Americans; 20 Chinese Americans killed (see text)
1898	Wilmington, N.C.	White attacks on blacks
1906	Springfield, Ohio, and Atlanta	White mobs attacked blacks (Boskin, 1969)
1908	Springfield, Ill.	Mass attacks by whites on blacks, black neighborhood burned; 2 blacks lynched, 4 whites killed by stray bullets (Crouthamel, 1969)
1917	East St. Louis, Ill., and other cities	Whites attacked blacks; 48 deaths (see text); disturbances also occurred in Philadelphia and Chester, Pennsylvania
1919	Chicago, Washington, D.C., and other cities	White attacks on blacks and interracial fighting; 39 deaths in Chicago (see text); 2 whites and 2 blacks killed in Washington. Other riots in Omaha; Knoxville; Charleston; Elaine, Arkansas; and Longview, Texas (Franklin, 1969; U.S. National Advisory Commission on Civil Disorders, 1968)
1921	Tulsa, Okla.	Mob attacks on blacks by whites, including, by some accounts, bombing from airplanes; 21 blacks, 9 whites killed (Franklin, 1969)
1943	Los Angeles, Detroit, and other cities	"Zoot-suit" riots; interracial fighting; 25 blacks and 9 whites killed in Detroit (see text; Franklin, 1969)

other times, race relations were still unequal and mostly segregated. Despite periods of relative fluidity and rigidity, the overall pattern changed little until after World War II: Segregation was still the rule. It has, however, changed dramatically since that time, a change that will be explored in the following sections.

A SHIFT TO FLUID COMPETITIVE RACE RELATIONS: AMERICA SINCE WORLD WAR II

Since World War II, dramatic changes have taken place in American race and ethnic relations. Debate continues over whether and to what degree race relations today are *better* than in the past, but there can be no question that race relations are substantially *different*. Today's majority–minority relations in the United States are an example of what Wilson (1973, 1978) calls fluid competitive race relations. Briefly, this can be classified as a system that is a mixture of caste and class, with more open and less restricted intergroup competition and decreasing amounts of overt or deliberate discrimination. In fact, such discrimination may even be illegal in such a system, as it is in the United States. In the next few pages, we outline some of the major characteristics of present-day American intergroup relations and see how they represent changes from the past.

A black woman is ushered onto a police truck after being arrested during the zoot-suit riot. In this riot, blacks and Chicanos attacked by white mobs were arrested, while police did little to control the white rioters. *UPI/Bettmann Newsphotos*

Changes in the Law: The Banning of Discrimination

As we have said, racial segregation and discrimination were the rule in most of the United States up to the time of World War II. In some areas, discrimination and segregation resulted from formal or informal practices in the private sector. Examples included unwillingness of many employers to hire blacks and other minority group members (or hiring them only for certain jobs), refusals of homeowners or realtors to sell to blacks, and segregated businesses, such as lunch counters. In other instances, discrimination was written into law. The laws of many southern states *required* discrimination in public facilities and education, and numerous state universities refused to accept blacks. These conditions remained largely in effect until the late 1940s to mid 1950s, and—in some cases—well beyond. In addition to this legally required discrimination, a great deal of private-sector discrimination operated with the support of the legal system. An example was the restrictive housing covenant. When a person purchased a house, she or he was frequently required—as a condition of purchase—to agree to a legally binding commitment not to sell the house to blacks, Jews, and/or other minority group members. This agreement had the backing of the law, so that it was actually illegal and punishable for the homeowner to sell to a minority group member. Without the backing of the law, the agreement would have been meaningless; accordingly, this private-sector discrimination was in fact made possible by the action of the public sector.

Beginning in the late 1930s, the law that at worst required and at best tolerated racial discrimination began to change. While not challenging segregation, court rulings in 1936 and 1938 did put some teeth in the "but equal" part of the old "separate but equal" doctrine. In 1936, the appellate court required that a black applicant be admitted to the University of Maryland Law School because there was no comparable state-supported facility for blacks. In 1938, the Supreme Court ruled the same way in a case involving the University of Missouri's Law School (Johnson, 1943). In 1946, federal courts ruled that segregation on interstate travel regulated by the federal government was illegal (Simpson and Yinger, 1985). In 1948, the Court ruled that states could no longer enforce restrictive housing covenants, though the writing of such agreements was not banned. The truly crucial ruling, however, came in 1954, in the *Brown* v. *Board of Education of Topeka* case. This ruling abolished the concept of "separate but equal," as the court ruled unanimously that separate schools could not be equal because segregating children on the basis of race "generates a feeling of inferiority as to their status in the community that may affect their hearts and minds in a way unlikely ever to be undone." In this and a related case, the Court ruled that the equal-protection clause of the Fourteenth Amendment and the due process clause of the Fifth Amendment forbade school segregation. Various legal rulings in the remainder of the 1950s and into the 1960s extended the *Brown* principle to all publicly operated programs and facilities, though some cities and states in the South defied these rulings well into the 1960s. In many cases, direct protest was a significant factor in getting local and state governments in the South to comply with the federal law. In general, the action of the courts was a critical factor in the elimination of segregation and overt discrimination by state, federal, and local bodies of government.

The banning of overt discrimination and segregation in privately owned businesses came later, and legislation and direct protest were both important factors in bringing about this change. Following the 1954 *Brown* decision, important civil rights laws were passed by Congress in 1957, 1960, 1964, 1965, and 1968. These laws protected the voting rights of blacks and other minorities, which in some parts of the country had been almost totally blocked by various tactics such as poll taxes and literacy tests. (At one time, tactics such as "grandfather clauses"—one could vote if his or her grandfather had been a voter—and the "white primary" had been used to restrict black voting, but these had been ended by earlier court decisions.) These laws also extended the protection against discrimination beyond the public sector to the private sector: Employers were not to discriminate in hiring, businesses were not to discriminate in the sales of goods or services, and real-estate owners and brokers were not to discriminate in the sale or rental of housing. These laws generally forbade discrimination on the basis of race, religion, color, or national origin. They did not, in general, deal with discrimination on the basis of other characteristics, such as sex, age, disability, or sexual orientation, with the important exception that the 1964 law did ban sex discrimination in employment. (More recent federal legislation, however, has banned many types of discrimination based on age and disability.) At the local level, numerous ordinances and laws were also passed against discrimination on the basis of race and ethnicity and, in some cases, other characteristics as well. Although these laws have not always been effective, it is indeed significant that by 1968 the clear position of American law was against racial and ethnic discrimination. This represents a near-total reversal of the situation twenty-five to thirty years earlier, when the position of American law had been somewhere between tolerating and requiring such discrimination. The change came about first by action of the courts and later through legislation by elected lawmaking bodies, with the help of court rulings legitimating and enforcing the legislation. It is important to stress that the court rulings and especially the legislation came largely in response to a powerful, articulate, and well-timed protest movement on the part of American minorities—a development that will be discussed at greater length in Chapter 7. (The stance of American government and law toward minorities past and present is discussed in Chapter 11.)

Changes in Economics: The Development of Substantial Middle Classes Among Minority Groups

While the status of minority groups in America will be discussed in greater detail in a later chapter, it should be stated here that one of the major changes in minority-group status since World War II is the presence of a sizable and growing middle class. There have always been some members of each American minority group who have attained middle-class or elite status. Until recently, however, pervasive racial discrimination in American society has kept the proportion attaining such status very small. In recent years this has changed. Now, substantial middle classes exist among blacks and Hispanics, though the majority would still be classified as either working class or poor. Among Chicanos, the educational gap with whites closed between 1950 and 1970, and the proportion of Chicanos in white-collar (professional, managerial, clerical, and sales) jobs increased, though improvement here was less extensive than in the educational area (Moore, 1976, pp. 64–67). Somewhat greater improvements were noted in the black population, especially in the job structure. Among black males, the percentage in white-collar jobs more than doubled from 8.6 percent in 1950 to 20.2 percent in 1970 (W. J. Wilson, 1978, p. 128). The comparable figure for Chicano males in the Southwest was 21.6 percent (Moore, 1976, p. 64), a rise from around 16 percent in 1950. Among both blacks and Hispanics, this figure rose further to about 26.9 percent in 1980 (computed by the author from U.S. Bureau of the Census, 1983a, pp. 45, 152). It should be pointed out that despite this substantial middle class among both groups, the comparable figures for white Anglos are much higher—over half of white males hold middle-class, white-collar jobs. Among Chinese Americans and Japanese Americans, who were also victims of segregation and discrimination—but against whom these patterns broke down earlier and more completely—the change has been such that by most criteria, both groups would be considered predominantly middle class today.

With the growth in minority middle classes has come an increase in social mobility among minorities. No longer are certain jobs reserved for whites or for minorities, as they frequently were before World War II. There is, in theory, free competition for jobs, unrestricted by rules of discrimination, although in reality, a considerable amount of informal discrimination persists. This continued pattern of informal discrimination has been demonstrated both by surveys of employers and housing providers (Kirschenman and Neckerman, 1991; Lake, 1981) and by testing studies in which socially similar whites and blacks apply for jobs or housing or attempt to make purchases (ABC News, 1991; U.S. Department of Housing and Urban Development, 1991; Ahmad, 1993). These studies show that blacks and whites are often treated differently when they shop, apply for jobs, or attempt to rent or buy housing—even though it is rare for anyone to openly say that they will not rent or sell to blacks.

Wilson (1978) has summarized changes in the class structure of the black population by noting that today there is more class stratification *within* the black population than ever before. In other words, we are moving—as is ordinarily true when competitive race relations become more fluid—from a *racial caste system* toward a *class system*. That is not to say, however, that we have moved all the way. Although Wilson sees race itself as declining in economic significance, he points out that there remains in the black population a large group, often called the *underclass,* that is not enjoying the benefits of this fluidity of race relations. Much the same is true of Chicanos and Puerto Ricans, despite their growing middle classes, and the underclass is even larger in the American Indian population. This impoverished underclass, which outnumbers the middle class among all four minorities, is trapped in poverty, apparently unable to move up. (We shall examine the reasons for this in later chapters.) Still, class stratification has increased within the black and Hispanic populations (but perhaps not in the American Indian population), and a portion of the black and Hispanic populations has experienced increased social mobility. (The debate over the relative importance of race and class as causes of minority group disadvantage are explored in greater detail in Chapter 15. For recent discussions of the urban underclass, see Wilson, 1987, forthcoming.)

Changes in Attitudes: Changes in the Kind and Degree of Prejudice Among Whites

Another clear trend in the past thirty to forty years has been an apparent substantial change in the kind and degree of racial and ethnic prejudice. These changes were discussed in greater detail in Chapter 3, but the major points can be restated here. First, racial prejudice of all three types discussed in that chapter has declined: Cognitive prejudice (stereotypical or racist beliefs about minorities) has decreased, as Americans today show less tendency to agree with stereotypical statements about racial and ethnic groups. Affective prejudice (dislike of minorities) has also declined, as people report more willingness to associate with minorities on a friendly basis. Finally, conative prejudice (desire to act in a discriminatory way) has declined, as fewer and fewer whites express support for segregation and discrimination. This does not, of course, mean that prejudice has been eliminated, and part of the change might be a result of greater "sophistication" or unwillingness to openly express feelings of prejudice. Still, the change in what people say, at least, has been quite dramatic. The second change is in the kind of prejudice, or, more precisely, the kinds of racist ideologies or beliefs that are accepted. Forty years ago, it was widely believed among whites that blacks and other minorities were *biologically* or *genetically* inferior. Today, those beliefs have greatly declined, despite the arguments in support of genetic racial intelligence differences by a few advocates such as Jensen (1969, 1973) and Shockley (1971a, 1971b). However, another form of racism, which W. J. Wilson (1978) calls *cultural racism,* has come to predominate. This view argues that minorities have developed cultural characteristics that in some way place them at a disadvantage. In more extreme forms, this view holds that groups are culturally inferior; in milder forms, minorities are believed to be at a disadvantage because of certain of their cultural characteristics. In other words, if people are poor (or a minority group is disproportionately poor), it is their own fault. Feagin (1972), Schuman (1975), and Kluegel (1990; see also Kluegel and Smith, 1986) have demonstrated that this view is very widespread among whites—even ones who consider themselves unprejudiced—and that it is specifically used by many whites to explain black poverty. This allows whites to escape the burden of responsibility arising from the facts that whites, by discrimination and exploitation, created minority poverty in the first place and that many of them continue to benefit from it (see, for example, Gans, 1971). This leads readily to the *symbolic racism* discussed in Chapter 3, which is marked by unwillingness to make the changes that would be needed to eliminate the disadvantages that blacks and other minorities in our society experience (Pettigrew, 1985; Kluegel, 1990).

FACTORS CAUSING THE CHANGES: THE EFFECTS OF URBANIZATION AND INDUSTRIALIZATION

The twentieth century has been a period of dramatic urbanization and industrialization in the United States. This process was already under way at the turn of the century, but at that time the United States was still a predominantly rural society. Today, it is overwhelmingly urban. Industry and technology have expanded tremendously in this century, and increasingly the productive capacity of the country has come to be owned by massive corporations. For minority groups, the transformation has been even more rapid. Early in the century, blacks and Mexican Americans were more rural than the white population; today, they are more urban. Much of the urbanization of these groups occurred between World War II and about 1970, though the process had begun earlier. Only Indians are less urban than the white population.

Urbanization, modernization, and industrialization have influenced majority–minority relations in numerous ways and can directly or indirectly explain much of the change. We have already noted that Van den Berghe and Wilson have argued that as urbanization proceeds, societies often move from castelike race relations toward increasingly classlike race relations. We have seen that this type of change has corresponded to urbanization and industrialization in the United States. That, of course, does not prove that they caused the change. Nonetheless, a number of consequences of urbanization and industrialization do seem to push in the direction of more fluid race relations. In this section, we shall enumerate and briefly discuss some of these factors.

Requirement of Greater Mobility and the Economic Irrationality of Discrimination

To operate effectively, industrial societies require greater mobility than do agricultural societies. Especially in the modern era of giant corporations and complex technology, employees are frequently recruited on a nationwide basis. Considerable geographic and social mobility is required to achieve the best match of person and job.

In addition, getting the best match of person to job suggests that such considerations as race, religion, and parentage—ascribed statuses—should not influence the hiring decision. Only job qualifications should matter, as considering ascribed statuses can only interfere with the best match. The same can be said of other kinds of activities and transactions. It does not make sense for a seller of goods or services to cut off potential buyers because of race, religion, or some other irrelevant factor. In short, a complex, modern society works at maximum efficiency when all irrelevant factors such as race are disregarded. This was recognized by the classic sociological theorist Max Weber (1968), who argued in the early twentieth century that such *rationalization* is the critical element in the emergence of industrial society. Many theorists of race and ethnic relations see such rationalization as a key force leading to the breakdown of discrimination as societies modernize.

If rationalization had been the only social force at work, however, it might not have been sufficient to cause the changes that have taken place. The social psychologist Herbert Blumer, in a widely cited article entitled "Industrialization and Race Relations" (1965), argues that the forces of modernization and rationalization do *not* always lead to more fluid race relations. Even with industrialization (and sometimes because of it), some elements within society perceive that they are gaining from the subordination of minorities, and these elements press for continued discrimination. We have already seen examples of white workers trying to shield themselves from black, Chicano, or Chinese competition. Thus, were it not for other changes that reduced majority demands for discrimination and created a situation conducive to the development of strong and effective minority group movements, the changes in majority–minority relations might never have occurred, even with industrialization.

Generally Rising Educational Levels

Another trend that has occurred throughout the twentieth century and become especially pronounced after World War II is a rising educational level. Among minority group members, this has tended to promote greater assertiveness, as we shall see in Chapter 7. Among whites it has undoubtedly led to some increase in tolerance, as the irrationality of prejudice is revealed. We have already seen in Chapters 2 and 3 that there is some tendency for prejudice to decrease at higher levels of education. Thus, the increasing educational level of the population has probably played some role in the education of prejudice and overt discrimination.

Postwar Economic Growth and Easing of Intergroup Competition

We have already seen that intergroup competition is an extremely important cause of intergroup prejudice, discrimination, and conflict. It therefore follows that when intergroup competition is reduced, intergroup relations should improve. Wilson (1978) makes a strong case that this is what happened during the 1950s and 1960s. In general, this was a prosperous time. The economy was growing rapidly, unemployment was for the most part fairly low, and the number of jobs was increasing, especially in the white-collar sector. This meant a number of things, all of which tended to bring about more fluid race relations. First, new opportunities were opened to blacks and other minorities in the expanding economy. Second, the position of minority-group members was more secure, so it was safer for them to make demands for more equality. Third, whites—especially middle-class ones—were less threatened by minority gains than in the past. This meant they could be less prejudiced, more receptive to the demands made by minorities, and more accepting of court rulings against discrimination and segregation. In short, the expanding economy and reduced intergroup competition of the postwar period made the climate favorable for easing the strict racial barriers of the prewar period.

Increased Assertiveness on the Part of Minorities

Probably very little if any of the changes in race relations would have come about were it not for one additional factor—the increased assertiveness of minorities, most notably the African American civil rights movement of the 1950s and 1960s and the legal efforts of the NAACP (National Association for the Advancement of Colored People). These changes, too, arose in large part from postwar urbanization, industrialization, and economic growth. Both in and of itself and as a means of understanding the changing pattern of race relations after World War II, the rise of minority group social movements is of special importance, and this is a major focus of Chapter 7.

SUMMARY AND CONCLUSION

In this chapter, we have seen that urbanization, industrialization, and the Civil War brought important changes in U.S. race relations. While slavery ended, racial inequality did not, and segregation became more widespread than ever, remaining so for well over half a century. White Americans clashed with African Americans, Asian Americans, and Mexican Americans in some of the worst domestic violence in U.S. history. As in earlier periods, economic factors continued to have an important effect on intergroup relations, as various groups of whites used segregation, minority group strikebreaking, and race riots to try to hold on to their economic advantage. Thus, competition and unequal power continued to be important forces shaping intergroup relations.

After World War II, however, formal policies of segregation began to be abolished. A number of factors contributed to this change. Among the most important were expansion of the economy and an upsurge in minority group social movements, which have continued to be a major force in American life ever since. These movements, and how they have changed over the past several decades, are explored in Chapter 7.

7

Minority-Group Movements, Values, and Contemporary Intergroup Relations

In the first part of this chapter, we shall explore the reasons that the black civil rights movement and other minority group movements became so influential in the 1950s and 1960s. Later, we shall consider how these movements have changed over time and some corresponding changes in the attitudes and beliefs of minority group members in America.

For any social movement, such as the civil rights movement, to emerge, people must decide that they want to make some change in society. Such a decision is only one of two major ways that people can respond when they find themselves in a situation that they do not like. These two responses are to *adapt* to the situation—to attempt to get along as best they can in a bad situation—or to try to *change* the situation. People can decide that they are not willing to put up with the situation and are therefore going to change it to something more favorable. Basically, the responses of minority-group members to the undesirable situation of being dominated or subordinated can be fit into one of these two approaches. Either they are *adaptive* strategies, which try to make the situation as tolerable as possible, or they are *change-oriented* strategies, which seek to change the situation for the better. In the following section, we shall discuss some responses that fit into each category.

ADAPTIVE RESPONSES

There are four common ways of responding to subordinate or minority status that are mainly adaptive. They are feigned or real *acceptance* of the status, *displaced aggression, avoidance* of the status, and *seeking assimilation* into the majority group. Each of these responses takes the system of unequal statuses as a given and attempts to adapt to or live with that system. Let us discuss each in somewhat more detail.

Acceptance

The response involving the greatest degree of resignation to a socially imposed position of disadvantage is to just accept it. When minorities choose to simply accept their lower status, several things may be happening. One possibility is that they really have become convinced of the ideology that whites are superior and minorities deserve an inferior role. Such a response is certainly not unheard of among relatively powerless people. Clark and Clark's (1958) doll studies (discussed in detail in Chapter 12) suggest that racism did result in a lower self-image among some black children during the 1950s. Many also point to the opposition of some women to the Equal Rights Amendment as an example of internal acceptance of a subordinate role.

More commonly, however, people do not accept that they should have a lower status or are inferior yet recognize the reality that they *do* have a lower status and believe that little can be done about it. In this case, the usual response is to put up with the situation and try to make the best of it.

A third response of this type is to *pretend* to accept the status, and play on majority-group prejudices. In effect, it says, If they think we're all stupid, then we'll pretend to be stupid, fool them, and use it to our advantage. It calls to mind the story (of unknown truth) about a southern sheriff who stopped a black man for running a red light. The man responded, "But sir, I didn't want to go on the white folks' light [green]. I thought us black folks was supposed to wait for the other one." The sheriff, completely fooled, responded, "Well, OK, I guess you meant well. But from now on, I'm going to let you go on the white folks' light," and got into his car and drove off.

Displaced Aggression

You will recall from Chapter 2 that when people feel frustrated, and consequently aggressive, but cannot take it out against the person or thing causing the frustration, they will take it out against some easier or more available target. This is called *displaced aggression,* or *scapegoating,* and as we have seen, it is a common cause of prejudice among majority group members. Such displacement of aggression also frequently occurs among minority group members. If they are oppressed by members of the dominant group and the power structure does not permit them to strike back, they may well displace the aggression. This helps to explain the tragic fact that minority group members frequently commit violence against other minority group members and, more generally, the fact that crime rates are frequently high among members of subordinate racial or ethnic groups. Most crimes are committed against others of the same racial group, and in recent years, as the plight of the urban underclass has worsened, rates of black-on-black and Latino-on-Latino crimes have risen in America's inner cities. This is particularly the case for certain types of street crimes, such as assaults and robberies. Much of this crime appears to represent displaced aggression, as feelings of hopelessness and frustration have worsened in areas of chronic, concentrated poverty (Anderson, 1990; Wilson, forthcoming). Such displacement of aggression may also explain high suicide rates among some ethnic minority groups, as feelings of frustration and aggression may even be turned against oneself.

Avoidance

Another way of dealing with a bad situation is to try to avoid reminders of it, or to try to escape reality entirely. One way minority group members may do this is to avoid contacts with majority group members, which may remind them of their subordinate status. Others may turn to a more generalized kind of avoidance or withdraw from one's role entirely. Such means as alcohol or drugs are sometimes used for this purpose. It is frequently true that alcoholism and drug abuse rates are high among subordinate ethnic groups; apparently, such substance abuse offers the hope of escape from an unhappy situation not of one's own making. In recent years in the United States, the percentage of minorities using illegal drugs has in fact been lower, not higher, than the percentage of whites using illegal drugs. However, the kinds of drugs that are more likely to be used by urban, low-income African Americans and Latinos are stronger and more addictive, and are thus more likely to result in serious problems of drug dependency. While young whites are most likely to use marijuana, stronger drugs including heroin, cocaine, and crack cocaine are much more commonly used by minority youth, particularly in areas of concentrated poverty. Such drug use is often a means of escape.

Seeking Assimilation

This response might best be classified as accepting the *system* but attempting to deny one's role within that system. In effect, the minority group member seeks either to become a member of the majority group or to become accepted in its culture and/or social institutions. In this case, no real attempt is made to change the system of majority–minority relations. Rather, the minority group individual attempts to change his or her individual position or role within that system.

The most extreme form of this response is the practice of "passing." Sometimes minority group members who are close in appearance to whites have presented themselves to the world as whites—or passed as whites. This has enabled them to enjoy the advantaged status that is reserved only for members of the majority group. It is not known how many people do this, but it does at least occasionally happen. (For discussions of the extent of the practice among American blacks, see Stuckert, 1958; Simpson and Yinger, 1985, pp. 139–140, 507.)

While members of racial minority groups sometimes engage in "passing," other, nonracial minority groups often engage in similar practices, and it can be easier for them to do so. For example, some homosexuals choose to remain "in the closet"—in other words, to deny to the outside world that they are homosexuals. In some societies, persecuted religious minorities have practiced their religions in secret to avoid discrimination. All of these closely related strategies have a disadvantage: They tend to produce great psychological stress because they force people to deny who they are. This constant denial of one's identity is both stressful and degrading—but some feel it necessary when they are faced with situations of intense discrimination. Even today, there are situations in which members of some nonracial minorities are virtually forced into such behaviors. The 1993 compromise policy on gays in the military, dubbed "don't ask, don't tell," in effect forbids gays in the military from publicly acknowledging their sexual orientation: Those who do so are supposed to be discharged from the armed forces.

More common than the above practices, however, is the practice of seeking cultural assimilation with the majority—adopting the lifestyles, fashions, and values of the majority group. Often, this is aimed at gaining acceptance with the majority group. This practice has been more common among the minority group middle classes than among the poor or working classes. In fact, minority middle-class people may attempt to put distance between themselves and poor people of the same minority group. It has been noted, for example, that some black middle-class neighborhoods have resisted the introduction of low-cost, subsidized housing as strongly as have any white middle-class neighborhoods. Other evidence may be seen in the popularity of straightened hair ("process" haircuts) among many blacks in the 1950s and early 1960s and the practice among a number of groups of "Americanizing" ethnic names. Although some people in minority groups still seek assimilation into the majority, there has been some movement away from this pattern since the mid 1960s. We shall examine the reasons for this change in a later chapter.

CHANGE-ORIENTED RESPONSES

The alternative to trying to live with an unpleasant position is trying to change that situation. Change-oriented responses to minority status attempt to change the nature of majority–minority relations in a society and/or to change the role or position of the minority group in that system. Such efforts vary in both their *goals* and *strategies*. The *goal* of such a movement may be to bring about a systemwide *assimilation*—to create a society and culture that is common, shared, and equal among the former dominant and subordinate groups. This results in a cultural and social coming together of the two groups, although in practice, the new culture and society usually resembles that of the old majority group more than that of the old minority group. Other change-oriented responses seek a different outcome—they seek to build alternative, minority-controlled institutions. This approach aims to preserve and strengthen minority group culture and to build an independent power base that will ultimately make the minority politically, socially, and economically stronger. To some degree, this encourages movement toward separate or distinct minority and majority group social structure rather than the single shared structure sought by assimilation. Of course, these goals are ideal types; real-life social movements most frequently fall somewhere between, with some elements of each approach.

The *strategies* of movements seeking change also vary. They may be legal and within the system, or they may go outside the system and use illegal strategies. Examples of within-the-system strategies include legal campaigns, such as lawsuits and judicial appeals, legislative campaigns (attempting to pass favorable legislation), voter-registration and election efforts, legal strikes and boycotts, and peaceful legal protests that appeal but do not disrupt. Outside-the-system strategies include peaceful but illegal protests aimed at disruption (nonviolent sit-ins are a good example) and violent forms of protest such as riots and bombings.

A SHIFT TOWARD CHANGE-ORIENTED RESPONSES

Minorities have always responded to subordinate status with both adaptive and change-oriented responses, and they continue to do so today. Nonetheless, there has been a shift in this century, particularly since World War II, *away* from adaptation and *toward* change. Largely because the power structure made it difficult or impossible to do otherwise, the earlier response by minorities to their socially imposed disadvantage fell more in the adaptive category than in the change-oriented one. This is not to say that most minorities were satisfied with their roles; they were not. Furthermore, important efforts aimed at changing the system had been made by all minorities. We have already discussed slave rebellions among blacks before the Civil War; here we shall briefly note some of the protest movements of the period between the Civil War and World War II. In the late 1860s, and again from 1900 to 1906, boycotts and protests were carried on against segregated streetcar systems in southern and border cities (Meier and Rudwick, 1969; Wilson, 1973). The first wave of protest ended such segregation in New Orleans, Louisville, Charleston, Richmond, and Savannah. The later campaign, though less successful, involved fully twenty-six cities. In the 1870s, the Negro Convention Movement became an important political force protesting violence against blacks and seeking civil rights enforcement of the Fifteenth Amendment, which forbade racial discrimination in voting. In the early twentieth century, the social movements led by Marcus Garvey and W. E. B. Du Bois were important. Garvey's separatist "Back to Africa" movement enjoyed widespread support among low-income blacks, and Du Bois' militant movement for racial integration and equality helped lead to the founding of the NAACP.

Among Mexican Americans, the amount of pre–World War II protest activity was less than among blacks (Simpson and Yinger, 1985, pp. 427–29) but still significant. In the 1880s, the Caballeros de Labor sought to unionize Chicano workers and protest the taking of Chicano land by Anglos. In the teens, twenties, and particularly the thirties, Chicano farmworkers struck in California; the movement to unionize farmworkers, then as now, was largely led and coordinated by Mexican Americans. In 1929, a number of organizations combined to form the League of United Latin American Citizens (LULAC). This organization combated segregated schools, exclusion of Mexican Americans from jury duty, and exploitation of farm labor (Meier and Rivera, 1972, pp. 241–43).

In comparison with these and other pre–World War II minority-group social movements, movements since World War II have been considerably more significant. Movements by African Americans, Latinos, Native Americans, and a number of other ethnic groups have been larger, more powerful, more widely supported, and more successful than before. Furthermore, more minority group people have rejected various ways of adapting to subordinate status. To these masses of people, adaptation is unacceptable because subordinate status is unacceptable. Since World War II, they have demanded change to an extent that has never been seen before.

THE RISING TIDE OF PROTEST

It is impossible here to provide a detailed history of the protest movements of minority groups during the postwar era; to do so would fill volumes. We shall, however, attempt to present a brief overview of some of the major events since World War II.

Among African Americans, the activity during and after the war centered largely in the courts. The NAACP began to pursue legal efforts against discrimination more vigorously and more effectively in the 1940s and 1950s, and this effort led up to most of the important court rulings discussed in Chapter 6, including the 1954 *Brown* decision. There were other efforts, too—most notably A. Philip Randolph's threat to organize a massive march on Washington if President Roosevelt did not ban job discrimination in military supply industries during World War II. (Under the threat of such an internationally embarrassing demonstration, Roosevelt did issue an order banning such discrimination.)

Gradually, as the 1950s gave way to the 1960s, such actions became more widespread. Court rulings were important, but their effectiveness was limited for two reasons. First, local governments—especially in the South—seldom complied promptly with the court orders. Typically, they stalled and looked for ways around the orders; sometimes they even defied those orders more or less openly. An example of this is the Little Rock, Arkansas, school desegregation case. Governor Orval Faubus defied a federal court order in 1957 to desegregate a high school in that city; President Eisenhower had to send federal troops to the city to carry out the order. A second limitation of the courts was that their orders—before the civil rights laws of the 1960s—generally applied only to public-sector discrimination, not discrimination perpetrated by private businesses or organizations. For these reasons, the civil rights movement had to change its tactics to include direct action.

A crucial event took place in 1955, that precipitated a move toward direct-action protest movements. A black woman named Rosa Parks refused to give up her seat on a bus in Montgomery, Alabama, to a white man. This led to a campaign to desegregate that city's bus system. The campaign was joined by a young minister named Dr. Martin Luther King. Months later and bolstered by a federal court order, the battle was won. This victory led to similar campaigns around the country and helped catapult Dr. King into a position of national leadership. Applying the principles and philosophy of nonviolent resistance developed in India by Mahatma Gandhi, King led similar campaigns around the country. Notable among these was the 1963 struggle in Birmingham, Alabama, in which hundreds of peaceful protesters were jailed, beaten, and fire-hosed by police, and in which the motel where Dr. King was staying was bombed, as was his brother's house. These protests and others, along with a massive demonstration by about 250,000 blacks and whites in Washington later that year, helped bring about the Civil Rights Act of 1964. It was at this demonstration that Dr. King gave his famous "I have a dream" speech. Other major events in the civil rights movement included the student sit-ins at lunch counters and various public facilities in the early 1960s and the freedom rides to protest segregated transportation facilities. In 1965, Dr. King's famous march from Selma to Montgomery, Alabama, helped to pass the 1965 Voting Rights Act.

Not all the action was in the South. Campaigns against discrimination were also carried on in a number of northern cities. A protest march against housing segregation led by Dr. King on Chicago's southwest side was attacked by a mob of angry whites, leading him to say he had never seen such racial hatred anywhere in the South. By the mid 1960s, white resistance to civil rights had grown sufficiently strong that many blacks felt new tactics were needed; furthermore, a repeated pattern of violent attacks against peaceful protesters was raising tensions to a critical point. The objectives of the protesters began to change; "black power" replaced desegregation as a goal. During this period, leaders with a new, more militant message began to emerge. These leaders, such as Malcolm X and Stokely Carmichael, began to stress survival, economic equality, and political power as the immediate goals of the black movement. These goals required changes far more drastic than civil rights laws, but they spoke directly to the immediate concerns of impoverished blacks in big-city ghettos.

At the same time, many blacks were beginning to question the value of non-violence in light of the strong and often violent resistance to change on the part of whites. The failure of civil rights laws to bring change in the day-to-day life of poverty-stricken urban blacks also led to a heightened frustration. Given the increasing anger and frustration of American blacks, it is not surprising that a wave of violent rebellions spread across the country during the period of 1964–1968. Violence broke out in hundreds of cities, and the rebellions resulted in scores of deaths (mostly blacks killed by law enforcement officials) and millions of dollars in property damage. The worst of these outbreaks were in the Watts district of Los Angeles in 1965 (thirty-four deaths), and in Newark (twenty-five deaths) and Detroit (forty-three deaths) in 1967 (U.S. National Advisory Commission, 1968). In 1968, Dr. Martin Luther King was shot to death on the balcony of a motel where he was staying in Memphis, Tennessee, to support a garbage collectors's strike. This violent attack on a man who had won the Nobel Prize for his advocacy of peaceful protest was, to many, the straw that broke the camel's back. Violent outbursts occurred in numerous cities, with especially severe ones in Washington and Chicago. More than ever, the effectiveness of peaceful protest was called into question. (For further discussions of the black civil rights and Black Power movements of the 1950s, 1960s, and early 1970s, see Killian, 1968, 1975; Meier and Rudwick, 1970b; Pinkney, 1975; Morris, 1984.)

Blacks were not the only groups turning to change-oriented movements during this era. After World War II, Mexican American veterans returning home to find discrimination formed the G.I. Forum, which became one of the most influential

The failure of the civil rights movement to bring increased economic opportunity to inner city blacks contributed to the growing influence in the 1960s of leaders such as Malcolm X, who offered a more militant message than earlier civil rights leaders. *Sygma/Ted Russell*

Chicano organizations of the 1950s and 1960s (Meier and Rivera, 1972, pp. 245–47). This organization fought discrimination at the local level and conducted voter-registration drives and lobbying efforts throughout the Southwest. In the 1960s, Chicanos increasingly turned to direct-action protest. Student walkouts and protests over discrimination, biased materials, and prejudiced teachers occurred in a number of areas. In California, a campaign begun by Cesar Chavez to unionize agricultural laborers led to massive strikes in 1965 and subsequent years and to nationwide boycotts of table grapes, lettuce, and certain wines. Like King, Chavez practiced Gandhian nonviolence and even went on an extended fast (with some damage to his personal health) to protest violence in his movement. Like King's, Chavez's efforts were met with considerable violence by Anglos. However, his efforts were also successful as never before in unionizing a sizable segment of farm labor.

Chicanos were carrying on other, more militant action. In New Mexico a movement seeking restoration of land to Mexican Americans claimed twenty thousand members in the mid 1960s. Its leader, Reies Lopez Tijerina, led an occupation of Forest Service land in which several Forest Service rangers were taken captive. Tijerina and several others were arrested, but on June 5, 1967, they were freed in an armed raid on a New Mexico courthouse by a group of their followers. A force of six hundred state troopers and National Guardsmen eventually captured them (Meier and Rivera, 1972; see also Knowlton, 1985a, 1985b). As with blacks, continuous resistance by Anglos was causing frustration and stimulating a move toward violence. The most serious outburst occurred in Los Angeles in 1970. A massive demonstration called the Chicano Moratorium was called to protest the Vietnam War and its effects on Chicanos. Violence broke out between protesters and police, spread across the barrio, and continued for hours. At least one person, a Chicano journalist, was killed by police fire, and property damage was heavy.

Among Indian people, too, social action and protest increased. The incidence of such protest gradually rose during the 1960s, frequently focusing on treaty rights to unrestricted fishing. This issue has led to conflicts in Michigan, Minnesota, and the Pacific Northwest. In 1968, the American Indian Movement (AIM) was founded in Minneapolis. It started out as a local organization but soon became national in scope and played a role in several major protests, most notably the 1973 occupation at Wounded Knee, South Dakota, which led to violent confrontations with federal authorities and two deaths. Other major protests by Native Americans included a takeover of Alcatraz Island, a former federal prison on San Francisco Bay, under an 1868 treaty providing that surplus federal property could be claimed by the Sioux. This takeover lasted nearly two years. Indian protesters also occupied Fort Lawton, a military base in Washington State, after it was declared surplus in 1970 and eventually were granted part of that property (Bahr et al., 1979). One of the most widely publicized protests took place in 1972, when various problems confronting a national protest in Washington, called the "Trial of Broken Treaties," led to a takeover of the Bureau of Indian Affairs building.

Some of these Native American protests were harshly repressed, particularly during the Nixon Administration and on South Dakota's Pine Ridge Lakota (Sioux) Reservation. Later investigations revealed concerted efforts to discredit Indian protest leaders, false charges of violence against AIM members, and cover-ups of violence by AIM opponents and government agents (Churchill, 1994, especially pp. 173–206; Matthiessen, 1983). Churchill (pp. 180–181), for example, notes incidents in which FBI officials made allegations about AIM activists that were widely reported in the press, then later admitted, sometimes in sworn testimony, that the statements were not true. In addition, from 1973 through 1976, there were dozens of unsolved murders—possibly as many as 70—of AIM supporters on the Pine Ridge Reservation (Churchill, 1994). Most of these murders were never investigated (Matthiessen, 1983; Churchill, 1994). At least 60 of these have been documented by name and date of death (Churchill, 1994, pp. 197–205; Johansen and Maestas, 1979). Counting only the murders of AIM supporters, the homicide rate on the Pine Ridge Reservation was eight times that of Detroit, the city with the highest homicide rate at the time.

Clearly, then, these three minority groups and others gradually changed their response to subordinate status from trying to adapt to it toward trying, with increasing insistence, to change it. Let us now examine some of the reasons why.

NECESSARY CONDITIONS FOR SOCIAL MOVEMENTS

If we are to explain why minority groups have turned to social movements seeking change as they have over the past forty years or so, a logical starting point is to ask, What are the conditions under which social movements get started? Social scientists have identified five major conditions that must be present for social movements to develop.

Dissatisfaction (Relative Deprivation)

The first condition that must be present for a social movement to form is dissatisfaction. People must *feel* that they are somehow being taken advantage of or that their situation is unsatisfactory. Such feelings of dissatisfaction are not always found where people are the worst off in absolute terms. Rather, they are found when people feel badly off *relative* to others or to what they feel they *should* have. This condition is called **relative deprivation.** This helps to explain why social movements develop most readily when poverty is found in the midst of wealth or when conditions begin to improve. In such situations, expectations and feelings of relative deprivation are the greatest (for further discussion of the notion of relative deprivation, see Geschwender, 1964).

Communication Network

The second condition needed for a social movement to develop is a network of communication within the dissatisfied group. It does not matter how dissatisfied people are if they cannot communicate their dissatisfaction to one another. Without communication, they cannot act collectively to change the source of their dissatisfaction. To form a movement, dissatisfied people must be able to share their dissatisfaction, develop a group consciousness, and decide what they are going to do to change the source of their dissatisfaction (see Morris, 1984, especially pp. 275–86).

Resources

A communication network is one example of a resource that can be used to organize social movements. A relatively recent approach to the study of social movements, known as *resource-mobilization theory*, addresses the concept of movement resources in a broader way (McCarthy and Zald, 1973, 1977). According to this theory, movements develop and spread when people who are dissatisfied have resources that they can use to build a social movement and, equally important, are aware that they have such resources and can use them in this way. Resources include money, influence, and personal-communication networks but also such things as modern mass media, which can be used both to facilitate communication among potential movement participants and to generate "bad publicity" about the groups or institutions that the movement opposes (Freeman, 1973, 1979; Lofland, 1985; Snow et al., 1986; McAdam, McCarthy, and Zald, 1988, pp. 722–23).

Sense of Efficacy

Assuming that a group is dissatisfied and has adequate means of internal communication, it must still have what social scientists call a *sense of efficacy*. Put simply, this means that people must feel that they have something to gain by protest and that the potential gains outweigh any possible negative effects that might come as a result of the protest. No matter how dissatisfied people are, they are unlikely to become involved in a movement if they think the consequence will be to make them even worse off than they already are. They have to see a net gain.

One factor that may influence people's sense of efficacy is the extent to which a social or political system is, in fact, vulnerable to protest. This is one of the main points of another fairly recent approach to the study of social movements, *political-process theory*. When people realize that the system is vulnerable to change through protest, they are much more likely to become involved in social movements (Jenkins and Perrow, 1978). For example, one study examined why the antinuclear power movement grew and prospered in Germany while it atrophied in France, even though it started similarly in both countries. The reason: German governmental review procedures provided opportunities for intervention by those opposed to nuclear power plants; French procedures did not (Nelkin and Pollack, 1981).

Leadership

The final condition that must be present for social movements to develop is leadership. Somebody has to plan strategies, inspire the rank-and-file participants, and do the day-to-day work behind most successful movements. There is some question whether this factor is as critical as the other four—some say that under those conditions effective leadership will emerge—but it is clear that leadership is important both in getting a movement started and in making it effective once it is under way.

DEVELOPMENT OF THESE CONDITIONS AND THE FORMATION OF MINORITY SOCIAL MOVEMENTS IN THE UNITED STATES AFTER WORLD WAR II

In the twentieth century, and particularly after World War II, a number of changes occurred that helped bring about these movement-facilitating conditions of dissatisfaction, communication, movement-related resources, sense of efficacy, and effective leadership among American minorities. The most important were the trend toward urbanization and industrialization, economic expansion, mass communications, rising educational levels, and international changes. Each helped in important ways to bring into being conditions favorable to the development of social movements among oppressed minorities.

Urbanization and Industrialization

The related trends of urbanization and industrialization were of great importance. We have already discussed the general trend of urbanization in the United States and the fact that most minority groups have undergone an even greater and more rapid transition from rural to urban than the white Anglo population (see Table 7.1). The pattern of rapid urbanization is particularly notable for blacks and Mexican Americans, who as recently as 1930 were more rural than the overall population but who today are more urban. Rapid urbanization is also notable among the Japanese American population and, since 1950, among the Native American population as well.

One of the effects of urbanization was to increase feelings of relative deprivation, or dissatisfaction. Minority group members arriving in large cities were exposed to affluence and lifestyles they often had not seen before, an experience that undoubtedly makes people more conscious of what they *could* have and, consequently, less satisfied when they have less than their share. The mobility that goes with urbanization and industrialization also helps to raise expectations (Williams, 1977, p. 28). If people enjoy greater freedom and have raised expectations but find that they must still accept a subordinate status, the potential for dissatisfaction becomes very great. In a society with racial inequality, urbanization has exactly this effect. Urbanization in the United States also increased competition between whites and minorities for the same jobs. Often whites were hired ahead of others or received higher pay than others for the same work. These experiences undoubtedly added to the feelings of dissatisfaction and relative deprivation among minority group members.

Urbanization also made it easier for minority group members to communicate their dissatisfaction to one another and to discuss what could be done. In the urban ghettos and barrios, masses of people with similar ethnic backgrounds were brought together with many others who had a similar sense of dissatisfaction. In the case of blacks, the urban ghettos established a base for black churches and colleges, which became key forces in organizing the civil rights movement (Morris, 1984, pp. 4–12). In addition, the greater freedom and independence of the urban setting made it safer to promote antiestablishment ideas. This presents a sharp contrast to

Table 7.1 Percentage Urban, 1910, 1930, 1950, 1970, and 1990, for Various American Ethnic Groups

YEAR	TOTAL POPULATION	BLACKS	CHICANOS	AMERICAN INDIANS	CHINESE AMERICANS	JAPANESE AMERICANS
1910	46%	27%	32%	4%	76%	49%
1930	56	44	51	10	88	54
1950	64	62	66	16	93	71
1970	74	81	85	45	96	89
1990	75	87	89	56	96	94

Source: U.S. Census of Population for the years 1910, 1930, 1950, 1970, 1990.

the rural setting (especially on large-scale plantations and fruit and vegetable farming operations), where close social control made even talking about protest risky. Thus, both the concentration of minority group members and the greater freedom of the city made it easier for minority people to communicate with one another about their dissatisfactions and what might be done about them (Morris, 1984, pp. 3–4).

It is also probably true that a social movement has, all else being equal, a greater chance of success in an urban setting than in a rural setting, partly because of the weaker social control in large cities. There are simply too many people for any authority to be aware of what everyone is doing. The large numbers of people mean that, almost by definition, there must be more variety of opinions and lifestyles. Thus, a social movement in an urban area is less likely to be repressed by authorities than a similar movement in a rural area. Furthermore, it is possible to mobilize large numbers of people in the city. People can vote; they can boycott businesses; they can pack public meetings; they can tie up city traffic. These actions are potentially a source of power for a social movement, and all are more effective when masses of people are involved. Thus, not only is a movement easier to organize in the city, it is also more likely to have some positive results. Undoubtedly, these factors go a long way toward explaining why social movements and protests are nearly always disproportionately urban events (Tilly, 1974).

All of the above considerations point to the same conclusion: A society that attempts to maintain a pattern of racial inequality when it is urbanizing is likely to experience considerable minority group protest. Urbanization helps to create most of the conditions necessary for social movements: feelings of dissatisfaction, ability to communicate among the dissatisfied, and a reasonable chance of success. It probably also helps to develop leadership; even movements occurring in rural areas, such as the United Farm Workers and the Wounded Knee protest, have had leaders with a largely urban background. Another look at Table 7.1 will show not only that minorities became much more urbanized in the twentieth century but that the period 1950–1970 was a time of particularly rapid urbanization among the black, Chicano, and American Indian populations. It is hardly surprising that this period was an era of social movements among groups seeking change in their subordinate status.

Economic Expansion

Although the trend toward urbanization and industrialization played an important role in facilitating ethnic protest movements, it has not been the only factor. Many experts feel that another reason for the postwar trend toward social movements can be found in the economic expansion of the time. It has been shown by Wilson (1973, 1978) that both the extent and militancy of racial protest and its degree of success tend to be greater in times of relative economic expansion. In times of economic decline, minorities have tended to protest less and often have difficulty protecting their status against attacks by members of the majority group.

The 1950s and early 1960s were generally a time of economic expansion in the United States. Given Wilson's historical observations, it is hardly surprising that this was a period of rising ethnic protest. In addition to the historical relationship, there are a number of other reasons to believe that this economic growth probably did facilitate minority group social movements. First, such expansion tends to raise minority group expectations by opening up new positions to minority group members. At the same time, it makes the minority groups less of a threat to the majority,

Contact among a great many people of diverse status and background occurs in urban settings. Frequently, this contact stimulates minority group protest by making people more aware of the inequalities that exist in society. *Charles Gatewood*

so that the majority group is more inclined to respond favorably to minority protest, increasing its chance of success. Thus, one of the important conditions necessary for social movements to develop is brought about: a belief that the movement can succeed. Wilson argues that one reason for both the size and effectiveness of the civil rights movement of the 1950s and 1960s is the fact that black leaders correctly perceived that the social and economic climate was favorable for a successful movement. Of course, once one campaign has been successful, others frequently follow, because people realize that the things they do *can* make a difference.

In addition to these factors, good economic times also tend to increase the resources that social movements can bring to bear. In the growing economy of the 1950s and 1960s, the civil rights movement was able to develop substantial resources such as money and legal assistance, receiving support from both the small but growing black middle class of that era and a sizable number of sympathetic whites (Zald and McCarthy, 1975; McAdam, 1982; Morris, 1984; Jenkins and Eckert, 1986).

Mass Communications

Williams (1977) and others have commented on the importance of mass communications in stimulating social protest. The media can easily raise feelings of dissatisfaction or relative deprivation by making people more aware of the contrasts between the haves and the have-nots. This can facilitate the exchange of ideas among dissatisfied people, if only by exposing more people to the ideas of protest leaders. Finally, it can stimulate protest by making people aware of movements elsewhere and the successes of those movements. In effect, it helps people to realize that "we could do that, too." Through the spread of radio and television, as well as the nearly universal availability of the telephone, mass communications since World War II have created a revolution in the ways people receive and exchange information. This change has very likely been an important stimulus for racial and other kinds of protest since World War II.

Rising Educational Levels

We have already discussed ways in which rising educational levels among both whites and people of color in the United States have contributed to the increasing fluidity of race relations in the twentieth century. More specifically, however, they have also contributed directly to the rising incidence of protest. For one thing, the increase in education among minority groups has helped in the development of leadership. As in all movements, the leaders of the civil rights and other minority group social movements have tended to be people of greater than average education. Increased education also has tended to increase feelings of relative deprivation as people in minority groups were made more aware of both the inequalities between them and the white majority and the ways in which minorities were treated unfairly or differently.

As we have suggested earlier, increasing levels of education in the population have also influenced the thinking of the white population. As we have seen, education tends to lower the level of prejudice. It also may make whites more aware of unjust treatment of minorities. This has undoubtedly made whites more responsive to minority demands (see, for example, Hall, Rodeghier, and Useem, 1986). Furthermore, it helps to explain the considerable involvement by whites in protest movements on behalf of minorities. Thousands of whites were involved in the civil rights movement, in protests to increase numbers of minority students in universities during the 1960s, in the United Farm Workers' boycotts of grapes and lettuce in the 1960s and 1970s, and in other efforts. In the 1980s and early 1990s, many white Americans were involved in the campaign against South African apartheid. In recent years, growing numbers of whites have been involved in efforts to promote diversity at work and school, and in various efforts opposing hate groups. In general, white college students and more highly educated whites have been most involved in these efforts.

International Changes

A final important factor enabling the development of minority-group social movements since World War II can be found in certain international changes. Most important is the emergence of independent nations in formerly colonized areas in Africa and other Third World areas. This trend has had two important effects. First, it has presented minority Americans with important examples, or role models, of the successful exercise of power and self-governance by people of color. The emergence of self-determination for black Africans, for example, has strengthened the hopes of African Americans for greater self-determination. A second major effect has been to force the American government to be more supportive of the demands for equality by people of color here. The United States is competing with other countries for friendship and economic relations with Third World nations. If it loses such friendship and economic ties, its position in the world may be seriously weakened. One important facet of our relationships with Third World countries is how people of color are treated in this country. If the United States discriminates against blacks, it can hardly expect to maintain good relations with African nations. If it mistreats Chicanos, it can hardly expect cooperation from Mexico. Thus, the position of people of color in the United States has been helped by these concerns. The U.S. government's concerns about international relations have undoubtedly made it somewhat more responsive to minority concerns. This was particularly the case from the 1950s to the 1980s, when the United States was in constant competition with the Soviet Union for influence in the world. Thus, the prospects for success by minority social movements have been enhanced and such efforts undoubtedly encouraged.

We have seen that a number of changes have helped bring about the conditions necessary for the development of minority-group social movements that seek change in the patterns of majority–minority relations. Among these changes, which have been particularly notable since World War II, are urbanization and industrialization, economic expansion, the spread of mass communications, rising educational levels, and international changes. Together, these changes have heightened feelings of relative deprivation among minority groups, enabled communication and planning among those groups, improved the hopes of success for minority movements, enhanced the resources of such movements, and facilitated the development of effective minority leadership. The result has been a turn toward change-oriented social movements among African Americans, Mexican Americans, American Indians, and other groups since World War II.

CHANGING VALUES AND GOALS: RACIAL AND ETHNIC GROUP MOVEMENTS AND ATTITUDES FROM THE 1960S TO THE 1990S

In the early stages of the civil rights movement and other minority group movements, the goals were, for the most part, (1) to eliminate the policies of open and deliberate discrimination that were widespread in the 1950s and earlier and (2) to eliminate barriers that kept minority group members from participating fully in American society. These movements were fairly successful in attaining the first goal, but the second proved much more elusive: Even with deliberate discrimination on the wane, blacks, Hispanics, and Native Americans did not come close to full participation in American society. As we shall see in greater detail in Chapter 9, all of these groups remain distinctly disadvantaged with respect to income, poverty, health, employment, education, political representation, housing, and a host of other indicators of the quality of life. In short, the mechanisms of inequality today are much more subtle than in the past, and there has been a clear decrease in some types of inequality—but a good deal of racial and ethnic inequality nonetheless remains.

As the mechanisms of intergroup inequality in American society have changed, both the tactics and goals of minority-group members have also changed. Indeed, the diversity of minority viewpoints has increased tremendously since the late 1960s. One example of this can be seen in the issue of school desegregation. In the era of de jure segregation in the 1950s, virtually all blacks in the United States favored integrated schools. Today, however, a significant number of blacks are skeptical about the benefits of integrated schools, and many more object to the methods that are proposed to bring about such integration. Thus, in the 1990s, blacks as well as whites are deeply divided over the issue of busing for the purpose of school desegregation.

The change in attitudes on school desegregation is just one of many examples. At least in part, it reflects a change in what some blacks consider to be an ideal or model pattern of race relations. In the remainder of this chapter, we shall turn our attention to such changes. We shall examine changes, and increasing diversity, in the goals and values of minority (and majority) group members concerning what constitutes a desirable pattern of intergroup relations. Specifically, we shall explore changing attitudes toward three ideal models as well as the arguments for and against each. The three models are *assimilation, pluralism,* and *separatism.*

THREE IDEAL MODELS OF INTERGROUP RELATIONS

Model 1: Assimilation

The general concept of assimilation was first introduced in Chapter 4 and has been referred to a number of times since. In this section, we discuss the concept in greater detail and delineate several distinct types of assimilation. By way of review, the general concept of **assimilation** refers to a situation in which (1) the dominant group accepts the minority group or groups (at least in some aspects of social life) and (2) the majority and minority groups become integrated into a common culture and social structure. In many cases, the common culture and social structure are for the most part those of the dominant or majority group, though they may incorporate some features of the minority group as well. In other cases, however, the minority group influence is quite substantial. Accordingly, the balance of dominant and minority group cultural influences varies considerably from society to society.

Sociologists distinguish between two major kinds of assimilation, *cultural* and *structural* (Gordon, 1964, pp. 70–71). **Cultural assimilation,** as the name suggests, occurs when two or more groups come to share a common culture. By this, we mean that they develop common attitudes, values, and lifestyles. Frequently, they also come to think of themselves increasingly as one common group. When cultural assimilation occurs, the common culture that evolves is often mainly that of the dominant group, though, as we have noted, certain aspects of minority group culture are usually also adopted.

Structural assimilation occurs when two or more social groups come to share one common social structure. By this we mean that they share common social institutions, organizations, and friendship networks. When structural assimilation is complete, the two or more groups share not only common institutions, organizations, and so on, but also hold relatively equal positions in those social structures. Partly for this reason, structural assimilation tends to be more difficult to achieve than cultural assimilation (Gordon, 1964, p. 77). A minority group may change its culture (attitudes, beliefs, lifestyles) to conform with the dominant society, but such conformity does not guarantee that the group will be accepted into equal-status roles in the society, which remains in the control of the dominant group. Furthermore, both majority and minority group members may prefer to develop friendships within their own group, even when cultural differences are not great. For these reasons, structural assimilation tends to occur to a significantly lesser degree than cultural assimilation.

Perhaps the most difficult type of structural assimilation is what Gordon (1964, p. 71) calls *marital assimilation*. Marital assimilation occurs only when there is widespread intermarriage between two racial or ethnic groups. If marital assimilation occurs and persists for an extended period of time, the assimilation of the groups involved becomes complete, and they gradually lose any identity as separate groups, an outcome known as **amalgamation.**

Although there has been much resistance in the United States to true structural assimilation, American ideology has always strongly supported the idea of cultural assimilation. Great emphasis has been placed on the idea of America as a "melting pot" in which citizens cease to think of themselves as "German," "Irish," "Polish," "Italian," "African," or "Mexican," and regard themselves instead as "American." Assimilation is also highly valued by the functionalist perspective in sociology because assimilation helps to bring about the common values and shared identity that functionalists believe are necessary in any society.

Assimilation can indeed lead to a system of racial and ethnic equality. For this to happen, however, there must be relatively complete *structural* assimilation as well as the often more superficial cultural type of assimilation. In addition, assimilation is more likely to lead to intergroup equality if it involves a true blend of the cultures and institutions of both groups. Unfortunately, because assimilation often means that the minority group for the most part adopts the culture and social structure of the dominant group, the process is unbalanced from the start. As we shall see in more detail later in the chapter, this has been largely true of assimilation in the United States, though in some other societies such as Mexico (see Chapter 8), the assimilation process has been much more balanced. For these reasons, the existence of cultural assimilation in a society does not at all guarantee that the society will have intergroup equality.

Model 2: Pluralism

A second model of intergroup relations is known as *pluralism* (Higham, 1974). In **pluralism,** some aspects of culture and social structure are shared in common throughout society; other aspects remain distinct in each racial or ethnic group. Under pluralism, there is a common culture and set of institutions throughout society, but only up to a point. To a large degree, each ethnic group maintains a distinct subculture; a distinct set of social institutions such as churches, clubs, businesses, and media; and a distinct set of *primary group* relations such as friendship networks and families. Thus, under pluralism there exists one society made up of a number of distinct parts. In contrast to the melting pot, the pluralist model is often compared with a *mosaic:* one unit made up of many distinct parts.

As was the case with assimilation, we can subdivide the concept of pluralism into *cultural pluralism* and *structural pluralism*. **Cultural pluralism** occurs when groups in society each retain certain sets of attitudes, beliefs, and lifestyles, while sharing others. Similarly, **structural pluralism** exists when groups retain some social structures and institutions of their own but share others. An example of this can be seen in the case in which several groups all willingly give allegiance to one government, speak the same language, and share the same monetary system but at the same time go to their own churches, have different patterns of occupations, and marry within their own group.

In recent years, *multiculturalism* has been widely advocated as a model for intergroup relations in the United States, Canada, and other countries. Because it emphasizes the preservation of the distinct cultural characteristics of different racial, ethnic, and religious groups, multiculturalism is similar in meaning to cultural pluralism.

In the sense that it involves the sharing of some common cultural and social-structural features throughout a society, the pluralist model is in part consistent with the functionalist perspective in sociology. In other respects, however, the pluralist model is more closely aligned with the conflict perspective. Specifically, it denies the need for complete consensus, suggesting instead that society can benefit from diversity and the opportunity for change that diversity can offer. Furthermore, the distinct cultures and distinct sets of institutions found in a pluralist society offer a power base for the various racial and ethnic groups in the society. In the view of conflict theorists, the various social groups in any society do not all share the same self-interests. By retaining its own culture and set of social institutions, each group potentially has a power base to protect its legitimate interests.

Like assimilation, a pluralist society can be a society of racial equality. This tends to occur if the power position of the various groups is relatively similar and if the institutions they control have relatively similar resources. If these conditions are *not* present, equality will not exist either, though some conflict theorists might well argue that the mere existence of distinct groups with distinct cultures and social institutions guarantees something of a power base, which makes social change more possible than it is when assimilation is complete.

Model 3: Separatism

A third model of intergroup relations, at the opposite end of the scale from assimilation, is racial or ethnic *separatism*. Under **separatism,** two or more racial or ethnic groups occupying an area each have their own cultures and their own separate sets of social institutions and primary group relationships. Little or nothing is held in common by the groups. If there is contact between them, it is the type of contact that occurs between two distinct societies or independent nations.

In many instances, separatism could occur only with *population transfer.* The reason is that separatism is virtually impossible unless each group involved has a distinct geographic base—a territory of its own. Therefore, unless the population distribution in a society is such that each group lives in distinct areas, it is necessary for many members of one or both groups to move in order to bring about separatism. Because people are often unwilling to do this, separatism can, as a practical matter, be very difficult to implement.

Like assimilation and pluralism, separatism may or may not act as a means of bringing about intergroup equality. If separatism is voluntary on the part of the minority group, as in secession, in which the minority group withdraws from the dominant group's society; if the two groups are able to gain similar levels of power; and if the geographic areas to which the groups move have similar resources, separatism can potentially offer an opportunity for intergroup equality. If, however, these conditions are not present, separatism may not only fail to bring equality but may lead to even more inequality. This is particularly true when separatism is imposed on the minority group against its will. A recent example of this is South Africa's policy in the 1970s of resettlement of the black population to bantustans, or "independent" black states. This policy inhibited any real movement toward black–white equality because (1) it was imposed on the black population by the dominant whites, (2) the areas assigned to the black population were small relative to the size of that population and were limited in resources, and (3) the bantustans were allowed the power associated with true independence. In effect, they existed at the pleasure of and subject to the restrictions of the white regime in South Africa. When majority rule was established in 1994, they were eliminated.

More broadly, the difficulties of separatism are illustrated by recent attempts to divide former Yugoslavia into separate territories for Yugoslavia's major ethnic groups, including Croatians, Serbs, Bosnians, and Macedonians. No matter how the country is divided, some ethnic groups are faced with the dilemma of moving, living under the rule of some other ethnic group, or fighting. The result is that it is impossible to draw any set of boundaries on which everyone can agree. A number of groups, but particularly Serbs, have engaged in a practice that has become known as "ethnic cleansing," an attempt to force other groups out of a territory so that the group with the numerical majority (or that is most powerful) in that area can control the territory. Murder, rape, destruction of cities and towns, and imprisonment in concentration camps have been among the tactics used to force out unwanted groups. While virtually all ethnic groups have engaged in these tactics to some extent, they have been used on by far the largest scale by Serbs and have been directed against Bosnian Muslims to a much greater extent than against any other group. Thousands of people have died as a result of these actions, and large portions of Sarajevo and other cities have been destroyed.

In general, sociologists of the functionalist viewpoint tend to frown on separatism because of the divisions within society that separatist movements create. Some conflict theorists, however, see merit in some forms of separatism, taking the view that, if it is voluntary on the part of the minority group, separatism can free the subordinate group from the control of the dominant group and give it the independent power base it needs.

Each of the three models we have outlined—assimilation, pluralism, and separatism—has had varying levels of support in the United States. In the following section, we shall explore changing attitudes toward the three models among the American population and, in particular, some ways that the goals of minority groups and their social movements have changed as they relate to assimilation, pluralism, and separatism.

ASSIMILATION, PLURALISM, AND SEPARATISM IN AMERICAN SOCIETY

Assimilation and Anglo-Conformity

There is no doubt that the dominant norm in the United States through nearly all of its history has been cultural assimilation. The dominant cultural group in the United States has been the so-called WASPs: white Anglo-Saxon Protestants. Such has been the influence of this group on American culture that many social scientists describe the cultural pattern of the United States as *Anglo-conformity:* All other groups in America have been expected to adopt the language, culture, and social structure of the white northern Europeans (Gordon, 1964, p. 85). As Feagin (1989, chap. 3) illustrates in a thorough chapter on English-Americans and the Anglo-

Saxon core culture, the most influential group has been British Protestants. A somewhat altered British Protestant culture came to be accepted as the dominant "American culture," and all ethnic groups in America have been expected to conform to this culture and its attendant institutions. Thus, though we are a "nation of immigrants," English remains the language that everyone has always been expected to learn and speak, regardless of what their native language is. In fact, a number of states and localities have passed legislation designating English as their only official language; California did so by public referendum in 1986. (As Latino political power has increased, however, some areas, such as Dade County, Florida, have subsequently repealed such legislation.) Bilingual education, an innovation of the 1960s originally aimed at improving the schooling of Hispanics and immigrants, has become highly controversial because many people feel it gives educational sanction to languages other than English.

Indeed, education has played a central role in the assimilation of a variety of immigrant groups into the so-called WASP culture. Not only was American education based largely on a British model and heavily under the control of elite English Americans during its formative years, it also placed intense pressure on children to conform to the dominant Anglo culture. In Feagin's (1989, p. 70) words, "whether the children were Irish, Jewish, or Italian did not seem to matter. Anglicization of the children was designed to ferret out the harmful non–Anglo-Saxon ways, to assimilate the children in terms of manners, work habits, and the Protestant Ethic."

Although we have seen that schools and other agents of socialization have placed a great deal of pressure on immigrant groups to culturally assimilate, not all that much pressure has been needed in many cases: Many immigrants have very much *wanted* to give up their old ways and assimilate into the dominant Anglo American culture. This has tended to be especially true of the children of immigrants, who generally have oriented themselves much more closely to the "American" ways of their peers and the school system than to the "Old World" culture of their parents (see Gordon, 1964, pp. 107–8). Still, these tendencies toward cultural assimilation among immigrant groups have largely been the result of the strong pressure to assimilate in American society (Gordon, 1978, chap. 7). In general, the view that cultural assimilation is *expected* of American immigrants has only rarely been challenged, and the overwhelming majority of immigrants have assimilated to a substantial degree.

Although cultural-assimilationist tendencies have always been strongest among immigrant minorities, such tendencies have also existed among colonized minorities. Such a theme can be seen, for example, in the Negro self-help movement of Booker T. Washington around the turn of the century. Washington—one of the very few blacks to gain widespread credibility among whites during that era—argued that rather than challenging white society, blacks should demonstrate their value to American society through improved education, hard work, and demonstrations of loyalty to that society (Hawkins, 1962). Washington hoped that by emulating the values and work habits of middle-class white society, blacks could eventually gain a greater degree of acceptance. Of course, part of the reason for such an emphasis on assimilation and accommodation was that, in Washington's era, a more direct challenge to the white power structure would probably not have been tolerated.

Even in the 1950s and early 1960s, when the civil rights movement developed to full blossom, assimilationist tendencies remained evident. True, the movement did seek to plead, pressure, or force whites to accept social change, and it challenged the power structure through civil disobedience and direct action. Nonetheless, if we examine the goals and objectives of the early civil rights movement, it is clear that the movement in many ways sought assimilation. The major issues of this era centered largely around desegregation—the elimination of "whites only" schools, lunch counters, buses, railroad stations, and so on. In effect, the demand was for full participation by black Americans in all aspects of the white-controlled society. The goal was not, during this period, to build new or radically different social institutions; rather, it was for blacks to be able to participate in American social institutions on the same basis as whites.

Although their continuing loyalty to the Spanish language reflects a significant tendency toward cultural pluralism, Mexican Americans have in many ways sought assimilation into American society as well. Alvarez (1973), for example, notes strong assimilationist tendencies in what he calls the "Mexican-American generation." These children of migrants from Mexico, born in the United States and coming of age during the 1950s and 1960s, generally lived an urban life somewhat better than that of their parents. Consequently, most of them began to think of themselves as more American than Mexican and as moving toward full participation in American life. Unfortunately, the acceptance by Anglos that would have been necessary for such full Chicano participation in American life was still missing.

Probably the one major racial or ethnic group that presents a clear exception to the pattern of seeking assimilation is Native Americans. The United States government has, over the years, used about every technique imaginable to get Indian people to give up their Indian ways and seek assimilation into white culture and society. Among these have been attempts to set up Indian people as small farmers, to isolate their children from native culture in white-controlled boarding schools, and to get them to leave the reservation to take industrial jobs in urban areas. Native rituals and languages have in some cases been banned (for further discussion of U.S. policy toward Indian people, see Chapters 5 and 6). All of these efforts, however, have been notably unsuccessful in getting Indian people to seek assimilation into white culture. In part, this is true because Indians have, until very recently, lived in predominantly rural and predominantly Indian social settings: Thus, they have been able to maintain much of their culture, even in the face of sometimes powerful attacks. Even recently, despite rapid urbanization of the Native American population, Indian people continue to resist pressures for assimilation. Steele (1972, 1985) has demonstrated the strong resistance by many urban Indians to white social and cultural influences. Apparently, an important reason for this is the close contact with nearby Indian reservations that maintain many urban Indians. Thus, Native Americans probably represent the one major exception to the general pattern whereby nearly all racial and ethnic groups in America have sought assimilation into the dominant culture and society during at least a significant portion of their history in the United States.

In one sense, even Native Americans have undergone considerable assimilation. A substantial number through the years have married whites, and to a large extent, people of mixed European and Native American ancestry have culturally blended into the white population. In the 1980 census, for example, nearly 6.7 million Americans reported some American Indian ancestry. Accounting for nearly 3 percent of the population, this was the eleventh largest ethnic ancestry group in 1980 (Farley, 1991). By 1990, it had increased to 8.7 million, and was the tenth largest ancestry group (U.S. Bureau of the Census, 1993, p. 51). In addition, the number of

Americans who reported some American Indian ancestry was nearly five times as great as the number who indicated their race was American Indian or Native American. Most of these people of mixed ancestry live in urban areas and have little or no knowledge of Native American culture or connection to the reservation. Until recently, most thought of themselves as white, though increasing numbers today are identifying with their Native American ancestry. This is one reason, for example, why since 1970 the census has indicated a rapid increase in the number of people stating that their race is American Indian or Native American. Some people answered the race question as "white" in 1970 but as "American Indian or Native American" in 1980 and/or 1990. It should be noted, however, that most of the highly assimilated people of mixed ancestry have substantially more white than Native American ancestry.

Critique: Have Social Scientists Exaggerated the Degree of Assimilation in American Society?

As we shall soon see, Americans from a wide variety of racial and ethnic groups have shown signs of turning away from assimilation since the mid 1960s. Some social scientists, however, have questioned whether there was *ever* as much assimilation in America as was widely believed. Glazer and Moynihan (1970, p. xxxiii), for example, found in their study of the six major ethnic groups of New York City (blacks, Puerto Ricans, Jews, Italians, Irish, and WASPs) that ethnic groups remained important throughout the twentieth century, developing and retaining "distinctive economic, political, and cultural patterns." These patterns may not have been particularly similar to the culture of the "old country," but they were distinct in American society.

To this we must add Gordon's (1964, 1978) reminder that *structural* assimilation occurs much less easily than cultural assimilation. Thus, for example, family and other primary group relations continue to be influenced to a substantial degree by race and ethnicity. Interracial marriage remains quite rare, and majority group members continue to associate and form friendships mainly within the majority group, while minority group members similar associate mainly with other members of their group. While *interethnic* marriage is not uncommon, the image of one great melting pot does not fit very well here, either. A study of eighty years of marriage data in New Haven, Connecticut, by Kennedy (1944, 1952) revealed that patterns of interethnic marriage were far from random. In fact, there seemed to be three distinct marriage pools: a Protestant one among British, Germans, and Scandinavians; a Catholic one among Irish, Italians, and Poles; and a Jewish one (see also Greeley, 1970). Although this tendency toward marriage within religioethnic groupings has decreased over time (see Yetman, 1985, pp. 233–234; Alba, 1981), it has not disappeared. Major occupational distinctions also exist, as can be seen in the well-known specialization of many Irish Americans in police work, manufacturing, and politics; of Greek Americans in fishing and the restaurant business; of Jewish Americans in small business; and of Chinese Americans in services, restaurants, and specialty shops. Research by Greeley (1974, pp. 51–55, 1977) and Cummings (1980) confirms that different ethnic groups have different occupational structures, although Neidert and Farley (1985) have shown that these differences decrease as time passes after immigration. Overall, indicators of structural assimilation such as occupation, marriage and friendship patterns, and religious affiliation do reveal a lower level of assimilation than we would expect if we considered only cultural assimilation. Thus, assimilation, although considerable, has definitely had its limits. This is especially true of structural assimilation. The latter has occurred to a significant, though not unlimited, extent among "old" immigrant groups (British, Scots, Germans, Scandinavians, Irish), less so among "new" immigrant groups (eastern and southern Europeans, Asian Americans), and only to a very limited extent among minority groups (blacks, Hispanics, Native Americans), who, as we have seen, remain largely outside the institutional power structure of America.

CHANGING ATTITUDES TOWARD ASSIMILATION AND PLURALISM

As we have seen, most racial and ethnic groups have sought cultural assimilation throughout most of American history. Even minority group social movements were substantially assimilationist in their goals until around the mid 1960s, although, as always, there were some exceptions to the rule. Since that time, however, important changes have taken place. In the remainder of this chapter, we shall examine both what those changes have been and the major reasons for the changes.

African Americans

1965–1975: The Black Power Movement and a Shift Toward Pluralism. Probably the earliest and most important indicator of a shift away from seeking assimilation was the Black Power movement, which began during the 1960s. Although the Black Power movement was never a cohesive, single, centrally organized movement with a totally agreed-on set of goals, certain viewpoints and objectives were fairly well agreed on by the various groups and individuals who identified with the general concept of Black Power. On the whole, there was a de-emphasis on black–white integration as a goal in itself. There was also something of a turn away from the old civil rights movement's objective of full participation by blacks in American social institutions. Rather than integration or participation, the major goals of the Black Power movement were (1) for blacks to have full control of their own lives rather than having their roles and statuses defined by whites and (2) full social and economic equality between blacks and whites. There was increasing skepticism among blacks that the goals of self-determination and equality could be achieved through assimilation. More and more blacks began to believe that as long as society's institutions remained under the control of white people, black people could not realistically expect to gain equality through participation in or integration into those white-controlled institutions.

As a result of these changing perceptions, Black Power proponents developed objectives and priorities quite different from those of the earlier civil rights movement. A central objective was that blacks should have much greater (in some cases, total) control over institutions affecting black people. Examples of this were the community-control movement in education and, in higher education, the widespread demand for black studies and black culture programs *under the control of blacks*. The Black Power movement also placed great emphasis on pride in the accomplishments and the culture of black people in America. This was considered important because of the value of black culture and the risk that much that was positive could be lost if blacks assimilated totally into white culture. It was also seen as important in building a positive self-concept among black people. More and more African Americans began to say, "We will determine our own reality and our own concept of ourselves as a people rather than having it defined for us by white people."

All this added up to a distinctly more pluralistic and less assimilationist set of goals than had existed in the past. A good deal of serious discussion about the idea of black people building their own institutions and organizations to serve their own interests occurred. At the same time, the distinct features of black culture attracted considerable interest, and there was renewed interest in the African heritage of American blacks. At the same time, many blacks (and some nonblacks) began to regard integration and assimilation as ways by which whites sought to preserve cultural domination of blacks and other minorities. In effect, many black people came to believe that, by promoting assimilation, many white people were seeking to impose white culture on blacks as a precondition for social equality. This perception, not surprisingly, aroused considerable opposition to assimilation.

The turn away from assimilation as a goal occurred to a sufficient extent that not only pluralist, but also separatist, goals enjoyed a sizable surge of support. Although never supported by the majority of black people, separatist movements such as Elijah Muhammad's Nation of Islam (commonly known as the Black Muslims) enjoyed greatly increased support from the middle 1960s into the 1970s. It should be pointed out that separatism was not a new idea in the 1960s. Marcus Garvey's Back to Africa movement had gained considerable support during the 1920s, though not on the scale enjoyed by the Muslims in the late 1960s and 1970s. The Nation of Islam, under Elijah Muhammad's leadership, existed as early as the 1930s (Pinkney, 1976, p. 156). It was not until the 1960s, however, that the movement began to enjoy widespread support among black people in the United States. By the 1970s, the membership of the group had reached somewhere between 100,000 and 250,000 (the organization does not release membership statistics), but its influence was broader than its numbers suggest: By the mid 1970s, its weekly newspaper, *Muhammad Speaks,* had a circulation of 600,000, the largest of any black-owned newspaper in the United States (Pinkney, 1976, pp. 159–60).

One area where the trend toward cultural pluralism since the 1960s is evident is in dress and hairstyles. Observe the African influence on the dress of this African American family celebrating Kwanzaa. *Stock Boston, Inc./Lawrence Migdale*

Throughout most of its history, the Nation of Islam has been distinctly separatist in both its goals and practices. Until a brief period beginning in the late 1970s, membership was limited to blacks, and Elijah Muhammad argued that whites constituted an evil and inferior race. The emphasis of the organization was always on building separate, membership-controlled institutions rather than relying on those of the dominant society. Thus, the organization has operated its own school system and financed its operations through ownership of numerous business enterprises including supermarkets, restaurants, a publishing house, and thousands of acres of farmland in several states (Pinkney, 1976, p. 162). During the 1960s and early 1970s, a major objective of the organization was to establish a separate, African American–controlled region in the United States. Though the Nation of Islam never came close to attaining this goal, it did succeed in amassing a good deal of wealth and property, the benefits of which were shared among the membership. One estimate by the *New York Times* (1973) placed the value of the organization's holdings in 1973 at $70 million. Since the late 1970s, there have been both divisions within the organization and changes in its direction. These more recent directions of the Nation of Islam are discussed in a later section on contemporary trends in African American thought and social action.

The Black Muslim movement gave rise to one of the most influential spokespersons for a new, more militant view rejecting assimilation as the route to success for African Americans—Malcolm X. Although Malcolm X eventually broke with the Nation of Islam over its separatist tendencies, he constantly spoke of the need for African Americans to develop their own institutions and their own power base. He argued persuasively that nobody else would do that for African Americans, and he was greatly admired for his willingness to stand up to threats from the police, the FBI, and his political opponents. In his autobiography, he pointed out that, from the standpoints of economics, quality of life, and political power, the civil rights movement had done little or nothing for impoverished, inner-city blacks (Haley, 1964). To make a difference in these areas, he argued, African Americans would have to build their own social institutions and their own power base. Malcolm X was assassinated while speaking at a rally in New York City in 1965.

Along with a shift away from assimilation as a goal among African Americans, important changes in the tactics used by the black movement were occurring. Although the civil rights movement of the 1950s and early 1960s frequently used civil disobedience as a tactic, it was in nearly all cases nonviolent. Dr. Martin Luther King, for example, carefully studied the philosophy and tactics of the great nonviolent leader of India's struggle for independence, Mahatma Gandhi. With the coming of the Black Power movement in the middle 1960s, however, some important changes in tactics occurred. Among younger black activists, particularly, there arose considerable dissatisfaction with the "turn-the-other-cheek" philosophy. The Black Muslims, the Black Panthers, and many leading individuals in the movement began to argue that when whites use violence against blacks, black people should fight back. Muslim leader Malcolm X, for example, said, "We should be peaceful, law-abiding, but the time has come to fight back in self-defense whenever and wherever the black man is being unjustly and unlawfully attacked." This statement was frequently quoted by Black Panther leaders Huey Newton and Bobby Seale, who explained that the black panther, chosen as the symbol of their movement, symbolized an animal that will not attack but will tenaciously defend itself (Hall, 1978, pp. 123, 124).

In spite of this philosophy, the white media often exaggerated the violent tendencies of the Panthers, Muslims, and other groups associated with the Black Power movement. The view of these organizations was, as we have seen, not that black people should *initiate* violence, but that they should defend themselves by whatever means necessary once violently attacked. The number of violent incidents involving either the Muslims or the Panthers was in fact relatively small, nearly always involving shootouts or other confrontations between group members and police, with some doubt regarding who initiated the violence. In some cases, there is good reason to believe that the police were the instigators, such as the incident in 1969 in which fifteen armed law officers raided the Black Panther office in Chicago, resulting in the deaths of party leaders Fred Hampton and Mark Clark and the wounding of four others. Subsequent investigations of the incident indicate that, contrary to police reports of a shootout, it is likely that the Panthers were attacked while sleeping. Ultimately, a lawsuit led to the payment of nearly $2 million in damages to the survivors of the raid and to relatives of Hampton and Clark (Simpson and Yinger, 1985, p. 424). Both the American Civil Liberties Union and a staff report of the National Commission on the Causes and Prevention of Violence concluded that police action against the Panthers was widespread, excessive, and frequently violated the group's rights (Pinkney, 1976, pp. 109–10).

Urban Racial Violence. Most of the violence committed by blacks in the 1960s was not initiated by any organized group such as the Muslims or Panthers but rather took the form of spontaneous ghetto uprisings with little organization or planning. That these uprisings were as widespread as they were between 1964 and 1968 indicates a major change in black attitudes toward violence. Indeed, nearly every city with a sizable black population (except some in the South) experienced at least one disorder during this period, and many had several. The worst outbreaks were in Los Angeles in 1965 and Newark and Detroit in 1967. According to the U.S. National Advisory Commission on Civil Disorders (1968), however, during 1967 alone, 164 disorders took place in all parts of the country. The following year also brought widespread violence. About 125 cities experienced disorders after the assassination of Dr. Martin Luther King in April 1968, and outbreaks of violence continued intermittently throughout the summer and early fall of that year. After 1968, the level of violence subsided, and the 1970s were relatively quiet, with the exception of widespread outbreaks of looting and arson in New York City's minority neighborhoods during a citywide power blackout in 1977.

The riots of the 1960s were different from earlier riots in the United States in several important ways. Most previous riots involved mass fighting between whites and blacks or other minorities. Nearly always, these earlier riots started when white mobs attacked minority group members. The main targets of the rioters were people, not property, as the mobs sought to beat and in some cases kill members of the opposite racial group. In the riots of the 1960s, however, the target of the rioters was mainly property, not people. The violence primarily took the forms of window-breaking, looting, and arson. Relatively few whites were involved, either as victims or participants. The instances of personal violence that did occur between blacks and whites took place mainly between white police and black rioters. Resentment of police by ghetto residents was a significant factor in the rioting of the 1960s, and a great many of the outbreaks began with incidents between police and black citizens (U.S. National Advisory Commission on Civil Disorders, 1968, chap. 11). Most of the deaths and injuries in the disturbances resulted from police action against citizens in the riot areas. Other than the confrontations with the police, personal violence between black and white citizens was rare during the urban violence of the 1960s (see Feagin and Hahn, 1973).

As urban violence spread during the 1960s, many frightened white Americans came to hold several beliefs that were proven incorrect by subsequent research. One such belief was that the disturbances resulted from "outside agitators" or some kind of nationwide black conspiracy (Campbell and Schuman, 1968). Numerous studies of the riots, however, uncovered no evidence of such a conspiracy (Williams, 1975, p. 147). Nearly all the rioters arrested lived in the city where they were arrested (Fogelson, 1971). Most of the riots were spontaneous uprisings by an angry and disillusioned black population; organized efforts to cause trouble apparently played little or no role in the disturbances.

Another widely believed but incorrect explanation of the trouble is the so-called riffraff theory. This view holds that most of the trouble was caused by a criminal element out to make trouble and that racial grievances were merely an excuse used by this small minority of blacks to make trouble. This explanation, too, has been soundly disproved by research. Lawless elements undoubtedly took advantage of the trouble for personal gain, but this was not the cause of the bulk of the trouble. A variety of studies suggest, instead, that rioting was a fairly generalized response among young urban blacks who had become deeply disillusioned with the slow pace of change in the status of black Americans. Research by Fogelson (1971) on a dozen cities experiencing serious disorders estimates that the proportion of blacks who participated actively in the disorders ranged from 2 percent to 35 percent, and averaged somewhere around 10 percent (see also Fogelson and Hill, 1968). Thus, a sizable minority of blacks participated in the disturbances. Furthermore, studies of participants indicated that those who participated in the violence were *not* more likely than other blacks of similar age to have criminal records (Fogelson, 1971, p. 42). Also contrary to popular belief, rioters in northern cities were *not* more likely than other black residents to have moved there from the South (Fogelson, 1971, pp. 41–42); in fact, if anything, the rioters were *more* likely than others to be lifelong residents of the riot city. In Detroit and Newark, for example, the majority of the rioters were lifelong residents, whereas the majority of the nonrioters had been born elsewhere (U.S. National Advisory Commission on Civil Disorders, 1968, pp. 130, 174). Also, rather than being concentrated among the poorest, most down-and-out blacks, participation in the disturbances occurred across the full range of income and occupational levels (Geschwender and Singer, 1968; Fogelson, 1971).

Attitude surveys of urban black Americans also indicate that the rioting had the support of far more than a tiny "riffraff" element of the black population. Research by Campbell and Schuman (1968), for example, revealed that about a third of blacks believed that the riots helped the cause of black rights, whereas only a quarter felt that they hurt. Most of the rest either thought they both helped and hurt, or thought they made no difference. The majority of ghetto residents felt that the riots had a purpose (Feagin and Hahn, 1973, p. 271). Thus, the position of the black majority appears ambivalent: the majority did not "favor" riots but did see them as resulting mainly from discrimination and unemployment (Campbell and Schuman, 1968), as having a definite purpose, and as being of at least some potential benefit. A sizable minority of blacks—about one-third in Los Angeles, for example—did "favor" the riots (Fogelson, 1971), and about 12 to 17 percent of blacks responding to surveys in 1968 regarded violence as "the best way for Negroes to gain their rights" (Campbell and Schuman, 1968; Feagin and Hahn, 1973, pp. 276–277). All this suggests rather clearly that rioting was not created by a criminal riffraff and was not caused by militant activists. Rather, it was an outburst of protest against what was, to a great many blacks, an intolerable situation that had not been much changed by earlier, more moderate forms of protest.

It is now clear that there were some fairly major changes in the thinking of black Americans during the 1960s. Many blacks, both those who were actively involved in protest and those who were not, turned away from assimilation as a goal and toward a more pluralist model. For some, the turn was more radical; as we have seen, support for separatism increased substantially. The turn away from universal acceptance of nonviolence indicates a similar change in attitudes and behavior, though the violence committed by blacks in the 1960s and since pales in comparison to the violence directed toward blacks by whites in earlier years.

The Reasons Behind the Changing Goals and Values of Black Americans. A number of reasons can be identified for the shift away from seeking assimilation and other changes in the thinking of black people during the 1960s. Among those most commonly mentioned are the inconsistent behavior of whites, who did not always live up to what they preached; the violent response by the white power structure to civil rights protest in the South; a growing realization that civil rights laws were not bringing real racial equality; a rejection of the culture-of-poverty and cultural-deprivation models that had become popular among white social scientists; and the continuing influence of black nationalism in Africa. Let us examine each of these factors in greater depth.

To blacks, the behavior of whites by the 1960s did not seem to reveal any serious or consistent commitment to the kind of open opportunity that true integration of black people in American society would have required. While white supporters of civil rights were urging other white people to open up their schools and businesses to blacks and telling black people that assimilation was the answer, other whites were doing everything possible to prevent any meaningful participation by black people in American society. By the mid 1960s, even the moderate policies of the federal government in support of civil rights (regarded as totally inadequate by most blacks) were under heavy attack from whites (Skolnick, 1969, p. 134). Furthermore, even whites who professed support for equal rights often did not live up to those ideals in their own behavior. An event that perhaps illustrates this as clearly as any was the failure of the Democratic National Convention in 1964 to seat the delegation of the Mississippi Freedom Democratic Party (Carmichael and Hamilton, 1967; Skolnick, 1969). This was an integrated delegation formed to challenge the all-white delegation of the regular party in Mississippi. In spite of the self-proclaimed position of the national Democratic party against racial discrimination, it seated the all-white delegation. The only so-called compromise was an offer—viewed by most blacks as an insult—to seat two members of the challenge delegation along with the segregated regular delegation. To many black people, actions spoke louder than words, and this was a clear message that even liberal whites could not be trusted to practice what they preached.

Closely related was the widespread violence by whites against civil rights workers in the South, and the inability or unwillingness of the federal government to do anything about it. As Skolnick (1969, p. 132) writes, "Freedom Riders were beaten by mobs in Montgomery; demonstrators were hosed, clubbed, and cattle-prodded in Birmingham and Selma. Throughout the South, civil rights workers, black and white, were victimized by local officials as well as by nightriders and angry crowds." In most cases, the federal government—notably the Justice Department, whose duty it is to enforce federal law—did little. Eventually, blacks in the South and elsewhere got tired of turning the other cheek or relying on the protection of a government that was not willing to protect them.

By the mid 1960s, it also was becoming clear to many black Americans that the passage of civil rights laws was not, as they had hoped, bringing about racial equality. Black unemployment continued to run twice as high as white unemployment, and black family income remained far below white family income. In the North especially, schools and neighborhoods remained as segregated as ever. To the poor or unemployed northern urban black, the civil rights movement of the 1950s and early 1960s had made almost no difference. Although this group had never been as involved in that movement as the black middle class and sympathetic whites, the poor urban blacks of the North had had their hopes raised by the promises to end discrimination and poverty that came with the civil rights movement and the Johnson administration's "War on Poverty." When these hopes proved to be false, this group was deeply disillusioned. It is accordingly not surprising that militant separatist organizations such as the Muslims gained most of their support from this segment of the black population. To the poor urban black, it did little good to integrate a lunch counter if you were unemployed and couldn't afford to buy a lunch. Leaders such as Malcolm X and groups such as the Muslims and the Black Panther party weren't talking about integrated lunch counters; they were talking about economic survival and self-defense, and these themes had great appeal to the urban black trapped at the bottom.

Among black intellectuals, important changes in thinking were also taking place. It was during the early and middle 1960s that culture-of-poverty and cultural-deprivation theories were gaining great popularity among white social scientists and intellectuals. What we have called the functionalist, or order, perspective was dominant in American social science at that time, and it seemed to offer a logical explanation of black disadvantage to the white social scientists of the era: Because of past discrimination, black Americans had never had the opportunity to develop the values, habits, and skills necessary to get ahead in American society. This seemed reasonable and not at all racist to most white social scientists, but black social scientists and intellectuals heard a different message. To them, this amounted to saying that blacks, because of their culture and attitudes, were at fault for their own disadvantages. (As we have seen, many avowedly racist whites did use the theories to make exactly that argument.) Furthermore, this explanation placed the burden for change on blacks: They had to change their ways before they could hope to enjoy the benefits of American society, even though the cause of their disadvantage, as admitted by white social scientists, was past discrimination *by whites*. This hardly seemed fair. Finally, all this seemed like a putdown of black culture precisely when blacks were proving their capabilities through the civil rights movement. Many blacks had a great need for pride in their race, and black accomplishments were becoming more visible than ever. (They had always been there but had been kept largely hidden by white society.) Nothing that seemed like an attack on the culture and accomplishments of blacks was going to be tolerated. By the mid 1960s, assimilation to many educated blacks seemed to be a message from whites that said, "Do it our way or don't do it." This was no longer acceptable.

A final factor that led to increased emphasis on black self-help and Black Power was the continuing development of independent black nations in Africa (Skolnick, 1969, pp. 137–39). This development served as a model to blacks in the United States: African Americans could, through their own efforts, throw off the domination and influence of whites, run their own affairs, and build their own power base. More than ever before, black people in the United States began to see this as a viable model for attaining black liberation here.

Recent Black Attitudes and Actions: 1975 to the Present. After the mid 1970s, the level of protest abated somewhat, and some but not all black Americans shifted for a time toward more assimilationist thinking. To some extent, this was undoubtedly the result of the 1960s civil rights legislation, which largely eliminated formal discrimination (Jewell, 1985), and of the fact that in some, if not all, areas of life, blacks experienced a real improvement during the 1960s and 1970s (R. Farley, 1984). Thus, a survey of black college students in the 1980s by Jewell (1985) found an increase in support for cultural assimilation as compared with their counterparts in the preceding decades. Similarly, Hall and Allen (1982) found that in 1981, race consciousness among graduate and professional students was lower among those most integrated into the system: those who had favorable interactions with their faculty, for example.

While protest abated and many blacks shifted toward more assimilationist thinking for a time during the 1970s and early 1980s, these trends began to reverse again around the mid 1980s. Since then, political action by African Americans has clearly increased again, and black opinion has again shifted away from assimilationist viewpoints. An early sign of renewed activism was a 1983 march on Washington on the twentieth anniversary of Dr. Martin Luther King's "I have a dream" speech, which drew a crowd at least as big as the one present when King gave the speech. In the mid 1980s, thousands of demonstrators, both black and white, participated in protests against South African apartheid on U.S. college campuses and at the South African embassy in Washington. In 1987, a major civil rights march occurred in Forsythe County, Georgia. Just one week after a small group of marchers commemorating Dr. King's birthday was attacked by Ku Klux Klan members in that all-white county, over twenty thousand people from all over the United States marched peacefully through the county. Similarly, racist incidents on college campuses in 1987 and subsequent years helped to spark a resurgent black student movement. After one such incident at the University of Michigan in 1987, two months of protest by black students and some white supporters led to a renewal of an unfulfilled 1970 commitment by the university to raise its black enrollment to the percentage of blacks in the state's population. In 1992, a massive protest at the University of North Carolina—the largest there since the Vietnam War—led to a commitment by that university to establish an African American cultural center.

Even violent protest was not unheard of during the 1980s, with major riots in Miami in 1980 and 1989. Racial polarization also was cited as a factor in annual outbreaks of arson in Detroit around Halloween in the mid 1980s. Urban violence reached a new peak in 1992, when the acquittal of four police officers in the videotaped beating of Rodney King led to the deadliest violence of the twentieth century in Los Angeles. More than fifty people died in Los Angeles, and serious violence spread to several other cities as well, including Atlanta, Las Vegas, San Francisco, and Seattle. These outbreaks of violence were in some ways similar to the ghetto rebellions of the 1960s, as they involved widespread looting, vandalism, and firebombing, as well as fighting between crowds of civilians and police. However, they differed in two important ways from the 1960s violence. First, the participants in the Los Angeles, San Francisco, and Seattle riots came from a variety of racial and ethnic backgrounds. Although the violence started in black neighborhoods, large numbers of Hispanics, substantial numbers of whites, and some Asian Americans, also participated. This led one Los Angeles sociologist to comment, "This was not a race riot. It was a class riot" (Joel Kotkin, quoted in Matthews, 1992).

The second difference between the recent riots and those of the 1960s, however, suggests that in some ways, the Los Angeles riot was a race riot. In the rebellions of the 1960s, most of the violence was directed against property and the police—few civilians were attacked. This presents a sharp contrast with the race riots earlier in the twentieth century, which involved mass attacks by whites against blacks and other minorities, and sometimes retaliatory attacks by the minority groups. Recent research by McPhail (1993) indicates that in the Miami riot of 1980 and the Los Angeles riot of 1992, something of a move back toward the earlier pattern took place, though this time, most of the crowd violence was committed by minority-group members. McPhail found that in Miami and Los Angeles, the percentage of deaths caused by crowd attacks against civilians was much higher than in the 1960s, though not as high as in the earlier race riots. This suggests that the violence of the 1980s and 1990s was targeted against civilians to a greater extent than in the riots of the 1960s, and much of this violence appears to have been racially motivated.

A store window is broken during the 1992 Los Angeles riot, the deadliest civil disorder of the twentieth century in the United States. *Bettmann/Reuters*

While both violent and nonviolent protest have increased again in recent years, the most important political trend among African Americans in the past decade or so appears to be increased political action through the ballot box. By 1986, four of the country's largest cities had black mayors, and by 1993, nearly all of the country's largest cities had at some time or other elected a black mayor. Recent years have brought the election of the first African American governor in any state (Douglas Wilder in Virginia) and the first African American female U.S. Senator (Carol Moseley-Braun of Illinois). The Reverend Jesse Jackson ran for the Democratic nomination for the presidency in 1984 and again in 1988, receiving as much as 95 percent of the black vote in some areas (Walton, 1985, p. 107). In 1988, he outlasted all but one of his white opponents, finished second in the delegate count, and won in a number of states through a combination of overwhelming black support and, in some states, a substantial part of the white vote as well (Farley, 1990). Both the Jackson campaign and some of the local election campaigns brought blacks to the ballot box as never before. The black turnout in the 1984 primaries was a record, and in some mayoral elections involving black candidates during the last decade, black voter turnout has exceeded white turnout, reversing the historical pattern.

The increased tendency of black voters to support black candidates in recent years and of voting when there is a black candidate are but two indications that the attitudes of African Americans today are less assimilationist than in the past.

This view is confirmed by studies of black public opinion. While there was something of a move back in the direction of assimilation during the 1970s and early 1980s, the trend has been in the opposite direction since around the mid 1980s. As early as the mid 1980s, surveys of black intellectuals showed that they were de-emphasizing issues such as school desegregation and placing greater emphasis on what could be called "Black Power," even though they did not use that specific term. Concerns included more black elected officials, more black-owned businesses, greater black political control, and greater support for predominantly black schools (Conyers, 1986). A series of surveys in the mid and late 1980s of African American students in black American studies courses at Southern Illinois University at Carbondale revealed a clear trend toward support for black political action and away from assimilationist thinking on some items (Tripp, 1992). For example, the surveys showed increased support for a black political party and for the idea of working to build "a separate black nation." The survey also showed that between 1984 and 1989 there was a shift away from a view that through reform, American society could accommodate the demands of black people for racial justice and equality. Instead, the view that the only real alternative for black people is a concerted effort to bring about radical change became more common. The percentage favoring the reform option fell from 64 percent to 38 percent, while the percentage favoring concerted effort for radical change rose from 36 percent to 62 percent.

A study of black and white college students at Stanford University revealed similar findings (Bunzel, 1991). On the one hand, most students reported feeling comfortable with those of other races and backgrounds, and half of the white students and three-quarters of the African American students had dated someone of another race. On the other hand, both black and white students observed that to a large extent, black students voluntarily withdrew from interactions with white students on campus, preferring to socialize mainly with other blacks. When asked why, one African American student commented,

> At a university like this, you fight against being manipulated by the system by gaining control yourself. For black students, a place managed by blacks is a safe place, free from the racial slurs and suspicions that exist everywhere else on campus. . . . In black-controlled arenas, blacks are freed from the pressure to evaluate themselves in comparison with whites. (Bunzel, 1991, p. 71)

While this comment was made by a student at Stanford University, I have heard similar comments from African American students at the campus where I teach, Southern Illinois University at Edwardsville. I suspect such comments reveal typical feelings of a good many black students on virtually all predominantly white campuses.

The recent trend in the attitudes of black college students apparently mirrors the attitude trend among African Americans in the larger society. The 1993–94 Black Politics Study, conducted by University of Chicago researchers, showed a sharp increase in support of black nationalism between 1988 and 1994. By 1994, about half the black population supported the idea of an independent black political party, which was the highest level of support ever observed in surveys (Michael Dawson, quoted in Strong, 1994). The reasons for this attitude change suggested by the Chicago researchers are similar to the comments of the Stanford University student quoted above: many blacks perceived that the mood and temper of the country was such that efforts at integration could not bring about true acceptance or social equality. Perceiving this to be the case, growing numbers of blacks have turned to black nationalist ideologies and separatist ideas such as the formation of a separate black political party.

An important contemporary movement reflecting this viewpoint is *Afrocentrism*. **Afrocentrism** can be defined as an effort by African Americans to emphasize African history, philosophy, and culture, particularly but not only in education. Afrocentrism has received strong backing from a number of leading black intellectuals in the early 1990s and has become a model for curricula in predominantly black schools in many parts of the country. Afrocentrism represents a rebellion against the Eurocentric aspects of much of American culture and education, with its emphasis primarily on the culture, philosophy, and history of Europeans and people of European ancestry. Those who favor Afrocentrism see Eurocentrism as both destructive to the collective self-image of African Americans (by sending a message that only that which is European is worthy of serious study) and irrelevant to peoples of African rather than European ancestry. (Afrocentrism as an educational movement is explored further in Chapter 12.) The emergence of Afrocentrism in the 1990s is one more indication that pluralist and separatist strains of thinking are once again gaining influence among African Americans.

In reviewing trends such as these, it is important not to get the impression that assimilationist or integrationist viewpoints hold no sway among African Americans today. In fact, public-opinion polls show clearly that most African Americans recognize the need to get along with and interact with white Americans and want to do so (Kilson and Cottingham, 1991). Moreover, most African Americans continue to favor neighborhood integration, oppose the idea that blacks should always vote for black candidates, and do not object to interracial dating (Kilson and Cottingham, 1991). Thus, in many ways, blacks continue to support integration to a greater extent than whites. Nonetheless, a substantial proportion of blacks, particularly in big-city ghettos, oppose these positions and instead support ideas such as learning an African language and patronizing black-owned businesses whenever possible. Furthermore, this trend is widespread and probably becoming more so. Thus, African American attitudes today as in the past reflect a mix of integrationist and pluralist/separatist ideas, but since the mid 1980s, there has again been something of a trend away from assimilationist and integrationist thinking.

This trend has led to an increased following for black leaders expressing militant or separatist themes, such as the Reverend Al Sharpton of New York City and Nation of Islam Minister Louis Farrakhan. In the mid 1980s, the Black Muslim movement experienced a split between Farrakhan's Nation of Islam and another segment of the movement led by Elijah Muhammad's son Warif, who adopted the beliefs of orthodox Islam and opened his group's membership to people of all races. Under Farrakhan's leadership, the Nation of Islam enjoyed a resurgence during the late 1980s and early 1990s. Although Farrakhan has at times been criticized for being antiwhite and anti-Semitic, he also gained recognition as the most outspoken advocate of black pride, black power, and black self-help in the 1980s (*New York Times*, 1985). For this reason, his movement gained a large following in big-city ghettos around the country, and his appearances reliably packed large arenas in major cities with sizable African American populations.

By 1993, Farrakhan and his followers were also drawing large crowds—and considerable controversy—on college campuses. At one such appearance at New Jersey's Kean College, a Nation of Islam official named Khallid Abdul Muhammad praised an individual who recently had gone on a shooting spree, systematically killing whites on a Long Island Railroad commuter train. In the same speech, Muhammad made comments seen by many as anti-Semitic and anti-Catholic, referring to Jews, for example, as "bloodsuckers of the black nation." Following the speech, Farrakhan removed Muhammad from his position in the Nation of Islam, but stated that in some regards, he had spoken the truth. In subsequent weeks, both Farrakhan and Muhammad (now acting on his own) continued to speak on college campuses and draw large crowds. Late in the spring of 1994, Muhammad was shot and slightly wounded after a speech on the University of California-Riverside campus. While many blacks rejected the anti-white, anti-Semitic, and anti-Catholic aspects of Muhammad's speeches, the ability of both Muhammad and Farrakhan to draw large supportive crowds indicates that their message of black empowerment and self-help, as well as anger at continuing racial inequality and discrimination, was striking a resonant chord among many African American young people.

Another leader expressing a separatist theme is Marcus Garvey, Jr., who spoke on numerous college campuses in the early 1990s, repeating his father's emphasis on the African roots and heritage of black people in the United States, to whom he refers as Africans in the United States. The increased usage of the term *African American* as an alternative to *black* in the late 1980s and 1990s reflects similar thinking.

Farrakhan, Garvey, and others have placed considerable emphasis in recent years on the themes emphasized by Malcolm X in the 1960s: African Americans cannot and should not count on whites or anyone else to take steps that will lead to the betterment of the black community. They argue that this can be accomplished only by blacks taking control of their own destiny by building their own institutions and power structure. While leaders with this viewpoint clearly do not have the unqualified support of the overall black community, it is clear that the viewpoint they espouse has substantial and probably growing support, even among the majority of

African Americans who do not entirely reject the concept of integration and who favor the idea of trying to get along with whites whenever possible. In summary, it is fair to say that assimilationist, pluralist, and separatist tendencies are all present to some extent in current African American thought, and the need for an independent black political and economic base is emphasized by a large and growing number of African Americans.

Pluralism and Militancy Among Chicanos, Latinos, and American Indians

During the 1960s, Mexican Americans also turned away from assimilation as a goal and began to emphasize such concepts as self-defense and building an independent power base. *Chicanismo*—pride in Chicano culture and heritage and a struggle to combat forced assimilation—became a widespread ideology, particularly among younger Mexican Americans. As we have seen in earlier chapters, there was growing emphasis during this period on the preservation of the Spanish language and of unique Chicano dialects that mixed Spanish and English. One manifestation of this trend was the demand for bilingual education. Many Chicanos have advocated bilingual education not only as a way of helping Chicano children to speak English but also as a vehicle to ensure the preservation of the Spanish language among young Mexican Americans.

Important changes also occurred during the 1960s in the tactics used by the Chicano movement. In the early 1960s, Chicano political involvement was marked by the *Viva Kennedy* movement, which was basically an effort to get Chicanos involved in the traditional American political process, which they have always shunned to some degree. This effort is frequently credited with carrying the crucial state of Texas for the Kennedy–Johnson ticket in 1960 (Acuña, 1972, p. 223). In the mid 1960s, Cesar Chavez's use of Gandhian nonviolence to unionize Mexican American and Filipino farmworkers was probably the most widely known segment of the Chicano movement. Though a more direct challenge to the system than the earlier voter-registration efforts, Chavez's movement retained a belief that Chicanos could be integrated into basic American institutions, in this case the labor movement. Today, both voter-registration and voter-turnout efforts and the United Farm Workers Union remain important parts of Mexican American political involvement. The UFW, for example, succeeded, at least for a time, in unionizing a sizable portion of California's agricultural labor force and led to significant improvements in wages and working conditions for Chicano farmworkers. Nonetheless, by the latter part of the 1960s, many Chicanos were starting to turn away from traditional electoral participation and Gandhian nonviolence. The year 1967 saw the formation of the Brown Berets, a group stressing militant self-defense tactics similar to those of the Black Panthers. A number of militant Chicano student groups were also formed in that year and subsequent years (Moore, 1976, p. 151). The imagination of younger Chicanos was captured by the militant actions of Reies Tijerina in New Mexico (see Chapter 6). By the late 1960s, many younger Chicanos in particular had given up on integration and sought to build an independent Chicano power base. Furthermore, at least some felt that violence or the threat of violence was the only way to get the Anglo power structure to take seriously the demands of Chicanos. Finally, the turn away from assimilationist tendencies can be seen in the formation of a Chicano political party—*La Raza Unida* party. This party won control of the school board and city

The late United Farm Workers Union president Cesar Chavez is interviewed at a rally in support of the union's lettuce boycott. The United Farm Workers have sought to improve the status of Chicano farmworkers through participation in the labor union movement and through efforts to establish a broad base of support in the American population for boycotts of producers who refuse to negotiate with their workers' union. This approach reflects a basic belief that with sufficient pressure, Chicanos can become integrated into basic American institutions. *AFL-CIO News*

council in Crystal City, Texas, and other nearby communities in 1970 and captured about 6 percent of the vote for governor in Texas in 1972 (Acuña, 1972, p. 236; Moore, 1976, p. 153). The party was also on the ballot in Colorado in 1970.

Moore (1976, p. 49) cites several factors that contributed to these changes in attitudes. A very important one was the development of the Black Power movement during this period. That movement provided a role model and both illustrated that legal equality did not guarantee social equality and "legitimized an ideology that rejected assimilation and fixed the blame on the larger society" for racial inequality. In addition, it demonstrated that blacks could at least get attention and promises by rioting, which at the time was more than Chicanos were getting. In addition to the Black Power movement, the antiwar movement and the general atmosphere of protest and rebellion helped to produce a situation conducive to a militant Chicano protest movement. The Chicano movement, however, was not merely a response to the Black Power movement or other social movements. It represented, as did the Black Power movement, a response to the failure of assimilation seeking to bring about equality. In the case of Chicanos, the frustrations may have even been greater than they had been with blacks. As with blacks, the promises of the Kennedy and Johnson administrations and the War on Poverty had led to raised expectations. Chicanos soon found out, however, that the government bureaucrats for the most part thought of poverty and intergroup relations in terms of blacks and whites. Chicanos were almost entirely forgotten in the early stages of the War on Poverty, and this proved an important stimulus for the militant Chicano movement (Acuña, 1972, pp. 226–27).

Today, the ideology of Chicanismo continues to have considerable influence among Mexican Americans. Such programs as bilingual education spread rapidly in the 1970s, and despite some efforts by the Reagan administration to curtail them in the 1980s, they remain quite widespread today. Indicators of continuing identification with Chicano culture include the continuing use of the Spanish language in the home by many Chicanos (Pachon and Moore, 1981) and widespread support for bilingual education, partly as a means of teaching English to non-English speakers, but also partly as a means of preserving Hispanic culture. For example, Latino advocacy groups such as the National Council of La Raza and the Puerto Rican organization Aspira have continued into the 1990s to support bilingual-education programs on the grounds that they enhance Latino culture, bolster self-esteem among Latino students, and help to serve as a corrective to the Eurocentric focus of many schools (Porter, 1991).

According to Pachon and Moore (1981), three factors tend to promote cultural pluralism among Hispanic Americans. These include proximity to the homeland (Mexico or Puerto Rico, for the large majority), the recent general emphasis among American racial and ethnic groups on cultural identity and roots, and bilingual education. Two other factors might be added. First, Hispanic Americans are very geographically concentrated—the great majority live in just five states. Second, the proportion of Spanish-speaking among current immigrants is larger than the proportion of immigrants speaking any one language at any time in our history (Domestic Policy Association, 1986). Both of these realities make it easier for Hispanics than for past immigrants to maintain their culture. Additionally, Chicanos and Puerto Ricans are, historically speaking, colonized minorities, and colonized minorities nearly always are more resistant to assimilation than immigrant ones (Blauner, 1972). In short, a number of factors suggest a continuing strong pattern of pluralism among Hispanic Americans now and in the future. Recent research by Yankelovich, Skelly, and White (1984) is enlightening on this point. These surveys found an *increase* during the early 1980s in commitment to Spanish language and culture.

An important new development in recent decades is the emergence of what Padilla (1985) has called *Latino ethnic consciousness.* This trend represents a move toward common identification among different Latino or Hispanic groups, particularly Mexican Americans and Puerto Ricans. Padilla sees this trend as partly the result of political necessity. Even combined, the various Hispanic or Latino groups make up only about 9 percent of the population, and are a numerical minority, even in places like Chicago where there are large populations of both Chicanos and Puerto Ricans. For a group (or set of groups) this size, Padilla argues, unity is essential, and he presents strong evidence that there was an increasing common identity among various Latino groups in the 1970s, at least in Chicago, where he conducted his study.

As has been the case with African Americans, activism among Chicanos appears to be on the increase in the 1990s. In 1993, a series of protests, including an extended hunger fast by a number of students and faculty as well as rallies and sit-ins, sought the establishment of a department of Chicano studies at UCLA. Hunger fasts by Chicano students spread to a number of other college campuses during the 1993–94 school year. Also, the United Farm Workers Union undertook a new grape boycott in the early 1990s, aimed at eliminating use of hazardous pesticides in the growing of grapes, after several cancer clusters developed among farmworker communities in California. This boycott was well under way when Cesar Chavez died in 1993, and his successor as president of the United Farm Workers, Arturo Rodriguez, vowed to continue it. By 1994, grape sales were falling, and several college campuses stopped serving grapes in residence halls.

Among Native Americans, the picture is somewhat different. The difference is that Indian people never sought assimilation to the degree that blacks or Mexican Americans did; thus, a turn away from assimilation was not possible. However, important changes did occur for Indian people during the 1960s and early 1970s. The most important was the upsurge in protest, which had been rare among Native Americans until the late 1960s. By 1970, Indian people had become much more involved in protest, and much of it took on a very militant tone. From the beginning, the protest was largely separatist in nature, as Indian people reasserted land claims and their historic status as independent nations. Thus, the thrust of Indian protest ever since the 1960s has been mainly the return of Indian land and the reassertion of treaty and fishing rights—*not* the elimination of barriers to participation in American society. As with the other groups, militant protest has had the greatest appeal among younger Indians. Throughout much of the 1970s, both legal means, such as lawsuits demanding the enforcement of old treaties, and illegal means, such as the various occupations of land and buildings discussed previously, have been used. Although these actions have not resulted in the return of large land areas to Indian ownership, Indians have had some important successes. For example, there have been some large cash settlements in lieu of land claims, and historic Indian fishing rights have been reestablished in a number of states, despite strong opposition from sport fishermen and state fish and game departments. Among the broader Indian population, a reemphasis of traditional culture emerged during the 1970s. By the early 1980s, nearly every tribe was making strong efforts to teach its younger generation its language, crafts, skills, and tribal history. This cultural revival extended to urban Indians, too: By the early 1980s, nearly every city with a sizable Native American population had an Indian center offering cultural and recreational activities (Deloria, 1981). These efforts continued into the 1990s. And during the 1980s and 1990s, AIM membership continued to grow, to the point that by the early 1990s, AIM existed in some form in almost every native community in North America (Churchill, 1994, p. 99).

An issue receiving new emphasis by all minority groups today, but particularly by Native Americans, is **environmental racism.** This term, coined in 1983 by Benjamin Chavis, president of the NAACP in the early 1990s, refers to the tendency for people of color to be placed at particular risk of suffering the harmful effects of environmental contaminants. We have already seen an example of this in the high incidence of cancer among Chicano farmworkers and their families, which apparently results from exposure to dangerous pesticides. For Native Americans, a major issue of environmental racism has been the disposal of radioactive and other hazardous wastes on Indian reservations. In many cases, government agencies and waste disposal companies who have encountered opposition to the disposal of such wastes elsewhere have sought to take advantage of the poverty of the reservations by offering tribal councils large sums of money in exchange for allowing disposal of this waste on reservations. This has generated considerable controversy and a strong movement against environmental racism on a number of reservations. In a number of cases, tribal councils have consequently rejected such monetary offers. In other cases, the acceptance of such offers has led to deep divisions on some reservations.

In addition to environmental racism, other issues that have come to the forefront among Native American activists in recent years include use of Indians as team mascots, abuse of Indian burial grounds and remains, and the often careless imitation of Native American religious rituals by non-Indians. Most Native Americans regard the use of their people as team mascots to be highly degrading, along with behaviors such as the "tomahawk chop" used by supporters of several teams, which Indian people see as mocking their culture and traditions. Ward Churchill (1994), for example, points out striking similarities between the appearance of the Cleveland Indians mascot and caricatures used in Germany in the 1930s to degrade Jews. He points out how silly it would sound to call a team the "Blacks," "Whites," "Jews," or "Hispanics"—yet many teams are called the "Indians," "Redskins," or "Braves." With respect to the burial grounds issue, Native American activists ask non-Indians how they would feel if their great-grandparents' bones were dug up and put in a display case for people to look at. This is exactly what has often been done in the case of Native Americans, though protests in recent years have largely curtailed the practice. As recently as June 1994, however, ground containing Indian bones was dug up and used as fill for construction of a freeway in Illinois, after state archeologists said the bones were of "no archeological significance."

Although the civil rights and Black Power movements played an important role in stimulating protest among American Indians (see Day, 1972), the distinctive history of Indian people also made a difference. This resistance among Indians to forced assimilation probably helps to explain why, although protest was slower to come among Indian people than to some other groups, it was more militant and separatist from the start once it did come.

The "Ethnic Revival" Among White Americans

The trend toward emphasizing ethnic distinctiveness was not limited to those groups that most clearly fit the definition of minority groups (blacks, Latinos, and Indians). White ethnic groups, as well, have placed a renewed emphasis on ethnicity since the late 1960s. Much has been written about the "ethnic revival" among various white ethnic groups. There is considerable debate over the nature and extent of this ethnic revival, but it seems clear that something has been happening. Outwardly, at least, Americans from a wide variety of groups have placed a greater emphasis on ethnicity and ethnic culture. This can be seen in the proliferation of ethnic festivals, the celebration of ethnic holidays, and so on. Much debate also centers on whether the change is superficial—relatively few participants (but some, nonetheless) have learned the language of their ethnic place of origin, for example. There is also debate over whether the changes are really based on ethnicity or whether they are mainly a class phenomenon (Gans, 1974, pp. xi, xii). The ethnic revival has been most notable among Catholic, Jewish, Eastern European, and predominantly working-class groups, and among these groups it has often taken on political overtones. In two ways, these changes seem to have grown out of the Black Power movement. First, the Black Power movement served as a role model. It showed all other groups that racial or ethnic group consciousness is a way of getting the political system to listen to the collective concerns of a group. Second, many white ethnic groups perceived blacks' gains as a threat: They believed that any gains made by blacks would come at their expense, not at the expense of the middle classes (Goering, 1971; Novak, 1971; Rieder, 1985). There was some basis in reality for this perception: Rarely were middle-class suburban white children bused, and rarely were middle-class neighborhoods blockbusted. Unfortunately, the anger of working class white ethnics was sometimes turned against blacks and the gains they made rather than against the larger power structure (see Ransford, 1972). Thus, it is ironic that a trend that is in part a product of the Black Power movement now threatens the position of blacks: The white ethnic working class, because of its greater numbers and economic and political resources, and because of its majority group membership, probably has the advantage in any struggle against blacks. Indeed, this group has vigorously opposed such programs as affirmative action and bilingual education (Kluegel and Smith, 1986; Lipset, 1992) and gave significant backing to efforts by the Reagan and Bush administrations to reverse these policies (for further discussion of this problem, see Patterson, 1977). Nonetheless, some observers such as Novak (1971) argue that the dominant thrust *is* against a power structure that has ignored the concerns of the working class white ethnics. Issues such as these suggest that the "ethnic revival" was at least partly a social class phenomenon, although ethnicity had at least symbolic importance.

Another school of thought suggests that the ethnic revival of the 1970s is not entirely an outgrowth of the Black Power movement. According to this school, it may have been partly a result of the length of time that some ethnic groups have been in the United States. Hansen (1952, 1966) developed a theory that an ethnic revival typically occurs in the third generation. The second generation, according to Hansen's view, seeks to get rid of all trappings of the ethnic background of its parents and to become fully assimilated. The third generation, generally more socially and economically secure, seeks to rediscover its ethnic culture and heritage. Hansen based his theory partly on his observations of Swedish Americans. Studies of other groups (see Sandberg, 1974; Abramson, 1975), however, call into question the universality of a third-generation ethnic revival. Nonetheless, Greeley (1971) sees the ethnic revival of the 1970s largely as an affirmation of Hansen's third-generation hypothesis. According to Greeley, the fact that many white ethnic groups had become more secure and affluent then they were in earlier years enabled them to assert their ethnicity and inquire into their origins. (Concerning the increased affluence of white ethnic groups, see also Greeley, 1974.)

Although there is debate about its degree (see, for example, Gans, 1974, 1979), there is little doubt that there has been a revived interest in ethnicity and group culture since the late 1960s. In greater or lesser ways, this is true for virtually every racial, ethnic, and cultural group in America. The blank in the statement, "I'm ___ and proud" could be filled in with *black, Chicano, Indian, Polish, German, Italian, Greek, Irish,* or numerous other labels. It could even go beyond ethnic groups and read *female, gay,* or perhaps *disabled* or *physically challenged.* The extent and meaning of the change may be debatable, but there can be little doubt that cultural pluralism became very fashionable in the United States in the late 1960s and early 1970s, and to a large extent has remained so since.

SUMMARY AND CONCLUSION

In this chapter, we have seen that cultural assimilation has been the dominant mode of adaptation for racial and ethnic minority groups in American society. The dominant group has always demanded it, and for the most part, minorities have gone along with it, though there have been notable cases of resistance. In the early stages of the black civil rights movement—which brought political action by blacks on an unprecedented scale in the 1950s and 1960s—the movement's goals were largely assimilationist. As some of those goals proved elusive, however, a shift toward more pluralist thinking emerged. Moreover, assimilation in American society has never been complete, particularly at the structural, as opposed to cultural, level. Indeed, substantial structural pluralism has been maintained, even when cultural assimilation has been quite general. Thus, the ideology of Anglo-conformity has probably led many to believe that America has been more of a melting pot than it in fact ever was. In addition, a noticeable shift away from cultural assimilation toward cultural pluralism has taken place since the 1960s. An important stimulus for this shift was the Black Power movement, which was at least partly the result of the failure of the assimilationist efforts of the civil rights movement to bring equality for black Americans.

We have also seen that assimilation occurs less readily for exploited minorities of the colonized type (Blauner, 1972) than for immigrant minorities. In the United States, this has meant that African Americans, Hispanic Americans, and Native Americans have experienced less cultural and structural assimilation than have immigrant groups from Europe such as Irish Americans, German Americans, or Polish Americans. As a general rule, racial minorities are also assimilated less easily than ethnic ones, because their distinct appearance makes discriminating against them easier. Both these factors suggest that a big reason blacks, Hispanics, and Indians have never been fully integrated into American society is that whites in large part have not wanted or permitted them to participate as equals. Another reason for a lack of assimilation is that colonized groups are likely to perceive the dominant group as an oppressor and for that reason to resist its culture. Colonized groups have also seen that group consciousness can build an important base for seeking political power.

Other factors not mentioned in this chapter (but discussed elsewhere; see Chapter 8) influence the likelihood of assimilation versus pluralism. Cultural and structural assimilation are less likely, for example, when a minority group is relatively large than when it is very small. A large group is both more likely to be perceived as a threat (and thereby resisted by the dominant group) and more capable of reinforcing and preserving its own culture. In the long run, however, this factor is probably less important than others: Irish Americans and German Americans are both more numerous and more assimilated than the typical ethnic group in America.

A final factor influencing the likelihood of assimilation is proximity to one's homeland. Groups that live near or on their homeland generally are more able to maintain their group culture than groups who are very distant from their homeland. In the United States, the two minorities living on or near their homeland are Chicanos and American Indians. It is striking that these are probably the two groups that have preserved their group cultures and institutions to the greatest degree in the United States.

America has been marked by substantial elements of both assimilation and pluralism. Separatist movements have occurred and exist today, but separation in the strict sense of minority groups choosing to live in separate territories from whites has never enjoyed the support of the majority of blacks or other people of color. While cultural assimilation mixed with a sizable amount of structural pluralism has been the norm, there have been important variations both from time to time and from group to group. The consequences of such shifts continue to be debated. Functionalist theorists see a serious threat to national unity in pluralism and thus urge a move toward assimilation and consensus (see A. Thernstrom, 1980). Conflict theorists, on the other hand, see a potential for a fairer power balance if pluralism can enhance the power base of minorities such as blacks, Chicanos, and Indians. They worry, however, that racial divisions could play off the white and minority working classes against one another, thus enhancing the power of the elite. (For further discussion of assimilation and pluralism in the United States, see Abramson, 1980).

8

Cross-cultural Studies of Majority–Minority Relations

In the previous three chapters, we have examined the changing patterns of majority–minority relations over the history of the United States and the earlier British colonies, and we have identified a number of basic principles about majority–minority relations. By studying different periods of American history, we have seen some of the conditions that lead to racial or ethnic inequality, and we have seen that the form of inequality varies with the social and economic conditions at the time. Although we have learned much about majority–minority relations, there is a limit to how much we can learn by looking only at American history. American society, and consequently American race relations, have been very different at different points in time, but we are still talking about one society. In a world with thousands of different societies, large and small, all kinds of social conditions exist that have never been seen in the United States. To fully understand the dynamics of race and ethnic relations, we must look at them in a wide range of social and cultural settings. We plan to accomplish two things in this chapter: (1) use international evidence to further test and refine major principles already identified in earlier chapters and (2) use cross-cultural comparisons to identify additional principles about the dynamics of majority–minority relations.

CROSS-CULTURAL EVIDENCE ON THE EFFECTS OF COLONIZATION

One principle we have identified in American race relations is that the racial or ethnic groups that have experienced the greatest disadvantage and that have had the greatest conflict with the majority are those whose initial entry into American society was through conquest or colonization. This would seem to suggest that one very important cause of both racial–ethnic stratification and conflict is the conquest or colonization of one group by another. That, at least, is what U.S. history suggests. But is it true throughout the world?

Consider for a moment the racial or ethnic conflicts that you have read or heard about in the last few years. Among the best known are conflicts between blacks and whites in South Africa; between Catholics and Protestants in Northern Ireland; between English-speakers and French-speakers in Quebec, Canada; among various groups in the former Soviet Union; among Serbs, Croats, and Bosnians in former Yugoslavia; and between Arabs (particularly Palestinian Arabs) and Jews in the Middle East. These groups and societies vary tremendously, but if we examine the situation closely, we find one common denominator: In each place, the intergroup conflict can be traced back to the colonization or conquest of one racial or ethnic group by another. Let us briefly examine the origins of ethnic stratification and conflict in each of these places.

South Africa

No other nation in recent world history has been known for a system of racial inequality as rigid as that which existed in South Africa until recently. By law, South Africans have been classified as black, white, Asian, or "colored" (that is, a mixture of black and white). Until very recently, South African law attached to these racial categories specified rights and restrictions affecting all aspects of life. In recent years, most of these restrictions were gradually repealed, but until 1994 the rights to vote and hold office were denied to blacks, who constitute over two-thirds of South Africa's population. An agreement was reached in mid 1993 to extend to blacks the rights to vote and hold office, and the country's first nonracial elections

Nelson Mandela is sworn in as South Africa's first black president in 1994, marking the end of decades of white minority rule in South Africa. *Bettmann/Reuters*

were held on April 27, 1994. In those elections, Nelson Mandela was elected South Africa's first black president, under the banner of the African National Congress (ANC) party. The election of a black president and a majority-black parliament in a free election in which all could vote represented a dramatic turnaround in a country in which the right to vote had been systematically denied to South Africa's black majority throughout the history of the country. However, a challenging task of undoing decades of institutionalized racial inequality remained following the 1994 elections: nearly all wealth in South Africa remained in the hands of the white minority, and the average income of blacks was a tiny fraction of that of whites.

During its forty-year history, beginning in 1949, South African apartheid, a legally mandated system of racial classification, segregation, and discrimination, restricted far more than the right to vote. It defined who could live where, who could work at what job, even who could be present in a given area at a particular time of day. For a long time, only the poorest jobs were open to blacks, though the need for labor changed that somewhat as time passed. Though constituting more than two-thirds of South Africa's population, blacks were limited to ownership of only 13 percent of the land, and the worst land at that. At one time, it was illegal to even conspire to have sex with someone of a different race, much less to actually do so. Whites, who number less than 20 percent of the population, used their total control of the political system to ensure that they continued to own virtually all the wealth, while the overwhelming majority of blacks remained segregated and trapped in poverty.

This severe racial inequality led to violent uprisings, particularly in the 1960s and thereafter, as well as an increase in underground actions, such as sabotage. Thus, South Africa is a nation whose history has been marked by gross racial inequality and extreme racial conflict.

The roots of this inequality and conflict originated with conquest of the indigenous black African population by white European populations. Although apartheid was the law only since 1949, racial inequality had been deeply institutionalized since the Dutch began to colonize the area in the mid 1600s. Although the first Dutch settlers were mainly interested in supplying their ships passing the area, agricultural settlers later began moving inland or "trekking," which brought conflict with the natives and ultimately their conquest. It also frequently brought genocide, or mass killing of the native population. Close to the coast, a paternalistic system of slavery was developed, though the slaves were usually imported from other parts of Africa. Gradually and after a series of conflicts, the British gained control of the area from the Dutch, and attempted to treat the native population more liberally. This was not the actual result, however, for several reasons. First, the Dutch were pushed inland in further "treks" to avoid the British, conquering and subordinating still more of the native population. Included in this group was the large and well-organized Bantu nation, which fought fiercely and effectively for many years before final conquest. Second, the British ultimately became as dependent as the Dutch on white supremacy, and their attempts at liberalization always stopped well short of a point that could have threatened the white power structure. In addition, the descendants of the Dutch settlers, known as Afrikaners, viewed the British as outsiders who threatened their way of life with their attempts at racial liberalism, and the Afrikaners responded by becoming even more repressive of the native population. Thus, the establishment of apartheid in 1949 when the Afrikaners regained full control was by and large a codification of what had already developed: a strict caste system of racial inequality that had changed mainly from paternalism to segregation (the rigid com-

After the 1994 South African elections a unity government was formed, including representatives of the predominantly white National Party as well as the majority African National Congress. *Sygma/Brooks Craft*

petitive pattern) as the society changed from agricultural to urban. The caste system actually became more rigid as the society urbanized, because whites came to see the black majority as an ever-greater threat to their supremacy. The more blacks were capable of doing work that allowed them to compete with whites and the more they become aware of their repression, the more of a threat they became to the dominant white minority. Despite these changes, and despite the conflict and shifting power balance between the British and Dutch, the presence of a racial caste system can be traced back to the conquest of the native population by the Dutch. In many ways, that conquest was similar to that of Indian people by whites in the United States. (For further discussion of South Africa, see Van den Berghe, 1965, 1978, chap. 5; Hunt and Walker, 1974, chap. 6.) Thus, while the pattern of conflict and inequality was changed and in many ways became worse, its origins can be directly traced to the country's colonial origins.

Northern Ireland

Not all instances of severe intergroup conflict or stratification in the world involve different races. In Northern Ireland, a violent intergroup conflict between Catholic and Protestant whites that flared in the late 1960s continued into the 1990s, and has showed no sign of resolution. Since 1968, approximately three thousand lives have been lost in that conflict (*New Statesman and Society,* 1992). Segregation and violence are so extreme that, by the mid 1980s, a Berlinlike wall had been built to separate the Catholic and Protestant sectors in Belfast. All participants are white and European. By all outward appearance, it is a religious conflict between Catholics and Protestants. A closer analysis of the situation shows, however, that there is much more to it than that. Indeed, the roots of today's conflict go all the way back to the sixteenth century, when Britain gradually asserted control over Ireland. Initially, an English colony was established in Ireland mainly for military and political reasons, since control of Ireland was advantageous in military conflicts with mainland European countries. Later, economic motivations also became important, as the English colonists established themselves as feudal landlords over the Irish population. It is important to note that the English colonists were Protestant (Anglican) and the Irish whom they conquered were Catholic. Later, the English settlers were joined by Scottish ones, who were also Protestant but Presbyterian. Many of the Scots settled in the six northern counties, which are today Northern Ireland. The Irish people never accepted domination by the British, and revolts and upheavals occurred intermittently. The Scottish Presbyterians, who occupied an intermediate position between the Anglicans from England and the Irish Catholics, also rebelled against the English periodically, but by the late eighteenth century, the two Protestant groups were drawn together by the threat of increased Irish Catholic political power (Moore, 1972). In addition, the British government played on the prejudice of the Presbyterians to assure that they would never form a coalition with Irish Catholics against the British crown (See, 1986, pp. 45–46). Eventually, polarization between the English and Scottish Protestants on one side and the native Irish Catholics on the other led to violent and bloody conflict, which resulted in the division of Ireland. The six northern counties, known as Ulster or Northern Ireland, remained under partial British control and Protestant domination. The remainder of the country, heavily Catholic, became the Republic of Ireland.

Since that time, the arena of conflict has been in the north. There the Protestants, a two-to-one majority, retain general control of the government and a position of social and economic advantage. Not all Protestants are wealthy or even middle class, but most of the wealth is in Protestant hands. The Catholics demand equality, but lacking effective political power, they are unable to escape the low status of a subordinate group. Being a third of the population, they *can* cause a great deal of disruption. Consequently, the situation has remained a violence-ridden stalemate. This necessarily brief and somewhat superficial discussion[1] is sufficient to illustrate one very important point: The roots of the conflict are to be found in colonialism. Today's Irish Catholics (North and South) are descendants of the native Irish who were conquered and colonized by British (Scottish and English) Protestants. Today's Irish Protestants are the descendants of the British colonizers and look on the Irish Catholics as an inferior but dangerous and treacherous people. The history of conquest, rebellion, and conflict is central in the mind of both groups in Northern Ireland. Finally, the two groups largely retain the statuses associated with colonizers and colonized minorities. As a result, majority–minority relations in Northern Ireland, even though between two white, European, and Christian ethnic groups, have in many ways closely resembled race relations between blacks and whites in such places as South Africa and the United States (Moore, 1972).

Quebec, Canada

Quebec Province in Canada is unique among the areas we have discussed; not only is the conflict between two white, European, and Christian groups (English- and French-speaking Canadians), but it is between two groups whose original pres-

---

[1]For more extensive discussions, see Barrit and Carter (1962), Rose (1971), Moore (1972), See (1986).

ence in Canada was that of colonizer rather than indigenous population. Neither the British nor French were native to Canada, and both (in somewhat different ways) colonized the native Canadian Indian population. The dominance of the English-speaking population (a 20 percent minority of Quebec's population) over the much larger French-speaking population originated with the conquest of the French colonists by the British colonists in 1759. Since that time, the English-speaking Canadians have had a dominant social, economic, and, until recently, political position. The great majority of the province's wealth, for example, is owned by the English-speaking population. Although English–French conflict has been muted by class divisions that exist within the French population (Ossenberg, 1975), the English–French conflict increased in the 1960s and 1970s. This led to violence by militant Quebec separatists in 1970 and later in the 1970s brought to power the *Parti Quebecois,* which advocated separation of Quebec from the Canadian confederation. In 1980, however, a referendum on separation failed, and the position of the *Parti Quebecois* weakened somewhat. A series of laws passed in the 1970s and 1980s, however, mandated increasingly strict rules that French was to be the province's only official language, despite Canada's official national policy of being bilingual (English and French). Quebec's language laws, for example, require that signs posted outside businesses be in French.

The question of separation again came to the fore in the late 1980s and early 1990s, as efforts were made to amend Canada's constitution in ways that would recognize Quebec as "a distinct society" within the Canadian confederation. In 1992, agreement was reached on such a constitution (which also provided for autonomy for Canada's native Indian population). The agreement failed, however, because it was not ratified by the required number of provinces: Quebec rejected it because it did not go far enough in guaranteeing Quebec's autonomy; a number of other provinces rejected it because in their view it went too far and gave Quebec (and/or the native population) special privileges that other provinces did not enjoy. The failure of this agreement raises some questions about Canada's long-term ability to function as a unified nation, though at the present there is no imminent likelihood of Quebec seceding. In 1994, however, the *Parti Quebecois* returned to power.

Once again, the example of Quebec shows that considerable ethnic stratification and ethnic conflict can result from conquest and colonization, even when one colonizing group conquers another colonizing group and the groups are of the same race and only moderately different in cultural values. As we shall see later, language differences such as those in Quebec can greatly aggravate ethnic conflicts, but in the absence of colonization or conquest, often do not do so. The inequality and conflict in Quebec arise largely out of a situation in which one group conquered and colonized another over two hundred years ago.

The Former Soviet Union

In 1991, the Soviet Union was abolished after the failure of a coup attempt against the government of Soviet president Mikhail Gorbachev, who had dramatically altered Soviet politics through the introduction of freedom of expression, a free press, and, to a limited extent, free elections. When freedom was introduced, many old ethnic rivalries came to the surface, and many of the fifteen ethnically-based republics of the Soviet Union began to seek independence. When the plotters of the coup attempt failed in their efforts to reestablish an authoritarian communist government, the end of the old Soviet Union came quickly, with all fifteen republics establishing themselves as independent countries; eleven of them choosing to remain very loosely connected as the Commonwealth of Independent States.

Given the freedom to pursue old ethnic rivalries, and now separated into fifteen countries based largely on ethnic groupings, the former Soviet Union plunged into a bewildering variety of ethnic conflicts, some of which became very violent. Two of the former republics, Armenia and Azerbaijan, immediately plunged into a war that to a large extent had already been under way before the breakup of the Soviet Union and that continued into 1993 with heavy casualties. The war was fought over an ethnically Armenian region, Nagorno–Karabakh, within Azerbaijan. The Armenian population of that region was opposed to living under Azerbaijani rule and sought to become part of Armenia. Moreover, Armenia wanted the territory and as a result went to war over it. In other parts of the former Soviet Union, disputes arose among former republics over control of nuclear weapons and of installations such as naval bases. In a number of former republics, ethnic minorities rebelled against the government, seeking to establish their own independent, ethnically based nations much as the former republics had done.

As recently as the late 1980s, the Soviet Union had been one of the two strongest military powers in the world. Its population had been the third largest of any country in the world, and its military and political influence extended to all parts of the world. For more than seventy years, the Soviet Union had ruled a vast, ethnically diverse territory extending from eastern Europe across northern Asia all the way to the Pacific Ocean—a bigger territory than any other country in the history of the world. How could it be that in a matter of just a few years, such a superpower could break up into fifteen countries, many of which were in conflict with one another and/or deeply divided within, each of which was ruled by a different ethnic group, and most of which were of relatively minor military or economic significance in the modern world?

To a large extent, the answer, as in other ethnic conflicts around the world, lies in a history of conquest and colonialism. When the Soviet Union was created in 1917, its territory coincided for the most part with that of the old Russian empire. The Russian empire was created through a series of annexations and conquests beginning in the sixteenth century and continuing into the late nineteenth century (Nahaylo and Swboda, 1989). Among the larger groups conquered or annexed were Lithuanians, Latvians, Estonians, Byelorussians, Ukrainians, Moldavians, Georgians, Armenians, Azerbaijanis, Tatars, Kazakhs, Kirghizes, Uzbeks, and Tadzhiks.

In 1917, the czar (the monarch of the Russian empire) was overthrown in the Bolshevik revolution, led by Vladimir Lenin. As little as a few months before the revolution, Lenin had reiterated his support of a nation's right to secede from the empire through a process of referendum (Nahaylo and Swboda, 1989, p. 15). Lenin also believed, however, that most could be induced to voluntarily remain in the new nation created by the revolution, the Soviet Union. He believed that this could be accomplished in part by allowing each ethnic region to retain its own language and culture. He wrote, "We want *free* unification; this is why we must recognize the right to secede (without freedom to secede, unification cannot be free)" (Lenin, 1960–70). At the same time, he believed that the advantages of having one national language would eventually lead most regions to voluntarily choose to speak Russian if it was not imposed on them against their will.

In reality, however, the right to secede was not respected by the Soviet

Union. The test came less than a month after the Bolshevik revolution, when the Ukraine announced it did not recognize Soviet rule and proclaimed independence. Although Lenin at first recognized its right to secede, the Soviet Union soon invaded the Ukraine after it refused to allow Russian Red Guards free passage through it. Russian troops with the support of ethnic Russians in the Ukraine occupied virtually all of the Ukraine and established Soviet rule within about three months. Soviet control was similarly established over virtually all former Russian territory in Europe. In the next few years, control was similarly established over Islamic regions of the former Russian empire. In effect, Soviet policy proclaimed the legitimacy of the various ethnic states in former Russian territory, while in reality it created a centralized, unitary state that denied them any opportunity for real independence (Rakowska-Harmstone, 1992).

The only real exceptions to the above patterns were the three Baltic States, Latvia, Estonia, and Lithuania. In part because they were or had been occupied by the Germans or Poles, these countries were able to become independent and remain so for about twenty years after the creation of the Soviet Union. Georgia also briefly gained independence but lost it ten months later when the Soviet army invaded. At the end of World War II, the Baltic States were brought back under Soviet rule. The Soviets also gained effective control of Poland and several other Eastern European nations that remained nominally independent.

In compelling more than one hundred ethnic groups—many of them living in clearly distinct territories—to live under a common state, the Soviet Union to a large extent sowed the seeds of its ultimate destruction and of the ethnic turmoil that erupted into violence in the 1990s (Rakowska-Harmstone, 1992, p. 523). An important part of this process was that it was very clearly Russians who were in charge, even though a sizable minority (about 50 percent by 1990) of the Soviet Union's population was non-Russian. Moreover, non-Russian minorities, for the most part, occupied a clearly subordinate economic position (Huttenbach, 1990). Thus, as in other places in the world that have experienced severe ethnic violence, non-Russian ethnic groups in the Soviet Union were, in effect, forced into a subordinate status under Russian rule, both under the old Russian empire and the more recent Soviet Union.

This pattern only intensified when Joseph Stalin gained control of the Soviet Union after Lenin's death. Demanding total loyalty, Stalin imposed a harshly dictatorial state that suppressed all signs of independent thought, including expressions of ethnic consciousness and practice of the traditional religions. Though himself Georgian, Stalin pursued a policy of Russian hegemony because he had seen how regional independence movements could threaten the power of the centralized government. This led to repeated purges of non-Russian, ethnic-oriented elements in the Communist Party and government.

The consequences of all this were to (1) make expressions of ethnic solidarity or independence as impossible as they had been under czarist Russia and (2) to build tremendous resentment of conquest and outside rule that simmered for years, then came to the surface once freedom of expression was finally allowed in the 1980s. As the country modernized, rising educational levels gave rise to better-educated elites among the various ethnic groups, who became leaders in the struggle for ethnic autonomy. After Stalin's death, the Soviet government tried to accommodate desires for ethnic autonomy by tolerating some increase in regional autonomy and allowing the leaders of the republics greater autonomy in their own affairs. Loyalty to the national government was still demanded, however, and any se-cessionist moves were harshly suppressed. Thus, true autonomy was impossible, and as soon as conditions allowed, the republics and ethnic groups rebelled against cen-tral rule. Increasingly, once the Soviet Union was abolished, they also rebelled in any situation, such as that in the Nagorno–Karabakh region of Azerbaijan, where one ethnic group lived in an area ruled or dominated by another. Armenians in that re-gion did not want to become free of Russian rule only to fall under Azerbaijani rule. With no powerful, authoritarian Soviet government to repress them, ethnic groups were free to use whatever means they had at their disposal to advance their causes, and in most cases they did.

In addition to the war between the former republics of Armenia and Azer-baijan, conflicts have flared in other ethnically mixed republics. In Russia, the largest of the former republics, this has been particularly intense as Tatars, Bashkirs, Yakuts, Buryats, Ossetians, and others have all rebelled against Russian rule, many declar-ing independence (Rakowska-Harmstone, 1992). An example of the complexity of ethnic tensions in Russia can be seen in the Chechen–Ingushetia region of southern Russia, which declared independence from Russia in 1991. Subsequently, Ingushetia broke away from Chechen and is now fighting over territory with neighboring North Ossetia (Elliott et al., 1993). In the former Russian republic, the potential for ten-sion is especially great because the group that continues to rule the minority groups there, the Russians, is the one that conquered them in the first place. Thus, in the former Soviet Union as elsewhere, the roots of today's ethnic violence and conflict lie in the past conquest and colonization of a host of ethnic groups. In this case, col-onization by the Russian empire came first, but it was followed by the continued im-position of a basically colonial model of Russian domination under the Soviet Union for seven decades (Huttenbach, 1990). The effect of these historical influences can be seen in a statement made at a rally of Tatars seeking independence from Russia in March 1993: "Russia occupied us in 1552 and must beg forgiveness. Now Russia is falling apart, and we must hurry to make them recognize our independence" (Marat Mulyakov, quoted in Elliott et al., 1993).

Former Yugoslavia

Even worse ethnic violence than in the Soviet Union has occurred in former Yugoslavia in the early 1990s. As in the old Soviet Union, a variety of new ethnic na-tions were created when the old country of Yugoslavia began to dissolve in 1991. One by one, the republics of Slovenia, Croatia, Bosnia–Herzegovina, Macedonia, and Montenegro each declared independence from Yugoslavia. The Serbian-dominated Yugoslav government at first intervened militarily to prevent Slovenia and Croatia from seceding, though these republics eventually succeeded at becoming indepen-dent. (Serbs, however, regained control of a substantial part of Croatian territory.) The most serious violence has been in Bosnia–Herzegovina, where the effort to es-tablish an independent Bosnian state met resistance not only from Serbia (as east-ern Yugoslavia again became known after the breakup) but also from ethnic Serbs and Croats within Bosnian territory. Bosnia is much more ethnically diverse than Yu-goslavia's other former republics. While a narrow majority of its population is Bos-nian and Muslim, sizable portions are composed of Serbs and Croats, both of whom are predominantly Christian, though of different denominations. As a result, Bosnia's move toward independence has been opposed not only by the Serbian government but also by ethnic Serbs and Croats in Bosnian territory who do not want to live under Bosnian rule. The result has been civil war and the worst case of ethnic genocide in Europe since World War II.

In Bosnia, where 30 percent of the population is ethnically Serbian, the Serbian army and militias composed of ethnic Serbs living in Bosnia began a campaign in early 1992 that they called "ethnic cleansing." This meant eliminating the Bosnian Muslim population from areas of Bosnia that had Serbian majorities and establishing Serbian control over these areas. This was accomplished through a variety of brutal techniques including concentration camps where Bosnians were tortured and sometimes killed and Bosnian women systematically raped; forced relocations of Bosnians, sometimes accomplished by burning their homes; and a series of sieges in which Bosnian cities and neighborhoods were blockaded, rocketed, and shelled. In some instances, Croats, who make up about 17 percent of Bosnia's population, used similar tactics against the Bosnian Muslims, though they did not refer to their actions as "ethnic cleansing." On occasion, too, Bosnians also used tactics of these types against Serbs, but this has been less common because for the most part embargoes and blockades kept the Bosnians from obtaining the weapons that would enable them to do so and because in former Yugoslavia as a whole, the Bosnians were badly outnumbered by the Serbs. By August 1993, it was estimated that between 140,000 and 200,000 people had been killed or were missing as a result of this ethnic warfare (*St. Louis Post-Dispatch*, 1993a). Many, perhaps most, of these were Bosnian civilians.

The roots of the ethnic conflict in former Yugoslavia, as elsewhere, are imbedded in past histories of domination and colonialism. For hundreds of years, the Croats were ruled by Hungary, and all of Yugoslavia's other ethnic groups were ruled by the Turks. In 1878, Montenegro and Serbia managed to gain their independence, but all of the other regions remained under foreign rule until Yugoslavia was formed in 1918 (McFarlane, 1988, pp. 3–4). From then until 1939, Yugoslavia was dominated politically by the Serbs, and economically by foreign (French, British, and German) capital investment (McFarlane, 1988). In 1939, a Serb–Croat coalition took over rule of the country until 1941, when disorder resulted from both a Nazi invasion and civil war. In 1943, under the leadership of Josip Broz Tito and with the backing of the Soviet Union, Yugoslavia was reconstituted as a socialist republic. Tito's army was the only one of the various factions in Yugoslavia during World War II that fought on the basis of equality of all of Yugoslavia's component ethnic groups.

During and just before World War II, ethnic massacres were committed by virtually all of Yugoslavia's ethnic groups against one another. In 1941, Croats, cooperating with the Nazis and angry over decades of being ruled by Serbs, undertook a campaign of extermination, with one of their military commanders proclaiming, "I have given orders for the total extinction of Serbs [on Croatian territory]. Annihilate them wherever you can find them" (Joffe, 1992). Another group known as the Chetniks, an alliance of Serbs and Montenegrins, similarly engaged in systematic extermination of both Croats and Bosnians. Tito's partisans did not have clean hands, either. After World War II, they engaged in mass executions; and in at least two cities, they massacred thousands of people. Although these actions were motivated more by politics than ethnicity, they added to the resentment and the feelings, which persisted into the 1990s, that every group in Yugoslavia had accounts to settle (Joffe, 1992).

In spite of Tito's ultimate victory, moreover, strains between Croatian nationalism and Serbian attempts at central rule occurred throughout the history of

The city of Mostar, Bosnia, one of the several cities nearly destroyed by ethnic warfare among Serbs, Croats, and Bosnian Muslims during the early 1990s. *Sygma/Nigel Chandler*

Yugoslav communism (McFarlane, 1988). In fact, Serbs dominated the government of Yugoslavia from World War II until the country disintegrated in 1991. While Tito himself was of Slovenian and Croatian ancestry, Serbs dominated the military, the government bureaucracy, and the secret police (Joffe, 1992). This domination was resented by Croats, Slovenians, and Bosnians, but given the power of Tito's government and his willingness to use the secret police to stifle dissent, this resentment was kept in check. An additional factor helped to hold Yugoslavia together throughout Tito's life and beyond: fear of its bigger and more powerful communist neighbor, the Soviet Union. Yugoslavia was the only communist country in Eastern Europe that was able to remain free of Soviet domination. It did so through a combination of being strong enough to put up a fight if it were militarily invaded and Tito's skills in leading a movement of "nonaligned" nations that played the Soviet Union and United States off against one another in a contest for influence. Since nobody in Yugoslavia wanted to be ruled by the Soviets, the fear of being conquered and ruled by them to a large extent kept internal tensions among Yugoslavia's ethnic groups in check. Tito died in 1980, however, and by a decade later, the Soviet Union was on the road to collapse and clearly no longer a threat to Yugoslavia's independence. With neither Tito's central power nor the fear of the Soviet Union to hold it together, Yugoslavia was torn apart in the early 1990s by its longstanding ethnic conflicts.

Several historical factors are important to keep in mind in understanding today's ethnic warfare in former Yugoslavia. First, *every* ethnic group in Yugoslavia had, through much of its history, been conquered by other groups and denied any rights of autonomy or statehood. Second, during the twentieth century, Serbians have, by force, dominated every other group in Yugoslavia—even as they themselves have been similarly dominated in the past and have come to see power and dominance as ways of preventing their own loss of independence. Third, all of these conflicts and resentments have been worsened by a twentieth-century history in which nearly all ethnic groups in Yugoslavia have been both perpetrators and victims of ethnic massacres and extermination campaigns. This has greatly deepened the resentments arising from past conquest and colonialism. Finally, ethnic groups are sufficiently scattered and mixed in some parts of Yugoslavia that it is virtually impossible to create ethnic nations in which some group does not end up becoming involuntarily ruled by another. For example, the 30 percent of Bosnia's population that is Serbian and the 17 percent that is Croatian do not want to live under Bosnian rule. Thus, they have sought to force out Bosnians and link themselves to Serbia or Croatia. But to Bosnians, the consequence of that would be to place large parts of Bosnia under Serbian or Croatian rule, an option that is equally unacceptable to them. Absent a history of conquest, colonialism, and massacre, these ethnic distinctions might not matter so much. But within such a history, each group sees these distinctions as matters of national and ethnic survival.

IRMA: THE STORY OF ONE BOSNIAN CHILD

While a textbook can help us to understand the causes of ethnic conflict in places like former Yugoslavia, no textbook analysis can begin to capture the horrors of a practice such as ethnic cleansing. These horrors have included such behaviors as repeatedly attacking neighborhoods in cities, then blockading those cities so that medical supplies can't be delivered. They have included placing people in concentration camps because of their ethnicity, and torturing some of them until they die. They have included organized and systematic raping of thousands of women who have been taken prisoner. They have even included people climbing into hills above their own neighborhoods and then shelling and rocketing those neighborhoods because the people remaining are the "wrong" religious or ethnic group. They have included thousands of deaths of civilian men, women, and children—some who were hit by shells as they went to cemeteries to bury friends and relatives killed in the war; others as they lined up to get the water they could no longer get from the faucets in their homes. By midsummer 1993, an average of three children were being killed in Bosnia every day.

Many television images and many heart-wrenching news reports were broadcast in the summer of 1993, but the shooting and killing and raping and burning went on. Perhaps no news story captured the horror and insanity of ethnic cleansing more poignantly than that of Irma, a young girl who was wounded in the same attack that killed her mother. She suffered an injury that could have been effectively treated in an almost routine manner anywhere but Bosnia. But there it threatened to kill her, as told in this news story:

Tiny Bosnian Life Flickers Under Weight of Bureaucracy

Irma's shoulder is the color of milk. It is sharp because she is skinny, and it looks a little awkward poking out from the sheets of her hospital bed. Suffering from shrapnel wounds in her back, stomach and spinal cord, her right arm thrashes. Her head is tilted against the back of her neck, locked in a contorting cramp.

"My head hurts," she gurgles between moans that sound bizarre coming from the mouth of a 5-year-old girl.

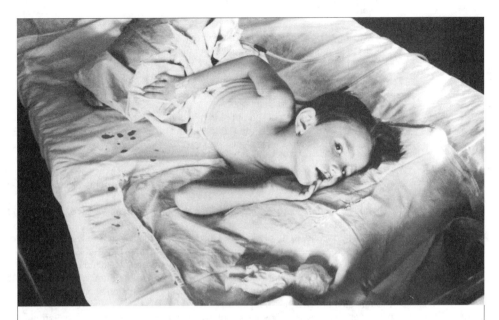

Irma Hadzimuratovic, 5, lying in her dirty hospital bed in Sarajevo. Doctors said she would die unless she received medical attention outside of Sarajevo. *AP/Wide World Photos/ Morten Hvaal*

Her doctor is fighting U.N. rules on emergency airlifts out of Sarajevo. "She is a very simple case," said her surgeon, Edo Jaganjac. "She will simply die here and survive [abroad]."

A senior U.N. official in Sarajevo said, "Everybody is passing the buck. No one wants to make a decision to save a life."

Irma was severely wounded July 30 by a Serbian mortar bomb that killed her 30-year-old mother, Elvira Hadzimuratovic. She has abdominal, spinal and head injuries that her doctor said may have caused either meningitis or brain damage.

The child was clinically dead for one minute after surgery last week and now lies on a soiled bed in Sarajevo's state hospital, her head thrown back at an ugly angle, mumbling pathetically and occasionally whimpering in pain.

A small plastic doll sits on her bed.

Irma's father, Ramis Hadzimuratovic, 36, said, "She was a very lively girl. She wanted to go out even if it was war."

Jaganjac said Irma's condition deteriorated Sunday when she began bleeding internally from a stress ulcer.

In any other country in Europe, her medical condition would not be grave. But in Sarajevo, under siege for months by Serb forces, Irma has little chance of surviving.

The hospital's only X-ray machine runs off a generator and doesn't produce clear pictures. Jaganjac says he believes there might be hemorrhaging or an infection in her brain, but he cannot prove it without better diagnostic equipment. Laboratory machines needed to test and monitor mineral imbalances in her blood and bring her damaged digestive system back to normal do not function because Serbian forces have cut power to the city.

A solution to the problem would be immediate medical evacuation by the office of the U.N. High Commissioner for Refugees, but that appears unlikely.

One U.N. official who is needed to make such a decision is on vacation; another, Donald Acheson, formerly Britain's chief medical officer, left Sarajevo on Sunday, refusing to comment on the case. A third is in Zagreb, Croatia, and couldn't be reached, while a fourth is based in Cambodia.

Under procedures established in March, a commission of four international doctors—from the U.N. refugees office, the World Health Organization, the U.N. Children's Fund, and the U.N. Protection Force—has the task of deciding which patients should be evacuated for treatment by specialists abroad.

But the doctors meet only every four to six weeks, and officials say that because of the bureaucracy, none of the 89 patients the commission has sent abroad so far has been an emergency case.

In addition to these requirements, besieging Serbian forces demand to see the names of civilians leaving on U.N. planes three days before their departure.

Manuel Fontaine, head of the U.N. Children's Fund office in Sarajevo, said he would do his best to "pull strings" to get Irma out if the committee decided to act.

But he said U.N. officials were worried that an emergency airlift procedure could lead doctors in the city to prepare wounded for evacuation rather than try to save lives.

Foreign hospitals also had to be ready to accept patients on short notice, a willingness that so far had been lacking.

U.N. officials say U.S. hospitals require up to three weeks' notice and German hospitals want money up front for treatment.

"They can find a million reasons not to take her out," Jaganjac said of the U.N. forces. "They say they are here to take care of general things and not personal problems. But what kind of general things have they taken care of?

"It's 16 months of war, and what have they really done? Why don't they just go home if they don't want to do anything? Thank you very much; we can die here by ourselves."

In a country where, as one news correspondent put it, "Attention from the media can make the difference whether a child lives or dies," Irma was, in one regard, one of the lucky ones. After news reports like this one generated international outrage, Great Britain's Royal Air Force provided an airplane to evacuate Irma, and she got the treatment she needed in a London hospital. News stories did not report, and perhaps nobody knows, how many other children died in Bosnia the day that Irma was flown out. However, Irma's case drew so much attention to the plight of injured persons unable to get adequate treatment in Bosnia that, in the following weeks, scores of others were flown out of Bosnia into European countries to receive medical treatment.

Source: *St. Louis Post-Dispatch*, August 9, 1993, pp. 1, 5.

The Middle East

Another potentially explosive area of intergroup relations in the modern world has been the Middle East. Conflict here is not entirely an issue of ethnic or racial relations, or even of majority–minority relations, because the conflict is in large part an international one between Israel and several of its Arab neighbors. It is, however, worth considering in a book on majority–minority relations for several reasons. First, the conflict is both internal and international—one fundamental question in the whole conflict is the status of Palestinian Arabs within the boundary of Israel, some of whom are even Israeli citizens. Second, the conflict is partly ethnic, in the sense that being Jewish or Arab will almost certainly determine where one stands in the conflict. Third, even the international aspect of the conflict centers around jurisdiction over one land area to which both Jews and Palestinian Arabs feel they have a historical and legitimate claim and which each group regards fervently as its true homeland.

The origins of this conflict are more complex than some of the others we have examined. First, both the dominant group (Jews) and the subordinate group (Arabs) in today's Israel had some historical claim to the land prior to the establishment of the Israeli state in 1948. Israel, or Palestine, was the historic home of the Jewish people and has been the focal point of their religion throughout history. Nonetheless, until modern times, no significant Jewish presence was there after the conquest of Jerusalem in A.D. 70 (Douglas-Home, 1968, p. 14). During this long period, the only Jewish population was a handful of students and scholars of the Holy Writings (Dodd and Sales, 1970).

The Arab dominance of the region can be traced at least to the establishment of the Turkish and Islamic Ottoman Empire's rule over the region in the sixteenth century, though some trace it further back to the spread of Islamic and Arabic culture to the region in the seventh and eighth centuries (Epp, 1970). In any case, the area had unquestionably been predominantly Arab for hundreds of years before the Zionist movement of the twentieth century, even though the area was often governed from outside and did not exist as a distinct Arab or Palestinian state. It should also be noted that the area has major religious significance for both Christians and Muslims as well as Jews. In any case, it is certainly fair to say that, at the time Israeli control of the area was established, both the Jewish and Arab populations viewed the area as their homeland and felt they had a legitimate claim to it. The same cannot be said for majority and minority groups in America or in the African colonies.

The Israeli situation also differs from the others we have studied in that the group that established dominance—the Jewish population—was in large part a displaced population that had experienced centuries of worldwide persecution. It had just suffered perhaps the worst incident of genocide in the history of the world—the murder of six million Jews in the Holocaust. Thus, the impetus for the Jewish settlement came not from the expansionist desires of a colonial power but in large part from the desire of a persecuted people for a safe homeland.

In these regards, then, the origin of the Israeli state and the present-day Arab–Jewish conflict differ from the patterns of colonialism and conquest we have seen in other societies. There are also important similarities, however. When Zionism first became a serious movement in the late nineteenth century, the population of what is now Israel was overwhelmingly Arab and had been for hundreds of years. Furthermore, the establishment of the Jewish state of Israel was imposed against the will of that indigenous Arab population. It was accomplished through the actions of the United Nations, European powers (notably Britain and France), and ultimately, the armed struggle of the Jewish immigrants against the indigenous Arab population. In the end, much of that population fled, and those who stayed behind have occupied a subordinate role in Israeli society (though not to nearly the extent as blacks in South Africa, for example). Thus, while there are important differences between the Israeli case and the pattern of colonialism we have examined in other places, there are some important similarities as well. Most important, the problem did arise as a result of an indigenous population coming under the domination of a new population through the use of force.

In 1993, an important step toward resoution of the bitter dispute in the Middle East was reached when, for the first time, Israel and the Palestine Liberation Organization (PLO) recognized one another diplomatically and in effect accepted that each had some historic claim to land in the Middle East. The Palestinians recognized Israel's right to statehood, and the Israelis, in addition to recognizing the PLO as the legitimate representative of the Palestinian people, also agreed to limited Palestinian self-rule in two territories that had long been occupied and controlled by Israel—the Gaza Strip and the portion of the West Bank in and around the city of Jericho. Moreover, the Israelis also agreed to enter negotiations for more extensive Palestinian self-rule throughout the occupied territories. This could occur in the form of a Palestinian state on the West Bank and Gaza Strip or a confederation of Palestinian territory with the neighboring state of Jordan. While the 1993 agreement was by no means certain to bring peace—in fact, it was promptly rejected by the more extreme elements on both sides—it was historic in the sense that it was the first time that Palestinians and Jews mutually acknowledged and accepted, however grudgingly, each other's aspirations for a homeland. For this reason, it laid a groundwork that could become the basis for a more extensive agreement and a more lasting peace.

Israeli Prime Minister Yitzhak Rabin and PLO Chairman Yasir Afafat shake hands at the White House after the PLO and the Israeli government reached an agreement to recognize one another. *Bettmann/Reuters*

Some Comparisons and Contrasts

Sociologist Stanley Lieberson (1961) has examined majority–minority relations both historically within certain societies and comparatively between a number of societies. Lieberson concluded that when an *indigenous group*—one that is established in or native to an area—is made subordinate to another group entering from the outside, the result is usually conflict and ethnic inequality. Assimilation and intergroup cooperation are very difficult in this situation. Of course, such situations usually originate with the conquest or colonization of the indigenous population. In the reverse situation, in which the indigenous group is dominant over the immigrant group, the situation is usually different. Unless the immigrant group was forced to immigrate, as in the case of slaves, a trend toward assimilation will usually emerge, with only mild and occasional ethnic conflict.

The societies we have examined in this section all fit Lieberson's first type, in which the indigenous group was made subordinate to an immigrant or outside group. With the possible exception of Israel, they all have a history of colonialism. And, as we know, they are all among the world's most volatile areas of intergroup conflict. A history of colonialism, conquest, or domination of an indigenous population by an immigrant population appears to be one of the factors most closely associated with cases of ethnic conflict and inequality in today's world. Not every country with such a history has a serious majority–minority problem, and not every country with such a problem has that type of history. The U.S. state of Hawaii and the countries of Mexico and Brazil, for example, all have a history of conquest of the native population by colonial powers but are all frequently cited as cases of better-than-average intergroup relations. On the other hand, one of the most brutal examples of ethnic oppression in history, Hitler's genocidal campaign against Jews, occurred in a situation with no colonial history. It is thus important to keep in mind that *no one factor* taken alone can explain the pattern of intergroup relations in any society. Nonetheless, if we examine the broad range of societies in the world, it does seem clear that, *all else being equal,* the presence of a colonial history does seem to be associated with greater-than-average amounts of intergroup inequality and intergroup conflict. (For further discussion of this issue, see Mason, 1971, pp. 81–86; Kinloch, 1974, 1979, pp. 175–88.)

Great Britain: Another Effect of Colonialism

The recent history of Great Britain illustrates another way that colonialism can lead to intergroup conflict and inequality. In Great Britain, about 4 percent of the population is composed of immigrants (or their children) from former British colonies, mainly in Asia, Africa, and the Caribbean (Richmond, 1986). These immigrants—nearly all people of color—have experienced some discrimination and considerable social inequality. In such key areas as housing, education, and employment, they experience disadvantages much like those of blacks and Hispanics in the United States. As in the United States, this racial inequality has at times resulted in violence. During the 1980s, a series of violent uprisings spread through major British cities, including Liverpool, Birmingham, Bristol, and London, which experienced several major outbreaks. Although the violence in the 1980s was unprecedented in extent, violent racial or ethnic conflict in Britain can be traced at least to the turn of the century.

Britain's immigrant groups, then, have not—at least yet—shared the experience of assimilation and rising status that is typical of immigrant groups most places. An important reason appears to be that, like Puerto Ricans in the United States, they do not fit the usual historical experience of immigrant groups. Rather, they were originally colonized elsewhere and eventually took advantage of their status as commonwealth citizens to immigrate to Great Britain. Once there, however, they were treated by many British as colonized peoples, and they found escaping the disadvantage associated with that status difficult. In this way, too, their experience is much like that of Puerto Ricans in the United States. (For a general discussion and review of several major works concerning contemporary intergroup relations in Great Britain, see Richmond, 1986.)

SOCIETIES WITH PEACEFUL INTERGROUP RELATIONS

The importance of history to contemporary intergroup relations can also be illustrated by looking at examples at the opposite end of the scale from those we have examined. One such example, cited by Hunt and Walker (1974, pp. 41–45) is Switzerland. That country has a number of different nationalities and religions, many of whom do not even speak the same language. Despite this diversity, relations between groups are for the most part harmonious. According to Hunt and Walker, an important reason is that each of the various and ethnically diverse parts of the country came into confederation voluntarily, largely to seek protection. One rare exception to this is the Jura region, which is the one part of Switzerland where intergroup relations are not harmonious. This area was taken from France and made a part of Switzerland in 1815, against the will of its residents. As recently as the 1960s and 1970s, a social movement to separate the area from Swiss rule sparked violence.

Another relevant example is Hawaii. Although Hawaii did experience external colonization, its colonization was quite different from that of South Africa, Ireland, or the mainland United States. Berry and Tischler (1978, pp. 158–63) discuss Hawaii as an example of a society with relatively harmonious intergroup relations. Hawaii has greater ethnic diversity than any other state, yet it sets an admirable example of racial and ethnic harmony for the rest of the country. This is not to say that there is *no* racial problem—native Hawaiians do occupy a position subordinate to that of several newcomer groups—but racial harmony and tolerance do seem more the rule than is the case in much of the rest of the United States. Certainly, the norms against prejudice and discrimination are much stronger there than on the mainland, and contact among various racial groups is more commonplace and more harmonious than on the mainland. According to Berry and Tischler, much of the reason for this can be found in the islands' history. The local population, although subject to colonial influences, was never conquered and subordinated in a manner similar to, for example, the native populations of the mainland United States or South Africa. While there was considerable outside interest in Hawaii from 1778 on, the native population was well organized and had effective leaders who represented their interests well to the outsiders. The whites who came to Hawaii, in turn, respected and cooperated with the leadership. Indeed, friendship and marriage between the two groups was common and socially supported. This was in part because the early contact was with whites interested in trade rather than conquest. A variety of groups such as Chinese, Japanese, and Filipinos arrived later to meet the islands' labor needs, but no outside group ever took control and dominated the indigenous population. Consistent with Lieberson's theory, Berry and Tischler argue that this history is an important factor in Hawaii's harmonious racial and ethnic relations.

The first general pattern, then, that we see from international examination of intergroup relations is that colonization or conquest of an indigenous population tends to leave a legacy of majority–minority inequality and conflict that can persist for years, even centuries. In countries where groups have come together peaceably, intergroup relations tend to be more harmonious. Of course, this is not the only factor influencing intergroup relations, and other factors can and often do create exceptions. Still, the general rule holds more often than not.

CROSS-CULTURAL EVIDENCE ON THE EFFECTS OF URBANIZATION AND MODERNIZATION

In our study of the history of majority–minority relations in the United States, we also examined the closely related trends of urbanization, industrialization, and modernization. In American history, these trends have been associated with a decrease in the rigidity in race relations. As we saw in detail in Chapters 6 and 7, this has been especially evident since World War II, though the shift from an agricultural society to an industrial one began to have important effects much earlier than that. In this section, we wish to explore the degree to which parallel changes have been taking place throughout the world. We cannot, of course, explore the history of every country in even the limited detail we have given to the United States. Nonetheless, some important worldwide trends have taken place that seem related to one another, and that may provide some answers to the question of whether and how modernization and urbanization affect intergroup relations.

Industrialized Countries

The first of these general kinds of changes involves those more developed countries of the world that have subordinate ethnic or racial minorities. In such countries, two changes have tended to occur. First, the minority groups have increasingly turned to protest and to social and political action to improve their position. We have already discussed this trend in some detail for the United States. It is equally evident in a number of other developed countries. In Canada, the French-speaking minority, about 30 percent of the population, became highly vocal in the 1960s and 1970s. Among the results were legislation making French the only official language in Quebec Province, where most of the French-speaking population lives, and the 1976 election victory of the Quebec separatist *Parti Quebecois*. Although Quebec voters have since voted against separation from the Canadian confederation and the *Parti Quebecois* was out of power from 1985 to 1994, its victories in 1976 and 1994, the passage of the language legislation, and continued pressure by Quebec for recognition in Canada's constitution as a "distinct society" all clearly indicate heightened assertiveness by Canada's French-speaking minority. We have also discussed the violence in Northern Ireland in the 1960s, 1970s, and 1980s. In Quebec, the causes underlying the recent protest and political change have existed for years, but the protest has surfaced only in the last thirty years. Although Northern Ireland has a long history of conflict, that conflict has substantially escalated since 1968. Other examples of minority groups that have become increasingly vocal in recent years include blacks and Asians in Great Britain; the Flemish in Belgium (who have become a numerical majority but have historically been a subordinate group); the South Moluccans, who have turned to terrorism in Holland; and the Jurans in Switzerland. In Great Britain, minority group dissatisfaction was an important contributing factor to widespread urban violence in several years during the 1980s.

The other, related trend in the more developed countries has been a reduction in overt discrimination and prejudice and a move toward legal protection of the rights of minorities. The United States, Great Britain, Canada, and other Western countries have passed legislation banning racial and ethnic discrimination. In these countries, the open expression of racial prejudice is generally frowned on, though most of them continue to have significant racial and ethnic inequality. In both Europe and North America, however, there has been increased opposition to immigration in recent years, as the number of immigrants identifiable by skin color has increased. In some countries, this opposition has become quite violent, and in many, a resurgence in hate-group activity has taken place. The worst violence has been in Germany, where right-wing, neo-Nazi mobs in 1992 and 1993 attacked Turks and other immigrants and refugees, resulting in a number of deaths, many injuries, and considerable homelessness as a result of arson attacks against immigrant housing. In a number of other countries, including the United States, Canada, and Great Britain, opposition to immigration has grown, though the type and level of violence found in Germany has not developed. Nonetheless, the intensity of opposition to immigration can be seen in proposals made in 1993 by the governor of California, who argued for harsh crackdowns on illegal immigration, including changes in the law to revoke automatic citizenship for children born in the United States if their parents are present illegally and to deny such children the educational and nutritional benefits they are entitled to under current law. And hate-group activity has increased not only in Germany but to a lesser but significant extent in France, Great Britain, the United States, and elsewhere.

The severity of these problems is greater in Germany than elsewhere, reflecting a combination of circumstances. First, Germany admits more immigrants than most Western countries, a number that was greatly increased by floods of refugees from Romania, former Yugoslavia, and elsewhere in the early 1990s. (Until 1993, Germany was extremely open in granting asylum to refugees, a policy designed to repay Germany's debt to other countries that accepted refugees from Germany during the Nazi era. However, opposition to immigration in recent years has led to some tightening of this policy.) Second, and at the same time, Germany experienced serious economic difficulties arising from attempts to absorb the unproductive East German economy and to some extent from worldwide recession in the early 1990s. Consequently, hopes on the part of East Germans that union with the West would bring rapid economic improvement were unfulfilled. When these hopes were unfulfilled, many began to look for scapegoats. Third, unlike other Western countries such as France, Canada, Great Britain, and the United States, Germany has never accepted or acknowledged the concept of a multicultural society. In the words of the German sociologist Erwin Scheuch (quoted in Nagorski, 1993), "Britain and France are former empires, but Germans are entirely European. Anything outside of Europe for them is close to Mars." In such demographic, economic, and cultural circumstances, it was easy to view immigrants as a threat and to make them into scapegoats for Germany's economic hardship. In a later part of this chapter, we shall examine how changes in the amount of immigration in a country may affect that country's intergroup relations.

Despite conflicts over immigration, discrimination today is illegal in most Western nations, and open discrimination and prejudice are relatively rare compared with the past. It is sometimes argued that discrimination is economically irrational in such societies because it interferes with hiring the most productive workers. Furthermore, as Kinloch (1979) points out, social differentiation in the more developed nations has become more complex, and based on a wide range of factors including class, sex, and lifestyle, with some decline in the importance of race and ethnicity.

Increasing Fluidity? Or Rigidity with Conflict?

In spite of these general patterns, it would be an overstatement to say that modernization always leads to increasingly fluid intergroup relations. The examples of South Africa and Northern Ireland, and to some extent Germany, show that rigid intergroup inequality and intergroup conflict can continue and even worsen in societies that have experienced considerable modernization and urbanization. A widely cited essay by Blumer (1965) suggests some of the reasons why. Blumer argues that industrialization is no guarantee of improved race relations because certain social forces tend to maintain inequality, even if discrimination is economically irrational in a modernizing society. First, important elements of the traditional structure remain, including a desire for discrimination on the part of many majority group members, some of whom benefit directly from discrimination. An example of this would be the white industrial laborers in the early-twentieth-century United States, who saw discrimination as a way of protecting themselves from competition from minority workers (for further discussion, see Chapter 6). Thus, in societies with a history of rigid discrimination, Blumer argues that dominant group members exert strong pressure for discrimination as a way of shielding themselves from potential competition from minority groups. As a result, it is often more economically rational for industrialists to continue discriminating than to put up with the conflict and protest they would get from elements of the majority group if they stopped discriminating. Thus, Blumer makes the point that it is by no means clear that discrimination is always economically irrational in industrial societies.

This suggests that there are two directions a country's intergroup relations can take as it modernizes. One possibility is that they may become increasingly fluid, though sometimes after a period of rigid competitive relations, as in the United States. The following conditions make such a pattern more likely:

1. Minority groups are in a position to generate effective protest. Among other factors, such protest is more likely to be a result of urbanization in countries allowing relatively great freedom of expression.
2. There is external pressure for more-equal race relations. Blumer cites the pressures of northern liberals and the federal government on the South as examples of this. The desire of the United States, Britain, and other Western countries for good relations with African countries is another example, since this exerted pressure on them to "get their own house in order" and improve race relations on the home front.
3. The economy and/or social system is such that gains by minority group members are not viewed as a threat by majority group members. W. J. Wilson (1978) argues that this was the case in the United States during the late 1950s and much of the

1960s because it was a period of economic growth with room for everyone to bene-fit. Thus, it was largely during this period that the United States moved from rigid to fluid competitive race relations. Bastide (1965, pp. 14–18) argues that one reason for Brazil's relatively harmonious intergroup relations is that until very recently, blacks were not seen as competitors by most whites. They largely did different kinds of work. Whites, for example, had little desire to work in crafts or manual labor, so there was little objection to the movement of blacks into such jobs (Mason, 1971, p. 314). Even when blacks *did* compete with whites, they were not seen as a real threat because whites could shield themselves from blacks in their family settings even if not in their work settings, and the family, not the economy, has historically been the central institution in Brazil's social system. Recently, as blacks and whites have begun to compete more in the work setting and as the family has declined somewhat in im-portance, there have been more noticeable instances of racial conflict.

4. The country does not have a history of highly rigid racial inequality. Blumer (1965, p. 23) suggests that ethnic distinctions in the United States and Canada have blurred more than racial ones in part because they did not have the same degree of rigidity to begin with. He cites the mingling of racial groups in Southeast Asia as another ex-ample of this.

The other possibility that can result from modernization, urbanization, and industrialization is continued rigid intergroup inequality but with rising levels of conflict, protest, and, often, violence. South Africa until very recently is probably the best example of this, though Northern Ireland is another example, and for a time, this was the pattern in the southern United States. Recently, elements of this pattern have developed in Germany also. The following conditions make this pattern most likely:

1. The dominant group has great power relative to the subordinate group(s).
2. The dominant group sees the subordinate group as a strong threat.
3. There is no effective source of external pressure for more fluid intergroup relations.
4. The country has a history of very rigid racial distinctions.
5. The dominant group is small in numbers relative to the subordinate group.

Not surprisingly, *all* these conditions have very clearly been present in South Africa. Historically, the power has always been on the side of whites, first through the possession of firearms and later through control of the government and the military. Blacks in South Africa had essentially no civil or political rights until the early 1990s. They did not enjoy rights to freedom of assembly, free speech, and free press, and, until the elections in 1994, they were never allowed to vote. Until 1984, when col-oreds and Asians were granted separate parliaments, coloreds and Asians also had no political rights. In fact, nobody of any race enjoyed truly free speech until around 1990. During much of the 1980s, government sanctions were often applied even to whites who opposed apartheid. It was only after the release of political prisoners in-cluding African National Congress leader Nelson Mandela in 1990 that South Africa began to move in the direction of allowing free expression and negotiating to bring about majority rule.

In spite of the harsh repression of dissent in South Africa until very recently, violent outbursts of protest did occur regularly from the 1960s on. Outnumbered four to one, whites came to see these protests as a very serious threat to their monopoly on power, and they repressed them severely for many years. Dominant whites have in fact felt threatened for a long time in South Africa. When the British ruled South Africa, their attempts at liberalization were seen by the majority Afrikaners (South African whites of Dutch ancestry) as a threat to the security of white rule. For many years under apartheid, whites tenaciously fought to protect apartheid because they saw its exclusion of blacks from the political process as the only way they could maintain power and status in a society in which they were outnumbered by such a great margin. As the forces of urbanization and modernization fed growing protests by black South Africans and as whites struggled to repress these protests and hang on to their advantaged status, the level of violence escalated. Even in 1993 and early 1994, as the government of President Frederick Willem de Klerk negotiated to bring about majority rule, a great many South African whites intensely opposed such moves. In 1993, a group of armed whites opposed to the negotiations broke into buildings and, for a time, held government officials hostage.

A final factor in this example is the absence, until quite recently, of any effective outside pressure on South Africa to change. In the southern United States, pressure from the North was an important cause of liberalization during the 1960s. In what was then known as Rhodesia (now Zimbabwe), pressure from Britain and the United States (along with an escalating civil war on the home front) helped to force the white-minority government there to give up power in 1978. Until the mid 1980s, however, no comparable pressure was placed on South Africa. Though opposed to its minority rule, its African neighbors were not militarily strong enough to interfere, though some supported the idea of economic sanctions by Western nations (see Mason, 1971, pp. 218–19; Legum, 1975, pp. 103–4).

The first real pressure came in the form of economic sanctions during the 1980s. After many Third World countries and several Scandinavian countries imposed economic sanctions, the U.S. Congress adopted strong sanctions during the 1980s, overriding the veto of President Ronald Reagan. Eventually—and despite some smuggling and breaking of the sanctions by some countries—most of the world joined the sanctions, creating significant economic pressure on South Africa. With the combination of rising internal violence and worsening economic difficulties because of the sanctions, South Africa's white-minority government began to feel increasing pressure for change. When President de Klerk took office in 1989, he began to dismantle apartheid and to support negotiations for majority rule. Major steps in this direction, which eventually led to the dropping of the sanctions by most countries, were the release of Mandela and other political prisoners in 1990 and the passage by white voters of a referendum in 1992 authorizing negotiations for majority rule—though there was, as noted, substantial white opposition to this idea, some of which was violent. Nonetheless, the negotiations were successful and as noted earlier, the elections were held, resulting in the election of President Nelson Mandela.

To summarize, change in South Africa came about when the combination of internal violence and external economic pressure became too strong for the white-minority government to withstand. But until that happened, apartheid was able to survive for more than forty years, despite modernization. The result was a rising tide of violence and internal conflict, as usually happens when societies try to maintain rigid systems of discrimination in the face of modernization. Ultimately, the system of apartheid was abolished, but South Africa will continue to feel its effects, particularly in the form of economic inequality, well into the future.

Third World Countries: Two Major Trends

In the Third World, the change has been more dramatic than in the West, though its direction has been perhaps less uniform. Here, two major trends can be observed. First, there has been a great movement away from colonialism toward national independence. The great colonial empires of the British, French, Portuguese, and Dutch have disappeared, or practically so, many of them since World War II. In some cases, the colonies were relinquished voluntarily, but in others independence came about only after long periods of warfare.

Closely related has been the change in those places still under colonial influence. Most such situations that remain today take one of two forms. Sometimes a small minority of people ethnically associated with the colonial power dominates an indigenous majority population, even though the country is legally no longer a colony. The dominance of the ethnically British whites until the late 1970s in Zimbabwe and of the descendants of Dutch and British colonialists in South Africa provide two examples of this pattern. In other countries, a government may be established and heavily influenced by a colonial power, even though the countries involved may never have been colonies of the power involved. Examples of this in recent history include the Thieu government in Vietnam and the monarchy of the shah in Iran, both of which were established by action of the U.S. CIA and heavily supported and influenced by the U.S. government. In both types of "pseudocolonial" situation, there has since World War II been a marked increase in indigenous-group opposition to the regimes. In all of these examples, there has been a change of government in which colonial governments or ones supported by European powers collapsed in the face of indigenous opposition.

These changes have come about during a period of rapid urbanization and modernization in the world. Certainly, many parts of the world remain rural and traditional, but even these parts are undergoing rapid change. By 1992, the world's population was 42 percent urban, and even the two most rural continents, Africa and Asia, were 30 percent and 31 percent urban, respectively (Population Reference Bureau, 1993). Even the predominantly rural countries today frequently have large cities. Bangladesh, for example, is only 14 percent urban, yet it has a city, Dacca, with a population of a million. China, India, Indonesia, Burma, and Vietnam all have cities among the world's fifty largest; none of these countries are more than one-third urban (Cousins and Nagpaul, 1979, pp. 9–11; Population Reference Bureau, 1993). Most of these cities have grown dramatically since World War II, as even the societies that are still predominantly rural have undergone considerable urbanization. Between 1950 and 1975, for example, the proportion of the world's population living in places with a population of twenty thousand or more increased by nearly 50 percent. In the less developed parts of the world, the increase was greater than that (Frisbie, 1977). Also notable during the period was social and technological modernization. The complexity of social organization increased throughout the world, mass communications such as radio and television spread to even some of the least developed parts of the world, and modern economic systems such as capitalism, and until the late 1980s, socialism continued to spread, supplanting agrarian feudal systems. In most parts of the world, there has been more and more influence from outside the local area, both national and international (Schermerhorn, 1978, p. 165).

Of course, the fact that the changes in majority–minority relations around the world have been happening at the same time as the urbanization and modernization trends does not prove that the changes were *caused* by those trends. Nonetheless, a thoughtful analysis of the issue does suggest some reasons for assuming they probably were, at least in part. One of the most important changes we have noted in majority–minority relations has been the move toward more minority assertiveness in developed countries and toward nationalism and anticolonialism in the Third World. We can identify a number of ways in which urbanization and modernization have brought these changes. Urbanization has brought people together in the cities where they can share ideas and organize protest. Mass communications have helped make people aware of inequalities and have contributed to rising expectations by showing subordinate peoples what life *could* be like. They have provided role models by showing people protests and revolutions over similar issues in other places. Finally, mass communications have facilitated communication and the use of propaganda by protest movements.

Industrialization and technological modernization have had more general effects. They have created demands for labor, thus opening new opportunities to members of the native or colonized population—at times when even the colonial leadership would rather not create such opportunities. The white leadership in South Africa, for example, had to face the question of whether to leave jobs unfilled and suffer lowered productivity or train and hire blacks for what were formerly "white jobs" (Hunt and Walker, 1974, pp. 187–91). Modernization and industrialization also created a need for rising educational levels. This increase in education has had a number of important effects, both on minorities in developed countries and on indigenous populations in less developed, colonial societies. One general effect has been to raise expectations by heightening awareness of inequalities. Another important effect, particularly in the Third World, has been to provide leadership for protest movements. It is not at all unusual for leaders in revolutionary Third World movements to have been educated in developed Western nations. Some of the leaders of the 1979 revolution in Iran, for example, had attended institutions of higher education in the United States.

Another important trend associated with modernization has been greater contact among the nations of the world. This has tended to expose people to a wider range of social, religious, and political ideologies than ever before. This alone is likely to have some unsettling effects. When combined with the presence of big-power competition in the world, the effect is even greater. As the United States, the Soviet Union, and, to a lesser extent, China and some European nations sought political, economic, and military advantage around the world in the 1960s, 1970s, and 1980s, they offered additional sources of aid to combatants in internal conflicts. The Soviet Union frequently aided revolutionary movements aimed at overthrowing governments friendly to the United States, though the ability of the Soviets to cause such events was always greatly exaggerated by political conservatives in the United States.

Finally, in this era of international contact and mass communications, the spread of minority and anticolonial protest since World War II has developed a momentum largely of its own. This is not unlike the "contagion effect" on domestic protest in the United States, which we discussed in the previous chapter. A successful protest or revolution in one place raises hopes for a similar action in another place where similar conditions exist. Thus, the rise of protest against one colonial or racist regime can, particularly if successful, lead to similar protest against others, given the amount of international contact and the extent of mass communications in today's world.

COMBINED EFFECTS OF COLONIALISM AND DEGREE OF MODERNIZATION

Kinloch (1979, chap. 12) has developed a useful model combining the effects of (1) whether a nation has a colonial history and (2) the degree of development or modernization in the country. Kinloch, along with most sociologists of race relations, argues that societies with a history of colonialism or conquest have more majority–minority inequality and more conflict than do countries without such a history. Within this group of societies, race and ethnicity are more important in the less developed, less modernized countries. As such countries modernize, they tend to become differentiated less on the basis of race and ethnicity and more on the basis of a wide range of factors including economics, behavior, sex, and age. Among countries without a colonial history—for example, Switzerland—there tends to be less division, and race and ethnicity are less important. Again, the degree of inequality and the lines along which society is divided vary with degree of development. Among underdeveloped societies with no history of colonialization, there may be very little stratification. There is barely enough to go around, and everyone shares fairly equally. As Kinloch notes, such societies are an extreme rarity in today's world: Only some scattered tribal groups really fit this pattern. More common is the noncolonial developed society, which has less racial or ethnic inequality than in the past but does tend to have inequalities based on class, behavior, sex, age, and so on.

NUMBER OF RACIAL AND ETHNIC GROUPS

Although many social scientists feel that the two most important factors in comparative studies of majority–minority relations are the nature of the original contact—whether or not it involved colonialism or conquest—and the degree of modernization and development of a society, other factors also seem to make important differences. One that many experts have emphasized is the number of racial or ethnic groups. In general, when a society has many groups that are generally recognized as distant, it tends to have less racial and ethnic conflict and less inequality than when it has only two groups (Hunt and Walker, 1974, p. 235). When there are several groups, there is often no *one* group large or powerful enough to dominate the others. Furthermore, any group that discriminates against or shows hostility toward outgroups runs the risk of being treated the same way itself. When there are only two groups, it is much easier for one to discriminate against the other. It is also common for each group to see the other as the enemy and the cause of its troubles in the "us-versus-them" mentality that can easily develop in the two-group situation.

Some of the places already mentioned as examples of harmonious race relations help to illustrate this principle. According to Smith (1942), one reason for Hawaii's harmonious race relations is that it has a large number of racial and ethnic groups rather than just two. As of the 1980 census, no racial group accounted for more than about 35 percent of the population, and the population included large numbers of whites, Japanese Americans, native Hawaiians, Filipino Americans, and Chinese Americans. Also present, in relatively small numbers, were blacks, Korean Americans, and American Indians. The fact that no group is a majority in Hawaii makes the situation there particularly conducive to harmonious racial and ethnic relations. To a lesser degree, the presence of multiple ethnic and linguistic groups in Switzerland probably helps to explain that country's relative racial harmony.

In other examples, complex racial classification systems recognizing a number of distinct classifications have been suggested as causes of relative racial and ethnic harmony in Mexico and in the French Antilles (Hunt and Walker, 1974, pp. 155–56, 235). In Mexico, a multiple-classification system that contained from ten to forty-six categories (Roncal, 1944, p. 533; Hunt and Walker, 1974, p. 139) became so confusing that it was generally disregarded, and the bulk of the population came to be regarded as mestizo (mixed Indian and white), or simply "Mexican." Ultimately, the result was considerable *amalgamation*—biological mixing that eliminated distinct racial categories. In the French Antilles (Guadalupe and Martinique), racial animosities were reduced as a result of a multiple-classification system treating persons of mixed black and white ancestry as a separate group. This practice, which is also common in Latin America, helps "to blur racial distinctions rather than to sharpen them" (Hunt and Walker, 1974, p. 214). In general, if a society has multiple racial and ethnic groups or multiple racial and ethnic classifications, it will—all else being equal—tend to have more harmonious intergroup relations.

Often, it is not so much the number of groups present as it is the number of classifications that is important. In the United States, persons of European, African, and North American ancestry are socially classified in three major groupings: whites, blacks, and American Indians. In Mexico, however, the same population would be divided into *at least* six groups: whites (*Hispanos*), blacks (*Negros*), Indians (*Indios*), *mestizos* (Indian and white), *lobos* (Indian and black), and *mulattos* (white and black). In fact, the Mexican classification system has tended to be more complex than that, with mixtures such as Indian–mulatto recognized as separate groups and with region—and birthplace—also related to classification. The importance of classification is further illustrated in the South African system. Each of the four official groups—whites, blacks, coloreds, and Asians—has within it important ethnic divisions. Nonetheless, the classification system has come to blur these ethnic distinctions and heighten the racial ones: The European population has come to think of itself as white rather than as British or Afrikans, and the native population has moved away from ethnic or tribal identity toward black nationalism. Significantly, however, as South Africa's strict racial-classification system began to break down in the early 1990s and the country moved toward majority rule, its old ethnic and tribal conflicts intensified. In 1992 and 1993, intense conflict erupted in South Africa between backers of Nelson Mandela and the African National Congress (ANC), and backers of Chief Mangosutthu Buthelezi and the Inkatha Freedom Party. In much of the country, this conflict was largely ethnic. In the townships around Johannesburg, for example, most Inkatha backers were Zulu, and Buthelezi often appealed to Zulu nationalism. On the other hand, many ANC backers were Xhohas, the second-largest ethnic group (Ottaway, 1992). In fact, through much of the early 1990s in South Africa, factional violence among blacks took more lives than violence between blacks and whites—a marked change from earlier decades. In 1994, however, a power-sharing agreement was reached, and Nelson Mandela's cabinet included members of both Inkatha and the predominantly white National Party.

The propensity for conflict may be especially great where the majority of the population falls into one of two classifications. Although both South Africa and the United States have multiple classifications, over 85 percent of South Africa's population is either black or white, and over 85 percent of the U.S. population is either white Anglo or black. Canada has many racial and ethnic groups, but in Quebec province, the great majority is either English or French. Finally, in Northern Ireland, nearly everyone identifies him- or herself as either Catholic or Protestant. Undoubtedly, this factor is less important than others, such as the balance of power and a history of colonialism, but the division of most of the population into two major groups does appear to heighten the potential for polarization, whereas a multitude of classifications—with no one or two groups forming a large majority—frequently seems to lead to a blurring and softening of intergroup divisions.

CULTURAL AND DEMOGRAPHIC CHARACTERISTICS OF MAJORITY AND MINORITY GROUPS: THE EXAMPLES OF BRAZIL AND MEXICO

The cultural and demographic characteristics of the groups involved in any situation of intergroup relations also help to determine the kinds of relations that develop between groups. We shall illustrate this general principle with two examples from Latin America: Brazil and Mexico.

Brazil has often been cited as an example of successful assimilation between diverse groups. Extensive assimilation, including widespread intermarriage, took place between the white population and the native Indian population and between blacks and whites, even though blacks were originally brought to Brazil as slaves. This is not to deny that there is racial stratification in Brazil: In general, darker skin color is associated with lower status. Brazil did have a long period of slavery, and both blacks and Indians were forced to live under a paternalistic system of race relations (Van den Berghe, 1978, pp. 63–65). The blacks were slaves on the *fazendas,* or feudal plantations, as were some Indians. Most of the Indians, however, experienced paternalism in the *aldeas,* or Jesuit mission villages. Although this system had more benevolent objectives than the slave plantations, it too was a despotic system that forcibly took children from their parents and resocialized Indians to what the Jesuits viewed as the ideal culture. Nonetheless, there is no U.S.-style segregation and little overt discrimination. Indeed, to Brazilians, the major "problem" in intergroup relations is concern about groups unwilling to assimilate (Berry and Tischler, 1978, pp. 156–58).

Several characteristics of the ethnic groups involved (the majority group in particular) help to account for Brazil's pattern of assimilation. One is the very uneven sex ratio among the Portuguese who settled Brazil: They were overwhelmingly male. This encouraged considerable intermarriage between the male settlers and Indian women. Later, when more women did arrive, the pattern of intermarriage had become well established. In addition, this mixing of groups led to a considerable blurring of racial distinctions. In contrast to the Brazilian pattern is that of the United States, in which English settlers much more frequently came over as families. As a result, intermarriage has been much less common in the United States.

Another factor noted by Pierson (1942) that supports a tendency toward assimilation in Brazil is the history of Moorish influence in Portugal. According to Pierson, this led to a tolerance of darker-skinned people, perhaps even a tendency to view dark skin as a source of prestige. In Brazil, for example, brown skin and straight hair are regarded as the standard of beauty, again reflecting the mixed composition of the population. To the degree that this was true, it certainly would have led the Portuguese colonists in Brazil to be more supportive of intermarriage and assimilation. Intermixing was also supported by the common Portuguese custom of concubinage, which often brought regular and somewhat institutionalized relationships between white males and racially mixed females.

A final important factor, noted by Kinloch (1974), was the Catholic religion of the Portuguese colonists. As in other parts of Latin America, the Catholic religion of the Portuguese led them to seek to assimilate the Indians and black slaves rather than to isolate and subordinate them. The Catholic religion emphasized human equality and the winning of souls. Consequently, an effort was made to convert the Indians and blacks and integrate them into the Catholic culture and society of the Portuguese colonists. Protestant religions, some of which include notions of a select people, often tended to view people as either having received the word of God or not having received it, with the prescription to avoid those who are seen as not having received it. This has often been suggested as a reason for the lack of acceptance of racial minorities and the much greater segregation in the United States as compared with countries such as Brazil.

These cultural characteristics have helped lead to a milder form of intergroup inequality and more harmonious intergroup relations than are found in many other countries with a history of colonialism. As we have suggested, they made possible a greater degree of cultural assimilation and more amalgamation than is typically found elsewhere. Such cultural assimilation and interbreeding with whites (called *blanchiment,* meaning "bleaching" or "whitening") became a potential route of upward mobility for blacks and mulattos (Bastide, 1965, pp. 15–17).

Assimilation has been a limited source of mobility, to be sure, and one that requires a loss of one's racial identity. Nonetheless, it has been sufficient to prevent widespread protest on the part of blacks and to preserve the widespread image of Brazil as a racial paradise. In reality, it is not a racial paradise, but racial inequality there *is* less rigid than in other countries with a colonial history, and there is notably less racial conflict (though both are probably on the increase as the country moves toward a competitive, industrial system).

Another country that is frequently cited as an example of successful assimilation is Mexico. Some of the reasons are the same as in Brazil: The colonizers (Spanish) were mostly Catholic, so they believed that Indians had souls and that, accordingly, there was an obligation to convert them. They were also mostly male, which encouraged racial mixing. There were, however, also, important characteristics of the indigenous or subordinate group that contributed to the pattern of assimilation. In Mexico, the Aztec Indians had a highly developed and in many regards modern culture before the Spanish *conquistadores* arrived. Their chief city, Tenochtitlan (now Mexico City), had a population of over three hundred thousand and must be regarded as one of the great cities of the world at that time. Although the Indian society was quickly crushed by Spanish military force, the influence of the highly developed Indian culture lived on. Mexico's unique mixture of Spanish and Indian culture became a national symbol, the more so with time as intermixing between those of Indian and Spanish ancestry continued. The evolution of a Mexican or mestizo culture that was neither Spanish nor Indian but a mixture of both became a symbol of national unity and helped to contribute further to the disappearance of distinct racial categories in Mexico. Thus, we see from the example of Mexico that cultural- and social-organizational characteristics of both the majority group and the minority group had important effects on the relationship between the two groups. In this case, it led in large degree to an amalgamation of the two groups into one new group that became a symbol of national unity.

Sunbathing in Sao Paolo, Brazil. Assimilation and amalgamation of racial groups has proceeded further in Brazil than in most societies. Nonetheless, there remains substantial class inequality and lighter-skinned people are overrepresented in the upper classes, darker-skinned people in the lower classes. *United Nations/J. Frank*

As a result, it became the rule in Mexico that one's group identity was determined by one's social roles and cultural attributes rather than one's genetic composition or physical appearance. Thus, a mestizo who married into a prominent Spanish family could come to be regarded as a Spaniard. An Indian who moved to the city and adopted the Spanish language, way of dressing, and customs would be regarded as a mestizo or Mexican, whereas one who remained in the rural village and kept the Indian culture would be regarded as a member of the *Indio* group. Today, the great majority of the Mexican population identifies with the mestizo, or simply Mexican, grouping, and it is this group that is regarded as representative of the Mexican culture. Nonetheless, despite a view that in Mexican history the Spanish are seen largely as villains and the Indians as heroes, higher status attaches to Spanish appearance and culture than to Indian (Mason, 1971, p. 249). Furthermore, the 15 percent or so of Mexico's population that retains the *Indio* identity is the least well-off and is looked down on somewhat by the rest of the population. Thus, in Mexico, as in Brazil, movement toward the European group's culture is an important requisite for upward mobility. On the other hand, the group boundaries in both countries have been greatly blurred, and Mexico is one of the closest approximations of the amalgamation model (loss of group distinctions through interbreeding) found anywhere in the world.

OVERLAPPING VERSUS CROSSCUTTING CLEAVAGES

Divisions, or *cleavages*, in society are sometimes described as being either *overlapping* or *crosscutting*. Overlapping cleavages occur when, for example, racial, religious, class, and language divisions all cut the same way. Imagine a fictitious society made up of blacks and whites. Assume that all the blacks are wealthy, Muslim, and speak Swahili and that all the whites are poor, Protestant, and speak German. In a society like this, the potential for conflict would be very high: No matter whether conflict occurred on the basis of race, religion, language, or economics, the division would always be the same. Nobody would be in a position of having mixed loyalties. Such a society would quickly divide into two mutually hostile and distrustful groups. The opposite kind of society is said to have crosscutting cleavages: There is little or no relationship among race, income, religion, language, and so on. In a society like this, knowing that a person was black would tell us nothing about his or her income, language, or religion. Divisions along the lines of religion would be different from divisions along the lines of income, and both would be unrelated to racial divisions. In this kind of society, there would be relatively little conflict because everyone would have mixed loyalties.

Of course, few societies are as closely delineated as those described here. Nonetheless, real-life societies do differ in the *degree* to which they have overlapping or crosscutting cleavages, and there is considerable evidence that crosscutting cleavages do tend to reduce intergroup conflict. This can be illustrated by two examples. We have already discussed the general pattern of ethnic harmony in Switzerland. That country has two religious groups, three nationalities, and four language groups. However, two of the three nationality groups, Germans and French, are religiously divided. Hunt and Walker (1974, p. 42) believe that these crosscutting cleavages are an important reason for Switzerland's relatively harmonious ethnic relations, since those united by religion are often divided by language.

Another society in which crosscutting cleavages have muted ethnic conflict is Canada. The conflict between English- and French-speaking Canadians heated up considerably in the 1960s and 1970s, but before that time it was very difficult for French-speaking Canadians to develop a unified movement. According to Ossenberg (1975), an important reason for this was the existence of class divisions within the French-speaking population. Although the French-speaking population as a whole was of lower socioeconomic status than the English-speaking population, and the latter controlled the wealth, there was also a fairly wide range of socioeconomic status within the French-speaking population. This tended to prevent a unified French position against the dominant English-speaking group and thereby reduced the amount of English–French conflict. Moreover, after the English gained control of Quebec, they exploited these class divisions by protecting the French-Canadian upper class, in what amounted to a tacit deal designed to avoid upper-class support of Quebecois nationalism. For the most part, this worked for a full century, until the worldwide social upheavals of the 1960s helped to create a social climate conducive to the growth of Quebec separatism. Significantly, when the English–French conflict subsided in the mid 1980s, economic issues had again become predominant in Quebec politics (Martin, 1985).

The contrasting case, overlapping cleavages, can be seen in the bloody conflicts in Northern Ireland and Bosnia–Herzegovina. In both of these countries, ethnic background, religion, and to some extent social class overlap in ways that have worked to heighten conflict. In Northern Ireland, nearly all of the Protestants are of British (that is, either English or Scottish) ancestry, and nearly all of the Catholics are of Irish ancestry. Furthermore, among the Protestants, those of English ancestry are mainly Anglican, and those of Scottish ancestry, Presbyterian. Finally, social class also overlaps with ethnicity to a large extent: The wealthy are mainly English and Anglican, while at the other end of the scale, nearly all of the Irish-ancestry Catholics are working class or poor. The Scottish-ancestry Presbyterians fall somewhere in the middle. Thus, whether the battle lines are drawn on the basis of ethnicity or religion, they are virtually the same, and class in many regards again divides the population similarly.

In Bosnia, somewhat similar conditions exist. Ethnicity overlaps strongly with religion: Croats and Slovenes are mainly Catholic, Bosnians are Muslims (in fact, they are often referred to as "Muslims" rather than "Bosnians"), and Serbs are Orthodox. As a practical matter, ethnic and religious identity in Bosnia are virtually indistinguishable. Whether people think in terms of religion or ethnicity, the divisions are identical. Thus, with respect to these two variables, divisions clearly overlap. Social class is not as strongly linked to ethnicity and religion as in Northern Ireland, but given Bosnia's history not only of conquest but also of brutal ethnic massacres as recently as World War II, the overlapping cleavages based on nationality and religion have proved sufficient to cause one of the worst outbreaks of intergroup conflict in recent world history.

TERRITORIAL ETHNIC BASE

Another factor that can influence the intensity of racial or ethnic conflict is whether ethnic minority groups are territorially based. When a subordinate group is concentrated in one part of a country and is a numerical majority in that area, its ability to mount an effective social movement is often strengthened. Its members are concentrated together and are frequently in a position to become dominant in their particular part of the country, even though they are subordinate in the nation as a whole. Accordingly, if ethnic conflicts exist, they may become more intense when the subordinate group is territorially based. Once English–French conflict in Canada came out into the open, the strength of the French-speaking group was enhanced by its concentration in Quebec Province. This enabled the French-speakers to elect leaders supportive of their cause and to change the province's language laws. As frequently happens when minorities are territorially based, a secessionist or separatist movement developed. Other minorities that have used a territorial base to develop powerful social movements include the Basques in northern Spain, the Flemish and Walloons in Belgium, and the Kurdish population in northwestern Iran.

Territorial ethnic bases also have obviously played an important role in the conflict in former Yugoslavia. Each former republic of Yugoslavia—Croatia, Slovenia, Serbia, Bosnia–Herzegovina, Montenegro, Macedonia—represents a territory historically occupied by a particular ethnic group. Undoubtedly, the fact that Yugoslavia's ethnic groups were so territorially distinct is one reason why its ethnic conflicts were able to persist through many decades of centralized Yugoslavian rule and resurface so intensely as soon as the Yugoslav national government lost its power to rule by force. Yugoslavia also illustrates the point that if ethnic groups are sufficiently geographically concentrated, severe conflict can occur even when there are many different ethnic groups, a condition that, as we have seen, usually mutes intergroup conflict.

One of the very few former Yugoslav republics that is *not* overwhelmingly composed of a particular ethnic group is Bosnia. Even today, the Bosnians, or Muslims, who live there are only a bare majority of Bosnia–Herzegovina's population, and in the past, Croats and Serbs together outnumbered them (Banac, 1984; Joffe,

1992). Within Bosnia–Herzegovina, however, there have always been different areas of Serbian, Croatian, and Bosnian settlement. Even though some areas such as the capital city of Sarajevo have been multicultural, each group has had its territorial base within Bosnia. This has fueled the conflict because (1) each group has a base from which it can organize and operate, and (2) those who live in the Serbian and Croatian ethnic territories do not want to live under Bosnian rule. Thus, the territorial base of ethnic groups in former Yugoslavia has added to the already explosive combination of social conditions there to contribute to that area's bloody ethnic conflict.

LANGUAGE

When two ethnic groups speak different languages, the potential for conflict between them increases. Language has been the major bone of contention between French and English Canadians; it has also been a major source of conflict between the Flemish and Walloons in Belgium. In the United States, a growing Hispanic population has increasingly demanded bilingual education; has tended to continue to use Spanish; and has increasingly demanded ballots, social-services materials, public documents, and product labels in Spanish. The intensity of debate on the issue observed by the author in his own race relations classes suggests that, as the Spanish population grows to become our largest minority group over the next twenty to thirty years, the potential for language-based conflict in the United States may greatly increase.

Evidence of this can be seen in the passage in the last fifteen years of official-language legislation in several places in the United States. In 1980, Dade County, Florida, voters reacted to the growing Latino influence in the area by voting to make English the county's only official language. Their objective was to end the county's practice of doing business on a bilingual basis. This legislation remained in effect for more than a decade, until it was repealed when Latinos gained a majority on the county's legislative board. Since 1980, however, similar laws have been established in several states, including California, where voters in 1986 overwhelmingly passed a law to make English the state's only official language.

INTERNATIONAL RELATIONSHIPS

Within any country, race and ethnic relations can be greatly influenced by international relations. In a nation that is in conflict with the country associated with one of its minority groups, members of that group are often in a very unenviable position. One of the clearest examples of this is the mass internment of Japanese Americans—many of whom were U.S. citizens—in detention camps in the United States during World War II. In addition to being imprisoned for up to two years without trial or hearing, many American citizens of Japanese descent lost most of their possessions. Other groups placed at a disadvantage because of international conflicts include Chinese in Vietnam, Arabs in Israel, and Jews in Arab countries. In 1979, a number of Iranians (as well as some Latin Americans mistaken for Iranians) in the United States suffered physical attacks or destruction of their property to avenge the taking of American hostages in Iran, even though some of the Iranians attacked did not even support the Iranian government.

Similar events occurred during the 1991 Persian Gulf War. Nationally, hate crimes against Arab Americans, as recorded by the Arab American Anti-Discrimination Committee, tripled in 1991 as compared with 1990 (*Belleville News–Democrat,* 1992). Incidents of harassment, death threats, and violence against Arab Americans took place in late 1990 (after Iraq's invasion of Kuwait) and in 1991 in Boston, Detroit, San Francisco, Washington, Toledo, the Los Angeles area, and elsewhere (Butterfield, 1990; Shaheen, 1990; Arnold, 1991; Stertz and Miller, 1991). In the Los Angeles area, an increase in attacks on Arab Americans after the 1990 invasion of Kuwait pushed hate crimes to a record level in 1990 (Katz, 1991). These incidents occurred in spite of the fact that nearly every Arab country besides Iraq sided *with* the United States in the Gulf War.

It is important to note that such incidents of violence toward and—sometimes—official harassment of groups associated with "the enemy" are more likely when the targeted group is one against which there is already significant racial or ethnic prejudice, as, for example, was true in the case of Japanese Americans during World War II and Arabs during the Gulf War (Farley, 1994b). This can be illustrated by the fact that there was no imprisonment of German Americans during World War II, even though the United States was also at war against Germany.

Surges of Immigration

Ethnic prejudice and violence against minorities can also be triggered by surges in immigration. In the United States, two major surges of immigration occurred in the twentieth century: one in the first two decades of the century, from around 1900 to about 1920, and another beginning around the mid 1970s and continuing to the present time. Both of these surges were accompanied by substantial opposition to immigration and particularly by opposition to immigration by non-Europeans. As is discussed in greater detail elsewhere in this book, concerns on the West Coast about growing numbers of Chinese and Japanese immigrants in the early twentieth century led to legislation completely banning immigration to the United States by Asians. By 1921, the Ku Klux Klan had nearly one hundred thousand member and had made opposition to immigration a central element of its program. In 1925, forty thousand Klan members marched through Washington, D.C. (Southern Poverty Law Center, 1988). Also around this time, President Herbert Hoover wrote a letter to an Italian American congressman (Fiorello La Guardia) stating that Italians are "predominantly our murderers and bootleggers . . . foreign spawn [who] do not appreciate this country" (Morganthau, 1993). By the mid 1920s, such views had shaped U.S. immigration policy to the point that immigration was almost entirely cut off.

Immigration began to increase again in the 1960s after immigration law was liberalized and rose sharply in the 1970s, owing in part to surges of refugees from places such as Vietnam, Cuba, Cambodia, and Haiti and in part to the burgeoning population in economically impoverished countries in Latin America, Asia, and the Caribbean. From 1971 to 1990, 10.5 million people—an average of about half a million a year—immigrated to the United States legally. If a conservative estimate of 3 million illegal immigrants is added to the total, the annual number of migrants during this period was about the same as in 1900–1920 (Morganthau, 1993). Relative to the size of the U.S. population, however, the present surge is smaller than the earlier one, because the population is much larger today. Nonetheless, immigration since the 1970s has been greater than for many decades, and the annual total has continued to climb, to over 800,000 legal immigrants annually by the early 1990s.

Again, as before, the growth in immigration since the 1970s has been accompanied by growth in opposition to immigration. In the 1970s, robed Ku Klux Klansmen harassed Vietnamese fishermen in Texas, and the growth of the Latino population as a result of immigration in parts of the country such as Florida and California sparked the passage of the official-language legislation discussed earlier. It is also in Florida and California, which together receive nearly half of all immigrants to the United States, where opposition to immigration has become the hottest political issue. In 1993, public-opinion polls clearly indicated rising opposition to immigration not only there but throughout the United States, much of it because most of today's immigrants come not from Europe but from Asia, Latin America, or the Caribbean. A 1993 *Newsweek* poll showed, for example, that while 59 percent of Americans agreed that immigration had been a good thing in the past, 60 percent also agreed that immigration is a bad thing today (Morganthau, 1993). The same poll also showed sizable majorities believing that immigrants take the jobs of American workers and often end up on welfare. Significantly, the poll showed much more opposition to immigration from Haiti, Asian countries, Africa, and Latin America than to immigration from Eastern Europe. The strongest opposition of all was to immigration from the Middle East. In this political climate, it is perhaps not surprising that in August 1993, the governor of California proposed harsh restrictive measures, including elimination of benefits to which children of even illegal immigrants had previously been legally entitled, as a means of controlling illegal immigration. It is also notable that the 1980s and early 1990s were marked by increased tension among different minority and immigrant groups, such as those between Latinos and African Americans in Miami and among Latinos, Asians, and African Americans in New York and Los Angeles. Tensions between African Americans and Asian Americans were dramatically illustrated by the targeting of Korean-American businesses during the 1992 Los Angeles riot. (U.S. policy toward immigration, as well as the social and economic consequences of immigration, is discussed further in Chapter 15. The purpose of the discussion here is to show how increases in immigration often lead to growth in nativism, prejudice, and ethnic tension.)

While growing immigration in the United States has led to growing opposition to immigration—particularly that of non-European people of color—the harshest response to immigration in recent years has been in Germany. Earlier in this chapter, we discussed the rise of neo-Nazism in Germany as well as the violent attacks against minorities and immigrants that cause scores of deaths and injured or rendered homeless thousands more. An important factor contributing to these attacks was growing opposition to immigration, which relative to the country's population was at an all-time high in Germany in the early 1990s and on that basis exceeded immigration in virtually all other industrialized countries, including the United States. Asylum seekers alone arrived in the early 1990s at a rate of over a thousand a day, nearly half the number of legal immigrants to the United States, whose population is more than triple that of Germany. Germany also has admitted a large number of guest workers, many from Turkey, who generally work at jobs most Germans do not want. All told, about 8 percent of Germany's population is legally classified as foreign, reflecting both a high rate of immigration and Germany's unwillingness to admit people of non-German ancestry to citizenship—neither refugees nor guest workers, nor even their children born in Germany, are admitted to German citizenship.

Increasingly, Germany's "foreign" population has been perceived as contributing to Germany's economic hardship, which in fact results mainly from the difficulties of absorbing the unproductive economy of former East Germany together with the effects of a worldwide recession. As neo-Nazi activity has increased, Turks, Gypsies, and other minority groups have increasingly been the targets of violence. In fact, opposition to immigration has been the primary organizing issue used by the neo-Nazi groups. While most Germans continue to reject Nazism, opposition to immigration has become widespread in the German population. In fact, such opposition had become so strong by 1993 that the German parliament moved to repeal Germany's liberal asylum provisions (Nagorski, 1993). Thus, both the German and American experiences would seem to suggest that large surges of immigrants breed both opposition to immigration and heightened hate-group activity and ethnic prejudice.

RACIAL VERSUS ETHNIC DIVISIONS

All else being equal, racial divisions tend to be more intense than ethnic divisions, if for no other reason than that race makes discrimination easier: It is possible to distinguish a racial group by appearance—something that is not possible with ethnic groups. Thus, the majority of the long, seemingly intractable intergroup conflicts in the world involve racial rather than ethnic divisions. This does not, of course, mean that ethnic conflicts can *never* become intense; Northern Ireland and Quebec clearly do have intense ethnic conflict. The point is that race, because of its visibility, can become a basis of discrimination and conflict more easily than ethnicity.

INTERNATIONAL PRESSURE

Finally, it is important to note another effect of international relations on majority–minority relations. In a highly complex world where no nation can afford to be isolated, international pressure can have important effects on race and ethnic relations within countries subjected to such pressure. Although just how effective such pressure can be is debatable, its importance cannot be totally discounted. Two cases in Africa show that such pressures can make a difference. One case is that of Zimbabwe (formerly Rhodesia), whose white minority government was replaced with a system of majority rule in the mid-1970s. In that case, the United States, England, and even to some extent South Africa applied strong pressures on the white minority government to negotiate a settlement, because they feared a bloody civil war that might well have resulted in a pro-Soviet government hostile to Western interests. These pressures were an important source of change, though the direct threat of internal revolt was probably an even greater factor. In South Africa, as already noted, international sanctions played a key role in bringing about the settlement that brought majority rule in 1994. However, the unwillingness or inability of international powers to apply effective pressure on South Africa until well into the 1980s is one reason that country's white minority government lasted as long as it did.

SUMMARY AND CONCLUSION

In this chapter, we have examined intergroup relations in a wide range of societies throughout the world. This examination has given rise to a number of generalizations. The most important is that *no one factor* can explain the pattern of intergroup relations in any society: The factors involved in shaping a society's intergroup relations are always multiple and complex. Thus, *none of the generalizations we have made will hold for all societies.* In any society, there are counterforces that modify the influence of any factor we might identify. Thus, while intense racial conflicts (that is, conflicts between groups different in appearance) develop more easily than intense ethnic conflicts, the particular history and social conditions present in Quebec and Northern Ireland have given rise to severe intergroup conflicts, even though both groups in both societies are white. With this caveat, we can summarize the generalizations arising from the societies we have examined in this chapter:

1. Societies in which the dominant group gained power through conquest or colonialism tend to have more racial or ethnic stratification and more intergroup conflict than societies without such a history. This is especially true if the subordinate group is indigenous to the area.
2. Modernization, urbanization, and development tend to facilitate the development of minority or indigenous group movements. This may, depending on a number of factors, lead either to increased fluidity of intergroup relations or to continued rigidity with rising levels of conflict. Typically, a move toward greater fluidity in race or ethnic relations leads to social differentiation on the basis of a wider range of characteristics.
3. Societies with a large number of racial and ethnic classifications tend to have more harmonious intergroup relations than societies in which the bulk of the population is classified into two major groups. This is especially true when no group is a numerical majority.
4. The cultural and demographic characteristics of the two or more groups involved in intergroup relations have important effects on the pattern of relations between the groups.
5. Societies with crosscutting cleavages experience less intergroup conflict than societies with overlapping cleavages.
6. Ethnic groups with a territorial base tend to be in a stronger power position and resort more readily to conflict strategies than do groups without a territorial base.
7. Ethnic conflicts tend to be more intense when the groups involved speak different languages.
8. International conflicts with a nation associated with a minority group tend to result in hostility toward and subordination of the minority group.
9. Surges of immigration often lead to increased ethnic prejudice and conflict and to heightened opposition to immigration.
10. Racial divisions tend to be more intense than ethnic divisions.
11. International pressure can cause dominant groups to change their treatment of subordinate groups, though the degree to which this is true is uncertain.

These generalizations help us to further evaluate usefulness of the social-psychological, functionalist, and conflict perspectives for understanding the dynamics of intergroup relations. Item 4 and, to a lesser extent, items 7, 8, and 10 do suggest that the patterns of attitude in a society are important, as the social-psychological perspective suggests. However, attitudes relevant to these generalizations are determined to a considerable degree by large-scale characteristics of the society. Clearly, much that is attitudinal is a product of society; only through an understanding of culture and social structure can the pattern of intergroup relations in any society be understood. Within the broad area of social-structural effects, some support is found in these generalizations for both the functionalist and conflict perspectives. In support of the functionalist view, generalization 2, insofar as it concerns a move toward more fluid intergroup relations in some modern societies, recognizes that patterns of intergroup relations that may be functional in modern societies differ from those that are functional in traditional societies. Items 4, 7, 8, and 10 implicitly recognize the importance of ethnocentrism, which is stressed by the functionalist perspective as a cause of ethnic inequality and conflict. On the other hand, there is also considerable support for the importance of competition and conflict in majority–minority relations, as stressed by the conflict theory. Generalization 1, which is crucial, recognizes the importance of one group's (the colonizer) opportunity to benefit at the expense of another (the indigenous group) in a context of unequal power. Items 2, 3, 6, and 11 all stress the importance of power as a variable shaping intergroup relations throughout the world. Thus, three general conclusions regarding the major perspectives seem warranted. First, variations in large-scale social structure and culture seem to be the most important factors determining what kind of intergroup relations a society will have. Second, both the order (functionalist) and conflict perspectives make important contributions to the understanding of intergroup relations in a worldwide context. Third, the power relationship between two groups and whether or not one has ever been in a position to gain at the expense of the other are probably the most important factors determining the kind of relations any two groups will have.

9

The Status of Majority and Minority Groups in the United States Today

MAJOR RACIAL AND ETHNIC GROUPS: OVERVIEW AND GENERAL STATISTICS

In this chapter we examine the major racial and ethnic groups in American society today—who they are, their numbers and geographic distribution, and their social status. We also explore the current debate over whether the status of minority groups in American society is improving and, if so, by how much and in what areas. In the first section, we present general information about a number of racial and ethnic groups in American society. Some closely fit the definition of *minority group* presented in Chapter 1; some fit the definition of *majority*, or *dominant*, group; and some fall somewhere between.

Minority Groups—African Americans, Latinos, and Native Americans

As we indicated in Chapter 1, the three groups that most closely fit the definition of *minority group* are blacks, or African Americans; Latinos, or Hispanic Americans (actually composed of several distinct subgroups); and Indians, or Native Americans (again, a larger grouping comprising many distinct subgroups). In the discussion that follows we present general information about each of these major groups.

Blacks. Blacks are the largest minority group in the United States. According to the 1990 census, there are 30 million black people in the United States, which constitutes 12.1 percent of the total population (U.S. Bureau of the Census,

1991a). For a number of reasons, this figure is probably somewhat low. The census has always missed a larger proportion of the black population than of the white population; it is estimated that the 1990 census missed about 4.4 percent of the black population, compared with about 1.6 percent of the overall population (O'Hare, 1992, p. 10). Thus, the true African American population in 1990 may have been over 31 million. The percentage of blacks missed has gradually declined since the 1960 census, when between 8 percent and 9 percent were unaccounted for (U.S. Bureau of the Census, 1979a, p. 10).

Today as in the past, the majority of African Americans live in the South. The percentage living there fell throughout much of the twentieth century until the early 1970s, reflecting migration of blacks out of the South and into other parts of the country. However, the percentage living in the South never fell below half of the black population. Since the early 1970s, at least as many blacks have moved into the South as have moved out, as a sizable number who had moved to other parts of the country returned to the South. Hence, the percentage of blacks living there has remained steady or risen slightly since the early 1970s. This return movement in recent decades reflects several factors. First, many blacks came to realize that the North was not the racial paradise some of them had believed. Also, many black migrants found it sensible to return to the South, where many of their families resided and where the mores, lifestyles, and, undoubtedly, the weather and climate were more familiar to them. Another important factor is the general nationwide pattern of jobs and population moving toward the Sunbelt. In recent decades, economic growth has been greater in the South than in the North, and blacks, as well as others, have moved south to take advantage of the newly created opportunities.

In 1990, 53 percent of all African Americans lived in the South. The remainder were fairly evenly divided between the Northeast and the Midwest, each of which was home to about 19 percent of the African American population, with a smaller number (9 percent) living in the West.

The black population is now highly urbanized, even though it was more rural than the population as a whole during the early twentieth century. As of 1990, 87 percent of blacks lived in urban areas, compared with 76 percent of whites (U.S. Bureau of the Census, 1992b). The black population is particularly concentrated in the large industrial cities of the Great Lakes and Northeast regions, as well as in the cities of the South (though there are more rural blacks in the South than anywhere else). Compared with the population as a whole, the black population is much more highly concentrated in large central cities and much less suburbanized. Over half (57 percent) of all blacks live in central cities, compared with just 31 percent of the overall population. In contrast, just 27 percent of all U.S. blacks live in the suburbs, compared with 46 percent of the total population. Reflecting the highly urban character of the black population, only 15 percent live in nonmetropolitan areas (U.S. Bureau of the Census, 1992b, p. 7). Although African Americans are less likely than other groups to live in the suburbs, the percentage that live there is rising. Among those blacks who live in metropolitan areas, the proportion who live in suburbs rose from 27 percent to 32 percent between 1980 and 1990 (O'Hare, 1992).

A final important observation can be made about the black population of the United States: It is younger than the population as a whole. In 1990, about 33 percent of all African Americans were under the age of eighteen, compared with about 25 percent of whites. The median age of blacks in 1990 was 28.1, compared with 34.4 for whites (U.S. Bureau of the Census, 1992b, p. 23).

Hispanic Americans.   The second-largest minority group in the United States is Hispanic Americans, also known as Latinos or Americans of Spanish origin (the Census Bureau's term). This umbrella label covers at least four distinct groups: Mexican Americans, or Chicanos; Puerto Ricans, or Boricuas; Cuban Americans; and Central and South Americans. There are also a number of Hispanic Americans who do not fit neatly into any of these categories. In March 1992, there were 24.1 million Americans of Spanish origin, or 9.5 percent of the U.S. population (O'Hare, 1992). This represents an increase from 14.6 million, or 6.4 percent of the population in 1980. As shown in Table 9.1, which is based on 1990 census data, the majority of Hispanic Americans are Chicanos, with Puerto Ricans being the next largest group. As is the case with Census Bureau statistics on blacks, it is known that these estimates are lower than the actual Spanish-origin population. For a number of reasons, including language barriers and the existence of illegal immigration from Latin American countries in recent years, the underestimate of the Spanish population is probably greater than the underestimate of the black population. About 5 percent of Hispanics were missed in the 1990 Census. If we correct for the census undercount, it appears that the true Hispanic population of the United States exceeds 25 million.

The Hispanic population is one of the fastest-growing population groups in the United States, partly because Latinos have a relatively high birthrate, and partly because their immigration rate, both legal and illegal, has been among the highest of any group in recent years. Officially, the Hispanic population increased by about 50 percent between 1970 and 1980, and again between 1980 and 1990. Most experts believe that within the next two decades, the Hispanic population will exceed the black population, making Latinos the nation's largest minority group.

The Hispanic population is even more urban than the black population. In 1990, fully 90 percent of the Spanish-origin population lived in metropolitan areas (U.S. Bureau of the Census, 1992b, p. 7). Though there is some variation among the various groups, all Hispanic groups are over 85 percent urban. Although many people associate them with agricultural labor, 89 percent of all Mexican Americans live in metropolitan areas. This percentage is higher than that of either the white or black population. Like blacks, Latinos are heavily concentrated in central cities; 52 percent of all Americans of Spanish origin lived in central cities in 1990, a figure that

Table 9.1   Americans of Spanish Origin, 1980 and 1990

	1980		1990	
Group	Number in Millions	Percentage of Total Spanish Population	Number in Millions	Percentage of Total Spanish Population
Chicanos	8.740	59.8	13.496	60.4
Puerto Ricans	2.014	13.8	2.728	12.3
Cuban Americans	.803	5.5	1.044	4.7
Other Spanish Origin	3.051	20.9	5.086	22.8
Total	14.609		22.354	

Source: U.S. Bureau of the Census, 1983b, pp. 20–21, 1992b.

is almost as high as that for blacks and well above the figure for whites. Hispanic Americans are more suburbanized than blacks but less suburbanized than whites; 38 percent of the Hispanic population lived in suburbs in 1990 (U.S. Bureau of the Census, 1992b, p. 7).

The Chicano population is heavily concentrated in five southwestern states: California, Texas, Arizona, New Mexico, and Colorado; 61 percent of all Hispanic Americans and 87 percent of all Chicanos live in these five states (U.S. Bureau of the Census, 1992c). There are, however, also sizable concentrations of Mexican Americans in several midwestern and northeastern states; Illinois and Michigan are notable examples. Illinois has the third-largest Chicano population of any state, numbering 624,000 (U.S. Bureau of the Census, 1992c).

The Puerto Rican population is heavily concentrated in the urban Northeast, particularly the New York City area, including nearby New Jersey. As a result of this concentration, about 10 percent of the total Latino population lives in New York State, which has the third largest Latino population of any state, behind only California and Texas (U.S. Bureau of the Census, 1993, pp. 31–32). There are also sizable Puerto Rican populations in several other northeastern cities; Boston is a notable example.

The Cuban American population, largely refugees from the Castro government and descendants of those refugees, is heavily concentrated in Florida, particularly the Miami area. According to the 1990 census, over 1.5 million Hispanic persons lived in Florida, the fourth-largest total of any state. About 675,000 of these were Cuban American. There are, however, also sizable numbers of Cuban Americans in some parts of the Northeast.

As a whole, Latinos are one of the youngest ethnic groups in the United States. As of 1990, 35 percent of all Hispanic Americans were less than eighteen years old, which is a higher proportion than for blacks and almost a time and a half as high as for whites. The median age of Hispanic Americans in 1990 was 25.5, more than seven years younger than for the American population as a whole (U.S. Bureau of the Census, 1992c).

Indian People.   Up-to-date and detailed statistics are more difficult to obtain for Indian people, because their relatively small numbers make it impossible to obtain reliable data on them from the Census Bureau's ongoing Current Population Surveys, the major source of current data on black and Hispanic Americans. The main source of data on Indian people is the U.S. Census, which is taken every ten years. The 1990 census revealed an American Indian and Alaskan native population of 1.96 million—up from about 1.5 million in 1980 and 800,000 in 1970 (O'Hare, 1992; U.S. Bureau of the Census, 1972a). In part this represents real growth, but much of the increase is probably the result of people of mixed parentage classifying themselves as Indian rather than white—the census determines race on the basis of self-reports. In recent years, people of mixed parentage have increasingly come to think of themselves as Indian. The 1.96 million total today nonetheless reflects substantial and real growth in the Indian population from a low point of around 250,000 just before the turn of the century (Driver, 1969). It is, however, no more than and probably substantially *less* than the Native American population before the decimation of the native population by warfare and, especially, European diseases that followed the arrival of whites on the continent (Kroeber, 1939; Dobyns, 1966; Driver, 1969).

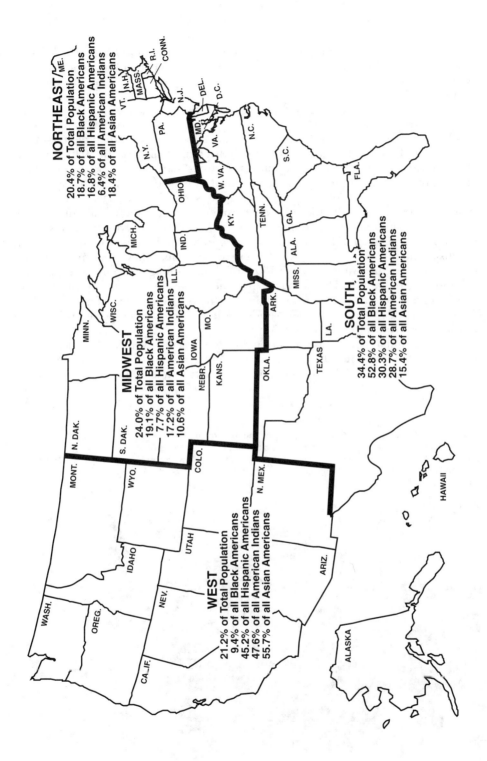

NORTHEAST
20.4% of Total Population
18.7% of all Black Americans
16.8% of all Hispanic Americans
6.4% of all American Indians
18.4% of all Asian Americans

MIDWEST
24.0% of Total Population
19.1% of all Black Americans
7.7% of all Hispanic Americans
17.2% of all American Indians
10.6% of all Asian Americans

SOUTH
34.4% of Total Population
52.8% of all Black Americans
30.3% of all Hispanic Americans
28.7% of all American Indians
15.4% of all Asian Americans

WEST
21.2% of Total Population
9.4% of all Black Americans
45.2% of all Hispanic Americans
47.6% of all American Indians
55.7% of all Asian Americans

Figure 9.1   Geographic Distribution of Minority Groups in the United States, 1990.   U.S. Bureau of the Census, 1992c, p. 21.

In 1990, 47.6 percent of the Indian population lived in the West, 28.7 percent in the South, 17.2 percent in the Midwest, and 6.4 percent in the Northeast. However, just three states, Oklahoma, California, and Arizona, account for fully one-third of the Indian population (O'Hare, 1992). (The regional distribution of all three minority groups we have discussed is illustrated in Figure 9.1.)

American Indians are the only minority group that is *less* urbanized than the population as a whole. In 1970, fewer than half, 45 percent, of Indian people in the United States lived in urban areas; 55 percent lived in rural areas. By 1990, a 56 percent majority of Indian people lived in urban areas—still a lower percentage than that of any other racial group. About one-third of Native Americans today live on reservations. The largest of these is the Navajo Reservation and Trust Lands in Arizona, New Mexico, and Utah, with a Native American population of about 150,000.

Not only are Indian people more rural than any other group, they also tend to become less permanently linked to the city even when they do move there. Urban Indians frequently live in cities near the reservation where they grew up. They tend to maintain close ties with the reservation, often remaining active in its cultural, social, and religious affairs. They also return to the reservation frequently for weekend visits and are visited by friends who still live on the reservation (Steele, 1972, 1985). Urban Indians also often view their residence in the city as a temporary sojourn after which they return to the reservation.

The Indian population is among the youngest of any major American racial or ethnic group. As of the 1990 census, 35 percent of all Indian people in the United States were under eighteen. The median age of Native Americans was 26.2 (U.S. Bureau of the Census, 1992c).

Although Chicanos are often associated in the public mind with agricultural labor (and it is true that many farm workers are Chicanos), the fact is that all three major Hispanic groups in the United States—Chicanos, Puerto Ricans, and Cuban Americans—are more urbanized than the American population as a whole. *Woodfin Camp & Associates/Michal Heron*

Blacks, Latinos, and Indian People as Minority Groups. We have said that the three major groups we have been discussing are those that best fit the definition of *minority group*. We will explore the present-day status of these groups later in this chapter, but it is important to note that these three groups, more than any others, today have less than their proportionate share of virtually all resources in American society. They have less wealth and lower incomes, less education, and less political power. They are accorded lower social status and live shorter lives than any other groups in American society. Although some other groups suffer low status in *some* of these areas, these are the only groups that, on the whole (there are many individuals who are exceptions to the general pattern), suffer low status across the board in *all* of these areas.

Groups with Intermediate Status: Asian, Jewish, and "White Ethnic" American

A number of racial and ethnic groups in the United States hold a status that is in some ways like that of a minority group but in other ways is not. These groups are near, or even in some cases above, the overall societal norm in some areas, such as income or education. However, each has in the past been or is now subject to widespread discrimination in American society. Furthermore, each of these groups has, to a large degree, been excluded from the upper echelons of American corporate power structure, or what Mills (1956) has called the power elite. Among these groups are the various Asian American groups, Jewish Americans, and a variety of "white ethnic" groups of eastern and southern European origin. We shall have more to say about the status of these groups later in this chapter; here we present general information about the numbers and geographic distribution of these groups.

Asian Americans. The six largest Asian American groups in the United States, as of the 1990 census, were Japanese Americans, Chinese Americans, Filipino Americans, Korean Americans, Asian Indians, and Vietnamese Americans. As shown in Table 9.2, each of these groups exceeded a half million in 1990, and all are growing rapidly. Together, Asians and Pacific Islanders totaled 7.3 million in 1990—double the 1980 total, and 2.9 percent of the U.S. population. The 1990 populations of the various Asian American groups are shown in Table 9.2.

These populations are heavily concentrated in the West, particularly in the

Table 9.2 1990 Population of Asian American Groups

Chinese Americans	1,645,000
Filipino Americans	1,407,000
Japanese Americans	848,000
Asian Indians	815,000
Korean Americans	799,000
Vietnamese Americans	615,000
5 Other Asian Groups Combined	558,000
Pacific Islanders	323,000

Source: U.S. Bureau of the Census, 1992c.

states of California and Hawaii. Over half of each of the groups live in these two states. There is also a large concentration of Chinese Americans in New York State, with a Chinese population of over 280,000. Lesser but substantial numbers of the other groups are also found in New York State, Illinois, and Texas. Overall, in 1990, 55.7 percent of Asian Americans lived in the West, 18.4 percent in the Northeast, 15.4 percent in the South, and 10.6 percent in the Midwest (U.S. Bureau of the Census, 1992c, p. 21).

All Asian American groups are highly urban. The precise percentage of the six nationalities ranges from 94 percent among Japanese Americans to 98 percent among Chinese Americans, with the other four groups falling in between. Chinese Americans predominantly live in central cities. Four urban areas account for the majority of the Chinese American population: San Francisco–Oakland, New York City, Honolulu, and Los Angeles–Long Beach. Many of these urban Chinese Americans live in the central-city neighborhoods known as the Chinatowns, although the Chinese population has suburbanized in recent decades. In addition to the cities mentioned, Chicago and Boston also have sizable Chinatowns.

Compared with the Chinese, other Asian Americans are more suburbanized, but more of them live in central cities than anywhere else. About 40 to 50 percent of each of the other groups live in central cities, compared with 30 percent of the total population (U.S. Bureau of the Census, 1992b, p. 7).

Japanese Americans are, on the average, older than the population as a whole, with a median age of 36.2. Chinese Americans and Filipino Americans, on the other hand, are somewhat younger than the population as a whole, with median ages of 32.1 and 31.1, respectively (U.S. Bureau of the Census, 1992b). In 1990, Asian Americans as a whole averaged about three years younger than the total population (U.S. Bureau of the Census, 1992c).

Jewish Americans.   Accurate data on Jewish Americans and other white ethnic groups are more difficult to obtain and less reliable than data on the other groups we have been discussing. The census does not ask people their religion, and only incomplete data (first- and second-generation immigrants) were obtained on nationality before the 1980 census.

The best guess is that the Jewish population of the United States is slightly above 6 million, or 3 percent of the U.S. population (Goren, 1980, p. 571). This is about half the world's Jewish population. The U.S. Jewish population is growing less rapidly than the population as a whole because of its relatively low birthrate.

The Jewish population is highly urbanized. In 1957, the last year for which good data are available, 96 percent of all Jewish Americans lived in urban areas (U.S. Bureau of the Census, 1958). In particular, a sizable proportion lives in the Greater New York City metropolitan area. This is reflected in the regional distribution of Jewish Americans: About 64 percent live in the Northeast. The remainder are somewhat evenly distributed throughout the Midwest, South, and West.

Eastern and Southern European "White Ethnics." The term *white ethnics* is applied to a wide variety of groups from eastern and southern Europe. As a general rule, these groups have immigrated to the United States somewhat more recently than the groups from northern and western Europe. The bulk of eastern and southern European migration took place after 1900, during the early part of the twentieth century. Much of the Italian population, for example, came in one decade,

Table 9.3 Persons of Eastern and Southern European Ancestry, 1980 and 1990

ANCESTRY[1]	1980 POPULATION	1990 POPULATION
Italian	12,184,000	14,715,000
	6.5%[2]	5.9%
Polish	8,238,000	9,266,000
	4.4%	3.8%
Russian	2,781,000	2,953,000
	1.5%	1.2%
Czech	1,892,000	1,615,000
	1.0%	0.6%
Hungarian	1,777,000	1,582,000
	0.9%	0.6%
Portuguese	1,024,000	1,153,000
	0.5%	0.5%
Greek	960,000	1,110,000
	0.5%	0.4%
Ukranian	730,000	741,000
	0.4%	0.3%
Slovak	777,000	1,883,000
	0.4%	0.8%
Lithuanian	743,000	812,000
	0.4%	0.3%

[1] Includes both single and multiple ancestry. Persons who reported more than one ancestry group may be counted in more than one category.

[2] In 1980, percentage of those who reported ancestry in that census. In 1990, percentage of total population.

Source: 1980: U.S. Bureau of the Census, 1983c, pp. 12–14. 1990: U.S. Bureau of the Census, *1990 Census of Population, Social and Economic Characteristics, United States,* p. 12.

1901–1910. In contrast, immigration from Ireland peaked in the 1850s and immigration from Germany peaked in the 1880s (Thomlinson, 1976).

The eastern and southern European white ethnics include, among others, Italian, Polish, Greek, Russian, Hungarian, Czechoslovakian, and Ukrainian Americans. The 1980 census—the first recent census to ask everyone a question about ancestry—indicated that the largest of these groups was Italian Americans. Next came Polish Americans and Russian Americans. Those remained the three largest groups in 1990. The populations of these and other groups are shown in Table 9.3.

The majority of these ethnic groups are concentrated in the Northeast and in the Great Lakes states. This is reflected in 1990 statistics, which show that Massachusetts, New York, Rhode Island, Connecticut, and New Jersey are all among the top ten states in the percentage of their population that is foreign-born (U.S. Bureau of the Census, 1992e). While some of the foreign-born population of these states is composed of recent, non-European residents, a sizable part of it is also composed of older immigrants from eastern Europe who arrived in the early decades of the twentieth century.

Eastern and southern Europeans also make up a substantial portion of the population of Illinois, Michigan, Wisconsin, and the northern parts of Ohio and Indiana. For the most part, these ethnic groups are highly urban; they are heavily concentrated in the large industrial cities of these regions.

A final important characteristic of these groups is that they generally belong to religions outside the Protestant majority in the United States. The majority of eastern and southern Europeans are Catholic. This is particularly true for Italians and Poles, though a sizable portion of the latter are Jewish. A large part of the Russian American population is also Jewish; much of the remainder is Russian Orthodox. The various Slavic groups tend to belong to one of the Eastern Orthodox churches, as do Greek Americans, who typically belong to the Greek Orthodox Church.

Whites from Western and Northern Europe: A Dominant Group Within a Dominant Group

In contemporary America, the groups that most clearly fit the definition of *majority* or *dominant group* are whites from western and northern Europe. Certainly, whites as a whole are in a dominant position relative to blacks, Chicanos, American Indians and, to a lesser degree, Asian Americans. Within that white population, however, the most advantaged groups are those from western and northern Europe. Table 9.4 shows the 1990 population of various western and northern European ancestries in the United States. By far, the three largest ancestry groups in the United States are the Germans, Irish, and English. In 1990, 58 million Americans, or 23 percent of the population, reported some German ancestry. Thirty-eight million, or nearly 16 percent of the population, reported some Irish ancestry, and 32 million, or 13 percent of the population, reported some English ancestry. At least one-third of the U.S. population can trace part or all of its ancestry to one or more of these three groups.

Besides the Germans, Irish, and English, there are a number of other groups of western or northern European ancestry. The largest of these are the French, Scottish, and Dutch, along with the Scandinavians (Swedish, Norwegian, and Danish). Together, Americans of western and northern European ancestry account for more than 60 percent of the US. population.

As a general rule, these groups immigrated earlier than most of the eastern and southern Europeans, though Scandinavians are something of an exception in this regard. Partly because of this, these groups tend to be more assimilated into American society and less conscious of ethnicity than other groups we have discussed, though some ethnic awareness persists in all American ethnic groups and may be on the rise in many.

The British groups (English, Scots, Welsh), a sizable proportion of the Germans, and the Scandinavians and Dutch are predominantly Protestant. These are the groups that form the core of the so-called WASP (white Anglo-Saxon Protestant) population. Most of the rest of the Germans and the majority of the Irish are Catholic, although many Irish, particularly in the South, belong to fundamentalist Protestant churches.

For the most part, these groups are quite widely distributed geographically. The most notable exceptions are the Scandinavian groups, which are largely concentrated in the upper Midwest.

As we have indicated, these groups are generally in a dominant socioeconomic position. They tend to have relatively high economic, educational, and occu-

Table 9.4 Persons of Western and Northern European Ancestry, 1980 and 1990

ANCESTRY[1]	1980 POPULATION	1990 POPULATION
English	49,598,000	32,556,000
	26.3%[2]	13.1%
German	49,224,000	57,986,000
	26.1%	23.3%
Irish	40,166,000	38,740,000
	21.3%	15.6%
French	12,892,000	10,321,000
	6.8%	4.1%
Scottish	10,049,000	5,394,000
	5.3%	2.2%
Dutch	6,304,000	6,227,000
	3.4%	2.5%
Swedish	4,345,000	4,681,000
	2.3%	1.9%
Norwegian	3,454,000	3,869,000
	1.8%	1.6%
Welsh	1,665,000	2,034,000
	0.9%	0.8%
Danish	1,518,000	1,635,000
	0.8%	0.7%
Swiss	982,000	1,045,000
	0.5%	0.4%
Austrian	948,000	871,000
	0.5%	0.4%
Finnish	616,000	659,000
	0.3%	0.3%
French Canadian[3]	780,000	2,167,000
	0.4%	0.9%
Canadian[3]	456,000	561,000
	0.2%	0.2%

[1] Includes both single and multiple ancestry. Persons who reported more than one ancestry group may be counted in more than one category.
[2] In 1980, percentage of those who reported ancestry in that census. In 1990, percentage of total population.
[3] Included because most Canadians and French Canadians are of western or northern European ancestry.

Source: 1980: U.S. Bureau of the Census, 1983c, pp. 12–14. 1990: U.S. Bureau of the Census, *1990 Census of Population, Social and Economic Characteristics, United States,* p. 12.

pational levels, and relatively low rates of poverty, though there is some variation by both nationality and religion. Data from large-scale surveys by the National Opinion Research Center indicate, for example, that among eleven white Catholic and Protestant ethnic groups, the four highest occupational prestige ratings were among British Protestants, Irish Catholics, German Catholics, and German Protestants, in that order (Greeley, 1977, p. 60). In urban areas outside the South, Scandinavian

Protestants also ranked close to these four groups (Greeley, 1977, p. 61; see also Greeley, 1974).

STATUS OF MINORITY GROUPS IN AMERICA TODAY

In the following sections, we focus in greater detail on the racial and ethnic groups in American society that we have identified as minority groups. We examine in detail the social and economic status of these groups, with special attention to the growing debate over whether the status of minority groups in the United States has improved significantly. We first present evidence of improvement in the status of minorities, then examine some evidence of continuing racial and ethnic inequality. We shall then attempt to see how the two balance.

Evidence of Improvement in Minority Status

Some social indicators suggest substantial improvement in the status of minorities between about 1940 and today. Some of the trends are fairly recent; others have been under way since around World War II.

One indication of improved status among minorities can be seen in their occupational structure. One indicator of a group's occupational status is the number or proportion of group members who hold professional or managerial positions. Among blacks, the number of persons in professional occupations more than tripled between 1960 and 1975. The number of blacks in management positions increased by about two-and-a-quarter times. Among whites, people in professional occupations increased by only about one-and-two-thirds times; people in managerial positions, by about one-and-a-quarter times (U.S. Department of Commerce, 1977, p. 377). In 1980, blacks held twice as large a share of the professional and managerial jobs as they did in 1960 (R. Farley, 1984, p. 194). In other words, the number of blacks in high-status jobs grew at a relatively faster rate than did the number of whites in such jobs. Latinos, too, experienced a more rapid growth in high-status jobs than did whites during this period (Moore, 1976, p. 64; U.S. Bureau of the Census, 1979c, p. 26). Thus, by 1980, a substantially higher proportion of the black and Latino populations held high-status occupations in the United States than ever before, though that proportion was still lower for both blacks and Latinos than it was for whites.

The growth in the percentage of African Americans and Latinos in higher-status occupations continued during the 1980s, but at a slower pace than in the 1960s and 1970s. By 1991, about 14 percent of employed black males and 19 percent of employed black females were in professional or managerial occupations—an improvement over the past but still well below the 27 percent of white males and 28 percent of white females in such occupations (U.S. Bureau of the Census, 1992f).

Among those who are employed, the gap in individual incomes between minorities and whites has decreased substantially since about 1950. In 1950, for example, the median hourly income of employed black males was about 60 percent that of whites. By 1979, it had risen to 74 percent. Racial differences in annual pay are greater than racial differences in hourly pay, however, because blacks and Latinos on the average experience more unemployment over the year than whites and may receive less opportunity for overtime work. Among males who worked full-time all year in 1990, the median annual income of African Americans was 73 percent that of whites, and the median annual income of Latinos was only 66 percent that of whites (computed from U.S. Bureau of the Census, 1991b). For African Americans (but perhaps not for Latinos), this represents significant improvement over the past, but the racial gap remains quite large. Among females, the gap between minorities and whites has closed more than it has among males. Among women who worked full-time all year in 1990, the median income of black women was 89 percent that of white women. Among Hispanic full-time working women, the gap was somewhat larger: Their median income was 78 percent that of comparable white women. Women of all races, however, continue to receive much lower incomes than white males.

Part of the remaining racial gap in income is a product of educational differences. If we examine only full-time workers with comparable educational levels, the gap in income is even smaller than it is in the overall population. Among recent college graduates with year-round, full-time jobs, for example, the median income of black males is 85 percent that of white males, and the median income of Latino males is 89 percent that of white males. Among women who have recently graduated from college, the incomes of black and white year-round, full-time workers are virtually identical, and that of Latinas is 90 percent that of whites. However, black, white, and Hispanic women all continue to receive only about three-fourths as much income as white males even among recent college graduates with full-time jobs (computed from U.S. Bureau of the Census, 1991b). While these figures do indicate a decline in racial inequality in income among comparably educated full-time workers, it is important to remember that both African Americans and Latinos are less likely to be college graduates and more likely to be unemployed. Thus, their representation within the category of college-educated, year-round, full-time workers remains quite low.

In the area of political representation, there is also substantial evidence of minority gain in recent years. Between 1970 and 1991, the number of black elected officials in the United States rose from fewer than fifteen hundred to more than seventy-four hundred. Between 1984 and 1991 the number of Latino elected officials rose from fewer than thirty-one hundred to more than forty-two hundred (U.S. Bureau of the Census, 1992c). There are more than three hundred black mayors and more than four hundred black state legislators. Nearly every major city in the United States has elected a black mayor at some time within the past two decades, including New York, Chicago, Los Angeles, Detroit, Philadelphia, Atlanta, Washington, New Orleans, St. Louis, and Birmingham, Alabama—a city that had been a symbol of resistance to black rights in the early 1960s. Another such city, Selma, Alabama, elected a black majority to its city council in 1993. In 1981, San Antonio became the first major city to elect a Latino mayor, Henry Cisneros (who later became Secretary of Housing and Urban Development in the Clinton administration). Two Hispanic governors were elected in the 1970s (in Arizona and New Mexico); the first African American governor (L. Douglas Wilder of Virginia) was elected in the 1980s, and the 1990s brought the election of the first black woman (Carol Mosely-Braun of Illinois) and the first native American (Ben Nighthorse Campbell of Colorado) to the U.S. Senate. The 1992 elections also brought the number of African Americans in Congress to a record high of forty, and of Hispanics to a record high of nineteen. Also that year, the first Puerto Rican and the first Korean American were elected to the U.S. Congress. Thus, it is very clear that minorities have made considerable gains in political representation over the past two decades or so.

Finally, it is important to reiterate that deliberate racial discrimination is today illegal and less common than in the past. This in itself is a dramatic change, considering that as recently as thirty years ago, such discrimination was not only legal and widespread but, in some parts of the country, required by law. This decline has, as we have indicated, been accompanied by some rather dramatic reductions in prejudice in the population.

It seems clear from these data, then, that in at least some areas there *has* been substantial improvement in the status of minority group members in America. An important factor in this improvement has been the rise of minority group social movements, discussed at length in Chapter 6.

Despite these apparent gains, some hard questions must still be asked. First, despite whatever progress has occurred, how much inequality and racism still persists? More specifically, what is the standing of minorities relative to that of whites in America today? The fact that minorities have gained in certain areas does not necessarily mean either that they have caught up or that *all* minority group members have gained at all. Finally, we must ask what is the absolute level of living among minorities today? We turn to these questions in the next section.

Evidence of Continuing Majority–Minority Inequality

Economics. Despite the progress we have seen among some segments of the minority population, the overall picture today continues to be one of serious majority–minority inequality in the economic arena. One important indicator of economic well-being is median family income. The median family income for all white, black, and Spanish-origin families in 1990 is shown in the top row of Table 9.5. These data clearly indicate that, whatever gains have been made, the family income of Latinos and, even more so, blacks, remains substantially below that of whites. Indeed, the figure for blacks represents only a small gain relative to whites over the past forty years: In the 1940s, median family income for blacks was about 50 percent of what it was for whites. Today, it is about 58 percent.

Table 9.5 Median Family Income, by Race, Hispanic Origin, and Type of Family, 1990

	ALL FAMILIES	MARRIED-COUPLE FAMILIES		MALE HOUSEHOLDER, NO WIFE	FEMALE HOUSEHOLDER, NO HUSBAND
		Wife in Paid Labor Force	Wife Not in Paid Labor Force		
U.S. Total	$35,353	$46,777	$30,265	$29,046	$16,932
White	36,915	47,247	30,781	30,570	19,528
Black	21,423	40,038	20,333	21,848	12,125
% of white	58.0	84.7	66.1	71.5	62.1
Hispanic	23,431	34,778	21,166	22,744	11,914
% of white	63.5	73.6	68.8	74.4	61.0

Source: U.S. Bureau of the Census, 1991b.

It has been commonly argued that the recent increase in female-householder families with no husband present is a major reason for the lack of improvement in median black family income, since such families have low incomes among all races (Bianchi, 1981; R. Farley, 1984, pp. 199–200). This is correct, but it is only part of the answer. As Table 9.5 shows, substantial racial differences in income exist within each type of family, although the gap is less among married-couple families in which both the husband and wife are employed than among all other types of families. Among married-couple families both of whose partners are employed, the median income of black families is about 85 percent of that of white families; this compares with about 72 percent in 1967, indicating that for this type of family, the income gap has narrowed over the past three decades or so, though it remains sizable (U.S. Bureau of the Census, 1992e). For all other types of families, including married-couple families in which only the husband is employed, the racial gap in income is far greater: Median black family income ranges from about 62 to 72 percent of median white family income among other types of families. In short, black families have low incomes compared to whites *regardless of family type,* but their economic situation is further worsened by their overrepresentation in the low-income, female-householder category. Hispanic families also have low incomes compared to Anglos in all types of families and, like blacks, have experienced no improvement in recent years. If anything, they have lost ground: In 1978, median Hispanic family income was 68 percent of the white median, compared with less than 64 percent today.

Another indicator of the economic position of a group is the proportion of its members who are below the federally defined poverty level (in 1991, approximately $13,900 for a family of four and $6,900 for a single individual, but adjusted annually for inflation). As shown in Table 9.6, African Americans, Latinos, and Native Americans all have far-greater percentages of their populations living below the poverty level than do white Americans. In fact, the poverty rates of blacks and of Indian people are about three times as high as that of whites, and the Hispanic rate is about two-and-one-half times as high. Poverty rates of all groups tend to rise during recessions, reaching high points, for example, during the 1982–1983 recession and the 1991–1992 recession, and falling somewhat during better economic times, such as the late 1980s. However, the poverty rates of African Americans and Native Americans have quite consistently been around three times the white rate over the past

Table 9.6 Percentage of Population Below Poverty Level, by Race, 1991

	ALL AGES	CHILDREN UNDER 18	PERSONS IN FEMALE-HOUSEHOLDER FAMILIES
Total Population	14.2%	21.8	39.7
White	11.3	16.8	31.5
Black	32.7	45.9	54.8
Hispanic[1]	28.7	40.4	52.7
Asian	14[2]		
American Indian	32[2]		

[1] Hispanics may be of any race.
[2] Data for Asians and American Indians are to the nearest whole percent.

Source: O'Hare, 1992; U.S. Bureau of the Census, 1992d.

decade or two, and the Latino rate has actually risen somewhat relative to the rate of non-Hispanic whites.

A final indicator of economic status is the unemployment rate. Here, too, substantial intergroup inequalities are evident. For the year 1991, the unemployment rate of whites was 6.0 percent. For blacks, it was 12.4 percent, and for Hispanics it was 9.9 percent. Among Hispanics, unemployment rates were even higher for Puerto Ricans (11.6 percent) and Mexican Americans (10.4 percent) (U.S. Bureau of the Census, 1992c). Unemployment data are less readily available for Native Americans, but in general, their unemployment rates have tended to be similar to those of African Americans.

Research by Snipp (1988) has shown that, even when valuable resources are developed on Indian reservations, Native American unemployment remains high. Even following the energy crisis of the 1970s, the unemployment rate on reservations with energy resources was about the same as the unemployment rate on reservations without energy. One reason for this is that, to date, it has been mainly non-Indians that have benefitted from development of resources on reservations. Coal is a good example of this. As the value of coal produced on reservations rose during the energy crisis, the rate of royalties fell—from 6.6 percent in 1972 to just 4.0 percent in 1979. Between 1978 and 1979, the value of coal produced on reservations nearly doubled, but the amount of royalties paid to Native Americans actually fell (Snipp, 1988, pp. 14–16). And on some reservations, such as that of the Navajo in Arizona, coal mining has resulted in the displacement of many Indians who had been engaging in agriculture.

Black unemployment has generally been about twice as high as white unemployment since the end of World War II. Before that time, during the 1920s and 1930s, blacks and whites had very similar unemployment rates (Wilson, 1978). Since the war, however, there has been a drastic reduction in the number of low-skill, low-pay jobs that many blacks had occupied. A sizable segment of the black population has continued to be excluded from the opportunity to learn skills necessary for better jobs, and the disappearance of unskilled jobs has left many of those individuals unemployed (Wilson, 1978, 1987).

The problem of minority unemployment becomes even clearer if we focus on particular segments of the minority population. Among young, black, urban males, for example, the unemployment rate is believed to be in the range of 40 percent to 50 percent.

Taken as a whole, these economic data indicate that very substantial inequalities between whites and minorities persist. While a segment of the black and Hispanic population today enjoys relatively high incomes and good jobs, a large segment of the minority population can be described only as trapped at the bottom of the socioeconomic structure. For this group, things are not getting better; indeed, relative to everyone else the situation is probably getting worse. If we examine the minority population as a whole, two conclusions are evident. First, among the black and Hispanic populations there is increasing stratification and a growing gap between a segment that is relatively well off and another segment that is impoverished and struggling for survival. Second, if we take the overall minority population, the *average* economic positions of blacks, Latinos, and Indians remain substantially lower than the average position of whites, and the average positions have improved only marginally relative to the position of whites.

In the United States today, there is a large and growing minority middle class. At the same time, however, other minority group members remain poor, and the proportion of minorities in the impoverished "underclass" is far greater than the proportion of whites in the underclass. *AT&T Photo Center/Marc Anderson*

Political Representation.   As we have seen, the political representation of black and Hispanic Americans has risen dramatically during the past decade. Nonetheless, it remains well below their share of the population. Even with the record numbers of minorities elected to Congress in 1993, the House of Representatives is less than 9 percent black and less than 4.5 percent Hispanic—even though blacks are 12 percent of the population and Hispanics 9 percent. When Carol Moseley-Braun was elected to the Senate in 1992, she became the only African American in that body and the first since 1978. And it is still true that only one black person has ever been elected governor of a state, and that, with the exception of one white female, Geraldine Ferraro, who was nominated for vice president by the Democrats in 1984 (her ticket lost), only white males have ever been nominated for president or vice president, much less elected. The closest any person of color has come was when the Reverend Jesse Jackson finished second to Michael Dukakis in the 1988 race for the Democratic nomination; Jackson also ran for president in 1984, when his delegate total fell well below the percentage of the vote that he received in the primaries and caucuses. In 1984, he won the popular vote in two states and the District of Columbia; in 1988, he improved this showing substantially, carrying about half a dozen states and the District of Columbia and outlasting all candidates except the eventual nominee, Michael Dukakis. Overall, however, only about 1.5 percent of all U.S. elected officials are African Americans and fewer than 1 percent are Latinos—even though, together, these groups make up more than 20 percent of the U.S. population. Thus, even though the number of minority elected officials has grown, people of color remain very unrepresented among U.S. elected officials.

Education.   Data on educational attainment in 1991 for whites, African Americans, and Latinos are shown in Tables 9.7 and 9.8. Table 9.7 shows the median number of years of school completed—a good overall measure of a group's educational status. These data indicate that in the population aged twenty-five and over, there is a gap of nearly half a year between the median educational attainment of blacks and that of whites, and almost a year between Latinos and whites. Among young adults, however, the gap between blacks and whites is smaller, suggesting a trend toward less black–white inequality in educational attainment. In 1991, for example, the median number of years of school completed among persons aged twenty-five to twenty-nine was 12.9 for whites and 12.7 for blacks—a difference of only two-tenths of a year. No such trend is evident in the case of Hispanics, however: Among Hispanics twenty-five to twenty-nine years old, the median was only 12.2 years of school, almost three-quarters of a year less than for whites.

Table 9.7   Educational Attainment by Race and Spanish Origin, Persons 25 and Over, 1991

	PERCENT HIGH SCHOOL GRADUATES	PERCENT WITH FOUR OR MORE YEARS OF COLLEGE	MEDIAN YEARS OF SCHOOL
Whites	79.9	22.2	12.8
Blacks	66.7	11.5	12.4
Hispanics	51.3	9.7	12.0

Source: U.S. Bureau of the Census, 1992c, p. 144.

Table 9.8 High School and College Graduation Rates by Race and Hispanic Origin, Young Adults and Population 25 and Over, 1991

GROUP	PERCENTAGE WITH 4 OR MORE YEARS OF HIGH SCHOOL	
	Persons 20–24 Years Old	Persons 25 and Over
White	85.2	77.9
Black	79.1	66.7
Hispanic	58.4	51.3
	PERCENTAGE WITH 4 OR MORE YEARS OF COLLEGE	
	Persons 25–29 Years Old	Persons 25 and Over
White	24.4	22.2
Black	11.0	11.5
Hispanic	9.2	9.7

Source: U.S. Bureau of the Census, 1992g.

Table 9.8 shows high school and college graduation rates for young adults and for the entire population over the age of twenty-five. This table shows that the gap in high school graduation rates between blacks and whites appears to be narrowing: There is a six-percentage-point difference between the graduation rates of young blacks and whites, compared with an eleven-point gap in the population over twenty-five. About four out of five African Americans in their early twenties are high school graduates, a substantially greater percentage than in the overall adult black population. On the other hand, young Hispanics are making no such gains: Their high school graduation rate is twenty-seven percentage points lower than that of the young white population, the same as is the case in the population over twenty-five. Even among the young, only 58 percent of Latinos are high-school graduates.

The data on college graduation in Table 9.8 indicate little gain on the part of either blacks or Latinos relative to whites. While blacks are now almost as likely as whites to attain four years of high school by their early twenties, they are less than half as likely to graduate from college by their late twenties. One out of four whites, but only one out of nine blacks, are college graduates by the time they are twenty-five to twenty-nine years old. Even fewer Hispanics, about one out of eleven, are college graduates by this age. Disturbingly, the gap is, if anything, widening. The percentage of college graduates for whites is higher among twenty-five to twenty-nine-year-olds than in the overall population over twenty-five; among both African Americans and Latinos, it is lower. This appears to reflect the decline in minority college enrollment between the mid 1970s and mid 1980s.

While less data are available on Native Americans and Asian Americans, an analysis of 1992 Current Population Survey data by O'Hare (1992) does provide some current, very useful information on this issue. The results of this study, which focused on adults between the ages of twenty-five and forty-four, are shown in Table 9.9, with data on whites, blacks, and Hispanics provided for comparison. They show that Native Americans are slightly less likely than blacks, and a good deal less likely than non-Hispanic whites, to graduate from both high school and college. Asian

Table 9.9   Educational Attainment, Persons 24–44, by Race and Hispanic Origin, 1992

GROUP	PERCENTAGE WITH			
	4 Years College	Some College	4 Years High School	Less than 4 Years High School
Non-Hispanic Whites	28	27	36	9
African Americans	14	26	41	19
Latinos	10	20	30	40
Asian Americans	47	20	25	8
Native Americans	11	30	37	22

Source: O'Hare, 1992, p. 29.

Americans, on the other hand, are more likely than any other group to graduate from both high school and college.

Data on current college enrollment are also instructive. In 1991, 10.2 percent of college students were black, which represents significant underrepresentation, since about 15 percent of the college-aged population is black (U.S. Bureau of the Census, 1992c). Also in 1991, just 6.3 percent of college students were Hispanic, compared with the more than 11 percent of the college-aged population that is Hispanic. This figure of 6.3 percent represents an all-time high, but it reflects growth of the Hispanic population not increased access to college among Hispanics. In 1991, 31.8 percent of black high school graduates between the ages of fourteen and twenty-four were enrolled in college. The corresponding figure for Hispanics was 34.6 percent (U.S. Bureau of the Census, 1992c). Both of these figures are substantially lower than the 42.0 percent of white high school graduates the same age who were in college, and both blacks and Hispanics are less likely to graduate from high school as well. Thus, the percentage of college-aged blacks and Hispanics who are in college is considerably less than that of whites. In general, the African American percentage among college students increased sharply in the early 1970s, peaked in the mid 1970s, fell until the mid 1980s, and began to rise again after about 1988 (National Center for Education Statistics, 1992a, 1992b). The 1991 percentage of undergraduate students who are black was the highest since 1976. It is also noteworthy that minority students are disproportionately likely to enroll in two-year colleges as opposed to four-year colleges. In 1990, for example, 9.8 percent of students in two-year schools were black and 8.0 percent were Hispanic, compared with just 8.4 percent and 4.0 percent, respectively, in four-year schools (National Center for Education Statistics, 1992b). The concentration of African Americans and Latinos in two-year schools is one reason why their college graduation rates are lower than those of whites.

Even fewer African Americans and Latinos are among graduate and professional (medical, law, dental, etc.) students. Among graduate students, just 5.9 percent were black and 3.2 percent were Hispanic in 1990 (National Center for Education Statistics, 1992a). As in undergraduate school, black enrollment in graduate school fell in the late 1970s and early 1980s but has been on the rise again in recent years. Still, the proportion of both blacks and Hispanics in graduate school is less than half what it is in the population as a whole. The picture is not much different in professional schools, where 5.9 percent of the students in 1990 were black and 3.9 percent Hispanic. And as low as these percentages are, both of them are record highs (National Center for Education Statistics, 1992a).

Taken together, these statistics indicate clearly that African Americans, Latinos, and Native Americans remain well behind whites and Asian Americans with respect to educational attainment. Of particular significance are the much smaller proportions of college graduates among minority groups, even among young adults. This indicates that, in an era when college graduation is increasingly a prerequisite for most of the better jobs, blacks, Hispanics, and American Indians all continue to have a much smaller chance of obtaining that important credential. Equally important, current data suggest that they are not even catching up—the gap is as great or greater among young adults as it is among adults of all ages.

Of course, statistics about educational attainment cannot begin to tell the whole story about how well or poorly any group is being served by the educational system. Quality of education is as important as quantity, and even statistics showing that young blacks' educational levels are growing closer to those of whites say nothing about the issue of educational quality. We know, for example, that black students are underrepresented in prestigious private colleges and major state universities and overrepresented in community colleges and smaller regional or commuter state colleges and universities. At major state universities, the decline in black enrollment in the late 1970s was in some cases quite sharp: At the University of Michigan, for example, it fell from 8.0 percent in 1976 to just 5.2 percent in 1980 (Allen, 1982). This decline led to renewed protests during the 1980s regarding the lack of minority students, and the university eventually recommitted itself to an unfulfilled 1970 promise to raise its black enrollment to the percentage in the state's population. After that, its African American enrollment began to rise again but still remains well below the 1970 goal. In Chapter 11, we shall explore the entire issue of how the operation of our educational system and the roles of minorities within that system shape the status of minority groups in America today.

Health and Mortality.   So far, we have seen evidence of continuing serious racial and ethnic inequality in the areas of economics, political representation, and education. In such situations, there is always the risk that such information will be seen by some as just so many more statistics in a world in which we are daily bombarded by more and more statistics. However, one area, probably more than any other, shows the human dimension—and indeed the human tragedy—of racial and ethnic inequality. In the United States today, the racial or ethnic group to which one belongs partially determines how long one will live. It also influences the amount that a person can expect to be ill in his or her lifetime and the likelihood that one or more of his or her children will die in infancy. As we shall see in considerably more detail in Chapter 10, these differences exist not because of biological racial differences but rather because of social inequalities associated with race or ethnicity. We turn now to the grim statistics.

On the average, African Americans live about seven years less than whites—actually a slight widening of the gap since the mid 1980s. In 1991, the life expectancy for white females was 79.6; for black females it was 73.8—a difference of nearly six years. Among males, the racial gap in life expectancy is wider. In 1991, life expectancy for white males was 72.9, compared with just 64.6 for black males—a difference of more than eight years (National Center for Health Statistics, 1993). This gap in life span has widened in recent years mainly due to a decline in the life expectancy of black males (O'Hare, 1992). Unfortunately, life expectancy data are not published for Hispanics or Native Americans, but the likelihood is that their life expectancies are less than those of non-Hispanic whites. In 1970, when data were published for Native Americans, their life expectancy was about six years less than that of whites.

Infant mortality is also higher among minority groups than it is among whites. The infant-mortality rate (number of deaths per year to infants under one year old per thousand live births) was 8.1 for whites in 1989 but 17.7—more than twice as high—for blacks (National Center for Health Statistics, 1992). Consistently for a number of years, black babies have been twice as likely to die in the first year of life as white babies. Among American Indians, the rate is slightly lower than among African Americans—13.5 in 1984–1986 (National Center for Health Statistics, 1992).

In addition to living shorter lives and experiencing a greater risk of infant death, African Americans experience more illness on the average than whites. In 1989, African Americans experienced an average of 17.1 days of restricted activity because of acute illnesses, compared with 15.0 days for whites. Hispanics, on the other hand, experienced an average of 13.2 days of restricted activity, fewer than either blacks or whites (U.S. Bureau of the Census, 1992c).

SUMMARY AND CONCLUSION

In this chapter we have seen that very serious racial and ethnic inequalities remain in the United States. It is true that racial and ethnic prejudice and discrimination have decreased a good deal since three decades ago, though they most certainly have not disappeared. It is also true that more African Americans and Latinos today have attained middle-class status, and some are wealthy and/or highly educated. There are, however, still large segments of the black, Hispanic, and American Indian populations that have not shared in that progress and that are trapped at the bottom of the socioeconomic ladder. For them, things are not getting better; indeed, in many regards, conditions are getting worse (Wilson, 1987; Massey and Denton, 1993). Consequently, the overall position of the minority population remains one of substantial disadvantage. In some aspects of the quality of life, the gap between the minority populations as a whole and the white population has narrowed only slightly, if at all. In a few aspects, such as life expectancy, the gap has actually widened in the last few years.

The facts in this chapter carry some important implications about the social forces influencing majority–minority relations in America today. Considering that deliberate discrimination has decreased, though not disappeared, it would appear that *open and deliberate* acts of discrimination are not as important as they once were as causes of continuing racial and ethnic inequality *today*. To a great extent, today's continuing intergroup inequality is the result of two factors. The first is the continuing effects of past discrimination. This has left a large portion of the minority population—particularly the "underclass," which is near or below the poverty level—without the resources necessary to enjoy a reasonable level of living or to offer their children much chance for upward mobility. The second factor involves a host of institutional, social, and economic processes that have the *effect* (though often not the intention) of maintaining and sometimes worsening the racial and ethnic inequalities in our society. These processes, which are the legacy of past discrimination and exploitation, impact on the underclass particularly heavily. Because these processes are so institutionalized and because some advantaged segments of the population benefit from them, there is frequently fierce resistance to any attempts to alter them in a way that would bring about greater equality. These institutional, social, and economic processes are a major concern of the remainder of this book.

10

The American Economic System and the Status of Minority Groups Today

As we have seen, a sizable gap remains between the average economic position of white people in America today and that of minority groups—most notably blacks, Indians, and Hispanic Americans. For some—particularly the younger, college-educated segments of the minority population—the racial disparity has decreased. Nonetheless, if we look at minority populations *as a whole,* the economic disparity is evident and not even greatly reduced from the past. A major part of this—discussed in greater detail in the previous chapter—is the existence within the minority population of a large, impoverished, and underemployed or unemployed underclass. More than one-fourth of the Latino population and about one-third of the African American population and Native American population have incomes below the federal poverty level. A smaller but sizable portion of each of these groups experiences the chronic, persistent poverty and unemployment characteristic of the underclass.

It is also highly significant that minority groups have been excluded from ownership or control of the major means of production in today's complex corporate economy. America's productive capacity today is overwhelmingly in the hands of a relatively small number of very large national or multinational corporations, exemplified by those included in the *Fortune 500*. Both the ownership and control of these organizations is in the hands of a relatively small elite, from which minority group members have been almost totally excluded. If, for example, we examine ownership of the corporations, we may think at first that ownership is fairly dispersed among the population. A great many Americans own corporate stock, including most certainly thousands of black and Latino Americans. Most of them, however, own only a small amount of stock. The great bulk of stock is owned by a small number of stockholders, and they are both very wealthy and overwhelmingly white. Recent studies have found that just 12 percent of the population owns between two-thirds and 90 percent of all corporate stock (U.S. Bureau of the Census, 1986c; Institute for Social Research, 1987). The majority of all wealth other than cars and houses is owned by just 5 percent of the U.S. population (Oliver and Shapiro, 1990). Precise data on stock ownership by race or ethnicity are not available, but the data just mentioned are instructive: Very few blacks, Latinos, or Indians fall in the very high income levels in which most of the corporate stock is owned. Thus, it appears safe to conclude that only a very small proportion of America's total corporate wealth is in the hands of minority-group members.

While corporate ownership is overwhelmingly white, minorities have found it difficult in the United States to attain ownership of even more commonplace forms of wealth such as houses. A recent study showed, for example, that the average white household in the United States is eleven times as wealthy as the average black household (National Research Council, 1989; Oliver and Shapiro, 1990). A major reason for this is that whites are far more likely to own their homes than African Americans. The 1990 census revealed, for example, that 67.5 percent of white Americans own their homes, compared with only 42.4 percent of blacks and 39 percent of Hispanics (U.S. Bureau of the Census, 1992a). Since owning a home is the major source of wealth for most households, these differences in homeownership add up to a huge gap in ownership of wealth. The Oliver and Shapiro (1990) study showed, for example, that one out of three African American households has zero or negative net worth, compared with just one out of ten white households.

Similarly, very few minority-group members are in positions of true power in the major corporations. As recently as 1970, a study by Egerton found *no* black senior executives or members of boards of directors among the nation's twenty-five largest industrial corporations, or among the largest retailing companies, transportation companies, and utilities, and just a handful among the largest banks and insurance companies. A study of five thousand positions on boards of directors and other positions of authority in 1976 found just fifteen blacks (Dye, 1979). During the 1970s, the number of blacks in such positions grew somewhat, but a recent study by Abraham Nad (reported in *Jet,* 1993a) found that among 801 large corporations, the combined percentage of blacks and Latinos on boards of directors was only 3 percent, the same as in 1987. About 2.3 percent were black; only 0.6 percent were Latino; however, the Latinos who were present had somewhat more prominent board seats than the blacks. These findings are particularly striking, considering that a very few prominent blacks serve on several different corporate boards. On the whole, it is not an overstatement to say that minority group members have been almost totally excluded from the boards of directors and senior executive positions that form the center of power in the corporate structure.

THE ECONOMICS OF DISCRIMINATION: THREE THEORIES

Because major racial inequalities persist in the area of economics, it is important to try to answer the question, What causes economic inequality or discrimination? In this section, we shall discuss and evaluate three major theories about the economics of discrimination.

Gary Becker's Theory

The first major effort to construct an economic theory of discrimination was made by Gary Becker (1957). Becker drew on some important insights from both the social-psychological and functionalist perspectives on race and ethnic relations. His starting point is that some people have a "taste for discrimination"—what we have called conative prejudice. This taste for discrimination on the part of employers, employees, or potential customers results in minority group members not being hired, or not being hired for certain (usually better) jobs. In effect, a *choice* is made to discriminate either because of the employer's prejudice or because of his or her concerns about the reactions of white employees or customers.

Such discrimination in hiring, however, is *dysfunctional* for both the employer and the society as a whole, because it stands in the way of getting the best-qualified employee. This harms the productivity or efficiency of both the employer's enterprise and of the society at large, and it wastes valuable human resources. It also, of course, directly harms minority workers, who end up underemployed, underpaid, or unemployed. The only potential beneficiaries are the white workers who get better jobs and more pay than they would in a rational, nondiscriminatory hiring system. Even they, however, are negatively affected by the lower overall productivity of the system.

Becker's theory implies that over the long run, discrimination in a complex industrial society should gradually disappear because it is dysfunctional both for the employer and for the overall society. Accordingly, firms that do not discriminate should gain a competitive advantage over those that do (Welch, 1967; Arrow, 1972; Masters, 1975). We would therefore expect the discriminatory firms to either stop discriminating or go out of business, with the overall result being a gradual reduction in the amount of discrimination.

In actual fact, this has happened, but only to a rather limited degree. Open, deliberate policies and acts of discrimination have become illegal over the past forty years and have become less common. However, less visible forms of discrimination, both intentional and unintentional, continue to occur. Kirschenman and Neckerman (1991) found substantial evidence of discrimination against blacks, particularly black males, in their study of Chicago-area employers. Much of this discrimination was based on stereotypes about black workers. Similarly, studies in which black and white testers, comparable in all regards except race, seek employment have found discrimination against blacks by employers and employment agencies (ABC News, 1991). White job seekers are told that jobs are available, while black job seekers are told that there are no openings. In addition, employers and employment agencies often interact differently with black and white applicants, lecturing the former but not the latter about laziness, drug use, and so forth. Testing studies have also shown discrimination against Latino job applicants (Bendick et al., 1993). In part because of discrimination such as this, the overall amount of economic racial inequality remains substantial.

In a critical evaluation of Becker's theory, we must also question the central role Becker attributes to *attitudes*. While studies such as Kirschenman and Neckerman's show that attitudes do frequently underlie discrimination, many other things besides attitudes can result in discriminatory practices and arrangements. We saw in earlier chapters that attitudes are often only weakly linked to discrimination. Economic motivations and pressures from workers and customers may be at least as important as a "taste for discrimination" in causing discrimination. We now turn our attention to two conflict theories that stress just that point: Perceived economic gain can motivate people to discriminate, whether they are prejudiced or not.

Split Labor Market Theory

One answer to the latter criticism of Becker's theory may be found in another theory of the economics of discrimination known as split labor market theory (Bonacich, 1972, 1975, 1976; W. J. Wilson, 1978; see also Blumer, 1965). This theory notes some of the same patterns as Becker's theory but attributes them to social structure rather than to individual preferences. It is a form of conflict theory in that it sees discrimination as a result of the clash of competing interest groups.

This model, unlike Becker's, argues that the business owner or capitalist *recognizes* that racial discrimination is dysfunctional for the business enterprise, and thus often prefers *not* to discriminate. The objective of the capitalist is to get the best worker for the cheapest wage, and it is therefore in the capitalist's interest *not* to discriminate, because discrimination limits the pool of workers available for the position. Accordingly, those doing the hiring discriminate not because they have a taste for discrimination but rather because they are forced or pressured to do so by another interest group that does benefit from discrimination. This interest group is white laborers. In the view of this theory, discrimination is the interest of white laborers because it insulates them from potential competition from minority-group workers. Accordingly, white workers, if they are powerful enough to do so, demand the exclusion of minority-group workers from certain more desirable jobs (or from industrial jobs altogether), in effect creating a system of "white jobs" with high pay and "black jobs" or "Latino jobs" with low pay.

In such a split labor market, the cost of white labor is higher than the cost of minority labor, still another reason why nondiscrimination would be in the interest of the employer or capitalist. But this is also largely why higher-paid white labor demands discrimination: Discrimination keeps white workers' wages high by protecting them from the competition of lower-paid minority labor. Higher-paid white labor may be able to impose a system of discrimination in a number of ways. It might prevent minority group labor from obtaining skills by demanding educational discrimination. It might seek to exclude minority group members from a territory entirely: If they cannot move into an area, they cannot compete (W. J. Wilson, 1978, p. 7). It may also attempt to keep minority laborers out of its segment of the labor market by, for example, keeping them out of labor unions. Exclusion of blacks from labor unions was commonplace in the United States before World War II (Wesley, 1927, pp. 254–281; Bonacich, 1975, p. 38). Brody (1960, p. 186) has also documented that in 1917 several steel firms refused to hire blacks because they were afraid of the reaction of white workers. In another part of the world, the system of apartheid in South Africa had its roots partially in the demands of white labor unions for the exclusion of black workers during the 1920s (Van der Horst, 1967, pp. 117–118; Wilson, 1973, p. 168).

Apparently, such strategies were effective for white laborers, at least in the short run (Marshall, 1965, pp. 22–23); over the long run, however, one must question their effectiveness: A frequent consequence of such discrimination was to so antagonize black laborers that they acted as strikebreakers, greatly weakening the position of the white workers' labor unions. This was especially common during the

1920s (Bonacich, 1976, p. 40; W. J. Wilson, 1978, p. 74), and it contributed significantly to the weakening of labor unions during that period (W. J. Wilson, 1978, p. 76). Thus, split labor market theory, too, appears to have some limitations, or at the very least, to describe some periods of history better than others.

Marxist Theory

A third theory, arising from a general Marxist perspective, differs from both theories we have examined thus far. It shares one element in common with split labor market theory: It is a conflict theory arguing that racial discrimination in employment is the result of the clash of competing interest groups. However, it disagrees with both of the other theories on who gains and who loses as a result of discrimination. Recall that both Becker's theory and the split labor market theory argue that white laborers gain and employers or capitalists lose as a result of discrimination. Marxist theory argues precisely the opposite: Employers or capitalists gain and white workers lose as a result of discrimination (Baran and Sweezy, 1966; Reich, 1986). This is mainly because racial antagonisms divide workers and thereby weaken their power relative to that of employers. A prime example can be seen in the strikebreaking of the early twentieth century. White unions excluded blacks, and blacks responded by acting as strikebreakers when the whites went on strike.[1] The consequence was the weakening of unions and lower wages for both blacks and whites. Eventually, many unions realized this (particularly the industrial unions of the CIO) and, with some encouragement from the Roosevelt administration, altered their policies to oppose discrimination. Reich (1986) argues that the theory continues to be relevant today, as conflicts over school busing and neighborhood racial change have mainly involved working-class blacks and whites (see also Anderson, 1990; Rieder, 1985). The consequence, according to Reich, is that working-class whites and blacks see each other as the enemy. Consequently, they fail to recognize their common self-interests and are unable to cooperate with each other to influence the political system or to protect their common self-interests against the opposing self-interests of their employers or, more generally, the wealthy elite.

A key assumption underlying Marxist theory is that class divisions have more to do with how well people live than do divisions between racial and ethnic groups. Thus, argue Marxists, the working class and the poor are disadvantaged relative to other groups regardless of their race. Race becomes significant in that it is used by the wealthy and powerful to divide the working class and the poor. Thus, if lower-income blacks and whites, for example, blame one another for their troubles, neither will challenge the wealth of the upper classes, and both will consequently remain poor. Hence, race becomes a means by which class inequality is perpetuated, allowing the wealthy to maintain their disproportionate wealth and income.

A Note on Internal Colonialism Theory.   Another conflict theory, which challenges Marxist theory's emphasis on the primacy of class divisions, is internal colonialism theory, discussed in Chapter 6. Internal colonialism theory views racial

---

[1]It is important, however, to note that this was not the *only* reason for black strikebreaking. Many did so out of desperation, and some took jobs in distant areas without being told that they were breaking a strike until they arrived at the job site. Of course, many whites were also strikebreakers, and most blacks never worked as strikebreakers.

divisions—particularly those between the dominant group and colonized minorities—as more important than class divisions, arguing that anyone in a colonized minority is at a potential disadvantage because, regardless of class, they are subject to discrimination and exploitation (Mirande, 1987). Moreover, proponents of this theory point out that entire groups, such as Native Americans and African Americans, have been made to suffer as a result of economic exploitation by the dominant group. Like Marxists and split labor market theorists, internal colonialism theorists believe that discrimination exists because someone benefits from it. Specifically, they hold that colonized minorities are exploited for the benefit of people in the dominant group. They do not, however, directly address the question of *who* within the dominant group benefits. Thus, internal colonialism theory is not directly relevant to the debate between Marxist and split labor market theories over who within the dominant group gains from racial discrimination. For this reason among others, the main discussion of internal colonialism theory appears in Chapter 6 rather than here.

Evaluating Theories About the Economics of Discrimination

Gary Becker's theory, split labor market theory, and Marxist theory each offer a different reason for the existence of economic racial and ethnic discrimination. According to Becker, discrimination occurs because some people have a taste for discrimination—in other words the cause lies in people's attitudes. According to split labor market theory, discrimination occurs because white workers benefit from it by eliminating minority competition. According to Marxist theory, discrimination occurs because capitalists benefit from the divisions it creates in the working class, which weaken the bargaining position of workers and lead black and white workers to blame each other rather than the capitalist class for their difficulties. With three such different explanations, who is right?

It would seem that, under different social conditions, each of the three theories can be correct. Discrimination *can* result from prejudiced attitudes, particularly when the culture is supportive. Certainly a culture that favored prejudice and discrimination led some employers to discriminate, regardless of the economic consequences, in the "Old South." Another example can be found in a personal experience of the author while conducting interviews in a survey of employers in the Detroit area in 1972. One plant owner claimed that if the government told him he had to hire a certain number of blacks (at the time, he had no black employees), he would simply close the plant and go out of business. It is hard to conclude that this employer was acting mainly on the basis of calculating his possible gains: He simply had a very strong opinion that made him willing (or so he said) to go out of business rather than change.

In other cases, however, individual attitudes are probably not the major cause of discriminatory behavior. We have noted cases in which pressures from white labor did cause employers to discriminate, and when white labor was able to effectively control the hiring process, the strategy appears to have worked. Marshall (1965, pp. 22–23) notes certain strong craft unions that were able to keep blacks out were able to maintain high wages and high membership during a period in the 1920s when most unions were losing ground. However, most unions do not have enough control over hiring to make such a strategy work. Both Reich (1986) and W. J. Wilson (1978, p. 78) have noted that in recent years, the one main element of white la-

This girl has suffered brain damage from eating lead-based paint. Lead poisoning is a common problem among children of impoverished families in urban areas. Sociologists of the conflict perspective believe that such poverty and suffering exists because, somewhere in the social system, some more advantaged group of people is benefitting from it. *United Nations/W.A. Graham*

bor that has been able to use discrimination to its advantage is the craft unions such as the building trades, which control hiring through the union hiring hall. A study by Mladenka (1991) has shown a second situation in which this can occur: In some cities, municipal labor unions have, in effect, largely kept blacks out of city employment. His study also showed, however, that this occurred only in unreformed city governments, those in which the unions were powerful enough to influence who got hired.

The majority of workers, however, do not have such control over hiring, and in these cases, Marxist theory may offer the best explanation of the causes and consequences of race discrimination. Racial divisions were disastrous for many unions during the 1920s, and since that time most unions (particularly industrywide unions such as the United Auto Workers) have taken an official stance against racial prejudice and discrimination. (Of course, white members do not always go along with the official position.)

There is also evidence that racial divisions continue to harm the economic position of the working and lower classes today. As we have seen, prejudice is strongest among these groups, at least by the usual measures of attitudes about intergroup relations. Social organizers, moreover, frequently lament the degree to which racial divisions keep poor blacks, whites, Latinos, and others from recognizing a common interest. Some empirical light is shed on the issue in a study by Reich (1981, 1986). Reich examined 1960 and 1970 census data on the forty-eight largest metropolitan areas in the Untied States. For each area, he determined the ratio of median black family income to median white family income as a measure of economic *racial* inequality or discrimination. He also obtained two measures of income inequality within the white population. His interesting finding was that where black–white inequality or discrimination was great, income within the white population was indeed more concentrated: The wealthier segment had higher income and the poorer segment lower income than in areas with less racial inequality. In Reich's judgment, this finding supports the theory that wealthy whites and employers benefit from racism and the less wealthy and working-class whites are hurt by it. Reich concludes that discrimination is largely a product of capitalism because it serves the interests of the dominant economic class in that system. There are, however, other possible interpretations of Reich's findings. All his variables could be measuring the same thing: the overall amount of inequality in an area, an inequality that falls along both class and racial lines. Accordingly, Reich's study should be seen as one piece of evidence supporting the Marxist theory of discrimination, not conclusive proof of it. Regardless of this, it does appear true that one of the major effects of discrimination is to create divisions that potentially weaken the bargaining position of the working class.

Studies by Glenn (1963, 1966), Dowdall (1974), and Farley (1987b) shed further light on the question and seem to support the view that both the Marxist and split labor market interpretations may be correct depending on the situation. These studies showed that, given the level of discrimination in American society, whites in areas with *more* blacks enjoyed higher occupational status, income, and/or employment rates. To the degree that this was true because blacks took the burden of unemployment and underpaid work, freeing whites for better jobs (and not being in much of a position to compete for those better jobs), the results would appear to support the split labor market theory. On the other hand, Dowdall (1974, p. 182) argues that the findings support Marxist theory, in that it seems to be those at the top who benefit most from discrimination. Finally, it must be pointed out that the findings do not directly bear on the question of who within the dominant group would be better off with or without discrimination. They merely show that, *taking discrimination as a given*, the dominant group appears to come out better off when large numbers of subordinate group members are present.

A more direct test of the effects of discrimination on the overall white population is provided by Szymanski (1976). Szymanski showed that in states with relatively high racial inequality in income, whites (1) had *lower* average incomes and (2) had a more *unequal* income distribution. This was especially true for those states with larger-than-average minority populations. This relationship was explained only partially by region; Szymanski's data indicated that the main reason for the pattern was that unions were weaker in states with great racial inequality. Similarly, Reich (1981, 1986) found that as income inequality between blacks and whites increased, white workers' wages decreased, and employers' profits increased. Like Szymanski, Reich found unions to be weaker in areas with greater racial inequality. These findings provide significant support for the Marxist theory of the economics of discrimination.

Even so, there is still room for debate. A study by Beck (1980), for example, found that comparisons made over time rather than across places suggest that to some degree the economy operates according to the split labor market model. Beck's study showed that comparing different points in time from 1947 to 1974, periods of relatively high unionization were accompanied by high black–white inequality, and vice versa. However, part of Beck's findings may result from the fact that changes in the job structure toward white-collar jobs have both reduced unionization and, as Wilson (1978) argues, opened new opportunities for the expansion of a black middle class.

Finally, we should mention a newer, emerging viewpoint among some sociologists and economists that the minority underclass is now so far out of the economic mainstream that it is almost irrelevant to the economic welfare of whites. In this view, the black and Hispanic underclass is so chronically unemployed and so completely excluded from opportunities to learn job skills that it can neither threaten the jobs of employed whites nor be used by employers to divide the white working class (Willhelm, 1980; see also Wilson, 1978, especially pp. 151–153, 1987). This observation probably has merit if one speaks strictly of the underclass, but several related points need to be made. First, not more than one-third of the black population and a smaller share of the Hispanic population can be considered part of the underclass, so the majorities of the black and Hispanic populations are anything but irrelevant economically. Second, if white workers *perceive* minorities as a threat— which they may well do during periods of relatively high unemployment—they may demand discrimination, even though discrimination may in reality raise corporate profits at the expense of white workers' wages. It is the perception, not the reality, that determines how people behave.

Discrimination and Economic Productivity

We conclude our discussion of theories about the economics of discrimination by returning to one idea raised in Becker's theory: Discrimination hurts the overall productivity of society. While we have thus far mainly emphasized debates about what interest groups get a bigger or smaller share of the pie as a result of discrimination, it is important to note that discrimination does reduce the size of the pie. This economic impact of discrimination arises in part from employment discrimination, which directly keeps minority-group members from contributing to the productivity of the economy. However, it also arises indirectly from racial inequality in the educational process, which can keep minority-group members from developing the skills they need to contribute to that productivity. By the early 1990s, 32 percent of children and 25 percent of the working-age U.S. population were people of color: African American, Latino, Asian American, or Native American (O'Hare, 1992). By about 2040—just forty-five years from now—it is projected that 53 percent of children and 44 percent of working-aged adults will be people of color. How well we educate this emerging majority and how well its members are given the opportunity to use their skills in the workplace in a productive manner will have a huge effect on the productivity of the U.S. economy in the next half century. Already, a number of countries have surpassed the United States in productivity. If the United States continues to relegate a large part of its black and Hispanic population to unemployment or underemployment and does not do a better job of developing high-tech skills in its minority population, this gap could easily widen. A number of studies and reports have warned about this risk, ranging from the *Workforce 2000* report (U.S. Department of Labor, 1987) to academic studies such as Schwartz and Disch's (1975) *White Racism: Its History, Pathology, and Practice.* The latter uses the example of Latinos to point out that if people are not allowed to develop and use their skills, productivity is hurt and, in addition, costs are imposed on society in the form of poverty and the social problems it brings. Thus, quite independent of whether or not some interest groups gain from discrimination, there is strong evidence that the society as a whole loses.

RECENT TRENDS AND THEIR EFFECTS ON RACIAL ECONOMIC INEQUALITY

Whatever the underlying causes of racial economic discrimination may be, there are some things we know about (1) the mechanisms that maintain racial economic inequality today and (2) the effects of recent social trends on patterns of economic inequality and discrimination along the lines of race. In the remainder of this chapter, these two closely related issues will be the focus of our concern.

Rising Educational Demands and the Employment of Minorities

As we have seen, the expansion of white-collar jobs has created the opportunity for a sizable minority middle class to develop. However, this expansion—because of the increase in educational requirements for employment that have accompanied it—has also created problems for a large segment of the minority population. These problems have been aggravated by the tendency of employers to demand higher levels of education for jobs, whether or not the education is actually needed for the job. The tendency of employers to make such demands increases as the average educational level of the population increases, as it has over the past few decades. It also increases during periods of high unemployment—and unemployment has been relatively high since the late 1960s. For a variety of reasons, an employer may want to hire a person with more education than is necessary to do the job. One very important factor—which will be discussed at greater length in a later chapter—is that employers frequently seek to hire workers with cultural values and work habits similar to their own. Thus, they prefer more-educated employees not because these employees know more about the job, but because they will "fit in" better.

This practice, though usually not deliberately racist, does end up being racist in its *consequences.* As we have seen, average educational levels among blacks, Latinos, and American Indians are well below the average educational level of whites. When more education is demanded than the job requires, many people quite capable of doing the job are excluded (Berg, 1971), and a disproportionate number of them are members of minority groups. Thus, inflated educational requirements can be identified as one cause of the relatively high levels of unemployment and poverty among the black, Hispanic, and American Indian populations. Considered along with the increase in jobs that *do* actually require higher educational levels and the reduction automation has effected in the number of unskilled jobs, this tendency helps to explain why the black unemployment rate rose to twice as high as the white unemployment rate after World War II and has been at least that high ever since.

In principle, practices that have the effect of discrimination, such as unnecessary education requirements, were recently banned by the 1991 Civil Rights Act. This law, which was passed in large part to reverse several Supreme Court decisions in the 1980s that made it harder for minorities to sue for job discrimination, also expanded the rights of minorities, women, and the disabled to take legal action against discriminatory policies and actions in the workplace. Specifically, it guarantees such groups the right to take legal action against requirements, such as educational requirements and strength requirements, that have the effect of discriminating, unless employers can show that the requirements are "job-related for the position in question and consistent with business necessity." The extent to which this legislation will actually prevent employers from engaging in practices that are discriminatory in effect but not intent remains to be seen and will probably depend on how many discrimination cases are brought under the law and how the courts interpret it.

Job Decentralization and Housing Segregation

As we have seen, the majority of black Americans and about half of Hispanic Americans live in the central cities of metropolitan areas—compared with only a little more than a quarter of the white population. The black and Latino populations became increasingly concentrated in the central cities between World War II and the 1970s.

During the same period and continuing into the 1980s and 1990s, however, employment opportunities have been moving *out* of those central cities. This is true for business and retail-sales jobs as well as for the industrial jobs that have been especially important as a source of relatively high paying jobs for blacks and Latinos. This is especially true for the larger metropolitan areas, which are the home of a disproportionate share of blacks and Latinos (Sternlieb and Hughes, 1976, p. 30). While the number of jobs has simply stopped growing in some of the smaller cities, it has actually fallen in many of the larger cities and in some smaller ones with large minority populations. New York City, for example, lost 600,000 jobs between 1970 and 1980, and Chicago lost 200,000 (Wilson, 1981). East St. Louis, Illinois, a relatively small industrial city that is overwhelmingly black, lost over half of its manufacturing jobs between 1950 and 1970 (Illinois Capital Development Board, 1977). Nationally, between 1947 and 1967, manufacturing employment in central cities declined by 4 percent; it rose by 94 percent in the suburbs during the same period. A similar movement to the suburbs can be seen in wholesale and retail trade (Barabba, 1976, p. 56).

The rate of overall job loss declined in some central cities during the 1980s, but in most cities there was a major shift away from the higher-paying industrial jobs that had been an economic mainstay for many blacks and Hispanics (particularly males) and toward much-lower-paying service jobs. The city of Chicago, for example, lost about 50,000 jobs between the 1977 and 1987 economic censuses—still a large number, but a considerably slower rate of loss than in the 1970s. However, there was a dramatic shift in the kinds of jobs available in the city, with about 90,000 fewer manufacturing jobs and about 80,000 more service jobs. Service jobs, however, pay only a small fraction of what manufacturing jobs pay, so the shift from manufacturing to service employment in the city contributed to the further impoverishment of Chicago's African American and Latino populations (Wilson, 1987, forthcoming). Chicago is typical in that only service jobs grew in the city. Between 1977 and 1987, the city lost more than 20,000 wholesale-trade jobs and nearly 25,000 retail-trade jobs.

While jobs continued to disappear in the city of Chicago, they continued to grow in the suburbs and fringe areas, which are overwhelmingly white. In the portion of the Chicago consolidated metropolitan statistical area outside the city, the number of jobs grew by about 150,000 between 1977 and 1987, even as it fell by about 50,000 in the city. This shift to the suburbs harms minority group members because, just as they are overrepresented in the central cities, they are underrepresented in the suburbs. The net effect is to take jobs out of areas where blacks and Latinos live and to move those jobs into areas where white Anglos live. Because a sizable segment of the urban minority population cannot afford to own an automobile and many cities lack adequate mass transportation, many minority workers cannot get employment unless they can move to the areas that are gaining the employment opportunities. Patterns of housing segregation, however, frequently make this impossible, restricting minorities to areas with increasingly fewer jobs. Studies of St. Louis, Chicago, Cleveland, and Detroit, for example, indicate that housing segregation has kept the numbers of blacks in the suburbs far below what would be expected on the basis of the black and white income distributions.[2] Over and above the restrictions resulting from housing discrimination, the high costs of moving and the exclusionary zoning practices make it even more difficult for lower-income minority people—the ones most in need of decent employment—to move to where the jobs are.

Although the evidence is mixed, several studies suggest that these factors are an important cause of high black unemployment. Research by Kain (1968) in Chicago and Detroit indicates that housing segregation in those cities may have cost black workers 25,000 jobs in Chicago and 9,000 in Detroit. Limited access to jobs also was identified as an important cause of black unemployment in studies by Mooney (1969), Hutchinson (1974), and Shanahan (1976). Studies by the author (Farley, 1981, 1987b) using data from all U.S. metropolitan areas showed that black and Hispanic unemployment in 1970 and 1980 was higher relative to white unemployment in areas where black and Hispanic populations were more concentrated in the central city, and where jobs were more suburbanized. In 1980, this remained true even after adjustment for racial differences in education. Moreover, research by Kasarda (1989a, 1989b, 1990) indicates that minority group members living in the central city have higher unemployment rates than minorities in the suburbs, and as increasing numbers of jobs have left the city, this gap has widened. These studies and others (e.g., Lichter, 1988) all indicate that today's high unemployment rates among blacks and Hispanics are in part the result of this growing geographic mismatch between where job opportunities are available and where most blacks and Hispanics live. The effects are particularly great for black and Hispanic males, many of whom once relied on manufacturing jobs for good-paying, stable employment. Today, many or most of those jobs have been eliminated or relocated out of the central city.

---

[2]These studies are discussed in detail later in this chapter.

Clearly, the movement of jobs from minority neighborhoods and the inability of these workers either to commute to distant jobs or to live near those jobs constitute one more major handicap imposed on many urban blacks and Latinos. Even if there were little or no deliberate racial discrimination on the part of employers, the result of the increasing separation of minority neighborhoods from areas with job openings may still be fewer opportunities for blacks and Latinos to obtain meaningful employment. Until recently, the main focus of research on geographic mismatches between minority populations and job opportunities has concerned disparities between cities and suburbs. Research now indicates that a similar pattern may be developing within suburbia: As black neighborhoods have developed and grown in suburban areas, job growth has tended to be greater in predominantly white suburbs than in suburbs with sizable black populations (Schneider and Phelan, 1990). If this pattern continues to develop, it may eventually place many suburban minority populations in a situation similar to their counterparts in the central cities: They may face rising unemployment because of separation from the areas that have the most job openings.

In addition to suburbanizing, manufacturing is also moving to rural areas, it is moving away from the Midwest and Northeast where it was once central to the economic base, and to some extent it is moving out of the United States to other countries where wages are much lower. These tendencies probably are hurting minorities disproportionately. Relatively few blacks or Latinos live in rural areas today, and Native Americans, though highly rural, do not benefit either, because they live on reservations far from the places where industries are relocating. Some jobs have shifted from the Midwest and Northeast into the South in recent decades, but the large African American population in the South has not benefited much from this shift: Industries that have relocated to the South have tended to locate in predominantly white areas, either in the suburbs or in rural areas (Thompson, 1976, p. 190; Firestine, 1977).

There is little doubt that job shifts in recent decades have resulted in reduced opportunities for minority group members. This pattern raises two important questions: Why have these changes detrimental to minority group members happened? What, if anything, can minority group members do to minimize the effects on them of these job shifts?

Reasons for Job Shifts.   There are numerous reasons why employment opportunities have moved out of central cities and into suburbs and rural areas. Some have absolutely nothing to do with race or ethnicity; others, however, suggest at least some race consciousness on the part of corporate decisionmakers.

One reason for the decentralization of manufacturing is that modern manufacturing is more efficient in sprawling, one-level factory complexes than in the once typical multistory factory. The one-story complexes require much more land than the old factories, and this land is available and affordable only in urban fringe areas and in rural areas. Nonetheless, the movement to rural and suburban areas would probably never have happened without the development of truck transportation and the interstate highway system. Because transportation is crucial to manufacturing, it was at one time necessary for industry to locate on a major waterway, at or near a rail junction, or both. Generally, this meant locating in a major city. Today, however, most industries can locate wherever there is an interstate highway, since much more shipping is done by truck. It is significant that the greatest growth in manufacturing activity and in population in rural areas has been in counties through which an interstate highway passes.

Other factors, however, may be more directly linked to race and ethnicity. Some movement is probably the result of prejudices and fears on the part of whites that make them reluctant to keep their businesses in predominantly black or Hispanic areas (Kirschenman, 1989, 1990; Kirschenman and Neckerman, 1991). Some employers have also complained about the work habits and lifestyle of inner-city employees, which may be significantly different from their own. Finally, some of the movement seems aimed at avoiding unionization, and in some cases, this probably means deliberately avoiding black areas. In the South, particularly, white workers are less prounion than black workers, and this may be one reason that companies moving to the South largely locate in white areas (Thompson, 1976, p. 190).

The movement of retail and wholesale trade to the suburbs appears largely to be the result of the movement of population—especially the wealthier (and mostly white) population with money to spend—to the suburbs. Fear of crime and the reluctance of white shoppers to shop in minority neighborhoods may also be a factor in the decentralization of these businesses.

Whatever the *intent* of those who decide to relocate business and industry out of central cities, the *result* clearly contributes to racial inequality by taking jobs out of the areas where minorities live and putting them into the areas where whites live. In the following section, we shall examine the alternatives available to minorities to adjust to this changing distribution of job opportunities.

Adjustment to Job Shifts. Two responses appear possible that might enable minority-group members to adjust to the shifting distribution of employment opportunities. One response would be increased commuting from city to suburb. Undoubtedly, some minority workers have responded in this way, but a great many others cannot. Only a few American cities have rapid-transit systems sufficient to permit such commuting by public transit, and for many minority group members, private transportation is simply not an alternative. A surprising number of minority group members cannot afford to own an automobile. In 1989, more than 43 percent of all families composed of people of color had *no* motor vehicle—up from about 35 percent in 1983 (U.S. Bureau of the Census, 1993, p. 476). Among those who do have cars, the cost of gasoline sometimes limits the feasibility of long-distance commuting.

The other alternative is to move to the areas where the jobs are located. In fact, a recent study in which impoverished black women were given an opportunity to relocate from the central city to subsidized housing in the suburbs showed that relocation produced significant improvements in employment rates (Rosenbaum and Popkin, 1991). The cost of moving to the suburbs is often prohibitive, however. Furthermore, restrictive zoning and public opposition to low-income housing have largely kept the minority poor out of the suburbs. There has been some increased migration of blacks to the suburbs in recent years, but much of it has been into "suburban ghettos," large concentrations of black population, mostly in the older parts of the suburbs, which are also losing employment opportunities. Much of it, too, has involved those blacks who have already attained middle-class status and are least in need of employment opportunities.

Probably the most important factor keeping minorities from moving to follow jobs, however, is the pervasive pattern of discrimination and segregation in housing. This issue is of such importance, both in and of itself and as a factor potentially reducing minority employment opportunities, that we shall discuss it separately in the next section.

Shifts in Job Type. Before turning to housing segregation, however, we must point out one additional trend. In addition to the movement of jobs, there are certain types of employment in which jobs have simply disappeared. This has been the case most clearly in heavy manufacturing and has happened for three reasons. First, manufacturing jobs had been lost to international competition. Second, U.S. multinational corporations have moved manufacturing jobs to foreign countries. Third, jobs have been eliminated by automation. The impacts of these trends have been greatest on blacks and Hispanics because these groups have been highly specialized in manufacturing employment. Thus, the kinds of jobs held by blacks and Hispanics are the most likely jobs to disappear (Wilson, 1987).

Let us now turn our attention to housing segregation, which elevates minority unemployment by largely excluding minorities from the areas where jobs are available.

HOUSING DISCRIMINATION AND SEGREGATION

When sociologists talk about housing segregation, they are referring to the tendency for people in any two groups or races to live in separate areas. When, for example, all the blacks in a city live in one neighborhood or set of neighborhoods and all the whites live in other neighborhoods, we would have a highly segregated situation. Sociologists have a number of measures of residential segregation, but probably the most widely used is the *index of dissimilarity,* sometimes called the *segregation index.* This index can range from 0 to 100, with 0 being no segregation and 100 being total segregation. This measure is based on city blocks or urban neighborhood areas called *census tracts.* For any two groups, such as blacks and whites, the segregation index tells us what percentage of a city's black *or* white population would have to move to another block or census tract to have no segregation at all.

Housing Segregation Between Blacks and Whites

This measure has been computed for every U.S. metropolitan area and for every city with a population over fifty thousand using census data from every population census from 1950 through 1990. In 1990, the average black–white segregation index for 219 metropolitan areas in the United States was 62, about the same as in 1980 (*USA Today,* 1991). For those cities for which data from every census from 1960 through 1990 were available, the average segregation index declined from about 76 in 1960 to about 68 in 1990 (Jakubs, 1986; *USA Today,* 1991). Virtually all of this relatively small decline occurred during the 1970s, with little change in levels of segregation during either the 1960s or the 1980s (Van Valey, Roof, and Wilcox, 1977; Jakubs, 1986; Harrison and Weinberg, 1992a, 1992b). These metropolitan areas, which contain the overwhelming majority of the nation's African American population, are, then, about two-thirds of the way toward the segregated end of the scale.

In general, levels of black–white segregation are higher in the Midwest and

Northeast and in larger, older cities with larger black populations (Jakubs, 1986; Massey and Denton, 1987, 1988, 1989; *USA Today,* 1991; Farley and Frey, 1994, 1992; O'Hare, 1992). Regionally, the lowest levels of segregation are found in the West (O'Hare and Usdansky, 1992; Farley and Frey, 1994), reflecting large declines in segregation in many western metropolitan areas during the 1970s. Data for selected metropolitan areas, from 1960 through 1990, are shown in Table 10.1. It should be noted again that these indices are based on census tract data. When segregation indices are computed based on smaller neighborhood areas, such as census blocks or block groups, segregation indices come out even higher. This is because data based on smaller areas permit the detection of patterns of segregation *within* the larger

Table 10.1 Segregation Indexes for Selected Metropolitan Areas, 1960–1990

METROPOLITAN AREA

	1990	*1980*	*1970*	*1960*
Atlanta	71	76.9	81.7	77.1
Birmingham	77	72.5	67.6	64.1
Boston	72	77.1	79.3	80.8
Buffalo	84	80.0	85.7	86.8
Chicago	87	87.2	91.2	91.2
Cincinnati	79	78.1	81.8	83.2
Cleveland	86	87.7	90.2	89.6
Dallas	68	77.5	86.9	81.2
Denver	66	68.5	84.7	84.6
Detroit	89	87.5	88.9	87.1
Indianapolis	78	78.8	83.8	78.7
Little Rock	66	64.2	70.8	65.0
Los Angeles	74	79.1	88.5	89.2
Louisville	73	73.6	82.8	80.4
Milwaukee	84	83.8	89.5	90.4
Newark	84	80.4	78.8	72.8
New Haven	73	69.6	67.0	65.4
New Orleans	72	71.0	74.2	65.0
New York	83	77.5	73.8	74.4
Philadelphia	81	78.3	78.0	77.1
Phoenix	54	59.6	75.4	81.1
Pittsburgh	—	72.9	74.5	74.4
Portland, Oregon	68	68.4	80.2	81.3
Richmond	63	64.4	76.6	74.9
Sacramento	58	55.4	66.1	72.1
St. Louis	80	81.9	86.5	85.9
San Diego	61	61.9	76.2	79.5
San Francisco	66	71.1	77.3	79.4
Seattle	50	67.4	78.1	83.3
Tucson	46	46.6	63.6	73.0

Source: 1960 and 1970 indices reprinted from Thomas L. Van Valey, Wade Clark Roof, and Jerome E. Wilcox, "Trends in Residential Segregation: 1960–1970," *American Journal of Sociology* 82:830–835, by permission of The University of Chicago Press. Copyright 1977 by The University of Chicago. 1980 indices prepared by John F. Jakubs and printed by permission. 1990 indices are from *USA Today,* "By the Numbers: Tracking Segregation in 219 Metro Areas," November 11, 1991, p. 3a.

neighborhoods that form census tracts. In 1990, for example, a study of 232 metropolitan areas using block-group data rather than tract data found an average segregation index of 65 (Farley and Frey, 1994, 1992), three points higher than was obtained in the *USA Today* study, which used census tract data.

As has been noted earlier, one result of housing segregation has been to
largely exclude African Americans from the suburbs. The percentage of African
Americans living in the suburbs rose more during the 1970s and 1980s than in previous decades, reaching nearly twenty-seven percent of the black population by 1990
(U.S. Bureau of the Census, 1992b). However, blacks are still very underrepresented
there relative to whites, about half of whom live in the suburbs. Increased black suburbanization has brought a little more interracial contact, since blacks and whites in
the suburbs are somewhat less segregated from one another than blacks and whites
in the central cities (Hwang and Murdock, 1983; Logan and Schneider, 1984; Farley, 1987c; Massey and Denton, 1988, 1992). Also, research based on the 1990 census indicates that in highly segregated metropolitan areas such as St. Louis, many
neighborhoods that had been all-white became at least minimally integrated (Farley, 1993). Nonetheless, many blacks in suburban areas still live in areas that are ex-
tensions of black neighborhoods in the central city (Farley, 1983; see also Winsberg,
1983).

It is obvious from these data that the level of housing segregation of blacks
and whites in most American cities is quite high and that in many cities there has
been little reduction in the extent of segregation over the past decade or two. How
can this persistence be explained? A number of possible explanations have been offered, and the topic has been researched widely enough to offer some fairly clear answers to some of the questions.

Economic Explanations of Housing Segregation

One explanation frequently offered for racial housing segregation is economic. As we have seen, the black population has a significantly lower average income than the white population. Accordingly, some people have argued that a major reason for housing segregation is that most blacks cannot afford to live in many
of the neighborhoods where whites live. It turns out that it is quite possible to measure the extent to which this is the case. Through use of a measure called *indirect
standardization,* sociologists can estimate quite precisely the number of blacks and
whites that one would *expect* to live in each neighborhood of a city based on the neighborhood's income distribution. From these estimates, it is in turn possible to com-
pute what the segregation index for the city would be if income differences between
blacks and whites were the only reason for housing segregation.

Using house value or rent as a substitute for income, Taeuber and Taeuber
(1965) calculated expected segregation indexes for fifteen major cities using 1960
census data and compared those with the actual segregation indexes. They found
that if economic inequality between blacks and whites had been the *only* reason for
segregation in these cities, the 1960 segregation indexes would have ranged from 8.5
to 30.4 and averaged 20.8. The *actual* segregation indexes for the fifteen cities ranged
from 67.8 to 87.1, and averaged 78.4 (Taeuber and Taeuber, 1965, p. 85). In other
words, if economic inequality had been the only reason for black–white segregation,
there would have been only a little more than one-fourth as much segregation as
there actually was. The continuation of this pattern is illustrated by a study con-

ducted by the author concerning racial segregation in the St. Louis metropolitan area (Farley, 1986). Using the technique of indirect standardization and working with 1980 census data, I computed the number of blacks who would have lived in St. Louis and each of 109 suburbs if differences in housing cost had been the only cause of segregation. These numbers were converted to percentages and compared with the actual percentage of blacks living in the suburbs. The results of this analysis are presented in Table 10.2. Both St. Louis and East St. Louis—an industrial satellite— have far *more* blacks than would be expected on the basis of income. Of the suburbs, 74 have far *fewer* blacks than would be expected. Indeed, 34 have essentially *no* black population—0.5 percent or less—even though based on their *income* distribution, we would expect these suburbs to be 10 percent to 18 percent black. Another 21 suburbs—mostly near the central city's black neighborhoods—had far more blacks than expected. Only 14 of the 109 suburbs had anything near the expected number of blacks. Had housing cost been the only factor influencing where blacks lived, the area's segregation index based on census tract data would have been 19; actually it was 80. More recently, I computed the same data for 1990, and found that if housing cost had been the only factor, the segregation index would have been about 12; actually, it was about 76.

This study, that of Taeuber and Taeuber, and others (see Hermalin and Far-

Table 10.2 Expected (based on housing cost distribution) and Actual Percent Black Population, St. Louis and Suburbs, 1980

AREA	EXPECTED PERCENTAGE OF BLACK HOUSEHOLDERS	ACTUAL PERCENTAGE OF BLACK HOUSEHOLDERS
St. Louis City	27.8	38.1
East St. Louis, IL	27.9	93.4
All suburban counties (excluding East St. Louis)	14.5	7.1
Inner suburban counties	14.5	8.8
Bridgeton	14.2	1.7
Clayton	15.0	0.8
Creve Coeur	10.0	1.4
Fenton	12.2	0.0
Florissant	13.4	1.7
Kinloch	26.0	99.6
Kirkwood	12.6	5.1
Normandy	16.9	29.8
St. Ann	17.5	2.3
University City	16.3	34.8
Webster Groves	11.6	6.4
Alton, IL	18.9	17.1
Belleville, IL	16.2	1.0
Edwardsville, IL	14.5	6.3
Granite City, IL	17.6	0.1
Venice, IL	26.0	66.3
Wood River, IL	16.5	0.1
Segregation index between all suburbs	Expected 10.4	Actual 71.0

Source: Analysis of 1980 census data by the author. Portions of this table appear in Farley, 1986.

ley, 1973; Farley, 1982, pp. 237–38) show clearly that (1) only a small portion, perhaps one-fourth, of racial housing segregation can be accounted for by income differences, and (2) housing segregation has largely restricted blacks to living in central cities, even though a great many of them can afford housing in the suburbs. The
author's data, for example, indicate that if income differences were the only reason
for housing segregation, over half of the St. Louis area's blacks would have lived in
the suburbs; in fact only 34 percent did. Similar findings have been obtained for Detroit and Cleveland in 1970 (Hermalin and Farley, 1973; Farley, 1982, p. 238) and
for Chicago and Kansas City in 1980 (Darden, 1985; Kain, 1987).

Black Preferences

Another explanation offered for housing segregation is that black people
prefer to live in all-black neighborhoods. Undoubtedly many do, but research suggests that this factor, too, probably cannot account for anywhere near the level of
segregation that really exists. A team of researchers headed by Reynolds Farley (Farley et al., 1978; Farley, Bianchi, and Colasanto, 1979) conducted a large-scale survey
of the housing and neighborhood preferences of blacks and whites in the Detroit
metropolitan area. Blacks and whites responding to the survey were shown cards depicting various combinations of blacks and whites in hypothetical neighborhoods
(see Figure 10.1). They were then asked about their willingness to live in the neighborhoods and their neighborhood preferences. Blacks expressed a clear preference
for integrated neighborhoods: 63 percent picked the 50 percent black and 50 percent white neighborhood as their first choice, and fully 85 percent of the blacks
chose integrated neighborhoods. Only 12 percent chose the all-black neighborhood,
and 2 percent chose an all-white neighborhood. The most common reason given for
preferring integrated neighborhoods was the need to get along with whites. A similar study done in New Jersey suburbs by Lake (1981, p. 132) also found that blacks
overwhelmingly preferred "integrated" neighborhoods over "mainly black" neighborhoods. More recent research by Clark (1991) also found that blacks in several
cities preferred neighborhoods with roughly equal numbers of blacks and whites.
Clearly, then, housing segregation cannot be explained primarily by black preferences, and the studies' findings are quite consistent with those of a number of previous studies (for a review, see Pettigrew, 1973, pp. 43–58).

White Preferences

Another commonly suggested explanation for housing segregation is that
white residents prefer all-white neighborhoods and behave in such a manner as to
exclude blacks from their neighborhoods. The two studies by Farley and his associates (1978, 1979) provide significant evidence for this explanation. When whites who
answered the survey in Detroit were shown cards depicting various neighborhood
racial mixes, they expressed preferences very different from those of blacks. Over
one-fourth (27 percent) of whites indicated that they would be unwilling to move to
a neighborhood with *one* black family, and fully half would not be willing to move
into a neighborhood that was 20 percent black. Almost three-fourths (73 percent)
of the whites indicated that they would not be willing to move to a neighborhood
that was one-third black, and 41 percent said they would try to move out of such a
neighborhood if they already lived there (Farley, Bianchi, and Colasanto, 1979). Fur-

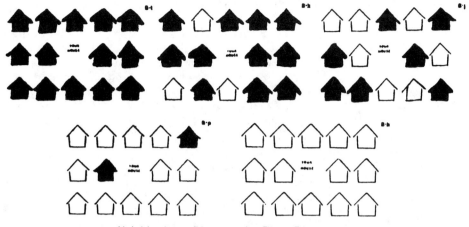

Neighborhood Diagrams for Black Respondents

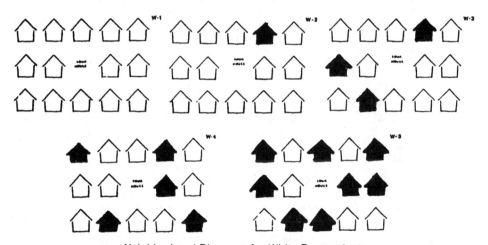

Neighborhood Diagrams for White Respondents

Figure 10.1 Pictures of neighborhood diagrams presented to black and white respondents. Source: Reprinted from "Barriers to the Racial Integration of Neighborhoods: The Detroit Case," by Reynolds Farley, Suzanne Bianchi, and Diane Colasanto in volume 441 of *The Annals of the American Academy of Political and Social Science.* Copyright© 1979 by the American Academy of Political and Social Science.

thermore, for each neighborhood racial mix, the number of whites who said they would feel uncomfortable if their neighborhood developed such a mix was almost as great as the number who said they would not move into such a neighborhood. Clearly, anything more than minimal integration in housing is unacceptable to the majority of whites, and a sizable minority rejects even minimal integration. Similar findings were obtained in suburban New Jersey by Lake (1981), though Lake's study found whites' expectations about the future racial mix of the neighborhood to be more important than its current mix.

These findings are instructive in several respects. While they do show that some whites are willing to live in minimally integrated neighborhoods, they also show that most whites prefer exactly the kind of neighborhood they live in—all-white or nearly all-white. Furthermore, they show that the integrated neighborhoods that blacks prefer to move *into* are exactly the kind of neighborhoods that whites want to move *out of,* and even more so, refuse to move into. This can be illustrated by find- ings from Clark's (1991) study. As noted, he found that most blacks prefer neigh- borhoods with roughly equal numbers of whites and blacks. He also found that a siz- able number of whites are favorable to living in "integrated" neighborhoods, but integration means something different to whites than it did to blacks. Most whites who indicated a preference for integrated neighborhoods wanted to live in an area about 20 percent black. Thus, neighborhoods with 30 or 40 percent black popula- tions are highly attractive to blacks but not attractive to whites, even whites who are favorable to living in integrated neighborhoods. In part because a large proportion of whites remain unfavorable to even this much integration, the actual neighbor- hood percentage of blacks that whites will accept is usually well under 20 percent. Based on actual patterns of residency, Massey and Gross (1991) argue that white re- sistance to living in mixed areas will result in the average white person living in a neighborhood that is not more than 5 percent black in most metropolitan areas. They go on to demonstrate from census data that segregation in most cases does not fall below the level required to limit the percentage of blacks in the average white person's neighborhood to about 5 percent or less.

It appears that once a neighborhood becomes integrated, the following se- quence of events usually happens: (1) The neighborhood becomes more attractive to blacks, so blacks move in at an accelerated rate. (2) Whites stop moving into the neighborhood. (3) In some neighborhoods, whites may move out at a faster than normal rate. Taken together, these processes tend to turn the neighborhood rather quickly from all-white to all-black, or nearly all-black. Because so many whites are un- willing to move into integrated neighborhoods, it becomes difficult for neighbor- hoods to remain integrated once they have become integrated: For the neighbor- hood to stay integrated, both blacks and whites must continue moving in. The data show that most blacks will continue moving into an integrated neighborhood; most whites will not. Even in the absence of sizable white flight, the failure of whites to move into the neighborhood guarantees that it will become resegregated, only now predominately black (see Molotch, 1972).

The inability of most neighborhoods to remain integrated is illustrated by several studies. A study by the author (Farley, 1983), for example, identified a num- ber of suburbs of St. Louis that were racially mixed and had low segregation indexes (below 50). However, nearly all of these suburbs were near the area's main sector of black population and underwent rapid changes in racial composition between 1970 and 1980. In fact, the average suburb in this group experienced a 27-point increase in its percentage black. These findings are consistent with an earlier study of ten cities by Taeuber and Taeuber (1965, pp. 105–114). Only six of the ten cities had *any* stable interracial neighborhoods where the racial mix stayed about the same be- tween 1950 and 1960, and in those six, only a small minority of the census tracts that had any sizable number of blacks were stably integrated.

It may be that whites have become somewhat less resistant to neighborhood integration in recent years. A study of St. Louis, one of the most segregated metropolitan areas in the country, found that between 1980 and 1990, much less change took place in the racial composition of mixed areas than had occurred in the preceding decade. During the 1970s, some municipalities in the St. Louis areas experienced increases in their black population of thirty, forty, or even fifty percentage points. During the 1980s, changes were much smaller; almost always less than twenty percentage points, and usually a good deal less (Farley, 1993). Similar results were also obtained in a recent study of five cities by Wood and Lee (1991): After 1970, racial turnover decreased and the stability of racially mixed neighborhoods increased compared with earlier decades. The St. Louis study also showed a dramatic decline in the proportion of whites living in areas that were less than 1 percent black, suggesting a real decrease in the number of all-white neighborhoods. In spite of these changes, however, the overall pattern in St. Louis and most other large, industrial cities in the Midwest and Northeast remains one of racial segregation.

Another factor that undoubtedly serves to preserve the pattern of housing segregation is harassment by whites of blacks who move into all-white neighborhoods. Incidents of this nature have been reported in most large metropolitan areas and continued to occur in various areas in the 1970s and 1980s and into the 1990s. Frequently such incidents are violent, with vandalism to homes, automobiles, and other property; in some cases, shots have been fired through windows and houses burned down. In the spring of 1993, for example, blacks living in or moving into predominantly white areas encountered vandalism, harassment, or cross burnings in nine cities in Ohio, California, Oregon, Alabama, Kentucky, and North Carolina (Southern Poverty Law Center, 1993b). Such incidents undoubtedly have had some effect of blocking the integration of all-white neighborhoods. The Detroit study (Farley, Bianchi, and Colasanto, et al., 1979) found that 90 percent of the blacks reluctant to move to all-white areas expressed the view that whites would not welcome them, and one-sixth expressed fears of serious violence against themselves or their house.

Practices in the Real-Estate Business

Not all racial segregation can be explained by the behaviors and preferences of white residents, however. Although many whites do not want to live in integrated neighborhoods, a significant minority of the white population clearly is willing and in some cases even desires to live in racially integrated neighborhoods (Farley, Bianchi, and Colasanto, 1979; Taylor, 1979; Lake, 1981). Furthermore, a significant portion of the white objection to living in integrated neighborhoods arises from fears that the neighborhood will "tip" and become all black (Taylor, 1979; Lake, 1981).

This suggests that there may be other important reasons for the pattern of housing segregation, and one that has been most often suggested is the behavior of some real-estate agents and speculators. Discrimination in the sale and rental of housing has been illegal in the United States since 1968, but there is ample evidence that such discrimination continues. One common practice is the selective showing of houses to blacks and whites, commonly referred to as *racial steering.*

Pearce (1976) showed that this practice was widespread in the Detroit area. She had couples with similar social characteristics except race approach a number of real-estate agents in the Detroit area. Each real-estate agent was approached a few weeks apart by a black couple and a white couple. The results of the study were striking: The white couples were shown more houses, on the average, and blacks and whites were shown houses in different areas. The whites were shown houses in white neighborhoods, usually in the same community as the real-estate agent's office. The black couples, on the other hand, were shown houses in either racially mixed or all-black neighborhoods, usually outside the community where the real-estate agent's office was located. A CBS news team conducting an investigation for the program *60 Minutes* found essentially the same pattern in the Chicago area, also by sending black and white couples to real-estate agents. Widespread discrimination and racial steering were found in both sale and rental housing in forty metropolitan areas in a study by the U.S. Department of Housing and Urban Development (1979). Even using a conservative approach, the researchers found that a black visiting six rental offices would have an 85 percent chance of encountering discrimination and that a black visiting four real-estate sales offices would have about a fifty-fifty chance of experiencing discrimination. A more recent national study conducted for the Department of Housing and Urban Development in 1989 was specifically designed to detect racial steering, and it showed that steering continues to be common (U.S. Department of Housing and Urban Development, 1991). This study found that black home seekers were directed toward neighborhoods with higher percentages of blacks than were white home seekers. African Americans also encountered other forms of discrimination, such as being kept waiting longer and being told about fewer houses available for sale.

Lake's (1981) survey of both homebuyers and real-estate agents uncovered considerable evidence of racial steering in New Jersey suburbs. The answers of the real-estate agents were especially enlightening. Most indicated that they would warn blacks about the prejudice they would encounter if they bought in white neighborhoods—clearly something that discourages blacks from buying in such areas. Real-estate agents' answers also indicated that they often provided more advice and assistance to whites than to blacks. Indeed, it is frequently difficult or impossible for whites wishing to buy in integrated or mostly black neighborhoods or blacks wishing to buy in all-white neighborhoods to do so: Real-estate agents actively discourage such home buying. Although illegal, racial steering is difficult to prove to a court or civil rights commission: To do so would require a careful and time-consuming study such as those of Pearce and the CBS news team, and of course, most potential complainants do not have the resources to do such a study. As an alternative, some communities (mostly in racially changing areas) have proposed affirmative marketing ordinances to require that people of all races be made aware of available houses in areas with the full range of racial composition. These have led to charges of reverse steering or discrimination by some whites and blacks, particularly those who are associated with the real-estate industry. However, unless effective measures are taken to curb the practice of racial steering, substantial reduction in the amount of housing segregation is unlikely.

Because of the difficulty of enforcing the 1968 Fair Housing Law, efforts began in 1979 to strengthen the law's enforcement mechanisms. After several unsuccessful attempts at legislation, these efforts came to fruition in the passage of the 1988 Fair Housing Act Amendments. The 1988 Fair Housing Act Amendments strengthen the enforcement mechanisms of the 1968 law in several ways. The new law makes suing for housing discrimination easier and increases the damages that can be collected in housing-discrimination cases. It also gives the Department of Housing and Urban Development increased authority to act to enforce fair-housing law. It does this by establishing a system of administrative-law judges to review discrimination complaints, which can be brought either by the Department of Housing and Urban Development or by an individual. If discrimination is found, the administrative-law judge can issue injunctions, order payment of damages, and impose civil fines of $10,000 to $50,000. Either party can appeal a decision to the federal courts. Finally, the 1988 Fair Housing Act Amendments contain new provisions protecting the rights of the disabled to accessible housing and forbidding discrimination on the basis of familial status. The latter means that it is now illegal to discriminate against families or individuals with children in the sale or rental of housing, except in the case of housing complexes developed specifically for senior citizens. Also, after the results of the 1989 Department of Housing and Urban Development study of steering were released in 1991, the Department of Justice announced that it would undertake a new program to investigate violations of fair-housing law and to enforce the law. In 1993, an investigation conducted under this program resulted in large fines for several Detroit-area apartment complexes that were caught in acts of illegal discrimination. The program also resulted in discrimination lawsuits by the Department in St. Louis, Los Angeles, and Sioux Falls, South Dakota.

Although enforcement of fair-housing law has improved somewhat, most acts of discrimination still go undetected. An inherent problem is that home seekers know only what they are told about, not what they are not told about or whether someone of a different race is treated differently. For example, an African American seeking an apartment may be told there are no vacancies. He or she has no way of knowing whether a white visiting the same rental office would be told the same thing or not. Similarly, black and white home seekers who are steered have no way to know that persons of a different race are being directed toward different housing. The only way to detect this is through testing studies like those of Pearce (1976), the CBS News team, and the Department of Housing and Urban Development (1991). More studies of this type, tied to enforcement actions against those caught discriminating, are clearly needed if fair-housing law is to be effectively enforced. The discrimination-testing movement is discussed in greater detail in Chapter 14.

Racial discrimination can be highly profitable to some people in the real-estate industry, as is shown by another practice known as *blockbusting*. Blockbusting is a practice whereby unscrupulous real-estate agents play on the fears of whites and the housing predicament of blacks to make a fast buck by encouraging the rapid turnover of a neighborhood from all-white to all-black. Typically, the process begins in an all-white neighborhood near a black neighborhood or a neighborhood undergoing change. Real-estate agents or real-estate speculators approach people living in the neighborhood and tell them that blacks are about to move into the neighborhood and that property values are going to go down. They tell the whites that they had better sell now, while they can still get their money out of the house. The object, of course, is to create panic so that the whites will sell their houses at a low price, often to a real-estate speculator. Commissions can be collected, and often a shrewd speculator can sell the house to a black family for more than it is worth: Blacks typically must pay more for the same-quality housing than whites because of the restricted housing market available. Of course, such practices are illegal under the 1968 and 1988 laws against housing discrimination. It is illegal for the real-estate agent to even volunteer information about the racial composition of the neighborhood, since that can be a form of racial steering. As a result, the incidence of open blockbusting has clearly been reduced since 1968. There are ways of getting around the law, however. In some cities, anonymous letters have been distributed in the middle of the night; anonymous phone calls saying "sell now" are not unheard of. In addition, both blockbusting and racial steering can be accomplished through subtler comments such as "You'll get better appreciation on the value of your house if you buy elsewhere than you will if you stay here" or "You really wouldn't be interested in looking south of the freeway."

The Marxist theory of the economics of discrimination (Reich, 1986) appears to be applicable to the issue of blockbusting. Both black and white homeowners are harmed by the practice: Whites sell their houses for less than they are worth, and blacks pay an inflated price. Furthermore, the practice would not work were it not for the fears and prejudices of the white population. If whites did not *believe* that blacks in the neighborhood lead to lower property values, they could not be frightened into the panic selling that creates falling property values. In short, racial prejudice appears to serve the interests of the real-estate speculators and unscrupulous real-estate agents at the expense of both black and white homeowners. Although blockbusting is less common today than in the past, its effects linger in the form of segregated neighborhoods and white fears about the consequences of neighborhood racial change.

To summarize briefly, we have seen that income differences between blacks and whites and the preferences of blacks are relatively unimportant as causes of housing segregation. The main causes appear to be the preference of most whites not to live in substantially integrated neighborhoods, and real-estate practices such as racial steering and blockbusting, which preserve the pattern of racial housing segregation.

Housing Segregation Among Latino and Asian Americans

Thus far, we have addressed only black–white housing segregation. Historically, though, Latino and Asian Americans have also encountered considerable housing discrimination and segregation, though not always on the scale encountered by African Americans. The limited number of studies based on the 1970 census showed that Hispanics were more segregated than other ethnic groups, and in the Northeast, Puerto Ricans were about as segregated as blacks (Guest and Weed, 1976; Hershberg et al., 1978; Kantrowitz, 1979). Mexican Americans, however, were less segregated than Puerto Ricans, and comparisons of the 1960 and 1970 censuses show that, unlike blacks, their segregation indices were already declining significantly during the 1960s. This decline continued in the 1970s, so that in Texas and California, where the largest proportion of the Mexican American population lives, Anglo–Latino segregation indices were averaging between 40 and 45 by 1980 (Lopez, 1981; Hwang and Murdock, 1982). Nationally, Massey and Denton (1989) found, based on the 1980 census, a similar level of Hispanic segregation in a sample of sixty large cities. In this study, the average segregation index between Hispanics and white Anglos was 44, compared with 69 for black–white segregation. Between 1980 and 1990, levels of Hispanic segregation did not change a great deal. Various studies show that in 1990, Latinos remained much less segregated from white Anglos than did blacks, although their levels of segregation were somewhat above those of Asian Americans (*USA Today,* 1991; Farley and Frey, 1992; Harrison and Weinberg, 1992a, 1992b; Alba and Logan, 1993). In 1990, for example, Anglo–Latino segregation indices exceeded 60 in just two of the thirty-three metropolitan areas where Hispanics are at least 20 percent of the population. In contrast, black–white indices exceeded that level in two-thirds of the metropolitan areas where they are at least 20 percent of the population (Usdansky, 1991). In some areas, Hispanic segregation may have decreased to a level (indices in the 30s and 40s) that could reflect voluntary self-segregation (Farley, 1987c; Clark, 1992). One point remains true, however: Puerto Ricans continue to be significantly more segregated than Mexican Americans and other Hispanic groups. This is reflected in the fact that in 1990, as in earlier years, Anglo–Latino segregation indices are higher in the Northeast than in other parts of the country (O'Hare, 1992, p. 27).

Although like Hispanics, Asian Americans were the targets of open housing discrimination in the past, they are today the least segregated groups among people of color in the United States. In metropolitan areas with large Asian populations, such as Los Angeles, New York, and Chicago, Asian-Americans are less segregated than Hispanics. In San Francisco, their segregation index is the same as that of Hispanics (*USA Today*, 1991). Nationally, though, their average levels of segregation are below those of both African Americans and Latinos (Harrison and Weinberg, 1992a, 1992b). One study of Asian Americans in the suburbs of New York City found that, for practical purposes, Asian Americans were fully integrated in suburban neighborhoods. Hispanics, in contrast, were only somewhat integrated, and blacks remained largely segregated (Alba and Logan, 1993).

In summary, Asian Americans and Hispanic Americans have become considerably less segregated in recent decades in a way that African Americans have not. In fact, both Asian Americans and Hispanic Americans are more segregated from blacks than they are from whites, again underlining the fact that housing segregation has increasingly become a pattern that applies distinctively to African Americans. This is consistent with a recent survey showing that whites indicate greater personal objection to black neighbors than to Japanese American neighbors, though the majority indicated no objection to either (Schuman and Bobo, 1988). Taken together, however, data on segregation, discrimination, and attitudes indicate that there is greater white resistance to black–white neighborhood integration than to integration involving either Hispanics or Asians, though Puerto Ricans (a significant number of whom are black) may be an exception in this regard.

Impacts of Segregation

When the topic of housing segregation was introduced earlier in this chapter, it was done so in the context of factors limiting the economic opportunities of blacks and other minorities. Obviously, housing segregation is in certain ways harmful in and of itself: It deprives people—especially black people—of their free choice of places to live. Furthermore, it restricts the market of housing available to blacks and other minorities. Beyond these factors, however, housing segregation can have an impact in two other important ways. First, it can lead to segregated schools, which are at the center of the busing controversy; this will be explored in a later chapter. Second, we have already seen that it can aggravate the minority unemployment problem by restricting minorities to living in exactly the areas where employment opportunities are disappearing (Kasarda, 1989a, 1989b, 1990). Both blacks and Hispanics have higher unemployment rates relative to whites in cities where they are more concentrated in the central city (Farley, 1987b).

In addition to whatever harmful effects housing segregation has on minority employment opportunities, it must be mentioned that it probably has affected the racial attitudes of both whites and minorities. It tends to greatly restrict the amount of day-to-day neighborly contact between the races, and contact can be an important source of improved race relations. In its absence, prejudices and stereotypes frequently go unchallenged. Furthermore, when housing is segregated, the racial contacts that *do* occur can be of a highly destructive type. Frequently, the racial composition of a neighborhood changes rapidly, as with blockbusting, creating a situation that is highly threatening to both blacks and whites and probably ends up making intergroup relations worse. Finally, as we have mentioned, the school desegregation and busing controversy is largely rooted in the pervasive pattern of housing segregation in American cities.

Recent work by Massey and his colleagues has identified two additional impacts of housing segregation. First, based on a study of Philadelphia in 1980, they conclude that segregation reduces the quality of life of the black middle class. Because of segregation, middle-class blacks must live in neighborhoods with fewer resources and amenities; poorer schools; and higher rates of poverty, crime, and mortality than do whites of comparable background (Massey, Condran, and Denton, 1987).

Second, a strong case can be made that residential segregation is a major reason poor blacks are so much more likely than poor whites to live in neighborhoods where many or most of their neighbors are poor. As is noted elsewhere in this book, black poverty is much more concentrated than poverty among other groups, especially whites. Massey argues that housing segregation is a major reason why. A residential location pattern that segregates any group with a high rate of poverty, such as African Americans, tends to produce concentrated poverty. Computer models suggest that black poverty is more concentrated than it would be were it not for housing segregation (Massey, 1990; Massey and Eggers, 1990; Massey and Denton, 1993). The fact that black poverty is concentrated produces additional problems: It deprives young, poor blacks of role models of economic achievement and subjects blacks to increased risks of problems associated with poverty, such as crime and drug abuse (Wilson, 1987, forthcoming). Many social scientists have argued that if poverty among African Americans were less geographically concentrated, it would be easier to escape.

For all the reasons outlined above, housing segregation is widely viewed as a problem that worsens race relations and adds to the difficulties faced by the black community. Not everyone agrees, however. Some point out that it enhances black political power by making possible majority-black cities and suburbs where blacks can elect their own political leaders. Also, some blacks clearly prefer to live in all-black or nearly all-black neighborhoods, though surveys show that most favor mixed neighborhoods. On the other hand, it is also true that, because of the concentration of poverty discussed above, majority-black cities often lack the tax base to be able to effectively address their problems. Cities such as Detroit; Gary, Indiana; and Newark have faced difficult economic situations requiring them to cut city services and lay off city workers because of a poor tax base—a condition that obviously limits the ability of black elected officials to improve the quality of life of their constituencies.

Ultimately, the key issue may turn out to be one of encouraging choice: making it possible for people to move to and live in a neighborhood with whatever racial composition they prefer, uninhibited by racial steering, sales and rental discrimination, and resistance to minorities from white neighbors. Judging from public-opinion polls, segregation would decline at least some if people were free to move where they wish, uninhibited by such practices. If the government were to expand recent efforts to enforce fair-housing laws, it would undoubtedly increase the ability of all to freely choose where to live. For a rather different approach to encouraging neighborhood integration, see the box "Supporting Integrative Moves: One State's Initiative."

THE FISCAL CRISIS OF CITIES AND ITS IMPACT ON MINORITIES

Thus far in this chapter, we have seen how a number of trends, practices, and patterns in contemporary society have contributed to the maintenance of economic racial and ethnic inequality. Among the important areas we have discussed are rising educational demands for prospective employees, the departure of jobs from the

---

SUPPORTING INTEGRATIVE MOVES: ONE STATE'S INITIATIVE

In response to the high interest rates of the early 1980s, the state of Ohio established a mortgage-revenue-bond program to offer low-interest home loans to first-time buyers. In 1983 and 1984, about $750 million of mortgage-revenue bonds were issued and used to finance such low-interest loans. By making loans available at rates of less than 10 percent (compared with rates of 15 percent and higher that were typical at that time), the program enabled people to buy homes who otherwise could not afford to. In the 1980s, many states established programs similar to the one in Ohio, but Ohio's program had one important difference: In response to pressures from the fair-housing groups that were and are very active in Ohio, along with support from the governor, the program had a component designed to encourage housing integration. In 1985 and again from 1988 to 1991, a portion of the money allocated for the program was set aside for "integrative moves." Integrative moves are moves that increase the diversity of a neighborhood, for example, when a black family moves into a predominantly white area, or vice versa. Because there were far more applicants than the number of loans that could be subsidized under the state program, a strong incentive for people to make integrative moves was created: A portion of the scarce mortgage-subsidy money could be obtained only by people willing to make such moves.

Evaluations of the program showed that it accomplished several things: It increased the proportion of black families participating in the mortgage-subsidy program, led black families to extend their housing search beyond traditionally black neighborhoods, and led white families to make moves that reinforced racial integration in areas where it existed (Bromley, 1992). Significantly, however, the program aroused the opposition of both white and black real-estate agents, who saw it as social engineering that infringed on their rights to do business as they saw fit. It was this opposition that led to the temporary elimination of the program in 1986 and 1987. In fact, were it not for the support of the governor and his staff and the ability of program supporters to generate data showing that the program worked, it would probably never have been reinstated (Bromley, 1992). Nonetheless, the Ohio program offers an interesting model for other states in that it supports the reduction of housing segregation by creating incentives for people to take voluntary actions that promote integration rather than relying exclusively on enforcement of laws against discrimination. Moreover, evaluations of the program indicate that its incentives were successful in encouraging integrative moves and reduced the previous underrepresentation of blacks among those receiving state-financed mortgage subsidies.

areas where minority-group members live, and the widespread pattern of housing segregation in major metropolitan areas. We shall next examine another significant economic pattern with especially dire implications for American minority groups: the fiscal crisis of American cities.

Over the next two decades, many large cities with substantial minority populations experienced serious fiscal difficulties, as revenue sources were unable to match expenditures. The most highly publicized cases have been New York City and Cleveland, both of which reached the brink of bankruptcy, but numerous cities have had similar problems, particularly in the Northeast and Midwest. In the 1970s, for example, Detroit was forced to lay off a large portion of its police force, Chicago was unable to meet payrolls in its school system, and Toledo was forced to close its school system entirely from Thanksgiving until after New Year's Day. In 1990, East St. Louis, Illinois, temporarily lost ownership of City Hall when the city lacked sufficient funds to pay a lawsuit against the city.

Almost all cities with large African American populations experienced worsening economic and fiscal crises during the 1970s (Bradbury et al., 1982; Bradbury and Ladd, 1987). Some of these cities, such as Baltimore, Chicago, Atlanta, and New York, experienced somewhat better economic fortunes during the 1980s (Fanstein and Fanstein, 1989). Generally, the cities that have fared better are the ones with corporate headquarters, as is illustrated by Chicago, Atlanta, and New York. A comparison of Buffalo and Pittsburgh by Koritz (1991) illustrates this: Pittsburgh, which had long been a major corporate center, experienced *restructuring*, while Buffalo experienced *destructuring*. In other words, when Pittsburgh lost its traditional industrial base, the loss was partially offset by growth in the corporate and service sectors, whereas Buffalo was not able to recoup its industrial losses. Thus, cities like Pittsburgh, Atlanta, New York, and Chicago were able in the 1980s to partially offset their fiscal declines of the 1970s; other cities like Buffalo, Detroit, Cleveland, St. Louis, and East St. Louis had a harder time doing so. In this latter group of cities, the best that happened was a slowing or cessation of fiscal decline (as in Cleveland and St. Louis); the worst was continuing deterioration (as in Detroit and East St. Louis); Detroit, for example, lost one-third of its jobs, while its poverty rate doubled between the early 1970s and the early 1990s (*St. Louis Post-Dispatch,* 1993b). The effect on this 75 percent black city's fiscal condition was predictable: Continued cuts in city services as the city's ability to generate tax revenue declined and its costs increased. But even in the cities that have been able to arrest the fiscal deterioration of the 1970s, today's fiscal conditions are usually worse than those of twenty or thirty years ago. They are also worse than those of the surrounding, more affluent suburbs. Taxes in today's central cities are higher than they were in the past and higher than in most suburbs, and city services are often less extensive.

The reasons for this fiscal crisis are complex, but to a large degree they arise from a tax system that requires local financing of city services and from the dual trends of industry and middle-class population leaving the city and of the lower-income population becoming increasingly concentrated in the city.

Cities receive significant state and federal financial aid, but because of the election of conservative national administrations and federal and state fiscal difficulties, this aid shrank during the 1980s. According to Wilson (forthcoming), federal funding to cities fell from 18 percent of city budgets in 1980 to just 6.4 percent in 1990. According to Wilson, this both reflected and reinforced economic and political inequalities between largely black and Hispanic central cities and largely white

Table 10.3 Sources of Municipal Revenue, United States

	PERCENTAGE OF TOTAL MUNICIPAL REVENUE		
Source	1970	1983	1990
General Revenue	81.4	77.8	78
Intergovernment	24.2	25.8	22
State	18.9	15.0	17
Federal and other	5.3	10.0	5
Local-government revenue	57.2	52.0	56
Taxes	41.7	32.0	34
Property	27.9	16.7	17
Sales	7.4	9.0	10
Income and other	6.4	6.4	7
Miscellaneous charges	15.5	20.0	22
Utilities	15.8	18.0	16

Source: U.S. Bureau of the Census, 1986b, p. 288; 1992c, p. 298.

suburbs. To an even greater extent than in the past, cities raise most of their revenue locally. As Table 10.3 shows, municipalities raise about 72 percent of their revenue locally, mainly through taxes, but also through utilities such as water, sewer, and, sometimes, electric power. School districts raise about half of their revenue locally. For both, the property tax is the most important source of local general revenue. In addition, both state and federal governments cut back on key local-government assistance programs during the 1980s, as they struggled to balance their own budgets.

Because cities must raise most of their revenue locally, a situation is created whereby the areas with the *greatest* need for services are the *least* able to raise the revenue to pay for those services. The ability, for example, of the property tax to raise revenue is directly dependent on the value of the property in the city. As we have seen, business, industry, and the middle-class population have all left central cities (especially in the Midwest and Northeast) in large numbers since World War II. Their departure has left less high-value property to tax in the city relative to the rate of growth in the cost of urban government. Consequently, many central cities have had to raise their tax rates per dollar of assessed valuation substantially yet are still less able to raise revenue than the wealthier suburbs, which have much more property to tax. One example of this can be seen in East St. Louis, a city whose population is 95 percent black and in large part poor. The city's tax effort (that is, the tax rate per total per-capita assessed valuation) is *six and a half times* as great as the average for the county in which it is located (Illinois Capital Development Board, 1977, p. 56). In spite of this the city's revenues fell well below that of neighboring communities, and in recent years the city has been chronically unable to raise enough revenue to meet its expenses, leading to the situation in which East St. Louis nearly lost ownership of City Hall.

Much the same problem exists with other local taxes, such as the local sales tax and local income tax. If retail business moves out of the city, there is less sales tax revenue. If the wealthier population moves out, there is less income tax revenue.

Thus, the need to raise revenue locally has become a crucial fiscal handicap to large cities with large minority populations, particularly in the Midwest and Northeast.

As local sources of revenue have been shrinking in large cities, the expenses of those cities have been rising, in large part because cities have increasingly become the home of the poor. This in turn has created a rising demand for welfare and for various programs and services aimed at reducing the harmful effects of poverty. In large part, too, this demand has increased because functions that once were performed by someone else have been left to the local government in recent decades. As Piven (1977, p. 134) notes, "In the era of the big city machine, municipal authorities managed to maintain a degree of consensus and allegiance among diverse groups by distributing public goods in the form of private favors. Today public goods are distributed through the service bureaucracies." In other words, they are distributed at the expense of local governments rather than at private expense, as they once were.

As a result of all this, it costs big-city governments more today than ever before to provide even a low level of services to the needy. At the same time, the sources of revenue have been drained to a greater degree than ever before in many cities. The consequence has been sizable cuts in services in the cities where much of the black and Latino population of the United States lives. Police and fire protection have been reduced, education has been cut back, library hours have been reduced, and day-care centers and public hospitals have been closed. Black and Latino Americans have been disproportionately harmed for a number of reasons. Most obviously, a disproportionate number of them live in the cities where the cutbacks have taken place. Beyond this, however, they tend—because they are disproportionately poor—to be more reliant on public services than are others who can buy services such as health care and education in the private sector. The recent tax-cutting mood of the American public has made the problem even worse, as the most fiscally fragile communities are most harmed by the revenue losses resulting from tax-slashing efforts such as California's Proposition 13 and similar measures that have followed in other states.

Again, all this may well have happened with no conscious and deliberate intent to discriminate. Nonetheless, it appears certain that as long as the current trend in the distribution of population, industry, and business continues, the present system of taxation will work against the interests of black and Hispanic Americans who are concentrated in America's central cities. They will continue to pay relatively higher tax rates and to receive lower levels of service. It appears that only some major change in the system of raising local revenue could meaningfully alter this pattern.

HEALTH CARE AND MINORITIES

As this book is being revised for a third edition, Congress is considering a proposal by the Clinton administration to make major changes in the American health-care system. If enacted, the Clinton proposal would, among other things, guarantee health-insurance coverage to all Americans. This would present a sharp contrast to the traditional American system under which health care has always been based, for the most part, on ability to pay. As sociologists who study race relations (for example, Wilson, 1987), have pointed out, reforms such as those proposed by Clinton, while attractive and beneficial to broad segments of the American population, would help to meet needs that are particularly acute among U.S. minority groups. This is because, as we will see in more detail shortly, minority-group members are far more likely than white Americans to either lack insurance entirely or to rely on governmental-assistance programs such as Medicaid for health-care coverage.

As we saw in Chapter 9, minority-group members suffer significant disadvantages relative to whites in health status. They live shorter lives, are more likely to die in infancy, and suffer more frequent and more serious illnesses. A brief review of the figures from that chapter will remind us that on the average, African Americans live about six years less than whites, as did Native Americans the last time statistics were available on their life expectancies. A black baby is more than twice as likely as a white baby to die in the first year of life, and the situation is almost as bad for American Indian babies, who are about a time and a half as likely to die in the first year of life as white babies. African Americans are also more likely to be disabled than whites and more frequently have illnesses that limit their normal daily activities.

There are, of course, many possible causes of health and mortality differentials between majority and minority groups, and some have nothing to do with the health-care system. Some jobs, for example, are more dangerous than others, and minority group members are overrepresented among many of the manual occupations that carry danger of injury or exposure to toxic substances. The latter is an example of **environmental racism,** a pattern whereby minorities are disproportionately exposed to hazardous substances both at work and at home. Examples of environmental racism abound. In California, farmworkers (most of whom are Chicanos) are routinely exposed to a variety of pesticides that are widely believed to cause cancer and the safety of which has never been established. Among farmworkers in recent years, there have been a large number of *cancer clusters,* unusual numbers of cases of cancer occurring in small localities. A disproportionate number of America's black communities are located adjacent to industrial facilities that release dangerous pollutants into the air and water. In urban America, both blacks and Hispanics are more likely than other groups to live in older housing, with its heightened risk of illness from lead-based paint. On America's Indian reservations, pressures have been strong in recent years for tribal councils to accept much-needed cash from major waste-disposal and energy companies in exchange for allowing the reservations to become dumping grounds for nuclear waste and other hazardous substances.

Other factors are the poor nutrition and inadequate shelter that are frequently associated with poverty. (As we have seen, blacks, Latinos, and Indians are much more likely than whites to be poor.) Life is frequently stressful for minority group members, and they frequently suffer from stress-related diseases such as ulcers and hypertension (high blood pressure). Among the black population, the problem of hypertension is especially widespread. Between the ages of twenty-five and forty-four, blacks are fifteen to seventeen times as likely as whites to die of hypertension (Cockerham, 1978, p. 34). Recent research suggests that anger over racism may be one cause of the high rate of hypertension among blacks. For example, a study of black college students watching racist scenes and other anger-provoking scenes found that their blood pressure rose three times as much when watching the racist scenes as when watching the other anger-provoking scenes. And doctors have reported black patients with no history of hypertension experiencing increases in their blood pressure after encountering situations in which they experienced racism, such as being assigned a racist supervisor (Goleman, 1990; Leary, 1991).

Among males, blacks are somewhat more likely than whites to smoke—behavior that may be a response to stress and that is known to be harmful to health. Finally, we have seen that minority-group members are more likely than whites to be the victims of violent crimes. Between 1960 and 1988, for example, homicide was by far the largest cause of death among black males between the ages of fifteen and twenty-four. At these ages, black males were six to seven times as likely to die as a result of homicide as white males (Snyder, 1991).

All of the above notwithstanding, there is considerable reason to believe that a good deal of the differences in health and mortality between minorities and whites do result from the ways these groups are treated by the health-care system. In the following sections, we shall examine some of the ways the health-care system treats majority and minority groups unequally.

Cost of Health Care

In the United States, health care is expensive. Furthermore, it has, until now, been in large part based on ability to pay. It is provided by the public sector only for the elderly through Medicare and for the poorest of the poor (about 7 percent of the population) through Medicaid. For the great majority of the population, including millions with low and moderate incomes, getting health care is a matter of buying or arranging for private-sector insurance, paying out of the pocket, or, most likely, some combination of the two. In this respect, the U.S. health-care system is virtually unique: Among the major industrialized nations of the world, only the United States and South Africa retain systems of health care based solely on ability to pay. The remainder of the industrial countries have either a system of socialized medicine, as does Great Britain, or of national health insurance, as does Canada. Under socialized medicine, doctors are essentially salaried employees who are paid out of tax revenues. This system is similar to a large-scale health maintenance organization (HMO), in which a group of people join together to pay the salaries of medical personnel who provide them with health-care services. The national health-insurance system retains the fee-for-service (that is, so much paid for each service, such as an office visit, lab test, or operation), but the fee is paid by a governmental insurance agency. Generally, the entire population is required to participate in this public-insurance program.

The universal health-coverage plan proposed by the Clinton administration would be somewhat different from approaches now used in other countries. In contrast to Canada's single-payer national health-insurance plan, for which the government operates as the only insurer, Clinton's plan would retain a limited number of large, private insurance plans. Employers would, by law, pay most of the premiums for those who are employed (including part-time workers, most of whom are not covered now) and their dependents; Medicare for the elderly would continue much as now under Social Security, and persons who are neither employed nor dependents of employed persons would be covered by public funds. Everyone would have a choice of several plans providing somewhat different levels of benefits at different costs, though most of the cost would be paid by government or employers regardless of the plan. The plan seeks to provide care for everyone while controlling costs by (1) creating large insurance pools with the power to negotiate favorable rates with groups of doctors and hospitals; (2) giving consumers choices of several insurance providers to encourage competition for the consumer's health-care dollar, and (3) setting national targets on health-care expenditures.

While we do not know precisely how much would be saved by a plan of this type, what is clear is that the United States today is spending more money per capita on health care than any other country in the world, even though as of 1992, over thirty-seven million Americans—nearly 15 percent of the population—lacked health insurance (*St. Louis Post-Dispatch,* 1993c) and statistics show that measures such as life expectancy and infant mortality in the United States are significantly worse than those of many other industrialized countries, all of which spend less on health care than the United States. In 1990, the United States spent 12.3 percent of its gross domestic product on health care, compared with 9 percent or less in all other industrialized countries (National Center for Health Statistics, 1992). On a per-person basis, the United States spends over 40 percent more than any other country.

This kind of system can be expensive for everyone—medical expenses, for example, are the top cause of personal bankruptcies (Blumenthal and Fallows, 1974). Furthermore, health care is rapidly becoming even more expensive: The rate of inflation in health-care costs has consistently outstripped the overall rate of inflation since the 1970s. The burden is especially heavy for groups with low incomes: In 1989, over 30 percent of the nonelderly with family incomes below $20,000 had no insurance, compared with less than 10 percent of those above that income level. The highest percentage of families lacking insurance, about 37 percent, is found in nonelderly families with incomes of $5,000 to $9,999 (U.S. Bureau of the Census, 1992c, p. 106).

Disproportionate rates of poverty, part-time employment, and unemployment among minorities are reflected in statistics on health insurance among minority groups. In 1990, 31.4 percent of Hispanic Americans and 18.4 percent of African Americans had no health insurance at all, compared with 12.7 percent of the white population (U.S. Bureau of the Census, 1992c, p. 105). Among those in minority groups who do have insurance, many encounter out-of-pocket expenses not covered by insurance (nationally, about 30 percent of health-care expenses are paid out of pocket), and many more rely on Medicaid. In 1990, 21.7 percent of the black population and 15.9 percent of the Hispanic population was covered by Medicaid, compared with just 5.2 percent of the white population. In contrast, 79 percent of whites have private health insurance, compared with just 56 percent of blacks and 50 percent of Latinos (U.S. Bureau of the Census, 1992c, p. 105).

To summarize the evidence presented here, it is clear that minorities are less likely to be covered by medical insurance, less able to afford to pay for health care out of pocket, but more likely to have to do exactly that. This represents a serious barrier to the ability of minority Americans, and poor Americans more generally, to obtain needed health-care services.

Frequency of Seeking Medical Care

An obvious factor influencing health is the frequency with which people seek medical care, including preventive care, which can keep them from getting sick when they otherwise might. Because of their poverty, minority-group members on the average receive medical care, and particularly preventive care, less frequently than whites. In the population as a whole, white people visit doctors about 10 to 15 percent more often than do blacks (National Center for Health Statistics, 1992; U.S. Bureau of the Census, 1992c). Strikingly, most of the racial difference in visits to doctors is among children: Black children visit doctors up to 45 percent less often than do white children (National Center for Health Statistics, 1986b, p. 113). For the poor person, it often comes down to a choice of what will be the greater burden: being sick or paying money that one cannot afford in order to see the doctor. This is especially true if the patient suspects that the doctor will merely tell him or her to "wait and see what happens" (Blumenthal and Fallows, 1974). The extent to which medical costs prevent people from seeking care is well illustrated by an experiment in Saskatchewan Province, Canada. As a way of deterring unnecessary visits to the doctor, the province instituted a $1.50 fee to visit the doctor (it had been free). Much to their surprise, provincial officials found that it did not reduce visits to the doctor; it merely changed the characteristics of those who came. Poorer patients, especially with large families, in large part stopped coming to the doctor. Wealthier patients, however, took up the slack and came more often, figuring that they would not have to wait as long. In short, all the fee did was keep poor people away. The fee was subsequently abolished (Blumenthal and Fallows, 1974). A similar experiment in California under Medicaid also showed that very small charges to the poor can have major effects on use of health care (Helms, Newhouse, and Phelps, 1978).

Factors other than money keep minority Americans from seeing doctors. Both blacks (Hines, 1972) and Mexican Americans (Moustafa and Weiss, 1968; Madsen, 1973) tend to avoid contact with professional medicine to some degree. This is in part cultural, as these groups tend to rely on folk medicine or on the advice of friends and relatives. Some African Americans utilize healers (sometimes also known as root workers, readers, or advisors), who do not make distinctions between religion and science in the treatment of illness (Snow, 1978). These healers view the symptoms of illness as relatively unimportant, emphasizing instead causes that are seen as either natural (consequences of abusing the body or the natural environment) or unnatural (often meaning the product of sorcery, evil influences, or curses). Some black folk religion is influenced by Caribbean approaches involving use of rituals, charms, herbs, and prayer aimed at healing the soul or spirit as well as the body. These forms of folk religion are more directly connected to native African beliefs and have arrived in the United States by way of the Caribbean's past slave culture (Cockerham, 1992). Similar beliefs and practices exist among Mexican Americans in the form of *curanderismo,* which centers around folk healers known as *curanderos.* Like black healers, curanderos address causes of disorders, not symptoms. Compared with black folk medicine, curanderismo uses religion to a greater extent. Suffering is seen as a worthwhile experience offered by God as a way of learning. Illnesses can also be seen as imbalances in the body, such as between "hot" and "cold" influences, or as the product of witchcraft. Herbs are prescribed for the former; the "good" power of the curandero is used to offset the latter (Kiev, 1968). Native Americans, too, often attribute illness to conditions such as loss of soul, evil spirits, or improper behavior. A study of Navajo medicine by Levy (1983) showed that it, too, classified diseases on the basis of such causes rather than symptoms. However, Native Americans also use medicines that have been shown by subsequent medical research to have demonstrable medical benefits.

The extent to which use of such traditional medicine keeps African Americans, Mexican Americans, and Native Americans away from doctors has probably been overstated. A study of small-town blacks in Mississippi by Roebuck and Quan (1976) and a study of Navajo Indians by Levy (1983) produced strikingly similar results: About half used only regular medical doctors, about 40 percent used a combination of traditional healers and physicians, and 10 percent or fewer used only traditional or folk medicine. Moreover, for those who believe in the effectiveness of traditional or folk medicine, this approach can be beneficial because of its positive effects on mental outlook: It is clear that a positive mental outlook does often contribute to improvements in health. Although minorities do use folk or traditional medicine to a greater extent than whites, other factors are probably more important causes of underutilization of scientific medicine by minorities. These include a lack of trust in some cases, resulting from impersonal treatment and/or cultural incompatibilities between minority poor patients and white, upper-middle-class health personnel. They also include shortages of medical facilities and personnel in areas where minorities live, an issue to which we now turn.

Availability of Health-Care Personnel

Once minority group members do decide to seek medical assistance, they sometimes find that medical services are not readily available. Inner-city neighborhoods with large minority populations usually have relatively few practicing physicians. Nationally, metropolitan areas have about one doctor per 500 people. In the inner-city ghettos, however, the picture is quite different. In the central district of Baltimore, there is only one doctor per 3,000 people and in one neighborhood with about 100,000 residents, the figure is one per 6,600 residents. In the South Bronx district of New York City, one of the nation's poorest areas, there was in 1968 only one doctor per 10,000 residents. Studies of Chicago and Los Angeles showed similar patterns of doctor shortages in low-income minority neighborhoods (Haynes and Garvey, 1969). A study of St. Louis in the early 1980s focused on *primary-care physicians*—the doctors people see first when they have health problems. In one poor neighborhood, it found only one such doctor per 34,000 residents, compared with the national average of one per 3,000. Several other poor neighborhoods had fewer than one per 10,000 (Confluence St. Louis, 1985).

There are a number of reasons for this shortage. In a system in which health care is based on ability to pay, a low-income ghetto is not an attractive place for doctors to locate: They can earn more money in middle- or upper-class (and often predominantly white) neighborhoods. In addition, health-care personnel in large part locate according to the availability of health-care facilities. The best-equipped hospitals tend to attract the most doctors and the best doctors, who prefer to locate where they can take advantage of the most up-to-date and elaborate technological innovations available. Such elaborate and well-equipped hospitals are rarely located in the ghetto or barrio. In fact, the hospital facilities available to the minority poor have recently *decreased* in many cities. In New York City, Philadelphia, St. Louis, and other cities, public hospitals serving minority populations were closed during the 1970s and 1980s as a result of the cities' fiscal problems.

Once established, the pattern of doctor shortages in minority neighborhoods tends to perpetuate itself. Frequently, physicians desire to locate their practice in proximity to other physicians, partly because of the convenience of referrals but also because physicians, like other professionals, enjoy interaction with professional colleagues and tend to avoid situations that deprive them of that opportunity.

Lack of Minority Physicians

There is another important reason for the lack of doctors in urban minority neighborhoods. Relative to the numbers of minority group members in the population, there are simply very few minority doctors. In 1991, 3.2 percent of doctors in the United States were African American, compared with just over 12 percent of the population. Hispanics represent 4.4 percent of doctors, compared with about 9 percent of the population (U.S. Bureau of the Census, 1992c, p. 392). Neither of these percentages has increased since 1983. Mexican Americans and Puerto Ricans are even more underrepresented in the medical profession than these figures suggest, since some Hispanic doctors are recent immigrants from a variety of countries, not Mexican Americans and Puerto Ricans, who are the most medically underserved portions of the Latino population. Data on medical-school enrollment confirm the underrepresentation of these groups: While 5.4 percent of medical students in the 1989–1990 school year were Hispanic, only 1.7 percent were Mexican American and only 0.7 percent were Puerto Rican (National Center for Health Statistics, 1992). These percentages are well below the percentages of Mexican Americans and Puerto Ricans in the overall population. The medical-school data do offer some hope for an increase in the proportion of African American physicians in the future: 6.4 percent of students in medical school were black, compared with just 4.4 percent of doctors. However, even 6.4 percent is far below the percentage of people in their twenties (the usual age of medical enrollment) who are black. These statistics are significant, because they show that, despite special efforts over the past two decades by a number of medical schools to recruit and admit more minority students, such students continue to be seriously underrepresented in medical school. Statistically, white males remain by far the most likely group to attend medical school.

Native Americans remain seriously underrepresented in the medical profession. While recent data on the number of Native American physicians are not readily available, the number of Indian physicians in 1970 was only one-eighth what would have been expected based on the size of the Indian population (U.S. Department of Health, Education, and Welfare, 1979, p. 10). Recent data are available on the number of Indian people enrolled in medical school, and they show underrepresentation similar to that of other minorities. In 1989–1990, just 0.6 percent of medical students were American Indians, compared with around 1 percent of the population in their twenties.

These figures indicate a serious need to increase the number of minority doctors. Such action would probably improve access to health care among black, Hispanic, and Native Americans, since minority physicians are more likely than others to locate in minority areas (though they, too, are subject to the same pressures that tend to keep physicians out of minority areas). Since anyone who wants to be a doctor must get into and through medical school, the participation of minority students in medical education today is a crucial determinant of the number of minority doctors in the future. This in turn has at least some bearing on access to health care among minority group members generally. Thus, legal decisions such as the *Bakke* case, which concerned minority admissions to medical school, may have important effects on the future health of minority Americans. The crucial issue of who is admitted to medical schools, as well as the legal and social implications of the *Bakke* case, will be discussed in Chapter 13.

Thus far, we have explored a number of factors related to the ability of black,

Hispanic, and Indian people in the United States to get needed health care. The cost of care, the availability of health-care facilities and personnel in minority areas, the cultural incompatibility between middle-class medicine and some minorities, and the lack of minority physicians have all combined to create a situation in which minority group members do not, on the average, get health care to the extent that members of the dominant white group do. However, even when they do get health care, the kind they get is sometimes quite different from that which the white middle class is accustomed to. We shall explore these differences next.

Places and Types of Care: Race and Class Differentials

Not everyone goes to the same kinds of places to get medical care, nor does everyone get care of comparable quality. Indeed, there are very important differences along the lines of social class both in where people go for care and in the kind of care that they get. Because minority Americans are so overrepresented among the lower-income groups, these differences also tend to occur largely along the lines of race and ethnicity.

Middle-class people are likely to have a private personal or family physician who is their regular source of medical assistance. This carries a number of advantages. First, the doctor's office maintains records containing a detailed medical history of the patients. This is helpful in diagnosis, as a new symptom may be related to a past problem and thus explained more readily than it would be if a medical history were not available. It is also helpful in treatment, since treatment for one condition can sometimes adversely affect another. The physician who has available a complete and detailed medical history is more likely to be aware of existing conditions that may be worsened by treatment for some new condition. Finally, the regular personal or family physician is more likely to get to know the patient as a person. Since we are becoming increasingly aware of the social, psychological, and emotional aspects of illness, we know that such personal knowledge and concern can be of great importance in the treatment of illness.

The poor, however, receive their treatment not from private physicians but from other types of facilities: emergency rooms, hospital clinics, public hospitals, and sometimes so-called Medicaid mills. We shall explore the treatment of the poor under the Medicaid program in a following section; our focus here is on the various hospital facilities in which the poor frequently receive medical treatment.

In 1990, 24.3 percent of physician contacts with African Americans occurred in hospital emergency rooms or outpatient clinics, compared with just 12.3 percent among whites. Low income and lack of insurance are a major reason why blacks are more likely to get care in emergency rooms than whites. Among Americans in families with incomes below $14,000, about 20 percent of doctor contacts occurred in emergency rooms or outpatient clinics, compared with less than 11 percent among Americans with family incomes of $35,000 or more (computed from National Center for Health Statistics, 1992, p. 219).

One problem common to emergency rooms and hospital clinics is that the patient tends not to see the same doctor on a regular basis and thus loses all the advantages of having a regular doctor. Emergency rooms present particular problems. Since they are readily available and one does not have to "know" a doctor to go there, they are becoming important sources of primary care, particularly among the poor (Gibson, Bugbee, and Anderson, 1970; Satin and Duhl, 1972; Satin, 1973; Cockerham, 1992). (*Primary care* means health care that is sought out by the patient as opposed to care that results from referral by a physician.) All in all, however, emergency rooms are far from ideal as a source of primary care. They tend to be concerned with relief of immediate symptoms and any seriously threatening conditions rather than the exploration of underlying causes of the problem. Detailed medical histories are not taken, and use of lab tests to diagnose problems is usually minimal. In addition, emergency-room physicians (often rotating interns or residents) usually have no medical history of the patient. Thus, emergency-room care is often fragmented and commonly fails to get to the root of the problem. Partly because of the kind of care they get—fragmented, with little or no explanation of what is being done, long waits, and limited if any preventive care—poor people are less likely than the nonpoor to seek treatment when they get sick. Thus, they are hurt both because of the quality of care they get and because their experiences discourage them from seeking care, even when they need it (Dutton, 1986; Rundall and Wheeler, 1979; Cockerham, 1992).

When their condition requires hospitalization, low-income patients frequently find themselves in public hospitals or Veterans Administration hospitals; middle-class patients are usually hospitalized in private hospitals. As a general rule, private hospitals are better staffed and better equipped than public hospitals, which must operate on very limited funds. Understaffing is a common problem in public hospitals, and the limited money available for salaries may keep the best-qualified medical personnel away. In addition, public hospitals often lack the sophisticated, up-to-date diagnostic and treatment equipment found in many private hospitals. In recent years, many public hospitals have closed. This has happened partly because of budget crises in the government units that support them and partly because Medicaid patients, who might have gone to public hospitals before Medicaid, now go elsewhere. Of course, when public hospitals close, another source of care for the poor who do not have Medicaid is eliminated. St. Louis provides a good illustration. Three large public hospitals there closed during the 1980s, two in the city and one in suburban St. Louis County. Those three were replaced with one publicly funded (but privately operated) regional hospital for the medically indigent, which had fewer beds than any one of the three hospitals it replaced.

Sometimes, when they are sick enough, low-income people are able to get admitted to university hospitals as ward patients. When this happens, they receive the most *technically* advanced treatment available. Even here, however, important differences exist between the way poor and nonpoor patients are treated. The nonpoor patient typically has a private or semiprivate room, and one physician is responsible for overseeing his or her care. Poor patients, on the other hand, are likely to be placed on a large ward shared with a number of other patients, and they are generally treated by interns and residents, sometimes on a rotating basis, rather than by a regular private physician. These practices led to a suit against one large midwestern university hospital for racial discrimination. The hospital put poor patients admitted through its clinic on certain floors and patients admitted by private physicians on others. The former were so predominantly black and the latter so predominantly white that a pattern of de facto floor-by-floor segregation of patients developed.

Attitudes of medical personnel toward low-income patients are also less than ideal. Indeed, in the hierarchy of roles within the hospital, the role of patient is generally at the bottom of the ladder with respect to esteem, regardless of class (Reynolds and Rice, 1971; Coe, 1978). The position of the lower-status patient is

A medical care facility in a minority neighborhood. Such facilities tend to be fewer in minority neighborhoods, and the type of care received there is often not the same as in the private facilities typically found in white middle-class neighborhoods. *Ken Karp*

even worse: Because of cultural differences between patient and practitioner, and because practitioners at the bottom of the hierarchy among physicians (interns and residents) are responsible for their treatment, low-income patients are often viewed as burdens and tend to remind interns and residents of their own low status within the hierarchy.

To summarize, the poor patient (and because of poverty, very often the black, Latino, or Indian patient) is generally hospitalized in a different kind of hospital, and within the hospital, in a different kind of setting. These differences frequently mean that the minority group patient receives lower-quality care, more fragmented care, or in some cases both. This, of course, happens once the patient reaches the stage of hospitalization. The lower-income patient, however, often goes longer before reaching the hospital, which sometimes makes the treatment of conditions more difficult because they become more advanced.

The Medicaid Program

In recent years, an important source of health care for lower-income Americans has been the Medicaid program. This program, established by the federal government in 1965 along with the Medicare program for the elderly, provides federal funding (with required state matching funds) for medical treatment of the poor. At a minimum, the program must cover persons receiving welfare; in some states, it is limited to such persons. Others may be included at the discretion of the states, subject to various limitations. The program is administered by the states, which of course means that there is considerable variation from state to state in the administration of the program. Basically, Medicaid is a program targeted at a small and very poor segment of the population. In 1989, fewer than 27 percent of persons in families with incomes below $14,000 were covered by Medicaid. A larger share of this group, over 37 percent, had no health insurance at all (National Center for Health Statistics,

1992, p. 291). In general, only a minority of the population below the poverty level is covered by Medicaid, and those with incomes just above the poverty level are even less likely to be covered. Thus, Medicaid, as presently established, fails to cover millions of needy Americans. This failing can only be made worse by the cutbacks in the Medicaid program initiated by the Reagan administration.

As in other areas we have examined, minority Americans, because of their disproportionate poverty, are more reliant on Medicaid than are white Americans. In 1990, 21.7 percent of black Americans and 15.9 percent of Hispanic Americans were covered by Medicaid, compared with only 5.2 percent of whites, who are much more likely than minorities to be covered by private insurance (U.S. Bureau of the Census, 1992c, p. 105). Even among the minority poor, many are not covered by Medicaid. Fewer than 60 percent of poor blacks and 50 percent of poor Hispanics are covered. Even so, the Medicaid program clearly is the main source of payment for health care for a sizable number of minority Americans.

It should be said from the start that the Medicaid program has clearly improved access to health care among the very poor over the three decades since it was established. In direct contrast to the past, people with incomes below the poverty level today see doctors more often than the nonpoor (Cockerham, 1992). In addition, indicators sensitive to the effects of health-care access, such as the infant mortality rate, showed dramatic improvements after Medicaid was established. In 1960, five years before Medicaid was established, the infant mortality rate in the United States was 26.0. By 1980, fifteen years after the program was begun, it had fallen to 12.6. In absolute terms, it fell by more than thirteen points; in relative terms, by more than 50 percent (National Center for Health Statistics, 1992, p. 141). Since 1980, however, gains have been more modest, particularly among minorities. The provisional 1990 infant mortality rate was 9.1. Among African Americans, infant mortality leveled off at around 18, more than double the white rate, and between 1988 and 1989, the black infant mortality rate actually rose slightly. The black infant mortality rate fell from more than 44 in 1960 to about 21 in 1980, but it remained near 18 in 1989 (National Center for Health Statistics, 1992, p. 141). There is no question that public-health improvements, such as the decline in the infant mortality rate result from a variety of factors, of which the Medicaid program is only one. Furthermore, it is equally clear that major inequalities remain, as we have seen. There is little doubt, however, that the Medicaid program has resulted in *some* improvement in access to health care among poor and minority Americans, and it has probably led to some improvement in their health status. Having said this, it must also be said that the program is far from perfect and that the care provided to the Medicaid patient is in many cases not as good as that provided to the middle-class patient. Let us examine some of the reasons for this.

To begin with, the Medicaid recipient must find a doctor willing to treat Medicaid patients. This is not always easy, since about half of the nation's physicians do not accept Medicaid patients. This is the case in part because Medicaid pays at lower rates than private insurance and does not allow doctors to bill their patients for the difference, since most cannot afford to pay. Thus, Medicaid patients are less profitable than other patients. This aspect would undoubtedly be substantially helped by a program such as the Clinton health-care proposal, which would eliminate distinctions between Medicaid patients and other patients, since all would be covered under the same overall system.

Among those physicians who do accept Medicaid, some operate "Medicaid mills," practices specializing in Medicaid patients. These practices attempt to offset Medicaid's lower rates of physician reimbursement by treating (and sometimes mistreating) large numbers of patients in an assembly-line fashion. In the mid 1970s, for example, it was estimated that there were five hundred such practices in New York State alone, each billing the government a half million dollars a year for services to Medicaid patients (*New York Times,* February 15, 1977, p. 35). These practices often try to give as much treatment as possible (sometimes, whether needed or not) to as many patients as possible in the shortest time possible. This often results in quick, superficial examinations and missed problems. Sometimes doctors specializing in Medicaid engage in outright fraud, such as charging for more-expensive procedures than the ones actually performed, double-billing for the same service, "ping-ponging" patients back and forth between different doctors for unnecessary visits, and ordering unnecessary visits and procedures (Jesilow, Geis, and Pontell, 1991). Such unnecessary procedures are bad for people's health and in some cases downright dangerous, and because of their disproportionate poverty, minorities are frequently the victims. One California ophthalmologist, for example, received $1 million from Medicaid recipients, many of whom he told that their cataracts, real or imagined, were contagious (cataracts are not contagious). After the doctor was imprisoned following the blinding of one of his patients in an unnecessary operation, the judge had this to say about the doctor and his attorney:

> They seem to think the whole trial is a contrivance by the attorney general's office. In not one of the letters has there been one word of sympathy for the true victims in this case, the uneducated, Spanish-speaking people, some of whom will never see a sunrise or sunset again. (Jesilow, Geis, and Pontell, 1991)

All this is profitable for doctors, who are paid once for each service they perform, but it is at best dehumanizing for the patient and at worst downright bad for the patient's health. Unnecessary operations and medical procedures are apparently fairly common in American medicine generally (Cockerham, 1978, pp. 140–41), but the problem is especially widespread among Medicaid patients. Not only does this waste public money; it threatens the lives and health of the Medicaid patients, since almost no medical procedure is entirely without risk. On the other hand, real problems may be missed because of the tendency of some Medicaid mills to run through as many patients as possible in a day. Thus, some Medicaid patients receive unneeded, costly, and potentially dangerous medical treatment; others fail to get treatment they really need. These problems result, in large part, because Medicaid retains the *fee-for-service* system that predominates in American medicine. By its nature, the fee-for-service system encourages doctors to perform as many services as possible in the shortest time (Jesilow, Geis, and Pontell, 1991). As third-party payments (by Medicare and private-insurance companies as well as Medicaid) have become more common, the fee-for-service system has led to more abuses, and complaints about quick, impersonal treatment and unnecessary procedures have become more common.

Not all Medicaid patients are treated in Medicaid mills, but among those who are, the above-mentioned problems frequently stand in the way of high-quality health care. In summary, we can say that the Medicaid program has made medical care available to millions of poor, largely minority Americans to whom it was not available in the past. The quality of that care, however, frequently does not match up to the quality of care enjoyed by middle-class Americans.

The American Health-Care Institution: A Conclusion

Health care in America, as we have seen, is economically and racially strati-fied for two main reasons. First, poor people generally, and therefore a dispropor-tionate number of black, Latino, and Native Americans, have a problem of *access* to medical care: They do not seek and/or cannot get care as readily as their white, mid-dle-class counterparts. Second, when they do get care, it is often more fragmented, more rushed, and less holistic than the care received by the middle class. Thus, the American health-care institution must be held at least partly responsible for the in-ferior health status of black, Hispanic, and Indian people in the United States as compared with the health status of white people.

It has been said that the American health-care system (or nonsystem, as some call it) has been designed to fit the needs of the physician more than those of the patient or the general public (see Stevens, 1971). This observation is strikingly similar to the more general position held by the conflict perspective: Social institu-tions tend to serve the interest of the dominant and powerful elite that controls them. In the United States, physicians have—at least until recently—wielded great political power through their national organization, the American Medical Associa-tion (AMA). This organization has vigorously resisted any governmental effort to regulate or control the fees that doctors charge for their services. In the 1980s, soar-ing medical costs led business and government (which pay many medical expenses through employee insurance, Medicare, and Medicaid) to assert greater control over American medicine. They did so mainly by limiting the kind and amount of care they pay for. Although this has reduced the power of doctors somewhat, it has done little for patients, particularly poor ones. Instead, it has made it harder for poor patients without insurance to get care, because cost-control measures have reduced the money that hospitals have to cover "charity care." As a result, the plight of poor peo-ple without medical care became significantly worse during the 1980s—and a large share of these medically indigent people are black, Hispanic, or American Indian.

For the great majority covered by neither Medicaid nor Medicare, health care remains based on ability to pay, either through private insurance or out of pocket. This system has led to a maldistribution of health care, with much of it in wealthy suburbs, little of it in the ghettos, barrios, and rural areas. It has also led to class and racial channeling in health care, as the nonpoor receive care from private personal or family physicians while the poor (disproportionately minorities) receive frequently inferior care from emergency rooms, hospital clinics, Medicaid mills, and, when hospitalization is required, public hospitals. The effects of all this are worsened by a system of medical education that produces few minority doctors and that attracts future doctors mostly from the upper social strata.

The limited reforms of Medicaid and Medicare, while helpful, have not been able to change these basic truths. It appears that to obtain racial and economic equality, the minimum necessary step would be the establishment of some form of national health insurance, as Canada and so many other countries have done. To de-velop a truly efficient system, one that places the needs of the patient on a par with those of the doctor, basic structural changes, such as elimination or reform of the fee-for-service system, may be necessary. While the Clinton plan and alternatives to it that have been proposed in Congress generally leave intact the fee-for-service plan (though with various mechanisms designed to control costs), the Clinton plan and some of the others do propose to guarantee health-insurance coverage to every

American, regardless of income, employment status, or health history. A plan of this type would help a wide variety of Americans with their health costs, since so many have no coverage, limited coverage, or preexisting conditions that their health plans do not cover. At the same time, these reforms would be particularly helpful in reducing the racial and ethnic inequalities that now exist in America's health-care system, since minorities are so disproportionately represented among those with no coverage and those who must rely on Medicaid. However, at the time of this writing, a well-financed campaign by insurance companies, employers, and others who have a stake in maintaining the present health-care system had generated sizable opposition in the U.S. Senate to proposals to guarantee universal health coverage. As a result, the prospects of attaining universal coverage remained uncertain.

SUMMARY AND CONCLUSION

In this chapter we began by examining competing theories on the causes of economic racial discrimination and on who benefits from such discrimination. The causes are complex, and the relative importance of various factors has changed with time. Although deliberate discrimination has decreased since the end of World War II, economic racial inequality has persisted. Clearly, minorities are harmed by such inequality, and a plausible argument can be made, based on studies like those of Reich and Szymanski, that many whites are also harmed by it.

Recognizing that the causes of inequality have changed, we then turned to examining practices and patterns that have become institutionalized in modern society and that harm the economic positions of minority-group members. Among such institutionalized patterns and practices are the use of inflated educational requirements in hiring, the movement of employment opportunities out of minority areas, and the pervasive pattern of discrimination in housing. The latter two, along with the system of raising revenue through local taxes, have helped to create a fiscal crisis in America's great cities, a crisis that has also been disproportionately harmful to the minority populations that are heavily concentrated in those cities. All of these processes have tended to preserve racial inequalities resulting from past discrimination. In the case of the large minority underclass described in the previous chapter, these processes have probably made matters worse. Finally, the problem of racial economic inequality is unlikely to be resolved until these institutionalized practices and patterns are altered. Eliminating deliberate discrimination, though necessary, does not appear to be enough: Further improvement in the status of minorities (and *any* real improvement in the status of the "underclass") will require more fundamental types of change.

Much the same is true of the health status of minority-group members. Certainly not all of the health disadvantages of minorities can be attributed to the health-care system. Nonetheless, it is clear that a health-care system based heavily on the ability to pay cannot serve the disproportionately low-income minority population as well as it serves the higher-income white population. Thus, it appears that to eliminate racial and ethnic inequalities in access to quality health care, it will be necessary to make fundamental changes in the system of health-care financing or, more basically, to eliminate substantial racial inequalities in income and wealth, or to do both. Thus, both the problem of economic racial inequality and the more immediate (but largely economic) problems of poorer health and higher mortality among the minority population would appear to require basic and far-reaching changes in our social institutions. Fortunately, such changes in the health-care system were under serious consideration in the 1990s, for the first time in more than forty years. This is a positive development for the health-care access of people of color and lower-income people of all races, even if the outcome of the health-care debate remains uncertain.

11

The American Political and Legal System and Majority–Minority Relations

In this chapter, we turn our attention to the American political and legal systems and examine their impact on majority–minority group relations in the United States. Although the chapter focuses on political and legal processes, it is important to recognize that these processes are closely intertwined with the economic processes described in the previous chapter.

To begin with, there is clearly some linkage between economic wealth and political power. Although the strength of this relationship is debated (see Reisman, 1953; Mills, 1956; Domhoff, 1967, 1983), clearly, those who are wealthy exercise considerably more power, both directly and indirectly, than those who are poor, and political power can enable a group to protect or advance its *economic* position. Thus, we see something of a vicious circle: If a group is generally poor, it will tend to have less than its share of political power, which will tend to further weaken its economic position, and so on.

Political processes are also linked to the economic process through the unintended economic effects of decisions made in the political arena. Such effects may work either to the advantage or disadvantage of minority groups. This can be illustrated by two examples from twentieth-century American history. Under the Roosevelt administration, various laws were passed to protect the rights of workers to organize into labor unions and to prohibit employers from engaging in unfair labor practices. According to Wilson (1978), these laws tended to reduce job discrimination against blacks and other minorities, even though this was not their main purpose. It happened because strikebreaking was made more difficult (and subsequently happened less often), so that discrimination associated with the use of minority-group members as strikebreakers decreased. In heavy industry particularly, a new environment developed in which white and minority workers cooperated in labor unions rather than struggled to undercut each other's position.

Government actions can also have a negative impact on economically disadvantaged minority groups. In the previous chapter, we discussed the impact of current urban fiscal difficulties on minority groups. A further analysis of these difficulties reveals that they are in part a product of federal governmental policies that sometimes had unforeseen consequences. Tax deductions, loan guarantees, and subsidies provided housing assistance to millions of middle-class (and mostly white) Americans after World War II and in large part made possible the flight of the middle class to the suburbs, which depleted central cities of their tax base. The construction of urban expressways, financed mainly by the federal government under the interstate highway program, had similar effects, contributing to suburbanization of both residences and jobs (Long and Glick, 1976, p. 40; Kasarda, 1976, p. 119). Furthermore, the costs of the freeway system have been disproportionately borne by blacks and other minorities, whose central city neighborhoods have frequently been bulldozed for freeway construction (Downs, 1970). Thus, the economic welfare of minorities was influenced both directly and indirectly by government housing, taxation, and highway construction policies that outwardly had nothing to do with race relations.

It is clear, then, that decisions made in the political system can influence the position of racial and ethnic minorities in a wide range of areas, and can do so for

An urban freeway. More often than not, it is poor people and minorities that are displaced by the construction of such freeways, and they are rarely if ever paid the full cost of their forced move. Furthermore, such freeways have enabled the middle-class populations to flee to the suburbs, leaving the central cities too fiscally poor to meet the needs of their growing low-income and minority populations. *Marc Anderson*

better and for worse. In the following section, we shall examine ways in which political decisions and the American political system itself have affected the well-being of American minority groups.

GOVERNMENT IN AMERICA: AGENT OF THE WHITE OPPRESSOR OR PROTECTOR OF MINORITY RIGHTS?

Historical Patterns: Governmental Policies of Discrimination

Throughout American history, Afro-Americans, Chicanos, and Native Americans have been directly affected by policies and actions of federal, state, and local governments. As was described in some detail in Chapter 5, the U.S. Army, acting upon the orders of the federal government, played a critical and central role in the conquest and subordination of both the Indian people and the Mexican citizens who lived in what is now the southwestern United States. Similarly, until the Civil War, the federal government recognized the legality of black slavery in the southern states, and a number of U.S. presidents themselves had slaves. For purposes of apportionment of Congress, the U.S. Constitution regarded each black slave as three-fifths of a person, one of many federal "compromise" decisions recognizing the legality and legitimacy of slavery in the southern states (Franklin, 1969, p. 142). Other such "compromises" provided for the return of runaway slaves to their owners, even when the runaways had established residence in states where slavery was illegal. Thus, it is no exaggeration to say that from the very beginning, the federal government played a central role in creating and maintaining racial and ethnic inequality in the United States. This was particularly true for the three colonized minority groups (see Chapter 6): blacks, Chicanos, and American Indians. In various ways the U.S. government has also clearly maintained formal policies of discrimination against people of Asian ancestry. Two of the most blatant examples are the ban on immigration from Asian countries, in effect in the early twentieth century, and the imprisonment of Japanese Americans during World War II.

In addition to the position of the federal government, state governments during the early history of the United States also took strong antiminority positions. In the South, all states had laws providing for black slavery. Furthermore, some had slave codes requiring freed slaves to leave the state and forbidding that slaves be taught to read or write or to conduct any business with whites.

Lest there be any confusion, however, we should recognize that openly racist state and local legislation was not limited to the South or to the pre–Civil War era. Pennsylvania, for example, denied the vote to blacks in 1838; Indiana did the same in 1851. In "liberal" New York, blacks were subjected to property ownership and length-of-residence voting requirements not required of whites (Franklin, 1969, p. 220). Indeed, the predominant stance of state and local legislation concerning race and ethnic relations was supportive of discrimination until around World War II, and in some areas it remained that way for a long while after the war.

As noted in Chapter 6, the one brief period that was something of an exception to this general pattern was the period immediately after the Civil War known as Reconstruction. During this short period, laws pertaining to race relations were liberalized in both the North and the South, though liberalization in the latter came mainly from federal intervention. During this period, the Fourteenth Amendment (equal protection) and Fifteenth Amendment (no denial of vote due to race) to the U.S. Constitution and federal civil rights laws were passed. Numerous blacks were elected to southern state legislatures, and between 1870 and 1901, twenty blacks were elected to the U.S. House of Representatives and two to the U.S. Senate (Johnson, 1943; Franklin, 1969, pp. 317–321). However, this period did not last long. Beginning with a political deal struck between Democrats and Republicans in 1876 (McWilliams, 1951, p. 265; Simpson and Yinger, 1985, p. 230), the control of the South was returned to white supremacists. A very important step in the process was the *Plessy* v. *Ferguson* ruling of the Supreme Court in 1896, which upheld the doctrine of "separate but equal" facilities. As a result, in many parts of the country, public facilities quickly became separate but rarely, if ever, equal. In addition, the federal Civil Rights Act of 1875, one of the civil rights laws passed during Reconstruction, had by now been declared unconstitutional, so that before the turn of the century, government had returned largely to the position of sometimes tolerating and other times requiring discrimination. Governmentally supported discrimination was most important in the first half of the twentieth century in the areas of voting rights, education, segregation of public facilities, housing, and immigration.

Voting Rights.   Although the Fifteenth Amendment to the U.S. Constitution, enacted in 1870, prohibited denial of the right to vote on account of race, many of the states, particularly in the South, developed ingenious ways of getting around the amendment and preventing minority group members from voting. Probably the earliest was the "grandfather clause," which provided that people could vote only if they, their father, and/or their grandfather had been entitled to vote at some date prior to emancipation (Simpson and Yinger, 1985, p. 230). These laws, passed by several southern states in the late 1890s, kept blacks from voting because they or their fathers or grandfathers had been slaves—and therefore ineligible to vote—on the date specified. These clauses had the effect of making previous condition of servitude (slavery) a condition of voting, which was forbidden by the Fifteenth Amendment, and in 1915 the Supreme Court declared them unconstitutional. In the meantime, however, they had been used to effectively eliminate black voting rights in a number of states for nearly twenty years.

Two other practices that were, for a time at least, accepted as constitutional, were the poll tax and the "white primary." Both practices became widespread in the South. In many southern states, the only real election during the first half of the twentieth century was the Democratic primary: These states were so heavily Democratic that whoever won the primary always won the general election. In Texas and several other states, voting in the Democratic primary was, with legislative permission, restricted to whites. This practice was based on a 1921 Supreme Court decision that primaries were not elections but rather party matters, and after two initial Texas laws were struck down, the Supreme Court approved in 1935 a decision by the Texas Democratic party convention to restrict the primary to whites, as long as the party, not the state, paid for it. In 1944, the Supreme Court reversed itself again and struck down all forms of the white primary, but by then the practice had been in effect in one or more southern states at virtually all times since 1923—a period of over twenty years.

Around the turn of the century, ten southern states instituted poll taxes, designed to keep blacks, who were disproportionately poor, from voting by attaching an unaffordable cost to voting (Simpson and Yinger, 1985, p. 230). In Texas the poll tax—in effect for about sixty years—also prevented Mexican Americans from voting (Moore, 1976, p. 142), as well, of course, as numerous poor whites. This discriminatory practice remained in effect in five states until 1964, when it was finally outlawed by the Twenty-fourth Amendment to the U.S. Constitution.

In addition to these measures, an important way of limiting minority voting in southern states has been to give voting registrars considerable discretion in deciding who to accept and who not to accept for voter registration. Scruggs (1971, p. 85) argues that this was one of the most important ways in which blacks were kept from voting.

Probably the most widespread requirement limiting minority voting has been the literacy test. This requirement has existed in various forms in numerous states in the South, West, and Northeast. Among the states that have required voters to pass literacy tests are New York, California, and Massachusetts. Literacy tests have tended to reduce voting opportunities for blacks, Hispanics, and Native Americans. All of these groups have suffered extensive educational discrimination, and consequently, a higher percentage of their adult populations are unable to pass the tests. The literacy tests in New York and in several southwestern states, because they were exclusively in English, had especially strong impacts on Puerto Ricans and Chicanos, respectively, though the New York test was revised to recognize Spanish in 1965. In many instances, too, literacy tests were applied unequally, with more stringent demands being made of minorities than of whites (see Chief Justice Warren's opinion in *South Carolina* v. *Katzenbach,* 383 U.S. 301, 1966; quoted in Dorsen, 1969).

These practices were largely ended by the Voting Rights Act of 1965. In 1975, this law was revised to require bilingual ballots in specified areas with large numbers of non–English speakers. Nonetheless, even during the late 1960s and 1970s, some states engaged in practices that reduce minority voter participation. Reports by the U.S. Commission on Civil Rights (1968, 1975) indicate that in some southern states, blacks were kept from registering by limited hours for registration, harassment by registrars, and more stringent identification requirements than were set for whites. Another common practice that has removed disproportionate numbers of minorities from the voting rolls is periodic purging of voters who do not vote. In Arizona, for example, this is done every two years (that is, every state/federal election), and this practice has had very disproportionate effects on Indian and Chicano voters (U.S. Civil Rights Commission, 1975, pp. 85–86).

It is clear from this review of the history of voting restrictions that numerous states have had policies governing voter registration that have made voting easier for whites than for minority group members. Especially but not only, in the South, the intent and effect of these policies has been partly or entirely to discriminate. During the past forty years, court rulings, the Twenty-fourth Amendment, and the 1965 Voting Rights Act have made discrimination in access to the ballot box considerably more difficult. Nonetheless, even in recent years the problem has not entirely disappeared, as the 1975 Civil Rights Commission report demonstrates. As a result, when the Voting Rights Act came up for renewal in 1982, Congress added new provisions prohibiting states from changing voting procedure in such a way that the *effect* would be to discriminate against minorities. In areas with a history of discrimination, such changes must be preapproved by the Justice Department or by a federal court. This is significant, since discriminatory effect is much easier to demonstrate than discriminatory intent.

Public Facilities.   Throughout the South and in some border states, such public facilities as libraries, museums, parks, swimming pools, golf courses, and public transportation were strictly segregated through most of the first half of the twentieth century. Such segregation was required by both state law and local ordinances (Myrdal, 1944, chap. 29). The length to which such rules of segregation sometimes went can be seen in examples presented by Woodward (1966, pp. 117–118). In 1932, Atlanta passed an ordinance forbidding amateur baseball clubs of different races to play within two blocks of one another. During the 1930s, Texas passed a law prohibiting "Caucasians" and "Africans" from boxing or wrestling together, and federal law was used to hinder the circulation of films showing interracial boxing. In Oklahoma, state law even required segregated fishing and boating. In general, segregation of public facilities was the law in the South and in some border areas until the 1950s.

State and local governments in the South were not always content with requiring segregation in publicly owned facilities. In many instances, legislation was also passed requiring the operators of privately owned facilities and services open to the public to discriminate. An example of this can be seen in the laws of Florida, Tennessee, and a number of other states, which required segregation of passenger trains (Scruggs, 1971, p. 84).

As a general rule, governmentally mandated segregation of public facilities was much more widespread in the South and border states than it was in the North (Myrdal, 1944, chap. 29). Nonetheless, the North was also highly segregated, and frequently the segregation existed with subtler forms of support and encouragement from state or local government. Although some northern states did have civil rights laws prior to the 1950s, others did not, and even where there were such laws, enforcement was frequently weak or nonexistent. Frequently, public facilities were de facto segregated by placing them in all-white or all-black areas rather than in borderline or racially mixed areas. In Chicago, police in some instances enforced segregation of city beaches even though there was no law or ordinance requiring such segregation (Drake and Cayton, 1945, p. 105). The absence of civil rights laws in some states made it perfectly legal for businesses to post signs such as "whites only," and many did (Myrdal, 1944, chap. 29). Such practices sometimes also occurred without interference even in states that had civil rights laws. Especially in smaller northern cities, rigid patterns of discrimination frequently existed without governmental interference. Lynd and Lynd (1929) noted a pervasive pattern of racial segregation in Muncie, Indiana, including a policy of segregation at the local YMCA. In his autobiography, Malcolm X (Haley, 1964, p. 3) reports telling Michigan State University students about his experiences while growing up in East Lansing, the town where that university is located. "In those days," he told the students, "Negroes weren't allowed after dark in East Lansing proper."

The best overall description of the stance of state and local governments toward discrimination in public facilities in the first half of the twentieth century would be something like the following. In the South, public-facility segregation and discrimination was generally required by law. In the border states, such discrimination was typically encouraged and often required. In the remainder of the country, the position of state and local governments varied. In some states, there was a formal prohibition of at least some types of discrimination, though enforcement was often weak. In many nonsouthern states, however, there was no law against discrimination in the private sector, and subtler forms of public-sector discrimination and segregation were frequently practiced, particularly at the local level and particularly in smaller communities. With the exception of an occasional Supreme Court ruling, the federal government did little or nothing to stop such discrimination before about World War II, and in some ways encouraged it.

Housing. In numerous ways, the actions of federal, state, and local government promoted discrimination in housing. Past actions of government are an important cause of the pervasive pattern of housing segregation that is found in the United States today. One of the most important things that governments did to promote housing segregation was to enforce restrictive housing covenants. As you will recall from Chapter 10, a restrictive covenant is a provision attached to a deed or sales contract in which the buyer must agree not to sell or rent to a member of a specified group, such as blacks, Chicanos, or Jews. To be enforceable, these restrictive covenants needed the backing of law. Until 1948 they got it: State courts, North and South, enforced these agreements by ordering a buyer of the "wrong" race or creed to give up the property. Thus, state enforcement was the crucial link that made the restrictive covenant an effective force maintaining discrimination. At one time, the practice of restrictive covenants was so widespread that it has been estimated that up to 80 percent of all vacant land in Chicago and Los Angeles was closed to blacks (Abrams, 1971, p. 218). In 1944, eleven square miles of Chicago and five and a half square miles of St. Louis were covered by restrictive covenants against blacks (Vose, 1959). In 1948, the Supreme Court ruled that state courts could not enforce such covenants, but the covenants themselves did not entirely disappear. Rather, they continued to appear on many deeds to older housing, as was vividly illustrated in 1986 when Senate hearings revealed that the chief justice-designate of the U.S. Supreme Court, as well as several U.S. senators, unknowingly owned houses that still bore restrictive covenants (unenforceable, of course).

Federal actions also contributed to housing segregation. The present-day pattern of predominantly minority cities and white suburbs is a legacy of the tax subsidies and the Federal Housing Administration (FHA) and Veterans' Administration (VA) programs that made suburban housing available to the middle-class masses after World War II. Most of the benefits of these subsidy programs went to whites; comparable levels of aid were not available to lower-income residents, who were more likely to be minorities. Thus, a situation was created that enabled whites to buy new housing in the suburbs and restricted minorities for the most part to poorer-quality housing in the central cities. There is, furthermore, evidence that this did not all happen by chance. The official manuals governing FHA policy from 1935 to 1950 contained warnings against "the infiltration of inharmonious racial and national groups," "a lower class of inhabitants," "the presence of incompatible racial elements," and "a lower level of society" (Larson and Nikkel, 1979, p. 235). In fact, FHA materials even included a model restrictive covenant, with the name of the unwanted group left blank to be filled in (Larson and Nikkel, 1979, p. 235)! Thus, federal housing policy emerges as a major culprit in the problem of housing discrimination and segregation.

Local governments also promoted housing discrimination. With the silent acceptance of the federal government, many local housing authorities used federal dollars to run segregated public-housing developments. According to Franklin (1969, pp. 537, 610), this practice was widespread until around the time of World War II. It was the rule in all southern cities that had public housing and in some northern and border cities as well. As late as the 1950s, formally segregated public-housing developments remained in some parts of the country.

Another approach widely used against minorities at the local level is zoning. Zoning has been used primarily in two ways that tend to discriminate against minorities. One is the use of rezoning to block proposed housing developments that would house minority group members, attempt to create an interracial environment, or be built for low-income populations. The other way is through what is known as snob zoning, which uses devices such as minimum lot sizes and prohibition of certain types of housing to keep out "undesirables." Both practices have been widespread in American local communities, and to a considerable degree both remain a problem today. Research shows, for example, that the larger the percentage of blacks is in nearby communities, the more likely a suburban community is to use zoning to restrict multifamily housing development (Burnell and Burnell, 1989). Moreover, such practices are legal, even in all-white communities, unless it can be proved than their *purpose* is to exclude minorities or that they are being applied differently to people of different racial groups.

Clearly, then, despite open-housing legislation in the 1960s and since, federal, state, and local governments have been actively and heavily involved in housing discrimination over the years. Although many of the discriminatory practices have been curtailed, some, such as snob zoning, continue to play a significant role in housing segregation today. Thus, government at all levels bears a significant responsibility for the pervasive pattern of segregation and inequality in housing found in American urban areas today.

Education. Although education is discussed in detail in a later chapter, we shall briefly show that in education, as in other areas, the orientation of governmental policies—particularly at the state and local level—generally ranged from accepting discrimination to requiring discrimination in education up to the time of the 1954 Supreme Court ruling against segregated schools. In the South and border states, school segregation was generally required by law. No less than seventeen states and the District of Columbia at one time had laws requiring segregation of schools (Myrdal, 1944, p. 632). In addition, many local school boards implemented a policy of segregation even where it was not required by state law. State-mandated educational discrimination has been used not only against blacks but against other minorities as well. An 1860 California law, for example, excluded Chinese and Indians, as well as blacks, from that state's public schools. In 1906, the city of San Francisco took action to segregate the Chinese and Japanese in its school system (Bahr, Chadwick, and Strauss, 1979, pp. 81, 85). In much of the Southwest, Chicanos were also segregated from Anglos in the school systems (Moore, 1976, p. 81). In at least some instances, school boards in Texas responded to court orders to desegregate schools by mixing black and Chicano students, leaving white Anglo students in all-Anglo schools (Moore, 1976, p. 81).

Another area of discrimination in the past was the refusal to provide bilingual teachers who could communicate with Spanish-speaking students. At one time, for example, it was against the law in California for teachers to use Spanish in the state's public schools. This issue could arise again as the result of passage by initiative and referendum in 1986 of a new law specifying English as California's only official language.

As we have seen in the preceding pages, there has been a widespread pattern of discrimination through much of American history involving, in various ways, the local, state, and federal levels of government. Although we have emphasized the areas of voting, use of public facilities, housing, and education, publicly supported or required discrimination has not been limited to these areas. In earlier chapters, we discussed legal restrictions on the freedom of travel of reservation Indians, laws forbidding Chinese and Japanese to enter the United States at times when other immigrants were accepted, the use of American law to deprive Mexican Americans of their land in the Southwest, and the blanket imprisonment of Japanese Americans during World War II. A careful examination of American history can yield only one answer: Government at all levels in the United States has engaged in discrimination in thousands of ways and must bear a substantial piece of the responsibility for racial and ethnic inequality in America today.

Contemporary Patterns: Government and Majority–Minority Relations Today

As was described in Chapter 6, the position of governments in the United States shifted gradually to an antidiscrimination stance, beginning around the time of World War II. The major legislation, presidential decisions, and court rulings against racial and ethnic discrimination are summarized in Table 11.1.

It is clear that the formal position of the federal government today, as well as state and local governments is, on the whole, opposed to racial and ethnic discrimination. Nonetheless, a strong case can be made that, in subtler ways, government continues to operate against the interests of minority group members. As we have seen, government has in the past played a major role in creating and maintaining the racial and ethnic inequality that is so widespread in American society today. In spite of this fact, governments today are doing very little to undo the effects of this discrimination. Analysis of a few areas of federal government action (or inaction) can clearly illustrate this point.

Government Spending.   One way to assess the priorities of any government is to see where it spends its money. Examination of governmental expenditures in recent years clearly shows that, contrary to popular opinion, programs to improve the status of minority Americans have not been given high priority. The recessions of 1974, 1980, 1982–1983, and 1991–1992 have reconfirmed the old adage that minority group members are the "last hired, first fired." From the 1970s to the 1990s, for example, the proportion of blacks unemployed has been two to two and a half times as high as for whites, with black unemployment soaring to 15 percent to 20 percent during the recessions. In spite of this, programs to provide jobs, which represent only a tiny fraction of the federal budget, were cut during 1980 as a way of combating inflation, even though defense spending was *increased* at the same time. These trends, already under way during the Carter administration, accelerated sharply after the Reagan administration took over in 1981 and continued throughout the 1980s. Despite governmental claims to the contrary, the efforts to combat inflation have been undertaken largely at the expense of the poor. In fiscal year 1990, for example, all programs providing cash and noncash benefits to low-income people amounted to less than 16 percent of the federal budget. By comparison, defense expenditures alone were about 21 percent (U.S. Bureau of the Census, 1992c). During the early 1980s, money was taken away from antipoverty programs and allocated

Table 11.1 Major Federal Actions Against Discrimination Since 1935

YEAR	ACTION
1938	*Missouri ex. rel. Gaines* v. *Canada,* 305 U.S. 337. Supreme Court rules that University of Missouri must admit a black applicant to law school because the state provided no comparable law school open to blacks
1941	President Roosevelt issues presidential order against discrimination in defense plants and governmental agencies
1946	Two federal courts rule that segregation in interstate travel is illegal
1948	President Truman issues a presidential order to integrate the U.S. armed forces
1948	*Shelley* v. *Kraemer,* 334 U.S. 1. Supreme Court rules that racially restrictive convenants in housing are not legally enforceable
1954	*Brown* v. *Board of Education,* 347 U.S. 483. Supreme Court ends "separate but equal" doctrine and rules that school segregation is illegal
1957	President Eisenhower orders federal troops into Arkansas to enforce a court order to desegregate Little Rock schools
1957	Civil Rights Act of 1957. Gave certain enforcement powers to a Civil Rights Division in the U.S. Department of Justice and provided penalties for failure to obey court orders in voting rights cases
1960	Civil Rights Act of 1960. Strengthened voting rights enforcement provisions of 1957 Civil Rights act
1964	Civil Rights Act of 1964. Banned racial, ethnic, and sex discrimination in employment and union membership. Prohibited discrimination by privately owned businesses providing public accommodations, such as hotels, restaurants, and theaters. Strengthened enforcement provisions against discrimination in education
1965	Voting Rights Act of 1965. Suspended use of literacy tests and permitted federal review of requirements attached to voting or registration. Authorized federal registration of voters where states discriminated
1968	Civil Rights Act of 1968. Banned discrimination in the sale and rental of housing
1975	Voting Rights Act expanded to protect linguistic minorities
1982	Ten-year extension and strengthening of Voting Rights Act of 1965
1988	Fair Housing Act Amendments of 1988. Strengthens fair-housing enforcement mechanisms of 1968 Civil Rights Act, bans discrimination based on familial status, and requires new housing to be accessible to disabled
1991	Civil Rights Act of 1991. Reverses several Supreme Court rulings in 1989 that made it more difficult for minorities to sue for discrmination. Bans job tests and practices that have the effect of excluding minorities or women, unless these requirements are demonstrably related to job performance and consistent with business necessity
1993	President Clinton eases military ban on homosexuals by no longer allowing recruits to be asked about their sexual orientation. However, a more restrictive policy than Clinton's original proposal is approved by Congress

to defense. Between 1980 and 1984, for example, federal spending on income maintenance programs and health care grew by less than 33 percent (without adjustment for inflation; substantially less if inflation is taken into account), despite a 35 percent increase in the number of poor people between 1979 and 1983 (U.S. Bureau of the Census, 1985b, 1986b). During the same period, defense spending grew by 77 percent (U.S. Bureau of the Census, 1985b). In response to the difficult economic conditions of the early 1990s, and to the severe inner-city conditions that gave rise to the

1992 Los Angeles riot, the Clinton administration proposed a jobs and economic-stimulus package of over $16 billion to Congress in early 1993. However, Congress cut this proposed jobs package to less than $2 billion. One part of the package that was cut was a summer-job program for inner-city teenagers; a sample of forty major cities revealed that more than twice as many eligible inner-city youths were registered for jobs as the number of jobs the reduced program was able to provide (Claiborne, 1993; Krauss, 1993).

Of course, the tendency to cut job-producing programs during times of economic difficulty is doubly devastating since (1) it is minorities who have the highest level of unemployment and (2) the cuts come precisely when jobs are most needed. Given the relatively low priority the problem has received, it is not surprising that black unemployment has consistently been twice (or more) as high as white unemployment, or that the employment situation in the 1990s in urban ghettos is worse than it was during the last major round of urban violence in the late 1960s.

A related pattern of government spending that is harmful to minorities can be seen by examining some geographic patterns of federal spending. Such an examination shows that the large urban areas, where the bulk of the minority population lives, have gotten less than their share of federal dollars. New York City, for example, paid the federal government $3.2 billion more in taxes than it got back in expenditures *each year* from 1965 to 1967, many times the $1 billion deficit that brought the city to bankruptcy. At the same time, other parts of the country were receiving *more* than they paid in (Melman, 1976). Generally, the growing areas of the West and South have done well in this regard, while the urban Northeast and Great Lakes states have fared poorly; New York, Michigan, and Illinois, for example—all urban industrial states with large minority populations—all paid in more in income and employment taxes alone than they got back in total federal spending in 1983. In cities with large minority populations such as Atlanta, Cleveland, Newark, and Detroit, fiscal problems have been chronic. In 1978, Cleveland became the first U.S. city since the depression of the 1930s to default on a debt payment.

By the early 1990s, ballooning federal deficits began to cause cuts even in the defense budget, which altered some of the geographic effects of federal spending. Defense cuts accelerated in the early years of the Clinton administration, but by then, the effects of tax cuts and massive defense spending in the Reagan era had brought about federal deficits so large that nearly all the savings from the defense cuts went to deficit reduction, not spending on antipoverty programs. Cuts in defense spending in the late years of the Bush administration and the early years of the Clinton administration appear to have had disproportionate effects on the West and South, which offset some of the advantage that those regions had enjoyed in the 1980s. Oil-producing regions, such as southern Texas, Louisiana, and southern California, were hit at the same time by falling oil prices, and in California, problems were further aggravated when the real-estate boom of the 1970s and early 1980s went bust, leading to drops in overinflated housing prices. The result was severe budget crises in states such as Louisiana and especially California, which were compounded by the long-term effect of tax-cutting measures such as California's Proposition 13. Because the low average incomes of minorities make them more dependent than whites on governmental assistance for everything from health care to student financial aid, minorities have suffered disproportionately from state and federal budget crises, though working-class people of all races have clearly been hurt.

Welfare Reform.   Another area in which the federal government has shown a lack of concern for minority needs in recent years is the welfare system. As it operates now, the system tends to keep poor people dependent and unable to become self-supporting. It does so in part by failing to provide incentives to work: Recipients lose their welfare if they work, so they end up little better and sometimes worse off for working. It is also not unusual for recipients to be denied welfare if they seek higher education, even though such training may be exactly what they need to become independent. Finally, it is widely accepted that the welfare system tends to break up families by taking needed aid away from women because of the presence of an adult male in the household. Despite awareness of all these consequences, efforts at a thoroughgoing reform of the welfare system, including the payment of a minimum subsistence level of income, have repeatedly failed in Congress since the years of the Nixon administration.

Moreover, what often passes as welfare reform frequently amounts to mean-spirited efforts at budget cutting. A 1993 experiment in two Wisconsin communities, approved by the Clinton administration as a way of trying out new ideas in welfare reform, is a good example. In these counties, anyone who does not find a job after receiving welfare for two years will lose welfare payments. The intent—to get people off welfare and into employment—is good. However, the program takes no account of job availability and thus has the effect of punishing people who try to find a job but cannot find one. Moreover, it also has the effect of hurting children because of their parent's actions or inability to find work. Clinton proposed a similar policy at the federal level in 1994, though the federal proposal was limited to younger women and included job training and child-care subsidies to make work more feasible. The fate of this proposal was uncertain at the time of this writing.

A more promising approach than merely cutting off welfare benefits after two years can be found in efforts to make work more feasible and attractive to welfare recipients. Until recently, welfare recipients in most states lost Medicaid if they went to work. This meant that a person who stayed on welfare would continue to get medical coverage, while a person who went to work would lose it. Recent federal legislation has sought to correct this by requiring that Medicaid coverage be continued for a period of time after a welfare recipient begins work. Because this was an unfunded mandate to state governments, however, many have had difficulty finding ways to pay for this extended coverage. A better solution to the problem lies in proposals advanced by the Clinton administration and others in 1993 for universal health coverage. Under this type of system, a person leaving welfare for work would continue to receive the same coverage as would a person switching from one job to another. Another factor that often inhibits welfare recipients from seeking employment is the high cost of day care. Although most other industrialized countries subsidize day care, in the United States it is usually available only on the basis of ability to pay. If a welfare recipient faces paying for both day care and health care if she or he goes to work, the costs may exceed the income provided by the job. Many of the low-skill service jobs in today's economy (which are particularly likely to be the kinds of jobs available in minority areas) pay minimum wage or little more and provide no medical benefits. Thus, the failure to provide help with day care and health care when welfare recipients take jobs makes it impossible for many of them to do so.

Public Transportation and Health Care.   Two other areas that the United States government has neglected are public transportation and health care. Among the industrialized nations of the world, the United States ranks near the bottom in these areas. The efficient subway systems of London, Paris, Stockholm, and Moscow present a striking contrast to the crowded freeways and the limited and financially insecure bus systems in many U.S. cities. In recent years, several major U.S. cities such as Pittsburgh, St. Louis, and Los Angeles have, with federal aid, built new mass-transit systems, and these have significantly improved access to employment for minority group members—many of whom lack cars—who are lucky enough to live near the transit lines. However, mass-transit systems in all but a handful of major cities such as New York, Boston, and Chicago are very small in scale compared with those found in most other industrialized countries. In the area of health care, one of the major supporters of national health insurance in the United States, Senator Edward Kennedy, is fond of pointing out that, aside from South Africa, the United States is the only industrialized nation in the world without some kind of national health-care coverage. This may change, however, as a result of proposals by the Clinton administration and others in 1993 and 1994 for various plans to provide universal health-insurance coverage in the United States. These proposals and the problems faced by minorities in the American health-care system are discussed in detail in Chapter 10.

Governmental failure to provide public transportation and health-care protection once again affects minority group members more than other Americans, because their disproportionate poverty leaves them less able than others to afford private transportation or health care. Statistics on auto ownership show that minority group members are less likely than whites to own automobiles (U.S. Bureau of the Census, 1984b), and health-coverage statistics show that they are also less likely to have health insurance (National Center for Health Statistics, 1992).

One may argue, of course, that the problems discussed here are economic rather than racial. In fact, W. J. Wilson (1978) has argued that class, rather than race, became the main reason for black disadvantage in the 1970s. Indeed, governmental policies are, as we have noted, nondiscriminatory when taken at face value. This line of reasoning, however, ignores two important facts. First, the economically disadvantaged position of minorities is in large part the result of past discriminatory actions by government. As an illustration, imagine the government as the organizer of a twenty-mile foot race. The race is started with one of the runners required to wear a ten-pound weight on each foot. Halfway through the race, the organizer decides that this is not fair and decides to remove the weights. By now, however, the runner with the weights is exhausted and far behind, but the organizer says that she must nonetheless continue the race from her present position. Because the weights are gone, says the organizer, there is no more discrimination. In your judgment, has the organizer run a fair race? Does governmental inaction today, in the context of a history of nearly two hundred years of governmental discrimination against African Americans, Native Americans, and Hispanic Americans, make for a "fair race" in society?

A second problem is that inequality continues to exist in certain institutions under the control of and funded by the public sector. The two best examples of this are probably the legal system and the educational system. The relationship of the legal system to majority–minority relations is discussed in the second half of this chapter, and education is covered in Chapter 12. The points to be made here, however, are these: (1) Governments have for the most part been unwilling or unable to undo the effects of their past discrimination on American minority groups, and (2) discriminatory practices continue in the legal and educational institutions that are funded by and to a greater or lesser degree controlled by the public sector. Thus, despite the passage of numerous laws against discrimination since World War II, government continues to operate in ways that contribute to the maintenance of racial and ethnic inequality.

Foreign Policy.   The foreign and military policies of the U.S. government have also tended to work against the interests of minority group members in certain ways. The Vietnam War, though it occurred during and after the period when the major civil rights laws were passed, is a case in point. First, the war shifted priorities away from the Johnson administration's antipoverty programs as more and more of the government's resources were turned to the war effort. Beyond this, however, minority group members fought and died in the war in numbers disproportionate to their share of the population. Among soldiers from the southwestern states, for example, over 20 percent of the casualties were Spanish-surnamed, though only about 15 percent of the area's population was Spanish-surnamed (Moore, 1976, pp. 55, 146; see also Guzman, n.d.). Black Americans also died in the Vietnam War disproportionately to their numbers in the population. Data gathered by the Harris Poll organization indicate that while blacks in the military were only slightly more likely than whites to go to Vietnam (55 percent versus 47 percent), they were over-represented among the casualties: 12.6 percent of those killed were black, while only 9.3 percent of those in the armed services were blacks. The pollsters correctly point out that this was the result of class inequity much more than any deliberate racial discrimination. Nonetheless, the *result* was racial inequality (see Harris Poll, 1980).

Similar concerns were raised about the 1991 Persian Gulf War, though it caused far fewer casualties. It was perceived by many minorities as a case in which the U.S. government was willing to expend great amounts of money and effort in a faraway place, while failing to address worsening conditions in America's own inner cities. African Americans and Latinos were disproportionately represented among the soldiers who fought that war, as they were in Vietnam. Perhaps for these reasons, minority-group members were considerably less supportive of the Persian Gulf War than were whites. For example, a *Newsweek* poll conducted by the Gallup Organization during the first week of the war showed that 82 percent of whites but just 55 percent of minorities supported the military effort (Adler, 1991).

Another example from the area of foreign policy can be seen in the government's past policies toward racist regimes such as South Africa. Despite decades of open discrimination against blacks and other people of color by that country, the U.S. government was slow to impose economic sanctions. When strong sanctions were finally applied in 1986, Congress had to override President Reagan's veto. This presents a sharp contrast with the quick imposition, by presidential order, of strict economic embargoes against other nations that the United States has disapproved of, such as Cuba since the 1960s and Nicaragua when it was ruled by the Sandinistas in the 1980s. Significantly, the economic sanctions that were finally imposed against South Africa by the United States and other countries appear to be an important reason why, by the early 1990s, that country had repealed many of its apartheid laws and negotiated a plan to allow majority-rule elections in 1994. These elections, in which South Africans of all races were allowed to vote, were held in April 1994 and resulted in the election of President Nelson Mandela.

Barriers to Greater Minority Political Power

Obviously, one reason a group's interests may be ignored by government is that the group has insufficient power to force the government to pay attention to it. Undoubtedly, minority groups have greater political power today than in the past; clearly their power is still quite limited. If we examine various sources of power, we can see some of the reasons why.

One way to gain power is through *influence:* gaining favor and popular support among groups other than one's own. When the issue was clear—that is, when the problem was defined as deliberate discrimination such as segregated lunch counters—minority group members had significant influence among the white population. During the 1950s and 1960s, when discrimination was open and blatant, it was possible to mobilize sizable numbers of whites against what they saw as an obviously unfair system of discrimination. (For greater detail, review Chapters 3 and 6.) However, as the issues became less clear-cut and many whites began to believe that the problem had been solved (or at least the white part of the problem had been solved) by the civil rights laws of the 1960s, minority influence began to wane. Since the late 1960s, various opinion polls have shown that whites no longer blame whites or our social institutions for racial problems and whites by and large do not favor any further major actions to solve the problem. One such example is Schuman's (1975) research showing that whites feel that, at least in their own towns, blacks are primarily at fault for their own disadvantages.

Research by Feagin (1972) shows similar results. Of eleven possible causes of poverty, a national sample of Americans ranked racial discrimination eighth. Low wages, poor schooling, lack of jobs, and exploitation by the rich ranked sixth, seventh, ninth, and tenth, respectively. Again, as in Schuman's research, the poor themselves were blamed for poverty. The top four causes of poverty according to those responding were lack of thrift and poor money management by the poor, lack of effort by the poor, lack of talent among the poor, and loose morals and drunkenness. The survey also showed that about 64 percent of the population favored a policy of guaranteed employment. But if such a policy required a tax increase to pay for it, only 35 percent would be willing to support it. Other proposals to combat racial inequality, such as preferential hiring and school busing, also met with opposition from a sizable majority of whites, according to most surveys taken in the past decade. It is apparent that the majority of whites from the 1970s on have felt little or no personal need to try to solve racial problems, and there has been limited support among whites for new governmental initiatives in that area. As was noted in Chapter 3, the unwillingness of most whites to support public policies aimed at eliminating the disadvantages of minority groups—or even to acknowledge that such disadvantages exist—has been referred to by social scientists as "symbolic racism" or "modern racism" (Kinder and Sears, 1981; McConahay, Hardee, and Botts, 1981; Kluegel and Smith, 1982, 1986).

A major cause of attitudes such as these is a perception among a majority of the white population that the American system, for the most part, offers equal opportunity to people of all races. National surveys show that it is widely believed by white Americans that minorities have much the same opportunity as whites (Kluegel and Smith, 1982, 1986; Kluegel, 1990). Apparently, such beliefs are based largely on the fact that laws against deliberate racial discrimination have been passed. The reality, however, is that, as is detailed in Chapters 10, 11, and 12, subtle and sometimes unintentional, but nonetheless real, forms of institutional discrimination persist in most major American social institutions. This discrimination results in reduced availability of jobs where minorities live; labeling of minority school children, which inhibits their achievement; lack of access to health care; living in areas of concentrated poverty; and other disadvantages. Moreover, discrimination testing studies have also showed a good deal of intentional individual discrimination, though hardly anyone openly proclaims that "we discriminate on the basis of race." However, these forms of discrimination are not experienced by most whites, nor are they easily visible. Thus, many white Americans are unaware of them, and it is relatively easy to deny that they exist. The significance of these beliefs is this: When whites incorrectly believe that minorities have the same opportunities in life that they do, they oppose policies designed to increase opportunities for minorities (Kluegel, 1990). Thus, the political constituency to support such programs is limited outside minority communities.

Voting and Political Participation

Another source of power is obtained through voting strength. This is particularly true if a group votes as a bloc, as minority group members sometimes do. This can be seen in several recent presidential elections. In 1964, 97 percent of the black vote went to the Democratic candidate, Lyndon Johnson. In 1972, 87 percent went to Democrat George McGovern, even though he lost badly in the total vote. In 1976, 82 percent of blacks voted for Democrat Jimmy Carter. In 1992, the black and Hispanic votes went heavily for Bill Clinton (80 percent and 62 percent, respectively), and as in relatively close elections in earlier years, they are a major reason why the Democratic ticket won. For example, John F. Kennedy in 1960 and Jimmy Carter in 1976 would have lost had it not been for the black vote, which provided more than the margin of victory in a number of big states. In 1992, the race between Bill Clinton and George Bush would have been a virtual dead heat among white voters; black and Hispanic voters, in contrast, went heavily for Clinton. In 1986, the black vote was the determining factor in a number of close U.S. Senate contests and was a major reason the Democrats regained control of the Senate that year. In spite of this, it is important not to overestimate the voting power of minorities. The combined racial/ethnic minority population in the United States is only 25 percent of the total population, less among the voting-aged population, and still less among those registered to vote. Thus, minorities have enough votes to make a real difference only when the election is relatively close, as was the case in 1960, 1976, and 1992. In landslide elections of 1964, 1972, 1984, and 1988, however, the minority vote made no difference. The black vote was not enough to save George McGovern in 1972 or Walter Mondale in 1984 from two of the worst defeats ever. Despite getting a large majority of the black vote, Michael Dukakis lost badly to George Bush in 1988. In 1964, Lyndon Johnson's win was so overwhelming that he would have won easily without any minority votes. Even in the relatively close election of 1968, an overwhelming black vote for Democrat Hubert Humphrey did not save him from losing to Richard Nixon. It is clear that any time the electorate divides racially (as it did to an unusual degree in 1972, 1984, and 1988), minorities will come out on the losing side.

One factor that does help strengthen the voting power of minorities is that, even though they are a relatively small percentage of the total population, they are concentrated in certain geographic areas, and in such areas, they may be a majority or near-majority of the population. In such cities as Washington, Atlanta, Detroit, and Newark, the black electorate has become large enough to control or heavily influence the local political apparatus. These cities and others like them have elected black mayors in recent years, and black majorities are beginning to appear on such elected bodies as city councils and school boards. Similarly, Chicanos have been able to gain control of the political apparatus in some towns and counties in south Texas where they are the majority of the electorate (Moore, 1976, pp. 153–154). In New Mexico, where Chicanos are not only numerous but have long been politically involved (although in a very conventional style), numerous Spanish-surnamed officials have been elected over the years, even to such high offices as governor and U.S. senator.

Even where they are in the majority and have elected members of their group to public offices, the power of minority group members is limited. One of the most important limitations is that the areas of concentrated minority population are typically low-income areas, which places severe restrictions on their tax bases. Consequently, these areas are often unable to provide needed services without outside help, and such help, if it is available at all, frequently comes with strings in which minorities are in solid political control, but where the cities have been in a more or less constant position of fiscal inadequacy. In such situations, a black mayor is ultimately confronted with the same choices as a white mayor in the same situation: Cut jobs and services to make the budget balance, accept outside aid with undesirable conditions attached to it, or both. Indeed, the white mayor of New York City, the black mayor of Detroit, and the Chicano mayor of a small southern Texas town are all faced with the same kind of unpleasant situation, and it must be recognized that this situation places a serious limit on the extent of black or Chicano political power, even when blacks or Chicanos are in the majority and have elected members of their own group to public office.

All of these factors combine to create a situation that leaves minorities seriously underrepresented in the political system, despite some improvement in recent years. The unwillingness of whites to support further major action to improve the position of minorities means, of course, that current officials have little or no incentive to pursue such policy. It also makes it very difficult for outspoken minority group members to be elected in areas where the electorate is mostly white. Black mayors have been elected in predominantly white cities such as Los Angeles; Spokane, Washington; Minneapolis; and Battle Creek, Michigan. A small number of minority-group members have been elected to statewide offices, which involve majority-white constituencies in every state. Edward Brooke, an African American, represented Massachusetts in the U.S. Senate during the 1970s, and in 1992, Carol Moseley-Braun of Illinois became the first African American woman elected to the U.S. Senate. That same year, the state of Colorado elected the first Native American U.S. Senator, Ben Nighthorse Campbell. In 1989, L. Douglas Wilder of Virginia became the first African American elected governor of any state. However, most of these officials have held quite moderate views on intergroup relations. More outspoken officials, such as Mayor Richard Hatcher of Gary, Indiana, or Coleman Young, who served for many years as mayor of Detroit, would have a difficult time getting elected without the large black electorates that exist in their cities. This is illustrated by 1984 and 1988 polls showing the majority of white Democrats unwilling to vote for the Rev. Jesse Jackson had he received the party's nomination for the pres-

idency. It is also illustrated by the fact that, when local politics become racially polarized, black elected officials with majority white constituencies are sometimes
voted out. In New York City in 1993, following rioting between Hasidic Jews and
African Americans, the city's first African American mayor, David Dinkins, was voted
out and replaced by a conservative white candidate, Rudolph Giuliani, whom he
had defeated in the previous election.

     In any case, an examination of the districts from which black officials have
been elected reveals that many have predominantly black constituencies. In 1985,
for example, about 40 percent of black big-city mayors and 70 percent of black congressional representatives were elected by majority-black constituencies (Joint Center for Political Studies, 1985). It is largely for this reason that, as noted in Chapter
9, only about 1.5 percent of all elected officials are black, even though around
12 percent of the U.S. population is black. The underrepresentation is especially severe at the state and federal levels, at which most of the important and far-reaching
decisions are made. Given current voting and belief patterns, it is unlikely that the
U.S. political system can soon produce any major change: Nearly all statewide offices,
and all but a handful of congressional districts, have electorates in which the majority of voters (usually a large majority) are white. In most cases, these voters simply
will not elect a minority group member who speaks out in favor of major policy
changes to improve the status of minorities. Thus, with the exception of a relative
handful of big-city mayors and congressional representatives from districts with large
minority populations, such input is nearly absent from the political system.

Sharon Pratt Dixon celebrates her election in 1990 as mayor of Washington, D.C. By the
1990s, most large cities had elected one or more African-American mayors. In some cases,
however, their ability to bring about needed changes has been hampered by the fiscal
poverty of the areas they govern. *Sygma*

In the search for alternatives to this pattern, one that comes to mind is suggested by the internal policies of the Democratic political party since 1972. To assure representation of women and minorities, the party established guidelines concerning the percentage of convention delegates that should be female and that should be minority. This led to a substantial increase in female and minority representation in the party's presidential nominating conventions beginning in 1972. By the 1984 convention, 18 percent of the delegates were black, and half were women, compared with just 5 percent black and 16 percent women in 1968 before the reforms. Such an approach or something similar might be possible in the larger political system as well (for example, by requiring parties to use such percentage guidelines in their nominations of candidates for public office). In fact, this is already done with respect to gender in Norway, where party rules specify that between 40 and 60 percent of people nominated to run for public office must be women (Schmidt, 1991). However, based on white reactions to such proposals as busing and preferential hiring for minorities, there would undoubtedly be intense opposition to such a proposal. In fact, when the Voting Rights Act was renewed, it specifically stated that such proportional representation was not required.

A few states have passed laws mandating diversity in appointments to state boards and commissions, but these laws have focused on gender, not race or ethnicity. Iowa, for example, requires equal numbers of men and women on state boards and commissions, and North Dakota requires equal representation "to the extent possible" (Gross, 1990). This legislation is effective in increasing diversity among public officials: The percentage of women in state appointive jobs rose from 30 percent to 49 percent after the Iowa law was passed. It is significant, however, that laws requiring proportional representation of women have passed only in states with small minority populations, like Iowa and North Dakota. In more diverse states, like California and Pennsylvania, they have bogged down amid debates over "quotas," and a campaign promise to support such a law contributed to Diane Feinstein's defeat when she ran for governor of California in 1990 (though she was later elected to the U.S. Senate). Experience with these laws tells us two things, however: First, they do succeed in making public officials more diverse, but second, they generate strong opposition in areas that are racially diverse, especially if racial representation as well as gender representation becomes an issue, as it did in California.

To summarize briefly, it is clear that the American political system still leaves much to be desired in its treatment of racial and ethnic minorities. Although deliberate discrimination is for the most part illegal today, government is doing relatively little to undo the effects of past discrimination, much of which was required or encouraged by laws and policies established by governments at various levels. Undoubtedly, part of the reason for this is that, despite considerable improvement, minorities are still seriously underrepresented among elected officials. Furthermore, there appears to be a definite limit to how much more this underrepresentation *can* improve, within the context of present white attitudes, the distribution of voting power, and the system by which we elect representatives. Thus, we must conclude that a sizable degree of institutional discrimination (though probably mostly of the nonconscious type) remains in the U.S. political system. Despite the ban against open and deliberate discrimination, that system continues to operate in a way that permits, and in some ways encourages, the continuation of the racial and ethnic inequalities it played a central role in creating.

THE AMERICAN LEGAL SYSTEM
AND MAJORITY–MINORITY RELATIONS

Closely related to and substantially influenced by the American system of government is the nation's legal system. In the remainder of this chapter, we shall examine the present-day treatment of minority group members by the American legal system. We shall attempt to answer the question, To what degree does the legal system serve to protect the rights of minority group members, or on the other hand, to keep them in a disadvantaged position.

As we have already seen, a number of important decisions by the federal courts in recent decades have gone against the legality of deliberate discrimination and have thereby worked to protect the rights of minority group members. Of course, it is important to point out that in the past, many decisions of the courts went the other way. We have already discussed the impact of these major, precedent-setting cases. Our concern in the remainder of this chapter is different: Here we shall examine the day-to-day operations of our criminal justice and judicial systems to see how they influence the well-being of black, Hispanic, and Indian people on a day-to-day basis. We shall emphasize two areas. First, we shall examine the criminal justice system and the process by which it accuses, assesses guilt, and assigns punishment. Second, we shall examine the effectiveness of the police and courts in protecting minority group citizens from crime and illegal exploitation.

The Criminal-Justice System and the Minority Accused

In any discussion of the detection and punishment of crime by the criminal justice system, it is important to stress that there are numerous steps in the process. At each of these steps, decisions musts be made, and at any such step, there is the potential for either fair and equal treatment under the law or for unfair and discriminatory treatment, whether intentional or not. Among the major steps in the criminal justice process are the following:

1. Detection of crime
2. Decisions by police to arrest a suspect
3. Setting and administration of bail for accused persons
4. Decision by police or prosecutor of whether to press charges in court, and if so, in what type of court
5. Decision of judge, judicial panel, or jury of whether accused is guilty or innocent
6. Sentencing, that is, decision concerning nature and severity of penalty for crime

In the following pages, we shall examine the experiences of majority and minority group Americans at each of these stages in the criminal justice process.

Detection. It may well be that in present-day American society, the greatest potential for unequal justice arises from the fact that the criminal justice system detects the crimes committed by some kinds of people but fails to detect the crimes committed by others. A look at conventional sources of data on crime, such as the FBI's *Uniform Crime Reports,* quickly confirms that the arrest and conviction rates of minority group members are far above those of whites. Other sources of data, such as criminal victimization surveys and self-report studies, seem to confirm that minority group members commit considerably more crime than do whites. However, all of these conventional sources of data on crime share one crucial limitation: They focus only on certain kinds of crime. The major crimes included in the FBI crime index (frequently referred to as index crimes), for example, include homicide, rape, robbery, assault, larceny, burglary, and auto theft. All are in the so-called "street crime" category. They are disproportionately committed by persons of relatively low socioeconomic status, and they are crimes with known and clearly identifiable victims. There is good reason to believe, however, that the importance of these and similar crimes may be overstated compared with other crimes that do not so often appear in the statistics. We are speaking here of white-collar and corporate crime, including tax fraud, bribery, embezzlement, violation of antitrust laws and laws on job safety, and the sale of products known to be unsafe or defective.

Although the costs of street crime in lives, injury, and dollars are huge, the costs of white-collar and corporate crime are even greater. For example, the dollar costs of consumer fraud alone have been estimated at five times those of all street crimes combined (Hagan, 1985, p. 103), and the annual economic impact of corporate crime has been estimated at more than $200 billion, over fourteen times the cost of street crime (Simon and Eitzen, 1993, p. 290). The human costs can be great, too. During the 1970s, for example, the A. H. Robins Company reduced its cost of production of the Dalkon Shield, an intrauterine contraceptive device, about 5 cents a unit by knowingly substituting less-expensive bacteria-conducive multifilament string for bacteria-resistant monofilament string. The result was almost two hundred thousand serious injuries and at least twenty deaths (Eagan, 1988, pp. 23–30).

Obviously, racial and ethnic minority group members are relatively uninvolved in crimes of this nature. As we saw in the previous chapter, they simply are not represented in the board rooms where the most costly crimes of this nature occur. Because of their relatively low socioeconomic status, minority group members are more likely to commit street crimes; whites, with their higher socioeconomic status, are more likely to commit white-collar and corporate crimes. As we have seen, most conventional measures of crime focus on street crimes rather than white-collar crimes. As a result, most conventional measures of crime focus on the crimes more likely to be committed by minority group members and de-emphasize the crimes more likely to be committed by whites.

There are a number of reasons for this. Certainly, to a large degree the cause is to be found in the economic and political institutions in our society and the supporting ideology. As the dominant economic institution in our society, the corporation exercises tremendous political power (Domhoff, 1967), which gives it substantial influence over the criminal justice system, including the reporting of crime. The values and beliefs of U.S. society are also heavily influenced by the dominant groups and institutions in the society, and this tends to direct the public's attention toward crimes committed by those from subordinate groups and away from crime in the dominant elements of our society (see Quinney, 1979, pp. 41–52; Barlow, 1993, pp. 256–62).

Beyond these considerations, the ease of *detection* plays an important role in differences in both public awareness of and punishment of white-collar and street crimes. When there is a murder, rape, robbery, burglary, or assault, there is usually little or no doubt that a crime has in fact taken place, and little or no question of who has been the victim. This is usually not true of white-collar or corporate crime.

Although we are all aware that we are continuously paying the cost of white-collar and corporate crime, we usually do not know when and where we have been victimized. If, for example, the price of a product is inflated because of price-fixing conspiracies in violation of the antitrust laws, we are usually unaware of it. Illnesses arising from exposure to pollutants encountered in the workplace, or the release of dangerous substances into the environment, may not be identified as such. Even when employers are the victims of white-collar crime, it frequently goes undetected. A good example of this is theft by computer, an increasingly common crime that is very difficult to detect.

Perhaps because of this greater awareness of the occurrence of street crimes, people are generally more *afraid* of street crimes than they are of white-collar and corporate crimes. In other words, people are more worried about the possibility of being robbed, shot, or raped than about the possibility of being exposed to dangerous chemicals, killed in an automobile that was known to be unsafe, or cheated by antitrust law violations. Not only are we more *aware* of being the victims of street crimes; such crimes also tend to be more sensational. Because of this greater public fear of street crime, law enforcement agencies are undoubtedly under more public pressure to control such crime. Nonetheless, this may be changing to some degree: Incidents such as the Love Canal and Times Beach toxic-waste disasters and the sale of autos with exploding gasoline tanks may have made the public more aware of the dangers they face from at least some types of corporate crime.

Difficulty of detection, combined with political, attitudinal, and ideological influences, has created a situation with important racial and ethnic implications. First, there is a greater public awareness of types of crimes committed disproportionately by minority-group members than of crimes committed disproportionately by whites. Because the crimes that people are most afraid of are the ones most likely to be committed by minority-group members, a racial dimension is added to the process. The fact that crime is seen as being perpetrated by blacks and Hispanics adds to the fears and concerns of many whites, because it reinforces fears that arise from racial prejudice and lack of experience with members of other racial groups. In the public mind, violent crime is often particularly associated with black males, an image that is reinforced by the sensationalistic manner in which the media often report street crime. This has led to a situation in which fears about violent crime have come to be highly focused on black males. This is illustrated by a number of recent events.

In the 1988 presidential campaign, a man named Willie Horton became the focus of a debate about crime between the major party presidential candidates. Horton was a convict in Massachusetts who had been released from prison under a furlough system much like that of other states. While he was out on furlough, he committed a murder. The Republican candidate, George Bush, attacked the Democratic candidate, Massachusetts governor Michael Dukakis, for being soft on crime and argued that his furlough program proved it. To underscore this point, Bush campaign ads repeatedly showed photos of Horton, a black male. Although this ad was widely criticized for playing on white fears about black crime and for reinforcing stereotypes about black males, it is evident that for many whites, the fears and stereotypes based on race were all too real, and the ad was effective.

The extent of these fears and stereotypes can be seen in another incident in Massachusetts in 1989, in which a young, white businessman, Chuck Stewart, called police on his car phone and reported that he and his pregnant wife had been shot by a black man in a jogging suit who invaded their car on a Boston street. She died, and he was admitted to the hospital with a gunshot wound. The press widely reported the case as another incident of out-of-control urban crime, and nobody in the media doubted the young white man's story. It later came to light, however, that he had murdered his own wife, shot himself to make himself look like an innocent victim, and made up the story about being attacked by a black man because he thought people would find that story believable (Martz, 1990). He was right.

In 1992 and 1993, two events occurred that dramatically illustrated white fears about black crime. One was the 1992 acquittal of police officers videotaped in the Rodney King beating in Los Angeles. Because of publicity, the trial had been moved to Simi Valley, an overwhelmingly white suburb northwest of Los Angeles. There, a jury with no black members found the police not guilty of beating King. Although a racially mixed jury in Los Angeles did later find some of the police officers guilty of federal civil rights violations in the beating, the actions of the white jury in Simi Valley were widely seen as reflecting the fears of white suburbanites about black and Hispanic crime. To many whites in Simi Valley, the police represented the "thin blue line" protecting them from the crime of the inner city, and their tendency was to give the police every benefit of the doubt.

The same dynamic was at work in Belleville, Illinois, a mostly white St. Louis suburb just east of the nearly all-black city of East St. Louis, Illinois. Investigations by the local newspaper and by the CBS News program *60 Minutes* in the early 1990s revealed that Belleville's all-white police force, on the orders of its chief, was systematically and selectively stopping cars driven by blacks in the west end of Belleville, the part of the city closest to East St. Louis. Rather than being outraged at the police for engaging in racial discrimination, most Belleville residents turned their anger on the media for exposing the police actions. Hundreds of people cancelled their subscriptions to the newspaper and criticized the *60 Minutes* program as unfair, even though the police chief had admitted on the air to a policy of stopping vehicles with two or more African Americans in them. Again, the police were viewed by white suburbanites as the line protecting them from inner-city crime, which they more or less automatically associated with African Americans.

Incidents such as these illustrate the extent to which public fear and concern about crime focuses on street crime and, in particular, on street crime committed by blacks and, in some parts of the country, Hispanics. Street crime committed by blacks and Hispanics is a serious problem, and it has undoubtedly been worsened by the increasing concentration of black and Hispanic poverty (Wilson, 1987, forthcoming). It is, however, just one part of the overall crime problem, and the statistics on white-collar and corporate crime show that it is not even the biggest part. Moreover, non-Hispanic whites are not the usual targets of crimes committed by blacks or Hispanics: In most crimes, the victim is of the same race as the offender. However, white *fears* about crime are heavily focused on street crime committed by minorities, and these fears have a strong influence on what is expected and demanded of the police. Moreover, it is easier to detect and "solve" the street crimes that are disproportionately committed by minorities than the white-collar and corporate crimes that are disproportionately committed by whites. As a result, more police effort is devoted to street crimes, with the result that the kinds of crimes committed by minorities get more attention from the criminal-justice system than the kinds of crimes committed by whites.

Social-class differences also influence the likelihood that crime will be detected. Activities such as drug violations and drunkenness are more likely to come to the attention of police when committed by the poor because they are more likely to occur in public settings. Surveys show that overall, whites are more likely to use illegal drugs than blacks (National Institute on Drug Abuse, 1989), but a disproportionate number of people arrested for drug violations are black. One reason may be that blacks are more likely to use more risky drugs such as heroin and cocaine, which attract greater police attention. Another reason, however, is that, because of their higher poverty rate, they are more likely to lack the access to private space that protects drug use by the middle and upper classes from easy detection. A study of marijuana arrests in the Chicago area, for example, showed that the proportion of blacks arrested for marijuana violations was more than double their proportion in the population (National Commission on Marihuana and Drug Abuse, 1972). Another example can be seen in arrests for drunkenness, a condition that—by itself—will usually only get one in legal trouble if it occurs in public. A study by J. Q. Wilson (1978) found that blacks were two to three times as likely as whites to be arrested for drunkenness. Again, racial differences in alcohol abuse rates are not large, but because of higher poverty rates, blacks are more likely to be drunk in public settings, which explains their higher arrest rates. Another reason appears to be a tendency in many cities for police to view black drunks, but not white drunks, as "homeless" or derelict (J. Q. Wilson, 1978, p. 160).

Decision to Arrest.   One of the most critical stages of the criminal-justice process is the police officer's decision whether to make an arrest when an illegal act is suspected. Unfortunately, this is also one of the most poorly understood stages of the process, since it is one of the most difficult to study. Clearly, the police can and do exercise considerable discretion in making such decisions. They cannot and do not arrest every person they suspect of committing an illegal act (see Goldstein, 1960; La Fave, 1965; Kadish and Kadish, 1973).

Apparently, *police expectations* concerning the behavior and motivations of suspects heavily influence their decision on whether or not to make an arrest. Such expectations are shaped by two major factors. First, there are *beliefs* about the kinds of people who may commit crimes and about how citizens should behave toward the police. Social class, race and ethnicity, age, dress, and appearance influence such judgments about citizens. Police will "find" and "solve" more crime among groups they are suspicious of, for example, at least partly because they investigate more closely the activities of people in these groups. Thus, if the police are generally suspicious of a particular racial or ethnic group, they will probably be more likely to investigate, stop, and/or arrest members of that group.

It is quite clear that police do stop and investigate people of color on the streets more than they stop whites (Moss, 1990; Barlow, 1993, pp. 358–61). This is evident both from personal-interview studies (Roddy, 1990; Feagin, 1991) and testing studies in which black and white testers have received different treatment from the police on public streets (ABC News, 1991). And, as mentioned above, one police chief admitted on national television that he had instructed his officers to stop all cars with two or more African Americans in them in certain parts of town. In fact, it appears that "by the time they are in their twenties, most black males, regardless of socioeconomic status, have been stopped by the police because 'blackness' is considered a sign of possible criminality by police officers" (Feagin, 1991). This is quite different from the experiences of whites and is a consequence of the basic fact that

The problem of bad relations between police and the black community was vividly illustrated by the videotaped beating of Rodney King and the riot that resulted when an all-white jury acquitted the officers involved in the beating. *Sygma*

police view blacks and other minorities as potential criminals, stop them more and investigate them more, and as a result of this greater attention, are more likely to find some violation that becomes the basis for an arrest.

The second major factor influencing police expectations about citizens is the demeanor and behavior of the citizens themselves toward the police. In one study (Piliavin and Briar, 1964), police officers themselves reported that in juvenile cases, the demeanor of the suspect was the main factor determining how they handled the situation in 50 percent to 60 percent of their cases. Of course, citizen demeanor toward the police is shaped by citizen perceptions of the police: Citizens who do not trust the police are more likely to behave in a negative manner toward them.

Unfortunately, racial, ethnic, and class factors can influence the ways in which both police and citizens perceive one another. Police, on the one hand, frequently have prejudiced or stereotypical attitudes and beliefs toward minority-group members (Black and Reiss, 1967, pp. 132–39). However, one should not be too quick to place all the blame on the individual police officers. The structure of the situation in which they must operate probably tends to make them prejudiced: The crimes they can most readily detect and are *expected* to detect are mainly street crimes, which are disproportionately committed by the poor and by members of racial and ethnic minority groups. This leads to a situation in which a "criminal stereotype" of certain class and ethnic groups easily develops.

The situation is worsened, of course, by the fact that minority groups are substantially underrepresented on many police forces in the United States, though in recent years court orders and increased minority voting power have begun to change that. Black and Hispanic representation on police forces has increased significantly in many cities. The police forces of Atlanta and Detroit are about 56 percent black; Washington's is about 41 percent black, St. Louis and Chicago about 23 percent black, and Los Angeles about 12 percent black. The Los Angeles police force is about 18 percent Hispanic, and Chicago's, about 5 percent Hispanic (U.S. Department of Justice, 1990). While these numbers generally represent improvements resulting from affirmative action programs, they are in nearly all cases well below the minority percentage of the city's population. One reason is that, as the minority proportion on police forces has risen, the minority percentage of the city's population also has risen. Thus, the percentage of minorities on the police force remains well below that of the city's population. Chicago is illustrative of this: The city's population is 39 percent black and 20 percent Hispanic. Thus, the percentage of blacks (23 percent) and Hispanics (5 percent) on the city's police force is far below that of its population. As a result of this underrepresentation, minority neighborhoods are still often patrolled largely by white police. Clearly, one effective way to combat police prejudice and stereotyping about minorities is to have more minority police.

Race and ethnicity also influence the ways in which minority-group citizens view the police. A survey of thirteen large American cities in 1975, for example, showed that blacks had a considerably less positive attitude about police effectiveness than whites (Parisi et al., 1979). These data are presented in Table 11.2. The survey also indicated that blacks were substantially more likely than whites to express dissatisfaction concerning inadequate amount of patrol or investigations in their neighborhoods, promptness, courtesy and concern, and discrimination. More recent survey data suggest that this continues to be the case (Louis Harris and Associates, 1989). After a series of unstructured interviews with African Americans, sociologist Joe Feagin (1991) concluded that, "It seems likely that most black men—including middle-class black men—see white police officers as a major source of danger and death." Notably, this was written *before* the Rodney King beating and *before* a 1992 incident in which a black man was beaten to death by white police officers in Detroit.

There are a number of reasons for these dissatisfactions. Minority-group members are well aware of the stereotyping and prejudice among police, and many have apparently experienced discourtesy or excessive use of force. There is a tendency, accordingly, for some minority group members to counterstereotype the police. This may lead to a mutual *self-fulfilling prophecy:* The white police officer and the black or Hispanic citizen, each expecting the worst of the other, speak or behave in

Table 11.2 Rating of Local Police by Race, 13 American Cities, 1975. Question: Would you say, in general, that your local police are doing a good job, an average job, or a poor job?

RACE	GOOD	AVERAGE	POOR	DON'T KNOW	NO ANSWER
White	47	37	9	7	0
Black and other	24	50	19	7	0

Source: Parisi et al., 1979, p. 301.

some negative way toward each other. This "confirms" the other's beliefs, "proving" the correctness of the stereotype (Kuykendall, 1970). Given this mutual distrust, it is easy to see how encounters between white police and minority citizens can more easily escalate into confrontations leading to arrest than, for example, encounters between white police and white citizens, particularly white middle-class citizens (for further discussion, see Bayley and Mendelsohn, 1968, pp. 162–66; Black, 1970).

Another factor creating hostility between police and minorities is the role of police as agents of control during minority protests. Regardless of the target of the protest, it is the police who must control it, and this frequently places them in an adversarial position to groups such as minorities seeking change through social and political protest. Because of their central role of controlling protest, the police become protectors of the status quo (Quinney, 1979, pp. 265–69), as indeed does the entire criminal justice system (see Balbus, 1973). In addition, police frequently overreact or treat people of different groups differently in situations of social unrest. We have already mentioned the tendency of police to arrest minorities but leave whites alone in the racial clashes of the teens and forties. In the riots of the 1960s, most of those killed died as a result of police action, frequently including indiscriminate firing into buildings. Conot's (1967) study of the 1964 Los Angeles riots, for example, showed that most of the people killed were black, were killed by police, and were unarmed. Such situations surely create considerable hostility toward police. Research on riots in Miami during the 1980s and in Los Angeles in 1992 shows that fewer of the deaths in these riots were caused by police actions, indicating that police may have learned some lessons from the riots of the 1960s (McPhail, 1993). It is also notable, however, that the Miami and Los Angeles riots, like many of the riots of the 1960s, were precipitated by incidents between the police and citizens: specifically, the acquittal of police officers who had been involved in violence against black citizens. It is significant that hostility toward police has been observed not only among minorities but among most groups seeking social change. It was notable, for example, among many labor unionists in the 1930s and among student and antiwar protesters in the 1960s.

Recent research suggests that these processes lead to disproportionate arrest rates for minorities in some situations, but not others. An observational study of twenty-four police departments in three metropolitan areas by Smith and Visher (1981) found that routine encounters between police and citizens did lead to arrests of minority group members more often than of whites, even adjusting for the seriousness of the crime and presence or absence of hostile behavior toward police. Surveys comparing self-reported juvenile delinquency to police arrest rates also indicate disproportionate arrests of black and Hispanic youths, although if the data are controlled for the frequency and severity of crime, the difference decreases (Elliott and Ageton, 1980). For the most serious street crimes included in the FBI Crime Index, it appears that blacks are not overrepresented at all among arrestees as compared with offenders: For these crimes, they are arrested more often because they commit the crimes more often (Hindelang, 1981). Keep in mind, however, that while blacks are especially likely to commit these crimes, whites, because of their middle-class status, are more likely to commit white-collar crimes, which less often lead to arrest. In short, minorities are more likely to be arrested in part because they are more likely to commit the index crimes and in part because for other, less serious types of crime and for juvenile delinquency they are arrested out of proportion to the amount of crime they commit.

Bail.   Another point in the criminal justice system where a potential for un-equal treatment exists is the setting and administration of bail. The purpose of bail is to guarantee that an accused person who has been released from jail will show up for his or her trial. It is a sum of money held by the court to assure appearance for trial. Once the defendant appears, the money is returned; however, if he or she does not appear, the bail is forfeited and kept by the court. In some states, law permits private bail bondspeople to collect fees of 10 or 20 percent of the bail amount to post bail for the defendant. In others, the defendant may be permitted to put up 10 percent of the bail amount. Regardless of how it is handled in any given jurisdiction, many people feel that bail is inherently discriminatory along lines of social class: The wealthier the accused person is, the more likely he or she will be able to afford the bail. Studies have shown that, depending on the crime, the locality, and the amount of bail, the proportion of persons unable to afford bail can range from 25 percent to 90 percent of the suspects (Foote, 1958; Silverstein, 1966; Bureau of Justice Statistics, 1991). Since black, Hispanic, and Indian people have lower incomes than whites, it is likely that members of these groups are overrepresented among those who cannot make bail.

Beyond the economic problem, there is apparently some more deliberate abuse of bail. As Barlow (1993, pp. 399–400) notes, numerous factors besides the likelihood that a defendant will fail to appear (the basic legal consideration) in fact influence the setting of bail. A study by the U.S. Commission on Civil Rights (1970a, pp. 48–52) demonstrated the widespread use of bail in the Southwest as a way of dis-criminating against Mexican Americans. Bail was sometimes used to harass people by keeping them in jail over the weekend: In one case, a group of Chicano students and a teacher were arrested on a Friday night, with bail set at $1,200 each. On Mon-day, the bail was lowered to $500 and eventually changed again to permit release on personal recognizance (no bail required). Similar tactics were used in Texas against United Farm Workers union organizers. In many cases, the bail set was much greater than the maximum fine for the violations the organizers were accused of. The com-mission also received similar complaints from Colorado and New Mexico. The fol-lowing passage from the Civil Rights Commission report indicates that the violations sometimes went far beyond mere harassment:

> Mr. Trujillo [an investigator for the Alamosa, County, Colorado District Attorney's Office] disclosed another and more serious problem resembling involuntary servi-tude or peonage [both of which are forbidden by federal law under a penalty of fine up to $5,000, up to five years' imprisonment, or both]. He stated that during the har-vest season local farmers would go to the jails in the towns of Center and Monte Vista, Colorado, on Monday mornings and inquire about the number of Mexican Ameri-can laborers arrested over the weekend. The farmers would select the best workers and pay their fines for them. Upon their release, the men would have to repay the farmer by working for him. According to Trujillo, in Monte Vista the men were told by the police magistrate that if they did not remain on the farm and work off the amount owed to the farmer, they would be returned to jail. In addition, he said, the police magistrate would sometimes give the farmer a "discount." If the fine was set at $40, he would only require the farmer to pay $25. The magistrate, however, would tell the worker that the fine paid by the farmer was $40 and that he owed the farmer $40 worth of work. According to Mr. Trujillo, once the worker was released from jail, he usually was at the mercy of the farmer and often was ill-treated while on the farm. The chief of police and a patrolman in Center, and the police magistrate in Monte

Vista confirmed the fact that workers are bailed out of jail or have their fines paid by local farmers and are obligated to work off the ensuing debt.

Another study by the commission (U.S. Commission on Civil Rights, 1965) showed that bail was also used to harass black civil rights workers in the South during the 1960s. Discrimination in bail is not always so blatant, however. Frequently, such factors as property ownership, employment, and middle-class status come into play. Apparently factors of this nature were significant in Korfhage's (1972) finding that in Seattle, whites were more likely than either blacks or Indians to be released on personal recognizance when charged with misdemeanors. More recent data demonstrate that such inequalities continue to occur. A national study of over 5,600 black- and white-male felony defendants by Albonetti et al. (1989) showed that, even after control for legally-relevant factors, white defendants fared better in bail decisions than black defendants.

Both because it inherently discriminates on the basis of income and because of racial discrimination ranging from subtle to blatant, it seems fair to conclude that the system of bail and pretrial release has generally served the interests of the white accused better than it has served the interests of black, Chicano, and Indian people accused of illegal behavior.

Prosecution and Conviction.   Another crucial decision in the criminal justice process that carries a great potential for discrimination is the decision whether or not to prosecute or refer a case to the court system. Such decisions are influenced by the police, by district attorneys or prosecutors, and when applicable, by juvenile delinquency officials and probation officers. At this stage of the criminal justice process, there seems to be significant discrimination in some places but little or none in others. Moore and Roesti (1980) found no effect of race on the frequency with which juvenile offenders in Peoria, Illinois, were referred to the court system, and Terry (1967) obtained similar findings with data from Racine, Wisconsin. Similar findings were also obtained in a study by Fagan, Forst, and Vivona (1987) of decisions to prosecute juveniles as adults. On the other hand, evidence that blacks accused of crimes are referred to the courts more often than whites accused of crimes has been found in a medium-sized southern city (Arnold, 1971), Philadelphia (Thornberry, 1974), New Jersey (Dannefer and Schutt, 1982), and a medium-sized northern city (Ferdinand and Luchterhand, 1970). A review of seventeen studies by Liska and Tansig (1979) revealed that a number, though not all, found evidence of racial bias in the decision to prosecute. These studies indicate that while racial inequality in prosecution is not a problem in *every* part of the country, it does exist in many areas, North and South, and therefore must continue to be regarded as a fairly widespread problem. Interestingly, one study in California (Petersilla, 1983) found the opposite result: Blacks and Hispanics were *less* likely than whites to be forwarded to the courts by the prosecutor. The apparent reason—prosecutors have a harder time building a case against minority arrestees than white arrestees. Similarly, Holmes, Daudistel, and Farrell (1987) found that, in two counties in Arizona and Pennsylvania, minorities were *less* likely to be convicted and *more* likely to have charges reduced. Much like the California study, the apparent reason was initial overcharging of minority arrestees as compared with white arrestees.

There is also evidence that racial inequality sometimes occurs in making judgments of guilt or innocence, although it may be less common than bias in the decision to prosecute (Dannefer and Schutt, 1982). Bias in conviction decisions may be especially likely when such decisions are made by juries rather than by judges (Bahr, Chadwick, and Strauss, 1979, pp. 393–94; see also Holmes and Daudistel, 1984). Underrepresentation of minorities on juries is a major reason behind the problem, and such underrepresentation is a major complaint of minority group members about the criminal justice system. All-white juries, the conviction of a prominent black educator, and the acquittal or nonfiling of charges in several cases of police violence against blacks were major precipitating issues in the 1980 Miami riots that took fifteen lives. Similarly, the acquittal of police officers in the Rodney King beating case by a jury with no black members was the precipitating factor in the worst riot of the twentieth century. The Los Angeles riot that followed the acquittal in May 1992 took over fifty lives.

Studies of jury composition show that minority group members are underrepresented in juries throughout the United States (Overby, 1972, pp. 268–70; Fukurai, Butler, and Krooth, 1991a). In Seattle, for example, juries are 89 percent white compared with 75 percent of the population; in Montgomery, Alabama, they are 78 percent white compared with 59 percent of the population, and in Dallas, 77 percent white compared with 55 percent of the population (Monagle, 1992). One reason for exclusion of minorities is that they often encounter socioeconomic barriers to jury participation because on the average their incomes are lower and their jobs are less flexible. Other reasons include jury selection criteria that exclude minorities, and the combined effects of racial housing segregation and the ways in which boundaries of court districts are drawn (Fukurai, Butler, and Krooth, 1991a, 1991b). At one time, it was common for lawyers to use peremptory challenges to potential jurors to exclude people from juries on the basis of their race, but this practice was struck down by a series of Supreme Court rulings beginning in 1986.

Sentencing. Probably the most widely studied aspect of the criminal justice process, as far as majority–minority inequality is concerned, is sentencing. Do black, Hispanic, and Native Americans receive longer or more severe sentences than whites in comparable circumstances? In many though not all areas, they apparently do. The studies by Arnold (1971) and Thornberry (1974) discussed in the previous section also showed black–white inequality in sentencing of juvenile offenders. Thomson and Zingraff (1978) obtained similar findings in a study of North Carolina sentencing patterns for assault and armed robbery using data from 1969 and 1977. There was, incidentally, little difference between the two years. Thomson and Zingraff (1981) also found evidence of more severe sentencing of blacks in Florida in 1977, and the difference *increased* during the 1970s. Petersilla's (1983) study of judicial decisions in California, Texas, and Michigan found that blacks and Hispanics received more severe sentences than whites. Hall and Simkus (1975) in a study of a western state, found that Indian people convicted of crimes tended to receive more severe sentences than did convicted whites. All of these studies showed that the sentencing of minorities was still disproportionately severe after controls for such factors as seriousness of the crime and past criminal record. In some areas, though, there is little evidence of such discrimination (see Welch et al., 1984). Hindelang's (1969) literature review suggests that the problem is more widespread in the South than in the North. More recent research by Humphrey and Fogarty (1987) suggests the same. Hagan (1974) reviewed seventeen studies published prior to that year (including some of the earlier ones cited above) and found that, while a number of them did indeed show racial effects on sentencing after control for other relevant factors, the effect in most cases was quite small. Some more recent studies, including ones in northern cities, have revealed larger effects. A study by Grams and Rohde (1976) of sentencing patterns in Minneapolis is especially striking in this regard. This study found that, among 3,390 convicted felons between 1973 and 1975, blacks and Indians were twice as likely as whites to receive straight jail sentences as opposed to some form of reduced sentence, even after control for such factors as type of crime, criminal record, and even education and occupation. Part of the reason is that minority group members are less likely to have their own private attorney than whites, relying instead on court-appointed attorneys from the public defender's office (see also Nagel, 1969). Grams and Rohde found that Minneapolis blacks and Indians represented by public defenders were three times as likely to get jail sentences as were blacks and Indians represented by private attorneys. In a similar study in Detroit, the Saul R. Leven Memorial Foundation (1959) found that defendants with court-appointed attorneys were twice as likely as others to get prison sentences. However, the Minneapolis study came up with an even more disturbing finding: *Blacks and Indians represented by public defenders were four times as likely to get straight jail sentences as whites represented by public defenders.* Thus, not only were minorities at a disadvantage because of their greater likelihood of having public defenders and the lesser effectiveness of such attorneys but also because minorities with public defenders apparently received less effective representation than did whites with public defenders.

While a number of studies do indicate racial discrimination in sentencing, a number of others find no discrimination, after controls for legally-relevant factors such as past record (Kleck, 1985). There is probably variation from place to place and from time to time in the extent of discrimination. As we have already seen, some studies suggest greater racial inequity in sentencing decisions in the South than elsewhere. Also, it appears that the trend toward determinate sentencing, that is, fixed rules about the penalties that reduce the discretion of judges to decide how severely a convicted defendant should be sentenced, may be reducing racial disparities in sentencing. When Petersilla (1983) studied sentencing disparities before California adopted determinate sentencing, she found evidence of racial inequities in sentencing. However, when Klein, Petersilla, and Turner (1990) studied sentencing again after implementation of the California Determinate Sentencing Act, they found that sentencing decisions were racially equitable after control for relevant legal factors such as past criminal record. They conclude that the reason for the more equitable decisions found in the more recent study may be determinate sentencing. Finally, useful information on sentencing disparities can be found in a study of convicted drug offenders in Miami by Unnever and Hembroff (1988). They found that when legally relevant or case-related attributes all point to probation, or they all point to imprisonment, then similar decisions are made for whites and minorities. However, when the case-related attributes are inconsistent, racial or ethnic inequities are likely to occur.

Apparently, the race of the *victim*, as well as the race of the offender, has some effect on severity of sentence in parts of the country. One would hope that things have changed since the early 1960s, when a southern police officer told a writer, "In this town there are three classes of homicide. If a nigger kills a white man, that's murder. If a white man kills a nigger, that's justifiable homicide. If a nigger kills a nigger, that's one less nigger" (Banton, 1964, p. 173). Studies in Virginia and

North Carolina (Johnson, 1941; Garfinkel, 1949) seem to confirm that many criminal justice officials took this view, finding that blacks accused of killing whites got the death sentence or life imprisonment about half the time, while whites accused of killing blacks never did. The problem is not entirely one of the past, however. A study of sentencing in Philadelphia by Zimring, Eigen, and O'Malley (1976) found that blacks who killed whites were twice as likely to receive life imprisonment or death sentences as were blacks who killed other blacks. A study of homicide cases in Florida from 1973 to 1977 found the most severe treatment of cases where blacks killed whites, and the least severe where blacks killed other blacks (Radelet and Pierce, 1985). Research by Paternoster (1983) in South Carolina produced similar results, indicating that (1) interracial murders were more likely to be treated as capital murders (eligible for death penalty) and to lead to death sentences than same-race murders and that (2) both whites and blacks were more likely to be charged with capital murder and to be given the death sentence when they killed whites than when they killed blacks. Capital-murder charges and the imposition of the death penalty were most likely when a black killed a white, next most likely when a white killed a black, somewhat less likely when a white killed a white, and least likely when a black killed a black.

In fact, the evidence that race of the victim makes a difference in homicide sentencing is so strong that the U.S. Supreme Court in 1986 agreed to hear a case arguing against the death penalty on the grounds that it is applied more often to people who kill whites than to people who kill blacks. By a five-to-four vote, however, the Court ruled in 1987 that overall patterns of bias in the application of the death sentence were not sufficient cause to overturn a death sentence in any given case. Studies also indicate that for types of crime that are frequently interracial, such as larceny and armed robbery, there is greater racial inequality in sentencing than for typically same-race crimes such as assault (Nagel, 1969; Thomson and Zingraff, 1978).

A final source of inequality in sentencing is related to the difference in *types* of crime committed by majority- and minority-group members, as discussed earlier in this section. White-collar crime, committed by the predominantly white middle and upper classes, is almost always prosecuted in *civil* court. Street crime, on the other hand, is usually prosecuted in *criminal* court. This is a very important difference, since only criminal court can put a person in prison and only criminal court can give a person a record that labels them for life as a criminal. The fact that white-collar and corporate offenders are usually white, whereas street offenders are more often black, Hispanic, or Indian, is another source of racial inequality in the definition and punishment of crime.

Conclusion

At each step of the criminal justice process, biases against blacks, Hispanics, and American Indians appear to occur in some situations but not others. Type of crime, whether the accused is an adult or juvenile, locality, and the particulars of judicial procedure in a given case all appear to make a difference (for an extensive listing of studies that do and do not show racial bias, see Unnever et al., 1980, pp. 197–99). At any given step, the degree of bias can be large, small, or nonexistent. However, there is enough bias in enough places at each step that, even though the effect at any step may be small or none, the cumulative effect over the entire course of the criminal justice process can be quite substantial (Thomson and Zingraff,

1981). As a result, some studies have found that the population of accused is quite racially mixed at the point of arrest but that the proportion of minority group members rises quite substantially as one moves through the criminal justice process to the point of examining the imprisoned population (Liska and Tansig, 1979). The effects of this can go far beyond the criminal-justice system itself, because of the *labeling* process associated with a criminal record. The person with a criminal record frequently experiences rejection in the areas of employment, credit, and social opportunity; this, in turn, can lead the person back to crime, and soon he or she is caught in a vicious circle. Thus, it is no exaggeration to say that inequality in the criminal justice system is a significant force tending to keep minority groups in an inferior social and economic position.

Protecting Minority Rights

In the previous section, we explored the treatment of majority and minority offenders (and accused offenders) in the criminal justice system. But what of the "average citizen," not accused of any crime but with certain fundamental rights as an American citizen that he or she relies on the police and legal system to protect? It is this concern to which we turn in the remainder of this chapter. Our emphasis is on three areas: police protection, courteous and legal treatment of citizens by the police, and protection of citizen rights by the civil courts.

Police Protection. As we have seen, among the most common complaints against the police among Americans of color are that the police fail to adequately patrol minority neighborhoods and they do not respond adequately to calls for assistance from minority citizens. J. Q. Wilson's (1978, pp. 158–66) study of police behavior indicates that this is indeed a problem in at least some cities. In Newburgh, New York, interviews with both black citizens and white police officers confirmed that officers were frequently slow or reluctant to intervene in response to complaints from the black community. This occurred partly because of police fears about intervening and partly because the police believed that blacks preferred to solve their problems themselves (a perception that interviews with black citizens suggest is frequently incorrect). A study in Denver by Bayley and Mendelsohn (1968) showed that black and Chicano citizens were less likely than whites to be satisfied with what the police did for them when called for help. Specifically, 47 percent of whites, 34 percent of blacks, and 31 percent of Chicanos were satisfied (Bayley and Mendelsohn, 1968, p. 177). It is difficult to assess to what degree these feelings reflect actual police behavior, because it is difficult without being an "insider" to observe just how police do respond to requests for assistance. However, from studies such as Wilson's and from observations like the one that follows, we do know that the problem is real. Grossman (1974) reports a case in which a police dispatcher decided not to send a car in response to a call for assistance in part because a caller's voice sounded Indian, and that group was known for its disproportionate use of police resources. Subsequently, an assault took place that might well have been prevented had police been sent. Although it is difficult to tell how widespread such incidents are, the widespread minority dissatisfaction with assistance received from police, as shown by the Denver study and the national survey cited earlier (Parisi et al., 1979), suggests that such inequalities may be fairly common.

A recent event quite consistent with the research described above occurred when Milwaukee police missed a chance to arrest mass murderer Jeffrey Dahmer. One of Dahmer's victims (most of whom were young African American or Asian American males) was a fourteen-year-old Laotian boy who managed to escape, with Dahmer in hot pursuit. A black woman reported to police that a man was attacking a teenaged boy. When the police arrived at the scene in Dahmer's predominantly black neighborhood, Dahmer (a white male) told them that he and the "young man" had been having a homosexual lovers' quarrel. He also said that the boy, who was wobbly from injuries he had already suffered at Dahmer's hand, was drunk. The police released Dahmer and allowed him to take the boy back to his apartment. Dahmer killed the boy that night and murdered several other people before he was eventually caught. The failure of the police to take seriously complaints from black women (others had also complained about Dahmer) and from the Laotian boy allowed Dahmer to continue murdering people.

In part because of inadequate police protection and in part because of the link between poverty and street crime, minority Americans are significantly more likely than white Americans to be the victims of crime. In 1982, minority group members were about twice as likely as whites to be victims of robbery, purse snatching, completed vehicle theft, and pocket picking. They were also more likely to be victims of aggravated assault, burglary, and household theft (McGarrell and Flanigan, 1985, pp. 294–312).

Police Brutality.   It is difficult to define exactly what is and what is not police brutality. Perhaps the most common definition is the use of force beyond what is necessary to make an arrest, subdue a violent suspect, or protect the police officer from injury. However, even this definition is imprecise, because in many instances there is a wide range of disagreement on how much force is necessary. Beyond this, many argue that brutality is not always physical: Such things as verbal abuse, racial epithets, and listening to only one side of the story are regarded by many people as a form of brutality (Bayley and Mendelsohn, 1968, pp. 122–25; Barlow, 1993, pp. 384–87) and at the very least as improper harassment of citizens. However defined, it is apparent that police brutality is a major issue among people of color throughout the United States. Indeed, untoward incidents between citizens and police have been the triggering incidents in many, if not most, outbreaks of racial violence from the 1960s through the 1990s (see, for example, U.S. National Advisory Commission on Civil Disorders, 1968). Complaints about police brutality are much more widespread among black, Hispanic, and Indian Americans than among white Americans (see Bayley and Mendelsohn, 1968, pp. 122–29; Parisi et al., 1979, p. 301). As is the case for arrest decisions, the structure of the situation surrounding minority–police encounters frequently contributes to an increased likelihood of violent police behavior in such situations. Such behavior on the part of police is especially likely when citizens challenge their authority or when the police hold citizens in low regard (Lundman, 1980, pp. 160–65).

As we have seen, the mutual feelings of mistrust and fear that frequently exist between police officers and minority citizens often create just such situations. In addition, there is a tendency for the incidence of police brutality to increase during periods of social unrest and political protest (Quinney, 1979, pp. 288–89). Since such protest has in recent decades involved minority group members more than whites, they have experienced more than their share of such police violence. In fact, a large proportion of the injuries and deaths during such disturbances are the result of police action, and such action is often far beyond that required by the situation.

Examination of the circumstances surrounding the deaths and injuries in two Los Angeles riots (Watts in 1964 and the Chicano Moratorium in 1970) confirms that police action was the main cause of death and injury, and that those killed or injured by police were frequently unarmed. In the Watts riot, indiscriminate police firing into buildings, at vehicles, and into crowded areas caused a large proportion of the thirty-four deaths in the riot (Conot, 1967, pp. 245–375). In the 1970 Chicano Moratorium, a massive protest by Chicanos against the Vietnam War, there is also evidence of excessive use of force by the police. The event had been mostly peaceful until police swept the park where the demonstration was being held in response to some minor incidents away from or on the fringes of the crowd. Most of the people in the crowd were not even aware of any trouble until the police moved into the crowd. The three deaths that occurred in the subsequent riot all resulted from the actions of police. One of those killed was a television reporter who had been critical of police action in previous incidents; he died when his head was pierced by a ten-inch tear gas projectile fired into the bar where he was sitting even though there had been no disturbance in the bar (Acuña, 1972, pp. 258–63).

While excessive use of force by the police is commonplace during civil disturbances, it is very important to keep in mind that disturbances are the exception rather than the rule, and that police brutality toward minority citizens is fairly widespread during times of tranquility as well. Reiss (1968), in a participant observation of police behavior in Chicago, Washington, and Boston, found that about 3 percent of alleged offenders in encounters with police suffered unnecessary violence at the hands of police. For a city of five hundred thousand, this rate of violence would suggest two thousand to four thousand incidences of police brutality per year. Both black and white suspects were victimized by police—indeed, white suspects at a somewhat higher rate than black suspects. But since, as we have seen, the black citizen is more likely to become a suspect than the white citizen, it is probable that, overall, blacks are somewhat more likely to suffer police brutality than whites.

If we consider the extreme use of police force, it is clear that minorities are more often the victim of police violence than are whites (Takagi, 1979). Of the more than forty-seven hundred persons killed by the police during the period from 1952 to 1969, over twenty-three hundred, or 49 percent, were nonwhite (Kobler, 1975). If the threat of death or severe injury to the police or to a third party is regarded as the criterion of justifiability, it appears that about 40 percent of killings by police are unjustified, and another 20 percent are questionable. Moreover, it appears that blacks are more likely to be shot in situations in which it is not obvious that such a threat to life exists (Fyfe, 1982).

Taken together, the various facts we have reviewed in this section suggest very strongly that minority group members, for a variety of reasons, experience more unnecessary violence at the hands of the police than do whites. It should be said again that individual police officers should not bear all the responsibility for this: The structure of the situations in which police officers come in contact with minority group members virtually guarantees that this will be the case, just as it guarantees that people of color will be *arrested* more frequently than whites. Until there is fundamental change in the ways wealth, income, and power are distributed between majority and minority groups, this is likely to continue.

Protection of Legal Rights in the Court System.   Ultimately, it is the judicial system that protects the rights of citizens in a democracy. If a citizen feels that his or her rights have been violated by another citizen or by an agent of the state, it is the court system that is called on to protect that citizen's rights. As we have seen, the laws of the United States today provide for equal rights regardless of race, creed, or color. As a practical matter, however, there is serious reason to question whether the judicial system actually operates that way. We have already seen considerable evidence of racial inequity in the courts in cases involving accused criminals. However, our concern in this section is not with accused criminals but rather with how the courts protect the legal rights of ordinary citizens who are accused of no crime.

An investigation of the civil court system by an individual who is himself a U.S. Court of Appeals justice suggests that there are serious inequities in the civil court system (Wright, 1969). Ordinarily, a citizen turns to the civil-court system when there is a reason to believe that her or his rights have been violated by another citizen or by the government. These courts have the power to award payments for damages and to issue injunctions against actions that illegally deprive citizens of their rights.

Wright's investigation of the civil-court system indicated that, in many ways, the courts have failed to protect the rights of poor Americans. One widespread problem is the failure of the courts to protect the minority poor from abuses by ghetto merchants. Wright describes one case in Washington involving the repossession of goods bought by an indigent mother of seven who was living on relief payments of $218 per month. In this case, a merchant sought to repossess $1,800 worth of goods bought over five years, most of which she had already paid for, because she failed to make her payments on a stereo she had subsequently purchased. This was based on a line of fine print on the sales contract that any unpaid balance on *any* item purchased from the store would be distributed among *all* items previously purchased. Although this arrangement allowed the taking without payment of items the woman had completely paid for, several lower courts upheld the contract and ordered the woman to return all the items. Only when the case reached the U.S. Court of Appeals did the court reverse and rule that only the stereo could be repossessed.

As disturbing as this case is, the woman was, for a number of reasons, more fortunate than a great many others in a similar position. Many poor people lack both the awareness of how the legal system operates and the money to hire a lawyer. To have any legal representation at all, they must be able to find a legal-aid lawyer who is willing and able to represent them. Unlike the criminal courts, civil courts in most cases make no presumption of the right to a lawyer, so indigent plaintiffs must often go unrepresented. Appeals through several levels of the court system such as the one described above are extremely expensive and time consuming. Accordingly, very few poor people ever have the resources to go as far as this woman was able to.

Wright (1969) notes that this woman was "lucky" in another regard. In her case, the store itself was attempting to make the repossession. Had the contract been sold to a finance company, the woman might have had an even more difficult time in the courts. Under the doctrine of "holder in due course," a finance company can in most jurisdictions purchase installment payments free of any responsibility for fraudulent practices by the dealers (this, again, is a standard clause contained in the fine print of sales contracts). Thus, the interests of the finance company are protected but those of the buyer are not. Unless the buyer can prove that the finance company *knew* the dealer was fraudulent (which is almost impossible to prove in most cases), he or she is out of luck, even if the dealer skips town.

Another widespread practice criticized by Wright and others is wage garnishment. Under this arrangement, it is possible under certain conditions in many states for a creditor to collect on past-due amounts by obtaining a court order to take up to one-half of the person's wages. This typically requires a deficiency judgment, which in effect is a legal declaration that the creditor was not able to resell a repossessed property at a sufficiently high price to cover the amount due. Once a wage garnishment order has been issued, the debtor frequently loses his or her job. The employer may be embarrassed by the garnishment orders or may simply consider the required procedure too much of a bother. Thus, a poor person who fails to make payment on a property may lose his or her job as well as the property—a condition that beyond doubt perpetuates poverty.

One innovation established in many areas as a way of better protecting the legal rights of the poor is the small-claims court system. In these courts, a citizen can, without legal counsel, sue for amounts up to a few hundred dollars. The idea behind the establishment of small-claims courts was to enable those too poor to hire lawyers to nonetheless receive legal protection when the amounts involved are not excessive. In practice, however, small-claims courts have often not worked that way: The great majority of those suing in small-claims courts have been landlords and businesses. Frequently, those sued in the courts have been poor. Thus, the system has had the opposite effect from that intended: It has largely helped wealthier interests extract debts from the poor, without helping to protect the poor from abuses by landlords and businesses, as had been intended. The apparent reason for this is that the wealthy are more aware of and used to operating in the system. Some landlords and collection agencies use it on a routine basis. Some states have acted to prevent this by limiting the number of times per year that a person can sue in small-claims court. In contrast to landlords and businesses, the poor are largely unaware of their rights and do not know how to sue in small-claims court.

Our discussion of the court system has, thus far, focused mainly on economic rather than racial factors. However, since black, Hispanic, and Indian people are so much more likely than white people to fall in the lower-income brackets, all of these class-related inequalities in the protection of legal rights create de facto racial and ethnic inequalities as well.

A final area in which the courts have in significant ways failed minorities in America is in protecting them against abuses by the state. Of particular salience here is the issue of police abuse of minority citizens. The failure of the judicial system to punish acts of violence by police against citizens has been a major source of tension from the 1970s through the early 1990s in Houston, Philadelphia, Los Angeles, and other cities. It was a major precipitating factor, as we have already noted, in the 1980 Miami riot and the 1992 Los Angeles riot. In Philadelphia, federal action against police violence failed in the courts in 1980. In Houston, a highly publicized case took place in which a Chicano man, Joe Campos Torres, was taken to a vacant area by police, beaten, and thrown or forced to jump into a swift-flowing stream, where he drowned. The verdict in the case was misdemeanor negligent homicide, and the sentence was one year in prison. Although the police involved were also convicted of felony violations of federal civil rights laws, the federal conviction added only one day to their sentence, although the law provided for a penalty of up to life imprisonment (*New York Times*, 1979, 1980). Although a few cases such as the Houston case and the Rodney King case in Los Angeles are highly publicized, they represent a much more widespread pattern. Kobler's (1975) study of fifteen hundred homicides

by police officers found only three cases in which *any* criminal punishment resulted—this despite the fact that about 40 percent of the killings appeared unnecessary. Since about half those killed were nonwhite, this must be regarded as a failure of the courts to protect the rights of minorities. Conot's (1967, pp. 396–409)
examination of the inquests into deaths resulting from the 1964 Watts riot also found
that homicides by police officers were rarely questioned. Virtually all cases involving
killings of citizens by police or national guardsmen were adjudicated justifiable,
though again, many in all likelihood were not. Much the same can be said of lesser
offenses by police against citizens: They are rarely tried, and convictions are even
rarer.

SUMMARY AND CONCLUSION

We have seen that a good deal of institutionalized racial inequality persists in the political and legal systems. Open and deliberate discrimination in these institutions has
been greatly reduced, if not totally eliminated. However, subtler and often unintentional forms of inequality remain, and these have had the effect of blocking most opportunities for blacks, Hispanic Americans, and Indian people to improve their
standing in the political and legal systems. Thus, minorities remain greatly underrepresented on juries and among political officeholders, the legal profession, and
police officers. They are overrepresented among those arrested, convicted, and imprisoned, and on the casualty lists of American wars. Often, this is because of institutionalized policies and practices that, though they are not openly discriminatory,
nonetheless have the effect of helping whites or holding down minorities.

As a result of this analysis we can offer some ideas about how to and how not
to go about trying to solve the problem of political, legal, and judicial inequality between the races. On the one hand, the more overt forms of prejudice and open acts
of discrimination seem less important today as causes of this inequality. On the other
hand, certain individual beliefs and actions remain important. Many whites continue, for example, to be reluctant to vote for African Americans and other minority candidates for public office, particularly when those candidates are outspoken in
their advocacy of minority-group interests. Similarly, a self-fulfilling prophecy continues to occur in which police officers and minority group civilians expect the worst
of one another and behave accordingly. In these regards, attitude change could
clearly make a difference.

However, much of the intergroup inequality in the political and legal systems is a product of institutional or systemic processes, not individual attitudes and
beliefs. How political boundaries such as those of congressional districts and city
wards are drawn makes a big difference in how well-represented minorities are, for
example. As a result of the 1982 extension of the Voting Rights Act, congressional
district boundaries drawn after the 1990 census were designed in a way that gave minorities a better chance to be elected to Congress, and the number of people of color
elected to Congress in 1992 rose significantly as a result.

Another example can be seen in our examination of the criminal justice system. That examination showed, for example, that no one stage in the process could
be identified as the main cause of racial inequality in treatment of accused criminals.
Rather, it was a number of sometimes small inequalities scattered throughout the
process, combined with differences in treatment of the types of crimes committed

by majority- and minority-group members, that *added up* to substantial racial differences in the punishment of crime. Thus, to eliminate the racial inequality in the punishment of crime, the entire process must undergo significant change, change that may threaten dominant elements of the majority group. One example would be to give the same emphasis to white-collar crime that is now given to street crime. While street crime is a serious problem, the costs of white-collar crime are even greater, yet it is not penalized in the same ways that street crime is. To do so would eliminate a significant source of inequality in the ways that crime is defined, prosecuted, and penalized in the United States. To do so would also threaten a much more powerful group of criminals than the ones whose crimes now receive the main emphasis in our judicial system. According to Feagin and Feagin (1978), it is because of such threats to the advantaged that there has not been a concerted attack on the problem of institutionalized racism. Privileged whites, and the owners of wealth in particular, do not want to think of themselves as racists—thus the reduction in openly expressed prejudice and open discrimination. Yet, Feagin and Feagin argue (p. 178), these dominant elements are unwilling to give up the advantages they enjoy as a result of discrimination and this is in large part why institutionalized racism, even though largely unintentional, persists. Put differently, changing our institutions in such a way as to eliminate processes that maintain racial inequality would harm the interests of the privileged, and for this reason, this group uses its considerable power to oppose such change. Given this persistence of institutional discrimination, it is unlikely that racial and ethnic equality in the political and legal processes will be attained until those processes and systems themselves undergo significant change.

12

Education and American Minority Groups

Continuing our examination of the roles of minority group members in American social institutions and the ways those institutions influence the status and welfare of minorities in American society, we now focus on the educational system.

As was discussed in Chapters 6 and 10, a series of court cases and federal actions, highlighted by *Brown* v. *Board of Education* in 1954, placed the legal position of the government clearly against segregated education. For a variety of reasons, however, these actions did not put an end to institutional discrimination in the educational system. To begin with, there was strong resistance to school desegregation in parts of the South, and actual change was slow to come in many areas. Second, the legal rulings applied only to relatively open and deliberate policies of school segregation. In both the North and South, residential segregation and subtler forms of discrimination in the drawing of school district boundaries have kept public schools de facto segregated, that is, segregated in fact if not by law. Third and most important, there are a number of ways schools can discriminate without being segregated. The debate over segregation, while important, has often turned public attention away from the numerous practices institutionalized in the educational system that may—often unintentionally—place minority students at a disadvantage. Also frequently ignored, but possibly very important, is the role of education in the larger social and economic structure in which it exists. In this chapter, we shall seek to understand these relatively subtle and complex issues in the education of minority groups in America as well as the more widely debated issue of school segregation (both deliberate and de facto).

A BRIEF HISTORY OF SCHOOL SEGREGATION SINCE 1954

As noted above, the Supreme Court's 1954 ruling requiring desegregation of public schools met widespread resistance in the South. Probably the most dramatic resistance came in 1957, when Arkansas governor Orval Faubus tried to use the state's National Guard to block court-ordered school desegregation in Little Rock. To enforce the law, President Eisenhower had to order U.S. Army paratroopers into the city and federalize the state's National Guard. In many other parts of the South, resistance took subtler forms. Legislation was passed in an attempt to avoid the jurisdiction of courts ordering desegregation; efforts were made to block the NAACP's desegregation drives (six states passed laws prohibiting the NAACP from providing legal aid); students were given "tuition grants" to attend segregated private schools; pupil assignment laws were written that provided access to desegregated schools only on request for reassignment; and compulsory attendance laws were repealed (Simpson and Yinger, 1985). Some districts went so far as to close their public schools entirely. Such resistance continued for years after the 1954 *Brown* decision. It was in 1963 that Alabama governor George Wallace (later a presidential candidate) declared, "I say segregation now, segregation tomorrow, and segregation forever!" in his inaugural address.

Despite such resistance, legally segregated education did gradually disappear in the border states during the late 1950s and early 1960s, and in the deep South later. By the mid 1970s about two-thirds of the nation's school districts had taken some action to desegregate their schools (U.S. Commission on Civil Rights, 1976). These efforts led to some decline in school segregation, though many children continue to attend schools that are quite segregated, even today. The percentage of black students in schools with more than 90 percent minority enrollment fell from 65 percent in 1965 to about 40 percent by 1974. After that, it fell more gradually, reaching 32 percent by 1988 (Armor, 1992). Thus, in 1988, about one out of three black students attended schools that could be classified as racially segregated. And nearly two out of three attended schools with student bodies that were over half minority that year (Armor, 1992).

Between 1988 and 1992, school segregation actually increased somewhat. The proportion of black students in schools with student bodies over half minority in 1992 was the highest it had been since 1968. In contrast to black students, who experienced some decline in segregation in the late 1960s and early 1970s, Latino students became steadily more segregated as their proportion of the population grew. Between 1968 and 1992, the percentage of Latino students with over half minority student bodies rose from 54 percent in 1968 to 73 percent in 1992—even higher than the percentage of blacks in such schools (Gary Orfield, quoted in *St. Louis Post-Dispatch*, 1993d). As we saw in Chapter 3, 84 percent of white Americans in 1972 agreed that white children and black children should attend the same schools. We are faced, then, with a perplexing question. If most school districts have tried to desegregate and if Americans overwhelmingly favor the principle of integrated education, why did one-third of the nation's black students still attend what amounted to segregated schools in 1988, and why did segregation increase between 1988 and 1992?

The problem is in large part what is commonly called **de facto segregation.** Unlike **de jure segregation,** which involves an official policy of segregated schools, de facto segregation results from subtler processes. One such process, sometimes called **gerrymandering,** involves drawing school attendance districts in such a manner that they are racially homogeneous. While such gerrymandering is illegal today if racial intent can be shown, present-day segregation in some cities is at least partly the result of past decisions about school attendance districts. (One example of this is Boston, where black students were at one time bused through a white neighborhood to attend a predominantly black school.)

Another major factor contributing to school segregation is housing segregation. Where housing is highly segregated, the system of neighborhood schools often amounts to a system of segregated schools (Wilson and Taeuber, 1978; J. Farley, 1984). Although housing segregation is largely produced by private-sector transactions (buying, selling, and renting of housing and the actions of the real-estate industry), it is produced at least partly by exclusionary zoning and housing policies in some suburban communities. Thus, even school segregation produced entirely by housing segregation must be regarded as *partly* the result of public action. Finally, school segregation may also contribute to housing segregation: Some whites select all-white neighborhoods or suburbs to avoid schools with large numbers of blacks (see Levin et al., 1976; Taeuber, 1979; Taylor, 1981). Among reasons cited by Orfield for the increases in segregation in the late 1980s and early 1990s are conditions we have discussed—ongoing housing segregation, and departure of white children from inner-city schools. Another factor has been a tendency of the federal courts in recent years to steer away from court orders (Gary Orfield, quoted in *St. Louis Post-Dispatch*, 1993d).

Although deliberate operation of segregated schools is illegal everywhere and although segregated schools are found in all parts of the country, there are significant regional differences in the level of segregation in schools today. In general, black–white school segregation is greatest in the Midwest and Northeast and lowest in the South and West (R. Farley, 1984, p. 30).

Segregation is *low* in the South apparently because much of the segregation there was of the de jure type. As we shall see later, de facto segregation is not illegal in and of itself. Accordingly, the de facto segregation of the North has been less changed by the 1954 *Brown* decision and subsequent events than has the de jure segregation of the South.

Although other minority groups, despite past patterns of segregation, are not as segregated as blacks, it is significant to note that their regional variations are similar to those for blacks. American Indians are more segregated in the Midwest than anywhere else, and Hispanic Americans are most segregated in the Northeast (U.S. Commission on Civil Rights, 1979, p. 20). Segregation also appears to be greatest in cities, particularly larger cities. In twelve of the twenty largest cities in 1978, the typical black student attended a school with 15 percent or fewer whites. In Cleveland, Chicago, and Washington, the figure was less than 2 percent (R. Farley, 1984, pp. 27–28). For both blacks and Hispanics, segregation levels are much higher in cities than in either suburban or rural school districts. It is important to note, however, that both groups are underrepresented in suburbs and rural areas, so that there may be relatively few minority students attending any schools in such areas. Furthermore, it must be kept in mind that all these statistics refer to segregation *within* school districts. Much of the segregation that exists today is *between* districts, such as exists when a city whose school population is 75 percent black borders on a suburban district that is 95 percent white.

To summarize, then, open and deliberate policies of segregation in schools have been illegal for over twenty-five years, yet actual segregation remains wide-

Table 12.1 Percentage of Black and Hispanic Students in Predominantly
Minority Schools, 1968–1992

| School Minority Percentage | BLACK STUDENTS | | | | | HISPANIC STUDENTS | | |
| | Year | | | | | Year | | |
	1968	1972	1980	1988	1992	1968	1980	1992
50+% Minority	76.6	63.6	62.9	63	67	54.8	68.1	73
90+% Minority	64.3	38.7	33.2	32		23.1	28.8	

Sources: 1968–1980 statistics are from Gary Orfield, 1983, *Public School Desegregation in the United States, 1968–1980* (Washington, DC: Joint Center for Political Studies), pp. 4, 10; 1988 statistics are from Gary Orfield and Franklin Monfort, 1992, *Status of School Desegregation: The Next Generation*; 1992 statistics are from Gary Orfield, quoted in *St. Louis Post-Dispatch*, December 14, 1993, "U.S. School Segregation Called Highest Since '60s," p. 3a.

spread. As shown in Table 12.1, segregation of black students decreased between 1968 and 1972 but has changed little since. Segregation of Hispanic students has actually increased. Furthermore, the mere fact that deliberate segregation is illegal does little to eliminate the kind of segregation that remains today. Only more drastic remedies, such as busing or redrawing of school districts to combine cities and suburbs, hold any real hope of further reducing segregation in U.S. schools. The reality is that few new busing programs have been established since the mid 1970s, and in some metropolitan areas, such as Oklahoma City and Dekalb County, Georgia, the courts have ruled that school districts have done all that they could reasonably do to reduce discrimination, so they can be released from court-ordered busing (Coughlin, 1991; Armor, 1992; Seligman, 1992). We shall return later in the chapter to these issues, exploring in particular the degree to which desegregation, through busing or otherwise, may offer improved educational opportunities to minority students. In the meantime, we shall explore other aspects of the educational system that influence the educational opportunities of racial and ethnic minority groups in the United States.

THE ROLE OF EDUCATION: TWO VIEWS

Before we explore some relatively specific aspects of organization and practice within education, it is important to explore briefly the role of the educational system in the larger American society. Sociology offers two contrasting viewpoints about the role of education in American society; we shall briefly explore each of them in this section.

The traditional view of American education, linked closely to the order, or functionalist, perspective in sociology, is that education provides a source of social mobility in society. In other words, it offers to all the opportunity to move up in society, and how far one moves depends on his or her ability and motivation. The educational system also serves as efficient way of allocating people to professions by providing them with the training they need. Thus, education provides employers with qualified workers, and it offers individuals the opportunity for mobility by rewarding them on the basis of what they know and what they can do (achieved characteristics) rather than on the basis of who they are or what their background is (ascribed characteristics). (For further discussion, see Davis and Moore, 1945; Parsons, 1959.)

A contrasting view that has gained increasing support among sociologists of education is that education does *not* operate in a way that offers much opportunity for upward mobility to the poor. Rather, education reflects and reinforces the social inequality in society. This viewpoint, more consistent with the ideas of the conflict perspective, challenges the popular view that "education is the answer." According to this view, education cannot be expected to bring about equality when the larger social and economic system is based on inequality. One strong proponent of this viewpoint is Christopher Jencks (Jencks et al., 1972). Jencks has argued that if society wants to move in the direction of social equality, the way to do it is not to "educate" everyone, but rather to pursue changes in the economic system that would bring about equalization of income. Jencks should not be misunderstood, as he sometimes has been, as opposing quality education for all. Rather, he argues that economic advantage is more important than mere access to education, and making everyone into a high-school or college graduate would not necessarily alter the basic forces that make for economic inequality in the United States.

Conflict theorists in the sociology of education argue that one reason education may not provide much opportunity for mobility is that the true function of the educational system is to *reinforce* and *preserve* the inequalities that exist in society. According to this view, education, as Marxist theory says is true of *all* institutions, exists to serve the interests of the dominant or advantaged elite that reaps most of society's benefits. The true purpose of education, then, is not to provide social mobility but rather to *channel* students into roles and statuses relatively similar to those of their parents. This serves two functions for the dominant group. First, it assures that they can pass along their advantages to their children. Second, it provides employers with "appropriately" socialized middle-class workers who will fit into their work organizations and not cause trouble.

There is some reason to believe that there is merit in this challenge to traditional views about education and social mobility. First, a wide range of studies show that predominantly middle-class and predominantly working-class or poor schools tend to stress different kinds of values. Schools with students predominantly from the lower classes mainly stress conformity and obedience; middle-class schools also stress control over one's situation and the ability to work independently, though within a context of hierarchical supervision (Friedenberg, 1965; Cohen and Lazerson, unpublished). These value differences between the social classes are already present to some extent when children enter school. They reflect the different experiences in life and work of middle-class and working-class or poor parents and the effect of these experiences on how parents raise their children (Miller, Kohn, and Schooler, 1986). However, the schools reinforce and enlarge these differences in ways that channel middle- and upper-class children toward more education and professional and managerial employment, and channel working-class and poor children toward less education and manual, clerical, or blue-collar employment (Bowles and Gintis, 1976). Furthermore, the higher one goes in the education system (from grade school to high school to college to graduate school) (1) the higher the average family income of the students and (2) the closer the educational approach approximates the middle-class model (Binstock, 1970). Thus, the educational system nurtures and reinforces the "appropriate" values of the middle class while it "cools out" the aspirations of working-class students and prepares them for lower-paying, manual jobs (Lauter and Howe, 1970).

This function of education can also be illustrated by the behavior and preferences of those who do the hiring for the better jobs in society. A variety of studies suggest that the *affective* characteristics gained in school (values and habits) are more linked to income and occupational status than is *cognitive* learning (the learning of skills and content). To begin with, a review by Gintis (1971) of a number of studies showed that while years of school were strongly related to a person's job status and income, measures of *what the person actually knew* added very little to the explanation of job status or income (see also Bishop, 1987; Rosenbaum and Kariya, 1991). Clearly, employers prefer educated workers for high-status jobs for reasons *other than* cognitive knowledge. Gintis argues strongly that the studies suggest that what employers are really looking for is middle-class values and work habits—exactly the kinds of things that the school system teaches. Also consistent with this observation is the fact that education pays off better for the white middle class than for minorities and the poor, and better for academic training (mostly middle class) than for vocational training (mostly working class) (Super and Crites, 1962; Weiss, 1968; Jencks et al., 1972; Harrison, 1972). Apparently, it is what is learned in the so-called *hidden curriculum* that employers are looking for in applicants for higher-status jobs: values and work habits that will "fit in" rather than any concrete factual knowledge.

Surveys of employers confirm that this is the case. Their preference for more-educated applicants for higher-status jobs is in many cases not related to what such applicants know in areas related to the job. In most cases, this is taught on the job. Rather, more educated employees are preferred because of their values, beliefs, and work habits (Hamilton and Roesner, 1972). Employers believe that such employees will adapt and fit in better to the work environment. As Berg (1975, p. 308) puts it, employers believe that with increased education, "the worker's attitude is better, his trainability is greater, his capacity for adaptation is more developed." It does not really matter that such employees are not necessarily more productive than other employees (Berg, 1971, 1975); it is the belief of employers that "desirable" values and work habits are found among more-educated employees that counts (Bowles and Gintis, 1976).

All this raises serious questions about the role of the educational system as a source of mobility in American society. Undoubtedly, it does operate that way for some individuals, but these studies suggest there is strong reason to believe that the overall effect of the American educational system is to preserve inequality rather than to reduce or eliminate it. Since economic inequality in the United States falls largely along racial and ethnic lines, education may well be acting in ways that preserve racial and ethnic inequality as well.

We have seen, then, that an increasing number of sociologists are arguing that the function of the school system is to preserve and pass along inequalities from generation to generation more than it is to break those inequalities down and to offer opportunities for mobility. They are able to present some significant data in support of this view, and the general relationship between such variables as race and class and the attainment of education (see Chapter 9) is also supportive of such a viewpoint. Data on the correlation between race and student achievement also support such a view, though there are some signs of change. As recently as 1990, data continue to show black students trailing behind white students on average scores on the National Assessment of Educational Progress. Among thirteen-year-olds, for example, black students on the average scored twenty points lower than white students in reading and twenty-seven points lower than in math. There has, however, been a considerable narrowing of this gap. In 1971, black thirteen-year-olds averaged thirty-nine points behind in reading and forty-six points behind in math. Thus, the gap has been cut nearly in half. Armor (1992) argues based on a variety of data that the decline in the gap can be attributed to social class, specifically the growth of the black middle class. This is, in fact, consistent with the foregoing argument: Educational success is strongly linked to class, such that opportunities are greater for the middle class than for others. Of course, despite the growth of the black middle class, there remain large differences between the average socioeconomic status of blacks and whites, and these continuing differences appear to be an important reason why a large part of the black–white achievement gap persists, despite significant improvement between 1971 and 1990.

If it is true that educational institutions reinforce patterns of social-class inequality—and by so doing also reinforce racial inequality—we face the question of what specifically is the means by which education does this. Two major possibilities have been suggested by educational sociologists. First, more money is spent, and thus the quality of education is greater, in areas where the students are white and middle class than in areas where they are black, Hispanic, Indian, and/or poor. The second possibility is suggested by our discussion of the functions of the educational system. This viewpoint holds that there are important cultural and behavioral differences between many minority students and the people who teach them and prepare their educational materials and that minority students are held back because of these cultural differences, which may be limited to either race or social class. In the following sections, we shall explore both of these general issues in greater detail.

FUNDING OF SCHOOLS

There is evidence that schools in which most of the students are black, Hispanic, or Indian are underfunded in comparison to schools in which most of the students are white. This is partly inherent in the way in which schools are funded. On the average, schools get about half of their revenue from state aid and most of the rest from the local property tax, although this varies considerably from state to state (Pisko and Stern, 1985). Since the amount that can be raised through the property tax depends on the value of property that is present in the community, this tax tends to bring in more revenue in wealthier communities and less in poorer ones. State funds are sometimes allocated according to matching formulas, which reward with state money those school districts that raise more money locally. Such matching formulas tend to reinforce the inequities that arise from unequal property tax bases. Thus, substantial disparities exist both within and between states in such measures as spending per pupil and number of teachers per thousand students. These inequities tend strongly to occur along the lines of income: Districts with higher incomes spend more per pupil on education than do districts with lower incomes.

Because minorities have lower incomes on the average than whites, one effect of this would appear to be that *less* money is spent per student on the education of minorities than on the education of whites. And although further investigation shows that expenditures in central cities, where the bulk of the minority population lives, are actually slightly higher than in other areas (Brown et al., 1978), these figures are misleading for two reasons. First, *costs* tend to be higher in such areas, so the greater expenditure does not necessarily mean better education. Second, the support of education is a greater burden in such areas: Relative to the value of their property, central-city residents must pay significantly higher tax rates. The severity of the problem is well demonstrated by cases of bankruptcy and consequent school closings in Chicago, Toledo, Cleveland, Boston, and other central cities: The limited property tax base and state aid simply cannot keep up with the soaring costs of urban education. The result: severe cutbacks and, in the most extreme cases, bankruptcy.

A recent book by Jonathon Kozol (1991) examined levels of school funding and the quality of school facilities in districts with large minority populations such as Detroit; East St. Louis, Illinois; and Camden, New Jersey. He found dramatic funding inequalities and woefully inadequate school facilities. In Detroit, for example, 1988 per-pupil school spending was $3,600 per year. In several affluent nearby suburbs, per-pupil funding ranged from $5,700 to $6,400. A 1994 report by the *St. Louis Post-Dispatch* found much the same in the St. Louis area, where per-pupil spending ranged from around $3,100 in the poorest districts to over $8,700 in the wealthiest. In several inner-city districts, Kozol found classrooms where students went weeks or months into the school year without receiving textbooks. And in East St. Louis, one physics lab teacher commented, "It would be great if we had water."

In some states, property tax equalization efforts have been made to try to eliminate some of the inequities arising from property taxation and state matching formulas. In about a half dozen states—notably California, Connecticut, Iowa, Maine, Oklahoma, Rhode Island, and Vermont—significant reductions in funding disparities were achieved between the 1969–1970 and 1976–1977 school years. However, in about the same number of states the situation became worse, and taking the nation as a whole, there was no improvement and possibly a slight worsening of educational funding disparities (Brown et al., 1978). By the late 1980s and early 1990s, the courts were paying increased attention to the fairness of state school-aid formulas. By the early 1990s, several states, including Texas, New Jersey, Missouri, and Montana, had been ordered by state courts to allocate more state aid to poorer districts (*Education Week*, 1989; Sullivan, 1990; *New York Times*, 1991). Similar suits had been filed in a number of other states. However, legislative efforts at such reform were also rejected in several states, and few if any states have taken the court orders as an opportunity to totally overhaul their school-funding systems.

An exception in this regard is Michigan, where the state legislature voted in 1992 to eliminate the local property tax as the primary source of funding for schools. After a long political battle, it was decided by referendum in 1994 to replace the property tax with a 50 percent increase in the state sales tax and a tripling of the cigarette tax. At the same time, minimum required per-pupil spending was increased from $3,277 to $4,200. However, wealthy districts were allowed to continue to fund their schools at a higher level. Thus, the Michigan reforms will reduce, but not eliminate, unequal funding of wealthy and poor school districts.

Another recent trend is an increase in many states in the state share of funding for education. This probably has reduced inequality among districts somewhat (Pisko and Stern, 1985), but substantial inequalities remain, and districts with large minority enrollments remain financially strapped in many parts of the country.

In addition to inequities *between* school districts, inequities also exist *within* school districts. Put simply, school boards allocate more money for some schools than they do for others. One study in Detroit, for example, compared spending for teachers' pay in schools that were 90 percent or more black to those that were 10 percent or less black in 1970. The finding: $380 per pupil in the mostly black schools; $432 per pupil in the mostly white schools (Michelson, 1972).

As serious as funding deficiencies in schools in many minority areas are, it will take more than money to bring about truly equal educational opportunity. Though a number of districts in which African American, Latino, and Native Americans attend school are clearly underfunded to the point that they lack necessities, there are also problems in education that cannot be addressed by money alone. An important source of evidence on this topic is a massive survey of 570,000 students and 10,000 teachers and principals in over 4,000 schools in the United States. This study, which has come to be known as the Coleman Report (Coleman et al., 1966), was mandated by the 1964 Civil Rights Act to explore the quality of education received by American minority students, and it revealed a number of startling findings. Among the most important was that traditional measures of educational quality—class size, educational level of teachers, facilities and programs available in the schools, and so on—explained relatively little of the variation in what students actually knew, as measured by tests of ability and achievement. Overall, these factors appear to explain about 5 percent of the variance—a bit more for "ability" measures, a bit less for the supposedly more schooling-related "achievement" measures. There was some racial difference, however: Such inputs explained from about 10 to 15 percent of the variance in achievement and ability for black students; they explained only about 2 to 6 percent of the variance for white students (Coleman et al., 1966, p. 294). In short, while school quality did make more difference in learning for blacks (and probably for other minorities as well) than for whites, it did not make a great deal of difference for anyone.

What *did* explain how much students learned? Coleman was able to identify two main factors. The first was a set of background factors, including urban/rural background, parents' education, family size and composition, facilities and educational resources available in the home, and parents' interests and desires concerning the child's education. These factors explained from 15 to 25 percent of the variance in student learning—more for whites than for blacks (Coleman, 1966, p. 300). The other important source of variation in student learning was the attitudes of the students themselves. Coleman measured three kinds of attitudes: interest in learning, self-concept, and belief that the individual can control his or her environment. Again, Coleman found a significant relationship: These individual attitudes explained 15 to 20 percent of the variation in learning for blacks, and 25 to 30 percent for whites. In the overall sample, these individual attitudes correlated more closely to student achievement scores than anything else Coleman measured (Coleman, 1966, pp. 319, 321). Although some differences were found for groups other than blacks or whites (see Table 12.2), Coleman's overall finding was quite clear: The background and attitudes of students were more strongly correlated to what they learned in school than was *anything* about the school that was measurable or that varied substantially from school to school.

The figures referred to above contain some overlap, that is, school characteristics, background factors, and student attitudes all tend to be associated with one another. Thus, it can be difficult to estimate just how much of the effect on student learning is a result of each variable. However, through a method known as stepwise regression, it is possible to add one variable at a time to the analysis and thus mea-

Table 12.2 Race/Ethnic Variation in Achievement Explained by Adding

GROUP	1 ALL SCHOOL-TO-SCHOOL VARIATION NOT LINKED TO BACKGROUND	2 SCHOOL-TO-SCHOOL VARIATION LINKED TO BACKGROUND	3 INDIVIDUAL VARIATION IN BACKGROUND	4 INDIVIDUAL VARIATION IN ATTITUDE	5 ALL FACTORS COMBINED
White	7.41%	2.08%	16.94%	13.38%	40.09%
Black	14.83	6.07	6.41	10.87	38.18
Puerto Rican	22.69	0.71	3.35	4.79	31.54
Indian	23.42	0.71	10.68	8.80	43.61
Chicano	17.75	2.32	6.02	8.24	34.33
Asian	2.20	0.13	19.66	10.05	32.04

Source: Coleman et al., 1966, p. 229, Tables 3.221.1 and 3.221.2.

sure, the *additional* effect of that factor after all others are taken into consideration. Using such methods Coleman was able to identify the effects of various factors on twelfth-grade verbal achievement, as shown in Table 12.2.

These data reveal that all variation between schools that was *not* related to the background of students attending those schools accounted for only 2 percent of the variation in achievement for Asian students, 7 percent for white students, and 15 percent for black students. Variation linked to backgrounds and attitudes was much more important for these groups. Attitude and background together accounted for 33 percent of the variation in achievement for whites, 30 percent for Asians, and 23 percent for blacks. Thus for these groups, which account for about 90 percent of all U.S. students, attitude and background factors correlated a lot more closely with achievement than did differences between schools. Thus, the importance of schools seems to be less than many believed, though undoubtedly greater for blacks than for whites. The other groups are a bit different. For Chicanos and Indians, variations between schools seems about as important as differences in attitude and background in explaining student learning. Only for Puerto Ricans did differences in schools seem more important than individual differences. Even when school differences were important, however, differences in the attributes of the student bodies of those schools seemed to make more difference than did either teacher quality or school facilities (Coleman et al., 1966, p. 302).

These results should not be taken to mean that school funding and quality of facilities and teachers are unimportant issues in minority education. For one thing, the Coleman Report did clearly show that these factors make more difference for minority students than for white students. This finding was confirmed a decade later in research by Summers and Wolfe (1977). Undoubtedly, one reason for this is that minority students are more likely to encounter serious inadequacies that could be addressed by better funding. Moreover, the Coleman Report did find one school resource that made a sizable difference, though it was not given great emphasis in the report: When teachers scored higher on a vocabulary test, their students did better (Thernstrom, 1991). The main message that is to be derived from the Coleman Report (and similar studies since, such as Jencks et al., 1972 and Bowles and Gintis, 1976) is that more money and better facilities will not *by themselves* solve all of the problems that are faced by American students, particularly students of color.

CULTURAL AND BEHAVIORAL FACTORS IN THE EDUCATION OF MINORITIES

The Coleman Report shocked the American educational establishment, because it seemed to suggest that schools do not make as much difference in how much students learn as had been previously believed. Regardless of the apparent quality of schools, it seems that students with certain kinds of attitudes and backgrounds were learning and those with other kinds of attitudes and backgrounds were falling behind. Subsequent research, however, has shown that schools can make more difference than one might be led to believe by the Coleman Report. However, what makes more difference than money alone (though money can be important when schools lack necessities, as many in minority areas do) is characteristics related to interaction between teachers and students. When teachers interact with students in certain ways, those students tend to learn, and when they interact with students in other ways, the students fall behind. Thus, even though more money and better facilities are needed by some schools, they will not by themselves completely solve the problems. What is also needed is greater attention to cultural, attitudinal, and interactional factors and the role these factors play in the learning process.

The finding that cultural and background factors are closely associated with learning in American schools can be interpreted in two quite different ways. One interpretation, aligned with the functionalist perspective, identifies the source of the problem in "dysfunctional" attitudes and beliefs among poor people and among racial and ethnic minorities. The other view, aligned with the conflict perspective, sees the source of the problem in the educational institution. According to this view, the educational system demands conformity to an arbitrary norm and punishes those who do not or cannot conform, and/or it expects poor performance from low-income and minority students, then treats them in ways that assure that this expectation comes true. In the following sections, we shall explore the evidence concerning the functionalist view that the problem is one of *cultural deprivation,* and the conflict theory view that the problem is *cultural bias.*

Cultural Deprivation?

Recall Coleman's finding that absence of facilities and educational materials in the home was associated with poorer performance in school. Specifically, Coleman found lower levels of achievement among children from homes that lacked such things as a television, a telephone, a record player, an automobile, or a vacuum cleaner. He also found that the lack of reading materials such as books, magazines, daily newspapers, encyclopedias, and dictionaries was correlated with lower levels of learning. This (along with other data on family structure and parental interest and encouragement of children's education) suggested to Coleman that children from certain kinds of homes entered school at a disadvantage. Put simply, they were deprived of many of the learning opportunities that other children enjoyed; thus, they could not compete on an equal footing with other children who enjoyed these advantages. Their disadvantage was in many cases worsened by the lack of parental encouragement of education and finally by the attitudes of the children themselves. Underachieving children, Coleman found, tended to (1) have a poor self-image, (2) be relatively uninterested in school, and (3) believe that they could not control their environment, that is, that success was a result of "good luck," not "hard work." Of these three, self-image and belief in control of environment had much stronger effects than interest in school, especially among black students; and for students from minority groups (and probably poor whites), the most important factor was belief in control over one's environment (Coleman et al., 1966, pp. 319–24).

To Coleman, this strongly suggested that the lack of facilities and encouragement in the home, *combined with* the attitudes that minority students brought to school, placed those students at a very substantial disadvantage to whites. The solution: Change the attitudes of disadvantaged students so that they could develop a positive self-image and believe that they *can* control their environment. Coleman was able to present one additional piece of evidence that lent further support to his argument. In his own words, he found that "as the educational aspirations and backgrounds of *fellow students* increase, the achievement of minority group children increases" (Coleman et al., 1966, p. 302). In short, he found that, all else being equal, a minority student attending school with students from advantaged backgrounds and who had positive attitudes did better than a comparable minority student attending school with students from disadvantaged backgrounds and who had negative attitudes. The apparent reason: The positive attitudes and study habits of the other students "rubbed off" and the minority student developed more positive attitudes and study habits. Of equal significance, the evidence did *not* show any harmful effect on the more advantaged students of attending school with students of less positive attitude and background. In fact, the white and Asian students, who on the average did better than others in school, were not much influenced by the characteristics of their fellow students. The influence of fellow students was mainly on black, Chicano, Puerto Rican, and, to a lesser degree, Indian students. A finding that was to have great political importance in later years, and that follows quite logically from what we have seen here, is that racially and socioeconomically integrated schools were associated with higher achievement among minority group children. The suggestion was clear: Desegregation of schools might lead to improved learning among minority students as they took on the attitudes and study habits of their more advantaged white middle-class peers. As we shall soon see, the findings of the Coleman Report became an important part of the battle over school busing for racial integration that began in the late 1960s and has continued into the 1990s.

Essentially, Coleman's interpretation of his findings was consistent with the functionalist perspective. He focused on the idea that minority students (and lower-income students in general) come to school with attitudes and backgrounds that do not "fit in" to the school system. Coleman's findings, and those of other studies showing background strongly linked to school achievement, have led to an emphasis on efforts aimed at helping minority students to fit in and develop the attitudes they need to get ahead in the school system. Such programs as Head Start have been designed to accomplish this, as has, in large part, the policy of school busing for the purpose of racial integration. The degree to which busing has been successful in improving the achievement of minority students will be explored in the final section of this chapter, which focuses on educational social policy. In the meantime, we shall turn to another interpretation of Coleman's findings that clashes with the functionalist viewpoint.

Cultural Bias?

Conflict theorists, including a number of minority group spokespersons, argue that the "cultural-deprivation" viewpoint reflects the biases of the white middle class, the group to which most social scientists belong. According to conflict theorists, the problem is not to be found in the characteristics of the minority groups but rather in the schools. The reason for low achievement among those with certain attitudes and backgrounds, according to this view, is that the schools demand certain values, attitudes, and habits and, in effect, punish those who do not conform. As we have seen, conflict theorists believe that schools operate this way for two reasons. First, it allows the dominant elements in society to pass their advantage along to their children. Second, it provides employers with a well-socialized workforce that will "fit in" and not cause trouble (Bowles and Gintis, 1976). Thus, the schools serve the interests of the advantaged, in spite of the widespread ideology that they serve everyone's interest. Social scientists who hold this viewpoint say that it is not surprising that Coleman's study and others found that more of the same kind of education does not do much for minority-student achievement: The problem is not the amount or quality (as traditionally measured) of education; rather, it is the *kind* of educational system we have and the role that system plays in the larger society.

If there is merit in this viewpoint, it should be possible to identify some specific ways in which the educational system penalizes minority students. In the following section, we shall examine the educational institution to see if we can identify practices or structures that do in fact work to hold down learning by minority students.

Biased or Limited Coverage of Minority Groups in School Materials

Both white and minority schoolchildren form important impressions about their own racial group and other racial groups based on what they are exposed to in educational settings. Until very recently, what most schoolchildren have been exposed to has been quite stereotypical and biased. Two distinct tendencies can be noted. One is simply to exclude minorities from materials discussing U.S. history, or from general educational materials, such as "Dick and Jane" grade-school readers. One study found that of forty-five social science textbooks, only eight even mentioned Spanish-speaking Americans. The largest Hispanic group, Chicanos, was mentioned in only two of the books (Kane, 1970). Research by Bowker (1972) indicates that Indian people were similarly neglected in history books and that the problem actually got worse between 1960 and 1972. One study of forty-nine major school textbook series from 1958 to 1976 showed that there was only a small increase in the number of minority characters (Britton and Lumpkin, 1977). Another study found African Americans underrepresented even in college psychology of women texts—a type of book one would expect to be sensitive to minority concerns (Brown et al., 1985). Furthermore, the Britton and Lumpkin study showed that minority characters were depicted in a much more limited range of occupational roles than were white characters. A more recent study of science books shows that this problem continues. Although minorities were generally rather well represented in the books, they were underrepresented in the pictures of adults in scientific occupations—thus missing the opportunity to present a positive minority role model (Powell and Garcia, 1985). Another problem was identified by McCutcheon, Kyle, and Skovira (1979)—a tendency to portray everyone, including minority characters, according to a white middle-class role model. Thus, skin color or names may be changed, but no real effort is made to display the great cultural diversity of the U.S. population.

The other major problem—which many view as more persistent than the one we have been discussing—is distorted or stereotypical presentations of Americans of color. Indian people, for example, have been referred to in many school textbooks with derogatory adjectives, including "filthy," "murderers," "lecherous," "dumb," "stupid," and "barely human" (Bahr, Chadwick, and Strauss, 1979, pp. 237–38). Chicanos have been similarly stereotyped. Kane's (1970) study showed, for example, that they were often portrayed as "wetbacks" crossing the border illegally, or as lawbreakers and bandits who are not wanted in this country. Another common stereotype is that of the migrant farmworker. Textbook portrayals of the Mexican American in this light undoubtedly help to explain why this image persists, even though Chicanos are actually more urbanized than the U.S. population as a whole. Similar stereotyping occurs in the presentation of blacks in educational materials. Too often, black Americans have appeared in low-status roles in textbooks, when they have appeared at all.

In the past fifteen to twenty years, awareness of these problems has been increasing, and minority-group members have begun to appear in school materials in greater numbers and in less stereotyped roles than in the past (Garcia, 1993). Most major textbook publishers, for example, have added recommendations to their authors' guides concerning inclusion of minorities and women in textbooks (Britton and Lumpkin, 1977). Over the past decade or so, a number of textbooks and other school learning materials have been specifically designed to be *multicultural,* that is, to represent the full diversity of groups, cultures, and traditions that make up the American population. This type of effort can be seen in California's mandate that the social-studies curriculum in its schools make a number of changes. The changes were designed to (1) increase emphasis on history and geography, (2) use a narrative approach designed to bring history to life and explain why things happened rather than memorizing names and dates, and (3) bring problematic issues such as race and religion to the forefront, with material on minority cultures woven into the mainstream narrative of history rather than being presented as peripheral to the main event of American history (Kirp, 1991). The latter meant that, for example, world history pays more attention to non-European regions; discussions of the United States deemphasize the "melting-pot" idea in favor of the image of a "mosaic" of distinct cultural traditions that continue to thrive; and American history gives major emphasis to the longstanding tension between the principle of equality and the reality of the oppression of minorities. Textbooks developed for the California curriculum have been adopted not only in California but also in Arkansas, Virginia, and other states (Kirp, 1991).

Despite the increased emphasis on cultural diversity in today's school materials, however, many critics argue that they are still *Eurocentric,* that is, they give undue emphasis to European historical and cultural influences or describe other groups from the standpoint of the European experience (Ratteray, 1988; Honeman, 1990). For example, Banks (1992) points out that African, Asian, and American histories are often studied under the topic "The Age of Discovery," meaning the time when Europeans first arrived in these continents. Similarly, debates among scholars about the extent to which African or Afro-Asian societies may have influenced the development of Western civilization are often kept out of the classroom, whereas Banks (1992) argues that in a truly multicultural educational system, such debates would be introduced and discussed. In a similar vein, some critics of the California curriculum have questioned its treatment of colonized minorities such as African Americans, Mexican Americans, and Native Americans under the rubric of America as a nation of immigrants, since none of these groups are voluntary immigrants.

In addition, even recent studies show that minorities are still sometimes absent or stereotypically portrayed in schoolbooks and materials. This is particularly the case for Native Americans and Hispanic Americans (Charles, 1989; Michigan State Board of Education, 1989; Romero and Zancanella, 1990).

The absence and/or distortion of minority groups in educational materials (coupled with similar omissions and distortions in the media) can have serious effects on both majority and minority group children. Among majority group children, the consequence can be to create or reinforce prejudices and stereotypes concerning members of groups other than their own. Among minority group children the result can be serious damage to the children's self-image or to their beliefs concerning the racial or ethnic group to which they belong. The symbolic-interactionist school of social psychology has shown that reality is socially constructed. In other words, we acquire our knowledge, beliefs, and self-images through what we are told by others (Cooley, 1964; Mead, 1967). For majority group children, this means that their beliefs about minority groups are formed on the basis of what they hear and read at home, at school, and in the media. This is especially true when, as very frequently happens, the children grow up in segregated neighborhoods and attend segregated schools. (For further discussion of the role of social learning in the perpetuation of prejudice among majority group members, see Chapter 2.)

The absence or distorted presentation of minorities in school materials also can seriously harm the self-image of minority group children. Cooley's (1964) concept of *looking-glass self* is highly relevant here. According to this concept, we develop beliefs about ourselves based on the messages we get from others. If these messages are negative, the self-concept will tend to be negative. It is not surprising, then, that a sizable body of evidence shows that black children have in the past developed serious problems in the area of self-image. Among the most widely cited studies in this area are the doll studies by Clark and Clark (1958) and by Radke and Trager (1950). These studies showed that, when given a choice of otherwise identical black and white dolls, black schoolchildren (as well as white children) showed consistent preferences for the white doll. In the Clarks' study, for example, two-thirds of the black children chose the white doll as the one they wanted to play with, and 60 percent said it was the doll that had a nice color. On the other hand, when asked which doll "looks bad," 59 percent of the black children chose the black doll. The study also showed that the children were aware of racial differences: 94 percent made the correct choice when asked which doll "looks white," and 93 percent when asked which doll "looks colored." Significantly, however, fully one-third of those same black children picked the *white* doll when asked which doll "looks like you"—an apparent denial of their own racial identity.

Another approach that has been used to assess self-image is to have children draw pictures of themselves or tell stories about themselves (Porter, 1971). Such studies have shown that black (and often poor white) children express less positive themes in their stories and pictures and are more likely to draw small pictures or pictures with missing limbs or features. Such findings are not limited to blacks. Rosenthal (1974), using pictures of white and Indian children, found that the preference for white children was even stronger among Indians than it was among other groups such as blacks and Asians, and that unlike some other groups, the pattern did not decrease with age (Rosenthal's data, however, apply only to Chippewa Indians and may not be true for other groups). Doll studies with Chicano children have also found a fairly widespread preference for white dolls (Werner and Evans, 1968).

In spite of this widespread evidence that the self-images of minority children have in the past been seriously harmed, there is also rather impressive evidence that this pattern is changing. A more recent doll study (Katz and Zalk, 1974) found that the preference among black children for the white doll no longer existed. In addition, when Rosenberg and Simmons (1971) administered paper-and-pencil self-esteem scales to both black and white school children, they found that the black children had self-images at least as positive as those of the white students. Other studies by Baughman (1971), Zirkel (1971), Zirkel and Moses (1971), Bachman and O'Malley (1984), Richman, Clark, and Brown (1985), and Solorzano (1991) suggest the same thing. Though the evidence is much more fuzzy and limited on Chicano and Indian children, such changes may quite possibly be occurring among them, too, since some studies show very little difference in self-esteem between them and white children (see Carter, 1968; Fuchs and Havighurst, 1972). It is undoubtedly true, however, that some of the conflicting findings for Chicano and Indian children result from the fact that different measures tend to produce different results. Nonetheless, there is little doubt that, at least for black children, self-esteem in the 1970s and 1980s has been significantly higher than in the past.

Why has self-esteem among black children improved? Undoubtedly, one factor has been the more balanced presentation of minorities in educational materials and the media, even though there remains much room for improvement. Of possibly greater importance, however, is the emphasis on black pride and self-identity that came with the Black Power movement in the 1960s and 1970s and again with the Afrocentrism movement of the 1990s, which emphasizes blacks' learning about and taking pride in their African cultural heritage. A major emphasis of both of those movements was a rejection of the negative black image presented by whites and a corresponding emphasis of the notion that black people can and should define their own identities. Considering the findings of studies in recent years, these movements appear to have succeeded in bringing about a distinctly more positive self-identity among blacks that has persisted into the 1990s. It appears likely that a similar process has taken place among Hispanic Americans, Native Americans, and Asian Americans. Of course, none of these positive changes can undo the harm that has been done to minority children in the past, but they do suggest that at least in the area of minority children's self-esteem, things are getting better.

Teacher Expectations and Tracking

Teacher Expectations.   In recent years, there has been increasing awareness of possible effects of *teacher expectations* on student performance. It is now evident that a **self-fulfilling prophecy** frequently operates in the classroom: Teachers expect more of some students and less of others, their expectations affect the way they interact with the students, and as a result, the expectations come true. The most widely known study of this process was published by Rosenthal and Jacobson (1968) in a book titled *Pygmalion in the Classroom*. In this famous experiment, the researchers began by giving a test to children in a California elementary school. The teachers in the school were told that the test was a new instrument designed to identify "academic spurters"—children who would greatly improve their performance in the coming academic year. Actually, the test was an ordinary IQ test, and the 20 percent of the children who were identified as academic spurters, supposedly on the basis of the test, were in fact randomly selected. The teachers, of course, did not know this.

At the end of the year, the children were given another IQ test. The results in the first and second grades were striking: The children who teachers thought were "spurters" showed improvements in IQ of 10 to 15 points relative to the other children. Recall that these children were in fact no different from the other children: They had been randomly selected. The only difference was that their teachers thought they were going to do better.

The effects of teacher expectations appeared to occur mainly in the first and second grades. Older children seemed less susceptible to such effects. This may be because they were more intellectually developed and therefore less subject to such influences or because they had by then established reputations with the teachers that affected teacher expectations more than did the supposed test results.

Apparently it is the content, not the amount, of teacher–student interaction that causes the expectancy effect. Teachers did not spend more time with the children identified as spurters, but they did apparently give them more positive messages. Another study by Brophy and Good (1970) also found that teachers were more critical of those they believed to be poorer students, and more praising and encouraging toward those they believed to be better students. These messages affect the students' self-images, which in turn influence their achievement (Brophy, 1983).

Research also shows that, when teachers believe their students to be disadvantaged or less capable, they teach in fundamentally different ways. They are more directive, more likely to walk students through tasks step by step, and give the student less opportunity to engage in higher-order thinking and to take on problem-solving tasks (Means and Knapp, 1991). While this may help students somewhat with basic skills, its most pronounced effect is to deprive them of opportunities to develop the skills of comprehension, problem solving, and reasoning. Moreover, there is growing evidence that most students labeled as disadvantaged are capable of such skills but are deprived of the opportunity to develop them because teachers don't think they can learn such skills and as a result don't try to teach them (Knapp and Shields, 1990). Moreover, a number of experiments to see what happens when efforts are made to teach students such skills have shown that when effort is made to teach higher-order problem skills and teachers believe that economically disadvantaged students can learn those skills, dramatic improvements in the students' achievement occur. These experiments have produced learning of problem-solving skills by minority and low-income students at grade levels from kindergarten to college—sometimes to the point that students in such programs surpass the average achievement of white, middle-class, suburban students (Selvin, 1992; see also U.S. Department of Education, 1987).

It should be pointed out that there have been methodological criticisms of the Rosenthal and Jacobson study (Thorndike, 1969) and that not all studies using similar methods have been able to replicate the findings (Boocock, 1978). Nonetheless, an impressive array of studies does suggest that teacher expectations influence student performance (see Beez, 1968; Brophy and Good, 1974; Nash, 1976, especially chap. 3; Brophy, 1983; Nolen and Haladyna, 1990). One of the most interesting (Rist, 1970) again reveals the sizable effects of labeling in early education. In the school observed by Rist, students were assigned to three tables according to their teacher's beliefs about their ability, during the first eight days of kindergarten. For many children, the assignments were inconsistent with reading-readiness scores. By second grade, not one of the children who remained in the class had moved to a higher group, and those in the low group had fallen far behind in reading and had become socially labeled as "the clowns." Thus, the initial assignment of children to groups, made largely without regard to available ability measures, had a longstanding effect on student performance. In effect, the students assigned to the "low" table never really had a chance.

In itself, the fact that student performance is influenced by teacher expectations may seem irrelevant to the issue of majority–minority relations. However, there is a large and growing body of evidence that teachers do in fact form their expectations of students at least partially on the basis of race and class. In a study by Harvey and Slatin (1975), for example, teachers were given photographs of children and asked to evaluate their chances of success. The result: Teachers had substantially higher expectations of white children and of children whom they perceived to be from the middle or upper classes. Research by Leacock (1969) similarly indicated

Teacher-student interactions have important effects on student learning. One example of this is the self-fulfilling prophecy; when teachers expect students to do well, they tend to actually do better. When teacher expectations are lower, student performance is not as good. *Liamute E. Druskis*

racial and class effects on teacher expectations, to the extent that teacher expectations of black students were actually negatively related to IQ. The study by Rist discussed above also showed that the students were placed at the "low" or "high" tables in kindergarten largely on the basis of social class—in spite of the fact that in this case both the students and teachers were black. To summarize, the studies that have been done to date have produced two clear findings. First, what teachers expect of students influences how much those students learn and the degree to which they progress in the school system. One literature review (Brophy, 1983) estimated the average effect on achievement at 5 percent to 10 percent, but, depending on the teacher and student in any given interaction, it is occasionally much larger. Second, such teacher expectations are formed at least partly on the basis of race and class, though the extent to which this is true varies greatly from classroom to classroom (Brophy and Good, 1974; Hurn, 1978; Brophy, 1983; Alexander, Entwisle, and Thompson, 1987; Didham, 1990; Gaines and Davis, 1990). Thus, it does seem clear that teacher expectations perpetuate racial and ethnic inequality in the American educational system.

Teacher expectancy effects can also occur on a schoolwide level. Often, teachers form generalized expectations about the learning potential of their entire class, and these affect student achievement. A more recent national study known as the *High School and Beyond* study illustrates this dramatically (Coleman, Hoffer, and Kilgore, 1982; Greeley, 1982; Hoffer, Greeley, and Coleman, 1987). This study included public, Catholic, and nonreligious private schools. It found that in both types of private schools, overall achievement exceeded that of public schools, and that in the Catholic schools, black, Hispanic, and low-income students did better relative to middle-class whites than they did in the public schools. Moreover, more recent research from the same sample has shown that this difference increased as students moved from the tenth to twelfth grade (Hoffer, Greeley, and Coleman, 1985; Haertel, 1987), though there is debate about the size of the difference (Jencks, 1985; Alexander and Pallas, 1987; Willms, 1987). Similar successes were also found in a small group of public schools. A key reason for the success of these schools is that they *expected* and *demanded* more of their students, and did so *regardless of race or social class* (Hoffer, Greeley, and Coleman, 1987). In short, low-income and minority students *are* doing very well in some schools, and the ones they do well in are the ones that expect them to do well. As a teacher told Fuerst in his (1981) study of successful all-black schools in Chicago, "The belief that children can succeed is more than half the battle." Unfortunately, the opposite belief that "students like these can't be expected to learn much" often develops among teachers in predominantly black, Hispanic, and/or low-income, central-city schools. For example, Kozol (1991) quotes a Chicago teacher as saying, "It makes no difference. Kids like these aren't going anywhere." And when Kozol asked an East St. Louis teacher if her class was preparation for employment, the teacher replied "not this class." When teachers expect and demand less from students, they usually get less, and ultimately, the learning of minority students is seriously impaired (Moore and Pachon, 1985). In a review of the literature on teacher-expectancy effects, Brophy (1983) concluded that such effects are maximized in racially and/or socioeconomically homogeneous schools, where low expectations often become generalized.

Tracking and Ability Grouping.

A closely related issue is that of tracking and ability grouping. Tracking and ability grouping are common educational practices whereby students believed to be similar in ability are grouped together either in separate classes with different curricula (tracking) or in different classes with the same curricula or different groups within a class (ability grouping). A survey of middle-school principals in the early 1990s revealed that 82 percent of the schools were using some form of tracking (*Jet*, 1993b). The idea behind tracking and ability grouping is to enable students to proceed at a pace consistent with their ability, preventing the better students from becoming bored and the poorer ones from being left behind. However, critics of tracking and ability grouping have claimed that they work to hold down the educational attainment of minority, poor, and working-class students by acting as a self-fulfilling prophecy, much like teacher expectations. Minority and lower-status students are placed into less advanced tracks, on the basis of race and/or class, and this inhibits their later learning and academic advancement. Research on the topic generally supports this viewpoint. Although again it is not clear just how strong the effects are, there appears to be fairly wide agreement in the literature that placement in tracks is influenced by race, Hispanic origin, and especially class (Schafer, Olexa, and Polk, 1972; Brischetto and Arciniega, 1973; U.S. Commission on Civil Rights, 1974; Alexander and Eckland, 1975; Alexander and McDill, 1976; Alexander, Cook and McDill, 1978; Boocock, 1978; Useem, 1991; Gamoran, 1992a; Oakes, Gamoran, and Page, 1992; England, Meier, and Fraga, 1988). Some of the reasons for the overrepresentation of minority and low-income students in lower tracks is that the tests used for placement produce scores that are correlated with race and class (Haller, 1985), but some studies show that even when the test scores are the same, lower-socioeconomic-status students are placed in lower tracks (Hallinan, 1992). One reason for this may be that college-educated parents are more likely to intervene to get their children placed in a higher track (Useem, 1992). A recent government report concluded that in about 10 percent of public middle schools, ability-grouping practices verged on outright racial discrimination (Armstrong, 1991).

Once students have been placed in a low track, their future educational experience is largely determined: They stay in the same track and have a significantly reduced opportunity to enter higher education, regardless of their initial ability (McGinley and McGinley, 1970; Schafer, Olexa, and Polk, 1972; Esposito, 1973; Rosenbaum, 1976; Bredekamp and Shepard, 1989; Gamoran, 1992a, 1992b).

The tendency for students to remain in the track where they are originally placed may be the most destructive aspect of tracking (Brophy, 1983; Gamoran, 1992b; Hallinan, 1992). In those rare cases where students move regularly from track to track, tracking may have positive effects. Fuerst (1981), for example, found that in all-black schools that used tracking and changed the track assignments yearly, student achievement was high. Usually, though, low track placement becomes a social label that stays with a student throughout his or her educational career. Thus, it is not surprising that Coleman, Hoffer, and Kilgore (1982) concluded that a major reason for the greater success of black, Hispanic, and low-income students in the Catholic schools is that these schools often lack the vocational tracks into which such students are frequently placed in the public schools. Research by Gamoran (1992b) reveals another reason for the success of minority and lower-income children in Catholic schools: When these schools do have tracking, they usually employ it in a more flexible manner. In both public and Catholic schools, schools with more mobility and flexibility in their tracking systems produce higher overall achievement and less inequality in achievement (Gamoran, 1992b).

The effects of track placement on children's performance and educational plans have also been noted. Effects on actual learning are probably greatest in the lower grades, where teacher expectations exert their greatest influence. In high school, on the other hand, tracking seems mainly to affect the self-expectations and plans of students: Those placed in lower tracks generally lower their expectations and do not plan on (and therefore do not attend) college. Track placement, then, has effects on future educational attainment that hold true even when we compare students who are in different tracks but have similar ability and achievement levels (Hauser, Sewell, and Alwin, 1976). Alexander, Cook, and McDill (1978, p. 60), for example, found that "enrollment in a college preparatory track increases by about 30 percent the probability that students will plan in their senior year to continue their education in comparison to equally able, motivated, and encouraged youth in nonacademic programs."

Taken as a whole, the literature raises serious questions about the usefulness of tracking unless the track placements are carefully reevaluated and changed on a regular basis. In addition, it must be stressed that the decision to place students in tracks is haphazard at best: Two studies of high school track placement found that ability, achievement, and background variables combined explained only 30 to 40 percent of the variation in track placement, leaving 60 to 70 percent unexplained (Hauser, Sewell, and Alwin, 1976, p. 318; Alexander, Cook, and McDill, 1978, p. 55). For a process that is supposed to be a rational decision based on student aptitude and performance, these figures are not impressive. Beyond this, however, we are talking about a process that contains racial and class biases, and that arbitrarily influences the future educational attainments of students. Viewed from this perspective, the practice appears highly questionable.

Linguistic Differences

Another area of difficulty has arisen from linguistic differences between minority students and their teachers. This has in various ways been a problem for black students, who frequently speak various forms of the dialect commonly called "Black

English," for Spanish-speaking students, and for Indian students, who may be penalized for speaking their native languages. The issue here is not whether students should be able to speak standard English—most educators, white and minority, would agree that not being able to speak standard English is a serious disadvantage in present-day U.S. society and that students should learn how to speak standard English if they do not know how. Rather, the issues concern negative and incorrect labels attached to minority children because they do not enter the school speaking standard English and in some cases, the *failure* of the school system to teach minority group children standard English.

We shall begin our examination of this issue with an exploration of Black English. Traditionally, Black English has been regarded by many educators as an inadequate or poorly developed version of English, linguistically inferior to standard English. Deutsch (1963, p. 174), for example, wrote ". . . It appears that speech sequences seem to be temporally very limited and poorly structured syntactically. It is thus not surprising to find that a major focus of deficit in the children's language is syntactical organization and subject continuity." More recently, however, sociolinguistic research on Black English has shown this viewpoint to be incorrect. In fact, Black English has standard rules (although there is some regional variation) concerning tenses, subjects and verbs, and so on. In the past, educators tended to see it as an inferior or incomplete language largely because their cultural and linguistic background did not give them the knowledge necessary to understand Black English. Put simply, Black English is *different from* standard English but equally regular in its rules (Baratz and Baratz, 1970). One difference is in the use of tenses: Black English has a wider variety of tenses than does standard English (Seymour, 1972; Dillard, 1972, pp. 39–72; Fickett, 1975, pp. 67–75). One example is the "habitual" tense, a pattern that exists in Black English but not in standard English. Apparently, this tense has its roots in West African languages. Silverstein and Krate (1975, pp. 146, 166) present two examples. In Black English, there is an important difference in meaning between "he workin" and "he be working." "He workin" (the present tense) means he is working right now, whereas "he be working" (the habitual tense) means he works regularly or habitually. Similarly, "she sick" means she is sick today but will probably be over it soon, whereas "she be sick" means she is seriously or chronically ill—the illness is likely to be of long duration.

Fickett (1975, p. 77) presents a similar example from research in a Buffalo high school. She found that nearly all the black students knew that "I been seen him" was longest ago, "I done seen him" more recent, and "I did see him" most recent. White students, on the other hand, either could not answer the question or guessed wrong. Interestingly, the black students were surprised that white students did not know the difference; some commented, "Those kids gotta be dumb." The findings of these and other studies, then, refute the traditional view that Black English is less developed or less capable of expressing concepts and ideas. The problem is that white educators did not understand Black English. (Some might say that these educators were "culturally deprived.")

Because of these misconceptions on the part of educators (including even some middle-class black ones who have adopted norms against Black English—see Gouldner, 1978), black children have frequently been, and sometimes still are, incorrectly labeled as "slow" or stupid—with all the consequences that carries—because of their use of Black English. This misperception is compounded in many cases by the fact that, in a white or middle-class environment where the norm is standard

English, black youngsters feel inhibited and consequently become withdrawn, answering questions from the teacher slowly and as briefly as possible. On the other hand, when given a less formal environment, a speaker who communicates with them in their own language, and topics they find more familiar and interesting, the same students become highly verbal and compete with one another for a chance to talk (Labov, 1972, pp. 60–62).

In addition to the labeling problem, many teachers apparently are not succeeding at teaching some of their black students standard English. This problem apparently is most serious for those black students who are toward the lower end of the socioeconomic scale. Middle-class black students frequently become adept at using both Black English ("everyday talk") and standard English ("school talk") (Wood and Curry, 1969). In fact, some middle-class blacks are a good bit more familiar with standard English than with Black English, indicating that such linguistic variation is at least partly based on social class. Many blacks—particularly in the middle class—use Black English among their friends and family but standard English in formal or work situations and other white-dominated settings. Wood and Curry's study indicated that middle-class black high-school students in Chicago were quite adept at this type of "code switching." Apparently, for many blacks who know standard English but prefer to speak Black English, the use of the dialect reflects an affirmation of black culture and a rejection of white cultural dominance (Taylor, 1978).

For black students from poor families, however, the picture is apparently different. It appears that many of these students *do* have trouble learning standard English. Wood and Curry (1969), for example, found that black students from poor families in the high school they studied were *not* adept at code switching: Even when asked to speak in "school talk," their responses more closely resembled Black English than standard English. One difference may be that the middle-class black child's parents speak both Black English and standard English; the poor child's parents speak only Black English. Some difference of this type has been noted in the literature (see Labov and Cohen, 1967). In any case, it appears that the schools are not too successful at teaching standard English to those black students who are not fa-

White teachers often incorrectly label black students as withdrawn, noncommunicative, or unable to verbalize, based on their behavior in the white-dominated classroom. If such teachers could communicate with their students in a more comfortable, less threatening setting, they would see a very different pattern. *Stock Boston, Inc./Billy E. Barnes*

miliar with it. One apparent reason for this is that a great many of the teachers who are trying to teach standard English to speakers of Black English do not themselves know how to speak in Black English (Baratz and Baratz, 1970; Fickett, 1975, p. 94). If a teacher cannot communicate with a pupil in language that the pupil understands, it is difficult for that teacher to explain to the student a new form of language. The situation is somewhat analogous to that of a person who knows absolutely no English attempting to teach an English-speaking person to speak Spanish. Although the linguistic differences between standard and Black English are less extensive, the difficulties involved are much the same. Thus, both inappropriate labeling of some black students because of the dialect they speak and the failure of the schools to teach some black students standard English have become important barriers to the education of black students. In 1979, the implications of this for equal educational opportunity became a legal issue, when a court ruling required the Ann Arbor, Michigan, school system to take steps to meet the educational needs of students who speak Black English. The court concluded that the previous failure of the school system to deal with this issue threatened the educational opportunities of the city's black students.

Much of what has been said about the difficulties imposed by the educational system also holds true (in some cases, even more so) for Hispanic students. The majority of Hispanics in the United States speak Spanish in their homes, though most also know English (Moore and Pachon, 1985, pp. 52, 119). Some schools, however, continue to strongly discourage *any* speaking of Spanish in school, and opposition to bilingualism in the schools was a big factor in the passage of a 1986 referendum making English California's official language. A related problem is the tendency of some teachers to look down on students who speak Spanish, contributing to the widespread negative labeling of Latino students (Moore and Pachon, 1985, pp. 149–49). This negative attitude in part reflects the development of dialogues that are neither distinctly English nor Spanish. Switching and mixing of the two languages is common among Hispanic Americans, as is the use of Spanish forms of English words (*pochismos*) such as *el troque* (the truck) or *huáchale* (watch it!) (Moore and Pachon, 1985, p. 121). This, too, has led to negative labeling on the part of English-speaking teachers and sometimes also on the part of educated Mexican Americans concerned with preserving standard Spanish. Nonetheless, this *caló* (mixed language) has come to be recognized by many in the Chicano movement as a symbol of a distinct Chicano culture that is neither totally Mexican nor totally American. In spite of this, it is clear that many Hispanic students have been held back by an educational system that labels them negatively because they speak Spanish or mixed Spanish–English dialects yet frequently fails to teach them standard English. As with black students, it appears that the nonlearning of standard English is most common among the lower classes.

Part of the problem is that some teachers attempting to teach Hispanic children to speak and write in English are not able to communicate with the children in Spanish. Since the late 1970s, this problem has received increasing attention through the development of bilingual-education programs. Such programs teach children in both English and Spanish; teachers, of course, must be proficient in both languages. Bilingual education has been used in different times and places for different purposes. Its primary *educational* purposes are to teach various subjects to students with limited knowledge of English in the language they know and to provide someone to teach them English who speaks their own language. In some cases, it has been used for the *social* purpose of promoting cultural awareness among Hispanic students through preservation of Spanish language and culture. This use has been controversial (see for example Thernstrom, 1980). People who favor cultural assimilation oppose it on grounds that it promotes divisions within society and often point to the linguistic conflict in Quebec, Canada. On the other hand, those who favor cultural pluralism argue that bilingual education contributes to a positive self-image among Hispanics and other linguistic minorities and to increased tolerance and increased appreciation of U.S. society's diverse heritage (Moore and Pachon, 1985, pp. 122, 153–55). Thus, where one stands on the social uses of bilingual education depends on one's values concerning assimilation and pluralism—an issue that will be explored further in Chapter 15.

In contrast, the effectiveness of bilingual education in achieving its *educational* purposes is a matter that can be tested scientifically. Long-term research on the effects of bilingual education as opposed to other methods of teaching non–English-speaking students to speak and write in English was conducted between 1983 and 1988 for the federal government by a California research firm. The study included about four thousand students, mainly Spanish-speaking. The study showed that strong bilingual-education programs were preferable to either partial bilingual-education or English-immersion (that is, trying to get students to learn English by teaching everything in English) programs: Students in the strong bilingual programs tend to become more proficient in English and receive stronger parental support (Lewis, 1991). The research suggests that students are most likely to become proficient in English when bilingual education continues for an extended period of up to five years. The findings of this study are consistent with earlier research results reported by Flores (1978). For bilingual education to be effective, the teacher must be fluent in *both* English and Spanish. Students must also be in the program long enough to benefit from it. Finally, students must be correctly selected for the program according to their language needs. Unfortunately, each of these conditions has not always been present in bilingual-education programs (see, for example, Schmidt, 1992).

Some studies seem to suggest that bilingual education is neither better nor worse than instruction in English (for example, Medina, Saldate, and Mishra, 1985; see also Baker and deKanter, 1981), while other research finds it superior in one or more regard (for example, Valenzuela de la Garza and Medina, 1985). One study that analyzed twenty-three earlier studies, making adjustments for various statistical inadequacies in the earlier studies, found modest positive effects on learning when students were tested in either English or their native language (Willig, 1985). The most thorough and definitive study is probably the federally funded one mentioned above involving four thousand students, and it, like the studies reviewed by Willig, found beneficial effects of bilingual education.

Despite these encouraging signs, bilingual education has encountered significant opposition from some who object to any use of languages other than English in the classroom. Federal support for bilingual education, which had reached $165 million in 1980 (Moore and Pachon, 1985), was temporarily cut during the Reagan administration, though some of the cuts were later restored. Officials of both the Reagan and Bush administrations expressed objections to bilingual education, and Bush's secretary of education, Edward Bennett, openly opposed it (Lewis, 1991). Congressional opposition existed, too, and Congress passed legislation allowing 25 percent of funding for bilingual education to be used for English-immersion programs if base funding reached a certain level (Lewis, 1991). The spate of state and local laws passed in the 1980s specifying English as the only official language suggests that this view is also common in the larger population. Thus, although there are signs that bilingual education, properly done, can be educationally beneficial to children who speak Spanish and other languages, its future remains uncertain.

Most of what has been said about language differences and the education of Hispanic Americans is also largely true of the education of Indian people in America. Through much of our history, Indian education emphasized the assimilation of Indian people in the dominant white culture. In practice, this has frequently meant placing Indian students in boarding schools, separating them from contact with their tribal culture, and allowing them exposure only to English in the schools. Such practices were common as recently as the 1940s and 1950s (Ogbu, 1978, p. 230).

Today, about two-thirds of all Native American students are in public schools, as opposed to BIA (Bureau of Indian Affairs) Indian Schools and other special schools (Bahr, Chadwick, and Strauss, 1979, p. 408). In response to the repeated failure of assimilationist educational programs in the past and to the increasing demands of Indian people for self-determination, Indian education has begun to change, and many schools attended by Indian students now have bilingual-education programs. Nonetheless, there is a long way to go, and Indian students in white-dominated schools frequently continue to be labeled as slow learners simply because of linguistic differences—just as many black and Latino students are.

Test Bias

One of the most controversial issues in the social sciences in recent years has centered around differences in ability and achievement test scores between whites and various minority groups in the United States. There is no question that, on the average, minority group members score lower than whites on standardized tests, though, of course, some individual members of *all* minority groups score far above the white average. Why are their average scores lower?

Some, most notably Arthur Jensen (1969, 1973), argue that the cause is genetic, but it is significant that those who hold this viewpoint have not been able to demonstrate any genetic factor associated with a racial difference in intelligence (Ogbu, 1978, p. 60). The large volume of research done on the topic indicates rather clearly that a more fruitful place to look for an explanation is in the tests themselves, the testing situation, and the wider environment. Among the important factors that are known to influence IQ test scores, for example, are the following:

Culture-specific content in the tests
The test situation
Teacher expectations
Health and nutritional factors
Perceived usefulness of doing well on the test

The differences that can be created by these factors appear to be more than enough to explain the average IQ score differences of about ten to fifteen points that have been noted between whites and various minority group members. Indeed, even identical twins (twins with the same genetic makeup) raised apart sometimes display IQ differences on this order. Let us explore the various factors influencing IQ test scores.

Culture-Specific Content. Although IQ tests are designed to assess ability (what one is capable of learning, not what one already knows), ability cannot in fact be directly measured (Vernon, 1969). All that any test can measure directly is knowledge or task performance—it can measure what the person knows or does but not what the person has the innate ability to know or do. It is hoped that the knowledge measured by IQ tests is associated with ability, but the strength of this association has come increasingly under question. What IQ tests in fact seem to measure is the knowledge, habits, and modes of thinking (all *learned* characteristics) that are valued by the dominant cultural group in any society (Berger, 1978; Ogbu, 1978, pp. 30–37). In other words, IQ tests are designed to predict school achievement, and they do correlate fairly well with later school achievement. The reason, however, is that they largely measure the knowledge, habits, and modes of thinking needed to get ahead in that school system—the cultural attributes of the dominant group. This can be illustrated in several ways. Today, the great majority of Americans would not take seriously the notion that persons of Italian, Russian, or Polish heritage are inherently less intelligent than persons of British or German heritage—nor do test scores suggest this. However, in the early twentieth century, when these immigrant groups were new arrivals unfamiliar with American culture, they *did* score lower on the tests. Furthermore, much of the intellectual community of the time believed that these groups were genetically inferior—a view obviously disproved by today's test scores. One author argued, for example, that 83 percent of Jewish and 79 percent of Italian immigrants were "feeble-minded" (Henry Goddard, cited in Kamin, 1974). Obviously, the reason for the low scores was cultural, not genetic.

Another example can be seen in the Goodenough Draw-A-Man IQ test. Although the test was designed to be culture-free, it—like all tests—has not turned out that way. In general, groups whose cultures stress art do well on this test. Southwestern Indians—who generally have highly developed arts—are generally shown by this test to be more "intelligent" than whites. The same Indians, however, tend to score lower than whites on verbal IQ tests, which are geared to the white culture. Thus, the differences in "intelligence" between whites and Indians as measured by these tests turn out to be cultural, not genetic (Ogbu, 1978, p. 218).

The cultural biases in intelligence tests, and the effects of these biases on blacks and other minority groups, are well illustrated by an example given by black psychiatrist Alvin Poussaint (1977) (see also Kagan, 1971, pp. 92–93). On one IQ test, there was a question, "Your mother sends you to the store to get a loaf of bread. The store is closed. What should you do?" The "correct" answer to this question was go to the next-closest store and get it there. Analysis of children's answers indicated that there were important group differences in response to this question. For one thing, rural children got it "wrong"—in their case, the next-closest store might be ten miles away. Inner-city black children also got the question "wrong." They answered that they would go back home and ask what to do. Poussaint argues that for these children, this was the right answer: Interviews with the children indicated that some felt going to another store might be unsafe because of dangers associated with gangs who controlled the "turf" around the next-closest store. Thus, these children were penalized, even though they gave what, *for them,* was the most intelligent answer. Pouissant, Kagan, and others argue that questions with interviews about why the student answered the way he or she did would give a more reliable measure of IQ than straight test items. Many in the field of intelligence testing agree, and some of the better tests follow this model. However, the time and expense limitations of mass testing do not always permit such a careful approach.

Although this item was removed from the test only in the last decade, many of the more discriminatory items are now gone from IQ tests. Supporters of the tests back this claim by showing that minorities and low-income children no longer do particularly poorly on any given items relative to their overall test scores (Sandoval, 1979; Sattler, 1982, pp. 357–58). Supporters of the tests also argue that the tests are not biased, because they do not underpredict minority achievement. In other words, a black with an IQ test score of 100 will do no better in school than a white with a score of 100—and if the tests were really unfair, he or she would do better.

Critics of the tests reply that this does not prove that the tests are unbiased—only that they may contain the same biases as the school system. In other words, the tests may simply be measuring the same knowledge, beliefs, and habits that the school system rewards. If this were true, the tests could be good predictors of school success but still far from being unbiased indicators of innate ability. In fact, even Sattler (1982), who generally supports the use of intelligence testing, acknowledges that (1) tests do not measure innate intelligence but rather an interaction of intelligence and environmental effects (p. 54), and (2) a number of factors associated with socioeconomic status and race, but unrelated to ability, do affect test scores (pp. 52–56). These include language models in the home, strictness of upbringing, and family emphasis on achievement and independent thinking, all of which have been shown to vary by social class.

Similar criticisms have been made of the standardized "readiness tests" that are sometimes used to determine whether young children should enter kindergarten, be delayed a year, or be assigned to a two-year developmental kindergarten program. To a large extent, these tests measure skills and knowledge that reflect past opportunity to learn, not inherent ability (Medina and Neill, 1988; Bredekamp and Shepard, 1989). Another criticism that has been made of both developmental and IQ tests is that, while they may predict school success better than some other measures, they nonetheless contain considerable error. One widely used kindergarten readiness test, for example, misidentified between one-third and one-half of the children said to be unready (Bredekamp and Shepard, 1989).

Within any group, inherent differences undoubtedly do account for part (not all) of the variation in IQ test scores. This does *not* follow when we are looking at differences in average IQ test scores *between groups,* however. Rather, group differences in familiarity with the culture-specific knowledge and modes of thinking measured by the test probably offer much of the explanation of such group differences in scores.

Differences in perception may also account for group differences in test scores, as pointed out by a group of sociologists known as phenomenologists. According to this view, people tend to emphasize different aspects of a situation: Some people will perceive one aspect, others a different one. Since both aspects are there, neither perception is "wrong"; both are simply different ways of seeing or organizing the same material. Furthermore, such perceptions and ways of organizing things vary from one cultural grouping to another. A child from a minority or lower-income family may attend to what the teacher or test designer regards as an irrelevant aspect of a question. The answer may be right in terms of the child's perception but wrong in terms of what the teacher intended to emphasize. Consequently, the child is mistakenly marked wrong (Keddie, 1971; MacKay, 1974; Mehan, 1974; Hurn, 1978, pp. 169–79).

Test Situation.   In addition to the content of the test itself, certain aspects of the test situation have also been shown to be in part responsible for the lower average scores of minority group members. Some studies have shown that the typical formality of the test situation tends to lower the scores of poor and/or minority group children. When the test is given in an informal, supportive setting or in the context of play, the IQ scores of such children rise significantly (Haggard, 1954; Golden and Birns, 1968; Palmer, 1970; Zigler, Abelson, and Seitz, 1973), and racial and social-class differences are reduced or eliminated. Even Jensen noted increases of eight to ten points in the IQ scores of low-income children as the result of play therapy. Apparently, minority and poor children are less comfortable in a formal test situation and consequently benefit more from a less threatening situation.

Another problem is that of linguistic differences, which can lead to testing bias as well as the types of general classroom bias we have already examined. Some Hispanic children, for example, have been labeled as having low intelligence because they were given intelligence tests in English rather than Spanish. Such imputation of low intelligence on the basis of linguistic differences is both inaccurate and harmful to the child.

Teacher Expectations.   We have already discussed this topic at some length, but it is important to remind ourselves that Rosenthal and Jacobson's (1968) classic study used IQ test scores as the dependent variable and found ten- to fifteen-point IQ differences in the first and second grades as a result of differences in teacher expectations. Although the particular test used by Rosenthal and Jacobson was one that is particularly sensitive to social influences, it seems reasonable to expect that when IQ tests or other kinds of standardized tests are given to students who have been in school a year or two (so that teachers have had some time to form and act on expectations), the results may be to some degree influenced by teacher expectations—which, as we have seen, are in turn related to the race and social class of children.

Health and Nutritional Factors.   Even primarily hereditary physical characteristics like height are significantly influenced by nutrition and other factors related to physical health. Thus, it hardly comes as a surprise that such factors can also influence IQ. Because minority groups are greatly overrepresented in the nation's impoverished population, they are more likely than others to suffer prenatal and childhood deficiencies in nutrition that can later inhibit their ability to do well on IQ and other tests.

Perceived Usefulness of High Test Performance.   Ogbu (1978) has raised another interesting factor that may help to explain low scores by minorities on standardized achievement tests. His theory centers around the fact—seen in our discussion of the work of Bowles and Gintis (1976) on education and mobility—that there is less payoff for education among minorities than among whites. Put simply, educational success provides a greater return in the form of high-paying jobs for whites than it does for minorities. Evidence of this can be seen in R. Farley's (1984, pp. 84–88) analysis of 1980 census data on income. Among the most poorly educated (those with less than a high-school education), black males received $2,800 less than whites per year—but among college graduates, blacks received $4,800 less than whites. Black-male income did increase with education, but more slowly than white-male income. Hence, going from elementary school through college was worth $2,000 *less* in increased income per year for black males than it was for white males. Affirmative action has improved the opportunities of very recent black college graduates, but among college graduates as a whole, blacks are paid much less than whites. Similarly, recent reseach by Tienda, Donato, and Cordero-Guzman (1992) has documented that, in terms of employment, women of color receive unequal returns to education as compared with white women. Moreover, analysis of data from 1960 through 1987 revealed that racial and ethnic inequalities in women's employment status widened over time. Ogbu argues that this affects the scores of minority students on all types of educational tests and tasks: "Doing well on these tests, like doing well on academic tasks generally, is not as rewarding for caste minorities as it is for the dominant group. Thus, caste minority children often do not take such tests seriously enough to try for the best scores they can get" (Ogbu, 1978, p. 37).

White Anglo parents, according to Ogbu (1978, pp. 235–36), teach their children to "persevere in school regardless of the boredom and unpleasantness involved *because they will be rewarded in the future with desirable social positions and jobs*" (emphasis Ogbu's). Minority children, on the other hand, will not be so encouraged by their parents, because the experiences of minority group parents "are different: education has not usually brought the same desirable social and occupational rewards." Ogbu (p. 37) notes that there is a real evidence of such underachievement on tests: Observations by psychologists generally indicate that minority children "communicate" with their peers, solve problems, and use concepts in ways typical of children who have IQ's of a Binet type ten to fifteen points higher than theirs.

Testing Bias: Summary

To summarize briefly, we have seen that numerous factors unrelated to ability tend to cause minority children to receive lower-than-average scores on intelligence tests and other kinds of standardized tests. If the tests are given to entire classes and used to compare children, serious harm is likely for two reasons. First, it leads to incorrect labeling of minority children as "slow learners," which, as we have seen, hurts their ability to learn, their self-image, and their relationships with their peers. Second, it leads to their placement in "slow" tracks or ability groups, with all the harmful consequences that has for their future development. Thus, if IQ tests are used, it should be a way of learning about and helping individual students who are already having problems—*not* as a way of screening, classifying, or comparing children (Sattler, 1982, p. 384).

In addition to the negative labeling and tracking of individual children, however, test bias has more general harmful implications for minority groups. First, it has tended to reinforce racist thinking about the intelligence of minority groups by creating the belief that it can be "scientifically proven" that some groups are genetically inferior to others. This is true in spite of the fact that there is absolutely no proof of genetic differences related to intelligence between races and that the test score differences can be well explained by the biases and situational factors we have discussed.[1] Unfortunately, the public is often not exposed to the scientific critiques of work such as Jensen's (and other more extreme materials such as those of Eysenck [1971], Hernstein [1971], and Shockley [1971a, 1971b], that have appeared following the publication of Jensen's 1969 article). Thus, claims based on tests purported to measure intelligence are often taken at face value by the public, even though there may be little basis in fact for such claims and/or widespread scientific criticism of them.

Another problem follows directly from Jensen's work. He argued that the supposed hereditary aspects of the racial IQ-score difference make any effort at compensatory education largely hopeless. While he is correct in pointing out that many compensatory-education programs have not been successful, it is quite another thing to argue that *no* program to improve the educational opportunities of minorities can be successful. An example of how the public can react to such arguments occurred just five days after Jensen's article was publicized by the popular press. In Virginia, it was used in a federal court case by opponents of school desegregation to "prove" that black students could not be helped by such integration (Brazziel, 1969). Thus, a real danger in the use of biased tests is that they will reinforce public beliefs that some races are superior to others and that efforts to improve minority education are doomed to failure.

However, other types of standardized testing with similar problems have become more widely used than in the past. In particular, there has been a dramatic increase in standardized testing of younger children from kindergarten entry through second grade since the 1970s (Perrone, 1991). This increased testing of younger children is a product of efforts to make schools more accountable for what children learn, but it creates problems for reasons outlined above. (Moreover, Perrone points out, there are more effective ways of assessment for purposes of accountability than standardized testing.) Standardized testing is particularly problematic when children are labeled on the basis of tests at such early ages, because group placements and decisions to retain children based on these tests have effects that can linger throughout a child's educational career. These effects occur because the tests misclassify many children and contain cultural biases, because tracking and grouping based on such tests is often inflexible, and because the effects of delayed entry into kindergarten or the increasingly common practice of flunking kindergarten are longstanding (Bredekamp and Shepard, 1989; Perrone, 1991). The result is that children who are negatively labeled by the tests are, in the long run, held back for reasons that often have little or nothing to do with their true ability to achieve. And, of course, it is low-income children and children of color who are most likely to be held back in this manner. It is perhaps time for an objective appraisal by more educators of what real benefits accrue from standardized testing and how these benefits, if any, compare with the very real harm done to minority and low-income students from the biases that are unavoidable in such tests.

---

[1] In addition, critics of the hereditary explanation note that neither blacks nor whites in America are genetically "pure," because there has been considerable racial interbreeding, and that the IQ scores of blacks and other minorities vary across the same range as those of whites.

Table 12.3   Representation of Blacks and Hispanics in the Teaching Profession,
1983 and 1991

Population	PERCENTAGE BLACK		PERCENTAGE HISPANIC	
	1983	*1991*	*1983*	*1991*
All employed persons	9.3	10.1	5.3	7.5
College teachers	4.4	4.8	1.8	2.9
High-school teachers	7.2	7.3	2.3	3.4
Elementary-school teachers	11.1	8.9	3.1	3.3

Sources: U.S. Bureau of Labor Statistics, 1984; U.S. Bureau of the Census, 1992c.

Lack of Minority Role Models

A final factor associated with the nature of the educational institution and relevant to the education of minorities is the lack of minority group role models. Minorities continue to be underrepresented among teachers, though there has been some improvement, particularly for blacks. As shown in Table 12.3, only among elementary-school teachers does the proportion of blacks approach that among all employed persons. Blacks and Hispanics at all levels of education are underrepresented in the teaching profession. At some levels, minority representation has actually declined in the teaching profession. Historically, compared with other professions, teaching was relatively open to minorities and women. As more opportunities have opened in other fields, growing numbers of talented minority members and women have turned to occupations other than teaching. The higher salaries available in occupations requiring no more education than teaching, such as accounting and management, have tended to draw talented minorities away from teaching. As Shenker (1992) points out, efforts to draw more minorities to the teaching profession are unlikely to succeed unless such efforts address societal forces that have made teaching relatively unattractive to people of color, including the relatively low salaries in teaching as compared with other alternatives now available.

It is also true that the higher the position in the educational system, the fewer the minority members there are. Thus, there are proportionately fewer minority principals and superintendents than minority teachers. Similarly, the percentage of minority teachers declines as one moves from elementary school to high school to college. Surely this gives an important message to both minority and majority group students about the roles to which they might aspire.

RACIAL BIAS IN THE EDUCATIONAL SYSTEM: AN EVALUATION

All of the evidence we have reviewed, when taken together, strongly suggests that the present educational system operates in certain ways that prevent minority students from achieving their full potential. This impression is supported by the findings of Coleman et al. (1966) and numerous others that the minority–white gap in learning starts out relatively small but increases over the course of the educational process.

As we have seen, a big piece of the problem is related to the fact that those who control our educational institutions and a great many minority students are, quite simply, *culturally different* from one another. To some degree, the problems of bias in educational materials and presentation of minorities in history, linguistic differences, teacher expectations, tracking, and testing *all* arise from such cultural differences. Given this reality, it is not so surprising that research shows that merely spending more money, or increasing the "quality" of minority education, will not do much good. The problem, at least in part, is that schools demand and reward certain values, beliefs, and habits and that they (often unconsciously and unintentionally) put down and hold back those who do not have those values.

How can we resolve the problem of incompatibility between the attitudes and habits demanded by the schools and the diverse cultures of American ethnic and socioeconomic groups? Several answers are possible, some associated with the functionalist perspective, some with the conflict perspective, and some falling somewhere in between. In part, the answer depends on whether or not one believes that middle-class values, such as belief that one controls one's own situation, self-motivation, and deferral of gratification, are necessary in society, and on whether one favors preservation of distinct cultural features, such as use of Spanish or nonstandard English along with English. One answer, of course, is that we *cannot* resolve the problem of incompatibility—and, curiously, this answer has been offered for different reasons by social scientists identifying with both the functionalist and conflict perspectives. Another answer—an *assimilationist* answer offered by some of those associated with the functionalist perspective—is that the schools must find ways to teach middle-class values and beliefs and must oppose symbols of diversity such as maintenance of distinct languages and dialects. This view counsels against any drastic changes in the educational system itself but suggests that the system do what it can to help minority and poor children learn the skills, attitudes, and habits they need to succeed. Yet another answer, which stands in opposition to the assimilationist view, is held by a variety of experts including some conflict theorists. This *multiculturalist* view holds that American society is composed of a variety of distinct cultures and group experiences and that students should not be made to conform to that of the dominant group, Anglo-Europeans. Thus, the distinct cultures and experiences of children from different groups must be recognized and valued by the schools. If this is done, achievement can be encouraged through role modeling and enhancement of self-esteem. Finally another view draws on insights from both the functionalist and conflict theories but is best classified as *interactionist* because it sees the source of the problem in interpersonal processes between teachers and minority and poor students. This view agrees with the conflict view insofar as it sees part of the problem arising from teachers and other school personnel making unfounded negative judgments about minority and poor students based on their culture. However, it agrees with the functionalist perspective in seeing certain middle-class values, such as achievement motivation and independent thinking, as socially useful. (It does not necessarily favor assimilation in other areas, however.) What is different about this view is that it sees the *process* of education as the critical factor. In other words, what really matters is how teachers think about and accordingly behave toward their students (which is shaped by the students' cultures and how school personnel react to them) and how students respond to that behavior by their teachers. In the remainder of this chapter, we shall explore the varying approaches to minority-group education as suggested by each of these four general viewpoints.

RESOLVING PROBLEMS OF MAJORITY–MINORITY INEQUALITY IN EDUCATION: FOUR APPROACHES

Approach 1: The Problem Does Not Lie in the Educational System

Conservatism: "Blaming the Victim." As we have seen, the unequal test scores of majority and minority group children, and the failure of some programs to improve minority education, have led some to conclude that it is hopeless to try to improve the educational opportunities of minority students by reforming the educational system. There is both a conservative and a radical version of this viewpoint. The conservative variant often makes the mistake of assuming that the tests are true indicators of ability—an assumption that, as we have seen, is largely incorrect because of various forms of bias in the process and content of "ability" testing. A slightly different version of this view holds that the *culture* of blacks and other minorities is the cause of the problem. They adopt the culture-of-poverty or cultural-deficit model, arguing—as do a wide range of functionalist theorists—that the values, beliefs, family structure, and so on of minority group members make it impossible for them to advance educationally and that there is little that can or should be done to change that situation (see Banfield, 1968, 1974). This view is clearly racist in the sense that it (1) blames minorities for their disadvantage, when the true source of that disadvantage is a long and continuing history of discrimination, and (2) regards as completely acceptable—perhaps even desirable—a continuing pattern of racial inequality in education and most other areas. Nonetheless, it would be a mistake to underestimate the popularity of this view: As we have seen before (see Feagin, 1972; Schuman, 1975), a great many Americans *do* believe that minorities are to blame for their own disadvantage.

Economics Versus Education. The radical version of the view that education can't make much difference holds that the attitudes and values of the minority underclass are a product of its situation, and because of the incompatibility between these attitudes and those of the school personnel, change through the educational system is unlikely. In essence, the roots of educational inequality lie in an economic system that produces great inequality. These scholars, including Jencks et al. (1972), Bowles and Gintis (1976), and Ogbu (1978), argue that the only way to bring meaningful change is to change the economic system, not education. As we will see shortly, however, other researchers, including conflict theorists, have shown that the educational system can make a difference.

Approach 2: Assimilation

Compensatory Education. While a great many social scientists do hold views consistent with the culture-of-poverty or cultural-deficit theories, many of them do not favor neglecting the problem of racial inequality. Instead, they favor programs to bring about *cultural assimilation:* to teach to minority students the values and habits they need to get ahead in school and in life. This viewpoint is clearly aligned with the order perspective in that it does not question the need to maintain consensus on dominant (middle-class) values and beliefs. It is, however, more liberal than the "blaming-the-victim" viewpoint because it seeks to bring about more equal educational outcomes rather than accepting racial and class inequality as a given. One approach arising from this liberal version of the order perspective is *compensatory education*. This approach consists of preschool programs for low-income and minority children and, in some cases, supplementary programs within the regular educational setting. The idea is to expose disadvantaged children to educational materials and to teach them skills, habits, and values related to education, compensating for what is believed to be missing in the home. The largest and best-known example of compensatory education has been the Head Start preschool program.

Early research concerning Head Start and similar compensatory education produced results that appeared to show that the programs were quite ineffective in bringing about improved learning among minority and poor children (Cicirelli et al., 1969; White, 1970; Little and Smith, 1971; Stanley, 1973; for a review see Ogbu, 1978). This led some conflict theorists to argue that such programs are ineffective because they do not change the basic operation of the educational system but simply offer "more of the same" (Baratz and Baratz, 1970; Bowles and Gintis, 1976; Ogbu, 1978). In other words, conflict theorists saw the programs as attempting to "teach" minority and/or poor people cultural characteristics that were contrary to their experiences, and failing for that reason.

More recent research, however, has found that the proclamations of failure in the 1970s were premature. Because one problem with early research was small samples, a number of researchers in early-childhood education in 1975 decided to pool their data to generate a much larger sample. At the same time, early studies were being reanalyzed with more sophisticated methodology, and a good deal of new data were being collected. By the late 1970s, these more comprehensive research efforts were generating different and more scientifically sound findings than earlier research (Brown, 1985). By 1978, a review of ninety-six valid studies revealed clear gains among students in early-childhood compensatory education programs compared with students not in such programs (Brown et al., 1978). Later research (Consortium for Longitudinal Studies, 1979, 1983; Lazar et al., 1977, 1982) showed that early education programs:

1. Reduce the number of children who need to be placed in special education, even among children of similar background and initial ability.
2. Reduce the number of children who have to repeat a grade.
3. Raise IQ and achievement, at least through the early years of elementary school.
4. Produce a higher achievement self-image and higher parental aspirations.

Studies of one program found such effects to be very long term, extending into adolescence and early adulthood in the form of reduced delinquency, unemployment, and teenage pregnancy (Berrueta-Clement et al., 1984; see also Weber, Foster, and Weikart, 1978; Lazar, 1981).

Nonetheless, there continues to be debate about the long-term effects of Head Start and similar programs as they are usually implemented. While there is no doubt that Head Start and similar programs have short-term benefits (Zigler and Muenchow, 1992), there has debate as to whether they have effects beyond about two years. Some studies, like those described in the preceding paragraph, have focused on the best-designed programs, and these programs do appear to have such benefits (Kramer, 1993). Long-term studies of more representative samples of Head Start programs generally show little if any effect on achievement-test scores after about two years, but they also show that students with Head Start experience are more likely to be in the proper grade (as opposed to being held back) and less likely to be placed in special education classes (McKey et al., 1985; Zigler and Muenchow, 1992). When they reach high-school ages and beyond, they are less likely to become involved in delinquency, more likely to graduate from high school, and more likely to be employed a year after high school graduation (Helmich, 1985). Thus, Head Start and similar programs as they typically operate may not increase test scores, but they do appear to increase the amount of education that their participants ultimately get and to have other benefits in areas of employment and delinquency.

As a result of Head Start's successes, it has been steadily expanded in recent years, growing to serve 450,000 children in 1985 and around 700,000 in 1993. As noted above, some of these children are better served than others. Among the suggestions to improve Head Start are to increase accountability, so that all programs function more like the best ones; to address attendance problems; to lengthen the average Head Start day from four hours to full-day to facilitate mothers' employment; and to increase the program from one year (as it is for many children) to two years, since research shows that two-year programs produce more long-term benefits than do one-year programs (Lewis, 1992; Zigler and Muenchow, 1992; Besharov, 1993; Kramer, 1993). It is also important to keep in mind that, despite its benefits, compensatory education alone has not fully broken down educational inequality along the lines of race and class, nor is there evidence that, by itself, it could reasonably be expected to do so (Zigler and Muenchow, 1992).

Desegregation Through Busing. Another, quite different, approach to minority education is the effort to combat urban de facto school segregation through busing. Although some see busing as a radical proposal, a thorough analysis of the theory underlying busing shows that it basically arises from the functionalist perspective's ideas on cultural deprivation and the need for assimilation of minorities. Much of the theoretical argument behind busing can be traced to the Coleman Report (Coleman et al., 1966) discussed earlier in this chapter. Let us turn our attention for a moment to that report and identify the parts that led to the suggestion that busing may be the route to equal educational opportunity for minority schoolchildren. You will recall that the study found that the background characteristics of *fellow students* were an important factor influencing the learning of minority and low-income students. Specifically, the more "advantaged" the background of their fellow students, the better the minority students did. When their fellow students came from homes in which parents were more educated and able to provide more materials such as books, newspapers, and television, minority and low-income students did better. When their fellow students had the attitudes and beliefs associated with educational success, minority and low-income students also did better (Coleman et al., 1966, pp. 302–5). Coleman's data also showed that, apparently for this reason, minority students generally learned more in integrated schools than they did in segregated schools (pp. 307–12, 330–31). At the same time, Coleman's data indicated that the learning of white students was *not* harmed by attending integrated schools and that the white students indeed generally appreciated the contact with students from groups other than their own. Coleman suggests that the reason that minority students do better when they attend school with white middle-class students is that minority students adopt the attitudes, beliefs, and study habits of their fellow students and consequently do better. In short, assimilation of minorities into the school system is accomplished through their contact with their "culturally more advantaged" white middle-class classmates. Thus, Coleman's suggestion fits well within the functionalist perspective and its emphasis on cultural assimilation.

Coleman's finding that minority students do better in integrated schools—coupled with a theory that explains why they did better—was seen by many as convincing proof that equal educational opportunity could come about only through the creation of an integrated school system. You will recall that de facto segregation remained widespread in the United States at the time the Coleman Report was issued. In other words, schools remained largely segregated even though deliberate policies of segregation were illegal. A large part of the reason for this was that schools are based on neighborhood attendance districts, and neighborhoods are, as we have seen, usually quite racially segregated. Therefore, the only way to bring about school desegregation in many urban areas was to bus minority children to schools in white neighborhoods and/or white children to schools in minority neighborhoods.

Because of its findings on integration and learning by minority students, the Coleman Report was frequently cited in court cases over school desegregation as "proof" that equal educational opportunity for minorities required that schools be integrated, by means of busing if necessary. Since the Coleman Report was published in 1966, busing for the purpose of school desegregation has been initiated, on varying scales, in many cities. In some, lawsuits by the NAACP or other groups favoring integrated schools have led to court rulings requiring busing. Frequently, such rulings have been based on findings that segregation resulted at least partially from actions of school officials, not entirely because of housing patterns. In other places, busing programs have been initiated without court action, either at the initiative of the local school board or in response to pressures from groups favoring desegregation. Most programs to desegregate schools through mandatory busing were established during the late 1960s and early 1970s, and many of these programs remain in effect today. In the late 1970s and 1980s, several metropolitan areas established desegregation programs based on school choice, in which parents of minority children in city schools could opt to have their children bused to suburban schools, and magnet schools—schools with special programs not available in most schools—were used to attract suburban whites to inner-city schools. Today, sufficient research has been done on school-busing programs that we can draw some conclusions about whether school segregation has benefited minorities in the ways the Coleman Report suggested it might.

The answer appears to be that it does have such benefits, but not to an unlimited degree, and only under certain circumstances. Of the many studies that have been done on school desegregation, some have shown that it has beneficial effects on the achievement and education of minority students, and some have not. Among the areas in which a number of studies show improvement are the academic achievement (and in some cases, also IQ scores) of minority students (Pettigrew et al., 1973; St. John, 1975; Crain and Mahard, 1982; Wortman and Bryant, 1985; Rossell and Glenn, 1988; Orfield et al., 1991) and the probability that minority students will go on to attend college and/or get better jobs (Armor, 1972; Braddock, 1985; Janyes and Williams, 1989). Not all studies show improvement in these areas, but few if any show minority students in desegregated schools to be less well off in these regards. When an expert panel convened by the National Institute on Education analyzed a number of studies of effects of school desegregation, it concluded that the best-designed studies showed an average two-month educational gain by black students when they went from segregated to desegregated schools (Wortman and Bryant, 1985). Moreover, the research is quite consistent in showing that the achievement of white middle-class students does not decline when they attend desegregated schools (Orfield et al., 1991). Another benefit of desegregation is that it often triggers beneficial reforms in curriculum and teaching methods (Center for Education and Human Development Policy, 1981; Beady and Slavin, 1980; Foley, 1993).

As noted above, studies find widely varying effects: Some show sizable effects of desegregation; some, small effects; some, no effects. One reason for this is that the effects of desegregation vary under different conditions. It appears that the success of desegregation in improving the achievement of minority students depends on (1) how the desegregation is carried out, (2) the racial and political climate in which it occurs, and (3) social and demographic characteristics of the urban area in which it occurs.

EFFECTS OF HOW DESEGREGATION IS CARRIED OUT.   In terms of how desegregation is carried out, some of the key issues are the age of the children in the schools that are desegregated, the geographic scope of the area included in the desegregation plan (particularly whether it includes both city and suburban schools or just city schools), and whether the plan involves mandatory busing or parental choice. Other key issues are the preparation of the school staff for desegregation and the degree of integration or segregation *within* schools whose student bodies have been desegregated. In general, desegregation appears to have the largest benefits for student achievement when it occurs in the early grades. For example, one review of the literature showed that *every* study of desegregated kindergarteners showed achievement gains (Crain and Mahard, 1982). Overall, it appears that the more grades that are covered, the better desegregation plans work (Orfield et al., 1991).

In general, metropolitanwide desegregation plans are more effective than plans that involve only central-city children, in part because they eliminate the opportunity for whites to flee to all-white suburban schools. Crain and Mahard's (1982) review of the literature also showed, however, that achievement and IQ gains are the greatest when schools are desegregated on a metropolitanwide basis. Based on findings such as these, a group of fifty-eight desegregation experts recommended to the Supreme Court in 1991 that desegregation plans should encompass as large a geographic area as possible (Orfield et al., 1991).

Research is also quite clear in showing that the degree of segregation *within* schools that have been desegregated has significant effects on minority-student achievement. If, for example, a formerly all-white school becomes racially mixed but practices such as inflexible tracking separate black and white students into different classes within the school, the benefits of desegregation may be lost. In desegregated schools with no tracking or with flexible tracking, mixed learning groups, and group rewards for learning, minority student achievement is enhanced (Epstein, 1985; Slavin, 1985). Pettigrew (1969a, 1969b) draws a distinction between mere desegregation—simply altering the proportion of white and black students attending the schools—and true integration. In true integration, not only are students reassigned to different schools but real efforts are made to bring about closer and more friendly relations between the races. Even seating arrangements in the classroom can reflect the presence or absence of true integration. The nature of materials used in the classroom can also affect the success of school integration. It is important that the materials reflect the degree of cultural diversity present in the classroom, and it is equally important that teachers avoid the use of materials that may either intentionally or subtly downgrade a minority group. In some cases, the use of materials that teachers did not realize were degrading to minority groups has caused problems in newly desegregated classrooms. It is also important that teaching staffs as well as students be integrated, so that there are minority teachers and principals as well as students. In short, true integration is much more than transferring pupils to different schools to achieve racial balance. It requires extensive planning, preparation, effort, and, in many cases, changes in established practices.

Overall, then, the effect of school desegregation on minority-student learning appears to range from negligible to positive. It has generally not harmed the achievement of white students, but, where implemented, it has certainly not *eliminated* racial inequality in learning, either. To improve the educational performance of minority students, *socioeconomic* desegregation as well as racial desegregation is desirable. The original findings of the Coleman Report strongly support this view: The habits and beliefs that relate to academic achievement were associated with social class just as they were with race and ethnicity. Subsequent experience has supported this, as the case of South Boston illustrates: Transferring poor black and poor white students between two schools that have always been characterized by low levels of learning can be expected to do little or nothing to help the learning of either black or white students. There is some reason to believe, based on the Coleman Report and other research, that socioeconomic integration may have benefits of its own even independent of racial integration. In the 1992–1993 school year, the nearly all-white LaCrosse, Wisconsin, school district became the first in the nation to implement a program designed to reduce socioeconomic segregation in its schools.

Recall from Chapter 3 that intergroup contact, when it is equal status, non-threatening, noncompetitive, and, ideally, interdependent, can improve intergroup relations. Recall also that when these conditions are not present, contact can make intergroup relations worse. A major purpose of school desegregation, besides bringing about more equal educational opportunity, has been to improve intergroup relations. And, of course, better intergroup relations in the school often means better education. Conflicts over school desegregation in some cases have been so intense as to disrupt the educational process, as in Boston, where tensions and violence continued throughout the school year in which busing was first implemented. Once again, the evidence on the effectiveness of school desegregation in improving intergroup relations seems mixed. In some cases, the short-term effects have been quite bad, but long-term positive effects are common. As our discussion of Boston's desegregation efforts in Chapter 3 showed, desegregation's success or failure in improving intergroup relations, particularly in the short term, depends largely on the presence of the conditions we have mentioned: equal-status contact, interdependency, and the absence of threat and excessive competition.

RACIAL AND POLITICAL CLIMATE OF THE COMMUNITY: THE ROLE OF LEADERSHIP. It goes without saying that learning cannot occur under conditions of endless disruption. In a few communities, opposition to busing has been so sustained, violent, and disruptive that, for a period of time, it was very difficult for anyone to learn anything in the schools affected by the conflict. (It is important to point out however, that even in cities where there is much disruption and conflict, most of the trouble often centers around only a few schools. In Boston, for example, there was serious trouble in only four of eighty schools involved in desegregation.) In com-

Minority teachers can serve as important role models for minority students, and can be helpful in breaking down stereotypes among majority-group students. *Ken Karp*

munities where busing has led to serious violence, such as Boston, and, several years earlier, Pontiac, Michigan, the actions of the leadership in the community apparently played an important role in creating the trouble. A national survey of 532 school districts (U.S. Commission on Civil Rights, 1976, p. 175) showed, for example, that in the 411 districts that had no serious disruptions associated with desegregation, 65 percent of the districts had business leaders who were generally supportive of or neutral toward segregation, and 67 percent had political leaders who were supportive or neutral. On the other hand, among the 95 districts that *did* have serious disruptions, only 27 percent had supportive or neutral business leaders, and only 30 percent had supportive or neutral political leaders. Boston, Louisville, and Pontiac were all to some degree marked by local leadership that emphasized its adamant opposition to busing rather than emphasizing the need to cooperate with the program (U.S. Commission on Civil Rights, 1976, pp. 179–83). In some communities the leadership, intentionally or not, gave people the misimpression that if only they "raised enough hell," the requirement of segregation would somehow go away. This apparently encouraged much more adamant opposition than would otherwise have developed. In cities where the local leadership took the view that, regardless of its popularity, busing was there to stay and that violent opposition to it would harm the schoolchildren and worsen the situation, even large-scale desegregation programs were implemented without serious disruption; Detroit and Columbus, Ohio, are two examples. Communities where the political, business, labor, and religious leadership make a vigorous effort to prepare the community for desegregation are less likely to experience difficulties.

SOCIAL AND DEMOGRAPHIC CHARACTERISTICS OF THE COMMUNITY. Some of the opposition to busing centers around problems associated with a long bus ride, which can require children to leave home for school earlier and get back later than they otherwise would or which can cut into the school day by using some of the time for transportation. There are also worries about the increased risk of accidents and the increased use of energy. However, except in the largest cities, these problems do not in fact appear sizable. In twenty-nine districts studied by the U.S. Commission on Civil Rights (1976), for example, there was only a small average increase in the percentage of students bused. For minority students, the numbers bused increased from 47 percent to 56 percent; for white students, from 50 percent to 53 percent. Furthermore, the bus rides were typically quite short. Even in one of the larger cities, Minneapolis, the average bus ride after desegregation was less than twenty minutes— about the same as it was before desegregation.

In a few very large cities with large minority populations, long and potentially disruptive bus rides are sometimes required. In the sprawling cities of Los Angeles and Detroit, for example, the length of the bus ride has become a major issue. In addition, there is another problem in some of these large districts that makes desegregation increasingly difficult: There are not enough white students to desegregate all the predominantly black schools. In general, the literature on school desegregation suggests that benefits of desegregation can be expected to be the greatest when the minority population is somewhere in the general range of 20 or 25 percent to 50 or 55 percent: enough to go beyond mere tokenism (Rist, 1978) but not so great as to represent a lack of true desegregation. In many large cities, however, the public school enrollment is 70 to 95 percent minority (Pisko and Stern, 1985)—too high to meaningfully integrate a sizable proportion of the city's schools unless schools from nearby suburban districts are also included in the desegregation plan. Minority enrollment (nearly all black) in Washington and Baltimore was 96 and 81 percent, respectively, in 1991; in Chicago, only 12 percent of the students were white Anglos (Hacker, 1992). Other cities with more than 70 percent minority enrollments include San Antonio, Newark, Phoenix, Birmingham, and New York City (Hacker, 1992, p. 235). As long ago as 1982, Detroit, Philadelphia, and St. Louis had minority enrollments (mostly African American) of more than 70 percent (Pisko and Stern, 1985), and this has remained the case since then. One solution that has been proposed to deal with this difficulty is busing between predominantly black central cities and nearby white suburbs. In the early 1970s, lower courts ordered such remedies in Detroit and Richmond, Virginia, but in 1975, the Supreme Court ruled that such cross-district busing was not required by law unless deliberate governmental action had been taken to create city–suburb segregation. There are a few areas, such as Louisville and St. Louis, where a history of such action has led to metropolitanwide desegregation plans, but more often, only the central city is included.

In several cities, including St. Louis and Hartford, metropolitanwide desegregation plans have used parental choice. Black parents in the central city have the option to have their children bused to the suburbs, and white parents in the suburbs may choose to have their children bused to magnet schools in the central city. This approach has generally aroused less opposition than mandatory city–suburb busing programs, but it also leaves many schools segregated, particularly when the minority percentage in the inner city is very high. There is some evidence however, that parental-choice programs bring greater integration than city-only busing programs. One study, in Cambridge, Massachusetts, even found that a parental-choice busing program led to greater integration than an earlier mandatory busing program (within Cambridge only) had done (Rossell and Glenn, 1988; Rossell, 1990).

An issue closely related to this that has received considerable attention from social scientists is the question of "white flight": Does desegregation through busing cause a substantial loss of white students from big-city school systems, thus leaving them even more segregated than they were before the desegregation program was put into effect? The argument was first raised by Coleman (1975), who had by now reversed his position and come out against mandatory busing for desegregation. Coleman presented data that, he said, showed that busing caused so many white students to be taken out of the central-city public schools—either through movement to the suburbs or enrollment in private schools—that the schools ended up even more segregated than when desegregation started. His study was incomplete, however, and critics such as Pettigrew and Green (1976) and Farley (1975) argued that methodological problems in the study prevented any such conclusion. It has been pointed out, furthermore, that white flight from public-school systems has been going on anyway, with or without busing. Therefore, busing at most can account for only a part of the "white-flight" problem.

Recent research has confirmed that white flight does occur. However, it occurs much more under some circumstances than others (Armore and Schwartzbach, 1978), and in most cases is not greatly larger, over the long run, than it would have been anyway, even without desegregation (Wilson, 1985). White flight because of school desegregation, when it occurs, usually happens in relatively large school districts (Farley, Richards, and Wurdock, 1980), and in districts with large minority enrollment (Armor, 1972; Wilson, 1985). Districts with large minority enrollment are especially likely to experience white flight if they are central-city districts surrounded by predominantly white suburbs and if the schools are desegregated only within the central city (Armor, 1972). Moreover, even in the large, suburbanized, predominantly minority school districts from which white flight does occur, Wilson's (1985) study and others indicate that much of the loss of whites, which typically happens in the first year the desegregation plan is put into effect, is made up by whites who later return to the city's school system.

In smaller cities without large minority populations, desegregation has proceeded more smoothly on all counts. Studies by the U.S. Commission on Civil Rights (1976) indicate that it is cities like Berkeley, California; Colorado Springs, Colorado; Kalamazoo, Michigan; Newport News, Virginia; and Waterloo, Iowa, that were able to desegregate their schools the most quickly and effectively. Despite their diversity in some regards, all these cities have relatively small populations (75,000 to 175,000), and small to moderate minority school enrollments (16 to 37 percent). Even large cities with relatively small minority enrollments can have very successful desegregation: Minneapolis (population 424,000; minority enrollment, 21 percent) has been cited as a city in which desegregation has been very successful (U.S. Commission on Civil Rights, 1976).

The problem of white flight—both that induced by desegregation and that which would have happened anyway—makes the desegregation of predominantly minority school systems in large suburbanized cities a more difficult case. Since a sizable proportion of the minority-student population lives in such cities, they are of considerable importance, even though relatively few cities are involved. One solution that might work is cross-district desegregation between city and suburbs. Armor (1972; Armor and Schwartzbach, 1978) presents some evidence that this would reduce the problem of white flight but downgrades it in favor of voluntary desegregation, in which those who choose could be bused to schools with a racial composition different from their own. It is for this reason that voluntary city–suburb parental-choice plans have been used in St. Louis, Hartford, and elsewhere. These plans reduce white flight and have been effective in integrating suburban schools, but they leave many central-city schools segregated because relatively few whites from the suburbs offer to be bused to the city, even when magnet schools are offered. In St. Louis, for example, fourteen times as many blacks have chosen to be bused from the city to the suburbs as the number of whites who have chosen to be bused from the suburbs to magnet schools in the city. Some critics of busing have pointed out that this is fairly typical of most desegregation programs in another regard: Most of those who end up riding the bus to schools outside their own neighborhood are black.

For two reasons, mandatory city–suburb busing for desegregation is unlikely to be implemented in many places besides the few metropolitan areas where it already exists. First, the Supreme Court has ruled that it can be ordered only in cases in which city–suburb school district boundaries had been drawn with an intention of racial discrimination. Second, busing for desegregation is not popular: 65 to 85 percent of the white population and up to half or more of the black population oppose it.

The Effectiveness of Busing: An Overview. We have seen that, if properly implemented, school desegregation can bring moderate improvement in minority-student achievement and in majority–minority relations in the schools. Such improvement, however, is not sufficient to eliminate the racial gap in learning. Furthermore, under present social and political conditions, desegregation is hard to accomplish in big cities with large minority populations and readily accessible suburbs. Indeed, for these reasons, black–white segregation in schools has not decreased very much since the early 1970s, and the segregation of Hispanic students has actually increased in recent years (Orfield, 1988; Orfield et al., 1989).

Two additional concerns have been raised about busing by a number of educators and social scientists concerned about possible negative impacts of school desegregation on the black community. One is that, when large numbers of black students are bused out of their neighborhoods, neighborhood stability is reduced and neighborhood institutions are weakened. For example, Dempsey and Noblit (1993) describe how one African American neighborhood in Milwaukee was disrupted by the closure of its neighborhood school as part of the effort to desegregate Milwaukee schools. A second concern is that black students are sometimes isolated and rejected by their peers when they are bused to mostly white schools (Miller, 1989; 1990). A common criticism is that the curriculum in such schools emphasizes and reflects the culture, values, and history of the white students and teachers who are the majority in those schools, leading to self-doubt and identity problems among black students (Gerard, 1988).

Because of these concerns, because of the difficulty of desegregating schools in large metropolitan areas with large minority populations, and because of continuing public opposition to busing, some educators are today asking whether other alternatives are available for improving the education of minority schoolchildren. Some hold that different institutional attitudes and teaching practices in all-black or all-Latino schools will benefit students of color more than desegregating those schools. We turn now to some educational approaches based on that premise.

Approach 3: Multiculturalism and Cultural Immersion

Some social scientists and educators criticize both compensatory education and busing for desegregation because they are based, in part, on a cultural-deficiency model. In effect, they are based on a "transmission-of-values" theory holding that, if blacks and other minorities are placed in a predominantly white middle-class setting, they will absorb the academically oriented values of that setting (Hacker, 1992, p. 165). This approach falls clearly within a functionalist or assimilationist model, as opposed to a pluralist or separatist one. As we have seen, a problem with this approach is that it can, at least under some circumstances, lead to isolation, rejection, self-doubt, and identity problems among students of color. Moreover, compensatory education and desegregation do nothing, in and of themselves, to alter the Eurocentric approach to education that is present in many schools. Such an approach, as was discussed earlier in this chapter, disregards the contribution of minorities, fails to discuss the uglier side of American history such as genocide against Indian people, and/or examines intergroup issues and history primarily from the perspective of people of European ancestry (Hilliard, 1988). The related but different approaches of *multiculturalism* and *cultural immersion* are efforts to correct this. Multiculturalism may be practiced in schools or preschool programs of any racial or ethnic composition; cultural immersion is an approach that is only practical in schools in which most or all students come from a common racial, ethnic, or cultural background. For these reasons, multiculturalism is sometimes seen as an approach placing relatively greater emphasis on cultural pluralism, whereas cultural immersion is sometimes seen as placing greater emphasis on separatism.

Multiculturalism. **Multiculturalism** can be defined as an approach that recognizes and values cultural differences, and attempts to (1) include all racial, ethnic, and cultural groups in the content and examples used in the classroom and (2) to teach history, literature, and other subjects from the perspectives of multiple groups rather than just the dominant group (Banks, 1992). Multiculturalism is different from traditional education in that it seeks cultural pluralism rather than cultural assimilation. The extent to which this should be done is a key source of debate among educators, however. There is an ongoing debate about how much stress should be placed on the experiences and traits that different groups have in common relative to those that are distinct to each group. And to some extent, this debate reflects an underlying disagreement about the extent to which different groups have similar experiences and traits. Some critics argue that multiculturalism goes too far when it questions the idea that the United States is "one nation, many peoples" or suggests that there is more than one history to be told (Kirp, 1991). These critics, influenced to varying degrees by a functionalist or assimilationist viewpoint, hold that when it questions a common national history, multiculturalism threatens to divide society on the basis of race, ethnicity, and culture and to inhibit cooperation by encouraging each cultural group to place its own concerns above the common interest.

Those who support the pluralist approach underlying multicultural education reply that colonized minorities—those who entered American society involuntarily, including African Americans, Native Americans, Mexican Americans, and Puerto Ricans—never have sought to assimilate to the extent that the larger society expected them to. Nor, for that matter, have they ever sought to assimilate to the extent sought by immigrant minorities who came to the United States voluntarily (Lieberson, 1980). In this view, multicultural education is seen as a much-needed legitimation of the values and experiences of groups that have been historically devalued and abused in American society. Moreover, it is not seen as divisive, because racial and ethnic divisions are already present in society as a result of past oppressive actions by the dominant group.

Such an approach is viewed as having three potential benefits. First, it is believed that this more positive approach to the cultures and experiences of people of color in the United States will lead to better self-images, stronger identities, and greater self-confidence among students of color. Second, it is intended to broaden the knowledge of all Americans about groups other than their own and to help students to understand how the different experiences of other groups have led to the development of different viewpoints. In this way, students will be better prepared for living in a society that is *in fact* multicultural, even if multiculturalism was not the approach favored by society in the past. Finally, it will correct a distorted presentation of American history and culture that has been present in the schools for too long. Rather than presenting these issues from the viewpoint of only European Americans, it will also present them from the sometimes very different views and experiences of non-European groups such as Native Americans and African Americans.

Cultural Immersion. Some argue that, particularly in areas of concentrated minority poverty, such as inner-city ghettos and Indian reservations, this is not enough (see, for example, Leonard Jeffries, quoted in A. Sullivan, 1990). In such areas, poverty has become more concentrated and jobs harder to find. And as traditional sources of institutional support have been eliminated through a variety of economic processes and cultural assaults, positive role models have become harder and harder to show to children. As was described in earlier chapters, Native American culture was systematically attacked by such means as taking children from their parents and placing them in boarding schools. In inner-city black neighborhoods, the combined forces of massive job exodus and the departure of the middle class (in many cases, both black and white) have undermined institutions and deprived many adults of the opportunity to serve as positive role models for their own and other neighborhood children through regular employment, organizational and religious participation in the neighborhood, and so forth (Wilson, 1987).

Some hold that job loss and unemployment, along with stereotypical images in the media and elsewhere, have subjected black males in particular to cultural attack and deprived young black males of positive role models (American Council on Education, 1988). Often, the harsh reality in the inner city is that it is easier in the short term to make money engaging in an illegal activity than a legal one. Yet the long-term consequences of such actions are devastating, and they further undermine the economic stability of the black community by directing young black males away from professional or managerial employment and often toward an ultimate outcome of imprisonment or even early death. By the early 1990s, more African American men were in jail or prison than were attending colleges and universities (Hacker, 1992, p. 177).

What is needed under such conditions as these, some claim, is an educational approach that directly promotes positive role models of the student's own racial or ethnic background and that promotes collective self-worth through teaching students to value their cultural heritage, which has been subjected to attack by the larger society. By establishing such role models and promoting collective self-worth, they argue, the achievement of students of color can best be enhanced (Bell, 1988).

In Milwaukee, Detroit, New York, Baltimore, and other cities, schools based on the cultural-immersion model have been developed and targeted toward black male students. One example is the Matthew A. Henson School in Baltimore, named for the African American man who served as Admiral Perry's navigator and directed him to the North Pole. In this school, black male teachers seek to serve as role models for their students, teaching their students on a variety of matters including self-defense, self-control, and personal appearance, using games as a way of learning in the classroom and taking their students on Saturday outings to museums and libraries (Farley, 1994a, p. 389). This and similar schools also emphasize achievements by African Americans (hence the naming of the school after Matthew Henson), and some of them use an *Afrocentric* curriculum—one centered around African history, culture, art, and literature. At Aisha Schule in Detroit, a private school using an Afrocentric curriculum, students learn about African American poets, greet one another in Swahili, and recite African folktales. At the same time, they also complete standard coursework in subjects such as geometry. There are about two hundred such private schools around the country targeted toward African American children (DePalma, 1990), and their approaches are increasingly being emulated in public-school systems with large numbers of black children.

Some people have criticized such schools for fostering racial and sexual segregation. In Detroit, plans for such schools in the public-school system were altered (but not eliminated) after the American Civil Liberties Union successfully sued the district for proposing a school that would admit only male students. However, the law does not prohibit having schools with curricula targeted toward or designed to enhance the achievement of black males, as long as admissions are not restricted on the basis of sex or race. And Hacker (1992, p. 174) points out two key differences between today's cultural-immersion schools and the segregated schools of the past: (1) Those proposing today's schools want those who enroll to sign up voluntarily, and (2) schools like those described above are under black control.

Does this approach work? Early signs are that it can indeed be effective. At the Matthew A. Henson School, for example, school attendance among black male students improved measurably. Graduates of Aisha Schule in Detroit include engineers and medical students. One of the longest-standing experiences with the cultural immersion approach to education comes from Hawaii, where the Kamahamena Early Education program was established in 1972 to deal with below-average performance of Native Hawaiian children on standardized tests. Students were allowed to speak spontaneously rather than raising their hands, in keeping with their more expressive culture. (This innovation has also been used in a number of immersion schools targeted to African Americans, for similar reasons.) They were also encouraged to assist one another in the tradition of the Hawaiian–Polynesian style of conversation and were allowed to answer questions in their native language, even though the questions were asked in English. Scores on achievement tests rose sharply (DePalma, 1990).

One factor that may contribute to the success of such schools is that the teachers and administrators have faith in the abilities of their students and expect and demand high levels of achievement. The fourth approach to improving the education of minority students centers around these features. We can loosely characterize that approach as an interactionist approach because it (1) focuses on student–teacher interactions and (2) it is based largely on the idea, arising from symbolic-interactionist theory, that the messages that we get from others about our abilities and personalities have major effects on how we in fact behave and achieve.

Approach 4: The Interactionist Approach

This approach has gained momentum as a result of research published in the late 1970s and 1980s. As we have seen, the approach is not altogether clearly associated with either the functionalist or the conflict approach. Like the conflict approach, it rests on the assumption that schools have failed minority students, but like the functionalist approach, it does not *necessarily* demand a substantial change in the organization or power structure of education. It does, however, require significant changes in the behavior of teachers and, ultimately, of minority students as well. This interactionist approach is based largely on the fact that, as we have seen, low teacher expectations lead to low student achievement. One reason for this is that when teachers have low expectations of students, they demand only a low quality of work. Thus, the solution is to (1) convince teachers that low-income and minority students *can* learn as well as anyone else and (2) get those teachers to demand such learning of their students. It is striking that essays advocating this approach have appeared in both the conflict-theory-oriented periodical *Social Policy* (Edmonds, 1979) and in the functionalist *Public Interest* (Coleman, 1981; Fuerst, 1981). These studies, along with other studies and experiences based on efforts at innovative education (Brookover and Lezotte, 1971; Weber, 1971; Means and Knapp, 1991; Selvin, 1992), strongly suggest that minority students do better when:

1. Teachers *believe* that the students are capable of success, and believe that their efforts can make a difference in what the students learn.
2. The class is a pleasant place, relatively quiet and orderly. The *most* effective teachers are those who can maintain reasonable order *without* spending a great deal of their time and effort on keeping order.
3. There is emphasis on the learning of basic reading and math skills, both in terms of how teachers spend their time and in terms of the level of performance that they require of their students.
4. There is also emphasis on the learning of higher-order skills, such as comprehension, composition, and mathematical reasoning.

A study by Fuerst (1981) of all-black schools in Chicago showed that the schools where black students excelled (in some of these schools, average reading scores substantially exceeded the norms in white suburban schools) displayed the patterns described above. Although different schools used various innovations, all demanded quality performance—students could not be promoted without it—and all had teachers who believed that black students could learn as well as anyone else, a pattern that, as we have seen, is not typical of most urban schools. Unfortunately, these patterns, according to Fuerst, existed in only a minority of Chicago's all-black schools. About 20,000 of Chicago's black public-school students were attending such schools, and another 10,000 were attending racially integrated schools and were also doing well. Unfortunately, about 145,000 other black students were in less advantageous settings, benefiting neither from these educational reforms nor from integration (Fuerst, 1981, p. 91).

Similar findings can be seen in the experiences of the Algebra Project, a program designed under a MacArthur Prize "genius grant" to Bob Moses, a civil rights activist who had become concerned because his daughter and other black children were not being taught algebra at as early a point in their schooling as white children typically are. Implemented in grades six through eight in a dozen school districts around the country, this program has demonstrated that supposedly disadvantaged children can be just as successful as others in early algebra education. The program is based on the concepts that its students can learn algebra as well as anyone else if given the opportunity to do so and that algebra is best taught in a step-by-step manner that builds on the students' real-life experiences. In a Kentucky school with 90 percent of its students below the poverty level, the percentage scoring above the national average on standardized math tests rose to 39 percent. In Cambridge, Massachusetts, where the program began, eighteen eighth-graders in a predominantly black school took a test to get credit for high-school algebra after participating in the program. Fifteen of them passed; no student from that school had ever passed the test before that (Selvin, 1992).

Results of this type were documented in schools throughout the country in a 1987 U.S. Department of Education report titled *Schools That Work: Educating Disadvantaged Children.* It documents numerous cases of schools in which high and uniform expectations, along with a belief that poverty need not be a barrier to achievement, have led to high levels of student achievement. Examples include a Dayton, Ohio, elementary school where a principal's insistence that all students can achieve led to rapid increases in the percentages of students performing at grade level; a public high school in the inner city of Los Angeles whose graduates are more likely to go on to college than the national average; and an all-black Catholic high school in Chicago where nine out of ten of its graduates go to college. The report also notes that such success can occur not just in one school but throughout a school system. In Jacksonville, Florida, a program called Blacks for Success in Education, which emphasizes critical-thinking skills, was begun after it was discovered that three-fourths of the nation's students were scoring above the average Jacksonville black student on the Stanford Achievement Test. By 1985, the typical Jacksonville black student got a score close to the national average.

Recall also the High School and Beyond study (Coleman, Hoffer, and Kilgore, 1982; Hoffer, Greeley, and Coleman, 1985, 1987; Haertel, 1987), which found that (1) minority students of comparable socioeconomic status do better in private schools than in public schools and (2) in Catholic schools, particularly, there is much less inequality in achievement along the lines of race and social class than in public schools. The reasons, according to Coleman et al. (1982) are that such schools expect and demand higher levels of achievement and that they maintain better order. Furthermore, public schools that have these characteristics are also marked by better student achievement. What all this suggests is that minority students *can* do as well as anyone in school and that, when teachers *expect* and *demand* it, they often will. According to Edmonds (1979), there are a variety of ways that such a situation can come about. It may be the result of an informed and dedicated teaching staff, or of a demanding principal. It may also be a result of parental pressure, so that it could be an outcome of an effective community-control program.

To summarize, the approach of increasing the rigor of minority education, like immersion, compensatory education, and desegregation through busing, shows promise where it has been implemented. On the other hand, it is also true that, just as there are very few schools that are truly integrated, there are—as Fuerst's (1981) Chicago study shows—few schools that really expect and demand high performance of minority students. Thus, in spite of this promising new development, most of our schools are continuing to fail in their quest to eliminate racial inequality in education.

SUMMARY AND CONCLUSION

In this chapter, we have seen evidence of educational inequality that has persisted despite the elimination of formal educational discrimination. We have also explored functionalist (cultural-deprivation) and conflict (cultural-bias) theories about the causes of educational inequality. We have seen a number of mechanisms by which schools subtly (and often unintentionally) discriminate against minority children, including culturally biased educational materials and tests, teacher-expectation effects, and tracking. We have also seen that, despite the very different theories and philosophies on which they are based, several approaches to improving the education of minority children have been shown to be effective if properly implemented. These include compensatory education, desegregation, multicultural education, cultural immersion, and higher teacher demands on and expectations of minority students. We know today that schools *do* make a difference, and we know a number of good ways to make them work better for minority students. Unfortunately, none of these approaches have been implemented on a scale sufficient to greatly reduce racial, social-class, and ethnic inequality in education, particularly in the biggest cities where most blacks and Hispanics live. The failure to institute large-scale reforms in education, along with the similar failure to reform the economic system (see Chapter 10) means continuing educational inequality for black, Hispanic, and Native Americans, despite the elimination of formal discrimination and official de jure segregation.

13

Majority–Minority Relations Based on Gender, Sexual Orientation, and Disability

Early in this book, we stated that the principles of majority–minority relations can be applied to social groups other than racial and ethnic ones. Women, the disabled or handicapped, and gay men and lesbians have been compared, in terms of their roles in society, to racial minority groups such as African Americans. In fact, a good deal of what has been said in this book about racial and ethnic groups could also be applied to these groups. All of them, for example, have been the targets of discrimination in such areas as employment and housing. On the other hand, there are differences in the nature and type of discrimination these groups encounter, as well as differences between their roles in society and those of racial minorities. In this chapter, we shall examine the nature of discrimination against women, the disabled, and gay men and lesbians, as well as the roles of each of these groups in society. We shall also examine legislation and court rulings concerning such discrimination. In addition, we will look at the ways that various minority roles intersect and interact, with particular attention to the intersection of race and gender. We shall see, for example, that the nature of racial discrimination varies by gender, and the nature of gender discrimination similarly varies by race.

THE NATURE OF GENDER INEQUALITY

From a sociological standpoint, women quite clearly fit the definition of a minority group. This is the case because the United States and many other societies are characterized by **gender inequality;** that is, different and unequal roles in society are defined on the basis of whether one is a man or a woman, with the result that men enjoy greater power, status, and economic security than women do. The different and unequal roles of men and women are called **gender roles**. Gender inequality is evident in a number of ways. On the average, women are paid less for the work they do (even when their level of education is the same as that of their male counterparts), and they have less autonomy on the job, less leisure time at home, and less political representation than men. So entrenched is the notion of male power in Western society that, until recently, marriage rituals typically included a promise by the bride to "love, honor, and *obey*" her husband. Even today, with deliberate sex discrimination forbidden by law, evidence of gender inequality in the United States continues to abound. In 1990, the average female, year-round, full-time worker received only about 70 percent of the income of her male counterpart. This did not vary much by education: At every level of education from eighth grade to five or more years of college, women were paid between 68 and 72 percent of what men were paid (U.S. Bureau of the Census, 1991b). Partly because of the low pay of women, people in female-householder families had a poverty rate in 1991 of almost 40 percent—nearly three times the overall poverty rate of 14.2 percent (U.S. Bureau of the Census, 1992d).

The power structure of the United States also remains heavily male-dominated. In both the public and private sectors, nearly all of the positions at the top, such as corporate officers, members of boards of directors, and high elected officials, are held by males. Even though the number of women in the U.S. Senate tripled between 1987 and 1993 and the number of women in the House nearly doubled, both remain overwhelmingly male. In the 1993–1994 session, only 6 out of 100 senators and only 48 out of 435 U.S. representatives were women.

Some critics of feminism—an ideology and movement supporting equal rights for women—have argued that the situation of women is not comparable to that of racial minorities in two senses. First, they have not been segregated in the same way, and second, their social-class composition is not very different from the overall population. From this view, some laws that are criticized by feminists for restricting the opportunities of women are seen differently. This viewpoint sees them as protecting women—from dangerous and "dirty" occupations, heavy physical labor, and military combat duty. People who feel this way often see the changing roles of women today as a threat to family life, noting that fewer mothers today have time to spend with their children and that the changing role of women has been accompanied by higher rates of divorce and nonmarital childbearing.

Feminists counter these arguments in a variety of ways. They point out that, while the class composition of women may not differ greatly from that of men, many women are dependent on their husband's income. When they get divorced, their economic standard of living quickly falls, while that of newly divorced men typically rises (Weitzman, 1985). Also, women who must support a family on their income alone have a far higher poverty rate than other families, including ones in which there is only one earner but that earner is male. Feminists also note that women have paid a high price in the form of low income and lack of power for whatever workplace protection is associated with traditional gender roles. They argue that women should be able to choose dangerous or physically demanding work if they want, the same as anyone else. Finally, they point out that while employed women do have a higher divorce rate than stay-at-home wives (Waite, 1981), research also shows that families with the wife in the labor force are just as happy as those in which she is not (Thornton and Freedman, 1984). It would appear that the higher divorce rate of employed women mainly reflects the fact that they are more financially able to leave bad marriages.

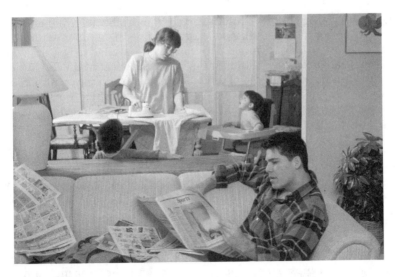

Research has shown consistently that married women spend many more hours a week on household work than their husbands, even when both the husband and wife are employed full-time. Photoedit/Tony Freeman

In fact, a good deal of research shows that unequal power between men and women remains a fact not only in the larger society but in the home as well. For example, families are far more likely to relocate for a job opportunity for the husband than for the wife; even women with good jobs must often put their husbands' jobs first when questions of relocation arise (Bielby and Bielby, 1992). Research has also shown consistently that women spend many more hours a week on household work than their husbands, even when both the husband and the wife work full-time (Peskin, 1982; Hochschild, 1989; Stockard and Johnson, 1992; Zhang and Farley, 1993). This unequal division of household labor has become an increasing source of conflict between husbands and wives in recent years (Townsend and Walker, 1990), and may be a factor in today's high divorce rates.

CAUSES OF GENDER INEQUALITY

A basic question that sociologists ask about gender inequality is, Why is there gender inequality? Why do men and women have different and unequal roles in society? As in other areas of sociology, the functionalist and conflict perspectives offer different answers to this question. We shall briefly examine the explanations of gender inequality offered by the functionalist and conflict perspectives.

Functionalist Explanations of Gender Inequality

Functionalists argue that having men and women play different roles in society may be useful to society in some ways, and certainly was in the past. Until about a century ago, most women spent much of their young-adult lives either pregnant or taking care of young children. Infant and child mortality was high, so to have two or three children survive to adulthood it was often necessary to give birth to five or six. Since there was no baby formula, all of these children had to be breast-fed. Thus, women had to stay near their children, which usually meant staying at home and avoiding activities such as hunting or any work that involved travel. Also, men are on the average larger and physically stronger than women. Much work done then required physical strength, making men, on the average, more able to do it. For these reasons, a gender division of labor made a certain amount of sense.

One view among sociologists is that gender roles survive today because of *cultural lag*—an arrangement that once was useful but no longer survives because it became engrained in the culture, so it persists even though its original purpose no longer exists. (Today, women have fewer children; overpopulation is a greater risk than underpopulation; alternatives to breast-feeding exist; and most jobs do not require great physical strength.) Another view within the functionalist perspective is that, in some ways, gender roles may still be useful today. Parsons and Bales (1955) argue that families benefit from the presence of both *instrumental leadership*, which focuses on getting things done, and *expressive leadership*, which addresses people's feelings and relationships. They argue that, in general, the husband/father fills the need for instrumental leadership, while the wife/mother fills the need for expressive leadership. Other sociologists have been quite critical of this formulation, however, pointing out that even if families do need both kinds of leadership, there is no clear reason why one type has to come from the husband and the other from the wife.

Some functionalists also hold that families are more stable when there are clear gender roles within the family. These sociologists point out, as noted earlier, that rates of divorce and nonmarital childbearing have risen as increasing numbers of women have left the home and entered the workforce. In turn, they argue, children have suffered, as they have received less adult attention, have encountered an increased risk of the disruptions of divorce, and have become increasingly likely to be born to a young single mother without the economic or personal resources to provide them with a good home environment (Moynihan, 1986; Popenoe, 1988). From this viewpoint, then, gender roles are useful to the family, and recent moves toward eliminating distinct gender roles have undermined the stability of the family.

In response to these arguments, however, other sociologists point out that many of the trends that seem to threaten the family have little to do with feminism or changing attitudes about the roles of women. The entry of women into the workforce, for example, is at least as tied to economic need as it is to feminism; the massive entry of women into the labor force is the only thing that kept most families from suffering a serious reduction in their standard of living during the 1970s and 1980s (Olsen, 1990). In addition, the notion that work keeps mothers from having close contact with their children is not well supported by research. A variety of studies show that full-time working mothers interact with their children about as much as full-time housewives do (J. Farley, 1977, pp. 197–202; Robinson, 1977; Goldberg, cited in Hodgson, 1979; Nock and Kingston, 1988; Benokraitis, 1983, pp. 318–19). Also, children in organized day care appear to develop about as well as children raised at home by their mothers (Hayes and Kamerman, 1983; Berg, 1986; Hoffmann, 1989). Children with less adequate day-care arrangements do less well, but this is more attributable to the unavailability of quality day care than to changes in the role of women per se. (Unlike the United States, most industrialized countries provide sub-sidized day care, available to any working parent who needs it.)

According to Thornton and Freedman (1984), social-science research pro-vides no evidence that families with the wife in the labor force are any less happy than families with stay-at-home wives. The former do have a higher divorce rate, but as noted, that is because employed wives are financially more able to leave bad mar-riages. And, as we saw in an earlier chapter, staying in a bad marriage is not neces-sarily any better for the children than getting a divorce. Finally, in response to Pope-noe's (1988) argument that adults often put their own priorities and concerns ahead of those of their children, it can be noted that this tendency exists among both men and women and cannot be simply tied to changing gender roles.

Conflict-Theory Explanations of Gender Inequality

From the standpoint of conflict theory, gender inequality, like other forms of inequality, exists because (1) an interest group benefits from it and (2) that in-terest group has the power to shape society in ways that suit its self-interests. In the case of gender inequality, the group that has benefited materially from the subordi-nate status of women is men (Collins, 1971; Reskin, 1988). Because of gender in-equality, men have greater incomes, more political power, and more spare time than women, as we have already seen. They also, on the average, enjoy greater status, au-tonomy, and authority on the job, and generally greater mobility and choice over how to spend their time. Thus, in all these ways, men clearly benefit in a material sense from gender inequality. It is true that there are also costs, mainly in socio-emotional areas: Men experience greater pressure to be "in control," expectations not to show emotion, greater difficulty sharing and expressing feelings, and lack of time to interact with their families and children. These, in turn, have costs in terms of health, as men are more subject to diseases such as high blood pressure, ulcers, and heart conditions—and partly for this reason, they live shorter lives. Nonetheless, the overall material benefits of sexism to men are quite clear in terms of time, money, power, and autonomy—and given that this is the case, it is not surprising that, through much of human history in many societies, men have used their power to maintain these benefits. Conflict theory, then, holds that gender inequality exists mainly because of the ways in which it materially benefits men and because men have the power to establish and maintain a system of inequality that benefits them in these ways.

What are the sources of male power that enable men to establish and main-tain a system of gender inequality? Conflict theorists point to several. One explana-tion, which draws on both the functionalist and conflict perspectives, is based on the fact that gender-role specialization, as we saw earlier, was once useful to society. It may have originally developed for that reason, but conflict theorists point out that once it did, it gave men certain kinds of power that women did not have, for exam-ple, greater freedom of movement and greater contact with the outside world. It also made women dependent on them for food, since it was men who did the hunting in most hunting and gathering societies. Once men had gained power through their mobility and outside contact and women's dependency on them for food, they be-gan to use that power to their own advantage. The result was that society became in-creasingly male-dominated. Eventually, the societal need for this gender role specialization largely disappeared, for reasons discussed earlier in this chapter. Because men benefited from these arrangements and because the arrangements gave men disproportionate power that they could use to their own advantage, however, men acted to maintain the system of gender roles, even after that system had outlived its usefulness to society as a whole.

Conflict theorists also point to another source of male power: their greater average size and physical strength. The fact that men can use force against women has been and continues to be a means by which men exercise power over women. In the earlier history of the United States, China, and a number of other societies, women were seen to a large extent as property of their husbands. Thus, rapes, assaults, and even in some cases killings of women by their husbands went unpunished and sometimes were not even recognized as crimes. This has changed in the legal sense, but as a practical matter the police and courts are often reluctant to become involved when violence occurs within the family. This reluctance was dramatically illustrated by the highly-publicized O. J. Simpson case in 1994. Police had been called to the Simpson home at least nine times prior to the murders of Nicole Simpson and her friend Ronald Goldman in June 1994, but only one of these calls resulted in an arrest. On that occasion, O. J. Simpson was convicted of assaulting Nicole Simpson, but his sentence consisted only of a public-service requirement that was not enforced, and a requirement that he see a counselor of his own choice. While Simpson's fame and popularity may have played some role in the relative uninvolvement of the police and courts, experts on family violence generally agreed that both the apparent pattern of abusive behavior and the official response to it in the Simpson case were fairly typical.

It remains true today that when a woman is assaulted or murdered, the most likely assailant is her husband or boyfriend. Fully one-third of all women who are murdered are killed by their husbands or boyfriends (Emery, 1989). Attacks on wives or girlfriends by husbands or boyfriends are far more common than the reverse (Straus, 1980; Makepeace, 1981). Thus, the use or threat of violence has historically been an important source of men's power over women, and this continues to be the case today.

Finally, it is important to note that the disproportionate economic and political power of men has a self-sustaining effect: Men use this power to assure continued advantage. As we have seen, Congress, the executive branches of state and federal government, and corporate board rooms and executive suites remain overwhelmingly male. It may be unreasonable to expect that public and private policies and arrangements that favor men over women, such as the system of unequal wages between predominantly male and female occupations, will change much as long as the key seats of power are so male-dominated. There are a few signs that male domination of positions of power may be starting to change. The Clinton administration appointed a record number of women to the executive branch of the federal government, including such important positions as that of attorney general. A handful of states (e.g., Iowa, North Dakota) have recently passed laws encouraging or requiring that about half of appointed state officials be female (Gross, 1990). Nonetheless, positions of power in both the public and private sector remain overwhelming occupied by males, and as long as this is the case, conflict theorists argue, it will be easy for men to maintain social policies and institutional arrangements that maintain the advantages they enjoy over women.

THE INTERSECTION OF RACE, GENDER, AND CLASS INEQUALITY

The Meaning of Gender for Women of Color

While gender inequality exists in the United States between men and women in virtually all social classes and all racial and ethnic groups, the form and meaning of this inequality varies among different groups and classes. The challenges and problems faced by working-class women, for example, are different from those faced by middle-class women. And African American and Latina women are confronted by different issues and different forms of gender inequality from those faced by most white, non-Hispanic women.

One way in which these experiences have been different is the extent to which the role of women has been linked to the home. Among middle-class women, the industrial era brought about a *housewife role*. The expectation was that the husband would be the breadwinner, while the wife would remain at home, raising the children and taking care of the home. From the emergence of the industrial era until two or three decades ago, this was the experience of most women in middle- and upper-income families (Degler, 1980). The justification provided for this role expectation was that it protected women from the dangers and the often difficult and strenuous labor of the workplace. With the emergence of the modern feminist movement in the 1960s and early 1970s, women rebelled against this role and entered the labor force in record numbers. (It should be noted again, though, that economic necessity played at least as big a role in the entry of women into the labor force as did feminism.) Even more fundamentally, women began to seek professional careers that had been male-dominated, attending law school and other forms of professional education in record numbers and dramatically changing the gender composition of some professions.

For low-income women and for many women of color, however, the housewife role never really became the norm as it did among white middle-class women (Seifer, 1973; Glenn, 1980; Jones, 1985). Low-income women and women of color never had the option of leaving the paid labor force to become housewives, because economic necessity demanded that they work for pay even at a time when most women did not. When most white middle-class women were housewives, for example, most African American women were working for pay, often in household-service jobs and other service occupations, or in low-paying industrial jobs in such places as textile mills. Thus, the rebellion against the confinement of the housewife role that characterized much of white middle-class feminism in the 1960s and early 1970s was never really an issue for poor women and women of color. Rather, their concerns focused on other areas, such as sexual harassment and abuse, racial and gender discrimination in hiring and pay, and the general low pay and powerlessness of women in service jobs and other working-class occupations typically held by women of color (Cotera, 1980; hooks, 1981). In many cases, African American and Latina feminists have criticized white middle-class feminists, who formed the core of the contemporary feminist movement during its early years, for not paying sufficient attention to these issues (Cotera, 1980; Zinn et al., 1986; Davis, 1989; Collins, 1991).

More recently, black and Hispanic women have increasingly been working in non-household-service occupations, such as fast-food workers and hotel housekeeping. These jobs have proliferated as the economy has shifted away from heavy industry and toward a service economy. As black and Hispanic males have been displaced from the better-paying industrial jobs, black and Hispanic women have often been able to find jobs in these service industries. The result has been that in recent years there has been somewhat less unemployment among women of color than among men of color in large urban areas. In fact, there is some evidence that women are preferred in some of these occupations because they are perceived as being less threatening and less likely than men to complain about the work situation (Kirschenman and Neckerman, 1991; Wilson, forthcoming). Another reason women may be preferred is that they are on the average paid less than men, making them an attractive source of cheap labor for jobs of this type.

While service employment has reduced the unemployment rate of women of color, it has also largely trapped them in low-wage employment (Collins, 1991, chap. 3). This is because most hotel and restaurant service jobs pay at or near the minimum wage. This has a particular impact on women of color, because the proportion of women who are single parents—and therefore the only source of income for their families—is higher among the Latina population than among the non-Hispanic white population and is even higher among the African American population. When a white non-Hispanic woman works at a low-wage job, it is more likely that she is either supporting only herself or is combining her income with her husband's (typically larger) income to support a family. Black and Latina women, on the other hand, are both more likely to work in low-wage service occupations and more likely to be the sole source of support for a family than is the case for white Anglo employed women.

Sexual harassment and violence against women have been matters of particular concern for African American women. Historically, black women were often expected to submit sexually to white males. Thus, they were sexual victims of both gender inequality and racial inequality (hooks, 1981). Slave women, for example, were required to submit to the sexual desires of white plantation owners. (This pre-

Many black and Latina women are employed in service industries such as fast food. While this service employment has lowered their unemployment rate relative to black and Latino men, it has also trapped many women of color in low-wage employment. *Photoedit/David Young-Wolff*

sented a sharp contrast to the inviolable taboo against sex between male slaves and white women; if this occurred, both partners were punished severely.) According to Collins (1991, p. 54), the sexual victimization of black women by white men "contributed to images of black women as fair game for all men." Sexual violence against African American women has in some cases been exacerbated by the anger and frustration of black men, many of whom have been largely deprived of opportunities to successfully play the traditional male role of economic provider and protector of their families. Culturally, this violence against women is both reflected and reinforced through the language of youth gangs, whose members often refer to women as "bitches" or "hoes," and by such media images as those contained in popular films about inner-city life and some forms of musical expression such as "gangsta" rap. For all these reasons, sexual violence has been a focus of major attention among African American feminists (hooks, 1981; Collins, 1991).

One special problem faced by black and Latina feminists is the question of how to advance the interests of women without threatening the position of black and Latino men, who are also highly disadvantaged in American society. When men of any race abuse, mistreat, or exploit women, it is always a problem from a feminist standpoint. Yet black and Latina feminists face important debates about the extent to which the subordinate role of women of color is related to the actions of men of color as opposed to actions of the majority group and institutional arrangements in the larger society. They must also face the reality that, even when black or Latino men behave in unacceptable ways toward women that must be confronted and addressed by feminists, the men, too, are victims of societal discrimination. This complicates the issue, adding a dimension not experienced by white feminists. For all these reasons, African American and Latina feminists have, to a greater extent than most white feminists, emphasized racial and class inequality as well as gender inequality as problems to be addressed by feminism (Davis, 1981, 1989; hooks, 1981, 1991; Collins, 1991; Higgenbotham, 1992; Lorde, 1992). More specifically, black and Latina feminists argue that race, class, and gender oppression, while they work in different ways and affect various groups of people in different ways, are part of an interlocking social relationship of domination, which oppresses various groups while giving unfair advantage to an elite, which is composed of white upper-class heterosexual males (hooks, 1989, p. 175; Collins, 1991, p. 226).

Black Males in American Society

While women of color face problems arising from both racism and sexism, there are also problems of particular concern to men of color. This is particularly the case for black males, whose situation has been the focus of growing concern in recent years. As noted earlier, one problem they face is that, because of racism, they have in many cases been denied the opportunity to fulfill the male role in the ways expected in American society. A long history of slavery, job discrimination, low wages, and high unemployment rates has made it difficult or impossible for many black males to be the economic provider for their families, as has been expected of males in American society. For some African American men, who have been fortunate enough to be part of the growing black middle class, economic hardship has eased in recent decades. At the same time, however, it has worsened for many other black men, particularly those who reside in central cities, where massive numbers of industrial jobs have been eliminated. As recently as 1974, nearly half of all young, employed black men worked at relatively well-paying jobs in manufacturing. By 1984, however, only about a quarter of employed black men were working in such jobs. During about the same period, between 1973 and 1984, the average earnings of black men under age thirty with four years of high school fell by more than 50 percent, largely because of this loss of manufacturing employment (Gordon Berlin and Andrew Sum, cited in Newport, 1992). As manufacturing jobs disappeared, black male unemployment rates soared, and many black males gave up looking for jobs and dropped out of the labor force (Wilson, 1987). More than 30 percent of young black men are out of the labor force entirely, about twice as many as among young white men (Newport, 1992).

Many young black males have responded to the loss of job opportunities by turning to crime or drugs. In many instances, young inner-city black males can make more money in an illegal activity than in any legal activity. As anthropologist Phillippe Bourgeois (quoted in Newport, 1992) put it:

> Crack has created a new Horatio Alger myth for inner-city kids searching for meaning and upward mobility. It's really their American dream. . . . Compared to earning chump change working for the white man at McDonald's, the drug trade can seem more realistic and even noble.

In short, the immediate economic incentives are to engage in illegal activity rather than legal. However, as we shall soon see, the long-term consequences of this have been devastating for inner-city African American males.

West (1993) points to another reason why growing numbers of young black males are turning to crime: The loss of job opportunities in the inner city, along with other recent changes, has exacerbated a longstanding problem in the black community that West calls *nihilism*. He defines *nihilism* as a "sense of psychological depression, personal worthlessness, and social despair that is so widespread in black America" (p. 13). The consequences of this nihilism include detachment from others, a self-destructive disposition, and a mean-spirited outlook that "destroys both the individual and others" (p. 15). West blames unrestrained capitalism and corporate market institutions for this problem. On the one hand, he argues, American capitalism has marketed the pursuit of pleasure in a variety of ways, constantly promoting products on the basis of comfort, fun, convenience, and sexual stimulation. Like all Americans, black Americans have been heavily influenced by this. At the same time, these same market forces have reduced job opportunities and elevated unemployment, worsening the social conditions faced by blacks in the inner city. Thus, blacks are subject to the hedonistic, pleasure-seeking tendencies of modern America but lack legitimate means to pursue these tendencies. And for inner-city blacks, objective conditions have worsened, leading to greater anger, more pressure in the direction of nihilism, and fewer means to legitimately pursue the pleasure that advertising constantly encourages all Americans to pursue.

According to West, the destructive consequences of nihilism in the black community were once held in check by strong black institutions and by fear of reprisals from whites if blacks expressed their anger. Today, however, many of those black institutions have been undermined by the loss of jobs in the black community and by the departure of the black middle class to the suburbs (on these points, see also Wilson, 1987). Also contributing to this, according to West, is the fact that re-

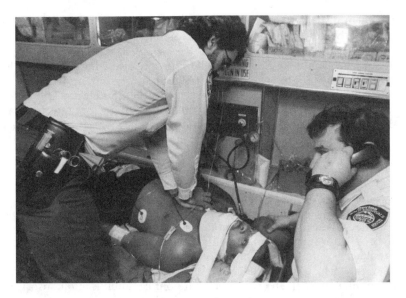

A black man receives emergency treatment for a gunshot wound. By the late 1980s, murder had become the most common cause of death for black men between the ages of 15 and 44. *Stock Boston, Inc./Christopher Brown*

cently many middle-class blacks have pursued individualistic goals of making more money and have focused less on service to the black community.

In addition, black anger, the expression of which was once held in check by fear of white reprisals, can today be more freely expressed, thanks to the results of the civil rights and Black Power movements of the 1960s and 1970s. The result has been that many young blacks, particularly males, have become more violent and more hedonistic. One of the few ways a young black man with little hope of employment can gain any feeling of power is by provoking fear in others. In West's (1993, p. 89) words, "to be 'bad' is good . . . because it imposes a unique kind of order for young black men on their own distinctive chaos and solicits an attention that makes others pull back with some trepidation." For the most part, violence by young black men has been directed toward other blacks, because they are the easiest targets. Black women have been particularly victimized (West, 1993, p. 18), often in the form of beatings and sexual assaults. On the other hand, fights and shootings among black men have become commonplace in poor, inner-city neighborhoods.

One consequence of this, of course, is that blacks are more likely to be victims of street crime. About half of the people murdered in the United States are black (compared with 12 percent of the population that is black), and violent crime has increased sharply since the early 1980s. Over a hundred U.S. cities had record homicide rates in 1993; in some of these cities, as many as 90 percent of those killed were black (and usually male). By the late 1980s, murder was the number-one cause of death for black males between the ages of fifteen and forty-four (Newport, 1992), and the homicide death rate among black males has continued to rise since then. Another consequence of this violence as well as the drug dealing mentioned earlier is that growing numbers of black men are imprisoned. A commonly cited statistic in recent years has been that more young black men are in prison than are in college.

The latter statistic points to another problem—declining educational attainment among black men. Since the 1970s, progressively fewer black males have been attending college. The proportion of black college students who are male fell from 50 percent in the 1960s to just 39 percent in 1990 (Sudarkasa, 1991). Reasons for the decline in black-male enrollment include some factors that have affected black enrollment generally—a series of economic recessions (which always hit minorities the hardest) and cutbacks in student financial aid since the mid 1970s. Other causes of the decline are specific to black males, however. As employment opportunities have worsened in the inner city, growing numbers of black men entered the military, or enrolled in private trade schools that promised (but rarely delivered) quick placement into attractive jobs (Sudarkasa, 1991). Some have been attracted by the temptation of easy money selling drugs and have ended up in jail. Finally, because of the lack of black-male role models and because of a variety of other problems, the proportion of black males with the academic qualifications to get into a four-year college is smaller than that of black females (Sudarkasa, 1991).

Several African American social scientists, including West (1993) and Wilson (forthcoming) have been critical of both political liberals and conservatives for the ways in which they have addressed (or avoided) behavioral problems among black males. Liberals (including many sociological conflict theorists) have said little about problems of crime and drug abuse among blacks for fear of contributing to stereotypes. Such stereotypes are a real problem: Despite the high crime rates, most black men are law-abiding citizens, yet they are often harassed by the police, tailed by store employees, and denied jobs because of the criminal stereotype (Anderson, 1990; Kirschenman and Neckerman, 1991). Nonetheless, West, Wilson, and others argue that we cannot address a problem if we do not discuss it, and they argue that liberals should acknowledge that conditions such as crime, substance abuse, and family disruption are genuine problems in the black community and are increasingly inhibiting the development of that community.

At the same time, West, Wilson, and others are even more critical of conservatives (again, including some sociological functionalists) for their tendency to speak simplistically about these conditions as if they are the only or ultimate cause of problems among African Americans. Both Wilson and West point out that while problems such as crime, drug abuse, and family disruption are very real among African Americans, they can be understood and addressed only as responses to the social conditions in which a large part of the African American community lives. As we have seen in this chapter, conditions such as job loss, lack of opportunity through legitimate channels, pressures for consumption and hedonism in the larger society, and role expectations that cannot be fulfilled have all created conditions that foster anger, crime, and substance abuse among inner-city black males. For example, if crime pays more than any available job in the short run, or if no job is available at all, it is not surprising that some people turn to crime. While it is necessary to directly address problems such as crime, family difficulties, and substance abuse, West and Wilson argue that this by itself is not enough. Society must also find ways to address the larger social conditions that have contributed to the growth and development of these problems. These include joblessness, low wages, unrestrained market forces, poor education, and the various forms of institutional discrimination that have been addressed in earlier chapters of this book.

OPPORTUNITY FOR INNER-CITY BLACK MALES:
THE DIFFERENCE A GENERATION MAKES

In 1992, *Time* magazine reporter Sylvester Monroe returned to the inner-city Chicago neighborhood where he had grown up. Like most young black men in the neighborhood today, Monroe grew up in a fatherless home. He lived in Taylor Homes, the nation's largest public-housing project. In large part because of encouragement from a mother who believed in the value of education and a high-school teacher who demanded the best from his students despite the disadvantaged background most of them came from, Monroe was able to succeed. He was chosen to participate in A Better Chance, a program that placed talented inner-city youngsters in exclusive private schools. (For more on this program and the life experiences of its graduates, see Zweigenhaft and Domhoff, 1991.) When Monroe returned to his old neighborhood, however, he found that many things had changed in ways that make it harder today to move up and out in the way that he was able to.

For one, government cutbacks have eliminated many of the programs and services that offered educational opportunities and kept kids out of trouble after school. Programs such as a 4-H club, student social centers, and a mentoring program that had been available to help Monroe no longer exist in his neighborhood today—they have fallen victim to budget cuts by the state and federal governments. From 1965 until the early 1990s, the Chicago public-school system operated Head Start in up to 120 schools. But in 1990, the school board voted to phase out the last 43 of these programs by 1993 because it could not afford to pay the salaries of the teachers.

Lack of money has hurt in other ways. In his national study of school funding, Jonathan Kozol (1991) found average spending per pupil in the city of Chicago to be about $5,500 per year—roughly half what it was in some affluent suburban districts near Chicago. In the ten years during the 1950s and 1960s when Monroe attended the Chicago public schools, not one day of class was canceled because of budget deficits or teachers' strikes. But in the decade between 1982 and 1992, school failed to open on time in five of the ten years. And as I write this in early 1994, the Illinois legislature still has not come up with a permanent solution to the chronic problem of budget deficits in the Chicago schools.

The neighborhood has also changed in ways that make life there more difficult today than they were in Monroe's day. Monroe points out that, while drug use and single parenthood were common then, too, other things have changed dramatically. For one thing, there has been a massive loss of population, which threatens the stability of the neighborhood's institutions. Enrollment at the high school Monroe attended has fallen from four thousand then to fewer than twelve hundred now, with the result that the school may have to be closed. With dropout rates already high, Monroe fears that many more students will leave if they no longer have a school in their own neighborhood. He notes that one good black male student that he interviewed expressed fears about having to run a gauntlet of hostile gangs in another neighborhood if the school is closed. As the population of the neighborhood has shrunk, the proportion of people who are poor has soared—from 36 percent in 1970 to 57 percent in 1990. This means that today's young people have less exposure to people earning money and supporting their families with steady jobs and more exposure to idleness and to crime, gang activity, drug abuse, and other problems associated with poverty. Monroe concludes his report on his visit to his old neighborhood by noting that if young African American males today succeed in moving up and out, they will do so only "by clearing hurdles that many black students of my generation never faced."

Source: Based on Sylvester Monroe, October 5, 1992, "Breaking Out, Then and Now," *Time:* 58–60.

Wilson, West, and others have recently argued for a two-pronged approach. One part of the approach would try to address behavioral problems among black males and to motivate them to pursue education and seek legitimate employment. School programs targeting black males, like the immersion schools discussed in Chapter 12 and black-male mentoring programs, are examples of this (Whitaker, 1991; Majors and Billson, 1992). Organizations such as Concerned Black Men, based in Washington, are being established to provide young fatherless black boys with monitoring and mentoring from adult black males who act as surrogate fathers (Dyer, 1992). At the same time, part of the approach must also be targeted to changing the social structure and institutions in ways that provide greater opportunities for employment and education and that meet basic needs, such as health care, that have gone unmet in the black community. (Examples of some ways in which lack of opportunity has worsened in inner cities in recent years are discussed in the box "Opportunity for Inner-City Black Males: The Difference a Generation Makes.") It may well be that such a two-pronged approach is the only hope for reversing the worsening plight of inner-city African American males.

We conclude this discussion with a cautionary note. While it is true that disproportionate numbers of black males face serious difficulties, it is important not to stereotype. Dunier (1992) argues that, in attempting to bring problems of racism and poverty to the attention of the public, many sociologists and journalists have inadvertently contributed to stereotypes of black males. Like all groups, black males vary widely in their attitudes, behaviors, and characteristics. In *Slim's Table*, Dunier studies a group of black men who meet regularly for lunch at a Chicago cafeteria. The men Dunier studied were not unemployed, not homeless, not in trouble with the law. Dunier reminds us powerfully that it is important to keep in mind that, while many black males do face real difficulties, most are law-abiding and employed and do not face poverty. This is important to keep in mind, since stereotyping appears to be a significant reason for discrimination against black males (Wilson, forthcoming). If discussion of the real problems of some black males turns into stereotyping that affects how people think about all black males, things could be made worse, not better.

PREJUDICE, INEQUALITY, AND DISCRIMINATION BASED ON SEXUAL ORIENTATION

Besides race and gender, prejudice, inequality, and discrimination occur on the basis of a number of other social characteristics. Two of the most important are sexual orientation and disability. In this section, we shall examine prejudice and discrimination based on sexual orientation; the final section of the chapter examines prejudice and discrimination against people with disabilities.

The Applicability of the Majority–Minority Model to Sexual Orientation

There is no question that prejudice and discrimination against homosexual men and women are widespread. So strong are prejudices against gay men and lesbians that laws protecting homosexuals from discrimination have been repealed by popular referendum in Miami, Colorado, several Oregon counties, and elsewhere, although many of these referendums have later been overturned by court rulings or legislation. Name calling and physical attacks against gay men and lesbians have long been commonplace, and the latter clearly appear to have increased in recent years (Southern Poverty Law Center, 1993a). For many years, a number of states had laws banning sexual relations between people of the same sex, and/or forms of sex other than vaginal intercourse, often referred to in legal terms as "sodomy." While some states have repealed these laws, they remain on the books in others (twenty-four in 1992, including nine that banned only homosexual sodomy). In important ways, federal law today still discriminates against gay men and lesbians, most notably by banning them from service in the military. (This ban has not always existed; it was instituted in 1943.) An attempt by President Clinton in 1993 to end this discriminatory policy was met with a firestorm of opposition in Congress and among some segments of the general population. In the end, the discriminatory law was retained, though softened by a "don't ask, don't tell" compromise policy that Congress weakened even beyond the initial compromise proposed by Clinton. While military recruits no longer have to state their sexual orientation, current policy still provides for discharge of military personnel who are found to be homosexual. Historically, one of the ugliest and deadliest cases of discrimination occurred during the Holocaust, when tens of thousands of homosexuals or suspected homosexuals were killed in Hitler's death camps (Humm, 1980; Plant, 1986; Muller, 1993). Although this deadly campaign against homosexuals is acknowledged more widely today than in the past, accounts of the Holocaust still often omit any reference to it. Yet the fact is that homosexuals were systematically targeted for imprisonment and brutalization, and, aside from Jews, probably suffered the highest death rate of any group the Nazis systematically imprisoned (Plant, 1986).

Efforts to combat discrimination on the basis of sexual orientation have been widespread since the gay and lesbian rights movement emerged in the 1960s. A galvanizing event was a raid by New York police in 1969 on the Stonewall Inn, a gay bar in Greenwich Village. This event resulted in a spontaneous protest by homosexuals, who felt that they were being singled out for police attention simply because of their sexual orientation. Since then, gay men and lesbians have organized to oppose discrimination and prejudice against homosexuals, and public support has grown

Jose Zuniga displays an award he won before being forced out of the U.S. military because of his homosexuality. Despite President Clinton's efforts in 1993 to end such discrimination, it has continued to occur under the "don't ask, don't tell" compromise, because anyone who openly acknowledges his or her homosexuality is still discharged. *Sygma/J. Patrick Forden*

for the idea that laws should be passed protecting homosexuals from discrimination. By the early 1990s, at least eight states, among them Massachusetts and Wisconsin, and more than fifty cities, including Minneapolis, Detroit, St. Louis, Washington, San Francisco and, in Canada, Toronto, had passed local ordinances forbidding discrimination on the basis of sexual orientation. Many, if not most, public colleges and universities have policies forbidding discrimination on the basis of sexual orientation. By the end of the 1980s, after a brief period of backlash attributable to AIDS, polls showed that the majority of Americans believed that discrimination against homosexuals is wrong. For example, by a margin of 71 percent to 18 percent in a 1989 Gallup poll, Americans agreed that homosexuals should have equal rights in terms of job opportunity (Gallup, 1990, pp. 215–18). Virtually identical results were obtained in a 1992 *Newsweek* poll (Turque, 1992, p. 36). However, when people were asked about hiring homosexuals for specific occupations, there responses were more variable. While large majorities felt that homosexuals should be hired as salespersons and as doctors, both polls showed that the public was about evenly divided on whether or not homosexuals should be hired as clergy and as high-school and elementary-school teachers. The *Newsweek* poll also showed that by a narrow majority, Americans rejected the notion that gay rights represent a threat to the American family and its values. However, just over half of those surveyed also rejected the idea that homosexuality is an acceptable alternative lifestyle.

In addition, it is clear that many Americans do not agree that homosexuals are a minority group that should be protected from discrimination by law. This is evident in the 1992 referendum passed in Colorado. This referendum sought to overturn laws that several Colorado cities had passed forbidding discrimination on the basis of sexual orientation. Although the referendum was later declared unconstitutional, the fact that it passed shows that the majority did not view homosexuals as a minority deserving of legal protection. Moreover, efforts were under way in mid-1994 to place similar proposals on the ballot in several other states. One argument commonly made by opponents of such legal protection is that, unlike racial or ethnic minorities, women, or the disabled, homosexuals are defined as a group on the basis of behavior, that is, sexual interest in and contact with people of the same sex. Therefore, they argue, homosexuality is a choice freely made (again, unlike race, sex, or disability) and therefore is voluntary. They argue that if people don't want to face disapproval, they should avoid behavior that is generally disapproved.

There is, however, one very fundamental flaw with this argument: Research does not back up the idea that homosexuality is a choice. While homosexual *behavior,* that is, sexual relations with a person of the same sex, is, of course, a choice in the sense that any sexual behavior is a choice, homosexuality or a homosexual *orientation,* that is, sexual attraction to people of the same sex, is not a choice. Rather, it is a condition that people more or less gradually discover that they have. Much research demonstrates this. For one, there has been no increase in the extent of homosexual behavior as homosexuality has become more accepted in American society (Karlen, 1971; Levin, 1975; McCary, 1978; Bell, Weinberg, and Hammersmith, 1981). In fact, some recent surveys have reported lower levels of homosexual behavior in recent years than were observed in the Kinsey studies in the 1940s, when social taboos against such behavior were much stronger than they are today (Barringer, 1993; Schmalz, 1993). If homosexuality were truly a freely chosen behavior, its frequency would likely increase as social support for it increased, as is the case with most forms of behavior. Even when young people know that a teacher or parent is gay, their own likelihood of becoming homosexual is not increased (McCary, 1978). Recent medical and biological research has discovered increasing evidence that sexual orientation is, at least to a large extent, biologically determined. These studies have found differences in the brains of homosexuals and heterosexuals (Levay, 1993) as well as evidence of genetic differences between homosexuals and heterosexuals for both men and women (Suplee, 1991; Bower, 1992; Wheeler, 1992; Hamer et al., 1993; Pool, 1993). Rather than *choosing* to be homosexual, it appears that gay and lesbian people gradually *discover* that they are homosexual. Based on this discovery, along with interaction with other people, both gay and straight, they gradually come to think of themselves as homosexual or lesbian (Cass, 1979, 1983–84, 1984).

It is true that while homosexual orientation is not chosen, people who are not primarily homosexual do at times engage in sexual relationships with people of the same sex. Some people are bisexuals; that is, they are attracted to and/or engage in sex with people of both sexes. While it may be true that a homosexual orientation, that is, being primarily or exclusively attracted to people of the same sex, is largely a product of biological and genetic factors, it is also true that how one behaves with respect to sexual preference is influenced by both sociocultural and biological/genetic influences. Nonetheless, it is becoming increasingly clear that, at least for many people whose primary sexual orientation is homosexual, biological or genetic factors are important influences, which further negates the idea that a homosexual orientation is a matter of choice.

It could, of course, be argued that even if homosexuality were a freely chosen behavioral pattern, which it is not, that it would be inappropriate to pass laws against homosexual behavior as long as it occurs between consenting adults. Thus, just as feminists argue that nobody has the right to tell women what role they must fill in society, advocates of gay and lesbian rights argue that nobody has the right to tell others what their sexual preference should be. And since—as we shall see later in more detail—norms against homosexuality in the United States have their roots largely in religious doctrine, antigay discrimination and rules against gay and lesbian sexual behavior can be seen as violations of the separation of church and state. In other words, such laws can be viewed as the state attempting to impose a particular religious viewpoint or set of beliefs on its citizenry. The dangers of this were evident in the eighteenth-century English society that many colonial Americans wanted to escape by coming to North America, and they can also be seen in Iranian society in the 1980s, when religious/political leaders such as Ayatollah Khomeini made strict Islamic codes the law of the land, imposing penalties up to and including the death penalty for those who refused to comply.

Since growing evidence refutes the notion that homosexuality is voluntary, it must in fact be viewed as an ascribed status much like race, ethnicity, sex, or disability. Nor is there evidence that homosexuals are less effective on the job. Despite the ban in the military, for example, there is no evidence that homosexuals are less effective soldiers than anyone else. On the contrary, homosexuals who have kept their sexual orientation secret have been serving effectively in the U.S. military for years (Shilts, 1993a, 1993b). Other countries that do not ban homosexuals from military service have not experienced difficulties, and some of history's most influential and effective military leaders, including the Roman emperor Hadrian, King Richard the Lion-Hearted, King Edward II, and the British soldier-author T. E. Lawrence, have been gay (Wallechinsky and Wallace, 1975, p. 1006; Boswell, 1980,

p. 25). In the United States, an early military leader who was gay was General William Frederick Wilhelm von Steuben, the army's first inspector general, one of the two most influential generals of the Revolutionary War, and the person who first conceptualized the idea of the West Point Military Academy (Shilts, 1993a).

The idea that homosexuals have an inclination toward molestation or sexual abuse, sometimes cited by people opposed to hiring them for jobs such as teaching, is also not well founded. The great majority of molestation and sexual abuse cases are heterosexual (usually males abusing females), just as the large majority of the population is heterosexual. Nor, for that matter, is there any evidence that having a homosexual teacher or clergyperson will make a child more likely to grow up gay or lesbian.

Given that homosexuality is not a freely chosen status and that it is not linked to ability to do a job, it would appear that the majority–minority model can be very appropriately applied to gay men and lesbians. Like minorities defined on the basis of race, ethnicity, and gender, they are the objects of prejudice and discrimination on the basis of a status they did not choose and are systematically denied opportunities to do things they are perfectly capable of doing. Given these realities, to fail to legally protect them from discrimination in the same ways that other groups are protected from discrimination seems patently unfair and, in fact, discriminatory. Sociologically, of course, we are faced with the question of *why* homosexuals are the objects of prejudice and discrimination, an issue to which we now turn our attention.

Causes of Discrimination Against Gay Men and Lesbians

Prejudice against homosexuals today (sometimes referred to as *homophobia* or, in its institutional form, *heterosexism*) is expressed more openly than most other kinds of prejudice. It is probably one of the few kinds of prejudice that remains socially acceptable to express in many circles, even though it is clearly less acceptable today than in the past. In this sense, prejudice against homosexuals is engrained in culture in the same way that prejudice against other minorities once was but no longer is to the same extent. One reason for the persistence of prejudice against homosexuals is linked to many people's religious beliefs. Most Christian religions condemn homosexual behavior, although some have changed in this regard in recent years. Virtually all of the more fundamentalist religions, however, continue to condemn any and all sexual contact between people of the same sex. Because the United States is more religious than most other Western countries, religion has played a stronger role in shaping norms about sex in the United States than, for example, in most of Europe (Jones et al., 1986). U.S. norms about homosexuality reflect this: While most U.S. states had laws against homosexual behavior and many still do, this is not the case in much of Europe. The Netherlands and Denmark, for example, have no law against it, and Holland has had no such law for over 170 years (Weinberg and Williams, 1974, chaps. 5–7). In some societies, it has even been valued, at least for parts of the population. The ancient Greeks, for example—who are today regarded as an especially civilized society—valued homosexuality among their leaders and in some ways institutionalized it (Licht, 1932).

The Christian ban on homosexual behavior, like other aspects of traditional American attitudes and rules about sex, can be traced to three historical periods: the Biblical era, early Christianity, and the Victorian era, which influenced British and American thought in the nineteenth century (Cohn, 1974; McCary, 1978). In each of these periods, but particularly the earlier two, a ban on forms of sex that did not result in pregnancy was functional, because there was a real risk that populations would not have enough children to replace themselves. In many societies, only about half of all babies born could be expected to live to adulthood, so a high birthrate was necessary for societies to replace themselves and survive. In this context, forms of sex that had no chance of leading to reproduction, including homosexual sex (also masturbation and heterosexual oral and anal sex), were dysfunctional in the sense that they potentially distracted people from forms of sex that could lead to reproduction. This was the source of the biblical concern about "wasting seed," and it explains why religions that developed in this time developed strong norms against homosexuality and other forms of sexuality that did not have the potential of leading to conception.

Because prejudice and discrimination against homosexuals is so strongly rooted in religious beliefs, it has been quite resistant to change, particularly in a highly religious country such as the United States. Nonetheless, there has been increased recognition that even if such discrimination may once have been functional, it no longer is today. The threat faced by today's world is not loss of population, but *overpopulation*. Thus, in the modern world, it can no longer be argued that homosexuality and other forms of sex that cannot lead to reproduction are dysfunctional. On the contrary, it could in fact be argued that they are functional, because they may help to reduce the birthrate in a world that is already overpopulated (Vidal, 1992). Nonetheless, because these norms and prejudices are so deeply rooted in religion and because a number of religions continue to proclaim and defend rules against homosexual behavior, the open expression of homophobic attitudes remains quite common today even as open expression of other kinds of prejudice has become distinctly less common.

It has also been argued that prejudice and discrimination against homosexuals is closely linked to gender inequality. For gay men, homosexuality involves rejection of a key element of the male role as it has traditionally been defined in our society—sexual relationships with women, often including elements of domination and sexual conquest. For men to reject this role involves an implicit threat to the dominant role in society that men enjoy, and men who reject it by being homosexual are seen by other men as traitors who have broken rank (Pharr, 1992). For this reason, males have historically exerted extremely strong peer pressure on any males who appear to reject a traditionally masculine, macho role that involves, among other things, the sexual conquest of women. This process starts at a young age: Peer condemnation is stronger for boys who are labeled "sissies" than for girls who prefer a "tomboy" role (Hartley, 1974; see also Avicolli, 1992). It has also been suggested that a major reason for the ban on gays in the military is to preserve "its image as the upholder of traditional notions of masculinity" (Shilts, 1993b).

Lesbianism, too, has been rejected by society for reasons linked to male dominance, and the role of male dominance in the rejection of lesbianism may have become more significant as lesbians have become more outspoken about their sexuality in recent years. By asserting a sexual orientation that does not include the need for a male partner, lesbians are viewed as sending a message that men are unnecessary to their sexual fulfillment or their economic support (Pharr, 1992). This threatens the traditional male role as the initiator and controller of sexual encounters and relationships, and the economic provider who through control of the purse strings has historically been able to keep women economically dependent. Thus, like male homosexuality, lesbianism may be socially disapproved largely because of the threat it poses to the traditional dominant-male role (Griscom, 1992; Pharr, 1992).

For a time, fear of AIDS played a major role in homophobia in the United States, and when the AIDS epidemic first broke out, some public opinion polls indicated that attitudes toward homosexuals became more negative. More recent polls, however, suggest that this trend has reversed, and that more people than in the past take positions against discrimination on the basis of sexual orientation (Gallup, 1990). While it is true that the risk of AIDS is often mentioned by people and groups who express prejudice against homosexuals, it appears that a growing proportion of the population has become aware that (1) AIDS cannot be transmitted through casual contact such as at school or work, (2) the disproportionate number of gay men among people with AIDS is specific to the United States but not the case in some other societies, and (3) AIDS can be transmitted through either homosexual or heterosexual sexual contact, as well as through contact with blood, such as when drug addicts share needles. For these reasons, homophobia linked to fears of getting AIDS from gay people appears to have subsided since the early days of the AIDS epidemic in the 1980s, though fears about AIDS undoubtedly do still contribute to homophobia for some people.

PEOPLE WITH DISABILITIES AS A MINORITY GROUP

Another group that has increasingly come to be viewed according to a minority-group model consists of people with disabilities. Although there is disagreement on the precise number of disabled or handicapped people in the United States, a compilation of various surveys suggests that from 13 to 16 percent of the U.S. adult population is disabled (see Nagi, 1972; Krute and Burdette, 1978; U.S. National Center for Health Statistics, 1979; Farley, 1980). In the early 1990s about one out of eleven freshmen entering college reported some type of disability (Jaschik, 1993). Increasingly, the disabled have come to believe that it is not mainly their physical disabilities that place them at a disadvantage, but society's *reaction* to their disability. Employers, for example, are often reluctant to hire the disabled, even when their disability in no way impairs them from doing the job. Physically disabled people must also frequently deal with nondisabled people who expect them to be *mentally* disabled as well and therefore talk down to them, talk about them in their presence, or assume that they cannot do things when they really can. Similarly, the nondisabled frequently view the disabled in a unidimensional manner—as *disabled* people rather than as whole people, so that the single characteristic of disability becomes foremost in their minds. Behaviors such as staring, uncomfortable silence, or endless questions about their disability continuously remind disabled people that they are "different" (Schuchardt, 1980). In effect, the stigma the rest of society places on persons with disabilities can often become a greater handicap than the disability itself. Even the physical disability is often more of a handicap than it need be because of actions of the larger society. It is not particularly difficult, for example, to design sidewalks and buildings so that most disabled persons can use them. Until recently, however, this was rarely done.

Because of various prejudices about people with disabilities and socially imposed handicaps such as hiring discrimination, many people with disabilities have come to view themselves as a minority group and to behave accordingly. Increasingly,

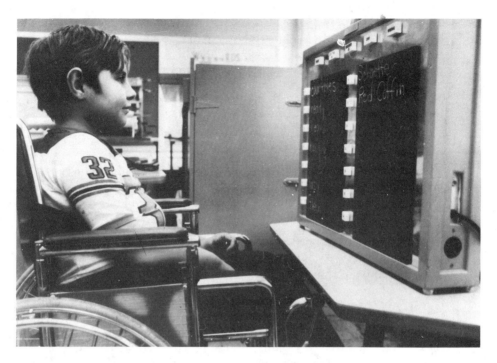

A speech-handicapped youngster undergoing therapy. Many sociologists feel that the disabled fit the definition of "minority groups" as well as do racial and ethnic minorities.
AT&T Co. Photo Center

they have been recognized by society as such. People with disabilities have held demonstrations in recent years and engaged in political lobbying similar to that done by racial and ethnic minorities and women. The threat of a lawsuit, for example, led to the captioning of part of the television broadcast of the 1980 Democratic National Convention for hearing-impaired viewers. Since then, closed-captioning systems have been developed and expanded to include a large proportion of television programming. Increasingly, legislation and labor–management contracts have forbidden discrimination on the basis of disabilities not related to job performance. Such discrimination was forbidden beginning in 1973, for example, in federal employment and among private employers under contract with the federal government (Bruck, 1978). Since 1990, this protection has been extended to most private employment. The disabled have also come to be regarded as a protected group under affirmative action programs, and many employers have made special efforts to hire and upgrade people with disabilities.

Nonetheless, such efforts cannot entirely eliminate the prejudices and fears of the nondisabled toward the disabled, and a big piece of the disadvantage that people with disabilities suffer in some way arises from one-to-one interactions with individuals who have such prejudices. Only a greater awareness of the perspectives of people with disabilities can solve this problem. Even good intentions are not enough; well-meaning expressions of concern often come off as paternalizing and end up making the disabled person feel powerless or unaccepted (Gliedman, 1979). As long as such problems exist, people with disabilities are likely to view themselves as a minority group and respond accordingly. For them, too, the black civil rights movement served as an important role model and provided some worthwhile lessons both about how society responds to groups who are "different" and how to deal with that response. (For further discussion of the problems of people with disabilities see Cohen, 1977; Stubbins, 1977; Bruck, 1978.)

Access and the Americans with Disabilities Act

As more overt forms of prejudice and discrimination against people with disabilities have diminished somewhat, and as legal protection against discrimination has been extended to the disabled, the efforts of people with disabilities have increasingly shifted to issues of *access*. The fact is that many public buildings, educational institutions, and retail stores are not designed in a way that makes them easily usable (or in some cases, usable at all) by people who are visually impaired, people whose activities are limited by chronic conditions such as arthritis or heart trouble, or people who are confined to wheelchairs. Such things as curbs without curb cuts for wheelchairs, signs that are printed but not in braille, and lack of places to park close to where people with disabilities want or need to go are additional design problems that limit access. For all of these reasons, it has been difficult in many cases for people with disabilities to gain access to education, work, shopping, and entertainment, even when their disabilities do not impair their actual ability to study, work, shop, or enjoy entertainment facilities. Rather, they are thwarted by design characteristics that make it hard or impossible for them to get in or move around once they are in.

In 1992, a major piece of legislation, the Americans with Disabilities Act, often referred to as ADA, was passed to deal with this and other problems faced by people with disabilities. This law broadens protection of the disabled against discrimination, and it requires that employers accommodate employees with disabilities and that public facilities be accessible to people with disabilities. Among the specific provisions is a ban on discrimination against the physically and mentally disabled in hiring and promotion. This ban applies to all employers with more than twenty-five employees. It also outlaws tests that have the effect of screening out job applicants with disabilities, unless it can be shown that the tests relate to a worker's ability to perform the job (Traver, 1990). Before the passage of ADA, people with disabilities were protected from discrimination by the Rehabilitation Act of 1973, but unlike ADA, this act applied only to organizations that receive federal funds (Jaschik, 1993). In addition to extending the ban on discrimination to all employers with more than twenty-five employees, ADA also allows people who are discriminated against to directly sue the organizations that discriminate. Under the old law, all they could do was file complaints to federal agencies, who then decided whether to take action and what action to take against the violators (Jaschik, 1993).

In addition to strengthening the ban on discrimination, ADA requires that workplaces and public accommodations be made accessible to people with disabilities. This includes physical accessibility, such as doors wide enough for wheelchairs and ramps or lifts for wheelchairs (Traver, 1990). Restaurants, colleges and universities, public-transportation systems, theaters, retail stores, and government offices are among the kinds of public facilities that are now required to be accessible. Employers must not only make their facilities accessible for employees with disabilities, but they are also required to make "reasonable accommodations" for such employees, such as providing readers for blind workers and signers or caption systems for the hearing-impaired, and arranging modified work schedules. Of course, the word *reasonable* is subject to various interpretations, and it will likely take some time and a number of court rulings to discover exactly what it means in a practical sense (Jaschik, 1993). Many people with disabilities have interpreted this and other provisions to mean that they are to be *integrated:* For example, in colleges, this would mean no separate classes, dorm rooms, or buses for the disabled. In some areas, the new law is quite explicit about this: ADA specifies, for example, that in public-transportation systems, *all* new buses must be accessible to people with disabilities; it is no longer enough to merely operate special "handi-van" service for the disabled, though such services may be provided in addition to making all new regular buses accessible (Traver, 1990).

It is too early to tell entirely what the effects of the ADA will be. Debates continue, for example, on how much of the costs employers and organizations providing public accommodations should incur to accommodate the disabled. But the passage of ADA does indicate one thing quite clearly: More than ever before, Americans recognize that people with disabilities can do many of the same things, and should have the same rights, as people without disabilities. Thus, they increasingly reject discrimination against people with disabilities, and this position has been written into law, recognizing people with disabilities as a minority group deserving of legal protection in the same way that legal protection has been afforded to racial, ethnic, and religious minorities by earlier legislation. As with the other groups, however, it remains to be seen to what extent such legislation is successful in bringing about truly equal opportunity for people with disabilities.

SUMMARY AND CONCLUSION

In this chapter, we have seen that the concepts of majority and minority groups can be applied to a wide variety of other kinds of groups besides those characterized by race and ethnicity: groups based on gender, sexual orientation, and disability, for example. It is clear that women, gay men and lesbians, and people with disabilities have been widely discriminated against in American society, and all of these groups continue today to be placed in a subordinate position with respect to wealth, income, status, and/or power, though the forms of discrimination vary among groups. We have seen, too, that there is a complex interaction among race, class, and gender inequality, so that while women of all races and social classes occupy a subordinate role in American society, the nature of that role and the issues faced by women vary among women of different racial and ethnic groups and different class backgrounds. Similarly, racial inequality has imposed unique difficulties on black men in the United States, who experience racial inequality in different ways than do black women. A particular problem has been increasingly difficult access to employment, which has made it impossible for many black men to play the male role as our society expects it to be played. The consequence has, in many cases, been self-destructive violence arising from frustration and lack of opportunity.

In recent years, Americans have been increasingly cognizant of these forms of intergroup inequality, though all of them persist today. Federal legislation has banned discrimination against women and against the disabled in employment and public accommodations, and several states and many cities have also extended such legal protection against discrimination to gay men and lesbians, However, there has been significant resistance, and the expression of opposition to such legislation has been particularly strong, in the case of laws banning discrimination on the basis of sexual orientation. One reason for this is that much of this opposition is based on religious beliefs, which remain a stronger influence in the United States than in other industrialized countries. In recent years, however, some religious denominations in the United States have reevaluated and altered their traditional position that homosexuality is sinful, and some have supported antidiscrimination legislation.

14

Current Trends in Majority-Minority Relations

In this chapter, we shall examine several issues and trends that have come to the fore-front in the area of intergroup relations in the 1990s. These include the diversity and multiculturalism movements in the workplace and in education, the recent resurgence of hate-group activity in the United States and elsewhere, and the growing debate over how to respond to such activity, which has centered on hate-crime legislation, speech codes, and so-called "political correctness." In this chapter, we shall also address the growing movement to combat discrimination by testing for discrimination in housing, lending, retail sales, and other business activities.

DIVERSITY AND MULTICULTURALISM IN WORK AND EDUCATION

As has been noted in earlier chapters, the population of the United States is becoming more diverse. Some population projections indicate that people of color will make up nearly half of the U.S. population by the year 2050 (Dovidio, 1993), and as the population is becoming more diverse, so are American workplaces and educational institutions. The *Workforce 2000* report (U.S. Department of Labor, 1987) noted that during the 1990s, about 85 percent of people entering the workforce will be people of color and women; only about 15 percent will be white males. Already at the beginning of that decade, more than half of the workforce was composed of minorities, women, and immigrants (Thomas, 1990). White males born in the United States, once a sizable majority of the labor force, were already a numerical minority by 1990, and the proportion of the workforce composed of this group will continue to decline through at least the first half of the twenty-first century. The younger segment of the population is even more diverse than the overall population, in part because birthrates among people of color in the United States are somewhat higher than among whites. Because of this greater diversity, the composition of students in schools is even more diverse than that of employees in workplaces, and as in the workplace, this composition will continue to become more diverse in coming years. The educational needs of these increasingly diverse students, along with the need to address the cultural conflicts and social tensions that sometimes accompany diversity, have led to a growing movement for *multiculturalism* in American education. This movement is discussed in some detail in Chapter 12, and for that reason, the main emphasis in this chapter's discussion of the diversity movement is on the workplace. Many of the trends and issues involved are similar in both work and education, however.

As the workforce continues to become more diverse, all Americans have a growing stake in equal opportunity and harmonious race relations. If racism, sexism, and other forms of discrimination prevent people of color, women, people with disabilities, and gay, lesbian, and bisexual people from becoming fully productive workers, then the entire economy will suffer. Moreover, this will occur in a global economy in which international competition demands efficiency and productivity. If the United States does not fully utilize the talents of its women, people of color, and other minority groups, then its productivity will suffer and it will lose out relative to international competition. In addition, any company that does not fully utilize the human resources of all of its diverse employees will similarly suffer.

For these reasons, increasing numbers of companies have come to view diversity as an issue they must address not merely out of principle but because the productivity and success of the company depends on it (Galagan, 1993). It is equally important for work organizations in the United States to address racial and cultural tensions and conflicts among their workers. These conflicts can disrupt the work

As illustrated by this meeting of corporate executives, America's work force is becoming more diverse. The most effective work organizations will be ones that create an environment in which diverse people work cooperatively and all feel that they are making a valued contribution. *Stock Boston, Inc./Stephen Agricola*

process, and they often lead to feelings of isolation and unwantedness among minority group workers, which in some cases result in unnecessary attrition among these workers. An example of this can be seen in a survey at Monsanto, where attrition rates of women and people of color were two to four times that of white males before the company initiated its diversity-management program. The survey revealed that the main reasons for this attrition included poor relations with supervisors and a perception among women and people of color that they were being given work that would not lead anywhere (Galagan, 1993).

Attrition among minority and female workers also occurs when they encounter **glass ceilings**—limited upward mobility within a company, which keeps them from moving into top executive and managerial positions. Such glass ceilings not only limit opportunity for minority and female employees, but they also deprive the company of the talents of women and people of color with the ability and experience to be good managers (Thomas, 1990). For example, among female professionals and managers who leave their jobs, 73 percent do so because they see limited opportunities for women in their companies (Morrison, 1993). The perception of limited opportunity among women and people of color appears to reflect reality: Much research shows that the higher the rank within an organization, the greater the disparities in promotions along the lines of race, ethnicity, and gender. Dovidio (1993) has shown this to be true for the U.S. armed forces, the federal government, and the one thousand largest corporations. Dovidio uses the U.S. Navy to illustrate this. African Americans make up 13 percent of the Navy but only 5 percent of the officers and 1.5 percent of the admirals. These differences cannot be explained by differences in the backgrounds of blacks and whites in the Navy. However, a survey conducted by Dovidio may offer the answer: When applicants have weak credentials, whites rank black and white applicants similarly—both are ranked low. However, when black and white applicants present strong credentials, but with the black and white applicant still having qualifications similar to one another, something quite different happens. In this situation, whites tend to rank both applicants positively, but they rank the white applicant higher than the black applicant (Dovidio, 1993, p. 56). This is consistent with a subtle form of modern racism in which whites do not assign negative characteristics to minority groups more than they do to whites, but they do assign whites more positive characteristics than they assign minorities. This behavior appears to reflect prejudice in the sense that difference is often equated with deficiency by majority group managers, and it also undoubtedly reflects the fact that managers have a greater comfort level dealing with people who are similar to themselves. Morrison (1993) lists such prejudices and "comfort-level" concerns as being among the greatest barriers to the advancement of women and people of color in the workplace.

Diversity Management in the Workplace

Because of such concerns, a growing number of employers have initiated *diversity management* programs in recent years. The objectives of such programs are to empower all employees, particularly women and people of color, to work, produce, and advance in the organization up to their full potential. They also aim to address intergroup tensions and conflicts in the workplace that interfere with productivity and often limit the opportunities of workers on the basis of their race, ethnicity, gender, disability status, or sexual orientation. According to a study in the early 1990s,

27 percent of companies in North America had initiated some type of diversity management program (*Jet*, 1993c). Similar programs have been established to address diversity among the employees of many governmental, nonprofit, and educational organizations, as well as the U.S. military. While the majority of work organizations still do not have such programs, many of the largest ones do. Among the work organizations that have been recognized for having particularly strong and effective diversity management programs are Monsanto, Corning, American Express, Xerox, DuPont, the Fairfax County (VA) public schools, the Palo Alto (CA) police department, Procter and Gamble, Avon, Digital, and U.S. West (Thomas, 1990; LaPorte, 1991; Morrison, 1993).

Diversity management programs are designed in a variety of ways, and it is quite clear that there is no one "right way" to go about managing and promoting diversity in the workplace. For example, there are debates about the extent to which programs should focus on attitudes as opposed to behavior. Some experts in the field argue that much of the problem lies in prejudices and that to be effective, programs must address such prejudices. For example Howard Ehrlich, director of the National Institute Against Prejudice and Violence (quoted in Solomon, 1992), points out that bad economic conditions and job loss in recent years have given rise to economic fears among many workers. Workers often focus their fears on competition from other racial, ethnic, or cultural groups. As will be discussed later in this chapter, these fears have given rise to a sharp increase in hate crimes and hate-group activities in recent years, and this trend is often manifested by prejudice and discrimination in the workplace: often by white-male workers who fear loss of their jobs and who feel threatened by improvements in the status of women, African Americans, Latinos, and others. Ehrlich argues that such feelings and prejudices must be dealt with directly, and that if employers do not deal with prejudice, it will likely be expressed in the form of hate acts and disruptive and potentially violent incidents in the workplace.

Others argue that the main focus of diversity management should be on behavior, not attitudes (Janet Himler, quoted in Solomon, 1992; Elsie Y. Cross, interviewed by Cutler, 1993). This argument is based on the fact that it is behavior that directly affects the opportunities of minority employees, as well as creating incidents and conflicts in the workplace. An employer can say, "Think whatever you want, but intolerant behavior will not be permitted in this workplace." An example of this is cited by Ehrlich (1990). At Ethcon, a company that developed a diversity management program in the late 1980s, an outside consultant at a sales meeting made fun of the company's diversity guidelines and told an off-color joke during his presentation. The consultant was dismissed on the spot by the sales manager, sending a powerful message that behaviors unsupportive of diversity would not be tolerated in the company. It may be, of course, that the most effective approach is one that clearly states that discriminatory or intolerant behaviors are unacceptable but also seeks to address the feelings, beliefs, and prejudices that give rise to such behaviors. In actual fact, that is what most diversity management programs do. It is also important to point out, as was discussed in Chapter 3, that changing behavior can often lead to changing attitudes. If people work cooperatively with individuals of different race, gender, ethnicity, disability status, or sexual orientation, their attitudes will often change to match their behavior. As they see that diverse groups can work cooperatively with each other, their attitudes toward working with others different from themselves will often change.

An example of addressing both behaviors and attitudes can be seen in the "consulting pairs" program developed at several establishments of the Monsanto company (Laabs, 1993). In this program, employees volunteer and are trained to serve as members of "consulting pairs," which have two main functions. One is to facilitate "join-up" meetings between supervisors and employees who are newly assigned to one another. The gender and ethnic composition of the consulting pair is matched to that of the employee and supervisor. In the join-up meeting, the consulting pair helps the employee and supervisor address mutual expectations and mutual understanding of developmental needs. The latter helps the supervisor to see what skills the employee would like to develop and where the employee would like to go in the company, and also helps the supervisor to identify interests and skills in the employee that can be utilized to the company's advantage. The join-up meeting also addresses organizational norms and personal "hot-button" issues of the supervisor and employee (such as annoyance when people show up late for meetings), so that inadvertent conflicts and misunderstandings can be avoided. This is important, because in a culturally diverse environment and in a polarized society, conflicts that may initially have nothing to do with race, gender, or culture quickly become defined in racial, gender, or cultural terms. This is probably inevitable as long as society remains deeply polarized and divided along the lines of race, gender, and culture.

This reality is demonstrated in a discussion by Monsanto diversity manager Tom Cummins of a case involving the other use of the consulting pairs—mediation and resolution of disputes in which diversity issues may play some role (quoted in Laabs, 1993). In this example, a dispute arose between a white-male senior manager and a black-male manager under his supervision. The white senior manager saw the black manager as unresponsive to his requests and consequently felt that the manager was not learning his job as he should be. The manager felt that his boss was watching him too closely and hovering over him in a way that would not be done with white managers. He saw this as interfering with his ability to work and take the initiative on his own, which he highly valued. When the consulting pair met with the two, it came to light that the white senior manager loved to teach and to get his hands on the work of middle-management employees under his supervision. It also came out that the black middle manager wanted to work independently and perceived the senior manager as interfering and not trusting him. It became clear that the issue did not have a racial basis at the start but simply reflected the different and somewhat conflicting work styles of the two managers. In a racially divided society, however, the conflict was quickly perceived in racial terms. Once the two managers understood that the basis of their conflict was a difference in their work styles, they were able to work out their differences, and from that point on, they worked well together without further conflict. Cummins points out that in the absence of the consulting pair, the conflict would have festered. The results of this could have been increased racial conflict and tension, a bad working relationship between the two managers, and possibly the loss of the black manager. With the consulting pair, none of this happened.

Characteristics of Effective Diversity Management Programs

While the specifics of different diversity management programs vary, the Monsanto example points out some key principles that are important in any diversity management program. One is that those involved in the diversity management program must themselves be diverse. One ingredient of the success of the consulting-pairs program at Monsanto is that the pairs are set up to match the characteristics of the people they assist. Thus, each party is assured of having someone with similar characteristics on the consulting pair. Also, diversity is important among diversity trainers because people sometimes will accept a message from a member of their own group that they would not accept from a member of another group. Thus, diversity training or management programs work best when those carrying out the program have the same mix of characteristics as the people in the organization.

Another key principle in managing diversity, also illustrated by the Monsanto example, is the importance of dealing with issues promptly rather than letting them fester. In fact, the opportunity to do that is one major advantage of having a diversity management program. Diversity consultant Bob Abrams (quoted in Solomon, 1992) illustrates this by describing a racial incident between a radio dispatcher and a truck driver who could not see one another. The driver informed the dispatcher that materials he was supposed to pick up were not ready, since the loading dock appeared to be empty. The dispatcher, who did not know the driver, replied, "Even a one-eyed nigger can see that. They certainly don't have the material ready to go." Nobody reported the incident, and it festered for more than four years until a diversity-training workshop, in which the truck driver, an African American, reported it and described the pain of living with such an ethnic slur, even though the dispatcher had not aimed it at him personally. According to Abrams, a good diversity management program would have given the driver an opportunity to report the incident and express the hurt that he felt, and to address the issue promptly. According to Abrams, "You can't let this stuff slide, because it impairs team ability to function. If you don't have a willingness to address these problems, you'll have serious problems in a team, working together." According to Solomon, such problems, if left unaddressed, often fester until they are expressed in diversity workshops, discrimination complaints, lawsuits, or exit interviews.

Another concept that is regularly cited as an element of successful diversity management programs is setting specific, clear, and quantitative goals, articulated and actively supported by top management. Morrison (1993) points out that accountability must be a feature of an effective diversity management program: There must be a way of determining whether or not the program achieved what it was supposed to, and there must be a message that it is important to top management that these goals are attained. Morrison says, "I believe that diversity efforts that don't have statistical goals are doomed. The reluctance of managers to hold themselves and others to some numbers has probably done more damage to diversity efforts than anything else" (p. 43). As Morrison's comment suggests, one way of achieving such accountability is to make diversity one of the criteria for evaluating organizational units and individuals: Are the units and individuals working to address diversity issues, and how effectively are they doing so?

Such accountability has received growing emphasis in both the business world and the world of education. In the business world, most of the companies with effective diversity management programs have moved to include diversity issues in annual employee evaluations. In higher education, diversity criteria have begun to be included in recent years in evaluations of schools for accreditation. In 1994, for example, the Western Association of Schools and Colleges approved the inclusion of diversity guidelines in its review procedure for accreditation of colleges and universities (Leatherman, 1994). The guidelines were designed to assist the association in evaluating the extent to which schools were complying with a 1988 standard requiring that colleges foster ethnic diversity on their campuses. Although fourteen member colleges protested the guidelines—sometimes quite loudly—as intrusions on their autonomy, 83 percent of the member colleges of the accreditation association supported the guidelines.

Finally, successful diversity management programs must both address the concerns of and raise the awareness of white males, who often feel threatened or attacked by such programs and frequently do not understand why such programs are needed. As has been discussed in other contexts earlier in this book, white males do not experience discrimination the way that other groups in society do, and consequently they often do not understand the realities of discrimination and inequality that people of color and women regularly encounter (see, for example, Kluegel, 1990). Thus, effective diversity management programs, such as that at Monsanto, place substantial emphasis on using examples to help white males become more aware of the realities experienced by other groups (Galagan, 1993, p. 49). As long as white males are not aware of these realities, there is a good chance that white males will behave in ways that counteract diversity efforts to support and develop minority and female employees and that they will fail to understand the reasons for diversity efforts and therefore oppose or feel threatened by such efforts. Thus, the effective diversity management program does two things: (1) It helps to develop minority employees by assuring that they get the support, encouragement, and opportunity that they are often denied in predominantly white-male organizations, and (2) it helps to prepare the majority-dominated work group to accept and work effectively with minority and female employees (Galagan, 1993).

Diversity Management and Multiculturalism

As we saw earlier with multicultural education, workplace diversity programs reflect a recognition that U.S. society is becoming more multicultural or pluralist and less assimilationist. In other words, racial, ethnic, and cultural groups today are placing a stronger emphasis on affirming and retaining their own distinctive cultures. This is reflected in the comment of one leading diversity manager that "as people begin to celebrate being different, they're no longer willing to get into that melting pot" (Roosevelt Thomas, quoted in Nicklin, 1992). Some people have criticized the tendency toward multiculturalism and pluralism on the ground that it creates divisions that inhibit cooperation in society. As we saw in earlier chapters, however, such pluralism is probably inevitable in a society such as the United States, where much of the population consists of minority groups, such as African Americans, Native Americans, Mexican Americans, and Puerto Ricans, whose initial entry into American society was involuntary. Moreover, there is growing evidence that over the long run, a more diverse work group is more effective, because it can offer a wider variety of ideas and ways of dealing with issues and problems and because it can often better address the needs of an equally diverse base of potential customers and clients. Evidence of the former can be seen in a recent study comparing homogenous and diverse work groups. The study found that, while the diverse groups did have more difficulty working together at first, they were more productive over the long term (Watson, Kumar, and Michealsen, 1993). The main reason was that diverse groups did a better job of examining different viewpoints and of devising possible responses. Matching the diversity of the workforce to that of customers can also be important. Livingston (1991) cites the example of Nadia Ali, southwest regional manager for the gift store chain Things Remembered. Ali discovered that, although nearly half the customers in her region were Spanish-speaking, nearly all the retail staff spoke only English. She addressed this by making the ability to speak Spanish a hiring criterion for new recruits and offering free Spanish lessons to present employees. The results both increased the diversity of the workforce and the effectiveness of the business. Sales rose by 13 percent, and employee turnover fell to less than one-fourth the companywide rate of turnover. Thus, as these examples show, diversity and multiculturalism in the workplace not only are inevitable realities but they also can often help a work organization become more adaptable and more in tune with its customers or clients.

HATE-GROUP ACTIVITY AND HATE CRIME IN THE 1990S

A disturbing trend in recent years has been the substantial increase in hate-group activity and hate crime in the United States (Levin and McDevitt, 1993). In 1992, the number of hate crimes in the United States was the highest since systematic records on hate crime were first kept in 1979 (Southern Poverty Law Center, 1993a). That year, there was a record thirty-one bias-motivated murders, compared with twenty-seven in 1991 and twenty in 1990. In 1993, there were 30 bias-motivated murders, and the overall level of hate crime remained at 1992's record level (Southern Poverty Law Center, 1994). Bias-related assaults also rose sharply in 1992, and acts of vandalism inspired by hatred rose by nearly 50 percent between 1991 and 1992. Hate crimes are targeted at a very wide variety of groups, but those most commonly targeted are African Americans, Arab Americans, Jews, and homosexuals. In the early 1990s, attacks against several of these groups were at or near record levels. The number of anti-Semitic incidents in 1991 was the highest since the Anti-Defamation League began its annual audit, and attacks against gay people rose 31 percent between 1990 and 1991 in five major cities (Solomon, 1992). The Arab American Anti-Discrimination Committee reported a similar surge in hate crimes against Arab Americans: Such crimes tripled in 1991 as compared with 1990 (*Belleville News–Democrat*, 1992).

Some examples may serve to illustrate the types of hate crime that have occurred in recent years, as well as the connection of organized groups such as the White Aryan Resistance (WAR), Church of the Creator (COTC), and some factions of the Ku Klux Klan to this violence. In Portland, Oregon, in 1988, a group of skinheads beat an Ethiopian college student to death. The courts later found that Tom Metzger, leader of WAR, had played a key role in inciting this crime and award $12.5 million in damages to relatives of the man who was murdered, to be paid by Metzger and WAR. A similar legal action by the Southern Poverty Law Center, a group that monitors and combats hate organizations, led to the disbanding of a Klan faction known as the Invisible Empire, after members of that group severely beat a group of civil rights marchers celebrating Martin Luther King's birthday in Forsythe County, Georgia, in 1987. In Japan, an enlistee in the U.S. Navy was beaten to death in 1992 by fellow sailors because he was gay. In St. Louis in 1993, two white men in a pickup truck chased, ran over, and killed a black man. A nearly identical incident also happened in 1993 in West Palm Beach, Florida, leading to the death of another black man. In 1993, gay men were stabbed to death in New Orleans and Everett, Wash-

Ku Klux Klan members are confronted by protesters at a recent march in Texas. Hate group activity increased in the late 1980s and early 1990s, and scenes like this became increasingly common. *Bettman/Reuters*

ington, and a gay man was beaten to death in Azusa, California. In 1992, a homeless black man was stabbed to death when a group of skinheads with connections to several hate groups, including a Klan faction and a renegade chapter of WAR, went out to "bash" minorities, homosexuals, and Jews following a drunken celebration of Adolf Hitler's birthday (Southern Poverty Law Center, 1993c). In 1991, a black naval officer was murdered by a minister in the COTC. In 1992, the Los Angeles riot and attacks on Arab and Muslim Americans during the Persian Gulf War added to the toll.

Groups such as the Klan (which is actually composed of about twenty factions that often compete with one another for membership and publicity), WAR, COTC, and others have also become increasingly visible in recent years. In 1994, for example, the Klan held rallies in about a dozen state capitals to protest the Martin Luther King holiday. In the fall of 1993, Klan and other white-supremacist rallies drew crowds in the hundreds in Illinois, Indiana, and Pennsylvania. Increasingly, hate groups have used modern communications technologies such as computer bulletin boards, telephone voice mail hotlines, and fax networks to spread their messages. For example, a fax newsletter dated October 7, 1993, defended two white supremacists who shot a policeman to death because he asked for their drivers' licenses: They felt that since they were from Florida, they should not have to show

David Duke is shown here in Klan garb giving a Nazi salute, and a few years later, running for governor of Louisiana. He won the Republican primary but lost in the general election. However, in the general election he did receive the majority of the white vote. *Sygma/Michael P. Smith/Lee Corkran*

their drivers' licenses in Alabama (*Outpost* fax newsletter, quoted in Southern Poverty Law Center, 1993d). One of the persons who did the shooting later said, "A man died because he defended bad policy, and because we were forced to defend our lives and our principles, against further submission to bad policy" (Southern Poverty Law Center, 1993d). The individual who made these statements had connections with Christian Identity and Posse Comitatus, white-supremacist groups with histories of violent clashes with law enforcement agencies and a variety of other legal problems. Computer bulletin boards are also widely used by white-supremacist and hate groups to communicate with one another and to promote events and rallies. Both locally and nationally, groups such as WAR operate telephone hotlines that allow callers to listen to messages full of racial epithets and to express interest in joining the organization, without permitting outsiders to know the identity of the people in the organization. In a similar vein, Klan factions, WAR, and a variety of skinhead groups have anonymously leafleted schools and colleges in recent years in an attempt to recruit young people and to exploit racial tensions in schools and colleges.

Nearly all white-supremacist organizations also use newsletters to communicate with their members and to recruit new members. Typically, these newsletters portray whites as an oppressed group in society, the victims of a conspiracy that is said to involve Jews, blacks, communists, homosexuals, and others. Often they use the language of religion to support their message. The Knights of the Ku Klux Klan (currently the largest Klan faction), for example, refers to itself as a "white Christian organization" and argues that the United States was founded as a "white Christian society." This is used to justify the segregation of blacks, Jews, Latinos, homosexuals, Arabs, Asians, and anyone else who does not fall within the Klan's definition of "white Christians." Some of these organizations have sought to become media savvy, denying that they are hate organizations while at the same time giving whites the message that their troubles in life are attributable to blacks, Latinos, Jews, Asians, homosexuals, and other minorities. Their newsletters reflect this viewpoint, and they actively seek interviews with the mainstream media to deny that they are hate organizations while spreading the message that working-class whites suffer because of gains by minority groups. Others advocate violence and hatred much more openly. An anti-Semitic diatribe in a December 1993 WAR newsletter, for example, called for guerrilla warfare, stating, "First, we have men willing to wage this war, though in a disassociated state. Second, we have free access to small arms and ammunition, again in a disassociated state. . . . In any case, where a Jew or an ally of the Jews is found, and they can be easily recognized by their class-distinctive possessions, he will be dispatched. . . . The last phase of the operation will be the use of heavy weapons against the enemy's citadels and residences. We will be in no hurry to negotiate with him in light of his treacherous nature."

Causes of Increased Hate-Group Activity

While there is no evidence that prejudice has increased since the early 1980s, it is clear that there is much more open expression of hatred and prejudice, more hate crime, more hate-group activity, and probably more people becoming involved in hate groups than was the case in the late 1970s or early 1980s. In some cases, these groups, particularly when they take the "media-savvy" route described above, have also been successful in drawing the support of a sizable segment of the white population. In 1991, for example, David Duke, a former leader of the Knights of the Ku Klux Klan, won the Republican primary election for governor of Louisiana and received the majority of the white vote in the general election. Only overwhelming opposition from black voters kept him from winning the general election. Why have these changes taken place?

There are a variety of reasons, including bad economic conditions, increasing socioeconomic inequality in the United States, a general increase in societal violence, and irresponsible statements and actions by many political leaders.

Bad Economic Conditions. In the 1980s and early 1990s, the economic situation of many Americans—particularly those in the middle, working, and lower classes—worsened. In part, this was because the productivity of the American economy has grown at a far slower pace in the past two decades than was the case in the 1950s, 1960s, and early 1970s (Farley, 1992b, p. 411). When productivity does not grow, neither can the standard of living. In 1988—around the time when the increase in hate crime began to be evident—real (that is, inflation-adjusted) hourly and weekly wages in the United States were lower than at any point since before 1970 (U.S. Bureau of the Census, 1990, p. 407). In part, people compensated for this by working longer hours, and in many families, wives entered the labor force (Olsen, 1990). This is particularly true for younger adults who have entered the workforce in recent years. Young adults and young families today receive less income, after adjustment for inflation, than did young adults twenty years ago.

Growing Economic Inequality. These conditions have been worsened by an increase in economic inequality. Especially for workers in the lower and middle ranges of income, wages have fallen after adjustment for inflation. This is because increasing economic inequality has shifted income away from those in the middle and lower income ranges toward those at the top. Between 1968 and 1988, for example, the share of total income received by the top 5 percent of U.S. families rose from about 15 percent to about 19 percent. During the same time, the share received by the bottom 20 percent of families—four times as many families—*fell* from 5.2 percent to 4.1 percent (Farley, 1994, p. 219). In other words, the lower 20 percent lost one-fifth of their share of income, while the share going to those at the top increased by nearly one-third. In plain terms, the rich got richer and the poor got poorer (Bartlett and Steele, 1992). In a practical sense, this redistribution of income from the poor to the rich worsened the effect of stagnant economic growth on those in the lower ranges of income. At the same time as the overall size of the economic pie was getting smaller, so was the share of the pie going to those on the bottom. Much of the reason for this growing economic inequality was that good-paying manufacturing jobs were being eliminated (Bartlett and Steele, 1992). Many Americans lost their jobs, and economists were increasingly telling people that they should expect to have several jobs or even careers over their lifetimes. In addition to job loss and declining real income, many Americans, particularly in the middle and working classes, have found it increasingly difficult to afford sending their children to college, which has become increasingly necessary for the better jobs. This is the case because tuition has risen faster than the cost of living, and financial aid has not kept pace.

In effect, what all this meant was more competition and greater scarcity. Many Americans could no longer be sure that they would be able to hang on to the standard of living that they had enjoyed in the past, or to help their children to enjoy a good standard of living when they grow up. This has had several effects. It has led people to perceive groups different from themselves as potential competitors, to be feared and seen as a threat. It has also led people to feel less secure and to look for scapegoats to blame for their declining fortunes. It is no coincidence that competition and perceived threat, feelings of personal insecurity, and a need to scapegoat have all been identified as factors contributing to prejudice (see Chapter 2). It is perhaps for these reasons that the highest levels of prejudice have generally been found in people experiencing downward economic mobility, that is, people whose economic situations are getting worse (Wilensky and Edwards, 1959). Similarly, whites who feel their positions to be the most threatened are the most opposed to desegregation (Smith, 1981). These reasons help to explain why, as was noted earlier in this book, support for hate groups such as the Ku Klux Klan has always been strongest among working-class and poor whites.

Given all this, it is not surprising that as the conditions of the white working and middle classes worsened in the 1980s, hate-group activity and hate violence rose. Many viewed minorities as the source of their economic difficulties, thinking that if only there were no civil rights laws and affirmative action, their economic lot would be better. In particular, many white males began to believe that white males are a persecuted group, being made to pay for past injustices to women and minorities.

In fact, there is no evidence that gains by minorities had anything to do with the worsening condition of the white working and middle classes. Statistics such as median family income reveal quickly that minorities have not, overall, gained economic ground relative to non-Hispanic whites. The ratio of the black median family income to that of whites has changed very little in recent decades, with black families receiving only about 60 percent of the median income of white families, with only minor year-to-year variations. In 1990, for example, the median income of black families was 58 percent that of white families (U.S. Bureau of the Census, 1991b). The median family income of Latinos in the United States, 63 percent that of white Anglos in 1991, has actually fallen relative to white Anglos. Thus, the reality is that the redistribution of income has *not* been from whites to minorities. Rather, it has been from lower-income people of all races to upper-income people, most of whom are white. Similarly, it is also true that whites remain more likely to be employed and more likely to attend and graduate from college than either African Americans or Latinos. Finally, there is no objective basis for the view that white males are being singled out and made to pay for "sins of the past." In fact, white males continue to enjoy higher incomes than any other group, even when comparisons are made between people with identical levels of education. They also remain greatly overrepresented in the political and corporate power structures. White males may not enjoy the same degree of advantage over other groups that they once did, but with respect to economics and political power, they remain advantaged compared with any other group. Reality does not matter as much as perception, however, and the perception of many whites (particularly white males) is that they are losing jobs, income, and opportunities for education, all of which are being gained by minorities.

Statements and Actions of Political Leaders. One reason for such perceptions lies in irresponsible statements and actions by political leaders, who have often used the economic fears of whites as a way of getting votes. This can be illustrated by several of the statements and actions of George Bush, who campaigned for the presidency in 1988 and served from 1989 through 1992. In his 1988 campaign, Bush supporters bought television ads showing Willie Horton, a black male who had committed a crime after being furloughed from the Massachusetts prison system. The photos, designed to make Horton look as threatening as possible, were used to tell voters that if Bush's opponent, the governor of Massachusetts, was elected, people like Horton could be running loose committing crimes everywhere. The Bush ads did not mention that nearly every state, including Bush's home state of Texas, which at the time had a governor of Bush's party, had a similar program. They also did not mention that at least half of the people furloughed under such programs were white. Rather, they played on the criminal stereotype of blacks that had been reinforced by the media for so long that much of the public believed it. The strategy worked, and Bush won the election.

Bush and other politicians used similar tactics in the following years. From 1989 until 1991, Bush referred to what eventually became the 1991 Civil Rights Act as a "quota bill." In fact, this law, discussed earlier in this book, at first said nothing at all about quotas. It was, instead, designed to reverse several Supreme Court decisions, including one that stated that job-qualification requirements with the effect of discriminating against minorities were entirely legal unless their *intent* was to discriminate. What the civil rights law actually said was that such discriminatory requirements would be made illegal unless it could be shown that they relate in some way to the employee's ability to do the job. When Bush, the U.S. Chamber of Commerce, and a number of conservative politicians argued that the bill would lead employers to use quotas to include minorities as a way of avoiding charges that they violated the law, the proposed law was changed. It was amended to state that quotas were *not* to be used in hiring. Even after this, however, Bush and a number of other politicians continued to call it a quota bill.

In a context such as this, when many whites were experiencing worsening economic conditions, the statements of Bush and others made it easy for whites to believe that the reasons for their economic hardships had to do with quotas that were allowing minorities to gain while they suffered. There was no factual basis in this belief, but hearing Bush and other politicians constantly talking about a "quota bill" made it easy for many whites to believe. Moreover, this viewpoint was constantly repeated by hate groups and their leaders. When David Duke, the former Klan leader, ran for the U.S. Senate in Louisiana, he made this a central part of his campaign. As noted above, he won the Republican primary and got the majority of the white vote in the general election.

After Duke won the primary, Bush reversed his position on the civil rights law, and it was finally enacted as the Civil Rights Act of 1991. Bush's explanation at the time was that the law had been changed in ways that made it acceptable, but the law Bush endorsed was virtually identical to the one he had opposed before the primary. It has been suggested that the real reason for the change is that Bush and other leaders realized that their position was similar to the one Duke was articulating when he won the Louisiana primary, and they did not want to be associated with someone like Duke, who as a former Klan leader was linked directly with racism in the mind of the public (Cohen, 1992). In spite of this, some politicians in the 1992 and 1994 elections continued to use racial "code words." This term refers to words that are used to indirectly refer to race and call on people's racial prejudice. This is done indirectly, because open racism is no longer socially acceptable and generates controversy. Less direct appeals to racial fears and prejudices, however, are less likely to generate controversy and may get votes.

An example of the use of racial code words can be seen in the 1992 campaigns for governor in Missouri, during which candidates in both parties used such tactics. The Republican nominee for governor, along with another candidate running for attorney general, both used the phrase "unfair desegregation payments" repeatedly in virtually every campaign commercial. They did not directly say that schools should be segregated, but by repeating the phrase were able to appeal indirectly to people who felt that way. In the Democratic primary, a white candidate tried to patch up past bad relations with the black community by using a reverse form of racial code—when campaigning in a black neighborhood in St. Louis, he referred to his opponent as the "redneck from Rolla," thus implying that the opponent's rural background meant that he would be prejudiced against blacks. When political leaders are willing to exploit racial fears and divisions in ways such as these to get votes, the fears, divisions, and tensions are often heightened. Given the common use of racial code words by politicians and distortions such as the "quota-bill" statements by Bush and a number of others, it is not surprising that racial tensions are sometimes heightened to the point that they boil over in the form of hate crimes and increased hate-group activity.

Reaction to Change? It may also be that, in some ways, the current surge in hate crime represents something of a reaction to progressive changes that are occurring in our society. This has happened in the past. The Ku Klux Klan enjoyed a surge in membership during the 1960s, for example, as whites reacted to the passage of civil rights legislation. Something of the same thing may now be occurring in response to renewed efforts in the 1990s to increase diversity in the workplace and in colleges and universities, as well as to the changing racial and ethnic composition of the population. For example, some workplaces and colleges that were once all-white have become more racially diverse in recent years (in part due to diversity efforts and in part because society has become more diverse). In response, people who do not want such change sometimes resist. Moreover, when people who have lived all their lives in a basically segregated society encounter diversity for the first time, some will respond with fear, and incidents may begin simply because people do not understand what behavior may or may not be acceptable to people of different backgrounds. Often, such incidents subsequently escalate as evidence of mutual misunderstanding mounts.

In a somewhat similar vein, efforts to promote greater sensitivity to people who are different from oneself have sometimes been derided as "political correctness" in recent years, and this reaction may be fueling a backlash. Both students and colleagues have suggested to me that one reason that some people engage in hate speech is because it has become socially taboo in some circles; hence, it becomes a form of rebellion. At the same time, however, there are many other forms of rebellion in today's society that do not involve hatred, and it appears likely that those who engage in hate speech as a form of rebellion have significant attitude differences from those who rebel in other ways. In some individuals, rebellion may combine with fears and prejudices like those described in preceding sections to produce hate speech, hate group activity, and in extreme cases, hate crimes. (The issue of hate speech codes and the "political correctness" debate is the next major topic discussed in this chapter, so a more detailed discussion of these issues is deferred until that section.) In others without such fears and prejudices, rebellion is more likely to take other forms.

Growing Societal Violence. Finally, it must be noted that violence of all types increased in the United States during the late 1980s and early 1990s. The total rate of violent crime had reached an all-time record by 1989 (Federal Bureau of Investigation, 1990), and many cities experienced record homicide rates in the early 1990s. It would appear that, as society became more violent in the late 1980s and early 1990s, so did the expression of racial and cultural prejudices and tensions (Southern Poverty Law Center, 1993a).

COMBATING HATRED: DEBATES OVER SPEECH CODES AND "POLITICAL CORRECTNESS"

As hate-group activity increased in the late 1980s and early 1990s, a number of debates arose about what is the best way to respond to such activity. A good deal of hate-group activity occurred on college campuses, leading to ugly and sometimes violent incidents. Consequently, much of the debate over how to respond has focused on colleges and universities. In many cases, this has happened because students, faculty, and administrators outraged by acts of hatred have insisted that something be done about the problem. One of the first such incidents occurred in 1987 at the University of Michigan, when a racist joke was told on the campus radio station, followed quickly by other incidents in which racist flyers were passed under the doors of black students' rooms in a dormitory. Outraged by these events, African American students and some white supporters staged a series of demonstrations that lasted nearly two months, leading to a renewal of an unfulfilled 1970 commitment by the university to raise black enrollment to the black percentage of the state's population. The incidents, however, continued to spread to other campuses. Some of the incidents have been violent: At the University of Massachusetts, a white mob beat several black students after they expressed support for the Boston Red Sox's opponent in the World Series, the New York Mets. Three Jewish students were attacked at Brooklyn College, and homosexual students were attacked on several campuses.

Other incidents did not involve violence but did involve threats, name calling, and other forms of ethnic harassment. At Dartmouth University, many people on campus were outraged when a conservative campus newspaper, the *Dartmouth Review*, wrote a derogatory article about an African American professor, among other things referring to him as a "Brillo pad." The paper also printed a sarcastic column in "Black English" and an anti-Semitic quote from Hitler's *Mein Kampf*. An African American homecoming queen was booed at the University of Alabama; thirteen Asian American faculty members received anonymous hate letters at the University of Minnesota; and at the University of Florida, a white student union was formed and quickly established contact with a former Ku Klux Klan official. Such groups usually seek to maintain the advantages whites enjoy in society, and are often fronts for hate groups. In addition to the Klan, WAR has also played a key role in the establishment of white student unions on several college campuses, particularly in the West (Levin and McDevitt, 1994).

Incidents like those described above have occurred on campuses throughout the United States and have been targeted against African Americans, Latinos, Asians, Jews, women, and gay and lesbian students. They have also occurred on a more or less continuous basis since the late 1980s. In the 1993–1994 school year, for example, conflicts erupted over a cartoon in the University of Iowa student newspaper that was widely seen as racist, a Ku Klux Klan tattoo worn by a worker at Iowa State University, and a column in the State University of New York at Stony Brook newspaper. In that column, the campus editor, who was Jewish, described incidents of anti-Semitic name calling by African American students, then described himself as "at times, downright revolted by African Americans."

In some cases, the offensive statements and actions have come not from students but from professors and administrators. At the University of Washington, the president of the university, while presenting an award for academic achievement to a Latino engineering student, commented that the student may have acquired his interest in the highway system "while driving down the highway at 70 miles per hour in the middle of the night to keep ahead of immigration officials." Later, a faculty member at the same university wrote a journal article alleging that the president had been unfairly criticized for this remark (Alexander, 1990). When role models such as university presidents and faculty members engage in behavior that says such stereotyping is all right, it may not be surprising that students sometimes express their own prejudices.

Because incidents such as these clearly make college and university campuses unwelcoming and unsupportive places for the groups against which they are targeted, many faculty, administrators, and students have undertaken efforts to prevent such incidents. The most controversial of these efforts involve *hate-speech codes*, which have sought to prevent people from use of racial, ethnic, or cultural slurs, insults, and name calling. After over 150 incidents, the University of Wisconsin decided to ban racist comments, pledging to provide students with an environment free of hostility and intimidation. Other campuses followed suit, and a number of local and state governmental units also passed laws against ethnic intimidation. These actions have been controversial, for two main reasons. First, many people believe that they improperly restrict free speech, setting a precedent that could be used against anyone who says something that someone else deems offensive. A related charge is that they involve an effort to enforce what many people have called "political correctness"—a term that is notoriously ill defined but often refers to efforts to ban anything that liberals, diversity advocates, minority groups, or feminists find offensive. (As we shall see shortly, conservatives, religious fundamentalists, and opponents of minority rights are at least as guilty of imposing their viewpoints on others, but to a large extent, they have successfully placed the "political correctness" tag on their opponents.) The second major reason that speech codes have been controversial is that it is very dubious whether or not they work.

As a result of the free-speech concerns outlined above, the American Civil Liberties Union filed suit against the University of Wisconsin speech code, and the code was overturned in court. From a legal standpoint, speech that clearly constitutes threat or intimidation (e.g., "If I see you here again, I'm going to shoot you") can be regulated, but the mere expression of prejudice cannot. At other campuses, political pressures have led to changes in speech codes. At the University of Pennsylvania, a white student was suspended after calling a group of black women "water buffalo." Supporters of the student argued that his free speech rights were violated and that the university was merely trying to enforce an arbitrary standard of political correctness. Eventually, the speech code was modified.

The outcry by conservatives that such speech codes restrict free speech and attempt to enforce arbitrary standards of political correctness may well be valid but it is worthwhile to ask why the "PC" (political correctness) label has been applied only in instances in which restrictions have been aimed at preventing insensitivity to minority groups. There are, after all, numerous other instances in which groups of all political viewpoints have attempted to impose their views on others and restrict views opposed to their own. In early 1994, for example, the Belleville, Illinois, school board banned a sex education book that had been used in the Belleville schools for a number of years when church groups objected that the book did not say that premarital sex and homosexual behavior were morally wrong. The book did not express what the church groups viewed as the politically correct viewpoint, but nobody referred to its banning as a case of enforcing PC. Other examples may be seen in efforts to prevent the National Institute for the Humanities from funding gay-oriented art and in efforts to ban popular music with lyrics some find offensive. Incidents such as these suggest that opponents of diversity may object less to the idea of enforcing political correctness than they object to efforts to promote sensitivity to diversity itself.

Having said this, there are valid questions both about the constitutionality of hate-speech codes and about whether they work. Some opponents of speech codes have argued, for example, that they in effect make martyrs of those who are charged with violations. The individual who made the "water buffalo" remark at the University of Pennsylvania, for example, gained considerable media attention and was often portrayed as a victim. To the extent that people who express prejudices come to be seen as victims of the system, speech codes may have the opposite effect from what is intended. For these reasons as well as the constitutional challenges such as at the University of Wisconsin, most of the speech codes that have been implemented have later been modified or relaxed.

An alternative approach to the problem, which has now been applied in some way in more than half of all colleges and universities in the United States, is to establish a requirement that all students must have some course dealing with diversity, minority groups, multiculturalism, or intergroup relations to graduate. This idea is based on research, discussed earlier in this book, showing that education about diversity and intergroup relations is often an effective way of reducing prejudice. A common and long-recognized problem is that people most in need of such education often avoid it (Allport, 1954), which is why such courses have been made mandatory on so many campuses: A requirement is seen as the only way to get the people into such courses who need them the most. On some campuses that have established or considered establishing such requirements, the political-correctness argument has come up: It has been argued that, rather than containing sound academic content, such sources aim mainly at getting students to think in a certain way about diversity issues or represent capitulation to politically motivated demands by activist

College students at a class on diversity. Coursework in diversity, multiculturalism, or intergroup relations is now required for graduation at the majority of colleges and universities in the United States. *Stock Boston, Inc./Joseph Nettis*

students and faculty (Leatherman, 1994b, 1994c). Such arguments have not prevailed at most campuses, however, in part because intergroup relations has long been recognized as an area of specialization within several traditional academic disciplines, including sociology, psychology, anthropology, and speech communications. If they are based on the substantial body of research on issues related to race, ethnicity, gender, and sexual orientation that has been developed in these disciplines, such courses are as academically valid as courses in any other area.

In addition to courses, many colleges and universities have developed conflict-resolution teams involving students in a manner somewhat similar to that of the consulting pairs at Monsanto, described earlier in this chapter. In some racial/ethnic incidents, both parties may feel that their ethnic group has been insulted or that they have been ridiculed or humiliated based on their ethnicity. Such perceptions were evident in the State University of New York at Stony Brook case noted earlier: The student who wrote the editorial felt that he had been insulted because he was Jewish; African American students felt that they had been insulted because they were black. Conflict-resolution teams generally acknowledge the validity of such feelings while helping the people involved to communicate in ways that meet one another's needs and do not lead others to feel that their ethnicity is being ridiculed or attacked.

While both intergroup-education and conflict resolution efforts have been shown to be effective, it is important to keep in mind that neither these strategies nor hate-speech codes are likely to entirely prevent incidents of harassment and hate-group activity on college campuses. To a large extent, the campus, like any other organization or institution, reflects the larger society within which it exists. If there are racial, ethnic, and cultural tensions in the larger society, they will likely surface on college campuses as well. Hate-speech codes appear to have been a well-intentioned effort to deal with these tensions and with the forces that lead minority students to feel uncomfortable on predominantly white campuses. However, both legal and practical problems have led to the repeal or relaxing of speech codes on many of the campuses that once had them. Mandatory courses on diversity or intergroup relations and conflict-resolution programs offer somewhat more hope and have been somewhat less controversial. However, as long as intergroup tensions run high in the larger society, campuses are unlikely to be entirely free of incidents or of hate-group activity.

THE DISCRIMINATION-TESTING MOVEMENT

Another important trend in majority–minority relations is the emergence in recent years of the *discrimination-testing* movement. Testing for discrimination is an important technique for determining whether or not discrimination on the basis of race, ethnicity, gender, or other characteristics is occurring in some situation. This technique can be used either for research purposes, to see whether, where, and to what extent discrimination is occurring; or for purposes of law enforcement, to detect and punish illegal discrimination. While the technique has existed for a long time (see, for example, Pearce, 1976), it has come into increasing use in recent years because it is the most effective tool to use when many people are engaging in discrimination but almost nobody will admit that they are doing so. Largely, this is the case today: Civil rights laws have driven discrimination underground, in that few will openly admit to discrimination because most forms of deliberate racial, ethnic, religious, gender, and disability discrimination are illegal. However, testing studies show that a good deal of it still occurs.

In a discrimination-testing study, two people are sent to whatever business or organization is being tested for discrimination. It might be a store, a real-estate office, a lending institution, an auto dealership, or an apartment-rental office. The two people are chosen to be as similar as possible except for the characteristic on which discrimination might be based. They are instructed to behave similarly and to carefully record what happens as soon as the test is completed. They might shop, try to rent or buy housing, or ask about a car for sale, depending on what type of business is being tested. In some cases, testers have been wired with hidden microphones or surreptitiously videotaped, so that there is direct audiovisual evidence of whether or not discrimination occurred.

The process can be illustrated by describing a fair-housing test for racial discrimination in rental housing. In a test of this type, a black tester and a white tester of the same gender and similar age might visit an apartment rental office about an hour apart. Both would request similar types of apartments, and both would report similar family characteristics (e.g., divorced, one child of which they have custody) and similar incomes. They would carefully observe what information they were given, whether or not they were shown apartments and if so how many and what kinds, what they were told about the availability of apartments, what rent and deposit rates they were quoted, and whether or not any information was volunteered about the neighborhood. After the test, a test supervisor or study director would review

A woman applies to rent an apartment. In a fair housing test, two individuals or couples of different races who are similar in other regards (age, gender, income) visit a rental office to see if they are treated similarly or differently. *Photoedit/Michael Newman*

their information to see whether they were treated similarly or differently. Since virtually everything about the two testers was the same except their race, discrimination on the basis of race would be suspected if the two were treated differently in any important way. Suppose, for example, that both testers were told that the kind of apartment they wanted was available, but the white tester was told that she could move in with a $100 damage deposit and the African American tester was told that she would have to deposit two months' rent, which would come to $550. This would be very strong evidence of racial discrimination.

The discrimination-testing movement began mostly with fair-housing tests and has since spread to a variety of other areas. As noted, testing can be done either to determine the extent of discrimination or to enforce antidiscrimination law. Testing studies to determine the extent of discrimination have been undertaken by sociologists (Pearce, 1976), the mass media (ABC News, 1991), and by the government and government-sponsored organizations (U.S. Department of Housing and Urban Development, 1979, 1991).

All of these studies have detected racial discrimination. Both Pearce (1976) and the Department of Housing and Urban Development (1991) detected considerable evidence of *racial steering* in the real-estate industry: Whites are more likely to be directed toward all or mostly white areas, while blacks are more likely to be directed toward racially mixed or predominantly black neighborhoods—even when both approach the same real-estate office on the same day and have similar income and family characteristics. All told, the Department of Housing and Urban Development study found that the majority of all African American home buyers and renters, the majority of Latino home buyers, and almost half of Latino renters encountered some form of discrimination. Two studies sponsored by the mass media, a *60 Minutes* study testing for housing discrimination in the Chicago area in the late 1970s and a *Prime Time Live* study testing for discrimination in retail sales, hiring, auto sales, and apartment rentals in St. Louis in 1990, found widespread evidence of discrimination. In the *Prime Time Live* study (ABC News, 1991), a black man and a white man, both young college graduates, conducted tests for two weeks in a variety of different businesses around the St. Louis area over a period of two weeks. The black man encountered clear-cut discrimination every day over the two-week period. In Washington, D.C., in 1988, the Lawyer's Committee for Civil Rights had testers hail Washington taxicabs and found that blacks were nine times as likely as whites to be passed by (Mathews, 1992). In the same city, tests by the Fair Employment Council of Greater Washington, D.C., for discrimination against Hispanic job applicants found that Hispanic applicants encountered discrimination 22.4 percent of the time (Mathews, 1992).

In recent years, testing has increasingly been used both by the government and by private civil rights and fair-housing organizations, to enforce civil rights laws. In 1991, the Fair Employment Council of Greater Washington, D.C., for example, sent male and female testers to an employment agency that had been accused of sexual harassment. The female tester was offered a job if she would let the director of the employment agency be her "sugar daddy," while a male tester encountered no harassment (Mathews, 1992). In the early 1990s, the U.S. Department of Justice undertook a series of fair-housing rental tests in several cities. By early 1994, housing-discrimination lawsuits had been filed by the department in Michigan, South Dakota, Missouri, Illinois, and California. In Detroit, two apartment complexes that had been caught discriminating against black testers were ordered to pay a total of

$350,000 in damages (Ahmad, 1993). In 1990, the Equal Employment Opportunity Council (EEOC), an agency of the federal government, began filing charges based on testing by private fair-employment organizations. In its first such case, the Miami chapter of the NAACP conducted tests for racial discrimination in eight department stores and found evidence of discrimination. At one store, white applicants with less experience and education were given offers that were not made to black applicants with more experience and education (Kennedy, 1992). By 1992, the EEOC was considering the possibility of conducting its own tests as a means of enforcing civil rights laws banning racial and sex discrimination in employment.

Sometimes, testing is done as a way of validating complaints about discrimination and is undertaken specifically in response to a complaint that a particular business has discriminated. Private fair-housing organizations, sometimes working cooperatively with the Department of Housing and Urban Development, have done this type of testing for years. Increasingly, however, testing is being done on a random basis. The rationale for random testing is that discrimination is usually done surreptitiously. In the ABC *Prime Time Live* program, for example, a rental agent and an auto dealer who have just been caught discriminating on videotape can be seen vigorously protesting that "we don't discriminate." When discrimination occurs in this manner, the victim of the discrimination often does not know that he or she has been discriminated against. Most businesses that discriminate know better than to say they won't do business with a person on the basis of race or gender or that they charge higher rates for blacks, Latinos, or women than for white males. Yet they often do: Research by the American Bar Foundation, for example, found that blacks and women are charged hundreds of dollars more for cars than are white males buying comparable cars. The only way to know whether or not discrimination has occurred is through a test in which otherwise similar people either are or are not found to have been treated differently on the basis of their race or gender.

U.S. Justice Department official James Turner (quoted in Ahmad, 1993) uses the Detroit case to illustrate this principle. Before the Justice Department began random testing in Detroit and found widespread evidence of discrimination, only seven racial housing-discrimination cases had been filed there in the first twenty years of the Fair Housing Act. This was the case in spite of the fact that Detroit has consistently ranked as one of the most segregated metropolitan areas in the United States. The Justice Department tests confirmed that discrimination was widespread, supporting the suspicion that such discrimination is an important reason why Detroit is so segregated. Yet until the department began its random testing there, almost none of that illegal discrimination was being detected and punished.

Some critics of the testing movement, particularly as it relates to enforcement of civil rights laws, have argued that testing constitutes entrapment because the testers do not really intend to rent an apartment, accept a job, or buy a car (Kennedy, 1992; Mathews, 1992). Supporters reply that this technique is no different from undercover techniques that have long been used to enforce a variety of other laws and question why civil rights laws should be treated any differently. They also point out that the legal definition of entrapment is to actively induce someone to break the law, then arrest him or her for the violation. An example would be to say, "Come on, smoke a joint with me!" and then charge the person with marijuana use if he or she did. This type of inducement is not used in a well-designed testing study. Testers do not try to get businesses to discriminate; they only apply for a job or housing or try to buy something and then note how they were treated. An example of legal entrapment would be for a white tester to say, "Rent to me; I'm white and won't cause you trouble like some of those other folks would." No properly trained tester would do this, and if one did, the test would probably be thrown out in court. From a legal standpoint, then, the entrapment issue carries no weight in well-designed testing programs. The use of testers has been approved by the courts in housing cases, though in employment cases, the issue appears to still be in dispute—not so much over the entrapment issue, but over the issue of whether or not testers have standing to sue since they do not really want to work at the places they are testing. However, the EEOC concluded in 1990 that testers do have standing to sue, because like anyone else, they have a right not to be discriminated against. If the courts follow the precedent they have set in housing-discrimination cases, it is likely they will agree.

Because of the difficulty of detecting subtle discrimination, the use of testing as a means of civil rights law enforcement has grown in recent years. Both private civil rights organizations and the federal government are using testing today to a greater extent than in the past. As the Clinton administration is giving civil rights law enforcement a higher priority than earlier administrations, testing initiatives begun under the Bush administration were expanded. The Department of Housing and Urban Development was, for example, to place increased emphasis on testing for mortgage-lending discrimination by 1994. Given the difficulty of detecting discrimination by any means other than testing, and given the continuing reality of widespread subtle or surreptitious discrimination, the likelihood is that the discrimination-testing movement will continue to grow in the 1990s.

SUMMARY AND CONCLUSION

In this chapter, we have examined current trends that include both the continuing reality of prejudice and discrimination and new ways in which people are trying to deal with those realities. Subtle and institutional discrimination continue to limit the opportunities of minorities in the workplace and to hurt productivity. But a growing number of work organizations with an enlightened sense of self-interest are dealing with these realities through diversity management programs.

Hate-group activity and hate crime have increased in recent years for a number of reasons. Even though evidence does not support the claim that people are more prejudiced today than in the 1970s or 1980s, the expression of prejudice has become more common, and hate groups have become more active, largely as a result of economic frustrations and fears, which have sometimes been manipulated for political purposes. Yet as hate activity has increased, people and organizations have struggled to come up with new ways of dealing with the problem. Some, such as speech codes, have been highly controversial and of dubious effectiveness. Other techniques, however, such as the growing tendencies of colleges to require courses on diversity and to encourage the development of conflict-resolution techniques, show promise. Nonetheless, colleges, work organizations, and local communities are likely to continue to experience some tension and divisiveness as long as intergroup inequality and racial segregation remain widespread in the larger society. Although hate-group activity has increased, most organizations and businesses today do not practice open discrimination. The discrimination that persists today has been largely driven underground by civil rights and fair-housing laws. For this reason, the testing movement has developed as an important tool for detecting, and sometimes punishing, more subtle forms of discrimination. For the reasons outlined in this chapter, diversity management, hate activity and how to respond to it, and discrimination testing have emerged as major trends and issues in intergroup relations in the 1990s and may well remain so through the rest of the decade.

15

Selected Issues for the Future of Majority–Minority Relations in the United States

In Chapter 14, we examined issues in majority–minority relations that are at the forefront in the United States in the 1990s. In this chapter, we turn to the future, focusing on issues that are not only current but are likely to continue to be issues in American intergroup relations well into the future. As we have seen throughout this book, racial, ethnic, and other forms of intergroup inequality remain very serious problems today and can be found in virtually every aspect of American society. As such, intergroup inequality raises numerous issues that will continue to demand attention and decisions for well into the future. No chapter—indeed, no book—can do justice to all of the issues and controversies that have grown out of various aspects of majority–minority relations. Hence, a chapter such as this must be selective. We shall focus on four issues that are likely to be at the center of debates about intergroup relations in coming years. These are the debate on the desirability of different models for intergroup relations (assimilation, pluralism, separatism), the controversy over affirmative action, the future immigration policy of the United States, and the relative importance of race and class in American society. We turn first to the debate over assimilation, pluralism, and separatism.

ALTERNATIVE MODELS FOR INTERGROUP RELATIONS

As we have seen in several previous chapters, one major debate in the area of majority–minority relations concerns the question, What is the ideal model or pattern of intergroup relations? To put it a little differently, What is the ultimate goal we are striving for when we try to bring about "better" race and ethnic relations? As we saw in Chapter 7, three major models have been proposed: assimilation, pluralism, and separatism. There continues to be much debate over which model we ought to be striving toward. In this section, we shall briefly explore the arguments for and against each of these models.

Assimilation

The Case for Assimilation.   In large part, the idea that cultural assimilation is desirable arises from the view that a society needs to share common values and beliefs, a common culture, to develop the sense of solidarity, unity, and cooperation that it needs to grow and prosper. This idea, as you probably recognize, is closely aligned with the functionalist, or order, perspective. The underlying premise is that a society with severe internal divisions along the lines of race, ethnicity, or religion cannot work well as a society. Too much energy goes into infighting, everyone places her or his own group ahead of the good of the larger society, and cooperation becomes impossible. A society in which everybody thinks in terms of one's own little group and nobody thinks about the good of the whole society is in trouble, they argue, and in the view of functionalists, such an outcome is inevitable unless all major groups develop an identity with the society as a whole and move toward a common culture. The increased support for pluralism in recent decades has been a matter of great concern to many functionalists, who argue that there are signs in the United States today of all the problems outlined above, for the simple reason that more and more Americans in recent years *have* been putting their own group needs ahead of the needs of the larger society. These sociologists believe that we are becoming a nation of special-interest groups, with nobody much concerned about the good of the larger society. (For an example of this viewpoint, see Thernstrom, 1980.)

Another reason for advocating assimilation is a belief by some that it is the only realistic way to obtain racial and ethnic equality (see Patterson, 1977). This viewpoint holds that people's tendency toward ethnocentrism is so strong that, wherever racial and cultural differences exist, prejudice and discrimination will occur. This, of course, is especially true in settings where there has been a long history of discrimination. This view argues that these evils can be eradicated only by eliminating the cultural differences that are the basis for prejudice and discrimination. In its most extreme form, it holds that *amalgamation*—the elimination through repeated intermarriage and interbreeding of distinct racial groups—is the most effective long-term solution to the problem. The advocates of this viewpoint sometimes point to certain Latin American countries where long-term mixing of the white, black, and Indian populations has largely erased racial distinctions and prejudices of a racial nature (although cultural differences not totally linked to race remain significant). Others argue, in a more moderate vein, that the widespread acceptance of racial intermarriage (which remains relatively infrequent today in the United States, although it is on the rise) would be a crucial step toward the solution of racial problems in this country.

The Case Against Assimilation.   A common argument against assimilation is that it amounts to forced conformity. Some advocates of assimilation view it, ideally, as a process of culture sharing, with the majority group adopting some aspects of minority group culture and the minority group adopting some aspects of the majority group culture. Thus, a new culture and social structure emerges that is neither that of the majority group nor that of the minority group or groups. Critics, however, argue that in reality, the process is seldom that balanced. As we saw in Chapter 7, the norm in the United States throughout most of its history has been Anglo conformity—a demand that all immigrant and minority groups conform to the expectations of the dominant WASP (white Anglo-Saxon Protestant) group. Other groups have certainly had some influence, but the influence of this dominant group has been quite disproportionate.

Other critics of assimilation see dangers in the promotion of cultural homogeneity rather than heterogeneity. First, a move toward homogeneity would bring a loss in freedom of choice: In a plural, or heterogeneous, society, a person has a wide range of values and lifestyles to choose from. To the degree that this heterogeneity is lost, freedom of choice is lost—there is no choice but to conform to the dominant values and lifestyle. The critics also argue that heterogeneity is an important source of adaptation and innovation in society. If we all become the same, the diversity that produces new ideas may be lost, and society may stagnate. An example of this can be seen in the research noted in Chapter 14, which shows that diverse groups, over the long run, are more productive than homogeneous ones.

Pluralism

The Case for Pluralism. Many of those who see in assimilation the dangers we have just discussed support cultural pluralism as the ideal model of intergroup relations. One reason is that they see a need in society for diversity or cultural heterogeneity, and pluralism facilitates this. In other words, a certain amount of diversity—as long as it does not create deep divisions—is good for society because it provides a basis for innovation and for adaptation to new situations. On the other hand, some critics such as Patterson (1977) have argued that *group* diversity can lead to *individual* conformity because of pressures to conform to group norms. While general societal benefits of diversity might be stressed by some functionalist sociologists, some conflict theorists see a different advantage in pluralism. This advantage is that racial- or ethnic-group awareness can form a power base through which an ethnic group can take action on behalf of its self-interest. Thus, if blacks, or Italian Americans, or Jews, or whoever develop a group identity, it can become a source of social and political power. This can occur through the ballot box (observe how candidates must court the vote of various racial and ethnic groups), or it can occur through collective protest. Either way, an ethnic or racial group can potentially gain power if it can develop a common identity and take some kind of political action. For groups not well represented in the traditional political process, the kind of group consciousness that leads to collective action and/or bloc voting may be the only real chance to gain political influence or power. Thus, by providing such a potential power base, cultural pluralism may be an important basis by which minority groups act on behalf of their self-interests. Furthermore, when a group has been subjected to widespread attacks on its culture, as have several minority groups in the United States, group identity can be an important source of self-esteem for its members.

A third argument in support of pluralism points out that it is desirable in and of itself to preserve the distinct cultures of various racial, ethnic, religious, and social groups. Such diversity provides a richness in society that would be absent if everyone were the same culturally. Furthermore, this view holds that it is nobody's business to tell a group that it must change its ways to conform to some dominant norm.

In recent years, support for pluralism has increased, at least among academics, for another reason: It is increasingly evident that it is simply unrealistic to expect complete assimilation. As was noted in Chapter 7, conquered or colonized minorities are particularly unlikely to assimilate (Blauner, 1972; Ogbu, 1978; Lieberson, 1980; Zweigenhaft and Domhoff, 1991). Immigrant minorities often do seek assimilation, at least up to a point, largely because by choice they have entered the society where they now live. In other words, they are there because they wanted to be, and in this situation, there will usually be some motivation to learn and fit into the new culture and society. However, colonized minorities involuntarily entered the society where they live, were brought into it in order to be exploited, and therefore have no automatic reason to wish to fit in. Hence, groups such as African Americans, Chicanos, and Native Americans have been more resistant to assimilation—and all of these groups are growing at a faster rate than the white Anglo population. However, as discussed in Chapter 7, support for assimilation has always had its limits even among immigrant groups, who have in fact sought to preserve some aspects of their culture. As a result of all this, there is a growing belief among experts on intergroup relations that some degree of pluralism in a society as diverse as the United States is inevitable.

The Case Against Pluralism. The major argument commonly made against pluralism is that it creates divisions in society. This can be harmful in several ways. To the functionalist, any significant division is potentially harmful, because it destroys the consensus and solidarity that society needs and inhibits cooperation. Furthermore, given the usual social tendency toward ethnocentrism, the existence of cultural differences makes prejudice and discrimination likely. While pluralism may sound like a good idea in the abstract, say the critics, it will not work in real life. As an example they point out that the emphasis in America in recent years on black culture, Italian culture, Jewish culture, and so on is dangerous because it emphasizes what is different about us (and therefore a potential basis for conflict and discrimination) rather than what is the same.

An example of this can be seen in the objections that some critics have raised concerning multicultural education, as discussed in Chapter 12. These critics have objected to forms of multicultural education that question the notion of a common national history shared among all ethnic and cultural groups. Such education stresses the idea that the experiences of different groups in American society (for example, English Americans and African Americans) are quite different. Thus, each group has a distinct national history that is not the same as that of other groups and that helps to explain the role, status, and values of each group today. Writers such as Kirp (1991) have criticized this view on the grounds that it tends to divide society on the basis of race, culture, and nationality. They argue, along the lines of the functionalist perspective, that such divisions inhibit societal cooperation by leading each group to place its own concerns above the common interest.

Some conflict theorists also see dangers in pluralism. For one thing, it is rarely true that different racial and cultural groups have equal power. Thus, if people organize and mobilize on the basis of racial or ethnic groups, the groups with greater political and economic resources are favored. Along this line, Patterson (1977) argues that the Black Power movement, by making ethnic political movements acceptable again, has made it easier, for example, for the Irish of South Boston to organize an ethnically based movement to keep the Irish in control of their community, which translates to keeping blacks out of the neighborhood.

A related argument can be seen in Marxist theory, which argues that growing awareness of racial and ethnic differences leads people to ignore the divisions in society that are really important. Thus, a working class in which people think of themselves above all as black or white, Anglo or Chicano, or perhaps (as in Northern Ireland) Catholic or Protestant, cannot act together on behalf of its interests as a class. Thus, the masses of blacks and whites (and so on) are *hurt* by ethnic awareness because it divides them and prevents them from acting on behalf of their larger common interests.

Racial/Ethnic Separatism

The Case for Separatism. Obviously, separation of the races is one mechanism by which a dominant group can maintain its advantages over a subordinate group—as the experience in the U.S. South during the Jim Crow era so clearly illustrates. For this reason, racial separation has often been advocated by racists as a way of maintaining dominant group advantage. In the modern era, two examples of this are the position of the Ku Klux Klan in the United States and, until recently, the system of apartheid in South Africa.

Other arguments made for separatism, however, do not arise from the desire of one group to dominate another. Historically, separatist movements have arisen among minority groups (especially those with a geographic base within the larger society) as a way of trying to escape the inequality they have experienced in their contacts with the dominant group. In this vein, black separatist movements in the United States were discussed in Chapter 7, and French separatism in Canada was discussed in Chapter 8. In cases such as these, the main argument for separatism is that it allows each group to control its own social institutions and to make its own political decisions, rather than having these things controlled by an outside group. This viewpoint can be seen in the results of a survey conducted as part of the 1993–1994 Black Politics Study at the University of Chicago. In a news interview before the release of the study, its coauthor Michael Dawson said, "We were stunned by the magnitude of change in support of black nationalism since 1988. Right now, half the black community supports the idea of an independent black political party. It has never been that high" (Dawson, quoted in Strong, 1994). Possible reasons suggested for the increase are that most blacks perceive the mood and temper of the country to be such that efforts at integration cannot bring about true acceptance or equality, so that the only viable mechanism is black nationalism, including the idea of a separate black political party (Strong, 1994).

In addition, separatism has been suggested by some as the only way of creating consensus out of a deeply divided society: create two separate societies, each with its own set of values and its own way of doing things. Thus, consensus and cooperation would be possible within each separate society, where they would not have been possible in the previous, larger society. The division of the Indian sub-continent into the separate and religioethnically distinct countries of India, Pakistan, and Bangladesh is sometimes cited as an example of this.

The Case Against Separatism. Those opposed to separatism counter that in theory the concept may work, but in practice it usually does not. They cite in support of this view examples such as the violent history of Ireland, which was partitioned, in effect, into a Catholic section and a Protestant section, or the situation in the Middle East, which arose out of an attempt to create separate Jewish and Palestinian states after World War II. Where conflict is deep, the two sides will in many cases merely become warring countries after the separation occurs. Furthermore, if the separation is not complete (for example, the continued presence of many Catholics in the "Protestant" section of Ireland, or of Serbs and Croats in Bosnia), internal conflict and violence are also likely. For this reason, separatism is nearly impossible to put into effect in any situation in which the minority group and majority group do not have distinct and nearly exclusive geographic bases. Canada approximates this model to some extent (Quebec is 80 percent French-speaking, and the rest of the country is almost totally English-speaking), and as discussed in Chapter 8, it has moved somewhat in the direction of separatism in recent years. However, the United States does not even come close to having such a geographic distribution.

Thus, despite growing advocacy of separatism among some African and Native Americans, full geographic separation would probably be virtually impossible to implement in the United States. What may well happen, however, is a move toward separate political organizations and perhaps economic institutions, as illustrated by the business network owned by the Nation of Islam. If such trends occur, the debate among people favoring assimilation, pluralism, and separatism will undoubtedly intensify and continue long into the future. Given the practical difficulties of obtaining either complete assimilation or complete separatism, however, it is likely that the true decisions faced by American society will center around the degree and type of pluralism. Whether we should have a type of pluralism in which much is shared in common and only a little is distinct or one in which relatively little is shared in common with different groups becoming more distinct and independent will likely be a matter of debate long into the future. Where people stand on this question will be influenced by their values, by their beliefs about how society operates, and, undoubtedly, by their group identities. This debate matters a great deal, because it will influence public thought on a number of other issues, including bilingual and multicultural education, school desegregation, workplace diversity, political organization, and immigration policy (discussed later in this chapter).

AFFIRMATIVE ACTION

A second major controversy in intergroup relations is more political, more concrete, and much more frequently seen in the headlines. This debate concerns *affirmative action*. The concept of affirmative action dates to 1965, when the term was first used in an executive order by President Johnson concerning enforcement of antidiscrimination requirements for agencies and businesses under contract with the federal government (Seabury, 1977, p. 99). The order said, "The contractor will not discriminate against any employee or applicant because of race, color, religion, sex or national origin. The contractor will take affirmative action to ensure that employees are treated during employment, without regard to their race, color, religion, sex or national origin." This meant, in effect, that contractors were supposed to make special efforts to ensure that they were not discriminating. In subsequent orders, the emphasis of affirmative action shifted toward the *result* of hiring practices and decisions. Specifically, a requirement was added for "goals and timetables to which the contractor's good faith efforts must be directed to correct the deficiencies and thus, to increase materially the utilization of minorities and women, at all levels and in all segments of his work force where deficiencies exist." Thus, the requirement was now added that contractors must not only avoid discrimination but must also (1) make an active effort to increase the number of female and/or minority employees where they are underrepresented and (2) develop a specific set of goals and timetables that would serve as targets and as a measure of a contractor's success in hiring more minorities and women.

These measures have been required of organizations doing business with the federal government (including most colleges and universities), and some businesses and unions have taken similar measures voluntarily. Similar affirmative-action programs exist in some colleges and universities in the area of student admissions. They are most common in professional schools, such as law and medical schools but exist in other areas as well. The objective of these affirmative-action admissions programs is to increase the number of students from underrepresented groups such as blacks, Chicanos, Indians, and women.

Affirmative-action programs in both hiring and college admissions became quite widespread during the 1970s and have remained so since. They have also been controversial, however, and became more so during the 1980s as they gradually came under attack during the Reagan and Bush administrations. After a long internal debate, during its second term, the Reagan administration dropped the requirement for goals and timetables. In the later years of the Reagan administration and throughout the Bush administration, Justice Department representatives were ordered to argue against affirmative-action preferences in several Supreme Court cases. These positions represented a reversal of positions that had been taken by every presidential administration, Democratic or Republican, from Lyndon Johnson through Jimmy Carter. In another reversal, the Bush administration also announced its opposition to minority scholarships for college students, no matter how underrepresented the targeted minority group might be in the college student population.

Increasingly, too, Reagan and Bush administration representatives sought to portray affirmative action as nothing but the use of "quotas." Partly because of these positions taken by political leaders and partly because of worsening economic conditions, public opposition to affirmative action intensified in the late 1980s and early 1990s, to the point that former Ku Klux Klan leader David Duke received the Republican nomination for governor of Louisiana in a 1991 campaign in which he strongly emphasized his opposition to affirmative action. In the general election, Duke received the majority of the white vote, but he lost the election because an overwhelming majority of the state's sizable African American population voted against him.

With the election of Bill Clinton, the position of the federal government on affirmative action changed again. The Clinton administration moved back to the pro-affirmative action position of the administrations before Reagan and Bush and also announced rather quickly that it was dropping all objections to minority scholarships. Despite the change in the position of the federal government, however, affirmative action remains controversial in the mid 1990s. In the next few pages, we shall explore arguments on both sides of this issue, which has been debated nearly everywhere in America over the past two decades—in classrooms, newspapers, union halls, and the U.S. Supreme Court.

Undoing Discrimination

The fundamental argument for making special efforts to hire more minority workers or to admit more minority students—even to the point of a preference for the minority applicant—is that such a practice is the *only* way to undo the harmful effects of past and present discrimination. Past discrimination has, according to this view, left minorities in a disadvantaged position, so that race-blind admission or hiring is *not* really fair: Minority applicants, after generations of discrimination, simply do not have all the advantages that white male applicants have. Recall the analogy used in Chapter 11 concerning the two runners, one of whom had to start with weights tied to her feet. Removing the weights halfway through did not make a fair race: The runner was by then far behind. Removing the weight of discrimination today, but doing nothing else to make the competition fair, will *not*, in the eyes of affirmative-action supporters, eliminate the disadvantages suffered by minority-group members.

The effects of past discrimination are not the only reason the supporters of affirmative action give for having such a program. In Chapters 10, 11, and 12, we explored a number of ways in which modern American social institutions discriminate, often without even being aware of it. Unless and until such subtle mechanisms of discrimination are eliminated, race-blind (as well as sex-blind) competition cannot really be fair: Minorities and women are held back by institutional discrimination in ways that whites and men are not. According to this view, the *only* way to get some semblance of racial or sexual equality *today* (until the effects of past and institutional discrimination can be eliminated) is to have some kind of racial or sexual preference in hiring and/or admissions. To fail to do this is to keep minorities and women in a position where, through no fault of their own, they have less than their proportionate share of jobs, education, political representation, and so on.

In effect, the supporters of affirmative action argue that the only way to break through the continuous cycle of discrimination is to pay attention to the *result*. They often point out that this was done in the South, where, for example, schools were given guidelines regarding what percentage of black and white students constituted an integrated school. In general, supporters of affirmative action see it as a temporary tactic for offsetting the effects of past and institutional discrimination. They argue that once the cycle of inequality has been broken and minorities and women enjoy the same educational and occupational advantages that white males do, the need for special consideration on the basis of race and sex will disappear.

Reverse Discrimination

As we stated, the concept of affirmative action is controversial. Many regard any preference for minority or female applicants as discrimination in reverse, just as unfair as is discrimination, for example, against blacks, Chicanos, or women (see Glazer, 1976). People with this viewpoint argue that preferential treatment of minorities is especially unfair when there is no evidence that the firm or school to which they are applying has deliberately discriminated in the past. They feel this practice forces many whites (or males) who are *not* guilty of discrimination to unfairly pay the price for past discrimination that they had nothing to do with. In short, it is seen as unfair to such people to be, through no fault of their own, passed over in favor of women and minorities who are no more qualified (and sometimes, it is charged, less qualified) than they are, at least by traditional measures of qualifications.

The question of qualifications has become a central issue in the debate over affirmative action. Those against affirmative action, in addition to the above arguments, say that affirmative action undermines the quality of workforces and student bodies by giving positions to persons other than the most qualified applicants. If one accepts the traditional measures of qualifications as reliable, it does appear that this happens sometimes. In many law schools and medical schools, for example, minority applicants have been accepted with admission-test scores and/or undergraduate grade point averages (GPAs) significantly lower than those generally required of whites (see Sindler, 1978).

Another barrage of criticism has been directed at affirmative action on the grounds that it amounts to an unfair quota system. This view holds that the goals and timetables used in affirmative-action programs end up as quotas that must be filled regardless of the qualifications of the candidates. Thus, if a firm has a goal of hiring so as to have a 10 percent black workforce in three years, it will end up having to hire some minimum number of blacks regardless of their qualifications. Perceptions that this is a problem have been increased by incidences of employers telling white male applicants that they have been passed over in favor of less qualified women or minorities to meet affirmative action goals (see Nisbet, 1977). The use of quotas is of special concern to some ethnic groups: Jewish Americans, for example, remember that many Jews were kept out of American colleges and professional schools by quotas that specified a maximum percentage of Jews. In part for this reason, many Jews and others see a dangerous precedent in what they view as a reintroduction of the use of quotas (see Raab, 1978).

Finally, affirmative action has come under attack from some African American conservatives in recent years. This can be seen, for example, in the writings of Steele (1990) and Sowell (1977, 1990) and in the legal opinions of Supreme Court justice Clarence Thomas. The main objection to affirmative action from this viewpoint is that it leads to the devaluation of minority and/or female employees and students. For example, black professionals and college students commonly encounter the view from some whites that "you're only here to fill a quota—you're not really qualified." Such a response by whites to affirmative action leads to questioning of the credentials of even the best-qualified minority employees or students. Steele argues that with affirmative action, no matter how good a minority student or employee is, some people will believe that he or she is there only because of affirmative-action preferences. In this way, he argues, affirmative action has the unintended effect of reinforcing negative stereotypes about minorities among the dominant group and creating self-doubt among minority-group members who constantly find their abilities and talents questioned. He also argues that the perception among whites that affirmative action amounts to reverse discrimination creates feelings of resentment that will be damaging to African Americans and other minorities in the long run.

Considering the Net Outcome

Supporters of affirmative action generally do not agree that a preference for women or minority applicants amounts to reverse discrimination, or that affirmative-action programs have brought about widespread use of quotas. On the issue of quotas, they argue that goals and timetables have never been intended as rigid quotas but rather as a target and a standard against which the performance of government contractors can be measured. It is acknowledged, for example, that there are sometimes good reasons why a goal cannot be met: The key criterion is good-faith effort and some indication of progress (Pottinger, 1972). Furthermore, it is argued that, unlike the quotas that limited the numbers of Jews in American universities in the 1950s and earlier, the purpose of affirmative action (whether it involves quotas or not) is to get people *into* employment or school, not to keep them out.

In this vein, supporters of affirmative action deny the claim that affirmative action leads to the hiring or admission of less qualified applicants. They acknowledge that women and minorities hired or admitted under affirmative-action programs may score lower on traditional criteria, but they deny that this indicates that they have lower potential as a student or employee. They cite two reasons. First, the minority applicant may score lower on these criteria because of disadvantages arising from past and institutional discrimination, not because of lesser ability. Society imposes handicaps on minorities that are not imposed on white males; thus, the criteria measure the effects of this discrimination better than they measure the applicant's true potential as an employee or student. The handicaps imposed on minorities by institutional discrimination are discussed in detail in Chapters 10, 11, and 12. Discriminatory processes in education, discussed in detail in Chapter 12, are particularly important in that they make it more difficult for minorities to become "qualified" according to the traditional measures. These discriminatory processes include unequal funding of schools, unequal expectations of student achievement, biased or Eurocentric content in educational materials, and tracking and ability grouping influenced by race, ethnicity, and socioeconomic status. All of these processes serve to reinforce and perpetuate racial inequalities already present in society and to make it more difficult for minority students to learn what they need to learn to do well on tests used for college admissions and for screening of applicants for employment.

The second reason that traditional measures of qualifications often do not accurately measure the potential of minority applicants has to do with the measures themselves. The tests and criteria may contain cultural biases that favor white middle-class male applicants and work to the disadvantage of others. (The issue of test bias is discussed in detail in Chapter 12.)

For both these reasons, traditional criteria may underestimate the potential of the minority applicant. Indeed, with the best criteria available, it is possible to make only rough estimates of how good a student or employee an applicant will turn out to be. Law school admission criteria, for example, typically explain only about 25 percent of the variation in first-year academic performance of law students (Sindler, 1978, pp. 115–16). In short, the use of traditional admission criteria for minority applicants is considered unfair because doing so does not compensate for the effects of discrimination (unintentional as well as intentional) that the applicant has previously experienced. People who support affirmative action believe that the *net effect of failing to consider race* in admissions and hiring decisions is to discriminate against minorities: Nothing is done to compensate for the effects of past discrimination and the subtle processes of institutional discrimination that have had the effect of placing the minority applicant at an unfair disadvantage. Under affirmative action, the white male applicant may suffer some disadvantage at the point of decision, but this is offset by disadvantages suffered by the minority applicant at earlier stages, such as primary and secondary education (see Chapter 12). Thus, according to this view, the only way to avoid net discrimination is through affirmative action.

Supporters of affirmative action offer several responses to the argument that affirmative action leads whites to label minorities as unqualified and to develop resentments that may lead to worse race relations in the future. It is true that some whites view minorities as unqualified no matter how well they do, and that affirmative action undoubtedly contributes to this viewpoint. However, a good many of today's minority professionals and managers point out that they would not have received the opportunity to prove themselves had it not been for doors opened by affirmative action. They acknowledge the problem of some whites refusing to recognize their abilities and accomplishments, but they also point out that the alternative would be worse: no opportunity to prove themselves at all. In other words, because of past and institutional discrimination, they would not have been given the opportunity to get in the door to the managerial or professional job and would not have had the opportunity to show that they could succeed in that job (Olojede, 1991). Thus, they argue that the answer to the problem is to make sure that the accomplishments of minority employees are recognized and known within the organization, not to close the doors opened by affirmative action.

A similar argument can be made with respect to white resentments about affirmative action. It was noted in earlier chapters that white opposition to affirmative action and other policies to increase opportunities for minorities is strongly linked to a belief that the system is fair. In other words, whites who believe that blacks and whites have essentially the same opportunities in American society (a clear majority of all white Americans) generally oppose affirmative action and similar measures (Kluegel and Smith, 1986; Kluegel, 1990). This opposition is based on the belief that the system already offers equal opportunity as it is, so it is an unfair advantage to have a preference for any particular group or groups. However, as has been amply demonstrated in Chapters 10, 11, and 12, as well as by discrimination testing as described in Chapter 14, American society has not yet attained the ideal of equal opportunity. Present-day individual and institutional discrimination, as well as lingering effects of past discrimination, still make it more difficult for African Americans, Native Americans, Latinos, and women to succeed in American society. The surveys by Kluegel and Smith (1986; Kluegel, 1990) show clearly that whites who recognize this reality of unequal opportunity understand the reasoning behind policies such as affirmative action and are much less likely to oppose them or see them as unfair. Moreover, there is also evidence that when people study and learn about the nature of racial inequality in the United States, they become more supportive of such policies (Davine and Bills, 1992). Thus, supporters of affirmative action, while acknowledging that some whites resent it, argue that the answer is not to eliminate affirmative action but instead to make people more informed about intergroup relations in the United States so that they better understand the reasons for maintaining affirmative action.

A final and related issue raised by the supporters of affirmative action is the need for minority professionals. As we saw in Chapters 10 and 11, a serious shortage of minority doctors and lawyers is one important reason why minority Americans have less access to medical care and legal representation. Without affirmative action in law and medical-school admissions programs, this condition would probably continue well into the future. A national study of law school admissions (Evans, 1977) showed, for example, that without affirmative action, not more than about 2 percent of all those admitted in 1976 would have been black, and only 0.75 percent would have been Chicano—compared with the actual figures of 5.3 percent black and 1.3 percent Chicano. Put differently, the number of minority students admitted would have been less than half what it was had there not been affirmative action. This almost certainly would have a substantial impact on the supply of minority lawyers, especially when repeated year after year. Although these figures pertain to the 1976 school year, more recent estimates indicate that things haven't changed much. In 1992, the dean of the University of Texas law school estimated that without affirmative action, there would have been only twenty to thirty minority students in the entering class of five hundred, instead of the hundred minority students that there actually were (Mark G. Yudof, quoted in Jaschik, 1992).

The situation is much the same in medical schools; a brief submitted in the *Bakke* case (discussed later in this chapter) by the Association of American Medical Colleges (Waldman, 1977) indicated that without affirmative-action programs, minority enrollment would have dropped from 8.2 percent to a "distressingly low" level of about 2 percent. And even with affirmative action, medical-school enrollment rates for minorities remain low. Between about 1975 and 1990, the proportion of medical students who are of minority groups increased more slowly than the proportion of the general population who are of minority groups, and the proportion of black medical students actually fell (Lee, 1992; Nickens, 1992; Sullivan, 1992). In addition, the notion that affirmative action leads to the admission of unqualified medical-school applicants is simply not supported by the data: More than 90 percent of all minority medical students graduate (Petersdorf et al., 1990; Lee, 1992).

As stated above, underrepresentation of minorities in law and medicine is an important reason why minorities lack access to medical care and legal representation. For example, minority physicians are more likely to have a high proportion of minority patients in their practices, are much more likely to locate in areas of low socioeconomic status, and are somewhat more likely to specialize in primary care (Nickens, 1992). They are also frequently more culturally sensitive to minority populations and more likely to schedule evening office hours so low-income working patients don't have to miss work to see the doctor (Nickens, 1992).

Practical Consequences of Affirmative Action: Empirical Evidence

Examining data on the employment and income of recent minority and white college graduates is helpful in assessing the actual effects of affirmative-action hiring programs in recent years. Such data suggest that among recent college graduates (and persons who have recently finished postgraduate work), African Americans and Latinos are earning incomes similar to those of whites but not greater than those of whites. A detailed examination of hourly earnings of whites and blacks by R. Farley (1984, p. 126) showed that in 1980, after a decade of affirmative action, the hourly earnings of black-male college graduates aged twenty-five to thirty-four were 96 percent those of white-male college graduates in the same age group. Although black-female college graduates did have annual incomes slightly higher than those of white females, women of both races lagged well behind white males.

More-recent comparisons based on annual income show that these patterns did not change much during the 1980s. As of 1990, comparisons among recent college graduates continued to show white males earning more than any other group. Among recent college graduates working full-time year-round, black and Hispanic males, and females of all races, continued to earn less than white males. Even among recent college graduates who were full-time workers, all of these groups except Hispanic males had median annual incomes at least $5,000 less than the median annual income of white males (U.S. Bureau of the Census, 1991b, Table 29). Thus, while affirmative action has moved things in the direction of equality among recent college graduates working full-time, white males continue to enjoy higher incomes than anyone else, even among this group. And it is among this group, recent college graduates, where minorities have benefited the most from affirmative action.

Among less educated minorities, the benefits of affirmative action have been less, although certain groups have nonetheless benefited. Minority workers of lower educational levels have made some gains as a result of affirmative action in a variety of public-employment positions, such as police and firefighters. Among building-trades contractors who are involved in government contracting, minority hiring has increased, in part because of set-aside programs designed to assure that some work is done by minority-owned construction firms. Gains have also occurred in some blue-collar manufacturing firms that have labor contracts calling for affirmative action; however, overall employment has declined sharply in such firms because of automation, relocation overseas, and international competition. Consequently, many minority workers who once had good jobs in manufacturing have lost those jobs despite affirmative action and antidiscrimination efforts.

As W. J. Wilson (1978, pp. 99–121, 1987) has pointed out, affirmative action has had almost no effect on low-income, poorly educated, chronically unemployed minorities. Thus, affirmative action has helped to offset the effects of discrimination for relatively more advantaged minorities, but it has neither given these groups an income advantage over the dominant white-male group nor made much difference at all for minorities in the impoverished underclass. Mainly for this reason, minority groups taken as a whole remain substantially disadvantaged in income, employment, and education compared with whites as a whole, in spite of affirmative action. Even minorities who have benefited from affirmative action may be less economically secure than whites (Collins, 1993). Middle-class blacks, for example, are more likely than comparable whites to be employed in government or in government-supported programs. Thus, they are more vulnerable to governmental cutbacks. Recent research by Collins (1993) has revealed a second reason why minority-group members with good jobs are often in a vulnerable position. Studying black executives in major white-owned corporations, she found that they are often employed in positions relating to human relations, affirmative action, urban affairs, or diversity management. To some extent, the amount of resources that corporations devote to activities of this type depends on the amount of social and political pressure there is to address problems of race relations and minority underrepresentation. As long as companies feel pressure to address these issues, they undoubtedly will do so. But if and when such pressures ease, as they did for a time during the 1980s, corporations may devote fewer resources to them, making such jobs vulnerable to cutbacks. In fact, many companies did make such cutbacks during the 1980s. To the extent that this occurs, black executives are more vulnerable than white executives because of their area of specialization (Collins, 1993).

The two black families in these photos depict the widening gap between affluence and poverty within the African-American population. Affirmative action has opened opportunities for minorities with sufficient education to take advantage of the opportunities, but has done little for poverty-level minority group members. *Stock Boston, Inc./Owen Franken/Jeffry W. Myers*

Legal Aspects of the Affirmative-Action Controversy

Not surprisingly, an issue as controversial as affirmative action has been widely debated in the courts as well as in other places. Those who are against it have argued that it violates the Civil Rights Act of 1964 and the equal-protection clause of the Constitution by discriminating against whites and/or males. Those who support it argue that affirmative action is not discrimination against anyone but rather an effort to *include* underrepresented groups, and thereby it is not illegal. In general, because of the equal-protection clause and the civil rights laws, the courts view race as a "suspect category." In effect, this means that anyone who in any way uses race as a basis of consideration must demonstrate that some compelling interest is served by doing so and that the purpose is not to discriminate against or exclude anybody on the basis of race. Since most affirmative-action programs do in some way involve a consideration of race, an early court test of their legality was inevitable. By 1971, affirmative action was beginning to find its way into the courts.

However, the Supreme Court did not rule on the legality and constitutionality of affirmative action until the *Bakke* case in 1978. Rather than settling the affirmative action issue, *Bakke* proved to be the first of a number of decisions the Supreme Court has been called on to make concerning affirmative action. What has emerged from these cases is that it makes a difference for the legality of various approaches to affirmative action whether the case involves student admissions, hiring, or layoff decisions, and, in the case of hiring, whether the hiring is done by a public or private employer or through a union hiring hall. The reasons for these differences include (1) the type of decision being made, and (2) the different decisionmakers and varying legal standards that apply to them. In all of the situations noted above except layoff decisions, the Court approved the use of preferences for underrepresented minorities under at least some circumstances. However, both the extent of the preference and the conditions that make it permissible vary according to the different situations.

In addition, support for affirmative action on the Supreme Court has waxed and waned as the composition of the Court has changed because of retirements and new appointments. During the 1980s, several appointments by presidents Reagan and Bush led to a Court less sympathetic to affirmative action. In 1989, several Court rulings were made that limited, but did not reverse, earlier Court support for affirmative action. However, some of these rulings were reversed by the 1991 Civil Rights Act as detailed below. Key affirmative-action rulings such as *Bakke* and *Weber* were never reversed by the Supreme Court during the Reagan–Bush era, despite several efforts by both administrations to press the Court to reverse its support for affirmative action. Given this, along with the prospect that Clinton administration appointees may make the Court again somewhat more favorable to affirmative action, it appears that the basic position of the law as it stood in the early 1990s is unlikely to change greatly in the near future. This position can best be described as legal approval of affirmative-action preferences in hiring, promotion, and higher-education admissions in both the public and private sectors. However, exactly what is permitted varies among hiring, promotion, and student admissions and between the public and private sectors. It also depends in some cases on the degree and type of discrimination that has taken place in the past. Let us now briefly examine the various situations and what the Court has ruled. (Major Supreme Court rulings on affirmative action are outlined in Table 15.1.)

Table 15.1 Summary of Major Supreme Court Decisions Concerning Affirmative Action

YEAR	CASE AND DECISION
1978	*Allan Bakke* v. *Regents of the University of California.* Racial preferences ruled legal in higher education admissions for educational purpose of having a diverse student body. Racial quotas forbidden by Constitution.
1979	*Weber* v. *Kaiser Aluminum and Chemical Corporation.* Racial preferences, including the use of quotas, are legal in private-employment hiring decisions as a means of compensating for societal discrimination.
1984	*Memphis Firefighters* v. *Stotts.* (Not discussed in text, because this case was clarified by later *Wygant* decision.) Seniority system for layoffs could not be abrogated to help individuals who were not proven victims of discrimination.
1986	*Wygant* v. *Jackson Board of Education.* Struck down minority preference in public-teacher layoff decisions for purpose of diverse role models for students. Ruled that stronger case was needed to justify layoff preferences than hiring preferences, but proof of individual discrimination against beneficiaries of preferences was not required.
1986	*International Association of Firefighters* v. *City of Cleveland.* Upheld racial preferences in public employment as a remedy for discrimination, and that court-approved settlement of discrimination lawsuits could include racial preferences.
1986	*Sheet Metal Workers* v. *Equal Employment Opportunity Commission.* Courts can order racial preferences, including goals and timetables for minority employment, if it is found that private employers have engaged in "egregious discrimination."
1987	*United States* v. *Paradise.* Use of minority quotas in hiring and promotion by public employers can be ordered by courts when employer has engaged in severe discrimination.
1987	*Johnson* v. *Transportation Agency.* Women or minorities can be hired or promoted by public employers ahead of slightly more qualified males or whites, for the purpose of making the workforce more representative of the area's population. (This ruling was made on the basis of the 1964 Civil Rights Act.)
1989	*Croson* v. *City of Richmond.* Ruled that governmental programs that set aside a certain proportion of contracts for minority-owned contractors must be based on documented patterns of past discrimination.
1989	*Wards Cove* v. *Antonio.* For an employer to be found guilty of discrimination, it must be proved that there is no business reason for imposing a job requirement that has the effect of excluding minorities or women. Makes it harder for women and minorities to win discrimination cases based on statistics showing employment disparities between minorities or women and white males. This decision was later reversed by the 1991 Civil Rights Act, which states that employers must prove there is a business reason for requirements that have discriminatory effects.
1989	*Martin* v. *Wilks.* Even when they have been previously approved by the courts, affirmative-action settlements can be reopened by white males who claim reverse discrimination.
1989	*Patterson* v. *McLean Credit Union.* Court ruled that, while the 1866 Civil Rights Act forbids racial discrimination in the making of contracts, it does not apply to racial harassment on the job or other forms of discrimination after a person has been hired. This part of the ruling was reversed by the 1991 Civil Rights Act.

Higher-Education Admissions. The major Supreme Court ruling governing higher-education admissions is *Bakke,* decided in 1978. In this case, a white medical-school applicant, Allan Bakke, challenged an affirmative-action plan at the University of California at Davis Medical School. The plan set aside sixteen of the schools one hundred admissions slots for "economically and/or educationally disadvantaged persons." Although whites were eligible for the special-admissions program, only minorities had actually been admitted under it. Bakke contended the program amounted to illegal discrimination against whites; the university argued it did not because its purpose was to promote the inclusion of groups that were underrepresented in the student body. The Court struck a middle ground in this, its first affirmative-action ruling, which had drawn tremendous attention from the media and from advocacy groups on both sides. It ruled, in a five-to-four vote, that the Constitution, which governed the actions of a public university, forbade quotas, and that the university was operating a quota system. Thus, it ordered Bakke's admission. However, it also ruled, by a different five-to-four vote, that public universities could, for the valid educational purpose of having a diverse student body, use racial preferences as long as race was considered along with other factors. Thus, racial preferences were legal; quotas were not.

Private Employment: Hiring Decisions. A year later, in 1979, the Court made another major affirmative-action decision in the *Weber* case. In this case, the suit was brought by a white employee against Kaiser Aluminum because of an affirmative-action plan that Kaiser and its union, the United Steelworkers, had agreed to. This agreement had provided that, when minorities were underrepresented in skilled labor positions relative to the local population, one half of the persons trained for placement in skilled positions would be minority until the racial mix of the skilled labor force approximated that of the local population (see Dreyfuss and Lawrence, 1979). The white employee, Brian Weber, claimed that this amounted to illegal discrimination against whites, but the Court ruled (by a five-to-two majority, with two justices not voting) that it did not. It ruled that if past societal discrimination has caused the underrepresentation of minorities in a workforce, racial preferences, including even a quota such as Kaiser's 50 percent provision, is legally permissible. It ruled differently in this case from the *Bakke* ruling because private employers are covered not by the Constitution (which regulates *government* bodies) but by the 1964 Civil Rights Act. Since the purpose of that law was to improve opportunities for minority Americans, actions consistent with that purpose are permissible (*New York Times,* 1979).

In a 1986 ruling, *Sheet Metal Workers,* the Court held that there are even circumstances in which courts may *order* employment racial preferences in private employment decisions. This case involved a situation in which hiring was done through a union hiring hall, and the union involved had been found guilty of racial discrimination. The union had been ordered by a lower court to establish a hiring goal of 29 percent minorities by 1987 to remedy that pattern of discrimination. The Supreme Court upheld that order, ruling six-to-three that where there had been a pattern of "egregious discrimination" the courts could order hiring preferences for minorities as a remedy. It also ruled five-to-four that such court-ordered preferences could include goals and timetables. Thus, not only are minority preferences, goals, and timetables in private employment legal under certain circumstances, but if there is sufficiently strong evidence of discrimination, the courts can even order them.

The 1989 Supreme Court rulings, along with the 1991 Civil Rights Act, which was passed to reverse certain aspects of those rulings, have brought further change to the legal situation with respect to affirmative action in private employment. The Court ruled in the *Martin* v. *Wilks* case that white-male employees could sue, for reverse discrimination, even when affirmative-action plans had been previously approved by the courts. Moreover, this court ruling placed no limits on how long after such court approval white-male employees could sue. This ruling opened the possibility that even when an affirmative-action plan had been previously approved by the courts, white-male employees could repeatedly go back to court to try to get the plan changed. Clearly, this could discourage employers from adopting affirmative-action plans, because of the threat of constant lawsuits (*Commonweal*, 1989). The same week as this ruling, the Court ruled in the *Patterson* v. *McLean Credit Union* case that minorities who experienced racial harassment on the job could *not* sue their employers under the 1866 Civil Rights Act. They ruled that while the law did ban racial discrimination in the making of contracts, it did not forbid discrimination *after* a person has been hired. The Court also ruled, in *Lorance* v. *AT&T Technologies*, that minority or female employees affected by discriminatory seniority systems must sue within three hundred days of when the program is adopted (Dingle, 1989). This had the effect of giving minorities and women claiming discrimination in seniority systems far more limited rights than white males claiming reverse discrimination: The latter could sue with no time limit, while the former had to sue within three hundred days of the establishment of the seniority system.

Another important ruling in 1989 was *Ward's Cove* v. *Antonio*. While this did not bear directly on affirmative action, it did have effects that many saw as antithetical to the goals of affirmative action. In part, affirmative action is designed to offset or eliminate subtle practices and employment requirements that have the effect of discrimination. But in the *Ward's Cove* case, the Court ruled that job requirements that have the effect of excluding minority or female applicants are illegal only if it can be proved that the intent of having such requirements is discriminatory. This ruling said that such requirements are legal unless the person claiming discrimination can prove that there is no valid business reason for having the requirements (Dwyer, 1989).

The *Ward's Cove* and *Patterson* rulings were reversed by the 1991 Civil Rights Act (Saltzman and Gest, 1991). This legislation states specifically that job requirements that have the effect of excluding minorities or women are legal only when it can be shown that they have a valid business purpose. The burden of showing that this is the case falls on any employer who has a job requirement that has such exclusionary effects. For example, if a college degree were required of someone being hired to wash dishes, this requirement might be called into question because it would have the effect of excluding minorities, who are underrepresented among college graduates. Unless it could be shown that having a college degree makes a person a better dishwasher, which is highly dubious, the requirement would be illegal. The 1991 Civil Rights Act also explicitly bans racial and sexual harassment on the job, thus reversing the *Patterson* ruling.

Public Employment: Hiring Decisions.   The Supreme Court made its first ruling concerning public-employment hiring decisions in the *Firefighters* v. *Cleveland* case in 1986. This case established that, under certain conditions, minority preferences are legal in public-employment hiring decisions. It also established that such preferences can be used as a court-mandated resolution of discrimination suits, if the two main parties agree to settle the suit in that manner. In this case, the city of Cleveland and a group of minority employees suing it for discrimination had agreed to give black and Hispanic firefighters preferences over whites, even if the whites had more seniority and/or higher test scores. The firefighters union sued against the settlement, but the Court ruled that it was a valid way to settle the suit as long as the two original parties agreed to it. The Court indicated, without specific rulings, that (1) stronger evidence of discrimination would be required for courts to *order* racial preferences than was needed to make such a settlement legal and (2) while minority preferences were a legal remedy to discrimination in cases involving public employment, racial quotas probably would not be. These rulings were further clarified by two more Supreme Court rulings in 1987. In the first, *United States* v. *Paradise,* the Court ruled that use of quotas in hiring and promotions by public employers *is* legal and can even be required, under at least one circumstance: a situation in which the employer (in this case, the Alabama State Police) had a past history of severe discrimination. A month later, in *Johnson* v. *Transportation Agency,* the Court ruled that either women or minorities could be promoted ahead of slightly more qualified white males to make the workforce more representative of the area's population. (This was the first ruling on affirmative action for women.)

> ***Public Employment: Layoff Decisions.***   Also in 1986, about two months before the *Sheet Metal Workers* and *Firefighters* cases, the Court ruled on racial preferences in layoffs. In the *Wygand* case, a group of white teachers sued over an agreement between the Jackson, Michigan, school board and its teachers' union. The agreement specified that minorities would receive special protection against layoffs. The reasoning was that most of the minority teachers had been recently hired, and if the district was to keep the teaching staff ethnically diverse in the face of layoffs, there would have to be some special protection for minorities. The legal justification used was that a diverse staff was necessary to provide appropriate role models for students. The Court found that this was not a sufficiently strong justification for racial preferences in layoffs, whose effect on innocent whites is more severe than that of hiring preferences. Thus, the Court established that stronger justification is needed in layoff cases than in hiring cases. It did, however, make the important ruling that the minority individuals benefiting from preferences did *not* have to be individual victims of discrimination by the employer—*societal* discrimination could be sufficient cause. This was a major blow to the Reagan administration's position, which sought to limit minority preferences to only persons the employer had specifically discriminated against. Had that position prevailed, the use of affirmative action to remedy past and institutional discrimination—its key purposes—would have been banned.

Minority Set-Aside Programs

Another method of affirmative action that came into common usage during the 1970s and 1980s was the minority set-aside program. Under programs of this type, state and local governments set aside a certain portion of their business for companies that are owned by minorities or women. For example, a city constructing a new municipal stadium might require that at least 10 percent of the expenditures on the project go to minority-owned companies and at least 10 percent to female-owned companies. These programs are designed to encourage the development of businesses owned by minorities and women, who have historically been largely excluded from business ownership. By 1989, when the Supreme Court first ruled on the legality of this practice, thirty-six states and 190 cities had some form of minority set-aside program.

In the *Croson* v. *City of Richmond* case, the Supreme Court struck down the set-aside program of Richmond, Virginia, on the grounds that the city had not presented sufficient documentation of the need for the program. To justify such programs, the Court ruled, it is necessary to document that there had been past history of discrimination that limited the opportunities of minorities for business ownership, or for minority-owned businesses to effectively compete for government business. Initially, it was believed that this ruling could eliminate many set-aside programs. In fact, during the first few weeks after the *Croson* decision, set-aside programs were dismantled in Georgia, Michigan, Delaware, and New Jersey (Dingle, 1989).

Over the longer run, however, most such programs have managed to survive, by developing ways to better document discrimination. Atlanta, for example, promptly commissioned a study to demonstrate a history of discrimination that limited the opportunities of minority-owned businesses (Thompson, 1989). In most cases, past discrimination is not all that difficult to document. Many set-aside programs pertain to construction, and construction is an industry with a long history of discrimination against both women and minorities. This discrimination has not only made it difficult for minorities and women to *own* construction companies; it has made it difficult for them to even work in such firms. An early affirmative-action program, called the Philadelphia Plan, was adopted more than twenty years ago under the Nixon administration to counteract a past history of exclusion in the construction industry. Since discrimination in this industry is fairly easy to document, many local and state governments ultimately responded to the *Croson* decision by developing better documentation rather than by eliminating their set-aside programs. Thus, in the mid 1990s, set-aside programs remained a commonly used method of affirmative action to increase opportunities for minority-owned businesses.

Overview. Despite some setbacks in 1989, some of which were reversed by the 1991 Civil Rights Act, the general position of the Supreme Court has been to support the legal validity of minority preferences as a tool to remedy the effects of societal discrimination. None of the 1989 rulings actually outlawed the use of affirmative action preferences in hiring or student admissions or of minority set-aside programs. Rather, the rulings placed limits on affirmative action. How far affirmative-action preferences can go depends on a variety of factors: whether hiring, student admissions, or governmental contracting is involved, and also the specific circumstances of any particular case. Many of the Court decisions on affirmative action have been divided. Often they have been based on five-to-four votes, and in some cases, as many as four or five different legal opinions have been written by Supreme Court justices. The degree to which the Court has been divided on this issue suggests that there is always a possibility that the balance could change in future affirmative-action cases. However, the election of Bill Clinton in 1992, whose Court appointees (Justice Ruth Bader Ginsburg was the first in 1993) are likely to be more favorable to affirmative action than were those of Ronald Reagan and George Bush, would appear to forestall any further shift by the Court away from support for affirmative action in the next few years.

Of course, the actual extent to which affirmative-action preferences are used depends on the extent of popular and governmental pressure on employers and educational institutions to use such preferences. Because the Reagan and Bush administrations viewed many forms of affirmative action as reverse discrimination, there was little such pressure from the government during the 1980s and early 1990s. In the more conservative atmosphere of that period, popular pressure also waned.

In the 1990s, however, the position of the Clinton administration, like those administrations before the Reagan administration, is more supportive of affirmative action, and minority-group social movements appear to be on the increase again in the 1990s. Under these conditions, colleges and employers may be under greater pressure to hire and admit increased numbers of minorities and women where they are underrepresented.

IMMIGRATION POLICY

A third major subject of controversy in the area of majority–minority relations is the immigration policy of the United States. As we have seen, immigration policy has long been controversial in the United States and has at times been used in more or less openly racist ways. For about the first half of the twentieth century, Oriental Exclusion Acts kept people from China, Japan, and other parts of Asia from migrating to the United States. Quota systems were also used until the 1960s to limit the number of southern and eastern Europeans entering the United States; such quota systems dated back to 1921. The discriminatory nature of this system can be seen in the fact that about 84 percent of the national quotas went to northern and western Europe (Great Britain and Germany alone accounted for about 60 percent), 14 percent to southern and eastern Europe, and 2 percent to the rest of the world (Thomlinson, 1976, p. 301). The reasons for these restrictions appear to have been twofold. First, there was resistance to the whole idea of immigration on the grounds that immigrants contribute to the unemployment problem, and that—because they are sometimes willing to work for lower salaries than Americans—they put Americans out of work and hold down their wages. Recent research, however, has shown that, by the money they spend, immigrants usually create more jobs than they take (Muller, 1985; McCarthy and Valdez, 1985). Immigrants are also low users of welfare, and with the possible exception of education, they pay more in taxes than they take back in the form of government services (McCarthy and Valdez, 1985). Second, much of the opposition to immigration arises from plain and simple ethnocentrism. Some Americans simply do not want to admit people who are "different from us," even though they or their ancestors were once immigrants, too. Thus, it is hardly surprising that anti-immigration groups such as the Know Nothing party and the Ku Klux Klan have been not only anti-immigration, but also anti-Jewish, anti-Catholic, and antiblack.

In 1965 legislation was passed that phased out the quota system over a three-year period. The annual limits on immigration were changed to 120,000 from the Western Hemisphere and 170,000 from the Eastern Hemisphere, with a maximum of 20,000 from any one country in the Eastern Hemisphere. This policy has obviously made immigration much more open to people from outside northern and western Europe than was previously the case. In 1978 the hemisphere distinction was dropped, and immigration was simply limited to 290,000 per year, with not more than 20,000 from any one country. Although the theoretical limit on immigration until recently was 290,000 per year, the actual number of legal immigrants per year has been larger because some immigrants are exempted from these limits. The parents, spouses, and unmarried children of U.S. citizens may enter the United States without numerical restrictions, and exceptions to the limits are also made for political refugees. Thus, legal immigration during the 1970s averaged close to 500,000 per year. In the 1980s, several influxes of refugees further elevated immigration, so that the average annual immigration for the period 1981–1990 was around 598,000, not counting people who were admitted under an amnesty approved in 1986 (to be discussed shortly) (U.S. Bureau of the Census, 1993, pp. 10–11). In 1991, about 704,000 immigrants were admitted, again not counting those admitted under the amnesty.

Part of the reason for the large number of immigrants admitted in 1991 was that the number of refugees that year was the largest in some time due to unrest in Haiti, El Salvador, and elsewhere. This was the case even though it was made very difficult for Haitians to obtain refugee status in the early 1990s. Had they been admitted according to the same criteria as Cubans and others in earlier years, the number admitted would have been significantly greater. In fact, the question of racial discrimination in immigration policy has again arisen in the context of resistance under both the Bush and Clinton administrations to the admission of Haitian refugees. Unlike refugees from Cuba, Nicaragua, Vietnam, and elsewhere, nearly all the Haitian refugees are black. It has been widely suggested that public opposition to Haitian immigration, which has been quite pronounced in Florida, where most Haitian immigrants arrive, is based partly on racism—and that government policy toward Haitian immigration has been largely shaped by the resultant political pressures (Page, 1994).

Today's immigrants are far more likely than in the past to come from non-European countries. In the 1990s, for example, more than 38 percent of all immigrants to the United States came from Asia. Another 35 percent came from Latin America, including Mexico (U.S. Bureau of the Census, 1993, p. 11). During the 1980s, there were more immigrants from the Caribbean than from Europe, even though Europe's population is fifteen times as large as that of the Caribbean. Throughout the 1980s, fewer than 10 percent of all immigrants to the United States came from Europe. Because most immigrants today come from Asia, Latin America, or the Caribbean, today's immigrants are more racially diverse than ever before, and immigration is one of the most important reasons for America's increasing diversity.

Illegal Immigration and the 1986 and 1990 Immigration Reform Laws

Although there are legal limits on immigration to the United States, we know that actual immigration into the United States is well above the legal limits, although we do not know by how much. Some estimates have held that illegal immigration is substantially greater than legal immigration—perhaps three or four million people per year. These estimates, however, are almost certainly too high. They are based on the fact that at the Mexican border alone, immigration authorities were catching and deporting about 700,000 illegal immigrants per year during the 1980s and on assumptions that this represents the "tip of the iceberg" in terms of the actual amount of illegal immigration. However, these estimates fail to consider two important realities. First, some of these people were caught more than once, so immigration authorities did not catch 700,000 different people. Second, most who enter illegally across the Mexican border return to Mexico on their own rather than remaining permanently in the United States. The best estimates are that, in 1980, a total of 2 million illegal immigrants were counted in that year's census (Warren and Passel, 1987). Perhaps that many more were missed by the census. If this were the case, the total number of illegal immigrants in the United States in 1980 would not have been more than 4 million. And of these, about 2.5 million were admitted as legal immigrants under an amnesty passed in 1986. Accordingly, the number of illegal immigrants in the United States today is probably not more than around 2 million, less than 1 percent of the U.S. population.

Illegal immigrants enter the United States in two main ways. One is the Mexican border, which at one time was not particularly well patrolled but which has become more so in recent years. The other, which may be of equal importance, is that people enter the United States legally and then overstay their visas, or, less often, present forged documents at ports of entry. The number of people who immigrate illegally by overstaying their visas is illustrated by a study by Vining (1979), who found that during the 1970s, about 500,000 to 700,000 more people were arriving by air in the United States than were departing each year. If every legal immigrant arrived by air (which is not the case), these figures would still suggest over 100,000 illegal arrivals each year, and they do not take into account people who arrive by land or sea and overstay their visas. Overall, the most reasonable estimates suggest that between 100,000 and 500,000 people per year immigrated illegally to the United States by all means during the 1980s—a sizable number, but well below estimates that were often reported by the popular press.

Because of the continuing problem of illegal immigration, adjustments were made in immigration laws in 1986 and again in 1990. The 1986 Immigration Reform and Control Act (IRCA) attempted to resolve the problem of illegal immigration in two ways: to legalize through an amnesty program those who were already here and to eliminate the main incentive for illegal immigration by preventing employers from hiring illegal aliens. As was already noted, about 2.5 million people were admitted under the amnesty provision between 1989 and 1991 (U.S. Bureau of the Census, 1993, p. 10). For the first time, IRCA established penalties for employers who knowingly hire illegal aliens and placed the burden on employers to attempt to ascertain that their employees are legally present in the United States. The idea behind this is that the main reason people come illegally to the United States is economic, and that if illegal immigrants cannot get jobs, they will have no reason to immigrate.

While the theory behind this provision is appealing, studies have shown that its effectiveness has been limited and its side effects substantial. A joint study by the Rand Corporation and the Urban Institute (1990) showed that illegal immigration fell by about 15 percent the first year IRCA was in effect but after that there was little decline, and the best estimate is that three years after the passage of IRCA, illegal immigration was only about 20 percent less than it had been before the law was passed (Stevenson, 1990). On the other hand, it appears that the law did lead to an increase in hiring discrimination. When the law was being debated, concern was expressed that it might lead to an increase in ethnic discrimination against people who looked or sounded "foreign." For this reason, Congress mandated a study to see to what extent this happened. The study found that, during the first year IRCA was in effect, about one in ten employers in the United States discriminated on the basis of foreign appearance or accent. In cities like New York, Los Angeles, and Chicago that have large Asian and Latino populations, 18 to 29 percent of all employers discriminated (General Accounting Office, 1990; Pear, 1990). Thus, the discouraging evidence about IRCA is that its ban on hiring illegal immigrants had only a small effect on the amount of illegal immigration but did lead to an increase in employment discrimination on the basis of ethnicity.

Why didn't the law have a greater effect on illegal immigration? There appear to be two reasons. First, some have argued that there are too many different forms of identification that job applicants can use to demonstrate legality—some of which are easily forged. Some have suggested the use of a national identification card as a remedy for this, but others have criticized this idea on the basis of civil liberties: Such a card could be used to keep track of political dissenters. There is, however, a more fundamental reason for IRCA's ineffectiveness at preventing illegal immigration. Given the great disparities in income and wealth between the United States and its neighbors to the south, there are very strong incentives for people to look for a better economic future in the United States. This is exacerbated by the rapid population growth of Mexico and other Latin American countries. Over the next thirty years, for example, Mexico's population is expected to soar from its present level of 90 million to nearly 138 million—an increase of more than 50 percent (Population Reference Bureau, 1993). As this population pressure increases, so will pressure for immigration to the United States. If the North American Free Trade Agreement (NAFTA), approved in 1993, succeeds in its goal of encouraging economic development in Mexico, some of this pressure could be offset. Even at the time that IRCA was passed in 1986, however, many of its critics argued that the immigration limits then in effect were too low, and that IRCA should have raised the limits. It did not, because of popular opposition to immigration in much of the United States.

By 1990, however, it was evident that IRCA had done little to reduce illegal immigration, and that legal immigration was continuing to rise. Consequently, in 1990 Congress passed amendments to the act to raise the limits on immigration. The 1990 approach was an attempt to set a realistic limit for immigration of all types. The new overall number of immigrants to be accepted each year was set at 700,000, which is higher than the numbers admitted annually throughout the 1980s. Provisions were also added to reserve some spaces for immigrants with occupational skills that are scarce in the United States or who are in a financial position to hire employees once they arrive here. Visas were also set aside for immigrants from thirty-five countries who had been largely shut out because priority had been given to people with families already in the United States, with a special provision for people from Ireland, many of whom had arrived illegally during the 1980s. The limit of 700,000 immigrants per year was to run through 1994, with the limit "permanently" set at 675,000 per year beginning in 1995 (Weeks, 1992).

While the 1990 legislation modestly increased the number of immigrants admitted legally each year to the United States, two facts remain true. First, not only the United States, but all affluent countries are experiencing increased immigration pressure. As long as a large and growing majority of the world's population lives in countries with high poverty rates and low standards of living, large numbers of people will seek to immigrate to countries like the United States, Canada, and most countries in western Europe. Many will try to enter illegally, and in a country with borders as extensive as those of the United States, it will be impossible to stop anywhere near all of them. Second, the limits on immigration in the United States, though relaxed recently, are quite restrictive compared with those in many other industrialized countries. During the 1980s, the legal-immigration rate to the United States was 3.1 per thousand—higher than any time since the 1920s but well below the rates that prevailed from 1830 through 1920. However, the immigration rate of the United States remains well below that of many other countries. In 1987, for example, the rate of legal immigration ranged from 5.9 to 8.4 per thousand in Canada, the Netherlands, Sweden, and Norway (computed from Europa Publications, 1989). With its liberal policy on admitting refugees and the widespread upheaval in Eastern Europe, Germany admitted 438,000 refugees in 1992—a rate of 5.5 per thousand population—and that does not include ordinary immigrants or the large number of guest workers it admits.

Should the legal level of immigration be raised further in the United States, to make it more consistent with the actual pressure for immigration and with policies of other industrialized countries? Some answer yes, based on both the difficulty of enforcing present laws and on the fact that immigration brings important benefits to society. Immigrants fill jobs for which trained workers are in short supply in the United States, and new jobs are created by the buying power of immigrants. Even some studies of illegal immigrants have shown that they have no downward effect on wages (Massey, cited in Bean and Tienda, 1987). As mentioned, immigrants generally pay more in taxes than they use in government services. For example, Simon (1990) found that the average immigrant family receives $1,404 per year in all forms of publicly funded assistance during the first five years, and $1,941 thereafter. In contrast, the average nonimmigrant family received $2,279. Studies also indicate that economic growth is correlated with population growth, and that immigration is one way to maintain population growth in the face of the low U.S. birthrate. Finally, many believe that the cultural diversity brought by immigrants is an important source of adaptability and innovation in society.

On the other hand, a great many Americans would like to see immigration

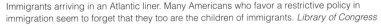

Immigrants arriving in an Atlantic liner. Many Americans who favor a restrictive policy in immigration seem to forget that they too are the children of immigrants. *Library of Congress*

reduced to a level lower than the present level. Indeed, this tendency is seen in nearly every country in the world that admits substantial numbers of immigrants—a fact that, if nothing else, certainly illustrates the near-universality of ethnocentrism. Assimilationists are concerned about both the overall number of immigrants and the fact that a few countries account for an especially large share. Large numbers from one country may mean it will be easier to retain their own culture rather than blend in. Nonetheless, it is important to keep in mind that the United States is a nation composed almost entirely of immigrants, and that—aside from sudden floods of immigrants that overwhelm an area's ability to absorb them—those who are here gain from immigration a number of benefits that are sometimes forgotten amid the worry about increased competition for jobs and the fears about cultures different from our own. Thus, it may well be that the benefits of immigration outweigh the costs. Finally, many argue that it is hardly fair for a nation with the great wealth of the United States, and a nation that consumes such a large share of the world's wealth, to post a "Keep Out" sign at its boundaries, particularly when that nation itself is populated by immigrants and the sons and daughters of immigrants.

THE RELATIVE IMPORTANCE OF RACE AND CLASS
IN AMERICAN SOCIETY

The final issue to which we now turn is an intellectual debate more than a policy debate, but it carries important implications for public policy as well. This debate concerns the relative importance of *racial discrimination* versus *social class* as causes of inequality in American society today.

The controversy began with the publication of William J. Wilson's (1978) *Declining Significance of Race,* parts of which have been discussed at some length in other parts of this book. The controversial part of Wilson's book was his conclusion, suggested by the title, that disadvantages linked to social class (income, education, occupation) have become much more important than *racial* discrimination as a cause of black social disadvantage today. He based this conclusion on the following major observations. First, there has been a substantial decline in deliberate employment discrimination in the United States since World War II. In other words, it has become much less common (as well as illegal) for employers to openly refuse to hire someone because he or she is black or to have a policy of paying blacks less for the same work. (This change, along with many of the reasons for it, including those suggested by Wilson, is discussed at greater length in Chapters 6 through 9 of this book.) Along with these changes have come an increase in enrollment and graduation of blacks in higher education, so that by the mid 1970s, according to Wilson, black enrollment rates in higher education were very close to white enrollment rates. As we saw in Chapter 9 and again in our discussion of affirmative action in this chapter, *recent black college graduates* are doing nearly as well as recent white graduates in terms of income and education, largely because previously closed opportunities have been opened by affirmative action. Thus, Wilson concludes that there is a growing black middle class and that the younger members of this middle class are doing quite well economically, though he acknowledges that they experience considerable discrimination in the residential, social, and educational arenas.

Totally apart from this, according to Wilson, is the large and perhaps growing black underclass. This group, mostly falling below the poverty level and living in the inner cities, is beset with problems of unemployment and underemployment and is, as we have seen in previous chapters, probably becoming *worse off*, not better off, in the 1970s and 1980s. Wilson argues, however, that it is not *racial discrimination* but poverty itself that is this group's main problem. Thus, while blacks are overrepresented in the group because of past discrimination, it is not present-day discrimination that is *keeping* them in their unfortunate position. Rather, it is changes in the economy that make this group in large part unemployable. (For a rather different analysis that reaches a somewhat similar conclusion, see Wilhelm, 1980, esp. pp. 108–9.) This has happened because as manufacturing employment has declined, the availability of low-skill jobs has also decreased. Because of *past* discrimination, however, lower-class, inner-city blacks lack the skills needed for jobs that *are* growing and have available fewer and fewer low-skill jobs for which they can compete. Thus, they experience high unemployment, often have to move from one short-term, dead-end job to another, and have little chance to escape this unfortunate situation. Thus, the problem is *not* the refusal of employers to hire such persons because they are black but rather their lack, because of past discrimination, of any marketable skills. Thus class, not race, is the primary cause of black disadvantage today, according to Wilson. (For elaboration of these arguments beyond those made in this book, see Wilson, 1979, 1980.)

In particular, Wilson has elaborated on this argument in *The Truly Disadvantaged* (1987), in which he argues that continuing losses of manufacturing employment, owing to the economic shifts described above, have had both direct and indirect effects on inner-city blacks, and to a sizable but lesser extent, on Latinos. In addition to the direct economic effects of job loss, there have been several important kinds of indirect effects. One is the disruption of social institutions in the inner city. As jobs have left and conditions have worsened in the inner city, the economic conditions of those living there have worsened, and the middle class—of all races—has fled. One effect of this has been to disrupt and undermine neighborhood institutions such as churches and businesses. For the same reasons, poverty and unemployment among African Americans and Latinos, who live disproportionately in the inner-city areas that are losing jobs, have become concentrated. In other words, if you are black or Hispanic and poor, it is far more likely that many or most of your neighbors will be poor than if you are white and poor, and far more likely that many of the people in your neighborhood will be out of work (Wilson, 1987). According to Wilson, this concentrates the problems associated with poverty and, for young people, reduces the number of role models they see working stable jobs. Concentrated poverty heightens the problems of the neighborhood and makes it harder for people to escape poverty. Finally, according to Wilson, it leads to other conditions, such as family disruption and nonmarital childbearing that—though they do not *cause* the problem of inner-city poverty—may well make it worse.

The *Declining Significance of Race* was, as noted earlier, a controversial book. One reason most certainly is that it is easily misinterpreted to suggest that America's racial problem is solved (Pettigrew, 1980). Certainly Wilson never intended such an interpretation, but some critics and some supporters of the book have given it that interpretation (Willie, 1979). As the critics emphatically point out, there is nothing approaching economic equality between the races in America (on this point, see the data presented in Chapter 9 of this text). A careful reading of Wilson, however, will clearly show that he certainly never intended to claim there is racial equality, though his choice of titles for the book does encourage misinterpretation (Payne, 1979,

p. 138; Pettigrew, 1980). As Willie (1979, p. 16) points out, such broad generalizations as "economic class is now a more important factor than race in determining job placement for blacks" (W. J. Wilson, 1978, p. 120) also encourage the interpretation (which many whites would like to make) that America's *racial* problem is largely solved and little more needs to be done. In the judgment of this author, a careful reading of Wilson's entire book would not support such an interpretation at all, but the title and some overly broad generalizations probably do.

The more empirical criticisms of Wilson's work, however, focus on somewhat different issues. Wilson does not disagree with his critics that blacks on the whole have lower incomes than whites[1] or that serious and rapid action is needed on the problem of black poverty (see Wilson, 1979, p. 175). The real argument, as has already been suggested, is over the *reasons* for black poverty and over the degree to which middle-class blacks have really gained a socioeconomic status comparable to middle-class whites. On the latter point, there is some evidence that while the income gap has narrowed for younger, highly educated blacks and whites, it has not necessarily disappeared. Willie (1979, pp. 53–54) reports that even black professional and managerial workers have incomes 20 percent below those of white workers in these areas and cites data from a U.S. Commission on Civil Rights study (1978) showing that *even after controls for age, education, and occupation,* both blacks and Chicanos typically received income substantially below that of white Anglos. A similar analysis by R. Farley (1984) using income data for 1979 showed that black males, even if they would have had the typical social characteristics of white males and worked the same number of hours, would still have received only 88 percent of the white-male income. The incomes of females of both races were substantially lower. This suggests significant racial inequality *independent of* class inequality (as Wilson's critics claim), though, in partial support of Wilson, Farley's analysis does show a narrowing over time since 1960 in black–white inequality. Furthermore, Farley found that a black–white gap persisted after controls for other factors even in the most highly educated group, though, again, the gap did narrow. Thus, evidence is found in this study for a declining *but continuing* "significance of race."

Like the racial difference in income, part of the racial difference in unemployment appears linked to race, not class. Educational differences alone cannot account for the disproportionate unemployment of either blacks or Hispanics. Part of it appears to be a product of segregation restricting minority groups to areas with limited job opportunities, and, for blacks, the potential gains to whites from keeping blacks unemployed may also be a factor (Farley, 1987b).

Edwards (1979), Collins (1993), and Marrett (1980) have pointed to another potential problem in Wilson's argument: Even though the black middle class *has* grown and narrowed the gap with the white middle class, the position of blacks and other minorities in the middle class is much less secure than that of the white middle class. Historically—as Wilson himself stresses—blacks and other minorities have tended to gain in good economic times and to lose in bad economic times. Given the economic uncertainty of the 1990s, as well as a possible conservative trend in the American populace, there is certainly a risk of minority losses. Wilson notes correctly that middle-class minorities did *not* lose ground in the recession of the mid 1970s, but over the longer term this may not continue to be the case if there

---

[1]Though he does argue that treating blacks "as a whole" masks important socioeconomic differences within the black population.

is a long period of economic difficulty. Indeed, with shortages of even middle-class jobs, white opposition to affirmative action has grown, and the Reagan administration has expressed considerable reluctance to press affirmative-action goals. A retreat on affirmative action would beyond doubt limit black entry into the middle class, and even with affirmative action, the principle of the last hired being the first to be laid off in a time of economic crunch still holds true. Thus, in Detroit for example, when layoffs became necessary in the city's police force, seniority rules required that most of those laid off be black, because it was blacks who were most recently hired under the city's affirmative-action program. Finally, Edwards (1979) correctly notes that black enrollment in a number of major universities declined in relation to that of whites in the latter half of the 1970s, a trend that continued irregularly through the mid 1980s. Thus, it seems a fair criticism of Wilson's work to warn that, however much race may have declined in importance relative to class, there is a very real danger that it could increase in importance again, especially given the intermittent economic difficulty the country has experienced in recent years and may well continue to experience.

Another point on which Wilson has received considerable criticism concerns the reasons for the disproportionate number of blacks in the impoverished underclass and the reasons that the people in this underclass cannot escape from that unfortunate status. It is Wilson's claim that blacks are overrepresented in the underclass because of past discrimination and that they are unable to escape the underclass (as is everyone else in the underclass) because of the lack of low-skill jobs in today's economy. Accordingly, Wilson argues that *present-day racial discrimination* is *not* very important as a cause of disadvantage among the black underclass. On this point, Wilson is vulnerable to considerable criticism. As we have seen in previous chapters, past racial discrimination and present-day class discrimination (including the institutionalized variety) *are,* as Wilson says, important reasons for continuing black (and other minority) overrepresentation in the impoverished underclass. However, Wilson is widely and correctly criticized for failing to note the importance of present-day *institutionalized racial discrimination* as a cause of the problem (Payne, 1979, pp. 134–37). Consider our own exploration of institutional discrimination in Chapters 10 to 12 of this book. There is no question that much of the discrimination discussed there does occur on the basis of social class, affecting minorities disproportionately because they are overrepresented among the poor. However, there is also a good deal of institutional discrimination specifically along the lines of *race.* In education, we have seen such problems as de facto school segregation, linguistic biases against minority students, low teacher expectations of minority students, distorted presentations of minorities in texts and materials, and racial inequities in tracking. Although there most certainly are strong class biases in the educational system (Bowles and Gintis, 1976), all of the inequities mentioned here are specifically *racial.* Since Wilson notes lack of quality education as playing a central role in the perpetuation of the minority underclass, it seems clear that institutionalized racial inequalities in education play an important role in the problem. The same is true in other areas. To cite one example, we can point to housing discrimination. Wilson himself (1980, p. 23) states that "the lack of opportunity for underclass blacks forces them to remain in economically depressed ghettoes," which along with poor ghetto education, "reinforce(s) their low labor market positions." Wilson is right about the effects of ghettoization on black employment when jobs have largely left the ghetto (see, for example, Farley, 1987b). He is incorrect, however, in that he ignores the crucial role of racial discrimination as a cause of ghettoization. As we saw in Chapter 11, economic differences between blacks and whites are less important than race as a cause of black–white housing segregation. The primary cause of such segregation is racial, not economic. Since such housing segregation restricts black opportunities in both employment and education, it is, as Wilson notes, an important cause of the problems of the minority underclass. However, Wilson fails to recognize the degree to which racial, as opposed to economic, factors produce that segregation. Thus, we see here, too, an example of the continuing significance of race.

These and other processes of institutional racial discrimination, then, *do* help to explain why blacks and other minorities are so overrepresented in the impoverished underclass and why they have so much trouble escaping from that underclass. Further evidence of racial discrimination can be seen in the fact that the minority underclass is worse off than the white underclass. Thus, we find that, at the lowest levels of occupation and education, blacks and other minorities have *substantially lower incomes than whites* (Willie, 1979, pp. 62–63), though this gap, too, has narrowed somewhat over time (R. Farley, 1984). On the other hand, black Americans are more than three times as likely as whites to fall below the poverty level, and this pattern has *not* changed significantly in recent years. In addition, the Hispanic poverty rate has *risen* relative to that of whites in recent years.

Wilson's critics also point out that deliberate employment discrimination, both individual and institutional, remains more common than appearances might suggest. While such discrimination is not usually open, it clearly still exists. As was described in Chapter 14, discrimination-testing studies in recent years have found racial discrimination to be quite common in employment as well as in other areas of life. Even members of Wilson's own research team at the University of Chicago have found considerable evidence of employment discrimination in surveys of major Chicago-area employers. Much of this discrimination was based on racial stereotypes, particularly about black males (Kirschenman, 1989, 1990; Kirschenman and Neckerman, 1991). Wilson (forthcoming) has argued that these stereotypes are based partly on reactions by employers to the angry response of black males to the joblessness they have encountered because of deindustrialization in the inner city. Thus, he argues that, to some extent, the social and economic forces that have taken jobs from the inner city play an indirect role in discrimination by employers. However, by anyone's definition, including Wilson's, these employers are engaging in racial discrimination.

Perhaps Payne (1979, p. 136) has hit on the best description of the process causing racial inequality in recent years with his statement that "it is entirely possible that the processes sustaining differentials in racial privilege have become a good deal more fragmented than they once were." In other words, there are a wider variety of factors causing racial inequality than there once were. At one time, deliberate acts of racial discrimination were the main cause of racial inequality in America. Today, deliberate acts of discrimination are not the sole cause and perhaps not the primary cause of racial inequality. Today's inequality is a product of a combination of acts of discrimination, the effects of past discrimination, economic disadvantages, *and* institutional discrimination. Thus, Wilson is right about the changes in the economy and the decline of open and deliberate discrimination, but he understates the continuing effect of institutional racial discrimination in perpetuating minority poverty. He is right, too, in pointing to increasing class differentiation within the minority population, through some measures show more of this than others (R. Farley,

1984, chap. 6). However, he understates the degree to which the position of the minority group middle class is insecure and could deteriorate in the hard economic times that may be coming. Thus, Wilson's *Declining Significance of Race* makes an important contribution to the understanding of majority–minority relations in America but at the same time underestimates the continuing importance of racial types of discrimination as a factor influencing the status of black (and other minority group) Americans today. Thus, both class *and* race continue to be economically significant, perpetuating a situation in which the overall position of minorities relative to whites is little if any better than in the past, despite increasing class differentiation within minority groups.

SUMMARY AND CONCLUSION

In this chapter, we have explored some of the issues in intergroup relations that face the United States today: affirmative action, assimilation versus pluralism, immigration policy, and the relative importance of racial discrimination and social class. These and a host of other issues relating to intergroup relations remain unresolved. The upsurge of racial violence in Los Angeles and other cities in 1992; the growth in poverty and homelessness in the 1980s, which hit blacks and Hispanics the hardest; the increased number of racial incidents around the country since the mid 1980s; and the increased racial polarization in voting in some recent elections all serve to remind us that problems of intergroup relations remain deeply rooted in American society and remain unsolved despite the deceptive calm of much of the 1970s and 1980s. An intelligent and effective response to these problems will require both compassion and informed knowledge on the part of the American public. Neither by itself is sufficient. It is hoped that this book will help in some small way to make people more informed about intergroup relations. People must be aware of the historical patterns and subtle institutional processes that keep minority groups in an inferior position in present-day American society. Furthermore, they must be able to look at the problem from a perspective other than that of their own group. If this book has helped to accomplish these two things, its author will regard it as a worthwhile endeavor. While knowledge and understanding are necessary, however, they alone are not enough. Americans must be *motivated* to solve problems of intergroup relations; they must *care* about what happens to people in groups less fortunate than their own. No book can make that happen. Only the American public, including you, the reader, can do that.

Glossary

achieved status A position of status attained by something a person does or accomplishes rather than by birth. In class systems, social standing is determined largely by achieved statuses, though *ascribed statuses* also have a sizable influence.

affirmative action Any deliberate effort to increase minority representation, such as in a workforce or student body. Affirmative action may be limited to more vigorous efforts to recruit minorities or may be extended to preferences in hiring or student admissions for *minority-group* members. This sometimes includes the use of specific goals and timetables for minority representation.

Afrocentrism An effort by African Americans to emphasize and value African history, philosophy, and culture, particularly (but not only) in education. In education, it often involves developing a curriculum centered around African experience and culture.

amalgamation The combination of two *racial* or *ethnic groups* into one through marriage or other sexual contact between the groups. Gradually, the distinction between the two groups becomes blurred, and they come to be regarded as a single group.

annexation An expansion of territory by one group to take control over territory formerly under control of another group. This may be through military conquest, in which the outcome is much the same as in *colonization*. It may also be voluntary, as when residents of an area ask to be annexed. Some cases, such as purchases, fall somewhere between.

anti-Semitism *Prejudice* and discrimination against Jewish people.

ascribed status Any characteristic or status determined by birth, such as race, sex, or who one's parents are. In *caste systems,* one's social standing is determined on the basis of ascribed statuses.

assimilation A process whereby a *minority group* and the *dominant group* gradually become integrated into a common culture and social system. Although the dominant group may adapt itself to the minority or absorb certain cultural characteristics of the minority group, it is more often the minority group that must adapt to fit into the culture and social system of the majority. See also *cultural assimilation* and *structural assimilation.*

attitudinal racism Racial or ethnic prejudice. See *prejudice.*

464

blockbusting A practice by real-estate agents or speculators that attempts to panic whites into selling their homes at a low price because blacks are supposedly moving into the neighborhood. The speculator purchases the house, then sells it to a black family, often at an inflated price. This practice exploits both black and white homeowners and encourages racial segregation and rapid racial turnover in urban neighborhoods.

caste system A system of social inequality with two or more rigidly defined and unequal groups, membership in which is determined by birth and passed from generation to generation. There is ordinarily no opportunity for a person in one group to move to another group of higher status.

class system A system of loosely defined, unequal groups in which there is significant but not unlimited opportunity to move to a higher or lower status.

cognitive dissonance theory A theory that says we strive to make our attitudes consistent with our behavior, frequently by developing attitudes to support or justify preexisting behavior. This theory suggests that nondiscriminatory behavior (for example, to comply with the law) may lead to unprejudiced attitudes. Similarly, racist behavior (for example, for personal gain) may lead to racist attitudes as a justifying mechanism.

colonization A form of intergroup contact that occurs when one group migrates into an area occupied by another group and subordinates that *indigenous group.*

colonized minority A *minority group* that initially became a part of the society it lives in through conquest or annexation. In addition to such forcible entry, colonized minorities are usually subjected to some form of unfree labor and to attacks on their culture and social institutions.

conflict perspective A sociological perspective that sees society as dominated by a powerful elite, which controls most of the wealth and power in the society, to the disadvantage of other, less powerful members of the society. Because of this inequality, society tends toward conflict and change, though the power and/or prestige of the dominant group may for a time lead to a consensus in society, or the appearance thereof. This consensus, however, is temporary: The long-term tendency is toward conflict and change.

crosscutting cleavages The situation in which societal divisions such as race, language, religion, and class all cut along different lines; there are, for example, religious divisions within racial groups. Crosscutting cleavages tend to hold down the amount of intergroup conflict because people have divided loyalties.

cultural assimilation A type of *assimilation* in which two or more groups gradually come to share a common culture, that is, similar attitudes, values, language, beliefs, lifestyles, and rules about behavior. Frequently, the shared culture is much more similar to that of the *majority group* than it is to that of the *minority group,* though this is not always the case.

cultural immersion An educational approach whereby children in a *minority group* are systematically exposed to positive role models of the student's own racial or ethnic background and that promotes collective self-worth by teaching students to value their cultural heritage. Schools based on the cultural-immersion model have most commonly been developed for black males because of the especially severe risk they face, particularly in impoverished inner-city neighborhoods.

cultural pluralism A pattern in which different racial, ethnic, or other groups retain cultural features that are distinct in each group but hold some others that are common to all groups in society.

de facto segregation School *segregation* that is the result not of an official policy of having separate schools for different racial groups but of other processes that tend to create segregated schools, even without an official policy to have segregated schools. The most important cause of de facto segregation is housing segregation, which leads to a situation in which neighborhood school attendance districts tend to be, for example, all-white or all-black.

de jure segregation School *segregation* that is the result of an official or deliberate policy of having separate schools for different racial groups.

displacement, or **displaced aggression** Similar in meaning to *scapegoating.*

diversity management Workplace programs designed to empower employees of all groups to work, produce, and advance in the organization to their full potential through addressing intergroup tensions and conflicts in the workplace that inhibit productivity and often limit opportunities of workers on the basis of their *race, ethnicity,* gender, disability status, or sexual orientation.

dominant group Similar in meaning to *majority group*.

environmental racism A tendency for *minority groups* to be placed at disproportionate risk of exposure to hazardous substances and environmental contaminants. Occurs because relatively powerless minority communities often become locations of hazardous-waste disposal sites and sources of labor for work involving exposure to dangerous substances.

ethnic group A group of people who are generally regarded by themselves or others as a distinct group, with such recognition based on social or cultural characteristics such as nationality, language, and religion. Ethnicity, like *race*, tends to be passed from generation to generation and is ordinarily not an affiliation that one can freely drop.

ethnic stratification, or **ethnic inequality** A pattern under which social inequality falls along the lines of *race* or *ethnicity*. In other words, one or more racial or ethnic groups enjoy an advantaged position over another group or groups with respect to income, wealth, power, prestige, and so on.

ethnocentrism A tendency to view one's own group as the norm or standard and to view outgroups as not just different but also strange and usually inferior. The ways of the in-group are viewed as the natural way or the only way of doing things and become a standard against which out-groups are judged.

false consciousness The acceptance—usually by a *subordinate group*—of values, beliefs, or ideologies that do not serve the self-interest of that group. In Marxist analysis, false consciousness frequently occurs when subordinate groups accept ideologies promoted by the wealthy elite to serve the interests of the elite at the expense of the subordinate groups.

fee-for-service system A system of health-care payment whereby a fee is collected by a physician for each service performed, such as an office visit, operation, or reading of an X-ray. Under such a system, the doctor is paid for each service in this manner regardless of whether the payment is made by the person receiving the treatment, a private insurance company, or a government program. This system can be contrasted with systems in which physicians receive fixed salaries, such as health maintenance organizations (HMOs) or systems of socialized medicine.

fluid competitive race relations A pattern of race relations best described as a *class system* with racial inequalities remaining from a past racial *caste system*. There is little official segregation but often much *de facto segregation*. Minority groups have middle classes but are disproportionately poor. Racial conflict is present but usually kept to a controlled level.

functionalist perspective A sociological perspective stressing the notions that society is made up of interrelated parts that contribute to the effectiveness of the society and that society tends toward consensus, order, and stability. These tendencies are seen as necessary if society is to be effective and efficient. According to this perspective, the absence of these conditions can pose a serious threat to the quality of life in the society and even to the society's ability to continue to function.

gender inequality Inequality between men and women in society, which results in men having greater power, status, and economic security than women.

gender roles Different and unequal roles of men and women. In other words, men and women are expected to behave differently and to carry on different kinds of activity in life, and men are typically accorded higher status and given greater economic rewards for what they do than are women.

gerrymandering The practice of drawing odd-shaped school attendance districts as a way of promoting racial or ethnic *segregation* in the schools.

glass ceiling An informal upper limit that keeps women and minorities from being promoted to the positions of greatest responsibility in work organizations. Glass ceilings may exist without any formal or deliberate attempt to discriminate and for a variety of reasons including *stereotypes*, cultural conflicts, and favoritism.

heterosexism *Institutional discrimination* against homosexuals (including gay men and lesbians) and bisexuals.

homophobia *Prejudice* and discrimination against homosexuals. Homophobia can be directed against either gay men or lesbians, or both, and is also usually taken to include prejudice and discrimination against bisexuals.

ideological racism, or **racist ideology** The belief that one *race* is superior to another biologically, intellectually, culturally, temperamentally, or morally. Such ideologies usually exist to rationalize or justify domination of one race or *ethnic group* by another, and tend to become institutionalized or widely accepted within a culture.

immigrant minority A *minority group* that voluntarily migrated into the country or society in which it lives. Ordinarily, these minorities are more readily assimilated into the dominant society than are colonized minorities.

immigration Migration of one group into an area controlled by another group. The entering group becomes a part of the *indigenous group's* society. Immigration may be either voluntary or, as in the case of slave importation, involuntary. Bonded or indentured laborers and political refugees are cases that fall somewhere between voluntary and involuntary.

index of dissimilarity A measure of the amount of housing *segregation* between any two groups, such as blacks and whites. It indicates the percentage of either group that would have to move to attain complete integration (the same mix of the two groups in every block or neighborhood). It can range from zero (fully integrated) to one hundred (totally segregated). It is also sometimes called the *segregation index*.

indigenous group A *racial* or *ethnic group* that is well established in an area before the arrival of some new group. An indigenous group may be, but does not have to be, native to the area in which it is established.

individual racial discrimination, or **individual behavioral racism** Any behavior by individuals that leads to unequal treatment on the basis of *race* or *ethnicity*. A restaurant owner's refusal to serve Chinese Americans would be an example.

in-group A group of which a person is a member or with which he or she identifies.

institutional racism, or **institutional discrimination** Any arrangement or practice within a social institution or its related organizations that tends to favor one *racial* or *ethnic group* (usually the majority group) over another. Institutional racism may be conscious and deliberate, as in discriminatory voting laws, or subtle and perhaps unintended, as in industrial location decisions that favor suburban whites over inner-city blacks.

intergroup education Any effort, by whatever means, to bring about factual learning about intergroup relations. Education is not primarily intended to change attitudes or opinions, although this may be a common result and is sometimes a latent objective.

internal colonialism A theory that argues that *colonized minorities* experience discrimination different in kind or degree from that experienced by *immigrant minorities,* and as a result experience less upward mobility and less assimilation. Also, a process whereby such minorities are exploited for the economic benefit of the *majority group* or some segment of the majority group.

majority group Any social group that is dominant in a society; that is, it enjoys more than a proportionate share of the wealth, power, and/or social status in that society. Although majority groups in this sense are frequently a numerical majority, this is not always the case.

Marxist theory of discrimination A theory based on the ideas of Karl Marx, it claims that discrimination hurts working-class whites as well as *minority group* members by creating racial divisions within the working class.

Medicaid Program A federally funded program administered by the states that provides medical care to the poor. The program is for the most part limited to the poorest of the poor, covering only welfare recipients in many states and covering some additional low-income population in other states.

Medicare Program A social-insurance program, funded under the Social Security System, that provides medical insurance for the elderly.

minority group Any group that is assigned to a subordinate role in society; that is, it has less than its proportionate share of wealth, power, and/or social status. Minority groups are frequently, but not necessarily, a numerical minority in society. Blacks in South Africa are an example of a minority group that is a numerical majority.

multiculturalism An approach, often in education, that explicitly recognizes and values cultural differences and attempts to be inclusive of all racial, ethnic, and cultural groups. In education, this inclusiveness applies with respect to course content and classroom examples and also includes the idea that history, literature, and other subjects can and should be taught from the perspectives of a variety of different groups rather than just that of the *dominant group*.

order perspective See *functionalist perspective*.

out-group A group to which one does not belong and with which one does not identify. Frequently, this group is culturally or racially different from and/or in competition with the in-group.

overlapping cleavages The situation in which societal divisions such as race, religion, class, and language all cut along the same lines. In this situation there tends to be a great deal of conflict because no matter what the issue, people are always on the same side.

paternalistic race relations A pattern of intergroup relations usually found in agricultural, preindustrial societies. It is a form of *caste system* characterized by clearly defined and well-understood racial roles, little outward conflict, much contact between races, but also with much ritual or etiquette denoting inequality and considerable paternalism.

perspective A general approach to or way of looking at an issue. A perspective consists of a set of questions to be asked about a topic, a theory or set of theories about realities concerning that topic, and a set of values concerning potentially controversial issues related to the topic.

persuasive communication Any communication—written, oral, audiovisual, or otherwise—that is specifically intended to influence attitudes, beliefs, or behavior.

prejudice A tendency to overgeneralize in some way, usually negative, toward an entire group. Prejudice can be cognitive (involving beliefs about a group), affective (involving dislike of a group), or conative (involving the desire to behave negatively toward a group).

projection A process whereby people minimize or deny characteristics they see as undesirable in themselves by exaggerating these same characteristics in others. Since such characteristics are often projected onto members of *outgroups*, projection appears to be a significant factor in the dynamics of prejudice.

race A grouping of people generally considered to be physically distinct in some way from others and regarded by themselves or others to be a distinct group.

racial group A group of people who develop a group identity and/or common culture based on *race*. The main difference between a racial group and a race is that one need not have a strong group identity or be part of a cultural group to be a member of a race.

racial steering A practice whereby real-estate agents show white customers houses in all-white areas and show black customers houses in all-black or racially mixed areas.

racism Any attitude, belief, behavior, or institutional arrangement that tends to favor one *racial* or *ethnic group* (usually a *majority group*) over another (usually a *minority group*). See also the four types of racism: *prejudice, ideological racism, individual racial discrimination,* and *institutional racism.*

rigid competitive race relations A pattern of race relations resembling an unstable *caste system.* Race largely but not totally defines roles and statuses; division of labor is more complex than in the *paternalistic* pattern, with majority and minority workers sometimes competing because they do similar work, though usually at different wages. Strict *segregation* usually accompanies this pattern, as a way the *majority group* protects its threatened social status. The potential for major conflict is nearly always present. This pattern is usually found in newly industrializing societies.

scapegoating A tendency to take out one's feelings of frustration and aggression against someone or something other than the true source of the feelings. Often, racial, ethnic, or religious *minority groups* are made the scapegoat for feelings of anger and frustration that have built up for reasons unrelated to the minority groups.

segregation The separation of two groups into separate neighborhoods, schools, workplaces, and so on. This may be the result of open and deliberate policies calling for segregation, as in *de jure segregation,* or of subtler processes as in *de facto segregation.*

self-fulfilling prophecy Any situation in which the expectation of some event or outcome contributes to the occurrence of that event or outcome. In education, for example, teachers frequently expect a lower quality of work from minority students than from white students. As a consequence, they treat minority students in ways that tend to produce the expected outcome.

separatism The establishment of, or attempt to establish, entirely separate societies made up of distinct racial, ethnic, or other groups that formerly existed within one society. Examples include efforts by some French Canadians to divide Canada into two independent countries, one English and one French, and efforts by some African Americans to establish separate black states in what is now the U.S. South.

social distance This term has two common uses or meanings. One refers to a preference among members of one group to avoid contact with members of another group. Social distance is said to be relatively small if only very intimate contact is resisted but greater when more superficial types of contact are also resisted. The other meaning of social distance is a pattern whereby the unequal status of two groups is clearly established and understood by both, no matter how closely they may interact, as in a master–slave relationship. Typically, rules governing interaction between two groups remind both groups that one of them is *dominant* and the other is *subordinate.*

social institution A well-established structure, form, or organization, with supporting norms and values, that performs a central function in society. Examples include religion, the family, and the economic, political, legal, educational, and health-care systems.

sociological, or **social-structural, approach** An approach to the study of majority–minority relations that emphasizes the characteristics of collectivities of people (e.g., groups, societies) rather than the characteristics of individuals. Issues of interest concern how a group or society is organized, its base of economic productivity, its power structure, its social institutions, and its culture.

split labor market A situation in which laborers are divided into two groups, one higher paid (often a *majority* or *dominant group*) and one lower paid (often composed of *minority group* members). The higher-paid group attempts to maintain an advantaged status by excluding the lower-paid group from certain kinds of employment.

stereotype An exaggerated belief associated with a category such as a group of people. It is a tendency to believe that anyone or almost anyone who belongs to a particular group will have a certain characteristic, for example, Jews are money-hungry.

structural assimilation A type of *assimilation* in which two or more groups gradually come to share a common social structure; that is, they share common institutions, organizations, and friendship networks and have relatively equal positions within these structures. If structural assimilation is complete, widespread intermarriage (marital assimilation) will also occur.

structural pluralism A situation in which two or more groups operate within a common social structure up to a point (e.g., a common government and economic system) but have some institutions, organizations, and patterns of interpersonal contact that are distinct and separate for each group.

subordinate group Similar in meaning to *minority group.*

theory A set of interrelated propositions about some topic or issue that are believed to be true. Ideally, a theory should be testable, that is, possible to evaluate in terms of its accuracy in describing reality.

value A personal preference or an opinion or moral belief concerning goodness or badness, right or wrong, and so on. A value, being a matter of personal preference, cannot be tested, proved, or disproved.

References _____

ABALOS, DAVID T. 1986. *Latinos in the United States: The Sacred and the Political.* Notre Dame, Ind.: University of Notre Dame Press.

ABC NEWS. 1991. "True Colors." *Prime Time Live.*

ABLER, THOMAS S. 1992. "Beavers and Muskets: Iroquois Military Fortunes in the Face of European Colonization." Pp. 151–74 in R. Brian Ferguson and Neil L. Whitehead (eds.), *War in the Tribal Zone.* Santa Fe, N. Mex.: School of American Research Press.

ABRAMS, CHARLES. 1971. *Forbidden Neighbors.* Port Washington, N.Y.: Kennikat Press.

ABRAMSON, HAROLD J. 1980. "Assimilation and Pluralism." Pp. 150–60 in Stephan Thernstrom, Ann Orlov, and Oscar Handlin (eds.), *The Harvard Encyclopedia of American Ethnic Groups.* Cambridge, Mass.: Harvard University Press.

ABRAMSON, HAROLD J. 1975. "The Religio-Ethnic Factor and the American Experience: Another Look at the Three-Generation Hypothesis." *Ethnicity* 2:163–77.

ABRAMSON, HAROLD J. 1973. *Ethnic Diversity in Catholic America.* New York: Wiley.

ACUNA, RODOLFO. 1972. *Occupied America: The Chicano's Struggle Toward Liberation.* San Francisco: Canfield Press.

ADAM, HERIBERT. 1971. *Modernizing Racial Domination.* Berkeley: University of California Press.

ADAY, LOU ANN. 1976. "The Impact of Health Policy on Access to Medical Care." *Milbank Memorial Fund Quarterly* 54:215–33.

ADLER, JERRY. 1991. "Prayers and Protest." *Newsweek* (January 28): 36–39.

ADORNO, THEODOR W., ELSE FRENKEL-BRUNSWICK, D. J. LEVINSON, and R. N. SANFORD. 1950. *The Authoritarian Personality.* New York: Harper & Row, Pub.

AHMAD, ISHMAEL LATEEF. 1993. "Redliners Better Beware: Discrimination in Housing Hits Pocketbooks." *St. Louis American* (July 1–7): 1A, 7A.

AJZEN, I., and M. FISHBEIN. 1980. *Understanding Attitudes and Predicting Social Behavior.* Englewood Cliffs, N.J.: Prentice Hall.

ALBA, RICHARD. 1981. "The Twilight of Ethnicity Among American Catholics of European Ancestry." *Annals of the American Academy of Political and Social Science* 454.

ALBA, RICHARD, and JOHN LOGAN. 1993. "Minority Proximity to Whites in the Suburbs: An Individual-Level Analysis of Segregation." *American Journal of Sociology* 98:1388–1427.

ALBONETTI, CELESTA A., ROBERT M. HAUSER, JOHN HAGAN, and ILENE H. NAGEL. 1989. "Criminal Justice Decisionmaking as a Stratification Process: The Role of Race and Stratification Resources in Pretrial Release." *Journal of Quantitative Criminology* 5:57–82.

ALEXANDER, EDWARD. 1990. "Race Fever." *Commentary* 90 5:45–48.

ALEXANDER, KARL L., MARTHA COOK, and EDWARD L. McDILL. 1978. "Curriculum Tracking and Educational Stratification: Some Further Evidence." *American Sociological Review* 43:47–66.

ALEXANDER, KARL, and BRUCE K. ECKLAND. 1975. "School Experience and Status Attainment." Pp. 171–210 in S. D. Dragastin and G. H. Elder (eds.), *Adolescence and the Life Cycle: Psychological Change and Social Context.* Washington, D.C.: Hemisphere.

ALEXANDER, KARL L., DORIS R. ENTWISLE, and MAXINE S. THOMPSON. 1987. "School Performance, Status Relations, and the Structure of Sentiment: Bringing the Teachers Back In." *American Sociological Review* 43:47–66.

ALEXANDER, KARL L., and EDWARD L. McDILL. 1976. "Selection and Allocation Within Schools: Some Causes and Consequences of Curriculum Placement." *American Sociological Review* 41:963–80.

ALEXANDER, KARL L., and AARON M. PALLAS. 1987. "School Sector and Cognitive Performance: When Is a Little a Little?" Pp. 89–112 in Edward H. Haertel, Thomas James, and Henry M. Levin (eds.), *Comparing Public and Private Schools.* Vol. 2: *School Achievement.* New York: Falmer.

ALLEN, MICHAEL A., and MICHELLE TOLLIVER. 1974. "Medical Delivery System for Urban Indians: Consumer and Providers Perceptions." Paper presented at the Southwest and Rocky Mountain Division of the American Association for the Advancement of Science, Laramie, Wyo.

ALLEN, WALTER. 1985. "College in Black and White: Black Student Experiences on Black and White Campuses." Summary of report prepared for the Southern Educational Foundation Monograph Series. Ann Arbor: Center for Afroamerican and African Studies, University of Michigan.

ALLEN, WALTER. 1982. "Black and Blue: Black Students at the University of Michigan." *LSA, The University of Michigan* 6, 1:13–17.

ALLPORT, GORDON W. 1954. *The Nature of Prejudice.* New York: Addison-Wesley.

ALVAREZ, RODOLFO. 1973. "The Psycho-Historical and Socioeconomic Development of the Chicano Community in the United States." *Social Science Quarterly* 53:920–42.

AMERICAN COUNCIL ON EDUCATION. 1988. *Minorities in Higher Education,* seventh annual status report. Washington, D.C.: American Council on Education.

ANDERSON, ELIJAH. 1991. "Neighborhood Effects on Teenage Pregnancy." Pp. 375–98 in Christopher Jencks and Paul E. Peterson (eds.), *The Urban Underclass.* Washington, D.C.: The Brookings Institution.

ANDERSON, ELIJAH. 1990. *Streetwise: Race, Class, and Change in an Urban Community.* Chicago: University of Chicago Press.

ANDREONI, HELEN, and VASILIKI NIHAS. 1986. "A Rationale for Intercultural Education." NACCME-commissioned research paper no. 4. Woden, Australia: National Advisory and Coordinating Committee on Multicultural Education.

APA Monitor. 1974. "Homosexuality Dropped as Mental Disorder." *APA Monitor* 5 (February).

ARMOR, DAVID J. 1992. "Why Is Black Educational Achievement Rising?" *Public Interest* 108:65–80.

ARMOR, DAVID J. 1972.. "The Evidence on Busing." *Public Interest* 28:90–126.

ARMOR, DAVID J., and DONNA SCHWARTZBACH. 1978. "White Flight, Demographic Transition, and the Future of School Desegregation." Rand Paper Series #P-5931. Presented to Annual Meeting of the American Sociological Association, San Francisco, California.

ARMSTRONG, LIZ SCHEVTCHUK. 1991. "Report Attacks Enforcement of Ability Grouping Practices." *Education Week* (May 1): 20.

ARNOLD, DAVID. 1991. "Increase in Bias Reported." *Boston Globe,* January 31, p. 17.

ARNOLD, WILLIAM R. 1971. "Race and Ethnicity Relative to Other Factors in Juvenile Court Dispositions." *American Journal of Sociology* 77:211–27.

ARROW, KENNETH J. 1972. "Models of Job Discrimination." In Anthony H. Paschal (ed.), *Economic Life.* Lexington, Mass.: Heath.

ASCH, SOLOMON E. 1956. "Studies of Independence and Conformity: A Minority of One Against a Unanimous Majority." *Psychological Monographs* 70, 9 (whole no. 416).

ASHMORE, RICHARD D. 1970. "Prejudice: Causes and Cures." Pp. 244–339 in Barry E. Collins (ed.), *Social Psychology.* Reading, Mass.: Addison-Wesley.

AVICOLLI, TOMMI. 1992. "He Defies You Still: The Memoirs of a Sissy." Pp. 201–7 in Paula S. Rothenberg (ed.), *Race, Class, and Gender in the United States: An Integrated Study.* New York: St. Martin's Press.

BABBIE, EARL. 1992. *The Practice of Social Research,* 6th ed. Belmont, Calif.: Wadsworth.

BACHMAN, GERALD G., and PATRICK M. O'MALLEY. 1984. "Black–White Differences in Self-esteem: Are They Affected by Response Styles?" *American Journal of Sociology* 90:624–39.

BAGLEY, CHRISTOPHER, and GAJENDRA K. VERMA. 1979. *Racial Prejudice, the Individual, and Society.* Westmead, England: Saxon Books. (Distributed in the United States by Lexington Books.)

BAHR, HOWARD M., BRUCE A. CHADWICK, and JOSEPH H. STRAUSS. 1979. *American Ethnicity.* Lexington, Mass.: Heath.

BAKER, KEITH, and ADRIANA DE KANTER. 1981. *Effectiveness of Bilingual Education: A Review of the Literature.* Final draft report. Washington, D.C.: U.S. Department of Education, Office of Planning, Budget, and Evaluation.

BALBUS, ISSAC D. 1973. *The Dialectics of Legal Repression: Black Rebels Before the American Criminal Courts.* New York: Russell Sage Foundation.

BALDRIDGE, J. VICTOR. 1976. *Sociology: A Critical Approach to Power, Conflict, and Change.* New York: Wiley.

BANAC, IVO. 1984. *The National Question in Yugoslavia: Origins, History, Politics.* Ithaca, N.Y.: Cornell University Press.

BANDURA, ALBERT, and RICHARD H. WALTERS. 1963.

Social Learning and Personality Development. New York: Holt, Rinehart & Winston.

BANFIELD, EDWARD C. 1974. *The Unheavenly City Revisited.* Boston: Little, Brown.

BANFIELD, EDWARD C. 1968. *The Unheavenly City.* Boston: Little, Brown.

BANKS, JAMES A. 1992. "Multicultural Education: For Freedom's Sake." *Educational Leadership* 49, 4 (December, 1991/January, 1992):32–36.

BANTON, MICHAEL. 1964. *The Policeman in the Community.* London: Tavistock.

BARABBA, VINCENT P. 1976. "The National Setting: Regional Shifts, Metropolitan Decline, and Urban Decay." Pp. 39–76 in George Sternlieb and James W. Hughes (eds.), *Post-Industrial America: Metropolitan Decline and Interregional Job Shifts.* New Brunswick, N.J.: Rutgers University Center for Urban Policy Research.

BARAN, PAUL A., and PAUL M. SWEEZY. 1966. *Monopoly Capital.* New York: Monthly Review Press.

BARATZ, STEVEN S., and JOAN C. BARATZ. 1970. "Early Childhood Intervention: The Social Science Base of Institutional Racism." *Harvard Educational Review* 40:29–50.

BARBER, JAMES. 1967. *Rhodesia: The Road to Rebellion.* London: Oxford University Press.

BARLOW, HUGH D. 1993. *Introduction to Criminology,* 6th ed. New York: HarperCollins.

BARLOW, HUGH D. 1987. *Introduction to Criminology,* 4th ed. Boston: Little, Brown.

BARRERA, MARIO. 1979. *Race and Class in the Southwest: A Theory of Racial Inequality.* Notre Dame, Ind.: University of Notre Dame Press.

BARRINGER, FELICITY. 1993. "Sex Survey of American Men Finds 1% Are Gay." *New York Times,* April 15, sec. A.

BARRITT, DENIS F., and CHARLES F. CARTER. 1962. *The Northern Ireland Problem.* London: Oxford University Press.

BARTH, GUNTHER. 1964. *Bitter Strength: A History of the Chinese in the United States, 1850–1870.* Cambridge, Mass.: Harvard University Press.

BARLETT, DONALD L., and JAMES B. STEELE. 1992. *America: What Went Wrong?* Kansas City, Mo.: Andrews and McMeel.

BASTIDE, ROGER. 1965. "The Development of Race Relations in Brazil." Pp. 9–29 in Guy Hunter (ed.), *Industrialisation and Race Relations.* London: Oxford University Press.

BAUGHMAN, E. E. 1971. *Black Americans: A Psychological Analysis.* New York: Academic Press.

BAUMEISTER, ROY F., and MARTIN V. COVINGTON. 1985. "Self-Esteem, Persuasion, and Retrospective Distortion of Initial Attitudes." *Electronic Social Psychology* 1: Article 8501014.

BAYLEY, DAVID H., and HAROLD MENDELSOHN. 1968. *Minorities and the Police: Confrontation in America.* New York: Free Press.

BEADY, CHARLES, and ROBERT SLAVIN. 1980. "Making Success Available to All Students in Desegregated Schools." *Integrateducation* 18, 5–6:107–8.

BEAN, FRANK D., and MARTA TIENDA. 1987. *The His-panic Population of the United States.* New York: Russell Sage Foundation.

BECK, E. M. 1980. "Labor Unionism and Racial Income Inequality: A Time-series Analysis of the Post–World War II Period." *American Journal of Sociology* 85:791–814.

BECKER, GARY S. 1957. *The Economics of Discrimination.* Chicago: University of Chicago Press (Revised edition 1971.)

BEEZ, W. V. 1968. "Influence of Biased Psychological Reports on Teacher Behavior and Pupil Performance." *Proceedings of the 76th Annual Convention of the American Psychological Association* 3:605–6.

BELL, ALAN P., MARTIN S. WEINBERG, and SUE KIEFER HAMMERSMITH. 1981. *Sexual Preference: Its Development in Men and Women.* Bloomington: Indiana University Press.

BELL, DERRICK. 1988. "The Case for a Separate Black School System." *Urban League Review* 11, 1–2:136–45.

Belleville News–Democrat. 1992. "Crimes Rise Against Arab Americans in 1991." February 21, p. 5a.

Bem, Daryl J. 1970. *Beliefs, Attitudes, and Human Affairs.* Belmont, Calif.: Brooks-Cole.

BENNETT, CHRISTINE. 1989. "Preservice Multicultural Teacher Education: Predictors of Student Readiness." Paper presented at the annual meeting of the American Educational Research Association, March 27–31, San Francisco.

BENOKRAITIS, NIJOLE V. 1993. *Marriages and Families: Changes, Choices, and Contrasts.* Englewood Cliffs, N.J.: Prentice Hall.

BERG, BARBARA J. 1986. *The Crisis of the Working Mother.* New York: Summit Books.

BERG, IVAR. 1975. "Rich Man's Qualifications for Poor Man's Jobs." Pp. 306–13 in Scott G. McNall (ed.), *The Sociological Perspective,* 4th ed. Boston: Little, Brown. (Reprinted from *Transaction* 6 [1969]).

BERG, IVAR. 1971. *Education and Jobs: The Great Training Robbery.* Boston: Beacon Paperbacks.

BERGER, BRIGITTE. 1978. "A New Interpretation of IQ Controversy." *Public Interest* 50:29–44.

BERRUETA-CLEMENT, J. R., L. J. SCHWEINHART, W. S. BARNETT, A. S. EPSTEIN, and D. P. WEIKART. 1984. "Changed Lives: The Effects of the Perry Preschool Program on Youths Through Age 19." *Monographs of the High/Scope Research Foundation* 8.

BERRY, BREWTON, and HENRY L. TISCHLER. 1978. *Racial and Ethnic Relations,* 4th ed. Boston: Houghton-Mifflin.

BESHEROV, DOUGLAS J. 1993. "Fresh Start." *New Repub-lic* (June 14): 14–16.

BESWICK, RICHARD. 1990. "Racism in America's Schools." *ERIC Digest Series,* no. EA 19. Eugene, Ore.: ERIC Clearinghouse on Educational Management.

BIANCHI, SUZANNE. 1981. *Household Composition and Racial Inequality.* New Brunswick, N.J.: Rutgers University Press.

BIELBY, WILLIAM T., and DENISE D. BIELBY. 1992. "I Will Follow Him: Family Ties, Gender Role Beliefs, and Reluctance to Relocate for a Better Job." *American Journal of Sociology* 97: 1241–67.

BIGGAR, JEANNE C. 1979. "The Sunning of America: Migration to the Sunbelt." *Population Bulletin* 34, 1.

BINSTOCK, JEANNE. 1970. "Survival in the American College Industry." Ph.D. diss., Brandeis University.

BISHOP, J. 1987. "Information Externalities and the Social Payoff to Academic Achievement." Working paper, School of Industrial and Labor Relations, Cornell University, Ithaca, N.Y.

BLACK, DONALD J. 1970. "The Production of Crime Rates." *American Sociological Review* 35:733–48.

BLACK, DONALD J., and ALBERT J. REISS, JR. 1967. "Patterns of Behavior in Police and Citizen Transactions." In President's Commission on Law Enforcement and Administration of Justice, *Studies in Crime and Law Enforcement in Major Metropolitan Areas*. Washington, D.C.: U.S. Government Printing Office.

BLAKE, R., and W. DENNIS. 1943. "The Development of Stereotypes Concerning the Negro." *Journal of Abnormal and Social Psychology* 38:525–31.

BLASSINGAME, JOHN W. 1972. *The Slave Community: Plantation Life in the Antebellum South*. New York: Oxford University Press.

BLAUNER, ROBERT. 1972. *Racial Oppression in America*. New York: Harper & Row.

BLOCH, HERMAN D. 1969. *The Circle of Discrimination: An Economic and Social Study of the Black Man in New York*. New York: New York University Press.

BLUMENTHAL, DAVID, and JAMES FALLOWS. 1974. "Health: The Care We Want and Need." Pp. 162–68 in Dushkin Publishing Group (eds.), *Annual Editions: Readings in Sociology '74–'75*. Guilford, Conn.: Dushkin Publishing Group.

BLUMER, HERBERT. 1965. "Industrialisation and Race Relations." Pp. 220–553 in Guy Hunter (ed.), *Industrialisation and Race Relations: A Symposium*. London: Oxford University Press.

BOLVIN, MICHAEL J., AMY J. DONKIN, and HAROLD W. DARLING. 1990. "Religiosity and Prejudice: A Case Study in Evaluating the Construct Validity of Christian Measures." *Journal of Psychology and Christianity* 9, 2:41–55.

BONACICH, EDNA. 1976. "Advanced Capitalism and Black/White Relations in the United States: A Split Labor Market Interpretation." *American Sociological Review* 41:34–51.

BONACICH, EDNA. 1975. "Abolition, the Extension of Slavery, and the Position of Free Blacks: A Study of Split Labor Markets in the United States, 1830–1863." *American Journal of Sociology* 81:601–28.

BONACICH, EDNA. 1972. "A Theory of Ethnic Antagonism: The Split Labor Market." *American Sociological Review* 37:547–59.

BOOCOCK, SARANE SPENCE. 1978. "The Social Organization of the Classroom." Pp. 1–28 in Ralph H. Turner, James Coleman, and Renee C. Fox (eds.), *Annual Review of Sociology—1978*. Palo Alto, Calif.: Annual Reviews.

BOSKIN, JOSEPH. 1969. *Urban Racial Violence in the Twentieth Century*. Beverly Hills, Calif.: Glencoe Press.

BOSKIN, JOSEPH. 1965. "Race Relations in Seventeenth Century America: The Problem of the Origins of Negro Slavery." *Sociology and Social Research* 49: 446–55.

BOSWELL, JOHN. 1980. *Christianity, Social Tolerance, and Homosexuality: Gay People in Western Europe from the Beginning of the Christian Era to the Fourteenth Century*. Chicago: University of Chicago Press.

BOUVIER, LEON F., and ROBERT W. GARDNER. 1986. "Immigration to the U.S.: The Unfinished Story." *Population Bulletin* 41, 4.

BOUVIER, LEON F., with HENRY S. SHRYOCK AND HARRY W. HENDERSON. 1977. "International Migration: Yesterday, Today, and Tomorrow." *Population Bulletin* 34, 2.

BOWER, BRUCE. 1992. "Genetic Clues to Female Homosexuality." *Science News* 142, 8:117.

BOWKER, LEE H. 1972. "Red and Black in Contemporary History Texts: A Content Analysis." Pp. 101–10 in Howard M. Bahr, Bruce A. Chadwick, and Robert C. Day (eds.), *Native Americans Today: Sociological Perspectives*. New York: Harper & Row.

BOWLES, SAMUEL, and HERBERT GINTIS. 1976. *Schooling in Capitalist America*. New York: Basic Books.

BRADBURY, KATHARINE L., ANTHONY DOWNS, and KENNETH A. SMALL. 1982. *Urban Decline and the Future of American Cities*. Washington, D.C.: Brookings Institution.

BRADBURY, KATHARINE L., and HELEN F. LADD. 1987. *City Taxes and Property Tax Bases*. Cambridge, Mass.: National Bureau of Economic Research.

BRADDOCK, JOMILLS HENRY. 1985. "School Desegregation and Black Assimilation." *Journal of Social Issues* 41, 3:9–22.

BRAZZIEL, WILLIAM F. 1969. "A Letter from the South." *Harvard Educational Review* 39:348–56.

BREDEKAMP, SUE, and LORRIE SHEPARD. 1989. "How Best to Protect Children from Inappropriate School Expectations, Practices, and Policies." *Young Children* (March): 14–24.

BREWER, MARILYN, and RODERICK K. KRAMER. 1985. "The Psychology of Intergroup Attitudes and Behavior." Pp. 219–43 in Mark R. Rosenzweig and Lyman W. Porter (eds.), *Annual Review of Psychology* 36. Palo Alto, Calif.: Annual Reviews.

BREWER, MARILYN B., and NORMAN MILLER. 1984. "Beyond the Contact Hypothesis: Theoretical Perspectives on Desegregation." Pp. 281–302 in Norman Miller and Marilyn B. Brewer (eds.), *Groups in Contact: The Psychology of Desegregation*. Orlando, Fla: Academic Press.

BRIMMER, ANDREW F. 1993. "The Economic Cost of Discrimination." *Black Enterprise* (November): 27.

BRISCHETTO, ROBERT, and TOMAS ARCINIEGA. 1973. "Examining the Examiner: A Look at Educators' Perspectives on the Chicano Student." In Rudolph O. de la Garza, Z. Anthony Kruzewski, and Tomas A. Arciniega (eds.), *Chicanos and Native Americans: The Territorial Minorities*. Englewood Cliffs, N.J.: Prentice Hall.

BRITTON, GWYNETH E., and MARGARET C. LUMPKIN. 1977. "For Sale: Subliminal Bias in Textbooks." *Reading Teacher* 31:40–45.

BRODY, DAVID. 1960. *Steelworkers in America: The Nonunion Era.* Cambridge, Mass.: Harvard University Press.

BROMLEY, CHARLES H. 1992. "The Politics of Race Reform of the Single Family Mortgage Revenue Bond Program in the State of Ohio, 1983–1988." Paper presented at the annual meeting of the Urban Affairs Association.

BROOKOVER, WILBUR, and L. W. LEZOTTE. 1977. "Changes in School Characteristics Coincident with Changes in Student Achievement." East Lansing: College of Urban Development of Michigan State University and Michigan Department of Education.

BROPHY, J. E., and THOMAS GOOD. 1970. "Teacher's Communication of Differential Expectations for Children's Classroom Performance: Some Classroom Data." *Journal of Educational Psychology* 61:365–74.

BROPHY, JERE E. 1983. "Research on the Self-fulfilling Prophecy and Teacher Expectations." *Journal of Educational Psychology* 75:631–61.

BROPHY, JERE, and THOMAS GOOD. 1974. *Teacher–Student Relationships.* New York: Holt, Rinehart & Winston.

BROWN, ANITA, BEVERLY J. GOODWIN, BARBARA A. HALL, and HUBERTA JACKSON-LOWMAN. 1985. "A Review of Psychology of Women Textbooks: Focus on the Afro American Woman." *Psychology of Women Quarterly* 9:29–38.

BROWN, BERNARD. 1985. "Head Start: How Research Changed Public Policy." *Young Children* 40:9–13.

BROWN, LAWRENCE L., ALAN L. GINSBERG, J. NEIL KILLALEA, and ESTHER O. TRON. 1978. "School Finance Reform in the Seventies: Achievements and Failures." Pp. 57–110 in Esther O. Tron (ed.), *Selected Papers in School Finance.* Washington, D.C.: U.S. Department of Health, Education, and Welfare.

BROWN, ROGER. 1965. *Social Psychology.* New York: Free Press.

BRUCK, LILLY. 1978. *Access: The Guide to a Better Life for Disabled Americans.* New York: Random House.

BUNZEL, JOHN H. 1991. "Black and White at Stanford." *Public Interest* 105:61–77.

BUREAU OF JUSTICE STATISTICS. 1991. *National Update.* Washington, D.C.: U.S. Department of Justice.

BUREAU OF LABOR STATISTICS. 1986. "Current Labor Statistics." *Monthly Labor Review* 109, 9:59–60.

BURGESS, JANE K. 1970. "The Single Parent Family: A Social and Sociological Problem." *Family Coordinator* 19:137–44.

BURNELL, BARBARA S., and JAMES D. BURNELL. 1989. "Community Interaction and Suburban Zoning Policies." *Urban Affairs Quarterly* 24:470–82.

BUTTERFIELD, FOX. 1990. "Arab-Americans Face Wave of Threats in U.S." *Los Angeles Times,* August 29, sec. A.

BYRNES, DEBORAH, and GARY KIGER. 1990. "The Effect of a Prejudice Reduction Simulation on Attitude Change." *Journal of Applied Social Psychology* 20:341–56.

CAMARILLO, ALBERT. 1979. *Chicanos in a Changing Society: From Mexican Pueblos to American Barrios in Santa Barbara and Southern California.* Cambridge, Mass.: Harvard University Press.

CAMPBELL, ANGUS, and HOWARD SCHUMAN. 1968. "Racial Attitudes in Fifteen American Cities." Pp. 1–67 in *Supplemental Studies for the National Advisory Commission on Civil Disorders.* Washington, D.C.: U.S. Government Printing Office.

CARMICHAEL, STOKELEY, and CHARLES V. HAMILTON. 1967. *Black Power: The Politics of Liberation in America.* New York: Vintage Books.

CARTER, THOMAS P. 1968. "The Negative Self-Concept of Mexican-American Students." *School and Society* 95:217–19.

CASE, CHARLES E., ANDREW M. GREELEY, and STEPHEN FUCHS. 1989. "Social Determinants of Racial Prejudice." *Sociological Perspectives* 32, 1:469–83.

CASS, VIVIENNE C. 1984. "Homosexual Identity Formation: Testing a Theoretical Model." *Journal of Sex Research* 20:143–67.

CASS, VIVIENNE C. 1983–84. "Homosexual Identity: A Concept in Need of Definition." *Journal of Homosexuality* 9:2–3.

CASS, VIVIENNE C. 1979. "Homosexual Identity Formation: A Theoretical Model." *Journal of Homosexuality* 4:219–35.

CATTON, WILLIAM J., JR. 1961. "The Functions and Disfunctions of Ethnocentrism: A Theory." *Social Problems* 8:201–11.

CENTER FOR EDUCATION AND HUMAN DEVELOPMENT POLICY. 1981. *Current Knowledge About the Effects of School Desegregation Strategies,* vol. 1, *Synthesis of Findings.* Nashville, Tenn.: Vanderbilt University.

CHACON, RAMON D. 1984. "Labor Unrest and Industrialized Labor in California: The Case of the San Joaquin Valley Cotton Strike." *Social Science Quarterly* 65, 2:336–53.

CHAMBER OF COMMERCE OF THE UNITED STATES. 1974. *A Handbook on White Collar Crime.* Washington, D.C.: National District Attorney's Association.

CHARLES, JAMES P. 1989. "The Need for Textbook Reform: An American Indian Example." *Journal of American Indian Education* 28, 3:1–13.

CHEBAT, JEAN CHARLES, PIERRE FILIATRAULT, and JEAN PERRIEN. 1990. "Limits of Credibility: The Case of Political Persuasion." *Journal of Social Psychology* 130:157–67.

CHURCHILL, WARD. 1994. *Indians R Us? Culture and Genocide in Native North America.* Monroe, Me.: Common Courage Press.

CICIRELLI, V. G., J. W. EVANS, and J. S. SCHILLER. 1969. *The Impact of Head Start: An Evaluation of the Effects of Head Start on Children's Cognitive and Affective Development,* vols. 1, 2. Athens, Ohio: Westinghouse Learning Corporation and Ohio University.

CIULLO, ROSEMARY, and MARYANN V. TROIANI. 1988. "Resolution of Prejudice: Small Group Interaction and Behavior in Latency-Age Children." *Small Group Behavior* 19:386–94.

CLAIBORNE, WILLIAM. 1993. "Labor Department Seeks Private Help as Summer Job Funds Fall Short." *Washington Post,* June 17, sec. A.

CLARK, KENNETH B., and MAMIE P. CLARK. 1958. "Racial Identification and Preference Among Negro Children." Pp. 602–11 in Eleanor Maccoby, Theodore M. Newcomb, and E. L. Hartley (eds.), *Readings in Social Psychology,* 3d edition. New York: Holt, Rinehart & Winston.

CLARK, WILLIAM A. V. 1992. "Residential Preferences and Residential Choices in a Multi-Ethnic Context." *Demography* 29:451–66.

CLARK, WILLIAM A. V. 1991. "Residential Preferences and Neighborhood Racial Segregation: A Test of the Schelling Segregation Model." *Demography* 28:1–19.

COCKERHAM, WILLIAM C. 1992. *Medical Sociology,* 5th ed. Englewood Cliffs, N.J.: Prentice Hall.

COCKERHAM, WILLIAM C. 1978. *Medical Sociology.* Englewood Cliffs, N.J.: Prentice Hall.

COE, RODNEY M. 1978. *Sociology of Medicine,* 2d ed. New York: McGraw-Hill.

COHEN, D., and M. LAZERSON. "Education and the Industrial Order." Unpublished manuscript.

COHEN, ELIZABETH G. 1984. "The Desegregated School: Problems in Status, Power, and Interethnic Climate." Pp. 77–96 in Norman Miller and Marilyn B. Brewer (eds.), *Groups in Contact: The Psychology of Desegregation,* Orlando, Fla.: Academic Press.

COHEN, ELIZABETH G. 1982. "Expectation States and Interracial Interaction in School Settings." Pp. 209–35 in Ralph H. Turner and James F. Short, Jr. (eds.), *Annual Review of Sociology,* vol. 8. Palo Alto, Calif.: Annual Reviews.

COHEN, ELIZABETH G., MARLAINE F. LOCKHEED, and MARK R. LOHMAN. 1976. "The Center for Interracial Cooperation: A Field Experiment." *Sociology of Education* 49:47–58.

COHEN, ELIZABETH G., and S. S. ROPER. 1972. "Modification of Interracial Disability: An Application of Status Characteristic Theory." *American Sociological Review* 37:643–57.

COHEN, RICHARD. 1991. "GOP Played Race Card and Won David Duke." *St. Louis Post-Dispatch,* (October 22): C3.

COHEN, SHIRLEY. 1977. *Special People.* Englewood Cliffs, N.J.: Prentice Hall.

COHN, FREDERICK. 1974. *Understanding Human Sexuality.* Englewood Cliffs, N.J.: Prentice Hall.

COHN, T. S. 1953. "The Relation of the F-Scale to a Response to Answer Positively." *American Psychologist* 8:335.

COLEMAN, JAMES S. 1981. "Public Schools, Private Schools, and the Public Interest." *Public Interest* 64:19–30.

COLEMAN, JAMES S. 1975. "Racial Segregation in the Schools: New Research with New Policy Implications." *Phi Delta Kappan* 57:75–78.

COLEMAN, JAMES S., ERNEST Q. CAMPBELL, CAROL J. HOBSON, JAMES MCPARTLAND, ALEXANDER MOOD, FREDERICK D. WEINFIELD, AND ROBERT L. YORK. 1966. *Equality of Educational Opportunity.* Washington, D.C.: U.S. Government Printing Office.

COLEMAN, JAMES S., THOMAS HOFFER, and SALLY KILGORE. 1982. *High School Achievement: Public, Catholic, and Private Schools Compared.* New York: Basic Books.

COLEMAN, JAMES S., THOMAS HOFFER, and SALLY KILGORE. 1981. "Public Schools and Private Schools." Paper presented to the conference on the High School and Beyond, National Center for Education Statistics, Washington, D.C.

COLLIER, JOHN. 1947. *The Indians of the Americas.* New York: Norton.

COLLINS, PATRICIA HILL. 1991. *Black Feminist Thought: Knowledge, Consciousness, and the Politics of Empowerment.* New York: Routledge.

COLLINS, RANDALL. 1971. "A Conflict Theory of Sexual Stratification." *Social Problems* 19:3–12.

COLLINS, SHARON M. 1993. "Blacks on the Bubble: The Vulnerability of Black Executives in White Corporations." *Sociological Quarterly* 34:429–47.

COMMITTEE ON THE BUDGET, U.S. HOUSE OF REPRESENTATIVES. 1976. *Working Papers on Major Budget and Program Issues in Selected Health Programs.* Washington, D.C.: U.S. Government Printing Office.

Commonweal. 1989. "Birmingham Firehouse." *Commonweal* (July 14): 387–88.

CONFLUENCE ST. LOUIS. 1985. *Health Care for the Indigent Population in the St. Louis Region: A Report of the Health Care Task Force.* St. Louis: Confluence St. Louis.

CONOT, ROBERT. 1967. *Rivers of Blood, Years of Darkness.* New York: Bantam Books.

CONSORTIUM FOR LONGITUDINAL STUDIES. 1983. *As the Twig Is Bent: Lasting Effects of Pre-School Programs.* Hillsdale, N.J.: Erlbaum.

CONSORTIUM FOR LONGITUDINAL STUDIES. 1979. *Lasting Effects After Preschool, Summary Report.* Washington, D.C.: U.S. Department of Health and Human Services. Administration for Children, Youth, and Families.

CONYERS, JAMES E. 1986. "Toward the Achievement of Racial Progress in America, According to Black Doctorates in Sociology." Paper presented at the annual meeting of the North Central Sociological Association, April, Toledo, Ohio.

COOK, STUART W. 1990. "Toward a Psychology of Improving Justice: Research on Extending the Equality Principle to Victims of Social Injustice." *Journal of Social Issues* 45:147–61.

COOLEY, CHARLES HORTON. 1964 [1909]. *Human Nature and the Social Order.* New York: Schocken.

COOPER, E., and MARIE JAHODA. 1947. "The Evasion of Propaganda: How Prejudiced People Respond to Anti-Prejudiced Propaganda." *Journal of Psychology* 23:15–25.

COOPER, JOEL, and ROBERT T. CROYL. 1984. "Attitudes and Attitude Change." Pp. 395–426 in Mark R. Rosenzweig and Lyman W. Porter (eds.), *Annual Review of Psychology,* vol. 34. Palo Alto, Calif.: Annual Reviews.

COTERA, MARTA. 1980. "Feminism: The Chicana and Anglo Versions, a Historical Analysis." Pp. 235–48 in Margarita B. Melville (ed.), *Twice a Minority: Mexican American Women*. St. Louis: Mosby.

COUGHLIN, ELLEN K. 1991. "Amid Challenges to Classic Remedies for Race Discrimination, Researchers Argue Merits of Mandatory School Desegregation." *Chronicle of Higher Education* (October 9): A9, A11.

COUSINS, ALBERT N., and HANS NAGPAUL. 1979. *Urban Life: The Sociology of Cities and Urban Society*. New York: Wiley.

COWELL, ALAN. 1986. "Eight Blacks Reported Slain in South African Violence." *New York Times*, July 29, sec. 1.

COX, OLIVER CROMWELL. 1948. *Caste, Class, and Race*. Garden City, N.Y.: Doubleday.

CRAIN, ROBERT L. 1981. *Some Social Policy Implications of the Desegregation Minority Achievement Literature*. Baltimore: Johns Hopkins University, Center for Social Organization of Schools.

CRAIN, ROBERT L., and RITA E. MAHARD. 1982. *Desegregation Plans That Raise Black Achievement: A Review of the Research*. Rand Note, June. Santa Monica, Calif.: Rand Corporation.

CRONBACH, L. J. 1946. "Response Sets and Test Validity." *Educational and Psychological Measurement* 6:475–94.

CROUTHAMEL, JAMES L. 1969. "The Springfield, Illinois, Race Riot of 1908." Pp. 8–19 in Joseph Boskin, *Urban Racial Violence in the Twentieth Century*. Beverly Hills, Calif.: Glencoe Press. (Reprinted from *Journal of Negro History*, [July 1960]: 164–75, 180–81.)

CUMMINGS, SCOTT. 1980. "White Ethnics, Racial Prejudice, and Labor Market Segmentation." *American Journal of Sociology* 85:938–50.

CUNNINGHAM, JEAN A., STEPHEN J. DOLLINGER, MADELYN SATZ, and NANCY S. ROTTER. 1991. "Personality Correlates of Prejudice Against AIDS Victims." *Bulletin of the Psychonomic Society* 29, 2:165–67.

CUTLER, BLAYNE. 1993. "When Cross Talks to the Boss." *American Demographics* 15, 5 (May): 12.

D'ALESSIO, STEWART J., and LISA STOLZENBERG. 1991. "Anti-Semitism in America: The Dynamics of Prejudice." *Sociological Inquiry* 61:359–66.

DANNEFER, DALE, and RUSSELL K. SCHUTT. 1982. "Race and Juvenile Justice Processing in Court and Police Agencies." *American Journal of Sociology* 87:1113–32.

DARDEN, JOE T. 1985. "The Significance of Race and Class in Residential Segregation." Paper presented at the annual meeting of the Urban Affairs Association, Norfolk, Va.

DAVINE, VALERIE R., and DAVID B. BILLS. 1992. "Changing Attitudes Toward Race-Related Issues: Is a Sociological Perspective Effective?" Paper presented at the annual meeting of the American Sociological Association, August 20–24, Pittsburgh, Pa.

DAVIS, ANGELA YVONNE. 1989. *Women, Culture, and Politics*. New York: Random House.

DAVIS, ANGELA YVONNE. 1981. *Women, Race, and Class*. New York: Random House.

DAVIS, DAVID BRION. 1966. *The Problem of Slavery in Western Culture*. Ithaca, N.Y.: Cornell University Press.

DAVIS, KINGSLEY, and WILBERT E. MOORE. 1945. "Some Principles of Stratification." *American Sociological Review* 10:242–49.

DAY, ROBERT C. 1972. "The Emergence of Activism as a Social Movement." Pp. 506–31 in Howard M. Bahr, Bruce A. Chadwick, and Robert C. Day (eds.), *Native Americans Today*. New York: Harper & Row.

DEBO, ANGIE. 1970. *A History of the Indians in the United States*. Norman, Oklahoma: University of Oklahoma Press.

DEBONO, KENNETH G., and RICHARD J. HARNISH. 1988. "Source Expertise, Source Attractiveness, and the Processing of Persuasive Information: A Functional Approach." *Journal of Personality and Social Psychology* 55:541–45.

DEFLEUR, MELVIN L., and F. R. WESTIE. 1958. "Verbal Attitudes and Overt Acts: An Experiment on the Salience of Attitudes." *American Sociological Review* 23:667–73.

DEGLER, CARL N. 1980. *At Odds: Women and the Family in America from the Revolution to the Present*. New York: Oxford University Press.

DEGLER, CARL N. 1959a. *Out of Our Past*. New York: Harper & Row.

DEGLER, CARL N. 1959b. "Slavery and the Genesis of American Race Prejudice." *Comparative Studies in Society and History* 2:49–66.

DELORIA, VINE. 1981. "Native Americans: The American Indian Today." *Annals of the American Academy of Political and Social Science* 454:139–49.

DEMO, DAVID H., and ALAN C. ACOCK. 1988. "The Impact of Divorce upon Children." *Journal of Marriage and the Family* 50:619–48.

DEMPSEY, VAN, and GEORGE NOBLIT. 1993. "The Demise of Caring in an African American Community: One Consequence of School Desegregation." *Urban Review* 25:47–61.

DENT, PRESTON L. 1975. "The Curriculum as a Prejudice-Reduction Technique." *California Journal of Educational Research* 26:167–77.

DEPALMA, ANTHONY. 1990. "The Culture Question." *New York Times*, November 4, 22–23.

DEUTSCH, MARTIN. 1963. "The Disadvantaged Child and the Learning Process: Some Social and Developmental Considerations." In A. H. Passow (ed.), *Education in Depressed Areas*. New York: Teachers Press.

DEUTSCH, MORTON, and MARY EVANS COLLINS. 1951. *Interracial Housing: A Psychological Evaluation of a Social Experiment*. Minneapolis: University of Minnesota Press.

DIDHAM, CHERYL K. 1990. "Equal Opportunity in the Classroom: Making Teachers Aware." Paper presented at the annual meeting of the Association of Teacher Educators, February 5–8, Las Vegas.

DILLARD, J. L. 1972. *Black English*. New York: Random House.

DINGLE, DEREK T. 1989. "Affirmative Action." *Black Enterprise* (September): 42–48.

DOBYNS, HENRY F. 1966. "Estimating Aboriginal

American Population: An Appraisal of Techniques with a New Hemispheric Estimate." *Current Anthropology* 7:395–416.

DOBZHANSKY, THEODOSIUS. 1962. *Mankind Evolving.* New Haven, Conn.: Yale University Press.

DODD, C. H., and M. E. SALES. 1970. *Israel and the Arab World.* London: Routledge & Kegan Paul.

DOMESTIC POLICY ASSOCIATION. 1986. *Immigration: What We Promised, Where to Draw the Line.* Dayton, Ohio: Domestic Policy Association.

DOMHOFF, G. WILLIAM. 1983. *Who Rules America Now? A View for the Eighties.* Englewood Cliffs, N.J.: Prentice Hall.

DOMHOFF, G. WILLIAM. 1967. *Who Rules America?* Englewood Cliffs, N.J.: Prentice Hall.

DORSEN, NORMA. 1969. *Discrimination and Civil Rights.* Boston: Little, Brown.

DOUGLAS-HOME, CHARLES. 1968. *The Arabs and Israel.* London: Bodley Head.

DOVIDIO, JOHN. 1993. "The Subtlety of Racism." *Training and Development* 47, 4 (April): 51–57.

DOWDALL, GEORGE W. 1974. "White Gains from Black Subordination in 1960 and 1970." *Social Problems* 22:162–83.

DOWNS, ANTHONY. 1970. "Losses Imposed on Urban Households by Uncompensated Highway and Renewal Costs." Pp. 192–229 in Anthony Downs, *Urban Problems and Prospects.* Chicago: Markham.

DRAKE, ST. CLAIR, and HORACE R. CAYTON. 1945. *Black Metropolis.* New York: Harcourt Brace Jovanovich.

DREYFUSS, JOEL, and CHARLES LAWRENCE III. 1979. *The Bakke Case: The Politics of Inequality.* New York: Harcourt Brace Jovanovich.

DRIVER, HAROLD E. 1969. *Indians of North America,* 2d ed. Chicago: University of Chicago Press.

DUNCAN, GREG J., with RICHARD COE, MARY E. CORCORAN, MARTHA S. HILL, SAUL D. HOFFMAN, and JAMES M. MORGAN. 1984. *Years of Poverty, Years of Plenty: The Changing Fortunes of American Workers and Families.* Ann Arbor: Institute for Social Research, the University of Michigan.

DUNIER, MITCHELL. 1992. *Slim's Table: Race, Masculinity, and Respectability.* Chicago: University of Chicago Press.

DURKHEIM, EMILE. 1965 [1912]. *The Elementary Forms of Religious Life.* Joseph Wald Swain (tr.). New York: Free Press.

DURKHEIM, EMILE. 1964 [1893]. *The Study of Society.* George Simpson (tr.). New York: Free Press.

DUSHKIN PUBLISHING GROUP, 1977. *The Study of Society,* 2d ed. Gilford, Conn.: Dushkin Publishing Group.

DUTTON, DIANA B. 1986. "Social Class, Health, and Illness." Pp. 31–62 in L. Aiken and David Mechanic (eds.), *Applications of Social Science to Clinical Medicine and Health Policy.* New Brunswick, N.J.: Rutgers University Press.

DWYER, PAULA. 1989. "Legal Affairs: The Blow to Affirmative Action That May Not Hurt That Much." *Business Week* (July 3): 61–62.

DYE, THOMAS R. 1979. *Who's Running America?* Englewood Cliffs, N.J.: Prentice Hall.

DYER, HERBERT, JR. 1992. "Why We Need Father Figures." *Essence* 23, 2:132.

DYER, JAMES, ARNOLD VEDLITZ, and STEPHEN WORCHEL. 1989. "Social Distance Among Racial and Ethnic Groups in Texas: Some Demographic Correlates." *Social Science Quarterly* 70:607–16.

EAGAN, ANDREA BOROFF. 1988. "The Damage Done: The Endless Saga of the Dalkon Shield." *Village Voice* (July 5).

EAGLY, ALICE H. 1992. "Uneven Progress: Social Psychology and the Study of Attitudes." *Journal of Personality and Social Psychology* 63:693–710.

EAGLY, ALICE H., and S. CHAIKEN. 1993. *The Psychology of Attitudes.* Fort Worth, Tex.: Harcourt Brace Jovanovich.

EDMONDS, RONALD. 1979. "Some Schools Work and More Can." *Social Policy* 9, 5 (March/April): 28–32.

EDMONSTON, BARRY, and JEFFREY S. PASSEL. 1992. "U.S. Immigration and Ethnicity in the 21st Century." *Population Today* 20, 10:6–7.

Education Week. 1989. "Tax Hike Needed, Chief Tells Montana House." *Education Week* (March 15): 21.

EDWARDS, HARRY. 1994. "The Sociology of Sport." Pp. 100–103 in John E. Farley, *Sociology,* 3d ed. Englewood Cliffs, N.J.: Prentice Hall.

EDWARDS, HARRY. 1979. "Camouflaging the Color Line: A Critique." Pp. 98–103 in Charles Vert Willie (ed.), *Caste and Class Controversy.* Bayside, N.Y.: General Hall.

EGERTON, JOHN. 1970. "Black Executives in Big Business." *Race Relations Reporter* 1, 17:5.

EHRLICH, ELIZABETH. 1990. "Anger, Shouting, and Sometimes Tears." *Business Week* (August 6): 55.

EHRLICH, HOWARD J. 1973. *The Social Psychology of Prejudice.* New York: Wiley Interscience.

ELKINS, STANLEY M. 1959. *Slavery: A Problem in American Institutional and Intellectual Life.* Chicago: University of Chicago Press.

ELLIOTT, DELBERT S., and SUZANNE S. AGETON. 1980. "Reconciling Race and Class Differences in Self-reported and Official Estimates of Delinquency." *American Sociological Review* 45:95–110.

ELLIOTT, DORINDA, ANDREW NAGORSKI, NATASHA LEBEDEVA, and CLINTON O'BRIEN. 1993. "After the Showdown: Yeltsin Survives a Power Struggle—but the Crisis May Only Speed Russia's Slide Toward a Crackup." *Newsweek* (April 5): 20–23.

ELLIS, ALBERT. 1992. "Rational-Emotive Approaches to Peace." *Journal of Cognitive Psychotherapy* 6, 2:79–104.

EMERY, ROBERT E. 1989. "Family Violence." *American Psychologist* 44:321–28.

ENGLAND, ROBERT E., KENNETH J. MEIER, and LUIS RICARDO FRAGA. 1988. "Barriers to Equal Opportunity: Educational Practices and Minority Students." *Urban Affairs Quarterly* 23: 635–46.

EPP, FRANK H. 1970. *Whose Land Is Palestine?* Grand Rapids, Mich.: Erdmans.

EPSTEIN, JOYCE L. 1985. "After the Bus Arrives: Resegregation in Desegregated Schools." *Journal of Social Issues* 41, 3:23–43.

ESPOSITO, D. 1973. "Homogeneous and Heterogeneous Ability Grouping: Principal Findings and Implications for Evaluating and Designing More Effective Educational Environments." *Review of Education Research* 43:163–79.

ESTRADA, LEOBARDO F., F. CHRIS GARCIA, REYNALDO FLORES MACIAS, and LIONEL MALDONADO. 1985. "Chicanos in the United States: A History of Exploitation and Resistance." Pp. 162–84 in Norman R. Yetman (ed.), *Majority and Minority: The Dynamics of Race and Ethnicity in American Life,* 4th ed. Boston: Allyn and Bacon.

EUROPA PUBLICATIONS. 1989. *Europa World Yearbook, 1989.* London: Europa Publications.

EVANS, FRANKLIN R. 1977. "The Social Impact of *Bakke." Learning and the Law* (Spring).

EWENS, WILLIAM L., and HOWARD J. EHRLICH. 1969. "Reference Other Support and Ethnic Attitudes as Predictors of Intergroup Behavior." Revised version of paper presented at the joint meetings of the Midwest Sociological Society and Ohio Valley Sociological Society, May, Indianapolis, Ind.

EYSENCK, HANS J. 1971. *The IQ Argument.* New York: Library Press.

FAGAN, JEFFREY, MARTIN FORST, and T. SCOTT VIVONA. 1987. "Racial Determinants of the Judicial Transfer Decision: Prosecuting Violent Youth in Criminal Court." *Crime and Delinquency* 33: 259–86.

FAIRCHILD, HALFORD H. 1985. "Black, Negro, or Afro-American? The Differences Are Crucial." *Journal of Black Studies* 16:47–55.

FANSTEIN, SUSAN S., and NORMAN I. FANSTEIN. 1989. "The Racial Dimension in Urban Political Economy." *Urban Affairs Quarterly* 25:187–99.

FANTINI, MARIO D. 1969. "Participation, Decentralization, Community Control, and Quality Education." *Record* 71:93–107.

FANTINI, MARIO D., and MARILYN GITTELL. 1973. *Decentralization: Achieving Reform.* New York: Praeger.

FANTINI, MARIO D., MARILYN GITTELL, and RICHARD MAGAT. 1970. *Community Control and the Urban School.* New York: Praeger.

FARLEY, JOHN E. 1994a. *Sociology,* 3d ed. Englewood Cliffs, N.J.: Prentice Hall.

FARLEY, JOHN E. 1994b. "Twentieth Century Wars: Some Short-Term Effects on Intergroup Relations in the United States." *Sociological Inquiry* 64:214–37.

FARLEY, JOHN E. 1993. "Racial Housing Segregation in the St. Louis Metropolitan Area: Comparing Trends at the Tract and Block Levels." *Journal of Urban Affairs* 15:515–27.

FARLEY, JOHN E. 1992a. "White Support for Black Political Candidates." Paper presented at the annual meeting of the Midwest Sociological Society, April, Kansas City, Mo.

FARLEY, JOHN E. 1992b. *American Social Problems: An Institutional Analysis,* 2d ed. Englewood Cliffs, N.J.: Prentice Hall.

FARLEY, JOHN E. 1990. "The White Vote for Jesse Jackson in 1988 Democratic Primaries and Caucuses."

Paper presented at the annual meeting of the Midwest Sociological Society, April, Chicago.

FARLEY, JOHN E. 1987a. *American Social Problems: An Institutional Analysis.* Englewood Cliffs, N.J.: Prentice Hall.

FARLEY, JOHN E. 1987b. "Excessive Black and Hispanic Unemployment in U.S. Metropolitan Areas: The Roles of Racial Inequality, Segregation, and Discrimination in Male Joblessness." *American Journal of Economics and Sociology* 46: 129–50.

FARLEY, JOHN E. 1987c. "Segregation in 1980: How Segregated Are America's Metropolitan Areas?" In Gary A. Tobin (ed.), *Divided Neighborhoods.* Newbury Park, Calif.: Sage Publications.

FARLEY, JOHN E. 1986. "Segregated City, Segregated Suburbs: To What Extent Are They Products of Black–White Socioeconomic Differentials?" *Urban Geography* 7: 180–87.

FARLEY, JOHN E. 1984. "Housing Segregation in the School Age Population and the Link Between Housing and School Segregation: A St. Louis Case Study." *Journal of Urban Affairs* 6, 4:65–80.

FARLEY, JOHN E. 1983. "Metropolitan Housing Segregation in 1980: The St. Louis Case." *Urban Affairs Quarterly* 18:347–59.

FARLEY, JOHN E. 1982. *Majority–Minority Relations.* Englewood Cliffs, N.J.: Prentice Hall.

FARLEY, JOHN E. 1981. "Black Male Unemployment in U.S. Metropolitan Areas: The Role of Black Central City Segregation and Job Decentralization." Paper presented at the annual meeting of the Society for the Study of Social Problems, Toronto, Ontario.

FARLEY, JOHN E. 1980. "Handicapped Persons in Madison County and Their Housing Needs." Report to Madison County, Illinois, Community Development Department. Edwardsville: Southern Illinois University at Edwardsville, Center for Urban and Environmental Research and Services.

FARLEY, JOHN E. 1977. Effects of Residential Setting, Parental Lifestyle, and Demographic Characteristics on Children's Activity Patterns. Ph. D. diss., University of Michigan.

FARLEY, REYNOLDS. 1991. "The Color Line and the Melting Pot: Racial and Ethnic Conflict in Twentieth-Century United States." Paper presented at Washington University, St. Louis, October 28.

FARLEY, REYNOLDS. 1984. *Blacks and Whites: Narrowing the Gap?* Cambridge, Mass.: Harvard University Press.

FARLEY, REYNOLDS. 1979. "Racial Progress in the Last Two Decades: What Can We Determine About Who Benefitted and Why?" Paper presented at the Annual Meeting of the American Sociological Association, Boston.

FARLEY, REYNOLDS. 1977. "Trends in Racial Inequalities: Have the Gains of the 1960's Disappeared in the 1970's?" *American Sociological Review* 42: 189–208.

FARLEY, REYNOLDS. 1975. "School Integration and White Flight." Unpublished paper. The University of Michigan, Population Studies Center.

FARLEY, REYNOLDS, SUZANNE BIANCHI, and DIANE CO-LASANTO. 1979. "Barriers to the Racial Integration of Neighborhoods: The Detroit Case." *Annals of the American Academy of Political and Social Science* 441 (January): 97–113.

FARLEY, REYNOLDS, and WILLIAM H. FREY. 1994. "Changes in the Segregation of Whites from Blacks During the 1980s: Small Steps Toward a More Integrated Society." *American Sociological Review* 59: 23–45.

FARLEY, REYNOLDS, and WILLIAM H. FREY. 1992. "The Residential Segregation of Blacks, Latinos, and Asians: 1980 and 1990." Paper presented at the annual meeting of the American Sociological Association, August 21, Pittsburgh.

FARLEY, REYNOLDS, TONI RICHARDS, and CLARENCE WURDOCK. 1980. "School Desegregation and White Flight: An Investigation of Competing Models and Their Discrepant Findings." *Sociology of Education* 53:123–29.

FARLEY, REYNOLDS, HOWARD SCHUMAN, SUZANNE BIANCHI, DIANE COLASANTO, and SHIRLEY HATCH-ETT. 1978. "Chocolate City, Vanilla Suburbs: Will the Trend Toward Racially Separate Communities Continue?" *Social Science Research* 7:319–44.

FEAGIN, JOE R. 1991. "The Continuing Significance of Race: Antiblack Discrimination in Public Places." *American Sociological Review* 56:101–16.

FEAGIN, JOE R. 1989. *Racial and Ethnic Relation*, 3d edition. Englewood Cliffs, N.J.: Prentice Hall.

FEAGIN, JOE R. 1984. *Racial and Ethnic Relations*, 2d ed. Englewood Cliffs, N.J.: Prentice Hall.

FEAGIN, JOE R. 1972. "Poverty: We Still Believe That God Helps Those Who Help Themselves." *Psychology Today* (November).

FEAGIN, JOE R., and CLAIRECE BOOHER FEAGIN. 1978. *Discrimination American Style: Institutional Racism and Sexism.* Englewood Cliffs, N.J.: Prentice Hall.

FEAGIN, JOE R., and HARLAN HAHN. 1973. *Ghetto Riots: The Politics of Violence in American Cities.* New York: Macmillan.

FEATHERMAN, DAVID L., and ROBERT M. HAUSER. 1978. *Opportunity and Change.* New York: Academic Press.

FEDERAL BUREAU OF INVESTIGATION. 1990. *Uniform Crime Reports: Crime in the United States, 1989.* Washington, D.C.: U.S. Government Printing Office.

FEDERAL BUREAU OF INVESTIGATION. 1979. *Uniform Crime Reports, 1978.* Washington, D.C.: U.S. Government Printing Office.

FENDRICH, J. M. 1967. "Perceived Reference Group Support: Racial Attitudes and Overt Behavior." *American Sociological Review* 32:960–70.

FENTON, RAY, and DOUGLAS NANCARROW. 1986. "When Good Will Isn't Enough: Prejudice and Racism—Reactions to a Multicultural Unit on Alaska Native Land Claims." Paper presented at the conference of Western Speech Communication Association, February 15–18, Tucson, Ariz.

FERDINAND, THEODORE N., and ELMER G. LUCHTER-HAND. 1970. "Inner City Youth, the Police, the Juvenile Court, and Justice." *Social Problems* 17:510–27.

FERNANDES, FLORESTAN. 1971. *The Negro in Brazilian Society.* New York: Atheneum.

FESTINGER, LEON. 1957. *A Theory of Cognitive Dissonance.* Standord, Calif.: Stanford University Press.

FESTINGER, LEON, and J. M. CARLSMITH. 1959. "Cognitive Consequences of Forced Compliance." *Journal of Abnormal and Social Psychology* 58:203–10.

FICARROTTO, THOMAS J. 1990. "Racism, Sexism, and Erotophobia: Attitudes of Heterosexuals Toward Homosexuals." *Journal of Homosexuality* 19, 1:111–16.

FICKETT, JOAN G. 1975. "Merican: An Inner City Dialect—Aspects of Morphemics, Syntax, and Semology." *Studies in Linguistics: Occasional Papers* 13.

FINEBERG, SOLOMON ANDHIL. 1949. *Punishment Without Crime.* New York: Doubleday.

FIREBAUGH, GLENN, and KENNETH E. DAVIS. 1988. "Trends in Antiblack Prejudice, 1972–1984: Region and Cohort Effects." *American Journal of Sociology* 94:251–72.

FIRESTINE, ROBERT E. 1977. "Economic Growth and Inequality, Demographic Change, and the Public Sector Response." Pp. 191–210 in David C. Perry and Alfred J. Watkins (eds.), *The Rise of the Sunbelt Cities*, vol. 14, *Urban Affairs Annual Review.* Beverly Hills, Calif.: Sage Publications.

FISHBEIN, M., and I. AJZEN. 1975. *Belief, Attitude, Intention, and Behavior: An Introduction to Theory and Research.* Reading, Mass.: Addison-Wesley.

FLORES, SOLOMON HERNANDEZ. 1978. *The Nature and Effects of Bilingual Education Programs for the Spanish-Speaking Child in the United States.* New York: Arno Press.

FLOWERMAN, SAMUEL H. 1947. "Mass Propaganda in the War Against Bigotry." *Journal of Abnormal and Social Psychology* 42:429–439.

FOGELSON, ROBERT. 1971. *Violence as Protest: A Study of Riots and Ghettos.* New York: Doubleday.

FOGELSON, ROBERT, and R. B. HILL. 1968. "Who Riots? A Study of Participation in the 1967 Riots." Pp. 217–48 in *Supplemental Studies for the National Advisory Commission on Civil Disorders.* Washington, D.C.: U.S. Government Printing Office.

FOLEY, DOROTHY M. 1993. "Restructuring with Technology." *Principal* 72, 3:22, 24–25.

FOOTE, CALEB. 1958. "A Study of the Administration of Bail in New York City." *University of Pennsylvania Law Review* 106.

FORD, W. SCOTT. 1973. "Interracial Public Housing in a Border City: Another Look at the Contact Hypothesis." *American Journal of Sociology* 78: 1426–47.

FORDHAM, SIGNITHIA, and JOHN U. OGBU. 1986. "Black Students' School Success: Coping with the 'Burden of Acting White.'" *Urban Review* 18:181.

FOSTER, WILLIAM Z. 1920. *The Great Steel Strike and Its Lessons.* New York: Huebsch.

FRANKLIN, JOHN HOPE. 1969. *From Slavery to Freedom: A History of Negro Americans,* 3d ed. New York: Vintage Books.

FRAZIER, E. FRANKLIN. 1966. *The Negro Family in the United States,* rev. ed. Chicago: University of Chicago Press.

FREEMAN, JO. 1979. "Resource Mobilization and Strategy." In Mayer N. Zald and John D. McCarthy (eds.), *The Dynamics of Social Movements.* Cambridge, Mass.: Winthrop.

FREEMAN, JO. 1973. "The Origins of the Women's Liberation Movement." *American Journal of Sociology* 78:782–811.

FREEMAN, RICHARD. 1978. "Black Economic Progress Since 1964." *Public Interest* 52:52–68.

FREUD, SIGMUND. 1962 [1930]. *Civilization and Its Discontents.* James Strachey (tr.). New York: Norton.

FREYRE, GILBERTO. 1946. *The Masters and the Slaves: A Study in the Development of Brazilian Civilization.* New York: Knopf.

FRIEDENBERG, E. Z. 1965. *Coming of Age in America.* New York: Random House.

FRISBIE, W. PARKER. 1977. "The Scale and Growth of World Urbanization." Pp. 44–58 in John Walton and Donald E. Carns (eds.), *Cities in Change: Studies on the Urban Condition.* Boston: Allyn and Bacon.

FUCHS, ESTELLE, and ROBERT J. HAVIGHURST. 1972. *To Live on This Earth.* Garden City, N.Y.: Doubleday.

FUERST, J. S. 1981. "Report Card: Chicago's All-Black Schools." *Public Interest* 64:79–91.

FUKURAI, HIROSHI, EDGAR W. BUTLER, and RICHARD KROOTH. 1991a. "Where Did the Black Jurors Go? A Theoretical Synthesis of Racial Disenfranchisement in the Jury System and Jury Selection." *Journal of Black Studies* 22:196–215.

FUKURAI, HIROSHI, EDGAR W. BUTLER, and RICHARD KROOTH. 1991b. "Cross-sectional Jury Representation or Systematic Jury Representation? Simple Random and Cluster Sampling Strategies in Jury Selection." *Journal of Criminal Justice* 19:31–48.

FURSTENBERG, FRANK F., THEODORE HERSHBERG, and J. MODELL. 1975. "The Origins of the Female-Headed Black Family: The Impact of the Urban Experience." *Journal of Interdisciplinary History* 6:211–33.

FYFE, JAMES J. 1982. "Blind Justice: Police Shootings in Memphis." *Journal of Criminal Law and Criminology* 73:707–22.

GAINES, MARGIE L., and MARGARET DAVIS. 1990. "Accuracy of Teacher Prediction of Elementary Student Achievement." Paper presented at the annual meeting of the American Educational Research Association, April 16–20, Boston.

GALAGAN, PATRICIA A. 1993. "Trading Places at Monsanto." *Training and Development* 47, 4 (April): 45–49.

GALLUP, GEORGE, JR. 1990. *The Gallup Poll: Public Opinion, 1989.* Wilmington, Del.: Scholarly Resources.

GAMORAN, ADAM. 1992a. "Is Ability Grouping Equitable?" *Educational Leadership* (October): 11–17.

GAMORAN, ADAM. 1992b. "The Variable Effects of High School Tracking." *American Sociological Review* 57:812–29.

GANS, HERBERT. 1979. "Symbolic Ethnicity: The Future of Ethnic Groups and Cultures in America." *Ethnic and Racial Studies* 2:1–20.

GANS, HERBERT. 1974. Foreword. In Neil C. Sandberg, *Ethnic Identity and Assimilation: The Polish American Community.* New York: Praeger.

GANS, HERBERT. 1973. *More Equality.* New York: Pantheon Books.

GANS, HERBERT. 1971. "The Uses of Poverty: The Poor Pay All." *Social Policy* (July/August).

GANS, HERBERT. 1967. "The Negro Family: Reflections on the Moynihan Report." Pp. 445–57 in Lee Rainwater and William L. Yancey (eds.), *The Moynihan Report and the Politics of Controversy.* Cambridge, Mass.: M.I.T. Press.

GARBARINO, MERWYN S. 1976. *American Indian Heritage.* Boston: Little, Brown.

GARCIA, JESUS. 1993. "The Changing Image of Minorities in Textbooks." *Phi Delta Kappan* 75:29–35.

GARFINKEL, HAROLD. 1949. "Research Note on Inter- and Intra-Racial Homicides." *Social Forces* 27: 369–81.

GARGAN, EDWARD. 1986a. "Whites Who Left Zimbabwe, Fearful of Future, Drift Back." *New York Times,* May 18, sec. 1.

GARGAN, EDWARD. 1986b. "For White Farmers in Zimbabwe, All's Well." *New York Times,* June 3, sec. 1.

GENERAL ACCOUNTING OFFICE. 1990. *"Report and Recommendations of the Task Force on IRCA-Related Discrimination."* Washington, D.C.: U.S. Government Printing Office.

GERARD, HAROLD B. 1988. In Phyllis Katz and Dalmas Taylor (eds.), *Eliminating Racism.* New York: Plenum.

GESCHWENDER, JAMES A. 1964. "Social Structure and the Negro Revolt." *Social Forces* 43:248–56.

GESCHWENDER, JAMES A., and B. D. SINGER. 1968. "Deprivation and the Detroit Riot." *Social Problems* 17:457–463.

GIBSON, GEOFFREY, GEORGE BUGBEE, and ODIN W. ANDERSON. 1970. *Emergency Medical Services in the Chicago Area.* Chicago: University of Chicago, Center for Health Administration.

GIBSON, JAMES L., and RAYMOND M. DUCH. 1992. "Anti-Semitic Attitudes of the Mass Public: Estimates and Explanations Based on a Survey of the Moscow Oblast." *Public Opinion Quarterly* 56, 1:1–28.

GIBSON, MARGARET A., and JOHN U. OGBU (eds.). 1992. *Minority Status and Schooling: Immigrant vs. Nonimmigrant.* New York: Garland.

GILBERT, G. M. 1951. "Stereotype Persistence and Change Among College Students." *Journal of Abnormal and Social Psychology* (April): 245–54.

GINTIS, HERBERT. 1971. "Education, Technology, and Worker Productivity." *American Economic Review* 61 (American Economic Association proceedings): 266–79.

GLASS, THOMAS E., and WILLIAM P. SANDERS. 1978. *Community Control in Education: A Study in Power Transition.* Midland, Mich.: Pendell.

GLAZER, NATHAN. 1971. "Blacks and Ethnic Groups:

The Difference, and the Political Difference It Makes." *Social Problems* 18: 444–61.

GLAZER, NATHAN. 1976. *Affirmative Discrimination*. New York: Basic Books.

GLAZER, NATHAN, and DANIEL PATRICK MOYNIHAN. 1970. *Beyond the Melting Pot*. Cambridge, Mass.: M.I.T. Press.

GLENN, EVELYN MAKANO. 1980. "Dialectics of Wage Work: Japanese American Women and Domestic Service, 1905–1940." *Feminist Studies* 6:432–71.

GLENN, NORVAL. 1966. "White Gains from Negro Subordination." *Social Problems* 14:159–78.

GLENN, NORVAL. 1963. "Occupational Benefits to Whites from the Subordination of Negroes." *American Sociological Review* 28:443–48.

GLIEDMAN, JOHN. 1979. "The Wheelchair Rebellion." *Psychology Today* (August).

GOBINEAU, ARTHUR DE. 1915 [1853–1855]. *The Inequality of Human Races*. Adrian Collins (tr.). New York: Putnam's.

GOERING, JOHN M. 1971. "The Emergence of Ethnic Interests: A Case of Serendipity." *Social Forces* 49: 379–84.

GOLDEN, MARK, and B. BIRNS. 1968. "Social Class and Cognitive Development in Infancy." *Merrill-Palmer Quarterly* 14:139–49.

GOLDSTEIN, JOSEPH. 1960. "Police Discretion Not to Invoke the Criminal Process: Low Visibility Decisions in the Administration of Justice." *Yale Law Journal* 69 (March).

GOLEMAN, DANIEL. 1990. "Anger over Racism Seen as Cause of Blacks' High Blood Pressure." *New York Times,* April 24: C3.

GOLUB, ELLEN. 1989. "Making 'A World of Difference.'" *Education and Society* 1, 1:5–9.

GONZALES, NANCIE L. 1967. *The Spanish Americans of New Mexico: A Distinctive Heritage*. Advance Report 9. Los Angeles: University of California, Mexican-American Study Project.

GORDON, MILTON M. 1978. *Human Nature, Class, and Ethnicity*. New York: Oxford University Press.

GORDON, MILTON M. 1964. *Assimilation in American Life*. New York: Oxford University Press.

GOREN, ARTHUR A. 1980. "Jews." Pp. 571–98 in Stephan Thernstrom, Ann Orlov, and Oscar Handlin (eds.), *Harvard Encyclopedia of American Ethnic Groups*. Cambridge, Mass.: Harvard University Press.

GOSSETT, THOMAS F. 1963. *Race: The History of an Idea in America*. Dallas: Southern Methodist University Press.

GOULDNER, HELEN, with MAYR SYMONS STRONG. 1978. *Teachers' Pets, Troublemakers, Nobodies: Black Children in Elementary School*. Westport, Conn.: Greenwood Press.

GRAMS, ROBERT, and RACHEL ROHDE. 1976. Unpublished report to Judges Committee. Hennepin County, Minnesota District Court.

GRANT, MADISON. 1916. *The Passing of the Great Race or the Racial Basis of European History*. New York: Scribner's.

GREBLER, LEO, JOAN W. MOORE, and RALPH C. GUZMAN. 1970. *The Mexican-American People*. New York: Free Press.

GREELEY, ANDREW M. 1982. *Catholic High Schools and Minority Students*. New Brunswick, N.J.: Transaction Books.

GREELEY, ANDREW M. 1981. "Minority Students in Catholic Secondary Schools." Paper presented at the Conference on the High School and Beyond, National Center for Educational Statistics, Washington, D.C.

GREELEY, ANDREW M. 1977. *The American Catholic: A Social Portrait*. New York: Basic Books.

GREELEY, ANDREW M. 1974. *Ethnicity in the United States: A Preliminary Reconnaissance*. New York: Wiley.

GREELEY, ANDREW M. 1971. *Why Can't They Be Like Us?* New York: Dutton.

GREELEY, ANDREW M. 1970. "Religious Intermarriage in a Denominational Society." *American Journal of Sociology* 75:949–52.

GREELEY, ANDREW M., and PAUL B. SHEATSLEY. 1971. "Attitudes Toward Racial Integration." *Scientific American* 225, 6:13–19.

GREEN, EDWARD. 1970. "Race, Social Status, and Criminal Arrest." *American Sociological Review* 35:476–90.

GREEN, MARK. 1982. *Winning Back America*. New York: Bantam.

GREENBERG, MICHAEL R., and NICHOLAS VALENTE. 1976. "Recent Economic Trends in the Major Northeastern Metropolises." Pp. 77–100 in George Sternlieb and James W. Hughes (eds.), *Post-Industrial America: Metropolitan Decline and Interregional Job Shift*. New Brunswick, N.J.: Rutgers University Center for Urban Policy Research.

GRIMSHAW, ALLEN D. 1969. "Three Major Cases of Racial Violence in the United States." Pp. 105–15 in Allen D. Grimshaw (ed.), *Racial Violence in the United States*. Chicago: Aldine.

GRIMSHAW, ALLAN D. 1959a. "Lawlessness and Violence in America and Their Special Manifestations of Changing Negro–White Relationships." *Journal of Negro History* 64:52–72.

GRIMSHAW, ALLEN D. 1959b. "A Study of Social Violence: Urban Race Riots in the United States." Ph.D. diss., University of Pennsylvania.

GRISCOM, JOAN L. 1992. "The Case of Sharon Kowalski and Karen Thompson: Ableism, Heterosexism, and Sexism." Pp. 215–25 in Paula S. Rothenberg (ed.), *Race, Class, and Gender in the United States: An Integrated Study*. New York: St. Martin's Press.

GRODZINS, MORTON. 1949. *Americans Betrayed: Politics and the Japanese Evacuation*. Chicago: University of Chicago Press.

GROSS, JANE. 1990. "Men and Women in Office: On Parity and Equality." *New York Times,* August 21, sec. A.

GROSSARTH-MATICEK, R., HANS J. EYSENCK, and H. VETTER. 1989. "The Causes and Cures of Prejudice: An Empirical Study of the Frustration–Aggression Hypothesis." *Personality and Individual Differences* 10:547–59.

GROSSMAN, BARRY A. 1974. "The Discretionary Enforcement of Law." In Sawyer F. Sylvester and Edward Sagarin (eds.), *Politics and Crime.* New York: Praeger.

GUEST, AVERY M., and JAMES A. WEED. 1976. "Ethnic Residential Segregation: Patterns of Change." *American Journal of Sociology* 81:1088–11.

GUILLEMIN, JEANE. 1978. "The Politics of National Integration: A Comparison of United States and Canadian Indian Administrations." *Social Problems* 25: 319–32.

GUTMAN, HERBERT. 1976. *The Black Family in Slavery and Freedom, 1750–1925.* New York: Pantheon.

GUZMAN, RALPH. "Mexican American Casualties in Viet Nam." *La Raza* 1 (n.d.): 12.

HACKER, ANDREW. 1992. *Two Nations: Black and White, Separate, Hostile, Unequal.* New York: Scribner's.

HAERTEL, EDWARD H. 1987. "Comparing Public and Private Schools Using Longitudinal Data from the HSB Study." Pp. 9–32 in Edward H. Haertel, Thomas James, and Henry M. Levin (eds.), *Comparing Public and Private Schools,* vol. 2, *School Achievement.* New York: Falmer.

HAGAN, JOHN. 1985. *Modern Criminology: Crime, Criminal Behavior, and Its Control.* New York: McGraw-Hill.

HAGAN, JOHN. 1974. "Extra-Legal Attributes and Criminal Sentencing: An Assessment of a Sociological Viewpoint." *Law and Society Review* 8:357–83.

HAGGARD, ERNEST A. 1954. "Social Status and Intelligence." *Genetic Psychology Monographs* 49:141–86.

HAIMOWITZ, MORRIS L., and NATALIE R. HAIMOWITZ. 1950. "Reducing Ethnic Hostility Through Psychotherapy." *Journal of Social Psychology* (May): 231–41.

HALEY, ALEX (ed.). 1964. *The Autobiography of Malcolm X.* New York: Grove Press.

HALL, EDWIN L., and ALBERT A. SIMKUS. 1975. "Inequality in Types of Sentence Received by Native Americans and Whites." *Criminology* 13, 2:199–222.

HALL, MARCIA L., and WALTER R. ALLEN. 1982. "Race Consciousness and Achievement: Two Issues in the Study of Black Graduate/Professional Students." *Integratededucation* 20, 1–2:56–61.

HALL, RAYMOND L. 1978. *Black Separatism in the United States.* Hanover, N.H.: University Press of New England.

HALL, ROBERT L., MARK RODEGHIER, and BERT USEEM. 1986. "Effects of Education on Attitudes to Protest." *American Sociological Review* 51:564–73.

HALL, THOMAS D. 1993. "Bound Labor: The Spanish Borderlands." Pp. 35–44 in Jacob Ernest Cooke (ed.), *Encyclopedia of the North American Colonies.* New York: Charles Scribner's Sons.

HALL, THOMAS D. 1989. *Social Change in the Southwest, 1350–1880.* Lawrence: University of Kansas Press.

HALLER, EMIL J. 1985. "Pupil Race and Elementary School Ability Grouping: Are Teachers Biased Against Black Children?" *American Educational Research Journal* 22:465–83.

HALLINAN, MAUREEN T. 1992. "The Organization of Students for Instruction in the Middle School." *Sociology of Education* 65:114–27.

HAMER, DEAH H., STELLA HU, VICTORIA L. MAGNUSON, NAN HU, and ANGELA M. L. PATTATUCCI. 1993. "A Linkage Between DNA Markers on the X Chromosome and Male Sexual Orientation." *Science* 261, 519:321–27.

HAMILTON, DAVID L. 1981. *Cognitive Processes in Stereotyping and Intergroup Behavior.* Hillsdale, N.J.: Erlbaum Associates.

HAMILTON, GLORIA, and J. DAVID ROESNER. 1972. "How Employers Screen Disadvantaged Workers." *Monthly Labor Review* (September).

HANDLIN, OSCAR, and MARY F. HANDLIN. 1950. "Origins of the Southern Labor System." *William and Mary Quarterly* 7:199–222.

HANE, MIKISO. 1990. "Wartime Internment." *Journal of American History* 77:569–75.

HANNERZ, ULF. 1969. *Soulside.* New York: Columbia University Press.

HANSEN, MARCUS L. 1966. "The Third Generation." Pp. 255–72 in Oscar Handlin (ed.), *Children of the Uprooted.* New York: Harper & Row.

HANSEN, MARCUS L. 1952. "The Third Generation in America." *Commentary* 14:492–500.

HARDING, JOHN, HAROLD PROSHANSKY, BERNARD KUTNER, and ISADOR CHEIN. 1969. "Prejudice and Ethnic Relations." Pp. 1–77 in Gardner Lindzey and Elliott Aronson (eds.), *The Handbook of Social Psychology,* 2d ed., vol. 5. Reading, Mass.: Addison-Wesley.

HARKINS, STEPHEN G., and RICHARD E. PETTY. 1987. "Information Utility and the Multiple Source Effect." *Journal of Personality and Social Psychology* 52:260–68.

HARRIS POLL. 1980. "Most Vietnam Veterans Glad They Served, Would Again, Poll Says." *St. Louis Globe Democrat,* July 2.

HARRISON, BENNETT. 1972. *Education, Training, and the Urban Ghetto.* Baltimore: Johns Hopkins University Press.

HARRISON, RODERICK J., and DANIEL H. WEINBERG. 1992a. "Racial and Ethnic Residential Segregation in 1990." Paper presented at the annual meeting of the Population Association of America, May, Denver, Colo.

HARRISON, RODERICK J., and DANIEL H. WEINBERG. 1992b. "Changes in Racial and Ethnic Segregation, 1980–1990." Paper presented at the annual meeting of the American Statistical Association, August 9–13, Boston.

HASSAN, M. K. 1987. "Parental Behavior, Authoritarianism, and Prejudice." *Manas* 34, 1–2:41–50.

HASSAN, M. K., and KHALIQUE, A. 1987. "Impact of Parents on Children's Religious Prejudice." *Indian Journal of Current Psychological Research* 2, 1:47–55.

HARTLEY, E. M. 1946. *Problems in Prejudice.* New York: King's Crown Press.

HARVEY, D. G., and G. T. SLATIN. 1975. "The Relationship as Hypothesis." *Social Forces* 54:140–59.

HAUSER, ROBERT M., WILLIAM H. SEWELL, and DUANE F. ALWIN. 1976. "High School Effects on Achievement." Pp. 309–41 in William H. Sewell, Robert M. Hauser, and David L. Featherman (eds.), *Schooling and Achievement in American Society*. New York: Academic Press.

HAWKINS, HUGH. 1962. *Booker T. Washington and His Critics: The Problem of Negro Leadership*. Boston: Heath.

HAYES, CHERYL D. 1987a. *Risking the Future: Adolescent Sexuality, Pregnancy, and Childbearing*. Report of the Panel on Adolescent Pregnancy and Childbearing, National Research Council, vol. 1. Washington, D.C.: National Academy Press.

HAYES, CHERYL D. 1987b. "Adolescent Pregnancy and Childbearing: An Emerging Research Focus." Pp. 1–6 in Sandra Hofferth and Cheryl D. Hayes (eds.), *Risking the Future: Adolescent Sexuality, Pregnancy, and Childbearing*, vol. 2, *Working Papers and Statistical Appendices*. Washington, D.C.: National Academy Press.

HAYES, CHERYL D., and SHEILA KAMERMAN (eds.) 1983. *Children of Working Parents: Experiences and Outcomes*. Washington, D.C.: National Academy Press.

HAYNES, M. ALFRED, and MICHAEL R. GARVEY. 1969. "Physicians, Patients, and Hospitals in the Inner City." Pp. 117–24 in John C. Norman (ed.), *Medicine in the Ghetto*. New York: Appleton-Century-Crofts.

HEAVEN, PATRICK C., and ADRIAN FURNHAM. 1987. "Race Prejudice and Economic Beliefs." *Journal of Social Psychology* 127:483–89.

HEER, DAVID H. 1980. "Intermarriage." Pp. 513–21 in Stephan Thernstrom, Ann Orlov, and Oscar Handlin (eds.), *The Harvard Encyclopedia of American Ethnic Groups*. Cambridge, Mass.: Harvard University Press.

HELMICH, EDITH. 1985. *The Effectiveness of Preschool for Children from Low-Income Families: A Review of the Literature*. Springfield: Illinois State Board of Education, Department of Planning, Research, and Evaluation.

HELMS, L. JAY, JOSEPH P. NEWHOUSE, and CHARLES E. PHELPS. 1978. *Copayments and Demand for Medical Care: The California Medicaid Experience*. Report no. R-2167-HEW Santa Monica, Calif.: Rand Corporation.

HERMALIN, ALBERT I., and REYNOLDS FARLEY. 1973. "The Potential for Residential Integration in Cities and Suburbs: Implications for the Busing Controversy." *American Sociological Review* 38:595–610.

HERNSTEIN, RICHARD J. 1971. "I.Q." *Atlantic Monthly* (September): 43–64.

HERSHBERG, THEODORE, HANS BURSTEIN, EUGENE P. ERICKSEN, STEPHANIE GREENBERG, and WILLIAM L. YANCEY. 1978. "A Tale of Three Cities: Blacks and Immigrants in Philadelphia: 1850–1880, 1930, and 1970." *Annals of the American Academy of Political and Social Science* 441 (January): 55–81.

HIGGENBOTHAM, ELIZABETH. 1992. "We Were Never on a Pedestal: Women of Color Continue to Struggle with Poverty, Racism, and Sexism." Pp. 183–90 in Margaret L. Anderson and Patricia Hill Collins (eds.), *Race, Class, and Gender: An Anthology*. Belmont, Calif.: Wadsworth.

HIGHAM, JOHN. 1974. "Integration vs. Pluralism: Another American Dilemma." *Center Magazine* 7 (July/August): 67–73.

HILL, ROBERT. 1972. *The Strengths of Black Families*. New York: Emerson Hall.

HILLIARD, ASA G. 1988. "Conceptual Confusion and the Persistence of Group Oppression Through Education." *Equity and Excellence* 24, 1:36–43.

HINDELANG, MICHAEL J. 1981. "Variations in Sex-Race-Age-Specific Incidence Rates of Offending." *American Sociological Review* 46:461–74.

HINDELANG, MICHAEL J. 1969. "Equality Under the Law." *Journal of Criminal Law, Criminology, and Police Science* 60:306–13.

HINES, RALPH. 1972. "The Health Status of Black Americans: Changing Perspectives." Pp. 40–50 in E. Jaco (ed.), *Patients, Physicians, and Illness*, 2d ed. New York: Free Press.

HITLER, ADOLF. 1940 [1925–1927]. *Mein Kampf*. New York: Reynmal and Hitchcock, 1940.

HOCHSCHILD, ARLIE. 1989. *The Second Shift: Working Parents and the Revolution at Home*. New York: Viking Penguin.

HODGSON, SUSAN. 1979. "Childrearing Systems: The Influence of Shared Childrearing on the Development of Competence." In William Michelson, Saul V. Levine, and Anna-Rose Spina (eds.), *The Child in the City: Changes and Challenges*. Toronto: University of Toronto Press.

HOFFER, THOMAS, ANDREW M. GREELEY, and JAMES S. COLEMAN. 1987. "Catholic High School Effects on Achievement Growth." Pp. 67–88 in Edward H. Haertel, Thomas James, and Henry M. Levin (eds.), *Comparing Public and Private Schools*, vol. 2, *School Achievement*. New York: Falmer.

HOFFER, THOMAS, ANDREW M. GREELEY, and JAMES S. COLEMAN. 1985. "Achievement Growth in Public and Catholic Schools." *Sociology of Education* 58:74–97.

HOFFMANN, LOIS WLADIS. 1989. "Effects of Maternal Employment in the Two-Parent Family." *American Psychologist* (February): 283–92.

HOLMES, MALCOLM D., HOWARD C. DAUDISTEL, and RONALD A. FARRELL. 1987. "Determinants of Charge Reductions and Final Dispositions in Cases of Burglary and Robbery." *Journal of Research in Crime and Delinquency* 24:233–54.

HOLMES, MALCOLM D., and HOWARD C. DAUDISTEL. 1984. "Ethnicity and Justice in the Southwest: The Sentencing of Anglo, Black, and Mexican Origin Defendants." *Social Science Quarterly* 65:265–77.

HOOKS, BELL. 1991. "Black Women Intellectuals." Pp. 147–64 in bell hooks and Cornell West, *Breaking Bread: Insurgent Black Intellectual Life*. Boston: South End Press.

HOOKS, BELL. 1989. *Talking Back: Thinking Feminist, Thinking Black*. Boston: South End Press.

HOOKS, BELL. 1981. *Ain't I a Woman: Black Women and Feminism.* Boston: South End Press.

HONEMAN, BOB. 1990. "Rationale and Ideas for Emphasizing Afrocentricity in the Public Schools." Paper presented at the Conference on Rhetoric and Teaching of Writing, July 10–11, Indiana, Penn.

HORTON, JOHN. 1966. "Order and Conflict Theories of Social Problems as Competitive Ideologies." *American Journal of Sociology* 71:701–13. Reprinted in Norman R. Yetman and C. Hoy Steele, 1975, *Majority and Minority,* 2d ed. Boston: Allyn and Bacon.

HOVLAND, CARL I., IRVING L. JANIS, and HAROLD H. KELLY. 1953. *Communication and Persuasion.* New Haven, Conn.: Yale University Press.

HUMM, ANDREW. 1980. "The Personal Politics of Lesbian and Gay Liberation." *Social Policy* 11, 2:40–45.

HUMPHREY, JOHN A., and TIMOTHY J. FOGARTY. 1987. "Race and Plea-Bargained Outcomes: A Research Note." *Social Forces* 66:176–82.

HUNT, CHESTER, and LEWIS WALKER. 1974. *Ethnic Dynamics: Patterns of Intergroup Relations in Various Societies.* Homewood, Ill.: Dorsey Press.

HUNTER, GUY. 1965. *Industrialisation and Race Relations.* London: Oxford University Press.

HURN, CHRISTOPHER. 1978. *The Limits and Possibilities of Schooling: An Introduction to the Sociology of Education.* Boston: Allyn & Bacon.

HUTCHINSON, PETER M. 1974. "The Effects of Accessibility and Segregation on the Employment of the Urban Poor." Pp. 74–96 in George M. von Furstenberg, Bennett Harrison, and Ann R. Horowitz (eds.), *Patterns of Racial Discrimination,* vol. 1, *Housing.* Lexington, Mass.: Lexington Books.

HUTTENBACH, HENRY R. 1990. "Conclusion: Towards a Multi-Ethnic Soviet State: Managing a Multinational Society Since 1985." Pp. 286–91 in Henry R. Huttenbach (ed.), *Soviet Nationality Policies: Ruling Ethnic Groups in the U.S.S.R.* London: Mansell Publishing.

HWANG, SEAN-SHONG, and STEVE H. MURDOCK. 1983. "Segregation in Nonmetropolitan and Metropolitan Texas in 1980." *Rural Sociology* 48:607–23.

HWANG, SEAN-SHONG, and STEVE H. MURDOCK. 1982. "Residential Segregation in Texas in 1980." *Social Science Quarterly* 63:737–48.

HYMAN, HERBERT H., and PAUL B. SHEATSLEY. 1964. "Attitudes Toward Desegregation." *Scientific American* 211:2–9.

ICHIHASHI, YAMATO. 1969. *Japanese in the United States.* New York: Arno Press and the New York Times. (First published by Stanford University Press, 1932.)

ILLINOIS CAPITAL DEVELOPMENT BOARD. 1977. *The East St. Louis Area: An Overview of State Capital Projects and Policies.* Springfield, Ill.: Illinois Capital Development Board.

INSTITUTE FOR SOCIAL RESEARCH. 1987. "Wealth in America." *ISR Newsletter* (Winter): 3–5.

JABIN, NORMA. 1987. "Attitudes Toward Disability: Horney's Theory Applied." *American Journal of Psychoanalysis* 47:143–53.

JACKMAN, MARY R., and MARIE CRANE. 1986. "'Some of My Best Friends Are Black . . .': Interracial Friendship and Whites' Racial Attitudes." *Public Opinion Quarterly* 50:459–86.

JAKUBS, JOHN F. 1986. "Recent Racial Segregation in U.S. SMSAs." *Urban Geography* 7:146–63.

JANYES, GERALD, and ROBIN WILLIAMS (eds.). 1989. *A Common Destiny: Blacks and American Society.* Washington, D.C.: National Academy Press.

JAQUET, CONSTANT H., JR. (ed.). 1979. *Yearbook of American and Canadian Churches, 1979.* Nashville: Abington Press.

JASCHIK, SCOTT. 1993. "Backed by 1990 Law, People with Disabilities Press Demands on Colleges." *Chronicle of Higher Education* (February 3): A26.

JASCHIK, SCOTT. 1992. "Education Department Says Affirmative Action Policies of Berkeley's Law School Violated Federal Anti-Bias Laws." *Chronicle of Higher Education* (October 7): A21, A25.

JENCKS, CHRISTOPHER. 1991. "Is the American Underclass Growing?" Pp. 28–100 in Christopher Jencks and Paul E. Peterson (eds.), *The Urban Underclass.* Washington, D.C.: The Brookings Institution.

JENCKS, CHRISTOPHER. 1985. "How Much Do High School Students Learn?" *Sociology of Education* 58: 128–135.

JENCKS, CHRISTOPHER, MARSHALL SMITH, HENRY ACLAND, MARY JO BANE, DAVID COHEN, HERBERT GINTIS, BARBARA HEYNS, and STEPHAN MICHELSON. 1972. *Inequality: A Reassessment of the Effect of Family and Schooling in America.* New York: Basic Books.

JENKINS, J. CRAIG, and CRAIG M. ECKERT. 1986. "Channeling Black Insurgency: Elite Patronage and Professional Social Movement Organization in the Development of the Black Movement." *American Sociological Review* 51:812–29.

JENKINS, J. CRAIG, and CHARLES PERROW. 1977. "Insurgency of the Powerless: Farm Workers' Movements (1946–1972)." *American Sociological Review* 42:249–68.

JENSEN, ARTHUR. 1980. *Bias in Mental Testing.* New York: Free Press.

JENSEN, ARTHUR. 1973. *Educability and Group Differences.* New York: Harper & Row.

JENSEN, ARTHUR. 1969. "How Much Can We Boost IQ and Scholastic Achievement?" *Harvard Educational Review* 39:1–123.

JESILOW, PAUL, GILBERT GEIS, and HENRY PONTELL. 1991. "Fraud by Physicians Against Medicaid." *Journal of the American Medical Association* 266:3318–22.

Jet. 1993a. "Minority Directors Scarce in Corporate Boardrooms." *Jet* 83, 11 (January 11): 16.

Jet. 1993b. "Many Schools Continue to Separate Kids by Ability." *Jet* 83, 18 (March 1): 22.

Jet. 1993c. "White Male Executives Haven't Changed Ways." *Jet* 84, 8 (June 21): 28.

JEWELL, K. SUE. 1985. "Will the Real Black, Afro-American, Mixed, Colored Negro Please Stand Up? Impact of the Black Social Movement, Twenty Years Later." *Journal of Black Studies* 16:57–75.

JOFFE, JOSEF. 1992. "Bosnia: The Return of History." *Commentary* (October): 24–29.

JOHANSEN, BRUCE, and ROBERTO MAESTAS. 1990. *Wasi'chu: The Continuing Indian Wars.* New York: Monthly Review Press.

JOHNSON, CHARLES S. 1943. *Patterns of Negro Segregation.* New York: Harper & Row.

JOHNSON, D. W., R. T. JOHNSON, and G. MARUYAMA. 1984. "Goal Interdependence and Interpersonal Attraction in Heterogeneous Classrooms: A Meta-Analysis." Pp. 187–212 in N. Miller and Marilyn B. Brewer (eds.), *Groups in Contact: The Psychology of Desegregation.* San Diego: Academic Press.

JOHNSON, GUY B. 1941. "The Negro and Crime." *The Annals of the American Academy of Political and Social Science* 217:93–104.

JOHNSON, STEPHEN D. 1992. "Anti-Arabic Prejudice in 'Middletown.'" *Psychological Reports* 70:811–18.

JOINT CENTER FOR POLITICAL STUDIES. 1985. *Black Elected Officials: A National Roster, 1985.* Washington, D.C.: Joint Center for Political Studies.

JOINT CENTER FOR POLITICAL STUDIES. 1977. *National Roster of Black Elected Officials,* vol 7. Washington, D.C.: Joint Center for Political Studies.

JONES, ELISE F., JAQUELINE DARROCH FORREST, NOREEN GOLDMAN, STANLEY HENSHAW, RICHARD LINCOLN, JEANNE I. ROSOFF, CHARLES F. WESTOFF, and DIERDRE WULF. 1986. *Teenage Pregnancy in Industrialized Countries.* New Haven, Conn.: Yale University Press.

JONES, JAMES M. 1972. *Prejudice and Racism.* Reading, Mass.: Addison-Wesley.

JONES, JAQUELINE. 1985. *Labor of Love, Labor of Sorrow: Black Women, Work, and the Family from Slavery to the Present.* New York: Basic Books.

JORDAN, WINTHROP D. 1968. *White over Black.* Chapel Hill: University of North Carolina Press.

JORDAN, WINTHROP D. 1962. "Modern Tensions and the Origins of American Slavery." *Journal of Southern History* 18:18–30.

JOSEPHY, ALVIN M. (ed.). 1992. *America in 1942: The World of the Indian Peoples Before the Arrival of Columbus.* New York: Alfred A. Knopf.

JOSEPHY, ALVIN M., JR. 1968. *The Indian Heritage of America.* New York: Alfred A. Knopf. (Bantam Edition, 1969.)

KADISH, MORTIMER R., and SANFORD H. KADISH. 1973. *Discretion to Disobey.* Palo Alto, Calif.: Stanford University Press.

KAGAN, JEROME. 1971. "The Magical Aura of the IQ." *Saturday Review of Literature* (December 4): 92–93.

KAIN, JOHN F. 1987. "Housing Market Discrimination and Black Suburbanization in the 1980s." In Gary A. Tobin (ed.), *Divided Neighborhoods.* Beverly Hills, Calif.: Sage Publications.

KAIN, JOHN F. 1968. "Housing Segregation, Negro Employment, and Metropolitan Decentralization." *Quarterly Journal of Economics* (May): 175–97.

KAMIN, LEON J. 1974. *The Science and Politics of IQ.* New York: Wiley.

KANE, MICHAEL B. 1970. *Minorities in Textbooks: A Study of Their Treatment in Social Science Texts.* Chicago: Quadrangle.

KANTROWITZ, NATHAN. 1979. "Racial and Ethnic Residential Segregation in Boston 1930–1970." *Annals of the American Academy of Political and Social Science* 441 (January): 41–54.

KARLEN, A. 1971. *Sexuality and Homosexuality.* New York: Norton.

KARLINS, MARVIN, THOMAS GOFFMAN, and GARY WALTERS. 1969. "On the Fading of Social Stereotypes: Studies in Three Generations of College Students." *Journal of Personality and Social Psychology* 13:1–6.

KASARDA, JOHN D. 1990. "Structural Factors Affecting the Location and Timing of Underclass Growth." *Urban Geography* 11:234–64.

KASARDA, JOHN D. 1989a. "Urban Industrial Transition and the Underclass." *Annals of the American Academy of Political and Social Science* 501:26–47.

KASARDA, JOHN D. 1989b. "Urban Change and Minority Opportunities." Pp. 147–67 in D. Stanley Eitzen and Maxine Baca Zinn (eds.), *The Reshaping of America: Social Consequences of the Changing Economy.* Englewood Cliffs, N.J.: Prentice Hall.

KASARDA, JOHN D. 1976. "The Changing Occupational Structure of the American Metropolis: Apropos the Urban Problem." Pp. 113–36 in Barry Schwartz (ed.), *The Changing Face of the Suburbs.* Chicago: University of Chicago Press.

KASPER, JUDITH A., DANIEL C. WALDEN, and GAIL R. WILENSKY. 1980. *NCHSR National Health Care Expenditure Study.* "Data Preview 1: Who Are the Uninsured?" Hyattsville, Md.: National Center for Health Services Research.

KATZ, DONALD, and KENNETH BRALY. 1933. "Racial Stereotypes of One Hundred College Students." *Journal of Abnormal Psychology.* (October/December): 280–90.

KATZ, DONALD, I. SARNOFF, and C. MCCLINTOCK. 1956. "Ego Defense and Attitude Change." *Human Relations* 9:27–46.

KATZ, JESSE. 1991. "Gulf Tensions Seen as Factor in Record Level of Hate Crimes." *Los Angeles Times,* March 2, sec. B.

KATZ, PHYLLIS A., and SUE R. ZALK. 1974. "Doll Preferences: Index of Racial Attitudes?" *Journal of Educational Psychology* 66:663–68.

KEDDIE, NELL. 1971. "Classroom Knowledge." Pp. 133–60 in M.F.D. Young (ed.), *Knowledge and Control.* London: Collier.

KELMAN, H. C. 1958. "Compliance, Identification, and Internalization: Three Processes of Attitude Change." *Journal of Conflict Resolution* 2:51–60.

KENDALL, PATRICIA L., and KATHERINE M. WOLF. 1949. "The Analysis of Deviant Cases in Communication Research." In Paul F. Lazarsfeld and Frank N. Stanton (eds.), *Communications Research, 1948–1949.* New York: Harper & Row.

KENNEDY, MARGARET A. 1992. "Testing to Uncover Unfair Hiring." *Nation's Business* (February): 36–37.

KENNEDY, RUBY JO REEVES. 1952. "Single or Triple Melting Pot? Intermarriage in New Haven, 1870–1950." *American Journal of Sociology* 58:56–69.

KENNEDY, RUBY JO REEVES. 1944. "Single or Triple Melting Pot? Intermarriage Trends in New Haven, 1870–1940." *American Journal of Sociology* 49:331–39.

KIEV, ARI. 1968. *Curanderismo: Mexican-American Folk Psychiatry.* New York: Free Press.

KILLIAN, LEWIS M. 1975. *The Impossible Revolution, Phase 2: Black Power and the American Dream.* New York: Random House.

KILLIAN, LEWIS M. 1968. *The Impossible Revolution?* New York: Random House.

KILSON, MARTIN, and CLEMENT COTTINGHAM. 1991. "Thinking About Race Relations: How Far Are We Still from Integration?" *Dissent* 38:520–30.

KINDER, D. R., and D. O. SEARS. 1981. "Symbolic Racism Versus Racial Threats to the Good Life." *Journal of Personality and Social Psychology* 40:414–31.

KINLOCH, GRAHAM C. 1979. *The Sociology of Minority Group Relations.* Englewood Cliffs, N.J.: Prentice Hall.

KINLOCH, GRAHAM C. 1974. *The Dynamics of Race Relations: A Sociological Analysis.* New York: McGraw-Hill.

KINSEY, ALFRED. 1953. *Sexual Behavior in the Human Female.* Philadelphia: Saunders.

KINSEY, ALFRED. 1948. *Sexual Behavior in the Human Male.* Philadelphia: Saunders.

KIRP, DAVID L. 1991. "Textbooks and Tribalism in California." *Public Interest* 104:20–36.

KIRSCHENMAN, JOLENE. 1990. "Tales from the Survivors: Business Relocation in a Restructured Urban Economy." Paper presented at joint annual meetings of the North Central Sociological Association and Southern Sociological Society, March, Louisville.

KIRSCHENMAN, JOLENE. 1989. "From Steel to Software, from Boardroom to Beyond the Expressway: Employers Consider the Inner City Economy." Paper presented at the annual meeting of the Midwest Sociological Society, April, St. Louis.

KIRSCHENMAN, JOLENE, and KATHRYN M. NECKERMAN. 1991. "'We'd Love to Hire Them, but . . .' : The Meaning of Race for Employers." Pp. 203–32 in Christopher Jencks and Paul E. Peterson (eds.), *The Urban Underclass.* Washington, D.C.: Brookings Institution.

KIRSCHT, JOHN P., and RONALD C. DILLEHAY. 1967. *Dimensions of Authoritarianism: A Review of Research and Theory.* Lexington: University of Kentucky Press.

KITAGAWA, EVELYN M. 1972. "Socioeconomic Differences in Mortality in the United States and Some Implications for Population Policy." Pp. 153–66 in Charles C. Westoff and Robert Parke, Jr. (eds.), *Demographic and Social Aspects of Population Growth* vol. 1. Commission on Population Growth and the American Future. Washington, D.C.: U.S. Government Printing Office.

KITAGAWA, EVELYN, and PHILIP M. HAUSER. 1973. *Differential Mortality in the United States: A Study in Socioeconomic Epidemiology.* Cambridge, Mass.: Harvard University Press.

KITANO, HARRY H. L. 1985. *Race Relations,* 3d ed. Englewood Cliffs, N.J.: Prentice Hall.

KLECK, GARY. 1985. "Life Support for an Ailing Hypothesis: Modes of Summarizing the Evidence for Racial Discrimination in Sentencing." *Law and Human Behavior* 9:271–85.

KLEIN, STEPHEN, JOAN PETERSILLA, and SUSAN TURNER. 1990. "Race and Imprisonment Decisions in California." *Science* 247:812–16.

KLOSS, ROBERT MARSH, RON E. ROBERTS, and DEAN S. DORN. 1976. *Sociology with a Human Face.* St. Louis: Mosby.

KLUEGEL, JAMES R. 1990. "Trends in Whites' Explanation of the Black–White Gap in Socioeconomic Status, 1977–1989." *American Sociological Review* 55:512–25.

KLUEGEL, JAMES R., and ELIOT R. SMITH. 1986. *Beliefs About Inequality: American Views of What Is and What Ought to Be.* Hawthorne, N.Y.: Aldine de Gruyter.

KLUEGEL, JAMES R., and ELIOT R. SMITH. 1982. "Whites' Beliefs About Blacks' Opportunity." *American Sociological Review* 47:518–32.

KNAPP, MICHAEL S., and PATRICK M. SHIELDS. 1990. "Reconceiving Academic Instruction for the Children of Poverty." *Phi Delta Kappan* (June):753–58.

KOBLER, ARTHUR L. 1975. "Police Homicide in a Democracy." *Journal of Social Issues* 31:163–84.

KOHLBERG, LAWRENCE. 1969. "Stage and Sequence: The Cognitive-Developmental Approach to Socialization." Pp. 347–480 in David A. Goslin (ed.), *Handbook of Socialization Theory and Research.* Chicago: Rand McNally.

KOOS, EARL. 1954. *The Health of Regionsville.* New York: Columbia University Press.

KORFHAGE, DARLENE W. 1972. "Differential Treatment in the Municipal Court System." Masters' thesis, Washington State University.

KORITZ, DOUGLAS. 1991. "Restructuring or Destructuring? Deindustrialization in Two Industrial Heartland Cities." *Urban Affairs Quarterly* 26: 497–511.

KOZOL, JONATHAN. 1991. *Savage Inequalities: Children in America's Schools.* New York: Crown.

KRAMER, BERNARD M. 1949. "The Dimensions of Prejudice." *Journal of Psychology* (April): 389–451.

KRAMER, MICHAEL. 1993. "Getting Smart About Head Start." *Time* (March 8): 43.

KRAMER, RONALD L. 1984. "Corporate Criminality: The Development of an Idea." In Ellen Hochs (ed.), *Corporations as Criminals.* Beverly Hills, Calif.: Sage Publications.

KRAUSS, CLIFFORD. 1993. "Senate Passes a Smaller Stimulus Bill." *New York Times,* June 23, sec. A.

KROEBER, ALFRED L. 1939. *Cultural and Natural Areas of Native North America.* University of California Publications in American Archeology and Ethnology 38.

KRUTE, AARON, and MARY ELLEN BURDETTE. 1978. "Disability Survey '72: Disabled and Non-Disabled Adults. Report 10-Chronic Disease, Injury, and Work Disability." Publication no. (55A) 78-11700. Washington, D.C.: Social Security Administration.

KUTNER, B., C. WILKINS, and P. R. YARROW. 1952. "Verbal Attitudes and Overt Behavior Involving Racial Prejudice." *Journal of Abnormal and Social Psychology* 47:649–52.

KUYKENDALL, JACK L. 1970. "Police and Minority Groups: Toward a Theory of Negative Contact." *Police* 15:47–56.

LAABS, JENNIFER J. 1993. "First Person: Employees Manage Conflict and Diversity." *Personnel Journal* (December): 30–36.

LABOV, WILLIAM. 1972. "Academic Ignorance and Black Intelligence." *Atlantic Monthly* (June): 59–67.

LABOV, WILLIAM, and P. COHEN. 1967. "Systematic Relations of Standard and Nonstandard Rules in the Grammars of Negro Speakers." In *Project Literacy Reports*, no. 8. Ithaca, N.Y.: Cornell University.

LA FAVE, WAYNE R. 1965. *Arrest: The Decision to Take a Suspect into Custody.* Boston: Little, Brown.

LAKE, ROBERT. 1981. *The New Suburbanites: Race and Housing in the Suburbs.* New Brunswick, N.J.: Rutgers University, Center for Urban Policy Research.

LAMMERMEIER, P. J. 1973. "The Black Family in the Nineteenth Century: A Study of Black Family Structure in the Ohio Valley, 1850–1880." *Journal of Marriage and the Family* 35:440–56.

LANDIS, JUDSON T. 1962. "A Comparison of Children from Divorced and Nondivorced Unhappy Marriages." *Family Life Coordinator* 11:61–65.

LA PIERE, R. T. 1934. "Attitudes Versus Actions." *Social Forces* 13:230–37.

LAPORTE, SUZANNE B. 1991. "Cultural Diversity: 12 Companies That Do the Right Thing." *Working Woman* 16, 1 (January): 57–59.

LARSON, CALVIN J., and STAN R. NIKKEL. 1979. *Urban Problems: Perspectives on Corporations, Governments, and Cities.* Boston: Allyn & Bacon.

LARSON, KNUD S., OMMUNDSEN, REIDAR, and ROBERT ELDER. 1991. "Acquired Immune Deficiency Syndrome: International Attitudinal Comparisons." *Journal of Social Psychology* 131:289–91.

LAUTER, PAUL, and FLORENCE HOWE. 1970. *The Conspiracy of the Young.* New York: Crowell.

LAZAR, IRVING. 1981. "Early Intervention Is Effective." *Educational Leadership* 38:303–5.

LAZAR, IRVING, R. DARLINGTON, H. MURRAY, J. ROYCE, and A. SNIPPER. 1982. "Lasting Effects of Early Childhood Education." *Monographs of the Society for Research in Child Development* 47, 1–2, serial no. 194.

LAZAR, IRVING, V. R. HUBBEL, H. MURRAY, M. ROSCHE, and J. ROYCE. 1977. *The Persistence of Pre-School Effects: A Long-Term Follow-Up of Fourteen Infant and Pre-School Experiments, Summary.* Washington, D.C.: U.S. Department of Health and Human Services, Administration for Children, Youth, and Families.

LEACOCK, E. B. 1969. *Teaching and Learning in City Schools.* New York: Basic Books.

LEARY, WARREN E. 1991. "Social Links Are Seen in Black Stress." *The New York Times,* February 6, sec. A.

LEATHERMAN, COURTNEY. 1994a. "All Quiet on the Western Front, at Least for Now: A West Coast Accrediting Group Approves Controversial Diversity Guidelines." *Chronicle of Higher Education* (March 2): A17.

LEATHERMAN, COURTNEY. 1994b. "Professors at U. of Oregon Will Try Again to Expand Multicultural Requirement." *Chronicle of Higher Education* (March 9): A18.

LEATHERMAN, COURTNEY. 1994c. "North Carolina A&T Decides to Require Black Studies Course." *Chronicle of Higher Education* (March 9): A19.

LEBERGOTT, STANLEY. 1976. *The American Economy: Income, Wealth, and Want.* Princeton, N.J.: Princeton University Press.

LEE, MIN-WEI. 1992. "'Programming' Minorities for Medicine." *Journal of the American Medical Association* 267, 17:2391, 2394.

LEGUM, COLIN. 1975. "Color and Race in the South African Situation." Pp. 98–105 in Norman R. Yetman and C. Hoy Steele (eds.), *Majority and Minority: The Dynamics of Racial and Ethnic Relations.* Boston: Allyn & Bacon. (Reprinted from *Daedalus* 96 [1967]: 483–95.)

LENIN, V. I. 1960–70. *Collected Works.* Moscow and London: Marx-Engels-Lenin Institute.

LESSING, ELISE E., and CHESTER C. CLARKE. 1976. "An Attempt to Reduce Ethnic Prejudice and Assess Its Correlates in a Junior High School Sample." *Educational Research Quarterly* 1, 2:3–16.

LEVAY, SIMON. 1993. *The Sexual Brain.* Cambridge, MA: M.I.T. Press (Bradford Books).

LEVIN, C. L., J. T. LITTLE, H. O. NOURSE, and P. B. REED. 1976. *Neighborhood Change: Lessons in the Dynamics of Urban Decay.* New York: Praeger.

LEVIN, JACK, and JACK MCDEVITT. 1993. *Hate Crimes: The Rising Tide of Bigotry and Bloodshed.* New York: Plenum Press.

LEVIN, R. J. 1975. "The Redbook Report on Premarital and Extramarital Sex." *Redbook* (October): 38–44, 190.

LEVY, JERROLD E. 1983. "Traditional Navajo Health Beliefs and Practices." Pp. 118–78 in J. Kunitz (ed.), *Disease Change and the Role of Medicine: The Navajo Experience.* Berkeley: University of California Press.

LEWIN, KURT. 1948. *Resolving Social Conflicts.* New York: Harper & Row.

LEWIS, ANNE C. 1992. "Head Start." *Education Digest* 57, 9 (May): 52.

LEWIS, ANNE C. 1991. "Washington News: Bilingual Education." *Education Digest* (January): 63–64.

LEWIS, OSCAR. 1965. *La Vida: A Puerto Rican Family in the Culture of Poverty.* New York: Random House.

LEWIS, OSCAR. 1959. *Five Families: Mexican Case Studies in the Culture of Poverty.* New York: Basic Books.

LIGHT, HANS. 1932. *Sexual Life in Ancient Greece.* London: Routledge.

LICHTER, DANIEL. 1988. "Racial Differences in Unemployment in American Cities." *American Journal of Sociology* 993:772–92.

LICHTER, DANIEL, FELICIA B. LECLERE, and DIANE K. MCLAUGHLIN. 1991. "Local Marriage Markets and the Marital Behavior of Black and White Women." *American Journal of Sociology* 96:843–67.

LIEBERSON, STANLEY. 1980. *A Piece of the Pie: Blacks and White Immigrants Since 1880.* Berkeley: University of California Press.

LIEBERSON, STANLEY. 1961. "A Societal Theory of Race Relations." *American Sociological Review* 26:902–10.

LIGHT, DONALD, JR., and SUZANNE KELLER. 1979. *Sociology.* New York: Knopf.

LINCOLN, C. ERIC. 1973. *The Black Muslims in America,* rev. ed. Boston: Beacon Press.

LIPSET, SEYMOUR MARTIN. 1992. "The Politics of Race: The Meaning of Equality." *Current* 343:10–15.

LIPSET, SEYMOUR MARTIN. 1959. "Democracy and Working Class Authoritarianism." *American Sociological Review* 24:498–501.

LIPSET, SEYMOUR MARTIN, and EARL RAAB. 1973. "An Appointment with Watergate." *Commentary* (September): 35–43.

LISKA, ALLEN E., and MARK TANSIG. 1979. "Theoretical Interpretations of Social Class and Racial Differentials in Legal Decision-making for Juveniles." *Sociological Quarterly* 20:197–207.

LITCHER, J. H., and D. W. JOHNSON. 1969. "Changes in Attitudes Toward Negroes of White Elementary School Students After Use of Multiethnic Readers." *Journal of Educational Psychology* 60:148–52.

LITTLE, ALLAN, and GEORGE SMITH. 1971. *Strategies of Compensation: A Review of Educational Projects for the Disadvantaged in the United States.* Paris: Organization for Economic Cooperation and Development.

LITWACK, LEON F. 1961. *North of Slavery: The Negro in the Free States, 1790–1860.* Chicago: University of Chicago Press.

LIVINGSTON, ABBY. 1991. "What YOUR Department Can Do." *Working Woman* (January): 59–60.

LOFLAND, JOHN. 1985. *Protest: Studies of Collective Behavior and Social Movements.* New Brunswick, N.J.: Transaction Books.

LOGAN, JOHN R., and M. SCHNEIDER. 1984. "Racial Segregation and Racial Change in American Suburbs, 1970–1980." *American Journal of Sociology* 89:875–88.

LONG, HARRY H., and PAUL C. GLICK. 1976. "Family Patterns in Suburban Areas: Recent Trends." Pp. 39–68 in Barry Schwartz (ed.), *The Changing Face of the Suburbs.* Chicago: University of Chicago Press.

LOPEZ, MANUEL MARIANO. 1981. "Patterns of Interethnic Residential Segregation in the Urban Southwest." *Social Science Quarterly* 62:50–63.

LORDE, ANDRE. 1992. "Age, Race, Class, and Sex: Women Redefining Difference." Pp. 401–7 in Paula S. Rothenberg (ed.), *Race, Class, and Gender in the United States: An Integrated Study.* New York: St. Martin's Press.

LOUIS HARRIS AND ASSOCIATES. 1993. *The Harris Survey Yearbook of Public Opinion.* New York: Louis Harris and Associates.

LOUW-POTGIETER, J. 1988. "The Authoritarian Personality: An Inadequate Explanation for Intergroup Conflict in South Africa." *Journal of Social Psychology* 128:75–87.

LOWENSTEIN, L. F. 1985. "Investigating Ethnic Prejudice Among Boys and Girls in a Therapeutic Community for Maladjusted Children and Modifying Some Prejudices: Can Basic Prejudices Be Changed?" *School Psychology International* 6:239–43.

LUNDMAN, RICHARD J. 1980. *Police and Policing: An Introduction.* New York: Holt, Rinehart & Winston.

LURIE, NANCY OESTREICH. 1991. "The American Indian: Historical Background." Pp. 132–45 in Norman R. Yetman (ed.), *Majority and Minority: The Dynamics of Race and Ethnicity in American Life,* 5th ed. Needham Heights, Mass.: Allyn & Bacon.

LURIE, NANCY OESTREICH. 1985. "The American Indian: Historical Background." Pp. 136–49 in Norman R. Yetman, *Majority and Minority: The Dynamics of Race and Ethnicity in American Life,* 4th ed. Boston: Allyn & Bacon.

LYNCH, FREDERICK R., and WILLIAM R. BEER. 1990. "'You Ain't the Right Color, Pal': White Resentment of Affirmative Action." *Policy Review* 51:61–67.

LYNCH, JAMES. 1988. "Pedagogical Strategies to Reduce Prejudice: Towards Middle Range Theories." Paper presented at the annual meeting of the American Educational Research Association, April, New Orleans, La.

LYNCH, JAMES. 1987. *Prejudice Reduction and the Schools.* New York: Nichols.

LYND, ROBERT S., and HELEN MERRELL LYND. 1929. *Middletown: A Study in Contemporary American Culture.* New York: Harcourt Brace Jovanovich.

MCADAM, DOUG. 1982. *Political Process and the Development of Black Insurgency, 1930–1970.* Chicago: University of Chicago Press.

MCADAM, DOUG, JOHN D. MCCARTHY, and MAYER N. ZALD. 1988. "Social Movements." Pp. 695–737 in Neil J. Smelser (ed.), *Handbook of Sociology.* Newbury Park, Calif.: Sage.

MCCARTHY, JOHN D., and MAYER N. ZALD. 1977. "Resource Mobilization and Social Movements: A Partial Theory." *American Journal of Sociology* 82:1212–41.

MCCARTHY, JOHN D., and MAYER N. ZALD. 1973. *The Trend of Social Movements in America: Professionalization and Resource Mobilization.* Morristown, N.J.: General Learning Press.

MCCARTHY, KEVIN F., and R. B. VALDEZ. 1985. *Current and Future Effects of Mexican Immigration in California.* Santa Monica, Calif.: Rand Corporation.

MCCARY, JAMES LESLEY. 1978. *McCary's Human Sexuality,* 3d ed. New York: Van Nostrand Reinhold.

MCCONAHAY, J. B. 1982. "Self-Interest Versus Racial Attitudes as Correlates of Anti-Busing Attitudes in Louisville: Is It the Busses or the Blacks?" *Journal of Politics* 44:692–720.

MCCONAHAY, J. B., B. B. HARDEE, and V. BATTS. 1981. "Has Racism Declined in America? It Depends on Who Is Asking and What Is Asked." *Journal of Conflict Resolution* 25:563–79.

McCutcheon, Gail, Diane Kyle, and Robert Skovira. 1979. "Characters in Basal Readers: Does 'Equal' Now Mean 'Same'?" *Reading Teacher* 32:438–41.

McFarlane, Bruce. 1988. *Yugoslavia: Politics, Economics, and Society*. London and New York: Pinter.

McGarrell, Edmund F., and Timothy J. Flanigan (eds.). 1985. *Sourcebook of Criminal Justice Statistics—1984*. U.S. Department of Justice, Bureau of Justice Statistics. Washington, D.C.: U.S. Government Printing Office.

McGinley, P., and H. McGinley. 1970. "Reading Groups as Psychological Groups." *Journal of Experimental Education* 39:36–42.

McGuire, William J. 1968. "Personality and Susceptibility to Social Influence." Pp. 1130–87 in Edgar F. Borgatta and William W. Lambert (eds.), *Handbook of Personality Theory and Research*. Chicago: Rand McNally.

MacKay, Robert. 1974. "Standardized Tests: Objective/Objectified Measures of Competence." In Aaron Cicourel (ed.), *Language Use and School Performance*. New York: Academic Press.

MacKinnon, William, and Richard Centers. 1956. "Authoritarianism and Urban Stratification." *American Journal of Sociology* 61:610–20.

McKey, Ruth, Larry Condelli, Harriet Ganson, Barbara Barrett, Catherine McConkey, and Margaret Plantz. 1985. *The Impact of Head Start on Children, Families, and Communities: Head Start Synthesis Project*. DHHS Publication no. (OHDS) 85-31193. Washington, D.C.: U.S. Government Printing Office.

McLanahan, Sara. 1988. "The Consequences of Single Parenthood for Subsequent Generations." *Focus* 11:16–21.

McLanahan, Sara, and Larry Bumpass. 1988. "Intergenerational Consequences of Family Disruption." *American Journal of Sociology* 94:130–52.

McPhail, Clark. 1993. Presidential address at the Annual Meeting of the Midwest Sociological Society, April 7–10, Chicago.

McWhirter, J. Jeffries, Rosie Paluch, and Rose M. Ohm. 1988. "Anytown: A Human Relations Experience." *Journal for Specialists in Group Work* 13, 3 (Special Issue: Group Work and Human Rights, vol. 2): 117–23.

McWilliams, Carey. 1951. *Brothers Under the Skin*, rev. ed. Boston: Little Brown.

McWilliams, Carey. 1949. *North from Mexico*. Philadelphia: Lippincott.

Madsen, William. 1973. *The Mexican-Americans of South Texas*, 2d ed. New York: Holt, Rinehart & Winston.

Majors, Richard, and Janet Mancini Billson. 1992. *Cool Pose: The Dilemmas of Black Manhood in America*. New York: Lexington Books.

Makepeace, J. M. 1981. "Courtship Violence Among College Students." *Family Relations* 30:97–102.

Mandelbaum, D. G. 1952. *Soldier Groups and Negro Soldiers*. Berkeley: University of California Press.

Mare, Robert D., and Christopher Winship. 1991. "Socioeconomic Change and the Decline of Marriage for Blacks and Whites." Pp. 175–202 in Christopher Jencks and Paul E. Peterson (eds.), *The Urban Underclass*. Washington, D.C.: The Brookings Institution.

Marmor, Judd. 1992. "Cultural Factors in the Darker Passions." *Journal of the American Academy of Psychoanalysis* 20:325–34.

Marrett, Cora Bagley. 1980. "The Precariousness of Social Class in Black America." *Contemporary Sociology* 9:16–19.

Marshall, Ray. 1965. *The Negro and Organized Labor*. New York: Wiley.

Martin, Douglas. 1985. "Parti Quebecois Is Ousted After Nine Years in Power." *New York Times*, December 3, sec. 1.

Martz, Larry, with Mark Starr and Todd Barrett. 1990. "A Murderous Hoax." *Newsweek* (January 22): 16–21.

Marx, Karl. 1971 [1859]. *A Contribution to the Critique of Political Economy*. Maurice Dobb (ed. and tr.). New York: International Publishers.

Marx, Karl. 1967 [1867–1894]. *Capital, a Critique of Political Economy*. Three vols., Friedrich Engels (ed.), Samuel Moore and Edward Aveling (trs.). New York: International Publishers.

Marx, Karl. 1964. *Selected Works in Sociology and Social Philosophy*. Thomas B. Bottomore and Maximilien Rubel (eds. and trs.). New York: McGraw-Hill.

Massey, Douglas S. 1990. "American Apartheid: Segregation and the Making of the Underclass." *American Journal of Sociology* 96:239–57.

Massey, Douglas S., Gretchen A. Condran, and Nancy A. Denton. 1987. "The Effect of Residential Segregation on Black Social and Economic Well-being." *Social Forces* 66:29–56.

Massey, Douglas S., and Nancy A. Denton. 1993. *American Apartheid: Segregation and the Making of the Underclass*. Cambridge, Mass.: Harvard University Press.

Massey, Douglas S., and Nancy A. Denton. 1989. "Hypersegregation in U.S. Metropolitan Areas: Black and Hispanic Segregation Along Five Dimensions." *Demography* 26:373–91.

Massey, Douglas S., and Nancy A. Denton. 1988. "Suburbanization and Segregation in U.S. Metropolitan Areas." *American Journal of Sociology* 94:592–626.

Massey, Douglas S., and Nancy A. Denton. 1987. "Trends in the Segregation of Blacks, Hispanics, and Asians, 1970–1980." *American Sociological Review* 52:802–25.

Massey, Douglas S., and Mitchell L. Eggers. 1990. "The Ecology of Inequality: Minorities and the Concentration of Poverty." *American Journal of Sociology* 95:1153–88.

Massey, Douglas S., and Andrew B. Gross. 1991. "Explaining Trends in Racial Segregation, 1970–1980." *Urban Affairs Quarterly* 27:13–35.

MASON, PHILIP. 1971. *Patterns of Dominance.* London: Oxford University Press.

MASON, PHILIP. 1960. *Year of Decision: Rhodesia and Nyasaland in 1960.* London: Oxford University Press.

MASTERS, STANLEY H. 1975. *Black–White Income Differentials: Empirical Studies and Policy Implications.* New York: Academic Press.

MATHEWS, JAY. 1992. "Undercover Bias Busters." *Newsweek* (November 23): 88.

MATHEWS, TOM. 1992. "The Seige of L.A." *Newsweek* (May 11): 30–38.

MATTHIESSEN, PETER. 1983. *In the Spirit of Crazy Horse.* New York: Viking Press.

MATUTE-BIANCHI, MARIA EUGENIA. 1986. "Ethnic Identities and Patterns of School Success and Failure Among Mexican-Descent and Japanese American Students in a California High School: An Ethnographic Analysis." *American Journal of Education* 95:233–55.

MAZÓN, MAURICIO. 1984. *The Zoot Suit Riots: The Psychology of Symbolic Annihilation.* Austin: University of Texas Press.

MEAD, GEORGE HERBERT. 1967 [1934]. *Mind, Self, and Society.* Chicago: University of Chicago Press.

MEANS, BARBARA, and MICHAEL S. KNAPP. 1991. "Cognitive Approaches to Teaching Advanced Skills to Educationally Disadvantaged Students." *Phi Delta Kappan* (December): 282–89.

MEDINA, MARCELLO, MACARIO SALDATE, and SHILALA P. MISHRA. 1985. "The Sustaining Effects of Bilingual Education: A Followup Study." *Journal of Instructional Psychology* 12:132–39.

MEDINA, Z., and D. M. NEILL. 1988. *Fallout from the Testing Explosion: How 100 Million Standardized Exams Undermine Equity and Excellence in America's Public Schools.* Cambridge, Mass.: National Center for Fair and Open Testing.

MEHAN, HUGH. 1974. "Accomplishing Classroom Lesson." In Aaron Cicourel (ed.). *Language Use and School Performance.* New York: Academic Press.

MEIER, AUGUST, and ELLIOTT RUDWICK. 1970a. *From Plantation to Ghetto: The Interpretative History of American Negroes,* rev. ed. New York: Athenium Publishers.

MEIER, AUGUST, and ELLIOTT RUDWICK (eds.). 1970b. *Black Protest in the Sixties.* Chicago: Quadrangle Books.

MEIER, AUGUST, and ELLIOTT RUDWICK. 1969. "The Boycott Against Jim Crow Streetcars in the South." *Journal of American History* 55:756–59.

MEIER, MATT S., and FELICIANO RIVERA. 1972. *The Chicanos: A History of Mexican Americans.* New York: Hill & Wang.

MELMAN, SEYMOUR. 1976. "The Federal Ripoff of New York's Money." Pp. 181–88 in Roger E. Alcaly and David Mermelstein (eds.), *The Fiscal Crisis of American Cities.* New York: Vintage Books.

MERTON, ROBERT K. 1949. *Social Theory and Social Structure.* New York: Free Press. (Reprint of *The Self-fulfilling Prophecy,* 1948. *Antioch Review* (Summer).)

MICHELSON, STEPHAN. 1972. "The Political Economy of School Finance." In Martin Carnoy (ed.), *Schooling in Corporate Society,* New York: McKay.

MICHIGAN STATE BOARD OF EDUCATION. 1989. *Michigan Social Studies Textbook Study (1988): A Review and Evaluation of Selected Middle School Textbooks.* Lansing: Michigan State Board of Education.

MIDDLETON, RUSSEL. 1960. "Ethnic Prejudice and Susceptibility to Persuasion." *American Sociological Review* 25:679–86.

MILLER, KAREN A., MELVIN L. KOHN, and CARMI SCHOOLER. 1986. "Educational Self-Direction and Personality." *American Sociological Review* 51:372–90.

MILLER, RANDI L. 1990. "Beyond Contact Theory: The Impact of Community Affluence on Integration Efforts in Five Suburban High Schools." *Youth and Society* 22:12–34.

MILLER, RANDI L. 1989. "Desegregation Experiences of Minority Students: Adolescent Coping Strategies in Five Connecticut High Schools." *Journal of Adolescent Research* 4:173–89.

MILLS, C. WRIGHT. 1956. *The Power Elite.* New York: Oxford University Press.

MIRANDE, ALFREDO. 1987. *Gringo Justice.* Notre Dame, Ind.: University of Notre Dame Press.

MIRANDE, ALFREDO. 1985. *The Chicano Experience: An Alternative Perspective.* Notre Dame, Ind.: University of Notre Dame Press.

MITTNICK, LEONARD, and ELLIOTT McGINNES. 1958. "Influencing Ethnocentrism in Small Discussion Groups Through a Film Communication." *Journal of Abnormal and Social Psychology* 56:423–41.

MLADENKA, KENNETH R. 1991. "Public Employee Unions, Reformism, and Black Employment in 1,200 American Cities." *Urban Affairs Quarterly* 26:532–48.

MOLOTCH, HARVEY. 1972. *Managed Integration: Dilemmas of Doing Good in the City.* Berkeley: University of California Press.

MONAGLE, KATIE. 1992. "Race and the Courts." *Scholastic Update* 125, 1 (Teachers' ed.): 3.

MONROE, SYLVESTER. 1992. "Breaking Out, Then and Now." *Time* (October 5): 58–60.

MONTAGU, M. F. ASHLEY. 1964. *Man's Most Dangerous Myth: The Fallacy of Race,* 4th ed. Cleveland: World.

MONTAGU, M. F. ASHLEY. 1963. *Race, Science and Humanity.* Princeton, N.J.: D. Van Nostrand.

MOONEY, JOSEPH D. 1969. "Housing Segregation, Negro Unemployment, and Metropolitan Decentralization: An Alternative Perspective." *Quarterly Journal of Economics* (May):299–311.

MOORE, JOAN W., with HARRY PACHON. 1976. *Mexican Americans.* Englewood Cliffs, N.J.: Prentice Hall.

MOORE, JOAN W. 1970. "Colonialism: The Case of the Mexican Americans." *Social Problems* 17:463–72.

MOORE, JOAN, and HARRY PACHON. 1985. *Hispanics in the United States,* 2d ed. Englewood Cliffs, N.J.: Prentice Hall.

MOORE, L. AUBREY, and PAUL M. ROESTI. 1980. "Race and Two Juvenile Justice System Decision Points: The Filing of a Petition and Declaration of Ward-ship." Paper presented to the annual meeting of the Midwest Sociological Society, Milwaukee, Wis.

Moore, Robert. 1972. "Race Relations in the Six Counties: Colonialism, Industrialization, and Stratification in Ireland." *Race* 14. (Reprinted in Norman R. Yetman, and C. Hoy Steele (eds.), 1975, *Majority and Minority: The Dynamics of Racial and Ethnic Relations.* Boston: Allyn and Bacon.)

Morgan, S. Philip, Antonio McDaniel, Andrew T. Miller, and Samuel H. Preston. 1993. "Racial Differences in Household and Family Structures at the Turn of the Century." *American Journal of Sociology* 98:798–828.

Morganthau, Tom. 1993. "America: Still a Melting Pot?" *Newsweek* (August 9): 16–23.

Morris, Aldon. 1984. *The Origins of the Civil Rights Movement: Black Communities Organizing for Change.* New York: Free Press.

Morris, John W., and Patrick C. Heaven. 1986. "Attitudes and Behavioral Intentions Toward Vietnamese in Australia." *Journal of Social Psychology* 126:513–20.

Morrison, Ann. 1993. "Diversity." Interview by Patricia Galagan. *Training and Development* 47, 4 (April): 39–43.

Moss, E. Yvonne. 1990. "African Americans and the Administration of Justice." Pp. 79–86 in Wornie L. Reed (ed.), *Assessment of the Status of African Americans.* Boston: University of Massachusetts, William Monroe Trotter Institute.

Moustafa, A. Taher, and Gertrud Weiss. 1968. *Health Status and Practices of Mexican Americans.* Advance Report II, Mexican-American Study Project. Los Angeles: University of California at Los Angeles.

Moynihan, Daniel Patrick. 1986. *Family and Nation.* San Diego: Harcourt Brace Jovanovich.

Muller, Thomas. 1985. "Economic Effects of Immigration." In Nathan Glazer (ed.), *Clamor at the Gates.* San Francisco: Institute for Contemporary Studies.

Murguia, Edward. 1975. *Assimilation, Colonialism, and the Mexican American People.* Austin: University of Texas at Austin.

Myrdal, Gunnar. 1944. *An American Dilemma: The Negro Problem and Modern Democracy.* New York: Harper & Row.

Nagel, Stewart. 1969. *The Legal Process from a Behavioral Perspective.* Homewood, Ill.: Dorsey Press.

Nagi, Saad Z. 1972. "Tabulations from the OSU Disability Survey—1972." Columbus: Ohio State University.

Nagorski, Andrew. 1993. "The Laws of Blood: Neo-Nazi Attacks Pressure Germany to Change Its Citizenship Rules." *Newsweek* (June 14): 38–39.

Nahaylo, Bohdan, and Victor Swoboda. 1989. *Soviet Disunion: A History of the Nationalities Problem in the Soviet Union.* New York: Free Press.

Nash, Gary B. 1970. "Red, White, and Black: The Origins of Racism in Colonial America." Chap. 1 in Gary B. Nash and Richard Weiss, *The Great Fear: Race in the Mind of America.* New York: Holt, Rinehart & Winston.

Nash, Roy. 1976. *Teacher Expectations and Pupil Learning.* London: Routledge & Kegan Paul.

National Center for Education Statistics. 1992a. *Digest of Education Statistics, 1992.* Washington, D.C.: U.S. Government Printing Office.

National Center for Education Statistics. 1992b. *The Condition of Education, 1992.* Washington, D.C.: U.S. Government Printing Office.

National Center for Health Statistics. 1993. *Monthly Vital Statistics Report.* Advance report of final mortality statistics, 1991. Hyattsville, Md.: Public Health Service.

National Center for Health Statistics. 1992. *Health, United States: 1991.* Hyattsville, Md.: Public Health Service.

National Center for Health Statistics. 1991a. *Monthly Vital Statistics Report.* Advance Report of Final Natality Statistics, 1990. Hyattsville, Md.: Public Health Service.

National Center for Health Statistics. 1991b. *Monthly Vital Statistics Report.* Induced Terminations of Pregnancy, Reporting States, 1988. Hyattsville, Md.: Public Health Service.

National Center for Health Statistics. 1987. *Monthly Vital Statistics Report,* vol. 35, no. 12. Births, Marriages, Divorces, and Deaths for 1986, Provisional Data. Washington, D.C.: U.S. Department of Health and Human Services.

National Center for Health Statistics. 1986a. *Monthly Vital Statistics Report,* vol. 34, no. 13. Annual Summary of Births, Marriages, Divorces, and Deaths: United States, 1985, Provisional Data. Washington, D.C.: Department of Health and Human Services.

National Center for Health Statistics. 1986b. Current Estimates from the National Health Interview Survey, United States, 1985. Series 10, no. 160. Washington, D.C.: U.S. Government Printing Office.

National Center for Health Statistics. 1984. *Health: United States, 1984.* Washington, D.C.: U.S. Government Printing Office.

National Center for Health Statistics. 1976. *Health Characteristics of Minority Groups.* Washington, D.C.: U.S. Government Printing Office.

National Commission on Marihuana and Drug Abuse. 1972. *Marihuana: A Signal of Misunderstanding,* Appendix, Part 4. Technical Papers of the National Commission on Marihuana and Drug Abuse. Washington, D.C.: U.S. Government Printing Office.

National Institute on Drug Abuse. 1989. National Household Survey on Drug Abuse, 1988. Rockville, MD: National Institute on Drug Abuse.

National Institute on Drug Abuse. 1976. *Young Men and Drugs—A Nationwide Survey.* Research Monograph Series 5. Rockville, Md.: National Institute on Drug Abuse.

National Opinion Research Center. 1991. *General Social Survey, 1990.* Press release issued January 8. Chicago: National Opinion Research Center.

NATIONAL OPINION RESEARCH CENTER. 1983. *General Social Survey 1972–1983: Cumulative Codebook*. Chicago: National Opinion Research Center.

NATIONAL RESEARCH COUNCIL. 1989. *A Common Destiny: Blacks and American Society*. Washington: National Academy Press.

NATIONAL RESEARCH COUNCIL, PANEL ON ADOLESCENT PREGNANCY AND CHILDBEARING. 1987. *Risking the Future: Adolescent Sexuality, Pregnancy, and Childbearing*. Washington, D.C.: National Academy Press.

NEIDERT, LISA J., and REYNOLDS FARLEY. 1985. "Assimilation in the United States: An Analysis of Ethnic and Generation Differences in Status." *American Sociological Review* 50:840–50.

NELKIN, DOROTHY, and MICHAEL POLLAK. 1981. *The Atom Beseiged*. Cambridge, Mass.: M.I.T. Press.

NEUHAUS, ROBERT, and RUBY NEUHAUS. 1974. *Family Crisis*. Columbus, Ohio: Merrill.

NEWPORT, JOHN PAUL, JR. 1992. "Steps to Help the Urban Black Man." Pp. 140–43 in John A. Kromkowski (ed.), *Race and Ethnic Relations 92/93*. Guilford, Conn.: Dushkin Publishing Group.

Newsweek. 1979. "A New Racial Poll." February 26, pp. 48, 53.

New York Times. 1991. "Texas Judge Backs Law on School Aid." April 16, sec. A.

New York Times. 1985. Editorial. September 30, sec. A.

New York Times. 1980. "3 Ex-Houston Policemen Begin Terms for Civil Rights Violations." April 12, p. 30.

New York Times. 1979. "A Tale of Two Cities," by Tom Wicker. November 2, p. 31.

New York Times. 1979. June 29. Pp. 14, 11B, 12B.

New York Times. 1973. February, 1973, p. 5.

NICKENS, HERBERT W. 1992. "The Rationale for Minority-Targeted Programs in Medicine in the 1990s." *Journal of the American Medical Association* 267, 7: 2390, 2395.

NICKLIN, JULIE L. 1992. "Helping to Manage Diversity in the Work Force." *Chronicle of Higher Education* (September 30): A5.

NISBET, LEE. 1977. "Affirmative Action: A Liberal Program?" Pp. 50–53 in Barry R. Gross (ed.), *Reverse Discrimination*. Buffalo: Prometheus Books.

NOCK, S. L., and P. W. KINGSTON. 1988. "Time with Children: The Impact of Couples' Work-time Commitments." *Social Forces* 67:59–85.

NOEL, DONALD L. 1972a. "Slavery and the Rise of Racism." Pp. 153–74 in Donald L. Noel (ed.), *The Origins of American Slavery and Racism*. Columbus, Ohio: Merrill.

NOEL, DONALD L. (ed.) 1972b. *The Origins of American Slavery and Racism*. Columbus, Ohio: Merrill.

NOEL, DONALD L. 1968. "A Theory of the Origin of Ethnic Stratification." *Social Problems* 16:157–72.

NOLEN, SUSAN BOBBITT, and THOMAS M. HALADYNE. 1990. "Personal and Environmental Influences on Students' Beliefs about Effective Study Strategies." *Contemporary Educational Psychology* 15, 2: 116–130.

NOSTRAND, RICHARD L. 1992. *The Hispano Homeland*. Norman: University of Oklahoma Press.

NOVAK, MICHAEL. 1971. *The Rise of the Unmeltable Ethnics*. New York: Macmillan.

O'HARE, WILLIAM P. 1992. "America's Minorities: The Demographics of Diversity." *Population Bulletin* 47, 4.

O'HARE, WILLIAM P., and USDANSKY, MARGARET L. 1992. "What the 1990 Census Tells Us About Segregation in 25 Large Cities." *Population Today* (September): 6–7.

OAKES, JEANNINE, ADAM GAMORAN, and R. N. PAGE. 1992. "Curriculum Differentiation: Opportunities, Outcomes, and Meanings." In P. W. Jackson (ed.), *Handbook of Research on Curriculum*. Washington, D.C.: American Educational Research Association.

OFFICE OF SPECIAL CONCERNS. OFFICE OF THE ASSISTANT SECRETARY, U.S. DEPARTMENT OF HEALTH, EDUCATION, AND WELFARE. 1974. *A Study of Selected Socio-Economic Characteristics of Ethnic Minorities Based on the 1970 Census*, vol. 2, *Asian Americans*. Washington, D.C.: U.S. Government Printing Office.

OGBU, JOHN U. 1988. "The Individual in Collective Adaptation: A Framework for Focusing on Academic Underperformance and Dropping Out Among Involuntary Minorities." Paper presented at the annual meeting of the American Educational Research Association, April 5–9, New Orleans.

OGBU, JOHN U. 1978. *Minority Education and Caste: The American System in Cross Cultural Perspective*. New York: Academic Press.

OLIVER, MELVIN L., and THOMAS M. SHAPIRO. 1990. "Wealth of a Nation: A Reassessment of Asset Inequality in America Shows At Least One-Third of Households Are Asset-Poor." *American Journal of Economics and Sociology* 49:129–51.

OLOJEDE, DELE. 1991. "Can I Quota You?" *Mother Jones* (July/August): 17, 19.

OLSEN, MARVIN E. 1990. "The Affluent Prosper While Everyone Else Struggles." Presidential address delivered at the 1990 Annual Meeting of the North Central Sociological Society, Louisville. (Reprinted in *Sociological Focus* 23:73–87.)

ORFIELD, GARY. 1988. "The Growth and Concentration of Hispanic Enrollment and the Future of American Education." Paper presented at the National Council of La Raza Conference, July 13, Albuquerque, NM.

ORFIELD, GARY. 1983. *Public School Desegregation in the United States, 1968–1980*. Washington, D.C.: Joint Center for Political Studies.

ORFIELD, GARY, ET AL. 1991. "Interdisciplinary Social Science Statement to U.S. Supreme Court Concerning Research on the Effects of School Desegregation." Submitted as appendix to friend-of-court brief in DeKalb County, Georgia, school desegregation case.

ORFIELD, GARY, ET AL. 1989. *Status of School Desegregation 1968–1986: A Report to the Council of Urban Boards of Education and the National School Desegregation Research Project*. Washington, D.C.: National School Boards Association.

ORGANIZATION FOR ECONOMIC COOPERATION AND DEVELOPMENT. 1977. *Public Expenditure on Health*.

Paris: Organization for Economic Cooperation and Development.

ORNSTEIN, ALLAN C. 1978. *Metropolitan Schools: Administrative Decentralization vs. Community Control.* Metuchen, N.J.: Scarecrow Press.

OSSENBERG, RICHARD J. 1975. "Social Pluralism in Quebec: Continuity, Change, and Conflict." Pp. 112–25 in Norman R. Yetman and C. Hoy Steele (eds.), *Majority and Minority: The Dynamics of Racial and Ethnic Relations.* Boston: Allyn & Bacon.

OSSENBERG, RICHARD J. 1971. *Canadian Society: Pluralism, Change, and Conflict.* Toronto: Prentice Hall.

OTTAWAY, DAVID. 1993. *Chained Together: Mandela, DeKlerk, and the Struggle to Remake South Africa.* New York: Times Books.

OVERBY, ANDREW. 1972. "Discrimination in the Administration of Justice." Pp. 264–76 in Charles E. Reasons and Jack L. Kuykendall (eds.), *Race, Crime, and Justice.* Pacific Palisades, Calif.: Goodyear.

OWEN, CAROLYN, HOWARD C. EISNER, and THOMAS R. McFAUL. 1981. "A Half-Century of Social Distance Research: National Replication of the Bogardus Studies." *Sociology and Social Research* 66:80–98.

PACHON, HARRY P., and JOAN W. MOORE. 1981. "Mexican Americans." *Annals of the American Academy of Political and Social Science* 454: 111–24.

PADILLA, FELIX M. 1985. *Latino Ethnic Consciousness: The Case of Mexican Americans and Puerto Ricans in Chicago.* Notre Dame, Ind.: University of Notre Dame Press.

PAGE, CLARENCE. 1994. "Clinton Clings to Shameful Policy Barring Haitian Refugees." *St. Louis Post-Dispatch* (March 20): B3.

PALMER, FRANCIS H. 1970. "Socioeconomic Status and Intellective Performance Among Negro Preschool Boys." *Developmental Psychology* 3:1–9.

PARENT, WAYNE. 1980. "A Liberal Legacy: Blacks Blaming Themselves for Economic Failures." *Journal of Black Studies* 16:3–20.

PARISI, NICOLETTE, MICHAEL R. GOTTFREDSON, MICHAEL J. HINDELANG, and TIMOTHY J. FLANIGAN (eds.). 1979. *Sourcebook of Criminal Justice Statistics—1978.* Washington, D.C.: U.S. Government Printing Office.

PARSONS, TALCOTT. 1959. "The School Class as a Social System." *Harvard Education Review* 29: 297–318.

PARSONS, TALCOTT, and ROBERT F. BALES. 1955. *Family, Socialization, and Interaction Process.* Glencoe, Ill.: Free Press.

PATERNOSTER, RAYMOND. 1983. "The Decision to Seek the Death Penalty in South Carolina." *Journal of Criminal Law and Criminology* 74:754–87.

PATTERSON, ORLANDO. 1977. *Ethnic Chauvinism: The Reactionary Impulse.* New York: Stein & Day.

PAYNE, CHARLES. 1979. "On the Declining—and Increasing—Significance of Race." Pp. 117–39 in Charles Vert Willie (ed.), *Caste and Class Controversy.* Bayside, N.Y.: General Hall.

PEAR, ROBERT. 1990. "Study Finds Bias, Forcing a Review of 1986 Alien Law." *New York Times,* March 3, sec. 1.

PEARCE, DIANA. 1976. "Black, White, and Many Shades of Gray: Real Estate Brokers and Their Racial Practices." Ph.D. diss., University of Michigan, Ann Arbor.

PEARL, D. 1954. "Ethnocentrism and the Self-Concept." *Journal of Social Psychology* 40:137–47.

PERRONE, VITO. 1991. "On Standardized Testing." *Childhood Education* (Spring): 132–42.

PESKIN, JANICE. 1982. "Measuring Household Production for the GNP." *Family Economics Review* (Summer): 16–25.

PETERSDORF, ROBERT G., K. S. TURNER, HERBERT W. NICKENS, and TIMOTHY READY. 1990. "Minorities in Medicine: Past, Present, and Future." *Academic Medicine* 65:663–670.

PETERSILLA, JOAN. 1983. *Racial Disparities in the Criminal Justice System.* Santa Monica, Calif.: Rand Corporation.

PETERSON, JAMES L., and NICHOLAS ZILL. 1986. "Marital Disruption, Parent–Child Relationships, and Behavior Problems in Children." *Journal of Marriage and the Family* 48:295–307.

PETTIGREW, THOMAS F. 1985. "New Black–White Patterns: How Best to Conceptualize Them." Pp. 329–46 in Ralph H. Turner and James F. Short (eds.), *Annual Review of Sociology,* vol. 11. Palo Alto, Calif.: Annual Reviews.

PETTIGREW, THOMAS F. 1980. "The Changing—Not Declining—Significance of Race." *Contemporary Sociology* 9:19–21.

PETTIGREW, THOMAS F. 1976. "Race and Intergroup Relations." Pp. 459–510 in Robert K. Merton and Robert Nisbet (eds.), *Contemporary Social Problems,* 4th ed. New York: Harcourt Brace Jovanovich.

PETTIGREW, THOMAS F. 1973. "Attitudes on Race and Housing: A Social-Psychological View." Pp. 21–84 in Amos H. Hawley and V. P. Rock (eds.), *Segregation in Residential Areas.* Washington, D.C.: National Academy of Sciences.

PETTIGREW, THOMAS F. 1971. *Racially Separate or Together.* New York: McGraw-Hill.

PETTIGREW, THOMAS F. 1969a. "The Negro and Education: Problems and Proposals." Pp. 49–112 in Irwin Katz and Patricia Gurin (eds.), *Race and the Social Sciences.* New York: Basic Books.

PETTIGREW, THOMAS F. 1969b. "Race and Equal Educational Opportunity." Pp. 69–79 in Harvard Educational Review Editors (eds.), *Equality of Educational Opportunity.* Cambridge, Mass.: Harvard University Press.

PETTIGREW, THOMAS F., and ROBERT L. GREEN. 1976. "School Desegregation in Large Cities: Critique of the Coleman 'White Flight' Thesis." *Harvard Educational Review* 46:1–53.

PETTIGREW, THOMAS F., ELIZABETH L. USEEM, CLARENCE NORMAND, and MARSHALL S. SMITH. 1973. "Busing: A Review of the Evidence." *Public Interest* 30:88–118.

PETTY, RICHARD E., JOHN T. CACIOPPO, and RACHEL GOLDMAN. 1981. "Personal Involvement as a Determinant of Argument-based Persuasion." *Journal of Personality and Social Psychology* 41:847–55.

PHARR, SUZANNE. 1992. "Homophobia as a Weapon of Sexism." Pp. 431–40 in Paula S. Rothenberg (ed.), *Race, Class, and Gender in the United States: An Integrated Study.* New York: St. Martin's Press.

PIAGET, JEAN. 1965 [1932]. *The Moral Judgment of the Child.* Marjorie Gabain (tr.). New York: Free Press.

PIERSON, DONALD. 1942. *Negroes in Brazil.* Chicago: University of Chicago Press.

PILIAVIN, IRVING, and SCOTT BRIAR. 1964. "Police Encounters with Juveniles." *American Journal of Sociology* 70:206–14.

PINKNEY, ALPHONSO. 1976. *Red, Black, and Green: Black Nationalism in the United States.* New York: Cambridge University Press.

PINKNEY, ALFONSO. 1975. *Black Americans.* Englewood Cliffs, N.J.: Prentice Hall.

PISKO, VALENA WHITE, and JOYCE D. STERN (eds.). 1985. *The Condition of Education, 1985 Edition.* Statistical Report, National Center for Education Statistics. Washington, D.C.: U.S. Government Printing Office.

PIVEN, FRANCES FOX. 1977. "The Urban Crisis: Who Got What and Why." Pp. 132–44 in Roger E. Alcaly and David Mermelstein (eds.), *The Fiscal Crisis of American Cities.* New York: Vintage Books.

PLANT, RICHARD. 1986. *The Pink Triangle: The Nazi War Against Homosexuals.* New York: Henry Holt.

POOL, ROBERT. 1993. "Evidence for Homosexuality Gene." *Science* 261, 5119 (July 16): 291–92.

POPENOE, DAVID. 1988. *Disturbing the Nest: Family Change and Decline in Modern Societies.* New York: Aldine de Gruyter.

POPULATION REFERENCE BUREAU. 1993. *1993 World Population Data Sheet.* Washington, D.C.: Population Reference Bureau.

POPULATION REFERENCE BUREAU. 1986a. *1986 World Population Data Sheet.* Washington, D.C.: Population Reference Bureau.

POPULATION REFERENCE BUREAU. 1986b. "New Projections of U.S. Hispanics." *Population Today* 14, 10:10.

PORTER, JUDITH D. R. 1971. *Black Child, White Child.* Cambridge, Mass.: Harvard University Press.

PORTER, ROSALIE PEDELINO. 1991. "Language Choice for Latino Students." *Public Interest* 105:48–60.

POTTINGER, J. STANLEY. 1972. "The Drive Toward Equality." *Change* 4, 8:24.

POUSSAINT, ALVIN. 1977. Presentation to Intergroup Relations Week Program, Concordia College, Moorhead, Minn.

POWELL, RICHARD R., and JESUS GARCIA. 1985. "The Portrayal of Minorities and Women in Selected Elementary Science Series." *Journal of Research in Science Teaching* 22:519–33.

PRESIDENT'S COMMISSION ON LAW ENFORCEMENT AND THE ADMINISTRATION OF JUSTICE. 1967. *Task Force Report: Crime and Its Impact.* Washington, D.C.: U.S. Government Printing Office.

PROTHRO, E. T. 1952. "Ethnocentrism and Anti-Negro Attitudes in the Deep South." *Journal of Abnormal and Social Psychology* 47:105–8.

PUBLIC BROADCASTING SERVICE. 1985. *Frontlines: A Class Divided.*

QUINNEY, RICHARD. 1979. *Criminology.* Boston: Little, Brown.

RAAB, EARL R. 1978. "Son of Coalition." Paper presented to the 28th Annual Meeting of the Society for the Study of Social Problems, San Francisco, Calif.

RAAB, EARL, and SEYMOUR MARTIN LIPSET. 1959. *Prejudice and Society.* New York: Anti-Defamation League.

RADELET, MICHAEL, and GLENN L. PIERCE. 1985. "Race and Prosecutorial Discretion in Homicide Cases." *Law and Society Review* 19:587–621.

RADKE, MARIAN J., and HELEN G. TRAGER. 1950. "Children's Perceptions of the Social Roles of Negroes and Whites." *Journal of Psychology* 29:3–33.

RAINWATER, LEE, and WILLIAM L. YANCEY (eds.). 1967. *The Moynihan Report and the Politics of Controversy.* Cambridge, Mass.: M.I.T. Press.

RAKOWSKA-HARMSTONE, TERESA. 1992. "Chickens Coming Home to Roost: A Perspective on Soviet Ethnic Relations." *Journal of International Affairs* 45:519–48.

RAND CORPORATION AND URBAN INSTITUTE. 1990. *The Effect of Employer Sanctions on the Flow of Undocumented Immigrants to the United States.* Report no. JRI-03. Santa Monica, Calif.: Rand Corporation.

RANSFORD, H. EDWARD. 1972. "Blue-Collar Anger: Reactions to Student and Black Protest." *American Sociological Review* 37:333–46.

RATTERAY, JOAN DAVIS. 1988. *Freedom of the Mind: Essays and Policy Studies.* Washington, D.C.: Institute for Independent Education.

RAVITCH, DIANE. 1973. "Community Control Revisited." *Commentary* (February): 70–74.

RAY, JOHN J. 1988. "Why the F Scale Predicts Racism: A Critical Review." *Political Psychology* 9:671–79.

RAY, JOHN J. 1980. "Authoritarianism in California 30 Years Later—With Some Cross-Cultural Comparisons." *Journal of Social Psychology* (June): 9–17.

REICH, MICHAEL. 1986. "The Political-Economic Effects of Racism." Pp. 304–11 in Richard C. Edwards, Michael Reich, and Thomas E. Weisskopf (eds.), *The Capitalist System: A Radical Analysis of American Society,* 3d ed. Englewood Cliffs, N.J.: Prentice Hall.

REICH, MICHAEL. 1981. *Racial Inequality: A Political-Economic Analysis.* Princeton, N.J.: Princeton University Press.

REIMERS, CORDELLA W. 1984. "Sources of the Family Income Differentials Among Hispanics, Blacks, and White Non-Hispanics." *American Journal of Sociology* 89:889–903.

REISMAN, DAVID. 1953. *The Lonely Crowd.* New York: Doubleday.

REISS, ALBERT J., JR. 1968. "Police Brutality—Answers to Key Questions." *Transaction* 5:10–19.

RESKIN, BARBARA F. 1988. "Bringing the Men Back In: Sex Differentiation and the Devaluation of Women's Work." *Gender and Society* 2:58–81.

REYNOLDS, ROBERT E., and THOMAS W. RICE. 1971. "Attitudes of Medical Interns Toward Patients and Health Professionals." *Journal of Health and Social Behavior* 12:307–311.

RHODES, N., and W. WOOD. 1992.. "Individual Differences in Influenceability: Self-Esteem and Intelligence." *Psychological Bulletin* 111:156–71.

RICHERT, JEAN PIERRE. 1974. "The Impact of Ethnicity on the Perception of Heroes and Historical Symbols." *Canadian Review of Sociology and Anthropology* 11, 2 (May): 156–63.

RICHMAN, CHARLES L., M. L. CLARK, and KATHRYN P. BROWN. 1985. "General and Specific Self-esteem in Late Adolescent Students: Race × Sex × Gender Effects." *Adolescence* 20:555–66.

RICHMOND, ANTHONY H. 1986. "Racial Conflict in Great Britain." Review Essay. *Contemporary Sociology* 15:184–87.

RIEDER, JONATHAN. 1985. *Canarsie: The Jews and Italians of Brooklyn Against Liberalism*. Cambridge, Mass.: Harvard University Press.

RIGBY, KEN. 1988. "Sexist Attitudes and Authoritarian Personality Characteristics Among Australian Adolescents." *Journal of Research in Personality* 22:465–73.

RIORDAN, CORNELIUS, and JOSEPHINE RUGGIERO. 1980. "Producing Equal Status Interracial Interaction: A Replication." *Social Psychology Quarterly* 43:131–36.

RIOUX, MARCEL, and YVES MARTIN (eds.). 1964. *French Canadian Society*. Toronto: McClelland & Stewart.

RIST, RAY C. 1978. *The Invisible Children: School Integration in American Society*. Cambridge, Mass.: Harvard University Press.

RIST, RAY C. 1970. "Student Social Class and Teacher Expectations: The Self-fulfilling Prophecy in Ghetto Education." *Harvard Educational Review* 40:411–51.

ROBERT WOOD JOHNSON FOUNDATION. 1983. *Special Report: Updated Report on Access to Health Care for the American People*. Princeton, N.J.: Robert Wood Johnson Foundation.

ROBERTSON, IAN, and PHILLIP WHITTEN. 1978. *Race and Politics in South Africa*. Edison, N.J.: Transaction Books.

ROBINSON, JERRY W., and JAMES D. PRESTON. 1976. "Equal-Status Contact and Modification of Racial Prejudice: A Reexamination of the Contact Hypothesis." *Social Forces* 54:911–24.

ROBINSON, JOHN. 1977. *How Americans Use Their Time: A Social Psychological Analysis of Everyday Behavior*. New York: Praeger.

RODDY, DENNIS B. 1990. "Perceptions Still Segregate Police, Black Community." *Pittsburgh Press,* August 29, sec. B.

ROEBUCK, JULIAN, and ROBERT QUAN. 1976. "Health-Care Practices in the American Deep South." Pp. 141–61 in R. Wallis and P. Morely (eds.), *Marginal Medicine*. New York: Free Press.

ROMERO, ANN, and DON ZANCANELLA. 1990. "Expanding the Circle: Hispanic Voices in American Literature." *English Journal* 79, 1:24–29.

RONCAL, JOAQUIN. 1944. "The Negro Race in Mexico." *Hispanic American Historical Review* 24:530–40.

ROONEY-REBEK, PATRICIA, and LEONARD JASON. 1986. "Prevention of Prejudice in Elementary School Students." *Journal of Primary Prevention* 7:63–73.

ROSE, R. 1971. *Governing Without Consensus*. London: Faber and Faber.

ROSENBAUM, JAMES E. 1976. *Making Inequality: The Hidden Curriculum of High School Teaching*. New York: Wiley.

ROSENBAUM, JAMES E., and TAKEHIKO KARIYA. 1991. "Do School Achievements Affect the Early Jobs of High School Graduates in the United States and Japan?" *Sociology of Education* 64:78–95.

ROSENBAUM, JAMES E., and SUSAN J. POPKIN. 1991. "Employment and Earnings of Low-Income Blacks Who Move to Middle-Class Suburbs." Pp. 342–56 in Christopher Jencks and Paul E. Peterson (eds.), *The Urban Underclass*. Washington, D.C.: The Brookings Institution.

ROSENBAUM, ROBERT J., and ROBERT W. LARSON. 1987. "Mexicano Resistance to the Expropriation of Grant Lands in New Mexico." Pp. 269–310 in Charles L. Briggs and John R. Van Ness (eds.), *Land, Water, and Culture: New Perspectives on Hispanic Land Grants*. Albuquerque: University of New Mexico Press.

ROSENBERG, MORRIS, and ROBERTA G. SIMMONS. 1971. *Black and White Self-esteem: The Urban School Child*. Washington, D.C.: American Sociological Association.

ROSENTHAL, BERNARD G. 1974. "Development of Self-identification in Relation to Attitudes Toward the Self in the Chippewa Indians." *Genetic Psychology Monographs* 90:43–141.

ROSENTHAL, D. 1970. *Genetic Theory and Abnormal Behavior*. New York: McGraw-Hill.

ROSENTHAL, ROBERT, and LENORE JACOBSON. 1968. *Pygmalion in the Classroom: Teacher Expectation and Pupils' Intellectual Development*. New York: Holt, Rinehart & Winston.

ROSSELL, CHRISTINE H. 1990. *The Carrot or the Stick for School Desegregation Policy: Magnet Schools or Forced Busing*. Philadelphia: Temple University Press.

ROSSELL, CHRISTINE H., and CHARLES L. GLENN. 1988. "The Cambridge Controlled Choice Plan." *Urban Review* 20, 2:75–94.

RUBIN, I. M. 1967. "Increased Self-acceptance: A Means of Reducing Prejudice." *Journal of Personality and Social Psychology* 5:133–238.

RUDWICK, ELLIOTT M. 1964. *Race Riot at East St. Louis, July 2, 1917*. Carbondale, Ill.: Southern Illinois University Press.

RUNDALL, THOMAS G., and JOHN R. C. WHEELER. 1979. "The Effect of Income on Use of Preventive Care: An Evaluation of Alternative Explanations." *Journal of Health and Social Behavior* 20:397–406.

RYAN, WILLIAM. 1971. *Blaming the Victim*. New York: Vintage Books.

RYAN, WILLIAM. 1967. "Savage Discovery: The Moynihan Report." Pp. 457–66 in Lee Rainwater and William L. Yancey (eds.), *The Moynihan Report and the Politics of Controversy.* Cambridge, Mass.: M.I.T. Press.

ST. JOHN, NANCY H. 1975. *School Desegregation: Outcomes for Children.* New York: Wiley.

St. Louis Post-Dispatch. 1993a. "British Take Ill Bosnian: Doctors Try to Save Girl Hurt in Attack." August 10, p. 3a.

St. Louis Post-Dispatch. 1993b. "Detroit Mayoral Contest Increasingly Centers on Race." October 22, p. 2c.

St. Louis Post-Dispatch. 1993c. "Ranks of U.S. Poor Grow by 1.2 Million." October 5, pp. 1a, 8a.

St. Louis Post-Dispatch. 1993d. "U.S. School Segregation Called Highest Since '60s." December 14, p. 3a.

SALTZMAN, AMY, and TED GEST. 1991. "Your New Civil Rights." *U.S. News and World Report* (November 18): 93–95.

SAMPSON, ROBERT J. 1987. "Urban Black Violence: The Effect of Male Joblessness and Family Disruption." *American Journal of Sociology* 93:348–82.

SANDBERG, NEIL C. 1974. *Ethnic Identity and Assimilation: The Polish-American Community.* New York: Praeger.

SANDOVAL, J. 1979. "The WISC-R and Internal Evidence of Test Bias With Minority Groups." *Journal of Counselling and Clinical Psychology* 47:919–27.

SATIN, GEORGE D. 1973. "Help? The Hospital Emergency Unit Patient and His Presenting Picture." *Medical Care* 11:328–37.

SATIN, GEORGE, and FREDERICK J. DUHL. 1972. "Help? The Hospital Emergency Unit as Community Physician." *Medical Care* 10:248–60.

SATTLER, JEROME M. 1982. *Assessment of Children's Intelligence and Special Abilities,* 2d ed. Boston: Allyn & Bacon.

SAUL R. LEVEN MEMORIAL FOUNDATION. 1959. Unpublished report of study of Detroit Recorder's Court over 20-month period, November 1, 1957 through June 30, 1959.

SCHAFER, WALTER E., CAROL OLEXA, and KENNETH POLK. 1972. "Programmed for Social Class: Tracking in High School." Pp. 34–54 in Kenneth Polk and Walter E. Schafer (eds.), *Schools and Delinquency.* Englewood Cliffs, N.J.: Prentice Hall.

SCHAICH, WARREN. 1975. "A Relationship Between Collective Racial Violence and War." *Journal of Black Studies* 5:374–94.

SCHERMERHORN, RICHARD A. 1978. *Comparative Ethnic Relations: A Framework for Theory and Research,* Phoenix ed. Chicago: University of Chicago Press.

SCHMALZ, JEFFREY. 1993. "Survey Stirs Debate on Number of Gay Men in U.S." *New York Times,* April 16, sec. A.

SCHMIDT, PETER. 1992. "Gap Cited in Awareness of Students' Home Languages." *Education Week* (April 29): 11.

SCHMIDT, WILLIAM E. 1991. "Oslo Journal: Who's in Charge Here? Chances Are It's a Woman." *New York Times* (May 22): A4.

SCHNEIDER, MARK, and THOMAS PHELAN. 1990. "Blacks and Jobs: Never the Twain Shall Meet?" *Urban Affairs Quarterly* 26:299–312.

SCHORR, LISBETH B., with DANIEL SCHORR. 1988. *Within Our Reach: Breaking the Cycle of Disadvantage.* New York: Anchor Doubleday.

SCHUCHARDT, THOMAS. 1980. "A Study of the Disabled in the Role of Social Deviant." Master's thesis, Southern Illinois University, Edwardsville.

SCHUMAN, HOWARD. 1975. "Free Will and Determinism in Public Beliefs About Race." Pp. 375–80 in Norman R. Yetman and C. Hoy Steele (eds.), *Majority and Minority: The Dynamics of Racial and Ethnic Relations.* Boston: Allyn & Bacon. (Earlier version appeared in *Transaction* 7, 2 [1969]: 44–48.)

SCHUMAN, HOWARD, and LAWRENCE BOBO. 1988. "Survey-Based Experiments on White Racial Attitudes Toward Residential Integration." *American Journal of Sociology* 94:273–99.

SCHWARTZ, BARRY, and ROBERT DISCH. 1975. *White Racism: Its History, Pathology, and Practice.* New York: Dell.

SCOTT, R. R., and J. M. MCPARTLAND. 1982. "Desegregation as National Policy: Correlates of Racial Attitudes." *American Educational Research Journal* 19:397–414.

SCRUGGS, OTEY M. 1971. "The Economic and Racial Components of Jim Crow." Pp. 70–87 in Nathan I. Huggins, Martin Kilson, and Daniel M. Fox (eds.), *Key Issues in the Afro-American Experience,* vol. 2. New York: Harcourt Brace Jovanovich.

SEABURY, PAUL. 1977. "HEW and the Universities." Pp. 97–112 in Barry R. Gross (ed.), *Reverse Discrimination.* Buffalo: Prometheus Books. (Earlier version appeared in *Commentary* [February, 1972].)

SEARS, D. O., R. R. LAU, T. R. TAYLOR, and H. M. ALLEN. 1980. "Self-Interest or Symbolic Politics in Policy Attitudes and Presidential Voting?" *American Political Science Review* 74:670–84.

SEE, KATHERINE O'SULLIVAN. 1986. *First World Nationalisms: Class and Ethnic Politics in Northern Ireland and Quebec.* Chicago: University of Chicago Press.

SEIFER, NANCY. 1973. *Absent from the Majority: Working Class Women in America.* New York: American Jewish Committee.

SELIGMAN, DANIEL. 1992. "Keeping Up: The Curious Case of the Missing Data." *Fortune* (June 15): 159–60.

SELVIN, PAUL. 1992. "Math Education: Multiplying the Meager Numbers." *Science* 28:1200–1201.

SEYMOUR, D. Z. 1972. "Black English." *Intellectual Digest* 2.

SHAHEEN, JACK G. 1990. "Our Cultural Demon—The 'Ugly Arab.'" *Washington Post* (August 19): C1.

SHAHEEN, JACK G. 1984. *The TV Arab.* Bowling Green, Ohio: Bowling Green State University Popular Press.

SHANAHAN, J. L. 1976. "Impaired Access of Black Inner-City Residents to the Decentralized Workplaces." *Journal of Economics and Business* 28, 2:156–60.

SHARMA, RAMA, and SAEEDUZ ZAFAR. 1989. "A Study of Prejudice in Relation to Feelings of Security–Insecurity." *Journal of Personality and Clinical Studies* 5:73–75.

SHEATSLEY, PAUL B. 1966. "White Attitudes Toward the Negro." *Daedalus* 95:217–38.

SHENKER, JOSEPH. 1992. "Preparing Teachers for Democratic Schools: A Response." *Teachers College Record* 94, 1:45–47.

SHEPPARD, B. H., J. HARTWICK, and P. R. WARSHAW. 1988. "The Theory of Reasoned Action: A Meta-Analysis of Past Research with Recommendations for Modifications and Future Research." *Journal of Consumer Research* 15:325–43.

SHERIF, MUZAFER, O. J. HARVEY, B. JACK WHITE, WILLIAM R. HOOD, and CAROLYN W. SHERIF. 1961. *Intergroup Conflict and Cooperation: The Robbers Cave Experiment.* Norman, Okla.: University Book Exchange.

SHILTS, RANDY. 1993a. "What's Fair in Love and War." *Newsweek* (February 1): 58–59.

SHILTS, RANDY. 1993b. *Conduct Unbecoming: Gays and Lesbians in the U.S. Military.* New York: St. Martin's Press.

SHOCKLEY, WILLIAM. 1971a. "Negro IQ Deficit: Failure of a 'Malicious Coincidence' Model Warrants New Research Proposals." *Review of Educational Research* 41:227–28.

SHOCKLEY, WILLIAM. 1971b. "Models, Mathematics, and the Moral Obligation to Diagnose the Origin of Negro IQ Deficits." *Review of Educational Research* 41:369–77.

SIEGEL, JACOB S., JEFFREY S. PASSEL, and J. GREGORY ROBINSON. 1980. Working paper on illegal immigration prepared for the Select Commission on Immigration and Refugee Policy.

SILVERSTEIN, BARRY, and RONALD KRATE. 1975. *Children of the Dark Ghetto—A Developmental Psychology.* New York: Praeger.

SILVERSTEIN, LEE. 1966. "Bail in the State Courts: A Field Study and Report." *Minnesota Law Review* 50.

SIMON, DAVID R., and D. STANLEY EITZEN. 1993. *Elite Deviance,* fourth edition. Boston: Allyn & Bacon.

SIMON, JULIAN. 1990. *The Economic Consequences of Immigration.* Cambridge, Mass.: Basil Blackwell.

SIMPSON, GEORGE EATON, and J. MILTON YINGER. 1985. *Racial and Cultural Minorities: An Analysis of Prejudice and Discrimination,* 5th ed. New York: Plenum.

SINDLER, ALLAN P. 1978. *Bakke, DeFunis, and Minority Admissions: The Quest for Equal Opportunity.* New York: Longman.

SKOLNICK, JEROME H. 1969. *The Politics of Protest.* New York: Simon & Schuster.

SLAVIN ROBERT E. 1985. "Cooperative Learning: Applying Contact Theory in Desegregated Schools." *Journal of Social Issues* 41, 3:43–62.

SMITH, A. WADE. 1981. "Racial Tolerance as a Function of Group Position." *American Sociological Review* (October):525–41.

SMITH, DONALD. 1984. *Saving the African American Child.* Report of the National Alliance of Black School Administrators, Inc.

SMITH, DOUGLAS A., and CHRISTY A. VISHER. 1981. "Street Level Justice: Situational Determinants of Police Arrest Decisions." *Social Problems* 29:167–77.

SMITH, W. C. 1942. "Minority Groups in Hawaii." *Annals of the American Academy of Political and Social Science* 233:41.

SNIDERMAN, PAUL M., THOMAS PIAZZA, PHILIP E. TETLOCK, and ANN KENDRICK. 1991. "The New Racism." *American Journal of Political Science* 35:423–47.

SNIDERMAN, PAUL M., and MICHAEL GRAY HAGEN. 1985. *Race and Inequality: A Study in American Values.* Chatham, N.J.: Chatham House.

SNIPP, C. MATTHEW. 1988. "Public Policy and American Indian Economic Development." Pp. 1–22 in C. Matthew Snipp (ed.), *Public Policy Impacts on American Indian Economic Development.* Santa Fe: Native American Studies, University of New Mexico.

SNIPP, C. MATTHEW. 1986a. "The Changing Political and Economic Status of American Indians: From Captive Nations to Internal Colonies." *American Journal of Economics and Sociology* 45: 145–57.

SNIPP, C. MATTHEW. 1986b. "American Indians and Natural Resource Development." *American Journal of Economics and Sociology* 45: 457–74.

SNOW, DAVID A., E. BURKE ROCHFORD, JR., STEVEN K. WORDEN, and ROBERT D. BENFORD. 1986. "Frame Alignment Processes, Micromobilization, and Movement Participation." *American Sociological Review* 78:537–61.

SNOW, LOUDELL F. 1978. "Sorcerers, Saints, and Charlatans: Black Folk Healers in Urban America." *Culture, Medicine, and Psychiatry* 2:69–106.

SNYDER, THOMAS D. 1991. *Youth Indicators 1991: Trends in the Well-being of American Youth.* Office of Research and Improvement, U.S. Department of Education. Washington: U.S. Government Printing Office.

SOLOMON, CHARLENE MARMER. 1992. "Keeping Hate Out of the Workplace." *Personnel Journal* (July): 30–36.

SOLORZANO, DANIEL G. 1991. "Mobility Aspirations Among Racial Minorities, Controlling for SES." *Sociology and Social Research* 75:182–88.

SOUTHERN POVERTY LAW CENTER. 1994. "Klanwatch Report: Violent Crime Remains at Record Levels Nationwide." *Intelligence Report* (March): 1, 4–5.

SOUTHERN POVERTY LAW CENTER. 1993a. "Klanwatch Reports Hate Violence at Record Levels Last Year." *SPLC Report* 23, 2 (April): 1, 5.

SOUTHERN POVERTY LAW CENTER. 1993b. "For the Record." *Intelligence Report* (September): 11–17.

SOUTHERN POVERTY LAW CENTER. 1993c. "Alabama Skinhead Convicted of Manslaughter for Slaying of Black Man." *Intelligence Report* (December): 6.

SOUTHERN POVERTY LAW CENTER. 1993d. "'Patriot' Fax Network Links Militant Anti-Government Extremists Nationwide." *Intelligence Report* (December): 1–4.

SOUTHERN POVERTY LAW CENTER. 1988. *Special Report: The Ku Klux Klan—a History of Racism and Violence* 3d ed. Montgomery, Ala.: Southern Poverty Law Center.

SOWELL, THOMAS. 1990. *Preferential Policies.* New York: Morrow.

SOWELL, THOMAS. 1977. "'Affirmative Action' Reconsidered." Pp. 113–31 in Barry R. Gross (ed.), *Reverse Discrimination.* Buffalo, N.Y.: Prometheus Books.

SPEAR, ALLAN. 1971. "The Origins of the Urban Ghetto, 1870–1915." Pp. 153–66 in Nathan I. Huggins, Martin Kilson, and Daniel M. Fox (eds.), *Key Issues in the Afro-American Experience,* vol. 2. New York: Harcourt Brace Jovanovich.

SPENCER, METTA. 1979. *Foundations of Modern Sociology.* Englewood Cliffs, N.J.: Prentice Hall.

STAMPP, KENNETH M. 1956. *The Peculiar Institution: Slavery in the Ante-Bellum South.* New York: Vintage Books.

STANGOR, CHARLES, LINDA A. SULLIVAN, and THOMAS E. FORD. 1991. "The Affective and Cognitive Dimensions of Prejudice." *Social Cognition* 9:359–80.

STANLEY, JULIAN C. (ed.). 1973. *Compensatory Education for Children, Ages 2 to 8, Recent Studies of Environmental Intervention.* Baltimore: Johns Hopkins University Press.

STAPLES, ROBERT. 1973. *The Black Woman in America.* Chicago: Nelson-Hall.

STEEH, CHARLOTTE, and HOWARD SCHUMAN. 1992. "Young White Adults: Did Racial Attitudes Change in the 1980s?" *American Journal of Sociology* 98:340–67.

STEELE, C. HOY. 1985. "The Acculturation/Assimilation Model in Urban Indian Studies: A Critique." Pp. 332–39 in Norman R. Yetman (ed.), *Majority and Minority: The Dynamics of Race and Ethnicity in America,* 4th ed. Boston: Allyn & Bacon.

STEELE, C. HOY. 1972. "American Indians and Urban Life: A Community Study." Ph.D. diss., University of Kansas, Lawrence.

STEELE, SHELBY. 1990. *The Content of Our Character: A New Vision of Race in America.* New York: St. Martin's Press.

STERNLEIB, GEORGE, and JAMES W. HUGHES. 1976. *Post-Industrial America: Metropolitan Decline and Interregional Job Shifts.* New Brunswick, N.J.: Rutgers University Center for Urban Policy Research.

STERTZ, BRADLEY, and KRYSTAL MILLER. 1991. "Chaldeans in Detroit Are Prime Targets of Threats, Violence." *Wall Street Journal,* January 21, sec. A.

STEVENS, ROSEMARY. 1971. *American Medicine and the Public Interest.* New Haven, Conn.: Yale University Press.

STEVENSON, RICHARD W. 1990. "Study Finds Mild Gain in Drive on Illegal Aliens." *New York Times,* April 21, p. 24.

STINNETT, NICK, and JAMES WALTERS. 1977. *Relationships in Marriage and Family.* New York: Macmillan.

STOCKARD, JEAN, and MIRIAM M. JOHNSON. 1992. *Sex and Gender in Society,* 2d ed. Englewood Cliffs, N.J.: Prentice Hall.

STODDARD, LOTHROP. 1920. *The Rising Tide of Color Against White World-Supremacy.* New York: Scribner's.

STOTLAND, E., DONALD KATZ, and M. PATCHEN. 1959. "The Reduction of Prejudice Through the Arousal of Self-insight." *Journal of Personality* 27:507–31.

STOUFFER, SAMUEL A., E. A. SUCHMAN, L. C. DEVINNEY, S. A. STAR, and R. N. WILLIAMS. 1949. *The American Soldier,* vol. 1, *Adjustment During Army Life.* Princeton, N.J.: Princeton University Press.

STRAUS, MURRAY A. 1980. "A Sociological Perspective on the Causes of Family Violence." In Maurice R. Green (ed.), *Violence and the Family.* Boulder, Colo.: Westview Press.

STRONG, JAMES. 1994. "The Resurgence of Black Nationalism." *St. Louis American* (March 10–16): 7A, 8A.

STUBBINS, JOSEPH (ed.). 1977. *Social and Psychological Aspects of Disability: A Handbook for Practitioners.* Baltimore: University Park Press.

STUCKERT, ROBERT S. 1958. "The African Ancestry of the White American Population." *Ohio Journal of Science* (May): 155–60.

SUDARKASA, NIARA. 1991. "Absent: Black Men on Campus." *Essence* 22, 7: 140.

SULLIVAN, ANDREW. 1990. "Racism 101." *New Republic* (November 26): 18–21.

SULLIVAN, JOSEPH F. 1990. "New Jersey Ruling to Lift School Aid for Poor Districts." *New York Times,* June 6, sec. A.

SULLIVAN, LOUIS W. 1992. "From the Secretary of Health and Human Services: The Need for Affirmative Action in Medical Education." *Journal of the American Medical Association* 267, 3:343.

SUMMERS, ANITA, and BARBARA L. WOLFE. 1977. "Do Schools Make a Difference?" In *Sociological Inventory Sample Issue.* Washington, D.C.: American Sociological Association.

SUMNER, WILLIAM GRAHAM. 1906. *Folkways.* Boston: Ginn.

SUPER, DONALD E., and JOHN O. CRITES. 1962. *Appraising Vocational Fitness.* New York: Harper & Row.

SUPLEE, C. 1991. "Brain May Determine Sexuality." *Washington Post,* August 30, sec. A.

SZYMANSKI, ALBERT. 1976. "Racial Discrimination and White Gain." *American Sociological Review* 41: 403–14.

TAEUBER, KARL E. 1979. "Housing, Schools, and Incremental Segregative Effects." *Annals of the American Academy of Political and Social Science* 441:157–67.

TAEUBER, KARL E., and ALMA F. TAEUBER. 1965. *Negroes in Cities.* Chicago: Aldine.

TAYLOR, D. GARTH. 1981. "Racial Preferences, Housing Segregation, and the Causes of School Segregation: Recent Evidence from a Social Survey Used in Civil Litigation." *Review of Public Data Use* 9:267–82.

TAYLOR, D. GARTH. 1979. "Housing, Neighborhoods, and Race Relations: Recent Survey Evidence." *Annals of the American Academy of Political and Social Science* 441 (January): 26–40.

TAYLOR, KARYN J. 1978. "A Black Perspective on the Melting Pot." *Social Policy* 8, 5:31–37.

TAYLOR, PAUL S., and CLARK KERR. 1935. "Uprising on the Farm." *Survey Graphic* 24:19–22.

TERRY, ROBERT M. 1967. "Discrimination in the Handling of Juvenile Offenders by Social Control Agencies" *Journal of Research in Crime and Delinquency* 4:218–30.

TESSER, ABRAHAM, and DAVID R. SHAFFER. 1990. "Attitudes and Attitude Change." *Annual Review of Psychology* 41:479–523.

THERNSTROM, ABIGAIL. 1991. "Beyond the Pale." *New Republic* 205, 25: 22–24.

THERNSTROM, ABIGAIL M. 1980. "E Pluribus Plura—Congress and Bilingual Education." *Public Interest* 60 (Summer): 3–22.

THERNSTROM, STEPHAN, ANN ORLOV, and OSCAR HANLIN (eds.). 1980. *The Harvard Encyclopedia of American Ethnic Groups.* Cambridge, Mass.: Harvard University Press.

THOMAS, R. ROOSEVELT, JR. 1990. "From Affirmative Action to Affirming Diversity." *Harvard Business Review* 68, 2 (March/April): 107–17.

THOMLINSON, RALPH. 1976. *Population Dynamics: Causes and Consequences of World Demographic Change,* 2d ed. New York: Random House.

THOMPSON, KEVIN D. 1989. "Atlanta: Keeping Affirmative Action Alive." *Black Enterprise* (September): 48.

THOMPSON, WILBUR. 1976. "Economic Processes and Employment Problems in Declining Metropolitan Areas." Pp. 187–96 in George Sternlieb and James W. Hughes (eds.), *Post-Industrial America: Metropolitan Decline and Interregional Job Shifts.* New Brunswick, N.J.: Rutgers University Center for Urban Policy Research.

THOMSON, RANDALL J., and MATTHEW T. ZINGRAFF. 1981. "Detecting Sentencing Disparity: Some Problems and Evidence." *American Journal of Sociology* 86:869–80.

THOMSON, RANDALL J., and MATTHEW T. ZINGRAFF. 1978. "A Longitudinal Analysis of Crime Sentencing Patterns." Paper presented at the annual meeting of the Society for the Study of Social Problems, San Francisco.

THORNBERRY, TERENCE P. 1974. "Race, Socioeconomic Status, and Sentencing in the Juvenile Justice System." *Journal of Criminal Law and Criminology* 64:90–98.

THORNDIKE, ROBERT C. 1969. "Review of Pygmalion in the Classroom." *Teachers College Record* 70:805–7.

THORNTON, ARLAND, and DEBORAH FREEDMAN. 1984. "The Changing American Family." *Population Bulletin* 38, 4.

THORNTON, RUSSELL. 1987. *American Indian Holocaust and Survival.* Norman: University of Oklahoma Press.

TIENDA, MARTA, KATHARINE M. DONATO, and HECTOR CORDERO-GUZMAN. 1992. "Schooling, Color, and the Labor Force Activity of Women." *Social Forces* 71:365–95.

TILLY, CHARLES. 1974. "The Chaos of the Living City." Pp. 86–108 in Charles Tilly (ed.), *An Urban World.* Boston: Little, Brown.

TOURNEY, GARFIELD, ANTHONY PETRILLI, and LON M. HATFIELD. 1975. "Hormonal Relationships in Homosexual Men." *American Journal of Psychiatry* 132:288–90.

TOWNSEND, LINDA, and ALEXIS J. WALKER. 1990. "American Women Get Mad: Women's Attitudes Are Changing—Here's What You Can Expect in the 1990s." *American Demographics* (August): 26–32.

TRAVER, NANCY. 1990. "Opening Doors for the Disabled." *Time* (June 4): 54.

TRIANDIS, HARRY C. 1971. *Attitude and Attitude Change.* New York: Wiley. Princeton, N.J.: Princeton University Press.

TRIPP, LUKE. 1992. "The Political Views of Black Students During the Reagan Era." *Black Scholar* 22, 3:45–52.

TUCH, STEVEN A. 1988. "Race Differences in the Antecedents of Social Distance Attitudes." *Sociology and Social Research* 72:181–84.

TUMIN, MELVIN M. 1953. "Some Principles of Stratification: A Critical Analysis." *American Sociological Review* 18:387–93.

TURQUE, BILL. 1992. "Gays Under Fire." *Newsweek* (September 14): 34–40.

UNESCO. 1952. "Statement on the Nature of Race and Race Differences—by Physical Anthropologists and Geneticists." New York: UNESCO. (Reprinted in Ashley Montagu, 1963, *Race, Science, and Humanity,* pp. 178–83. Princeton, N.J.: D. Van Nostrand.)

UNESCO. 1950. "The UNESCO Statement by Experts on Race Problems." New York: UNESCO. (Reprinted in Ashley Montagu, 1963, *Race, Science, and Humanity,* pp. 172–78. Princeton, N.J.: D. Van Nostrand.)

U.S. BUREAU OF LABOR STATISTICS. 1986. "Current Labor Statistics." *Monthly Labor Review* 109, 9:59–60.

U.S. BUREAU OF LABOR STATISTICS. 1984. *Employment and Earnings, January.* Washington, D.C.: U.S. Government Printing Office.

U.S. BUREAU OF LABOR STATISTICS. 1979. "Current Labor Statistics: Employment Data from the Household Survey." *Monthly Labor Review* 102, 12:67–71.

U.S. BUREAU OF THE CENSUS. 1993. *Statistical Abstract of the United States, 1993.* Washington, D.C.: U.S. Government Printing Office.

U.S. BUREAU OF THE CENSUS. 1992a. *Current Population Reports, Consumer Income.* Series P-60, no. 175. Poverty in the United States, 1990. Washington, D.C.: U.S. Government Printing Office.

U.S. BUREAU OF THE CENSUS. 1992b. *1990 Census of Population.* General Population Characteristics, United States. Report no. 1990CP-1-1. Washington, D.C.: U.S. Government Printing Office.

U.S. BUREAU OF THE CENSUS. 1992c. *Statistical Abstract of the United States, 1992.* Washington, D.C.: U.S. Government Printing Office.

U.S. BUREAU OF THE CENSUS. 1992d. *Current Population Reports, Consumer Income.* Series P-60, no. 181. Poverty in the United States, 1991. Washington, D.C.: U.S. Government Printing Office.

U.S. Bureau of the Census. 1992e. *1990 Census of Population.* Summary Social, Economic, and Housing Characteristics, United States. Report no. CPH-5-1. Washington, D.C.: U.S. Government Printing Office.

U.S. Bureau of the Census. 1992f. *Current Population Reports, Population Characteristics.* Series P-20, no. 464. The Black Population in the United States, March, 1991. Washington, D.C.: U.S. Government Printing Office.

U.S. Bureau of the Census. 1992g. *Current Population Reports, Population Characteristics.* Report P-20, no. 462, Educational Attainment in the United States: March, 1991 and 1990. Washington, D.C.: U.S. Government Printing Office.

U.S. Bureau of the Census. 1991a. *1990 Census of Population.* Public Law Counts. Washington, D.C.: U.S. Bureau of the Census.

U.S. Bureau of the Census. 1991b. *Current Population Reports, Consumer Income.* Series P-60, no. 174. Money Income of Households, Families, and Persons in the United States, 1990. Washington, D.C.: U.S. Government Printing Office.

U.S. Bureau of the Census. 1990. *Statistical Abstract of the United States, 1990.* Washington, D.C.: U.S. Government Printing Office.

U.S. Bureau of the Census. 1986a. *Current Population Reports: Consumer Income.* Money Income and Poverty Status of Families and Persons in the United States: 1985. Advance data from the March 1986 Current Population Survey. Series P-60, no. 154. Washington, D.C.: U.S. Government Printing Office.

U.S. Bureau of the Census. 1986b. *Statistical Abstract of the United States, 1986 Edition.* Washington, D.C.: U.S. Government Printing Office.

U.S. Bureau of the Census. 1986c. United States Department of Commerce, Bureau of the Census News Release, July 18.

U.S. Bureau of the Census. 1985a. *Current Population Reports: Consumer Income.* Money Income and Poverty Status of Persons and Families in the United States: 1984. Advance Data from the March, 1985 Current Population Survey. Series P-60, no. 149. Washington, D.C.: U.S. Government Printing Office.

U.S. Bureau of the Census. 1985b. *Statistical Abstract of the United States, 1985 Edition.* Washington, D.C.: U.S. Government Printing Office.

U.S. Bureau of the Census. 1984a. *1980 Census of Population.* Characteristics of the Population, Detailed Population Characteristics. Report no. PC80-1-D1-A. Washington, D.C.: U.S. Government Printing Office.

U.S. Bureau of the Census. 1984b. *1980 Census of Housing.* Housing Characteristics, U.S. Summary. Report no. HC80-2-1. Washington, D.C.: U.S. Government Printing Office.

U.S. Bureau of the Census. 1983a. *1980 Census of Population.* Characteristics of the Population, General Social and Economic Characteristics, United States Summary. Report no. PC80-1-C1. Washington, D.C.: U.S. Government Printing Office.

U.S. Bureau of the Census. 1983b. *1980 Census of Population.* Characteristics of the Population, General Population Characteristics, United States Summary. Report no. PC80-1-B1. Washington, D.C.: U.S. Government Printing Office.

U.S. Bureau of the Census. 1983c. *1980 Census of Population.* Ancestry of the Population by State: 1980. Supplementary Report no. PC80-S1-10. Washington, D.C.: U.S. Government Printing Office.

U.S. Bureau of the Census. 1983d. *Current Population Reports, Population Characteristics.* School Enrollment: Social and Economic Characteristics of Students (Advance Report). Washington, D.C.: U.S. Government Printing Office.

U.S. Bureau of the Census. 1981. *1980 Census of Population.* Age, Sex, Race, and Spanish Origin of the Population by Regions, Divisions, and States: 1980. Report no. PC80-51-1. Washington, D.C.: U.S. Government Printing Office.

U.S. Bureau of the Census. 1980a. *Current Population Reports: Consumer Income.* "Money Income of Families and Persons in the United States: 1978." Series P-60, no. 123. Washington, D.C.: U.S. Government Printing Office.

U.S. Bureau of the Census. 1980b. *Current Population Reports: Population Estimates and Projections.* "Estimates of the Population of the United States by Age, Sex, and Race: 1976 to 1978." Washington, D.C.: U.S. Government Printing Office.

U.S. Bureau of the Census. 1979a. *The Social and Economic Status of the Black Population in the United States: An Historical View, 1970–1978.* Current Population Reports, Special Studies. Series P-23, no. 80. Washington, D.C.: U.S. Government Printing Office.

U.S. Bureau of the Census. 1979b. *Current Population Reports: Population Characteristics.* "Persons of Spanish Origin in the United States: March, 1978." Series P-20, no. 339. Washington, D.C.: U.S. Government Printing Office.

U.S. Bureau of the Census. 1979c. *Current Population Reports: Consumer Income.* "Money Income in 1977 of Families and Persons in the United States." Series P-60, no. 118. Washington, D.C.: U.S. Government Printing Office.

U.S. Bureau of the Census. 1979d. *Current Population Reports: Consumer Income.* "Characteristics of the Population Below the Poverty Level: 1977." Series P-60, no. 119. Washington, D.C.: U.S. Government Printing Office.

U.S. Bureau of the Census. 1977. *Current Population Reports: Population Characteristics.* "Educational Attainment in the United States: March, 1977 and 1976." Washington, D.C.: U.S. Government Printing Office.

U.S. Bureau of the Census. 1973a. *1970 Census of Population.* Characteristics of the Population, vol. 1, United States Summary. Washington, D.C.: U.S. Government Printing Office.

U.S. Bureau of the Census. 1973b. *Current Population Reports: Population Characteristics.* Characteristics of the Population by Ethnic Origin: March, 1972 and 1971. Series P-20, no. 249. Washington, D.C.: U.S. Government Printing Office.

U.S. BUREAU OF THE CENSUS. 1972a. *1970 Census of Population*. General Characteristics: United States Summary. PC(1)-B1. Washington, D.C.: U.S. Government Printing Office.

U.S. BUREAU OF THE CENSUS. 1972b. *1970 Census of Population and Housing*. Census Tracts: Final Report PHC(1)-181: St. Louis, Missouri-Illinois SMSA. Washington, D.C.: U.S. Government Printing Office.

U.S. BUREAU OF THE CENSUS. 1971. *1970 Census of Population*. Number of Inhabitants: United States Summary. PC(1)-A1. Washington, D.C.: U.S. Government Printing Office.

U.S. COMMISSION ON CIVIL RIGHTS. 1979. *Desegregation of the Nation's Public Schools: A Status Report*. Washington, D.C.: U.S. Government Printing Office.

U.S. COMMISSION ON CIVIL RIGHTS. 1978. *Social Indicators of Equality for Minorities and Women*. Washington, D.C.: U.S. Government Printing Office.

U.S. COMMISSION ON CIVIL RIGHTS. 1976. *Fulfilling the Letter and Spirit of the Law: Desegregation of the Nation's Schools*. Washington, D.C.: U.S. Government Printing Office.

U.S. COMMISSION ON CIVIL RIGHTS. 1975. *The Voting Rights Act: Ten Years Later*. Washington, D.C.: U.S. Government Printing Office.

U.S. COMMISSION ON CIVIL RIGHTS. 1974. *Toward Quality Education for Mexican Americans*. Mexican American Study Report no. 4. Washington, D.C.: U.S. Government Printing Office.

U.S. COMMISSION ON CIVIL RIGHTS. 1970a. *Mexican Americans and the Administration of Justice in the Southwest*. Washington, D.C.: U.S. Government Printing Office.

U.S. COMMISSION ON CIVIL RIGHTS. 1970b. *Racism in America and How to Combat It*. Clearinghouse Publication, Urban Series no. 1. Washington, D.C.: U.S. Government Printing Office.

U.S. COMMISSION ON CIVIL RIGHTS. 1968. *Political Participation*. Washington, D.C.: U.S. Government Printing Office.

U.S. COMMISSION ON CIVIL RIGHTS. 1965. *Law Enforcement: A Report on Equal Protection in the South*. Washington, D.C.: U.S. Government Printing Office.

U.S. DEPARTMENT OF COMMERCE. 1977. *Social Indicators 1976*. Washington, D.C.: U.S. Government Printing Office.

U.S. DEPARTMENT OF EDUCATION. 1987. *Schools That Work: Educating Disadvantaged Children*. Washington, D.C.: U.S. Government Printing Office.

U.S. DEPARTMENT OF HEALTH, EDUCATION, AND WELFARE. 1979. *Minorities and Women in the Health Fields*. Publication no. (HRA) 79-22. Washington, D.C.: U.S. Government Printing Office.

U.S. DEPARTMENT OF HOUSING AND URBAN DEVELOPMENT. 1991. *1989 Housing Discrimination Study*. Washington: U.S. Government Printing Office.

U.S. DEPARTMENT OF HOUSING AND URBAN DEVELOPMENT. 1979. *Measuring Racial Discrimination in American Housing Markets: The Housing Market Practices Survey*. Washington, D.C.: U.S. Government Printing Office.

U.S. DEPARTMENT OF JUSTICE. 1990. *Sourcebook of Criminal Justice Statistics, 1990*. Washington, D.C.: U.S. Government Printing Office.

U.S. DEPARTMENT OF LABOR. 1987. *Workforce 2000: Work and Workers for the 21st Century*. Washington, D.C.: U.S. Government Printing Office.

U.S. DEPARTMENT OF LABOR. 1965. *The Negro Family: The Case for National Action* (The Moynihan Report). Washington, D.C.: U.S. Government Printing Office.

U.S. NATIONAL ADVISORY COMMISSION ON CIVIL DISORDERS. 1968. *Report of the National Advisory Commission on Civil Disorders*. New York: New York Times Company, Bantam Books.

U.S. NATIONAL CENTER FOR HEALTH STATISTICS. 1979. Current Estimates from the Health Interview Survey: U.S., 1978. *Data from the National Health Survey*. Series 10, no. 130. Washington, D.C.: U.S. Government Printing Office.

U.S. SENATE SELECT COMMITTEE. 1972. *Report: Toward Equal Educational Opportunity* Washington, D.C.: U.S. Government Printing Office.

USA Today. 1991. "By the Numbers, Tracking Segregation in 219 Metro Areas." *USA Today*, November 11, p. 3a.

UNNEVER, JAMES D., CHARLES E. FRAZIER, and JOHN C. HENRETTA. 1980. "Race Differences in Criminal Sentencing." *Sociological Quarterly* 21:197–205.

UNNEVER, JAMES D., and LARRY A. HEMBROFF. 1988. "The Prediction of Racial/Ethnic Sentencing Disparities: An Expectation States Approach." *Journal of Research in Crime and Delinquency* 25:53–82.

USEEM, ELIZABETH L. 1992. "Middle Schools and Math Groups: Parents' Involvement in Children's Placement." *Sociology of Education* 65:263–79.

USEEM, ELIZABETH L. 1991. "Tracking Students Out of Mathematics." *Education Digest* (May): 54–58.

VALENTINE, CHARLES A. 1968. *Culture and Poverty: Critique and Counter-Proposals*. Chicago: University of Chicago Press.

VALENZUELA DE LA GARZA, JESUS, and MARCELLO MEDINA. 1985. "Academic Achievement as Influenced by Bilingual Instruction for Spanish-Dominant Mexican-American Children." *Hispanic Journal of Behavior Science* 7:247–59.

VAN DEN BERGHE, PIERRE L. 1978. *Race and Racism: A Comparative Perspective*, 2d ed. New York: Wiley.

VAN DEN BERGHE, PIERRE L. 1965. *South Africa: A Study in Conflict*. Middletown, Conn.: Wesleyan University Press.

VAN DEN BERGHE, PIERRE L. 1958. "The Dynamics of Racial Prejudice: An Ideal-Type Dichotomy." *Social Forces* 37:138–41.

VAN DER HORST, SHEILA T. 1967. "The Effects of Industrialisation on Race Relations in South Africa." Pp. 97–140 in Guy Hunter (ed.), *Industrialisation and*

Race Relations: A Symposium. London: Oxford University Press.

VAN VALEY, THOMAS L., WADE CLARK ROOF, and JEROME E. WILCOX. 1977. "Trends in Residential Segregation: 1960–1970." *American Journal of Sociology* 82:826–44.

VERNON, P. E. 1969. *Intelligence and Cultural Environment.* London: Methuen.

VIDAL, GORE. 1992. "Get Gay and Save the Planet." *New Statesman and Society* 5, 215:12–13.

VINING, DANIEL R. 1979. "Net Migration by Air: A Lower-Bound on Total Net Migration into the United States." Working papers in Regional Science and Transportation, no. 15. Philadelphia: University of Pennsylvania.

VOSE, CLEMENT E. 1959. *Caucasians Only.* Berkeley: University of California Press.

WADE, MASON. 1968. *The French Canadians, 1760–1967.* Toronto: Macmillan.

WAITE, LINDA J., and LEE A. LILLARD. 1991. "Children and Marital Disruption." *American Journal of Sociology* 96:930–53.

WAITE, LINDA J. 1981. "U.S. Women at Work." *Population Bulletin* 36, 2.

WALDMAN, B. 1977. "Economic and Racial Disadvantage as Reflected in Traditional Medical School Selection Factors: A Study of 1976 Applicants to U.S. Medical Schools." Study reported in *Amicus* brief, U.S. Supreme Court, *Bakke,* Association of American Medical Colleges.

WALKER, SAMUEL. 1985. "Racial Minority and Female Employment in Policing: The Implications of 'Glacial' Change." *Crime and Delinquency* 31:555–72.

WALLECHINSKY, DAVID, and IRVING WALLACE. 1975. *The People's Almanac.* Garden City, N.Y.: Doubleday.

WALLERSTEIN, JUDITH S., and SANDRA BLAKESLEE. 1989. *Second Chances: Men, Women, and Children a Decade After Divorce.* New York: Ticknor and Fields.

WALLERSTEIN, JUDITH, and JOAN B. KELLY. 1980. "California's Children of Divorce." *Psychology Today* 13, 8: 67–76.

WALTON, HANES, JR. 1985. *Invisible Politics: Black Political Behavior.* Albany: State University of New York Press.

WARNER, W. LLOYD, and LEO SROLE. 1945. *The Social Systems of American Ethnic Groups.* New Haven, Conn.: Yale University Press.

WARREN, ROBERT, and JEFFREY S. PASSEL. 1987. "A Count of the Uncountable: Estimates of the Undocumented Aliens Counted in the 1980 U.S. Census." *Demography* 24, 3: 375.

WATSON, WARREN, KAMALESH KUMAR, and LARRY MICHEALSEN. 1993. "Cultural Diversity's Impact on Interaction Process and Performance: Comparing Homogeneous and Diverse Task Groups." *Academy of Management Journal* 36:590–602.

WEBER, C. U., P. W. FOSTER, and D. P. WEIKART. 1978. "An Economic Analysis of the Ypsilanti Perry Preschool Project." *Monographs of High/Scope Educational Research Foundation* 5.

WEBER, G. 1971. *Inner City Children Can Be Taught to Read: Four Successful Schools.* Washington, D.C.: Center for Basic Education.

WEBER, MAX. 1968 [1922]. *Economy and Society: An Outline of Interpretive Sociology.* Guenther Roth and Claus Wittich (eds.), Ephriam Fischoff et al. (trs.). New York: Bedminster Press.

WEEKS, JOHN R. 1992. *Population: An Introduction to Concepts and Issues,* 5th ed. Belmont, Calif.: Wadsworth.

WEINBERG, MARTIN S., and COLIN J. WILLIAMS. 1974. *Male Homosexuals: Their Problems and Adaptations.* New York: Oxford University Press.

WEISS, RANDALL. 1968. "The Effects of Scholastic Achievement on the Earnings of Blacks and Whites." Honors thesis, Harvard University.

WEITZMAN, LENORE. 1985. *The Divorce Revolution: The Unexpected Social and Economic Consequences for Women and Children in America.* New York: Free Press.

WELCH, FINIS. 1967. "Labor Market Discrimination in the Rural South." *Journal of Political Economy* 75:225–40.

WELCH, SUSAN, JOHN GRUHL, and CASSIA SPOHN. 1984. "Dismissal, Conviction, and Incarceration of Hispanic Defendants: A Comparison with Anglos and Blacks." *Social Science Quarterly* 65:257–64.

WERNER, NORMA E., and IDELLA M. EVANS. 1968. "Perceptions of Prejudice in Mexican-American Pre-School Children." *Perceptual and Motor Skills* 27:1039–46.

WESLEY, CHARLES H. 1927. *Negro Labor in the United States: 1850–1925.* New York: Vanguard.

WEST, CORNELL. 1993. *Race Matters.* Boston: Beacon Press.

WHEELER, D. L. 1991. "Studies Linking Homosexuality to Genes Draw Criticism from Researchers." *Chronicle of Higher Education* (February 5): A7–A9.

WHITAKER, CHARLES. 1991. "Do Black Males Need Special Schools?" *Ebony* 23, 1:17–22.

WHITE, SHELDON. 1970. "The National Impact of Head Start." *Disadvantaged Child* 3:163–84.

WILDER, D.A., and J. E. THOMPSON. 1980. "Intergroup Contact with Independent Manipulations of Ingroup and Out-group Interaction." *Journal of Personality and Social Psychology* 38:764–72.

WILENSKY, HAROLD L., and HUGH EDWARDS. 1959. "The Skidder: Ideological Adjustments of Downward Mobile Workers." *American Sociological Review* (April): 215–31.

WILHELM, SIDNEY M. 1980. "Can Marxism Explain America's Racism?" *Social Problems* 28:98–112.

WILLIAMS, CHARLES. 1992. "The Relationship Between the Affective and Conative Dimensions of Prejudice." *College Student Journal* 26, 1:50–54.

WILLIAMS, ROBIN. 1977. "Competing Models of Multiethnic and Multiracial Societies: An Appraisal of Possibilities and Performances." Paper presented at the plenary session of the American Sociological Association, 72nd Annual Meeting, Chicago.

WILLIAMS, ROBIN. 1975. "Race and Ethnic Relations." Pp. 125–64, in Alex Inkeles, James Coleman, and Niel Smelser (eds.), *Annual Review of Sociology.* Palo Alto, Calif.: Annual Reviews, Inc.

WILLIE, CHARLES VERT. 1979. *The Caste and Class Controversy.* Bayside, New York: General Hall.

WILLIG, ANN. 1985. "A Meta-Analysis of Selected Studies on the Effectiveness of Bilingual Education." *Review of Educational Research* 55:269–317.

WILLMS, J. DOUGLAS. 1987. "Patterns of Academic Achievement in Public and Private Schools: Implications for Public Policy and Future Research." Pp. 113–34 in Edward H. Haertel, Thomas James, and Henry M. Levin (eds.), *Comparing Public and Private Schools,* vol. 2, *School Achievement.* New York: Falmer.

WILNER, DANIEL M., ROSABELLE P. WALKLEY, and STUART W. COOK. 1955. *Human Relations in Interracial Housing.* Minneapolis: University of Minnesota Press.

WILSON, FRANKLIN D. 1985. "The Impact of School Desegregation Programs on White Public Enrollment, 1968–1976." *Sociology of Education* 58:137–53.

WILSON, FRANKLIN D., and KARL E. TAEUBER. 1978. "Residential and School Segregation: Some Tests of Their Association." Pp. 51–78 in F. D. Bean and W. Parker Frisbie (eds.), *The Demography of Racial and Ethnic Groups.* New York: Academic Press.

WILSON, JAMES Q. 1978. *Varieties of Police Behavior: The Management of Law and Order in Eight Communities.* Cambridge, Mass.: Harvard University Press.

WILSON, WILLIAM JULIUS. Forthcoming. *A Broader View.* Chicago: University of Chicago Press.

WILSON, WILLIAM JULIUS. 1991. "Public Policy Research and *The Truly Disadvantaged.*" Pp. 460–81 in Christopher Jencks and Paul E. Peterson (eds.), *The Urban Underclass.* Washington, D.C.: The Brookings Institution.

WILSON, WILLIAM JULIUS. 1987. *The Truly Disadvantaged: The Inner City, the Underclass, and Public Policy.* Chicago: University of Chicago Press.

WILSON, WILLIAM JULIUS. 1981. "The Black Community in the 1980s: Questions of Race, Class, and Public Policy." *The Annals of the American Academy of Political and Social Science* 454:26–41.

WILSON, WILLIAM JULIUS. 1980. "A Response to Marrett and Pettigrew." *Contemporary Sociology* 6:21–24.

WILSON, WILLIAM JULIUS. 1979. "The Declining Significance of Race: Revisited But Not Revised." Chapter 14 in Charles Vert Willie (ed.), *Caste and Class Controversy.* Bayside, New York: General Hall (Reprinted from *Society* [July/August, 1978].)

WILSON, WILLIAM JULIUS. 1978. *The Declining Significance of Race: Blacks and Changing American Institutions.* Chicago: University of Chicago Press.

WILSON, WILLIAM J. 1973. *Power, Racism and Privilege.* New York: Free Press.

WINSBERG, MORTON D. 1983. "Changing Distribution of the Black Population: Florida Cities, 1970–1980." *Urban Affairs Quarterly* 18:361–70.

WITT, L. ALLEN. 1989. "Authoritarianism, Knowledge of AIDS, and Affect Toward Persons with AIDS: Implications for Health Education." *Journal of Applied Psychology* 19:599–607.

WOOD, PETER B., and BARRETT A. LEE. 1991. "Is Neighborhood Racial Succession Inevitable? Forty Years of Evidence." *Urban Affairs Quarterly* 26:610–20.

WOOD, BARBARA SUDENE, and JULIA CURRY. 1969. "Everyday Talk and School Talk of the City Black Child." *Speech Teacher* 18:282–96.

WOOD, W., and A. M. EAGLY. 1981. "Stages in the Analysis of Persuasive Messages: The Role of Causal Attribution and Message Comprehension." *Journal of Personality and Social Psychology* 40:246–59.

WOODWARD, C. VAN. 1971. *American Counterpoint: Slavery and Racism in the North-South Dialogue.* Boston: Little, Brown.

WOODWARD, C. VAN. 1966. *The Strange Career of Jim Crow,* 2d rev. ed. New York: Oxford University Press.

WOOLBRIGHT, LOUIE ALBERT. 1987. "The New Segregation: Hispanics in the West and Sunbelt." In Gary A. Tobin (ed.), *Divided Neighborhoods.* Newbury Park, Calif.: Sage Publications.

WORTMAN, PAUL M., and FRED B. BRYANT. 1985. "School Desegregation and Black Achievement: An Integrative Review." *Sociological Methods and Research* 13:289–324.

WRIGHT, J. SKELLY. 1969. "The Courts Have Failed the Poor." *New York Times Magazine* (March 9).

WU, CHENGHUAN, and DAVID R. SHAFFER. 1987. "Susceptibility to Persuasive Appeals as a Function of Source Credibility and Prior Experience with the Attitude Object." *Journal of Personality and Social Psychology* 52:677–88.

YANKELOVICH, SKELLY, and WHITE. 1984. *Spanish USA 1984.* New York: Yankelovich, Skelly, and White, Inc.

YETMAN, NORMAN R. 1985. *Majority and Minority: The Dynamics of Race and Ethnicity in American Life,* 4th ed. Boston: Allyn & Bacon.

YINGER, J. MILTON, and GEORGE EATON SIMPSON. 1974. "Techniques for Reducing Prejudice: Changing the Prejudiced Person." Pp. 96–144 in Peter Watson (ed.), *Psychology and Race.* Chicago: Aldine.

ZALD, MAYER N., and JOHN D. MCCARTHY. 1975. "Organizational Intellectuals and the Criticism of Society." *Social Service Research* 49:344–62.

ZHANG, CUI-XIA, and JOHN E. FARLEY. Forthcoming. "Gender and the Distribution of Household Work: A Comparison of Self-reports by Female College Faculty in the United States and China." *Journal of Comparative Family Studies.*

ZIGLER, EDWARD, E. F. ABELSON, and V. SEITZ. 1973. "Motivational Factors in the Performance of Economically Disadvantaged Children on the Peabody Picture Vocabulary Test." *Child Development* 44:294–303.

ZIGLER, EDWARD, and SUSAN MUENCHOW. 1992. *Head Start: The Inside Story of America's Most Successful Educational Experiment.* New York: Basic.

ZIMRING, FRANKLIN E., JOEL EIGEN, and SHIELA O'MALLEY. 1976. "Punishing Homocide in Philadelphia: Perspectives on the Death Penalty." *University of Chicago Law Review* 43:227–52.

ZINN, MAXINE BACA, LYNN WEBER CANNON, ELIZABETH HIGGENBOTHAM, and BONNIE THORNTON DILL. 1986. "The Costs of Exclusionary Practices in Women's Studies." *Signs* 11:290–303.

Index

Abalos, David T., 59
ABC News, 53, 145, 254, 320, 429
Abelson, E. F., 364
Ability grouping, 355–56
Abler, Thomas S., 108
Abrams, Bob, 414
Abrams, Charles, 303
Abramson, Harold J., 189, 190
Acceptance, 151
Achieved status, 87
Acock, Alan C., 81
Acuna, Rodolfo, 183, 185, 331
Adaptive responses, 150–53
Adler, Jerry, 310
Adorno, Theodor W., 16–22, 26, 31
Affective prejudice, 14, 30, 146
Affirmative action, 438–53
African Americans
    Afrocentrism movement of, 182
    age distribution of, 230
    Black English spoken by, 356–59
    black nationalism, change in support for, 437
    Black Power movement of, 155–56,
        172–79, 185, 188, 436
    changing attitudes toward assimilation, 172–84
    civil rights movement of, 149,
        154–56, 160, 162, 169–70
    class stratification within population of, 145–46
    college tuition and, 11
    as colonized minorities, 122–23
    corporate executive positions and, 253
    corporate ownership and, 252–53
    criminal activities of, 319–20, 323,
        394–96
    criminal justice system and,
        318–29, 396
    criticisms of affirmative action by, 441
    cultural-immersion model and,
        380–81
    culture of poverty theory and,
        75–85
    drug use by, 152, 396
    educational attainment of, 241,
        246–49, 261
    family disruption and juvenile crime and, 81
    family structure of, 76–82
    geographic distribution of, 230,
        233
    governmental policies of discrimination against, 299–304
    hate-group activity and hate crime against, 416–27
    health care and, 285–95
    health status of, 250, 283–84
    housing segregation and, 266–76
    income status of, 79, 240–42, 259,
        445, 460
    initial contact with whites, 95–96,
        122–23
    IQ test bias and, 362–63, 365–66
    job decentralization and, 262–66,
        393–94

    job discrimination against, 126–27,
        136–37, 155, 254–56, 260
    male, problems of particular concern to, 393–98
    measurement of prejudice against,
        17–18
    median income by type of family,
        79
    medical students, 444
    middle class, 145, 278, 322, 342,
        393–94, 445, 460–61, 463
    mortality status of, 249–50, 292
    occupational status of, 240
    origins of inequality of, 95–106
    physicians, 288
    police brutality and, 330–31,
        333–34
    police officers, 322
    police protection, dissatisfaction with, 329
    police rating by, 322
    politicians, 181, 241, 246, 313–14
    population size of, 3, 229–30
    poverty of, 243–44, 278, 459–62
    prejudices of, 41–42
    rigid competitive race relations with whites, 125–39
    school desegregation and, 38–40,
        47, 155, 164–65, 371–78
    school segregation and, 337–39
    seeking of assimilation by, 170
    self-image of children, 351, 352
    slavery, 89, 95–106, 111–12, 299
    social-distance scores for, 50, 52
    stereotyping of, 15, 48, 349, 396
    student achievement, variations in,
        344–46
    teachers, 35, 367
    teenage pregnancy among, 82–84
    tension between Asian Americans and, 225
    trends in prejudice against, 50
    unemployment rate of, 244,
        261–63, 305, 392, 459
    urban population, 147, 160, 230,
        262–68, 280
    in U.S. Navy, 411
    violence against, 1–2, 126, 138–39,
        155, 175, 273, 284, 331, 333–34
    violence by, 156, 174–80
    voting power of, 312–13
    war casualties, 310
    white attitudes and inequality of,
        52–54
    white fears about, 318–19, 421–23
    women, 391–93
African American-white relations
    evolving patterns of, 125–39
    intergroup contact, 39–40
    symbolic racism, 51
African National Congress (ANC)
    party, 193
Afrikaners, 193, 213
Afrocentric curriculum, 381
Afrocentrism, 182
Age distribution
    African American, 230
    Asian American, 236

    Hispanic American, 232
    Native American, 234
Ageton, Suzanne S., 323
Aggression, displaced, 151–52
Ahmad, Ishmael Lateff, 145, 430
AIDS, 404
Aisha Schule, 381
Ajzen, I., 45
Alba, Richard, 171, 276, 277
Albonetti, Celesta A., 325
Alcohol use and abuse, 152
Alexander, Edward, 425
Alexander, Karl L., 354–56
Algebra Project, 382
Ali, Nadia, 416
*Allan Bakke v. Regents of the University of
    California* (1978), 288, 444,
    447–49
Allen, Walter R., 179, 249
Allport, Gordon W., 14, 23–25, 27, 28,
    31, 43, 141, 426
Alvarez, Rodolfo, 113, 114, 170
Alwin, Duane F., 356
Amalgamation, 166, 217, 219, 434
American Bar Foundation, 430
American Civil Liberties Union
    (ACLU), 33, 175, 381, 425
American Council on Education, 380
American Indian Movement (AIM),
    157–58
American Indians (*see* Native Americans)
American Legion, 33
American Medical Association (AMA),
    294
Americans with Disabilities Act (ADA)
    of 1992, 406–7
Anderson, Elijah, 82, 151, 256, 396
Anderson, Odin W., 289
Andreoni, Helen, 36
Anglo-conformity, 168–71
Annexation, 94
Antebellum North, race relations in,
    126
Anti-Catholicism, 139
Anti-intraception, 19, 43–44
Antipoverty programs, 305–6
Anti-Semitism, 17, 18, 24, 31, 139
Apartheid, 7, 193–94, 213
Arab American Anti-Discrimination
    League, 224, 416
Arab Americans, 224
Arab/Israel conflict, 204–6, 223, 438
Arafat, Yasir, 206
Arciniega, Tomas, 355
Armor, David J., 337, 339, 342, 372, 377
Armstrong, Liz Schevtchuk, 355
Arnold, David, 224
Arnold, William R., 325, 326
Arrest decision, 320–23
Arrow, Kenneth J., 254
Asch, Solomon E., 25
Ashley Montagu, M. F., 10
Ashmore, Richard D., 36, 38, 43
Asian Americans
    age distribution of, 236
    educational attainment of, 247–49

geographic distribution of, 233, 235–36
housing segregation and, 277
initial contact with whites, 123–24
population size of, 3, 235
poverty rate of, 243
rigid competitive race relations with whites, 139–40
self-image of children, 351
stereotyping of, 15
student achievement, variations in, 345, 346
tension between African Americans and, 225
violence against, 139–40
Asian Indian Americans, 235
Aspira, 186
Assertiveness, increase in, 149
Assimilation, 165–90
Anglo-conformity and, 168–71
bilingual education and, 360
case against, 434–35
case for, 434
changing attitudes toward, 172–90
concept of, 165
conflict perspective and, 71, 72, 119–20
cultural, 165, 168–71, 190
cultural and demographic characteristics and, 218–20
education and, 368–78
extent in American society, 168–72
as goal of social movements, 153
order (functionalist) perspective and, 68
seeking of, 152–53, 169, 170
structural, 165–66, 171–73, 190
Association of American Medical Colleges, 444
Atlanta, Georgia, 280, 322
Attitudes
toward assimilation and pluralism, changing, 172–89
behavior and, 46–47
changes in kind and degree of prejudice, 146–47
intergroup inequality and, 51–55
toward school desegregation, change in, 164–65
student learning and, 344–47
Austrian Americans, 238, 239
Authoritarian aggression, 19
Authoritarian personality, 18–21, 26, 44
Authoritarian Personality, The (Adorno et al.), 16
Authoritarian submission, 19
Autobiography of Malcolm X (Haley, ed.), 36
Avicolli, Tommi, 403
Avoidance, 152
Aztec Indians, 219

Babbie, Earl, 22
Bachman, Gerald G., 351
Bagley, Christopher, 28
Bahr, Howard M., 126, 157, 304, 325, 349, 361
Bail, 324–25
Baker, Keith, 360
Bakke, Allan, 448–49
Balbus, Isaac D., 323
Baldridge, J. Victor, 69
Bales, Robert F., 388
Banac, Ivo, 222
Bandura, Albert, 24
Banfield, Edward C., 369
Bangladesh, 214
Banks, James A., 350, 379
Banton, Michael, 327
Barabba, Vincent P., 262

Baran, Paul A., 256
Baratz, Joan C., 357, 359, 370
Baratz, Steven S., 357, 359, 370
Barlow, Hugh D., 317, 324, 330
Barrera, Mario, 123
Barringer, Felicity, 400
Barrit, Denis F., 195n
Barth, Gunther, 124, 139
Bartlet, Donald C., 420
Bastide, Roger, 212, 219
Batts, V., 51, 311
Baughman, E. E., 351
Baumeister, Roy F., 33
Bayley, David H., 323, 329, 330
Beady, Charles, 373
Bean, Frank D., 457
Bear Flag Revolt of 1846, 115
Beck, E. M., 260
Becker, Gary S., 253, 257
Beer, William R., 29
Beez, W. V., 353
Behavior, attitudes and, 46–47
Bell, Alan P., 380, 400
Belleville News-Democrat, 416
Bem, Daryl J., 47
Bendick, 254
Bennett, Christine, 36
Bennett, Edward, 360
Benokraitis, Nijole V., 388
Berg, Barbara J., 388
Berg, Ivar, 261, 341
Berger, Brigitte, 362
Berlin, Gordon, 394
Berrueta-Clement, J. R., 370
Berry, Brewton, 208, 209, 218
Besherov, Douglas J., 371
Beswick, Richard, 36
Bianchi, Suzanne, 76, 243, 270, 271, 273
Bias, cultural, 348–68
Bielby, Denise D., 387
Bielby, William T., 387
Bilingual education, 169, 184, 185, 223, 359–61
Bills, David B., 37, 443
Billson, Janet Mancini, 398
Binstock, Jeanne, 340
Birmingham, Alabama, 155
Birns, B., 364
Birthrates
African American, 82, 410
Hispanic American, 231
Jewish American, 236
Bishop, J., 46
Black, Donald J., 321, 323
Black Codes, 126–27
Black English, 356–59
Black Muslim movement, 173–75, 178, 183
Black nationalism, 437
Black Panthers, 174–75
Black Power movement, 155–56, 172–79, 185, 188, 436
Blacks (see African Americans)
Blake, R., 25
Blakeslee, Sandra, 81
"Blaming the victim," 369
Blauner, Robert, 72, 94, 121–23, 186, 190, 436
Bloch, Herman D., 126
Blockbusting, 275–76
Blumenthal, David, 285, 286
Blumer, Herbert, 148, 211, 212, 255
Bobo, Lawrence, 49, 277
Bogardus, Emory, 49, 50
Bolvin, Michael J., 28
Bonacich, Edna, 72, 137, 255, 256
Boocock, Sarane Spence, 353, 355
Boskin, Joseph, 97, 142
Bosnians, 168, 199–200, 202–4, 221–23

Boswell, John, 401
Bourgeois, Phillippe, 394
Bower, Bruce, 401
Bowker, Lee H., 349
Bowles, Samuel, 340, 341, 346, 348, 364, 369, 370, 461
Bradbury, Katherine L., 280
Braddock, Jomills Henry, 372
Braly, Kenneth, 15
Brazil, 212, 218–19
Brazziel, William F., 366
Bredekamp, Sue, 356, 363, 366
Brewer, Marilyn, 27, 41
Briar, Scott, 321
Brimmer, Andrew F., 3
Brischetto, Robert, 355
British Protestant culture, 169
Britton, Gwyneth E., 349, 350
Brody, David, 255
Brooke, Edward, 313
Brookover, Wilbur, 382
Brophy, J. E., 353–56
Brown, Bernard, 349, 370
Brown, Kathryn P., 351
Brown, Lawrence L., 342, 343
Brown, Roger, 23, 27
Brown Berets, 184
Brown v. Board of Education of Topeka (1954), 144, 306, 336
Bruce, Blanche K., 127
Bruck, Lilly, 405, 406
Bryant, Fred B., 372
Buffalo, New York, 280
Bugbee, George, 289
Bumpass, Larry, 77, 81
Bunzel, John H., 181, 182
Burakumin, 124–25
Burdette, Mary Ellen, 404
Bureau of Justice Statistics, 324
Burma, 214
Burnell, Barbara S., 304
Burnell, James D., 304
Bush, George, 312, 318, 421–22, 447, 452
Busing, desegregation through, 371–78
Buthelezi, Mangosutthu, 217
Butler, Edgar W., 326
Butterfield, Fox, 224
Byrnes, Deborah, 42

Caballeros de Labor, 154
Cacioppo, John T., 33
California
Asian American population of, 236
budget crisis in, 307
educational discrimination in 1860, 304
English as only official language of, 169, 223
environmental racism in, 283
illegal immigrants in, 210
literacy test in, 301
opposition to immigrants in, 225
origins of ethnic stratification in, 114–17
Camarillo, Albert, 118, 119
Campbell, Angus, 176, 177
Campbell, Ben Nighthorse, 241, 313
Canada, 210, 217, 221–23, 284, 294, 438, 456
Canadian Americans, 238, 239
Cancer clusters, 283
Carlsmith, J. M., 46
Carmichael, Stokeley, 10, 156, 177
Carter, Charles F., 195n
Carter, Jimmy, 312
Carter, Thomas P., 352
Case, Charles E., 28, 29
Cass, Vivienne C., 401
Caste systems, 87, 125, 141, 193–94

Catton, William J., Jr., 68
Cayton, Horace R., 302
Center for Education and Human Development Policy, 373
Centers, Richard, 27
Chacon, Ramon D., 118
Chadwick, Bruce A., 304, 326, 349, 361
Chaiken, S., 32, 47
Change-oriented responses, 153–54
Charles, James P., 350
Chavez, Cesar, 157, 184, 186
Chavis, Benjamin, 187
Chebat, Jean Charles, 33
Chicago, Illinois
    Asian American housing segregation in, 277
    fiscal crisis in, 280, 343
    housing segregation in, 263
    loss of jobs from, 262–63
    physician shortages in, 287
    police force of, 322
    public transportation in, 309
    riot of 1919, 138
Chicanos (see Mexican Americans)
Chinese Americans, 44–45
    economic status of, 145
    geographic distribution of, 236
    initial contact with whites, 123–24
    population size of, 235
    rigid competitive race relations with whites, 139
    stereotyping of, 15, 47
    urban, 160
Christian Identity, 418
Churchill, Ward, 157, 158, 187, 188
Church of the Creator (COTC), 416, 417
Cicirelli, V. G., 370
Cisneros, Henry, 241
Cities
    fiscal crisis of, 279–82, 307
    funding of schools in, 342–43
    job shift away from, 262–66
    (See also names of cities; Urbanization; Urban population)
Ciullo, Rosemary, 42
Civil court system, 332–34
Civil Rights Act of 1964, 155, 306, 344, 447
Civil Rights Act of 1968, 306
Civil Rights Act of 1991, 262, 306, 422, 450, 452
Civil rights laws, 144, 178, 427–28
Civil rights movement, 149, 154–56, 160, 162, 169–70
Civil War, 125, 126
Claiborne, William, 307
Clark, Kenneth B., 151, 351
Clark, M. L., 351
Clark, Mamie P., 151, 351
Clark, Mark, 175
Clark, William A. V., 270, 272, 277
Clarke, Chester C., 35, 37
Classification systems, racial, 217
Class stratification, 146
Class system, 87
Cleavages, overlapping vs. crosscutting, 220–22
Clinton, Bill, 283, 284, 308, 312, 399, 436, 452
Cockerham, William C., 283, 286, 289–90, 292, 293
Code switching, 358
Coe, Rodney M., 290
Coffman, Thomas, 48
Cognitive behavior therapy, 43
Cognitive dissonance theory, 46
Cognitive prejudice, 14, 30, 47–48, 146
Cohen, 422
Cohen, D., 340

Cohen, Elizabeth G., 39, 42
Cohen, P., 358
Cohen, Shirley, 406
Cohn, Frederick, 402
Cohn, T. S., 22
Colasanto, Diane, 270, 271, 273
Coleman, James S., 344–47, 354–56, 367, 371–72, 377, 382, 383
Coleman Report, 344–48, 371–72, 374
College admissions, affirmative action and, 438–49
College campuses, debate over hate groups and, 424–27
College courses, prejudice reduction and, 35–37
College graduates, 241, 246–49, 365, 445
College teachers, 367
College tuition, 11
Collier, John, 106
Collins, Mary Evans, 37
Collins, Patricia Hill, 389, 391–93, 445, 460
Colonialism
    cross-cultural evidence on effects of, 191–208, 216
    internal, 73, 121–25, 256–57
Colonization, 94
Colonized minorities, 122–25, 436
Commonweal, 450
Communication network development, as condition for social movements, 158
Compensatory education, 369–71
Competition
    ethnic stratification origins and, 95, 109, 112, 116–17, 119, 120
    in global economy, decline in, 3
    prejudice and, 28–29
    reduction in, changing patterns of race relations and, 148
Competitive race relations (see Fluid competitive race relations; Rigid competitive race relations)
Conative prejudice, 14, 30, 49–51, 146, 254–55
Concerned Black Men, 398
Condran, Gretchan A., 278
Conflict perspective
    assimilation and, 71, 72, 119–20
    compared with order (functionalist) perspective, 63, 75–85
    concept of, 60–62
    economics of discrimination and, 255–57
    education and, 340, 348–49, 368, 378–81
    ethnic stratification and, 65–66, 69–73, 94–95, 119–20
    gender inequality and, 389–90
    pluralism and, 190
    social problems and, 64–65
    synthesis with order (functionalist) perspective, 74
    varieties of, 72–73
Conflict theory (see Conflict perspective)
Conflict vs. value consensus, 91–92
Conformity
    forced, assimilation as, 434–35
    pressure for, 24–27
Conot, Robert, 323, 331, 334
Conservatism, 18
Consortium for Longitudinal Studies, 370
Contact between racial/ethnic groups
    initial (see Initial contact between race/ethnic groups)
    prejudice reduction with, 37–42, 278

Conventionalism, 19
Conviction process, 325–26
Conyers, James E., 181
Cook, Martha, 355, 356
Cook, Stuart W., 41
Cooley, Charles Horton, 351
Cooper, Joel, 34
Cordero-Guzman, Hector, 365
Corporate crime, 317
Corporate executive positions, 253
Corporate ownership, 252–53
Correlation coefficient, 18n
Cotera, Marta, 391
Cottingham, Clement, 182
Coughlin, Ellen K., 339
Court system, 332–34
Cousins, Albert N., 214
Covington, Martin V., 33
Cox, Oliver Cromwell, 66, 72
Crain, Robert L., 372, 373
Crane, Marie, 38
Crime
    African Americans as victims of, 395
    committed by African Americans, 319–20, 323, 394–96
    hate, 1, 2, 416–27
    street, 317–20, 394, 395
    white-collar, 317
Criminal justice system, 316–29, 396
Crites, John O., 341
Croatians, 168, 199–202, 222, 223
Cronbach, L. J., 22
Croson v. City of Richmond (1989), 448, 451–52
Cross, Elsie Y., 412
Cross-cultural studies, 191–228
Crosscutting vs. overlapping cleavages, 220–22
Crouthamel, James L., 142
Croyle, Robert T., 34
Cuban Americans, 231, 232 (See also Hispanic Americans)
Cultural assimilation, 165, 168–71, 190
Cultural bias, 348–68
Cultural characteristics of majority and minority groups, 218–20
Cultural deprivation, 347–48
Cultural immersion, 380–81
Cultural lag, 388
Cultural pluralism, 166, 379–80
Cultural racism, 146–47
Culture
    of poverty, 75–85, 369
    sociological approach and, 58
Cummings, Scott, 171
Cummings, Tom, 413
Cunningham, Jean A., 23
Curanderismo, 286
Curry, Julia, 358
Cutler, Blayne, 412
Cynicism, 1927
Czech Americans, 237

Dahmer, Jeffrey, 330
Dahrendorf, Ralf, 60
D'Alessio, Stewart J., 28
Danish Americans, 238, 239
Dannefer, Dale, 325, 326
Darden, Joe T., 270
Darling, Harold W., 28
Dartmouth Review, 424
Daudistel, Howard C., 325, 326
Davine, Valerie R., 37, 443
Davis, Angela Yvonne, 391, 393
Davis, David Brion, 98
Davis, Kenneth E., 50
Davis, Kingsley, 67, 69, 340
Davis, Margaret, 354

Dawson, Michael, 182, 437
Day, Robert C., 188
Debo, Angie, 108
DeBono, Kenneth G., 33
Declining Significance of Race (Wilson), 458–60
De facto segregation, 337–38
Defense spending, 305–7
DeFleur, Melvin L., 26
Degler, Carl N., 96, 391
De jure segregation, 337
DeKanter, Adriana, 360
de Klerk, Frederick Willem, 213
Demo, David H., 81
Democratic party, 300, 315
Demographics
    cross-cultural studies of Brazil and Mexico, 218–20
    U.S. minority groups, 229–40
Dempsey, Van, 378
Dennis, W., 25
Dent, Preston L., 37
Denton, Nancy A., 79, 80, 83, 250, 267, 268, 276, 278
DePalma, Anthony, 381
Desegregation
    changing attitude of African Americans toward, 164–65, 173
    school, 38–40, 47, 155, 164–65, 304, 337, 348, 371–78
Destructiveness, 19
Detroit, Michigan
    busing in, 376
    fiscal crisis in, 280
    housing preferences in, 270–71
    housing segregation in, 263, 430
    police force of, 322
    racial steering in, 273–74
    riots in, 138, 142, 156, 176
    school funding in, 343, 344
    tax base of, 278
Deutsch, Martin, 37, 357
Didham, Cheryl K., 354
Dillard, J. L., 357
Dillehay, Ronald C., 23
Dingle, Derek T., 452
Dinkens, David, 314
Disch, Robert, 261
Discrimination, 2
    affirmative action and, 438–53
    banning of, 143–45, 210, 242
    based on foreign appearance or accent, 455
    as cause of poverty, 311
    criminal justice system and, 316–29
    against disabled, 404–7
    diversity management and, 409–16
    dual-wage system, 126, 140, 141
    economics of, 3, 147–48, 253–61, 276
    in education (*see* Education)
    federal government actions against, 306
    federal government policies of, historical, 299–305
    gender-based, 385–98
    hiring, 253–60, 341, 400, 402, 406, 438–51, 455, 462
    against homosexuals, 2, 18, 152, 153, 398–404, 410
    housing, 50, 143, 263, 265–79, 303–4, 336, 338, 429–31, 461–62
    institutional (*see* Institutional discrimination)
    job decentralization and, 265
    prejudice and, 44–55
    protest movements against, 150–65
    reverse, 440–41
    segregation (*see* Segregation)

vs. social class as cause of inequality, 458–63
    testing for, 427–31, 462
    types of, 10–11
Displaced aggression, 20–21, 23, 151–52
Dissatisfaction, as condition for social movements, 158, 160
Diversity management, 409–16
Divorce, 80–81, 386
Dixon, Sharon Pratt, 314
Dobyns, Henry F., 232
Dobzhansky, Theodosius, 5
Dodd, C. H., 205
Doll studies, 351
Domestic Policy Association, 186
Domhoff, G. William, 94, 124, 125, 297, 317, 436
Dominant groups, 8
Donato, Katharine M., 365
Donkin, Amy J., 28
Dorn, Dean S., 137
Dorsen, Norma, 301
Douglas-Home, Charles, 205
Dovidio, John, 409, 411
Dowdall, George W., 259
Downs, Anthony, 298
Drake, St. Clair, 302
Dreyfuss, Joel, 449
Driver, Harold E., 232
Drug dealing, 394–96
Drug use and abuse, 152, 320, 396
Dual-wage system, 126, 140, 141
Du Bois, W. E. B., 154
Duch, Raymond M., 28
Duhl, Frederick J., 289
Dukakis, Michael, 246, 312, 318
Duke, David, 418, 419, 422, 439
Dunier, Mitchell, 398
Durkheim, Emile, 59, 68
Dushkin Publishing Group, 62
Dutch Americans, 238, 239
Dutton, Diana B., 290
Dwyer, Paula, 450
Dye, Thomas R., 253
Dyer, Herbert, Jr., 398
Dyer, James, 28, 29

Eagan, Andrea Boroff, 317
Eagly, Alice H., 32, 45
Eastern European white ethnics, 139, 236–38
East St. Louis, Illinois
    fiscal crisis in, 280
    loss of jobs from, 262
    riot of 1917, 138, 142
    tax rates in, 281
Eckert, Craig M., 162
Ecklund, Bruce K., 355
Economic growth
    changing patterns of race relations and, 148
    social movement formation and, 161–62
Economic insecurity, prejudice and, 28–29
Economic productivity, discrimination and, 260–61
Economic status
    continuing inequality in, 242–44
    vs. discrimination as cause of inequality, 458–63
    hate crime increase and, 420–21
    improvements in, 240–41
    middle class, development of, 145–46
    (*See also* Economic system)
Economic system, 252–96
    corporate ownership, 252–53
    economics of discrimination, 3, 147–48, 253–61, 276

education vs., 369
    fiscal crisis of cities, 279–82
    health care, 282–95, 308–9
    housing discrimination, 263, 265–79
    job decentralization, 262–66
    patterns of race relations and, 89–90
    political system and, 297–98
    sociological approach and, 58
Edmonds, Ronald, 382, 383
Edmonston, Barry, 3
Education, 3, 309–10, 336–84, 461
    affirmative action and, 438–49
    approaches to resolving inequality problems in, 368–83
    assimilation and, 169
    bilingual, 169, 184, 185, 223, 359–61
    Black Power movement and, 172
    cultural bias in, 346–68
    desegregation of schools, 38–40, 47, 155, 164–65, 304, 337, 348, 371–78
    discrimination in, 143, 144
    funding of schools, 342–46
    government policies of discrimination and, 304
    multicultural, 36, 350, 368, 378–80, 436
    prejudice and, 27–28, 31, 34–37
    role of, 339–42
    segregation of schools, 144, 337–39 (*See also* Schools)
Educational attainment
    African American vs. white returns to, 365
    changing patterns of race relations and, 148
    employment and rising demand for, 261–62
    improvements in, 241
    social class and, 342
    social movement formation incidence and, 163
Education Week, 343
Edwards, Harry, 15, 460, 461
Edwards, Hugh, 420
Efficacy, sense of, as condition for social movements, 159
Egerton, John, 253
Eggers, Mitchell L., 278
Ehrlich, Elizabeth, 25
Ehrlich, Howard J., 21, 26, 412
Eigen, Joel, 328
Eisenhower, Dwight D., 155, 337
Eisner, Howard C., 50
Eitzen, D. Stanley, 317
Elder, Robert, 18
Elementary-school teachers, 367
Elkins, Stanley M., 96
Elliott, Delbert S., 323
Elliott, Dorinda, 199
Elliott, Jane, 42
Ellis, Albert, 43
Emergency room treatment, 289–90
Emery, Robert E., 390
Employment
    affirmative action and, 438–53
    federal job-producing programs, 307
    hiring decisions, 253–60, 341, 400, 402, 406, 438–51, 455, 462
    housing discrimination and, 263, 265–66, 277
    job decentralization, 262–66, 393–94
    rising educational demands and, 261–62
England, Robert E., 355

English Americans, 238, 239
English/French conflict in Quebec, Canada, 195–96
Entwisle, Doris R., 354
Environmental racism, 187, 283
Epp, Frank H., 205
Epstein, Joyce L., 373
Equal Employment Opportunity Council (EEOC), 430, 431
Equal status, 38–39
Esposito, D., 356
Estrada, Leobardo, 114
"Ethics of Living Jim Crow, The" (Wright), 130–36
Ethnic group, defined, 6
Ethnic inequality (see Ethnic stratification)
Ethnic relations, reasons for study of, 1–3
"Ethnic revival" among whites, 188–89
Ethnic stratification (ethnic inequality), 2, 86–120
    attitudes and, 51–55
    caste vs. class systems of, 87
    competition and, 95, 109, 112, 116–17, 119, 120
    conflict perspective and, 65–66, 69–73, 94–95, 119–20
    cross-cultural studies of, 191–228
    current status of minority groups (see Status of minority groups)
    defined, 66
    development of, 92, 94–95
    discrimination and (see Discrimination)
    economic cost of, 3
    economic system and (see Economic system)
    education and (see Education)
    ethnocentrism and, 67–71, 95, 97–98, 105, 107–9, 111, 112, 116–17, 119, 120
    initial contact and (see Initial contact between race/ethnic groups)
    intergroup contact and, 38–39
    legal system and (see Legal system)
    order (functionalist) perspective and, 66–69, 94, 95, 119
    origins of, 94–100
    patterns of race relations and (see Fluid competitive race relations; Paternalistic race relations; Rigid competitive race relations)
    political system and (see Political system)
    social-psychological approach and, 94
    unequal power and, 95, 98, 106, 109, 112, 116–17, 119, 120
Ethnic vs. racial divisions, 226
Ethnocentrism
    defined, 17
    ethnic stratification and, 67–71, 95, 97–98, 105, 107–9, 111, 112, 116–17, 119, 120
    immigration opposition due to, 453
    in personality theory of prejudice, 17–18
    war and, 69
Eurocentrism, 350
European Americans, 123
    Eastern white ethnics, 139, 236–38
    Southern white ethnics, 236–38
    Western and Northern, 238–40
Evans, Franklin R., 351, 443
Ewens, William L., 26
Exhortation, 31–32

Expectations, teacher, 352–55, 364
Expenditures, government, 280–81, 305–7, 342–46, 360–61
Expressive leadership, 388
Eysenck, Hans J., 43, 366

Fagan, Jeffrey, 325
Fairchild, Halford H., 49
Fair Employment Council of Greater Washington, D.C., 429
Fair Housing Act Amendments of 1988, 274–75, 306
Fair Housing Act of 1968, 274
Fallows, James, 285, 286
False conciousness, 62
Family structure, African American, 76–82
Fanstein, Norman I., 280
Fanstein, Susan S., 280
Farley, John E., 54, 64, 138, 181, 224, 259, 263, 269, 273, 277, 338, 381, 388, 420, 461
Farley, Reynolds, 49, 170, 240, 243, 267–71, 273, 276, 338, 365, 377, 444, 460, 462–63
Farmworkers, 154
Farrakhan, Louis, 183
Farrell, Ronald A., 325
Fascism, 19, 22
Faubus, Orval, 155, 337
Feagin, Clairece Booher, 335
Feagin, Joe R., 52, 94, 146, 168, 169, 176, 311, 320, 321, 335, 369
Featherman, David L., 81
Federal Bureau of Investigation (FBI), 157–58, 316, 317, 323, 423
Federal government (see Political system)
Federal Housing Administration (FHA), 303
Fee-for-service system, 293
Feinstein, Diane, 315
Female-householder families, 76–82, 242, 243
Feminism, 386
Fendrich, J. M., 26
Fenton, Ray, 36
Ferdinand, Theodore N., 325
Ferraro, Geraldine, 246
Festinger, Leon, 46
Ficarrotto, Thomas J., 18
Fickett, Joan G., 357, 359
Fifteenth Amendment, 300
Filiatrault, Pierre, 33
Filipino Americans, 124, 235, 236
Fineberg, Solomon Andhil, 35
Finnish Americans, 238, 239
Firebaugh, Glenn, 50
Firestine, Robert E., 264
Fishbein, M., 45
Flanigan, Timothy J., 330
Flores, Solomon Hernandez, 360
Flowerman, Samuel H., 32
Fluid competitive race relations, 87, 89–93, 142–49, 211–12
    attitude changes, 146–47
    banning of discrimination, 143–45
    economic changes, 145–46
Fogelson, Robert, 176
Foley, Dorothy M., 373
Foote, Caleb, 324
Ford, Thomas E., 14
Ford, W. Scott, 41
Fordham, Signithia, 125
Foreign policy, 310
Forst, Martin, 325
Foster, P. W., 370
Foster, William Z., 137
Fourteenth Amendment, 299–300

Fraga, Luis Ricardo, 355
Franklin, John Hope, 96, 98, 127, 129, 130, 142, 299, 300, 303
Frazier, E. Franklin, 81
Freedman, Deborah, 386, 389
Freedom Riders, 177–78
Freeman, Jo, 159
French
    conflict with English in Quebec, Canada, 195–96
    contact with Native Americans, 107, 108
French Americans, 238, 239
French Antilles, 217
French Canadian Americans, 238, 239
Frenkel-Brunswick, Else, 16
Freud, Sigmund, 21
Freudian theory, 21, 26
Frey, William H., 267, 268, 276
Friedenberg, E. Z., 340
Frisbie, W. Parker, 214
Fuchs, Estelle, 352
Fuchs, Stephen, 28, 29
Fuerst, J. S., 355, 356, 382, 383
Fukurai, Hiroshi, 326
Functionalist perspective (see Order perspective)
Furnham, Adrian, 23
Furstenburg, Frank E., 82
Fyfe, James J., 331

Gadsden Purchase of 1853, 115
Gaines, Margie L., 354
Galagan, Patricia A., 410, 411, 415
Gallup, George, Jr., 400, 404
Gamoran, Adam, 355, 356
Gandhi, Mahatma, 155, 174
"Gangsta" rap, 393
Gans, Herbert, 65, 75, 80, 81, 147, 188, 189
Garbarino, Merwyn S., 106–8, 111
Garcia, Jesus, 349, 350
Garfinkel, Harold, 328
Garvey, Marcus, 154, 173
Garvey, Marcus, Jr., 183
Garvey, Michael R., 287
Gay men (see Homosexuals)
Geis, Gilbert, 293
Gender inequality, 385–98
Gender roles, 386, 389–90
General Accounting Office (GAO), 455
Genocide, 2
Geographic distribution
    African Americans, 230, 233
    Asian Americans, 233, 235–36
    Eastern and Southern European white ethnics, 237–38
    Hispanic Americans, 232, 233
    Native Americans, 233, 234
Geographic mobility, patterns of race relations and, 90–91, 147
Gerard, Harold B., 378
German Americans, 238, 239
Germany
    anti-Semitism in, 24
    guest-worker program, 67
    immigration to, 457
    Nazism in, 10, 18, 226
    opposition to immigrants in, 210, 225–26
Gerrymandering, 337–38
Geschwender, James A., 158, 176
Ghettoization, 462
G.I. Forum, 156–57
Gibson, Geoffrey, 289
Gibson, James L., 28
Gibson, Margaret A., 124
Gilbert, G. M., 15
Ginsburg, Ruth Bader, 452

Gintis, Herbert, 340, 341, 346, 348, 364, 369, 370, 461
Giuliani, Rudolph, 314
Glass ceilings, 411
Glazer, Nathan, 6, 171, 440
Glenn, Charles L., 372, 376
Glenn, Evelyn Makano, 391
Glenn, Norval, 259
Glick, Paul C., 298
Gliedman, John, 406
Gobineau, Arthur de, 10
Goddard, Henry, 362
Goering, John M., 188
Golden, Mark, 364
Goldman, Rachel, 33
Goldstein, Joseph, 320
Goleman, Daniel, 284
Golub, Ellen, 36
Gonzales, Nancie L., 116
Good, Thomas, 353, 354
Goodenough Draw-A-Man IQ Test, 362
Gorbachev, Mikhail, 196
Gordon, Milton M., 6, 165, 166, 168, 169, 171
Goren, Arthur A., 236
Gossett, Thomas F., 127
Gouldner, Helen, 357
Grams, Robert, 327
Grant, Madison, 10
Great Britain, 107–8, 207–8, 210, 213, 284
Grebler, Leo, 114, 116, 117
Greek Americans, 237, 238
Greeley, Andrew M., 28, 29, 49, 171, 189, 239, 240, 354, 355, 383
Green, Robert L., 377
Grimshaw, Allen D., 136, 138
Griscom, Joan L., 404
Grodzins, Morton, 140
Gross, Andrew B., 272
Gross, Jane, 315, 390
Grossarth-Maticek, R., 43
Grossman, Barry A., 329
Group size, patterns of race relations and, 90
Group therapy, 43–44
Guadelupe Hidaldo, Treaty of, 114–16
Guest, Avery M., 276
Guillemin, Jeane, 109, 111
Gutman, Herbert, 82
Guzman, Ralph C., 114, 116, 117, 310

Haaladyne, Thomas M., 353
Hacker, Andrew, 376, 379–81
Haertel, Edward H., 354, 383
Hagan, John, 317, 326–27
Hagen, Michael Gray, 52
Haggard, Ernest A., 364
Hahn, Harlan, 176
Haimowitz, Morris L., 43
Haimowitz, Natalie R., 43
Haitian refugees, 454
Haley, Alex, 36, 174, 302
Hall, Edwin L., 326
Hall, Marcia L., 179
Hall, Raymond L., 174
Hall, Robert L., 163
Hall, Thomas D., 107
Haller, Emil J., 355
Hallinan, Maureen T., 355, 356
Hamer, Dean H., 401
Hamilton, Charles V., 10, 177
Hamilton, David L., 23
Hamilton, Gloria, 341
Hammersmith, Sue Kiefer, 400
Hampton, Fred, 175
Handlin, Mary F., 96
Handlin, Oscar, 96
Hane, Mikiso, 140
Hansen, Marcus L., 189

Hardee, B. B., 51, 311
Harding, John, 36, 40, 54
Harkins, Stephen G., 34
Harnish, Richard J., 33
Harrison, Bennett, 341
Harrison, Roderick J., 266, 276, 277
Harris Poll, 310
Hartley, E. M., 16, 403
Hartwick, J., 45
Harvard Encyclopedia of American Ethnic Groups (Thernstrom et al.), 4n
Harvey, D. G., 353
Hassan, M. K., 23, 25, 27
Hatcher, Richard, 313
Hate crime, 1, 2, 416–27
Hate-speech codes, 425–27
Hauser, Robert M., 81, 356
Havighurst, Robert J., 352
Hawaii, 208–9, 216
Hawkins, Hugh, 169
Hayes, Cheryl D., 83, 388
Hayes, Rutherford B., 127
Haynes, M. Alfred, 287
Head Start program, 370–71
Health care, 282–95, 308–9
Health maintenance organizations (HMOs), 284
Health status, 250, 283–84
Heaven, Patrick C., 23, 28
Helmich, Edith, 371
Helms, L. Jay, 286
Hembroff, Larry A., 327
Henson, Matthew A., School, 381
Hermalin, Albert I., 269–70
Hernstein, Richard J., 366
Hershberg, Theodore, 82, 276
Hidden curriculum, 341
Higginbotham, Elizabeth, 393
Higham, John, 166
High-school graduates, 246–49
High-school teachers, 367
Hill, R. B., 176
Hill, Robert, 81
Hilliard, Asa G., 379
Himler, Janet, 412
Hindelang, Michael J., 323, 326
Hines, Ralph, 286
Hiring decisions, 253–60, 341, 400, 402, 406, 438–51, 455, 462
Hispanic Americans
    age distribution of, 232
    bilingual education and, 169, 184, 185, 223, 359–61
    class stratification within population of, 146
    college tuition and, 11
    corporate executive positions and, 253
    corporate ownership and, 252–53
    criminal justice system and, 318–29
    drug use by, 152
    educational attainment of, 241, 246–49, 261
    geographic distribution of, 232, 233
    governmental policies of discrimination against, 299
    health care and, 285–95
    health status of, 250
    housing segregation and, 276–77
    income status of, 79, 240–42, 445, 460
    job decentralization and, 262–66
    median income by type of family, 79
    occupational status of, 240
    physicians, 288
    pluralism among, 184–86
    police brutality and, 330–31, 333
    police officers, 322
    police protection, dissatisfaction with, 329

politicians, 241, 246
population size of, 2, 3, 231
poverty rate of, 243, 459
school segregation and, 337–39
self-image of children, 351–52
stereotyping of, 48, 49, 350
street crime by, 319
student achievement, variations in, 344–46
teachers, 35, 367
teenage pregnancy among, 83, 84
unemployment rate of, 244, 260–61, 263, 459
urban population of, 231–32, 262–66, 280, 282
voting power of, 313
war casualties, 310
women, 391–93
(*See also* specific groups)
Historical conditions, sociological approach and, 58
Hitler, Adolf, 6, 10, 207
Hochschild, Arlie, 387
Hodgson, Susan, 388
Hoffer, Thomas, 354–56, 383
Hoffmann, Lois Wladis, 388
Holmes, Malcolm D., 325, 326
Homeland, assimilation and proximity to, 190
Homeownership, 253
Homophobia, 402–4
Homosexuals, 2, 18, 152, 153, 398–404, 410
Honeman, Bob, 350
hooks, bell, 391, 392, 393
Hoover, Herbert, 224
Horton, John, 60
Horton, Willie, 318, 421
Hospitals, 290
Hovland, Carl I., 32
Howe, Florence, 341
Hughes, James W., 262
Humm, Andrew, 399
Humphrey, Hubert, 312
Hungarian Americans, 237
Hunt, Chester, 194, 208, 215–17, 221
Hurn, Christopher, 354, 364
Hutchinson, Peter M., 263
Huttenbach, Henry R., 198
Hwang, Sean-Shong, 268, 276
Hyman, Herbert H., 49
Hypertension, 283–84

Ichihashi, Yamato, 124, 140
Ideological racism, defined, 9–10
Illegal immigration, 210, 454–56
Illinois Capital Development Board, 262, 281
Immigrant minorities
    assimilation of, 436
    in Germany, 210, 457
    in Great Britain, 207–8, 210
    illegal, 210, 454–56
    refugees, 454
    in U.S., 122–25, 139, 140, 169, 172, 224–25, 231
    U.S. policy toward, 139, 453–58
Immigration, defined, 94
Immigration Reform and Control Act (IRCA) of 1986, 455, 456
Income
    affirmative action and, 444–45
    continuing inequality in, 242–44, 259, 460
    gender differences in, 386

Income (*cont.*)
    housing segregation and, 268–70
    improvement in minority status,
      240–41
    median, by race, Hispanic origin,
      and type of family, 79, 242
India, 214
Indirect standardization, 268–69
Individual discrimination, defined,
    10
Indonesia, 214
Industrialization, 90
    changing patterns of race relations
      and, 147–49
    cross-cultural evidence on effects
      of, 209–16
    social movement formation and,
      160–61
"Industrialization and Race Relations"
    (Blumer), 148
Inequality
    of the disabled, 404–7
    ethnic (*see* Ethnic stratification)
    gender, 385–98
    sexual orientation, 2, 18, 152, 153,
      398–404
    social class vs. discrimination as
      cause of, 458–63
Infant mortality, 250
Influence, 311
In-groups, 15
Initial contact between racial/ethnic
    groups, 94, 216
    African Americans, 95–96, 122–23
    internal colonialism theory, 121–25
    Mexican Americans, 113, 122–23
    Native Americans, 106–8, 122–23
Institute for Social Research, 253
Institutional characteristics, sociologi-
    cal perspective and, 58
Institutional discrimination, 461
    defined, 10–11
    (*See also* Economic system; Legal
      system; Political system)
Institutionalization of paternalistic
    caste relations, 98–100
Instrumental leadership, 388
Integration
    in housing, 270–73
    (*See also* Desegregation)
Interactionist approach to education,
    368, 382–83
Intergroup contact, 37–42
Intergroup inequality (*see* Ethnic strati-
    fication)
Intergroup-relations courses, 36–37
Intermarriage, 50, 51, 171, 218–19
Internal colonialism theory, 73,
    121–25, 256–57
Internalization, 25
International Association of Firefighters v.
    City of Cleveland (1986), 448,
    450–51
International changes, social move-
    ment formation and, 163–64
International pressure, 226
International relationships, 223–26
IQ tests, 361–66
Iran, 214, 223
Irish Americans, 123, 238, 239
Israel/Arab conflict, 204–6, 438
Italian Americans, 123, 236–38

Jabin, Norma, 23
Jackman, Mary R., 38
Jackson, Jesse, 246, 313–14
Jacobson, Lenore, 352, 364
Jahoda, Marie, 34
Jakubs, John F., 266, 267
Janis, Irving L., 32

Japanese Americans
    age distribution of, 236
    economic status of, 145
    initial contact with whites, 124
    internment during World War II,
      140, 223
    population size of, 235
    rigid competitive race relations
      with whites, 139
    social-distance scores for, 50, 52
    urban, 160
Jaschik, Scott, 404, 406
Jason, Leonard, 36, 41
Jaynes, Gerald, 372
Jeffries, Leonard, 380
Jencks, Christopher, 81, 340, 341, 346,
    354, 369
Jenkins, J. Craig, 159, 162
Jensen, Arthur, 146, 361, 364, 366
Jesilow, Paul, 293
Jet, 253, 355, 412
Jewell, K. Sue, 179
Jews
    anti-Semitism and, 17, 18, 24, 31
    Hitler and, 6
    Israel/Arab conflict and, 204–6,
      223
    measurement of prejudice against,
      17, 18
    quotas and, 441
    stereotyping of, 15, 47, 48
    in U.S., population statistics on,
      236
Job decentralization, 262–66, 393–94
Job discrimination (*see* Hiring deci-
    sions)
Job-producing programs, 307
Joffe, Josef, 200, 201, 221–22
Johansen, Bruce, 157
Johnson, Charles S., 144, 300
Johnson, D. W., 37, 41
Johnson, Guy B., 328
Johnson, Lyndon Baines, 312, 438
Johnson, Miriam M., 387
Johnson, R. T., 41
Johnson, Stephen D., 23, 28
Johnson v. *Transportation Agency* (1987),
    448, 451
Joint Center for Political Studies, 314
Jones, Elise F., 84, 402
Jones, James M., 9
Jones, Jaqueline, 391
Jordan, Winthrop D., 96–98
Jorgensen, 111
Josephy, Alvin M., 106–9
Jury composition, 326

Kadish, Mortimer R., 320
Kadish, Sanford H., 320
Kagan, Jerome, 362–63
Kain, John F., 263, 270
Kamerman, Sheila, 388
Kamin, Leon J., 362
Kane, Michael B., 349
Kantrowitz, Nathan, 276
Kariya, Takehiko, 341
Karlen, A., 400
Karlins, Marvin, 48
Kasarda, John D., 263, 277, 298
Katz, Donald, 15, 43
Katz, Jesse, 224
Katz, Phyllis A., 351
Keddie, Nell, 364
Kelly, Harold H., 32
Kelly, Joan B., 81
Kendall, Patricia L., 34
Kennedy, Edward, 309
Kennedy, John F., 312
Kennedy, Margaret A., 430
Kennedy, Ruby Jo Reeves, 171

Kerr, Clark, 118
Khalique, A., 23, 25, 27
Kiev, Ari, 286
Kiger, Gary, 42
Kilgore, Sally, 354, 356, 383
Killian, Lewis M., 156
Kilson, Martin, 182
Kinder, D. R., 51, 54, 311
King, Martin Luther, Jr., 155, 156, 175,
    179
King, Rodney, 179, 319, 321, 333
Kingston, P. W., 388
Kinloch, Graham C., 207, 211, 216, 219
Kirp, David L., 350, 379, 436
Kirschenman, Jolene, 145, 254, 265,
    392, 396, 462
Kirscht, John P., 23
Kitano, Harry H. L., 139
Klanwatch program, 1
Kleck, Gary, 327
Klein, Stephen, 327
Kloss, Robert Marsh, 137
Kluegel, James R., 51–53, 146, 147,
    189, 311, 312, 415, 443
Knapp, Michael S., 353, 382
Knowlton, 157
Know Nothing party, 10, 453
Kobler, Arthur L., 331, 333–34
Kohlberg, Lawrence, 25
Kohn, Melvin L., 340
Korean Americans, 124–25, 225, 235,
    241
Korean immigrants, 124, 225
Korfhage, Darlene W., 325
Koritz, Douglas, 280
Kotkin, Joel, 180
Kozol, Jonathon, 343, 355
Kramer, Bernard M., 14, 371
Kramer, Roderick K., 27
Krate, Ronald, 357
Krauss, Clifford, 307
Kroeber, Alfred L., 232
Krooth, Richard, 326
Krute, Aaron, 404
Ku Klux Klan, 1, 10, 29, 40, 127, 128,
    179, 224, 225, 416, 417, 419,
    421, 423, 424, 453
Kumar, Kamalesh, 415
Kutner, B., 44, 45
Kuykendall, Jack L., 323
Kyle, Diane, 349

Laabs, Jennifer J., 413
Labeling
    of students mixing Spanish and
      English words, 359
    of students speaking Black English,
      357–58
Labor
    Black Codes and, 126–27
    division of, patterns of race rela-
      tions and, 90
    exploitation of Mexican Americans
      for, 117–19
    in postbellum North, 136–37
Labor unions, 140, 154, 257–59
Labov, William, 358
Ladd, Helen F., 280
La Fave, Wayne R., 320
La Guardia, Fiorello, 224
Lake, Robert, 145, 270–74
Lammermeier, P. J., 82
Language
    bilingual education, 169, 184, 185,
      223
    effects of differences in, 220–23,
      356–61, 364
La Piere, R. T., 44, 45
LaPorte, Suzanne B., 412
La Raza Unida party, 184–85

Larson, Calvin J., 116, 303
Larson, Knud S., 18
Latino ethnic conciousness, 186
Latinos (see Hispanic Americans)
Lauter, Paul, 341
Lawrence, Charles, III, 449
Law school admissions, 442–44
Lawyer's Committee for Civil Rights, 429
Lazar, Irving, 370
Lazerson, M., 340
Leacock, E. B., 353–54
Leadership
    community, busing and, 374–75
    development of, as condition for
        social movements, 159
    family, 388
League of United Latin American Citi-
    zens (LULAC), 154
Leary, Warren E., 284
Leatherman, Courtney, 414, 427
LeClere, Felicia B., 79
Lee, Barrett A., 273
Lee, Min-Wei, 444
Legal system, 309–10, 316–35
    affirmative action and, 447–52
    banning of discrimination, 143–45,
        210, 242
    criminal justice system, 316–29
    disabled and, 405–7
    homosexuals and, 399, 400
    protection of minority rights,
        329–34
    real-estate business practices and,
        274–76
Legum, Colin, 213
Lenin, V. I., 197, 198
Lesbians (see Homosexuals)
Lessing, Elise E., 35, 37
Levay, Simon, 401
Level, Saul R., Memorial Foundation,
    327
Levin, C. L., 338
Levin, Jack, 416, 424
Levin, R. J., 400
Levy, Jerrold E., 286, 287
Lewin, Kurt, 35
Lewis, Anne C., 360, 361, 371
Lewis, Oscar, 75
Lezotte, L. W., 382
Licht, Hans, 402
Lichter, Daniel, 79, 263
Lieberson, Stanley, 81, 124, 137, 140,
    207, 379, 436
Life expectancy, 249–50, 283
Lillard, Lee A., 79
Lipset, Seymour Martin, 27, 44, 64, 189
Liska, Allen E., 325, 329
Litcher, J. H., 37
Literacy tests, 301
Lithuanian Americans, 237
Little, Allan, 370
Little Rock, Arkansas, school desegre-
    gation case, 155
Litwack, Leon F., 126
Livingston, Abby, 416
Local government (see Political system)
Lofland, John, 159
Logan, John R., 268, 276, 277
Long, Harry H., 298
Looking-glass self, 351
Lopez, Manuel Mariano, 276
Lorde, Andre, 393
Los Angeles, California
    Asian American housing segrega-
        tion in, 277
    busing in, 376
    physician shortages in, 287
    police force of, 322
    riots in, 2, 139–42, 156, 176,
        179–80, 323, 331, 333, 419

Louw-Potgieter, J., 26
Lowenstein, L. F., 43
Luchterhand, Elmer G., 325
Lumpkin, Margaret C., 349, 350
Lundman, Richard J., 330
Lurie, Nancy Oestreich, 107–11
Lynch, Frederick R., 29, 36
Lynd, Helen Merrell, 302
Lynd, Robert S., 302

MacKinnon, William, 27
Madsen, William, 286
Maestas, Roberto, 157
Mahard, Rita E., 372, 373
Majority groups, defined, 6–8
Majors, Richard, 398
Makepeace, J. M., 390
Malcolm X, 156, 174, 178
Managerial occupations, 240
Mandela, Nelson, 7, 192–94, 212, 213,
    217, 310
Mandelbaum, D. G., 37
Manifest Destiny, 117
Mare, Robert D., 76, 79
Marital assimilation, 166
Marmor, Judd, 29
Marrett, Cora Bagley, 460
Marriage, interracial, 50, 51, 171,
    218–19
Marshall, Ray, 255, 257
Martin, Douglas, 221
Martin v. Wilks (1989), 448–50
Martz, Larry, 319
Maruyama, G., 41
Marx, Karl, 60, 61, 71
Marxist theory, 61, 62, 71, 72, 256, 257,
    259, 260, 276, 340, 437
Mason, Philip, 207, 212, 213, 220
Mass communications, social move-
    ment formation and, 162–63
Massey, Douglas S., 3, 79, 80, 83, 250,
    267, 268, 272, 276, 278, 457
Masters, Stanley H., 254
Mathews, Jay, 429, 430
Matthews, Tom, 180
Matthiessen, Peter, 157, 158
Matute-Bianchi, Maria Eugenia, 125
Mazon, Mauricio, 139, 140, 141
McAdam, Doug, 159, 162
McCarthy, John D., 158, 159, 162
McCarthy, Kevin F., 453
McCary, James Lesley, 400–402
McClintock, C., 43
McConahay, J. B., 51, 52, 311
McCutcheon, Gail, 349
McDevitt, Jack, 416, 424
McDill, Edward L., 355, 356
McFarlane, Bruce, 200, 201
McFaul, Thomas R., 50
McGarrell, Edmund F., 330
McGinley, H., 356
McGinley, P., 356
McGinnes, Elliott, 34
McGovern, George, 62, 312
McGuire, William J., 32
McKay, Robert, 364
McKey, Ruth, 371
McLanahan, Sara, 77, 81
McLaughlin, Diane K., 79
McPartland, J. M., 38
McPhail, Clark, 2, 180, 323
McWhirter, J. Jeffries, 41
McWilliams, Carey, 116n, 141, 300
Mead, George Herbert, 351
Means, Barbara, 353, 382
Medicaid, 284, 285, 289–94, 308
Medical school admissions, 444
Medicare, 284, 294
Medina, Marcello, 360
Medina, Z., 363

Mehan, Hugh, 364
Meier, August, 127, 154, 156
Meier, Kenneth J., 355
Meier, Matt S., 113–16, 157
Melman, Seymour, 307
Mendelsohn, Harold, 323, 329, 330
Merton, Robert K., 15, 45–46
Metzger, Tom, 416
Mexican Americans
    bail setting abuse and, 324–25
    class stratification within popula-
        tion of, 146
    as colonized minorities, 122–23
    curanderismo and, 286
    environmental racism and, 283
    geographic distribution of, 232
    housing segregation and, 276
    initial contact with whites, 113,
        122–23
    job discrimination against, 117–19,
        254
    middle class, 145
    mixed language of, 359
    origins of inequality of, 113–19
    physicians, 288
    pluralism among, 184–86
    population size of, 231
    rigid competitive race relations
        with whites, 140–41
    seeking of assimilation by, 170
    self-image of children, 351–52
    social-distance scores for, 50, 52
    social movements of, 154, 156–57
    stereotyping of, 349
    urban, 147, 160
    violence against, 140–41
    voting power of, 313
    voting rights of, 301
Mexican illegal immigrants, 454, 455
Mexican Revolution of 1909–1910,
    117–18
Mexican War, 115
Mexico, 113–14, 217, 456
Miami riot of 1980, 180, 323, 333
Michealson, Larry, 415
Michelson, Stephan, 344
Michigan, University of, 424
Michigan State Board of Education,
    350
Middle class minorities, 145–46, 153,
    278, 322, 342, 393–94, 445,
    460–61, 463
Middle East, conflict in, 204–6
Middleton, Russel, 34
Military service, homosexuals in, 399,
    401–2
Miller, Karen A., 340
Miller, Krystal, 224
Miller, Norman, 41
Miller, Randi L., 378
Mills, C. Wright, 60, 235, 297
Minority groups
    defined, 7–8, 229, 235
    social movements of, 150–65
    status of (see Ethnic stratification;
        Status of minority groups)
Minority set-aside programs, 451–53
Mirande, Alfredo, 114, 115, 117, 119,
    123, 257
Mishra, Shilala P., 360
Mitnick, Leonard, 34
Mladenka, Kenneth R., 258
Modeling, 24, 25
Modell, J., 82
Modernization (see Industrialization)
Modern racism, 51, 311
Molotch, Harvey, 272
Monagle, Katie, 326
Mondale, Walter, 312
Monroe, Sylvester, 397

Monsanto Company, 412–14
Mooney, Joseph D., 263
Moore, Joan W., 114, 116, 117, 123, 145, 184–86, 240, 301, 304, 310, 313, 355, 359, 360
Moore, L. Aubrey, 325
Moore, Robert, 195
Moore, Wilbert E., 67, 69, 340
Morgan, S. Philip, 82
Morganthau, Tom, 224, 225
Morris, Aldon, 156, 158, 160–62
Morris, John W., 23, 28
Morrison, Ann, 411, 412, 414
Mortality status, 249–50, 263, 292
Moseley-Braun, Carol, 54, 181, 241, 246, 313
Moses, E. G., 351
Moses, Bob, 382
Moss, E. Yvonne, 320
Moustafa, A. Taher, 286
Moynihan, Daniel Patrick, 76, 77, 80, 84, 171, 388
Moynihan Report, 76, 80
Muenchow, Susan, 370, 371
Muhammad, Elijah, 173, 174
Muhammad, Khallid Abdul, 183
Muhammad Speaks, 173
Muller, Thomas, 399, 453
Multiculturalism, 167
   in education, 36, 350, 368, 378–80, 436
   in the workplace, 415–16
Mulyakov, Marat, 199
Municipal revenue, 280–82
Murdock, Steve H., 268, 276
Myrdal, Gunnar, 302, 304

Nad, Abraham, 253
Nagel, Stewart, 327, 328
Nagi, Saad Z., 404
Nagorski, Andrew, 210, 226
Nagpaul, Hans, 214
Nahaylo, Bohdan, 197
Nancarrow, Douglas, 36
Nash, Roy, 112, 353
National Assessment of Educational Progress, 341–42
National Association for the Advancement of Colored People (NAACP), 33, 149, 154, 155, 337, 372, 430
National Commission on the Causes and Prevention of Violence, 175
National Council of La Raza, 186
National Institute for the Humanities, 426
National Institute on Drug Abuse, 320
National Institute on Education, 372
National Opinion Research Center, 48, 50, 239
National Research Council, 82, 83, 253
Nation of Islam, 173, 174, 183, 438
Native Americans, 3
   age distribution of, 234
   as colonized minorities, 122–23
   educational attainment of, 246–49, 261
   education of, 361
   environmental racism and, 283
   geographic distribution of, 233, 234
   governmental policies of discrimination against, 299
   health care and, 286–95
   initial contact with whites, 106–8, 122–23
   IQ test bias and, 362
   life expectancy of, 283
   origins of inequality of, 106–12

police brutality and, 330
population size of, 3, 170, 232
poverty rate of, 243–44
protest by, 186–88
resistance to assimilation by, 170–71, 187
school segregation and, 338
self-image of children, 351–52
social-distance scores for, 50, 52
social movements of, 154, 157–58
stereotyping of, 349, 350
student achievement, variations in, 344–46
unemployment rate of, 244, 261
urban population of, 160, 170, 234
violence against, 157, 158
voting rights of, 301
Nazism, 10, 18, 226
Neckerman, Kathryn M., 145, 254, 265, 392, 396, 462
Neidert, Lisa J., 171
Neill, D. M., 363
Nelkin, Dorothy, 159
Newark, New Jersey, 175, 176, 278
Newhouse, Jospeh P., 286
New Jersey suburbs
   neighborhood racial mix preferences in, 271–72
   racial steering in, 274
New Mexico, 114–17
Newport, John Paul, Jr., 394, 395
Newsweek, 400
Newton, Huey, 174
New York City, New York
   Asian American housing segregation in, 277
   federal spending and, 307
   fiscal crisis in, 280
   loss of jobs from, 262
   physician shortages in, 287
   public transportation in, 309
New York Times, The, 174, 183, 293, 333, 343, 449
Nickens, Herbert W., 444
Nicklin, Julie L., 415
Nihas, Vasiliki, 36
Nihilism, 394
Nikkel, Stan R., 303
Nisbet, Lee, 441
Nixon, Richard, 312
Noblit, George, 378
Nock, S. L., 388
Noel, Donald L., 95, 97–99, 106, 116
Nolen, Susan Bobbitt, 353
North, the
   antebellum race relations in, 126
   postbellum race relations in, 136–39
North American Free Trade Agreement (NAFTA), 456
Northern European Americans, 238–40
Northern Ireland, 194–95, 209, 212, 217–18, 221–22, 226, 437, 438
Norwegian Americans, 238, 239
Nostrand, Richard L., 114, 116
Novak, Michael, 188, 189
Number of racial and ethnic groups, 216–18

Oakes, Jeannine, 355
Occupational specialization, 171
Occupational status, 240, 391–92
Ogbu, John U., 124, 125, 361, 362, 364–65, 369, 370, 436
O'Hare, William P., 3, 230–32, 234, 247, 248, 250, 260, 267, 277
Olexa, Carol, 355, 356
Oliver, Melvin L., 253
Olojede, Dele, 443

Olsen, Marvin E., 388, 420
O'Malley, Patrick M., 351
O'Malley, Shiela, 328
Ommundsen, Reidar, 18
Order (functionalist) perspective
   compared with conflict perspective, 63, 75–85
   concept of, 59–60
   education and, 339, 347–48, 368–78
   ethnic stratification and, 65–69, 94–95, 119
   gender inequality and, 387–89
   pluralism and, 190
   social problems and, 64–65
   synthesis with conflict perspective, 74
Orfield, Gary, 337–39, 372, 373, 378
Oriental Exclusion Acts, 453
Ossenberg, Richard J., 196, 221
Ottaway, David, 217
Out-groups, 15
Overby, Andrew, 326
Overcategorization, 13
Overlapping vs. crosscutting cleavages, 220–22
Owen, Carolyn, 50

Pachon, Harry, 186, 355, 359, 360
Pacific Islander Americans, 235
Padilla, Felix M., 186
Page, Clarence, 454
Page, R. N., 355
Palestinian Arabs, 205–6
Pallas, Aaron M., 354
Palmer, Francis H., 364
Parent, Wayne, 52
Parisi, Nicolette, 322, 329, 330
Parks, Rosa, 155
Parsons, Talcott, 59, 340, 388
Parti Quebecois, 209
Passel, Jeffrey S., 3, 454
"Passing" as white, 152
Patchen, M., 43
Paternalistic race relations, 87–93, 98–100, 111–12
Paternoster, Raymond, 328
Patterson, Orlando, 189, 434–36
Patterson v. McLean Credit Union (1989), 448, 450
Payne, Charles, 459, 461, 462
Peaceful intergroup relations, societies with, 208–9
Pear, Robert, 455
Pearce, Diana, 273–75, 427, 429
Pearl, D., 43
Peculiar Institution, The: Slavery in the Anti-Bellum South (Stampp), 100–105
People's Republic of China, 214, 215
Perrien, Jean, 33
Perrone, Vito, 366
Perrow, Charles, 159
Persian Gulf War, 224, 310, 419
Personality theory of prejudice, 16–24, 26–27
Perspectives
   defined, 58–59
   (*See also* Conflict perspective; Order perspective)
Persuasive communications, 31–34
Peskin, Janice, 387
Petersdorf, Robert G., 444
Petersilla, Joan, 325–27
Peterson, James L., 81
Pettigrew, Thomas F., 26, 147, 270, 372, 373, 377, 459, 460
Petty, Richard E., 33, 34
Pharr, Suzanne, 403, 404
Phelan, Thomas, 264

Phelps, Charles E., 286
Physicians, 287–94
Piaget, Jean, 252
Pierce, Glenn L., 328
Pierson, Donald, 218
Piliavin, Irving, 321
Pinkney, Alphonso, 156, 173–75
Pisko, Valena White, 342, 343, 376
Piven, Frances Fox, 282
Plant, Richard, 399
Plantation system, 89, 96–99, 111–12
Plessy v. *Ferguson* (1896), 127, 300
Pluralism, 166–67
    among Mexican Americans, 184–86
    bilingual education and, 360
    Black Power movement and shift
        toward, 172–79
    case against, 436–37
    case for, 435–36
    changing attitudes toward, 172–90
    cultural, 166, 379–80
    multiculturalism (*see* Multicultural-
        ism)
Police
    brutality, 330–31, 333–34
    crime detection by, 316–20
    decision to arrest by, 320–23
    minorities as, 322
    minority rating of, 322
    protection of minorities by, 329–30
    Rodney King beating and, 319
    violence between African Ameri-
        cans and, 175–76
Polish Americans, 237, 238
Political action
    African American, 181
    Mexican American, 184–85
Political correctness, 425–27
Political leaders, economic fears of
    whites and, 421–23
Political-process theory, 159
Political system, 297–315
    affirmative action, 438–53
    barriers to greater minority power,
        311–12
    continuing inequality in represen-
        tation, 246, 313–14, 386
    economic system and, 297–98
    foreign policy, 310
    government spending, 280–81,
        305–7, 342–46, 360–61
    health care, 308–9
    historical pattern of discrimination
        policies, 299–305
    immigration policy, 139, 453–58
    improvements in representation,
        241, 313
    public transportation, 308–9
    sociological approach and, 58
    voting power, 312–15
    voting rights, 130, 144, 299–301
    welfare reform, 308
Polk, Kenneth, 355, 356
Pollack, Michael, 159
Poll taxes, 300–301
Pontell, Henry, 293
Pool, Robert, 401
Popenoe, David, 77, 388, 389
Popkin, Susan J., 265
Population Reference Bureau, 214, 456
Population statistics
    African Americans, 3, 229–30
    Asian Americans, 3, 235
    changing composition, 2–3
    Eastern and Southern European
        white ethnics, 236–38
    Hispanic Americans, 2, 3, 231
    Native Americans, 3, 170, 232
    Western and Northern European
        whites, 238–39

Population transfer, 167
Populist party, 128–29
Porter, Judith D. R., 351
Porter, Rosalie Pedelino, 186
Portuguese Americans, 237
Posse Comitatus, 418
Postbellum race relations
    in the North, 136–39
    in the South, 126–36
Pottinger, J. Stanley, 442
Poussaint, Alvin, 362–63
Poverty, 3
    culture of, 75–85, 369
    vs. discrimination as cause of in-
        equality, 459–62
    extent of, by race, 243–44
    housing discrimination and, 278
    public opinion on causes of, 311
Powell, Richard R., 349
Power
    concern with, 19
    unequal, ethnic stratification ori-
        gins and, 95, 98, 106, 109, 112,
        116–17, 119, 120
    voting, 312–15
Prejudice, 13–29
    affective, 14, 30, 146
    causes of, 16–30
    changes in kind and degree of,
        146–47, 210, 211
    cognitive, 14, 30, 47–48, 146
    conative, 14, 30, 49–51, 146,
        254–55
    defined, 13
    against disabled, 404–6
    discriminatory behavior and, 44–55
    education and, 27–28, 31, 34–37
    ethnocentrism (*see* Ethnocentrism)
    forms of, 14, 30
    hate groups and, 419–23
    intergroup contact and, 37–42
    personality theory of, 16–24, 26–27
    persuasive communications and,
        31–34
    among police, 322–23
    prevalence of, 47–51
    projection, 19–23
    racial, defined, 9
    reducing, 30–44
    scapegoating, 20–21, 23
    sexual orientation and, 402–04
    simulation exercises and, 42
    social learning-conformity theory
        of, 24–27
    socioeconomic status and, 27–29
    stereotyping, 14–15, 19, 47–49,
        146, 349, 350
    symbolic racism, 51
    therapy and, 31, 43–44
Preston, James D., 41
Primary group relations, 166
Productivity, decline in, 3
Professional occupations, 240
Projection, 19–23
Propaganda, 31–32
Prosecution decision, 325–26
Protestants, 194–95, 221–22, 238–39,
    438
Protest movements, 150–65
Prothro, E. T., 26
Public Broadcasting Service, 42
Public employment
    hiring decisions, 450–51
    layoff decisions, 451
Public facilities, segregation of, 302–3
Public policy, 52
Public transportation, 308–9
Puerto Ricans
    as colonized minority, 122, 123
    education of, 345, 346, 348

geographic distribution of, 232
housing segregation and, 277
literacy tests and, 301
physicians, 288
pluralism among, 186
political representation of, 241
population size of, 231
underclass of, 146
unemployment rate of, 244
Punishment, socialization and, 24–25
Pygmalion in the Classroom (Rosenthal
    and Jacobson), 352

Quality of life, housing discrimination
    and, 278
Quan, Robert, 287
Quebec, Canada, 195–96, 209, 217,
    221, 222, 226, 438
Quinney, Richard, 317, 323, 330

Raab, Earl, 44, 64, 441
Rabin, Yitzhak, 206
Race, defined, 5–6
Race relations, reasons for study of,
    1–3
Racial-classification systems, 217
Racial code words, 422–23
Racial group, defined, 5–6
Racial inequality (*see* Ethnic stratifica-
    tion)
Racial prejudice
    defined, 9
    (*See also* Prejudice)
Racial steering, 273–74, 429
Racial vs. ethnic divisions, 226
Racism
    cultural, 146–47
    defined, 8–9
    environmental, 187, 283
    symbolic, 51, 311
    types of, 9–11, 146–47
Racist ideology, defined, 9–10
Radelet, Michael, 328
Radke, Marian J., 351
Rakowska-Harmstone, Teresa, 198, 199
Rand Corporation, 455
Randolph, A. Philip, 155
Ransford, H. Edward, 28, 188
Rational-emotive therapy, 43
Rationalization, 148
Ratteray, Joan Davis, 350
Ray, John J., 22, 23
Readiness tests, 363
Reagan, Ronald, 310, 312, 447, 452
Real-estate business practices, 273–76
Reconstruction, 127, 136, 299–300
Reference others, conformity to, 25
Rehabilitation Act of 1973, 406
Reich, Michael, 256–59, 276
Reimers, Cordella W., 76, 80
Reisman, David, 297
Reiss, Albert J., Jr., 321, 331
Relative deprivation, as condition for
    social movements, 158, 160
Religion
    of Eastern and Southern European
        white ethnics, 238
    effects of differences in, 220–22
    prejudice against homosexuals
        and, 402–3
Reservations, Native American, 109–12
Reskin, Barbara F., 389
Resource-mobilization theory, 158–59
Restrictive covenants, 303
Revels, Hiram R., 127
Reverse discrimination, 440–41
Reward, socialization and, 24–25
Reynolds, Robert E., 290
Rhodes, N., 32
Rice, Thomas W., 290

Richards, Toni, 377
Richert, Jean Pierre, 25
Richman, Charles L., 351
Richmond, Anthony H., 207, 208
Rieder, Jonathan, 188, 256
Riffraff theory, 176
Rigby, Ken, 23
Rigid competitive race relations,
    87–93, 112, 125–42
    African American-white, 125–39
    Asian American-white, 139–40
    cross-cultural studies of, 211–13
Riordan, Cornelius, 42
Riots
    in antebellum North, 126
    in Los Angeles, 2, 139–42, 156,
        176, 179–80, 323, 331, 333, 419
    in Miami, 180, 323, 333
    in postbellum North, 138
    social movements and, 156, 175–77
Rist, Ray C., 353, 354, 376
Rivera, Feliciano, 113–16, 157
Robbers cave experiment, 40–41
Roberts, Ron E., 137
Robins, A. H., Company, 317
Robinson, Jerry W., 41
Robinson, John, 388
Roddy, Dennis B., 320
Rodeghier, Mark, 163
Rodriguez, Arturo, 186
Roebuck, Julian, 287
Roesner, J. David, 341
Roesti, Paul M., 325
Rohde, Rachel, 327
Role models, lack of, 367
Roman Catholics, 194–95, 219, 221–22,
    238, 239, 438
Romero, Ann, 350
Roncal, Joaquin, 217
Roof, Wade Clark, 266
Rooney-Rebek, Patricia, 36, 41
Roosevelt, Franklin D., 155
Roots, Part II, 15
Roper, S. S., 42
Rose, R., 195n
Rosenbaum, James E., 265, 341, 356
Rosenbaum, Robert J., 116
Rosenthal, Bernard G., 351–53, 364
Rossell, Christine H., 372, 376
Rubin, I. M., 43
Rudwick, Elliott, 127, 137, 138, 154
Ruggiero, Josephine, 42
Rundall, Thomas G., 290
Russian Americans, 237, 238
Ryan, William, 65, 75, 80

St. John, Nancy H., 372
St. Louis, Missouri
    fiscal crisis in, 280, 287, 290
    housing segregation in, 268–69, 273
    police force of, 322
    public transportation in, 309
    school funding in, 343
St. Louis Post-Dispatch, 200, 202–4, 280,
    285, 337–39
Saldate, Macario, 360
Sales, M. E., 205
Sampson, Robert J., 77, 81
Sandberg, Neil C., 189
Sandoval, J., 363
San Francisco, California, 140, 277
Sarnoff, I., 43
Satin, George D., 289
Sattler, Jerome M., 363, 365
Scandinavian Americans, 238–40
Scapegoating, 20–21, 23
Schafer, Walter E., 355, 356
Schaich, Warren, 138
Schermerhorn, Richard A., 63, 74, 94,
    214

Scheuch, Erwin, 210
Schmalz, Jeffrey, 400
Schmidt, Peter, 360
Schmidt, William E., 315
Schneider, Mark, 264, 268
Schooler, Carmi, 340
School materials, biased or limited cov-
    erage of minority groups in,
    349–52
Schools
    ability grouping in, 355–56
    desegregation of, 38–40, 47, 155,
        164–65, 304, 337, 348, 371–78
    funding of, 342–46
    linguistic differences in, 356–61
    prejudice reduction and, 35–36
    segregation of, 144, 337–39
    teacher expectations, 352–55, 364
    test bias in, 361–66
    tracking in, 355–56
    (See also Education)
Schools That Work: Educating Disadvan-
    taged Children, 383
Schorr, Lisbeth B., 83
Schuchardt, Thomas, 404
Schuman, Howard, 49, 51, 52, 146,
    176, 177, 277, 311, 369
Schutt, Russell K., 325, 326
Schwartz, Barry, 261
Schwartzbach, Donna, 377
Scientific racism, 9–10
Scott, R. R., 38
Scottish Americans, 238, 239
Scruggs, Otey M., 301, 302
Seabury, Paul, 437
Seale, Bobby, 174
Sears, D. O., 51, 52, 54, 311
See, Katherine O'Sullivan, 195
Segregation, 91
    of Asian Americans, 140
    housing, 50, 143, 263, 265–79,
        303–4, 336, 338
    of Mexican Americans, 140
    in Northern Ireland, 194
    in postbellum North, 138
    in postbellum South, 126–28,
        130–36
    public facilities, 302–3
    school, 144, 337–39
    in South Africa, 7, 193–94, 213
Segregation index, 266–68
Seifer, Nancy, 391
Seitz, V., 364
Selective exposure, 24, 25
Self-fulfilling prophecy, 322–23, 352
Self-image of children, 351–52
Seligman, Daniel, 339
Selvin, Paul, 353, 382, 383
Sentencing, 326–28
Separatism, 167–68, 183–84, 190,
    437–38
Serbians, 168, 199–202, 222, 223
Set-aside programs, 451–53
Sewell, William H., 356
Sexual "goings-ons", exaggerated con-
    cern with, 19–20
Sexual harassment, 392–93
Sexual orientation, 2, 18, 152, 153,
    398–404, 410
Seymour, D. Z., 357
Shaffer, David R., 32, 33, 45
Shaheen, Jack G., 224
Shanahan, J. L., 263
Shapiro, Thomas M., 253
Sharma, Rama, 22
Sharpton, Al, 183
Sheatsley, Paul B., 47, 49
Sheet Metal Workers v. Equal Employment
    Opportunity Commission (1986),
    448, 449

Shenker, Joseph, 367
Shepard, Lorrie, 356, 363, 366
Sheppard, B. H., 45
Sherif, Muzafer, 40
Shields, Patrick M., 353
Shils, Randy, 401–3
Shockley, William, 146, 366
Silverstein, Barry, 324, 357
Simkus, Albert A., 326
Simon, David R., 317
Simpson, George Eaton, 23, 27, 31, 32,
    68, 139, 152, 154, 175, 300,
    301, 337
Simpson, Nicole, 390
Simpson, O. J., 390
Simulation exercises, 42
Sindler, Allan P., 441, 442
Singer, B. D., 176
Single-parenthood, 76–82
Skolnick, Jerome H., 49, 177–79
Skovira, Robert, 349
Slatin, G. T., 353
Slavery, 89, 95–106, 111–12, 299
Slavin, Robert, 373
Slovak Americans, 237
Small-claims court system, 333
Smith, A. Wade, 421
Smith, Douglas A., 323
Smith, Eliot R., 51–53, 146, 189, 311,
    443
Smith, George, 370
Smith, W. C., 216
Sniderman, Paul M., 18, 52
Snipp, C. Matthew, 244
Snow, David A., 159
Snow, Loudell F., 286
Snyder, Thomas D., 284
Social class vs. discrimination as cause
    of inequality, 458–63
Social Darwinism, 9–10
Social distance, 49–50, 52, 128
Social institutions, 10–11
Socialization, 24–25
Socialized medicine, 284
Social learning theory of prejudice,
    24–27
Social mobility, 90–91, 146, 147,
    339–41
Social movements
    in industrialized countries, 209–10
    in U.S., 150–65, 399–400
Social problems, sociological perspec-
    tives and, 63–65
Social psychology
    approach to race and ethnic rela-
        tions, 56
    ethnic stratification and, 94
    (See also Attitudes; Prejudice)
Social-structural approach (see Socio-
    logical approach)
Socioeconomic mobility, patterns of
    race relations and, 90
Socioeconomic status
    defined, 27
    prejudice and, 27–29
    (See also Status of minority groups)
Sociological approach, 56–85
    conflict perspective (see Conflict
        perspective)
    cross-cultural studies, 191–228
    defined, 56–57
    features examined by, 57–58
    order (functionalist) perspective
        (see Order perspective)
    perspectives, defined, 58–59
    vs. social-psychological approach,
        56
Solomon, Charlene Marmer, 412, 414,
    416
Solorzano, Daniel G., 351

South, the
  African American population in, 230, 233
  Asian American population in, 233
  governmental policies of discrimination in, 299–304
  Hispanic American population in, 233
  job decentralization in, 265
  Native American population in, 233, 234
  postbellum race relations in, 126–36
  prejudice and discrimination decline in, 47
  school segregation in, 337, 338
  slavery in, 95–106
South Africa, 212–15
  apartheid in, 7, 193–94, 213
  bantustan policy of, 167–68
  caste system of, 87
  effects of colonization in, 192–94, 214
  health care system of, 284
  international sanctions on, 226
  protest movements in, 212–13
  racial-classification system of, 217
  U.S. policy towards, 310
  "white jobs" in, 215
South Carolina v. *Katzenbach* (1966), 301
Southern European white ethnics, 236–38
Southern Poverty Law Center, 1, 224, 273, 399, 416–18, 423
Soviet Union, former, 196–99, 201
Sowell, Thomas, 441
Spanish contact with Native Americans, 107, 219, 220
Spear, Allan, 136
Spencer, Metta, 5
Split labor market theory, 72–73, 255–57, 260
Srole, Leo, 6
Stalin, Joseph, 198
Stampp, Kenneth, 97, 100–105
Stangor, Charles, 14
Stanley, Julian C., 370
Staples, Robert, 81
State government (*see* Political system)
Status of minority groups, 229–51
  adaptive responses to, 150–53
  change-oriented responses to, 153–54
  continuing inequality in, 242–50
  demographic, 229–40
  economic, 240–44
  educational attainment, 241, 246–49
  health and mortality, 249–50
  improvement in, 240–242
  political representation, 241, 246
Steeh, Charlotte, 51
Steele, C. Hoy, 170, 234
Steele, James B., 420
Steele, Shelby, 441
Stereotyping, 14–15, 19, 47–49, 146, 349, 350, 396
Stern, Joyce D., 342, 343, 376
Sternleib, George, 262
Stertz, Bradley, 224
Steuben, William Frederich Wilhelm von, 402
Stevens, Rosemary, 294
Stevenson, Richard W., 455
Stewart, Chuck, 318–19
Stockard, Jean, 387
Stoddard, Lothrup, 10
Stolzenberg, Lisa, 28
Stotland, E., 43
Stouffer, Samuel A., 37, 41

Straus, Murray A., 390
Strauss, Joseph H., 304, 326, 349, 361
Street crime, 317–20, 394, 395
Strikebreakers, African Americans used as, 137
Strong, James, 437
Strong, Mayr Symons, 182
Structural assimilation, 165–66, 171–73, 190
Structural pluralism, 166
Stubbins, Joseph, 406
Stuckert, Robert S., 152
Subordinate groups, 8
Suburbs, job shift to, 262–66
Sudarkasa, Niara, 396
Suicides, 152
Sullivan, Andrew, 380
Sullivan, Joseph F., 343
Sullivan, Linda A., 14
Sullivan, Louis W., 444
Sum, Andrew, 394
Summers, Anita, 346
Sumner, William Graham, 68
Super, Donald E., 341
Superstition, 19
Suplee, C., 401
Swedish Americans, 238, 239
Sweezy, Paul M., 256
Swiss Americans, 238, 239
Switzerland, 208, 216, 221
Swoboda, Victor, 197
Symbolic racism, 51, 147, 311
Szymanski, Albert, 259

Taeuber, Alma F., 268–70, 272
Taeuber, Karl E., 268–70, 272, 338
Takagi, 331
Tansig, Mark, 325, 329
Taxes
  cuts in, 307
  fiscal crisis in cities and, 280, 281
  funding of schools with, 342–43
  poll, 300–301
Taylor, D. Garth, 338
Taylor, Karyn J., 358
Taylor, Paul S., 118, 273
Teachers
  African Americans as, 35, 367
  expectations of, 352–55, 364
  Hispanic Americans as, 367
  linguistic differences and, 356–61
  prejudice and, 35
Teenage pregnancy, 82–84
Territorial ethnic base, 222–23
Terry, Robert M., 325
Tesser, Abraham, 32, 45
Test bias, 361–66
Texas
  bail setting abuse in, 324
  governmental discrimination policies in, 300–302
  origins of ethnic stratification in, 114
  political action by Mexican Americans in, 184–85
Thematic Apperception Test (TAT), 21
Therapy, 31, 43–44
Thernstrom, Abigail, 190, 346, 360, 434
Thernstrom, Stephan, 4n
Third World nations, 163–64, 214–15
Thomas, R. Roosevelt, Jr., 409, 411, 412, 415
Thomlinson, Ralph, 237, 453
Thompson, J. E., 38
Thompson, Kevin D., 452
Thompson, Maxine S., 354
Thompson, Wilbur, 264, 265
Thomson, Randall J., 326, 328
Thornberry, Terence P., 325, 326

Thorndike, Robert C., 353
Thornton, Arland, 386, 389
Thornton, Russell, 106
Tienda, Marta, 365, 457
Tijerina, Reies Lopez, 157
Tilly, Charles, 161
Tischler, Henry L., 208, 209, 218
Tito, Josip Broz, 200, 201
Torres, Joe Campos, 333
Toughness, concern with, 19
Townsend, Linda, 387
Tracking, 355–56
Trager, Helen G., 351
Transmission-of-values theory, 378–79
Transportation, public, 308–9
Traver, Nancy, 406, 407
Treaties with Native Americans, 108–10
"Trial of Broken Treaties," 157
Triandis, Harry C., 14, 32, 33
Tripp, Luke, 181
Troiani, Maryann V., 42
Truly Disadvantaged, The (Wilson), 459
Tuch, Steven A., 49
Turks
  German opposition to immigration by, 225–26
  stereotyping of, 15, 47
Turner, James, 430
Turner, Susan, 327
Turque, Bill, 400
Twenty-fourth Amendment, 301

Ukranian Americans, 237
Underclass, 146, 250, 260, 458–63
Unemployment, 3, 80, 82, 83, 178, 244, 260–63, 285, 305, 392, 459, 460
UNESCO, 10
Uniform Crime Reports, 316
United Farm Workers, 161, 184, 186, 324
U.S. Bureau of the Census, 3, 76, 79, 145, 170, 229–37, 239–44, 246–48, 250, 253, 265, 268, 281, 285, 286, 288, 292, 305, 306, 309, 367, 386, 420, 421, 445, 454, 455
U.S. Commission on Civil Rights, 9, 301, 324–25, 337, 338, 355, 375–77, 460
U.S. Department of Commerce, 240
U.S. Department of Education, 353, 383
U.S. Department of Health, Education, and Welfare, 288
U.S. Department of Housing and Urban Development, 145, 274–75, 429, 431
U.S. Department of Justice, 275, 322, 429, 439
U.S. Department of Labor, 3, 76, 79, 261, 409
U.S. National Advisory Commission on Civil Disorders, 142, 156, 175, 176, 330
U.S. National Center for Education Statistics, 248–50
U.S. National Center for Health Statistics, 82, 83, 285, 286, 288, 289, 291–92, 309, 404
U.S. Supreme Court, 11, 127, 144, 300, 303, 304, 328, 376, 378, 439, 447–52
United States v. *Paradise* (1987), 448, 451
Unnever, James D., 327, 328
Urban Institute, 455
Urbanization, 90
  changing patterns of race relations and, 147–49
  cross-cultural evidence on effects of, 209–16

Urbanization (*cont.*)
  social movement formation and, 160–61
Urban population
  African American, 147, 160, 230, 262–68, 280, 282
  Asian American, 236
  Hispanic American, 231–32, 262–66, 280, 282
  Native American, 160, 170, 234
USA Today, 266–68, 276, 277
Usdansky, Margaret L., 267, 277
Useem, Elizabeth L., 163, 355

Valdez, R. B., 453
Valentine, Charles L., 75
Valenzuela de la Garza, Jesus, 360
Values, 59
  changing, social movements and attitudes and, 164–65
  consensus of, vs. conflict, 91–92
Van den Berghe, Pierre L., 6, 87, 93, 194, 218
Van der Horst, Sheila T., 255
Van Valey, Thomas L., 266, 267
Vedlitz, Arnold, 28, 29
Verma, Gajendra K., 28
Vernon, P. E., 362
Veterans Administration (VA), 303
Vetter, H., 43
Vidal, Gore, 403
Vietnam, 214
Vietnamese Americans, 124, 224, 225, 235
Vietnam War, 310
Vining, Daniel R., 455
Violence
  against African Americans, 1–2, 126, 138–39, 155, 175, 178, 273, 284, 331, 333–34
  by African Americans, 156, 174–77, 179–80
  of all types, increase in, 423
  against Arab Americans, 224
  against Asian Americans, 139–40
  against civil rights workers, 177–78
  correlation with war, 138–39
  genocide, 2
  in Great Britain, 207
  hate crime, 1, 2, 416–27
  against homosexuals, 2, 399
  against Mexican Americans, 140–41
  by Mexican Americans, 157
  minority group on minority group, 151–52
  against Native Americans, 157, 158
  by police, 330–31, 333–34
  resurgence in, 1, 2
  surges in immigration and, 224–26
  against women, 390, 392–93
  (*See also* Riots)
Visher, Christy A., 323
Vitenam War, 138
Viva Kennedy movement, 184
Vivona, T. Scott, 325
Vose, Clement E., 303
Voting power, 312–15
Voting rights, 130, 144, 299–301
Voting Rights Act of 1965, 155, 301, 306

Wage garnishment, 333
Wages of women and minority groups, 80, 81
Waite, Linda J., 79, 386
Waldman, B., 444
Walker, Alexis J., 387
Walker, Lewis, 194, 208, 215–17, 221
Wallace, George, 337
Wallace, Irving, 401
Wallechinsky, David, 401
Wallerstein, Judith S., 81
Walters, Gary, 48
Walters, Richard H., 24
Walton, Hanes, Jr., 181
War
  ethnocentrism and, 69
  racial violence correlated with, 138–39
Wards Cove v. *Antonio* (1989), 448, 450
Warner, W. Lloyd, 6
War on Poverty, 178, 185
Warren, Earl, 301
Warren, Robert, 454
Warshaw, P. R., 45
Washington, Booker T., 169
Washington, University of, 424–25
WASP culture, 168–71, 435
Watson, Tom, 129
Watson, Warren, 415
Weber, Brian, 449
Weber, C. U., 370
Weber, G., 382
Weber, Max, 148
Weber v. *Kaiser Aluminum and Chemical Corporation* (1979), 448, 449
Weed, James A., 276
Weeks, John R., 456
Weikart, D. P., 370
Weinberg, Daniel H., 266, 276, 277
Weinberg, Martin S., 400, 402
Weiss, Gertrud, 286
Weiss, Randall, 341
Weitzman, Lenore, 386
Welch, Susan, 254, 326
Welfare reform, 308
Welsh Americans, 238, 239
Werner, Norma E., 351
Wesley, Charles H., 255
West, Cornell, 394–96, 398
Western Association of Schools and Colleges, 414, 414–15
Western European Americans, 238–40
Westie, F. R., 26
Wheeler, D. L., 401
Wheeler, John R. C., 290
Whitaker, Charles, 398
White, Sheldon, 370
White Aryan Resistance (WAR), 1, 416, 417, 419, 424
White-collar crime, 317
White-collar jobs, 145, 240, 260
White ethnics, Eastern and Southern European, 139, 236–38
"White flight," 376–77
Wilcox, Jerome E., 266
Wilder, D. A., 38
Wilder, L. Douglas, 54, 181, 241, 313
Wilensky, Harold L., 420
Wilhelm, Sidney M., 260, 459
Williams, Charles, 14
Williams, Colin J., 402

Williams, Robin, 63, 68, 74, 160, 162, 176, 372
Willie, Charles Vert, 459, 460, 462
Willig, Ann, 360
Willms, J. Douglas, 354
Wilner, Daniel M., 37
Wilson, Franklin D., 338, 377
Wilson, James Q., 297, 320, 329
Wilson, William Julius, 3, 10, 76, 79, 80, 82, 87, 96, 98, 99n, 126–29, 138, 142, 145–46, 148, 151, 154, 161, 162, 211, 244, 250, 255–58, 260, 262, 263, 266, 278, 280, 283, 309, 319, 380, 392, 394, 396, 398, 445, 458–63
Winsberg, Morton D., 268
Winship, Christopher, 76, 79
Wisconsin, University of, 425, 426
Witt, L. Allen, 23
Wolf, Katherine M., 34
Wolfe, Barbara L., 346
Women
  African American, 391–93
  discrimination against, 385–93
  educational attainment of, 241
  Hispanic American, 391–93
  income status of, 241–43, 386, 445
  single-parenthood, 76–82, 242, 243
  as sociological minority, 7
Wood, Barbara Sudene, 358
Wood, Peter B., 273
Wood, W., 32
Woodward, C. Van, 127, 128, 302
Worchel, Stephen, 28, 29
Workforce, diversity management and, 409–16
Workforce 2000 report (U.S. Department of Labor), 3, 409
Working-class prejudice, 28–29, 259
World War I, 138
World War II, 138, 140, 155
Wortman, Paul M., 372
Wounded Knee, South Dakota, 157, 161
Wright, J. Skelly, 332, 333
Wright, Richard, 130–36
Wu, Chenghuan, 33
Wurdock, Clarence, 377

Yankelovitch, Skelly, and White, Inc., 186
Yetman, Norman R., 8, 9, 171
Yinger, J. Milton, 23, 27, 31, 32, 68, 139, 152, 154, 175, 300, 301, 337
Young, Coleman, 313
Yudof, Mark G., 444
Yugoslavia, former, 168, 199–204, 222

Zafar, Saeeduz, 22
Zald, Mayer N., 158, 159, 162
Zalk, Sue R., 351
Zancanella, Don, 350
Zigler, Edward, 364, 370, 371
Zill, Nicholas, 81
Zimbabwe, 213, 214, 226
Zimring, Franklin E., 328
Zingraff, Matthew T., 326, 328
Zinn, Maxine Baca, 391
Zirkel, P., 351
Zoning, 304
Zuniga, Jose, 399
Zweigenhaft, 94, 124, 125, 436